FIFTH EDITION

Introduction to Criminal Justice

PATRICK R. ANDERSON

Florida Southern College

DONALD J. NEWMAN

Late Professor Emeritus
State University of New York at Albany

McGRAW-HILL, INC.

New York   St. Louis   San Francisco   Auckland   Bogotá   Caracas
Lisbon   London   Madrid   Mexico   Milan   Montreal   New Delhi
Paris   San Juan   Singapore   Sydney   Tokyo   Toronto

INTRODUCTION TO CRIMINAL JUSTICE

1 2 3 4 5 6 7 8 9 0 DOW DOW 9 0 9 8 7 6 5 4 3 2

ISBN 0-07-001958-4

This book was set in Stempel Garamond by Better Graphics, Inc.
The editor was Phillip A. Butcher;
the designer was Joan Greenfield;
the photo editor was Elsa Peterson.
Project supervision was done by The Total Book.
R. R. Donnelley & Sons Company was printer and binder.

Library of Congress Cataloging-in-Publication Data

Anderson, Patrick R., (date).
    Introduction to criminal justice / Patrick R. Anderson, Donald J.
Newman. — 5th ed.
        p.   cm.
    Newman's name appears first on the 4th edition.
    Includes bibliographical references and index.
    ISBN 0-07-001958-4
    1. Criminal justice, Administration of—United States.
2. Criminal procedure—United States.   I. Newman, Donald J.
II. Title.
KF9223.N5   1993
345.73′05—dc20
[347.3055]   92-19224

About the Authors

Patrick R. Anderson is Professor and Chair of the Department of Sociology and Criminology at Florida Southern College in Lakeland. Prior to coming to Florida Southern in 1986, he was a professor in the Department of Criminal Justice at Louisiana State University in Baton Rouge and, before that, professor of criminal justice at Florida Junior College in Jacksonville and Program Coordinator at the Northeast Florida Criminal Justice Training and Education Center.

Professor Anderson has a varied academic background, with degrees in English literature, philosophy, and theology in addition to a Ph.D. in criminology from Florida State University. He has been a jail officer, a juvenile probation case worker and casework supervisor, a police and corrections trainer, and an expert witness. He has been a professor since 1972.

Professor Anderson has been awarded research grants in prison design and architecture, criminological aspects of legalized gambling, effects of drunk driving statutes, and prisons in antiquity, among other topics. He has served as expert, researcher, speaker-lecturer, and consultant for several state legislatures, police departments and jails, the Justice Department's Law Enforcement Assistance Administration, and the National Institute of Corrections. During the past few years he has traveled extensively in Eastern Europe, especially Romania, and has consulted with several police departments there. He has published numerous articles in scholarly journals on various subjects, including prison overcrowding, expert witnessing, police high-speed chase, and postconviction due process. His books include: *An Architectural Program for the Design of a Prototypical State Correctional Facility* (1985) and *Expert Witnesses: Criminologists in the Courtroom* (1987). Professor Anderson is a member of numerous professional and academic societies including the American Society of Criminology and the Academy of Criminal Justice Sciences. He is currently an associate editor of *Justice Quarterly*.

Donald J. Newman was Professor of Criminal Justice at the State University of New York at Albany. Prior to his appointment at SUNY in 1967, he was on the faculty at St. Lawrence University and at the University of Wisconsin. He received his Ph.D. in sociology from the University of Wisconsin, Madison. Professor Newman passed away in 1991 after a long and productive career.

Throughout his career, Professor Newman was awarded research grants by prominent research organizations in the United States. He was a pioneer in the study of plea bargaining and was a consultant to many organizations concerned with criminal justice, including maximum security prisons, metropolitan police departments, the Department of Justice's Law Enforcement Assistance Administration, the Council of Graduate Schools, the New York Special Commission on Attica (McKay Commission), the Ministry of Justice of Japan, and others. He was instrumental in the planning and growth of many criminal justice programs of higher education, and with his colleague Frank Remington was largely responsible for developing the concept "criminal justice" as an academic discipline. On television he appeared as an expert on criminal justice on *60 Minutes* and *Today*. He authored numerous articles in leading criminal justice journals, law reviews, and other scholarly publications. His books include *Conviction, the Determination of Guilt or Innocence without Trial* (1966); *The Administration of Justice* (1969, 1982); and *Elderly Criminals* (1984).

To the memory of Donald J. Newman, scholar and friend

Contents

PART FOUR CORRECTIONS

PART FIVE: THE JUVENILE JUSTICE SYSTEM

16 JUVENILE CRIME AND JUVENILE JUSTICE   421

Preface

Few textbooks survive to a fifth edition. When Donald Newman originally conceived this one, it was the first introductory text in the field of criminal justice, and it quickly became the standard. The emphasis on the decision network, the scholarly approach to the subject, and the writer's skill set the book apart from those by other authors that followed. This edition keeps the strengths of previous editions, but is dramatically different.

First, its text is more concise. The fourth edition had twenty-one chapters, this one has sixteen. The chapters themselves are more direct, compact, and lively. Although we have attempted to cover the field thoroughly, we have not attempted to describe every tree in the forest. Rather, we have presented the broad sweep of the forest, the full landscape. We assume that other courses exist in the criminal justice curriculum, courses which examine in greater detail each subject introduced in this text. Therefore, we have written a text which explores for the beginning student the entire subject of criminal justice, and which pays more attention to the interrelatedness of the components of the criminal justice system, and to its underlying principles and values of justice, than to the infinite details of the separate police, court, and correctional systems themselves.

Second, this text is the first and only soft-cover introductory book in the field, at least as far as we can tell. We agreed with the editors at McGraw-Hill that cost-conscious students today deserve a break from the escalating prices of textbooks. A soft-cover edition is an attempt to satisfy what we perceive to be a desire by students and professors to be provided with more for less.

Third, this edition uses the "Conservative Crime Control Model" and the "Liberal Crime Control Model" throughout as a framework for students' understanding of the underlying values and value conflicts in criminal justice. We hope professors will use this didactic device to enliven lectures, discussions, and other classroom activities. And we hope students will be drawn to the issues associated with criminal justice by this thesis-antithesis approach.

Fourth, in response to many requests from reviewers and friends, we have included a chapter on criminological theory. The intention behind this chapter is to relate criminological theory to criminal justice, to show the relevance of theory to practice. We have not intended to provide an exhaustive analysis of criminological theory, but we believe the students' understanding of criminal justice decisions will be enhanced by this theoretical overview. And, as with the other chapters, our intention is to whet the appetite of students for further learning, for subsequent courses in the criminal justice curriculum.

Fifth, we begin each chapter with a vignette, a brief introductory case which brings the subject of the chapter vividly to life. These vignettes come from *real* life—from the pages of daily newspapers, from history, or from the personal experience of the author. Then, in each chapter we have added boxed material which highlights interesting areas discussed in the chapter. The subjects for boxes also come from current events, well-known cases, and history. These Field Practice and Criminal Justice System in Action boxes, we believe, help students focus on the subject, the real world of criminal justice. Various segments or quotes from well-known documents such as the Constitution should give each student an appetite for learning more. And the pictures herein complement the text in substantive ways, rather than merely providing visual interest or shock value.

Finally, this edition was written by only one author, half of the team, because Donald Newman passed away before the writing began. Although the major contributions of the Newman approach have been maintained, including the decision network analysis and the emphasis on democratic principles and values, readers familiar with the previous editions will quickly see that this one is a dramatic departure from the first four. Don and I discussed many of the changes, but others came at later stages of the writing and could not have been anticipated. I have to say that I miss Don a great deal, and I hope he would have liked what I have done with the book.

The belief Don and I shared, and the approach taken in the preparation of this text, is that criminal justice is the most interesting course in a college curriculum. Students are naturally drawn to the subject, and scholars find endless subjects to explore in their efforts to understand crime and criminal justice better. Therefore, this book attempts to present the subject in a way that is in keeping with its natural attractiveness—to make criminal justice as interesting to the student as it has always been to the book's authors.

In any project of this magnitude, expressions of gratitude should properly be made to many people. My family has paid a significant price by having to live with two monsters, the book and me. Carolyn, Chris, Scott, and Amy have been patient, supportive, and loving throughout it all. Also, certain close friends have been understanding and encouraging, and to each I express thanks.

Several colleagues and friends in criminal justice read early drafts of the text, criticized, made suggestions, and otherwise helped. John Scheb, Lorie Fridell, Tom Phelps, Bernie McCarthy, Jim Fyfe, Larry Wollan, Rolando del Carmen, Bill Pelfrey, Price Foster, and others have offered advice and assistance, some of which I accepted. Most important, they have been good friends.

The McGraw-Hill editorial team assigned to this edition has been wonderful. Phil Butcher, senior editor, put together a magnificent group of specialists who have treated this project with love and care. Sylvia Shepard first planned the production of this edition and set the project in motion. Valerie Raymond, has worked with me as the Developmental Editor, offering suggestions, pressing me to honor deadlines, encouraging me with her enthusiasm for the manuscript. She performed her tasks with great professional skill, but more than that she went beyond the call of duty by treating the manuscript as her own. Annette Bodzin has been the project supervisor and has managed the final production of the text with great tact and patience, keeping us all ahead of schedule and producing a truly first-class book. Safra Nimrod and Elsa Peterson discovered and chose the photos with attention to the unique needs of the text. The copy editor, Lester Strong, diligently scrutinized every line, offering professional assistance of the highest caliber.

Special appreciation is due to Marianne W. Zawitz of the Bureau of Justice Statistics, who helped greatly by securing the most recent statistics possible, often sharing prepublication data with me and pointing me in the proper direction to locate hard-to-find statistics.

Finally, a group of reviewers who read the fourth edition and each manuscript of this text carefully have been anonymous to me during the revision process. But now I am happy to be able to officially and publicly express appreciation to Steven G. Brandl, Georgia State University; Stephen Brodt, Ball State University; Barbara A. Carson, Ball State University; Lorie A. Fridell, Florida State University; Jay Livingston, Montclair State College; Bernard J. McCarthy, University of Central Florida; Robert J. McCormack, Trenton State College; G. Larry Mays, New Mexico State; William V. Pelfrey, Western Carolina University; Thomas R. Phelps, California State University, Sacramento; Gerald Rigby, Bowling Green University and Stan Stojkovic, University of Wisconsin. Their insights, criticisms, suggestions, and encouraging statements have been invaluable. Thanks to all of you.

Of course, I wish to also express appreciation to the hundreds of students who have sat in my classes during the past 20 years, always challenging me to do better, and inspiring me to teach the most interesting of all subjects, criminal justice.

Patrick R. Anderson

The System

1

The Crime Problem in the United States

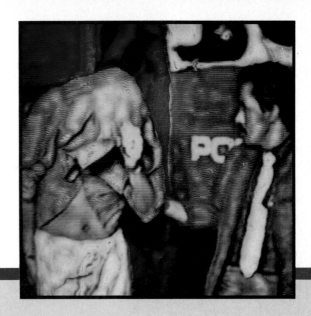

Early in 1990, leaders of a local victims' rights organization met with the Chief of Police to discuss the problem of rape in the city. Although the number of rapes reported in the city during the current year was relatively small, even fewer than the previous year, concern was expressed that only a fraction of rape victims reported the crimes to the police. Some scholars had estimated that as many as eight rapes occurred for every one reported to the police, and several reasons for this underreporting were identified. Rape victims, it was said, were reluctant to report the crime to police because the police department and prosecutors assigned to rape cases were men who did not treat rape victims with sympathy and understanding. Also, it was pointed out that rape victims were not informed about how to report the crime to police, and were often treated in an uncaring way by prosecutors.

The chief responded to the concerns expressed and began to work on the problem. He called for a meeting with the mayor and the state's attorney, the prosecutor. Together they devised a plan of action. First, the police chief selected three women detectives to work in the rape unit. They were trained in crisis intervention and taught to handle rape investigations with tact and skill. Also the prosecutor assigned well-trained prosecutors to rape cases. And the victims' rights group provided trained counselors to assist the police and prosecutors by giving the victims moral support through the entire process, including any possible court appearances.

Second, after the first step was accomplished, the Chief of Police began a public campaign to encourage rape victims to report the crimes to the police. A special "hot line" telephone number was established, and posters were printed and placed throughout the city to inform people that the new rape intervention program was in place. The telephone number was publicized on television and radio.

Almost immediately the number of rapes reported to the police increased, and by the end of the first year the number of reported rapes doubled. The next year, when year-end crime statistics were reported by the police department, a local television station's news department noticed the dramatic increase in rapes, calling the increase a "crime wave." The reasons for the increase in the number of reported rapes were not mentioned. A local politician who had announced his intention to run for Chief of Police in opposition to the incumbent began to make public accusations of poor leadership in the criminal justice agencies. He charged that the current police chief was "asleep at the switch" while the citizens of the city were "terrorized by crime in the streets." The police chief was angered by the charges, and privately told a friend, "If we had done nothing about the rape issue, the statistics would not have changed a bit from one year to the next, and I would have been considered a successful police administrator, I guess."

About this chapter

This story demonstrates some of the difficulties in crime measurement and reporting. Did the actual number of rapes change from one year to the next? Or did the criminal justice system change, thereby resulting in an improved ability to know about rapes? Since the number of reported rapes increased, and the statistical data indicated the rise dramatically, apparently a "crime wave" had occurred. Right?

No. This story demonstrates that sometimes official crime data reflect what the police are doing, or not doing—not what the criminals are doing. In other words, the actual number of rapes in the city may not have changed at all, or may have changed very little, but the new emphasis by the criminal justice agency resulted in a different statistical result.

Is it possible that a city which reports a low crime rate actually has as much crime or more than a city which reports a high crime rate? Could a low crime rate result from a passive, poorly trained and equipped police department while a high crime rate reflects an aggressive, well-trained and equipped police department?

This chapter discusses the definition and measurement of crime in the United States. What do we expect our criminal justice agencies to do? What purposes do they achieve or attempt to achieve?

CRIME DEFINED

The best place to begin is at the beginning. Although the term "crime" is used casually in conversation ("The price of new cars today is a crime!"), crime technically is what a legislature defines as crime. To be sure, certain forms of deviance have more or less consistently been defined as crime throughout history, for example, theft, murder, and kidnapping. These crimes are part of the **common law**, which is that body of law which has existed for centuries by general agreement without necessarily being codified in written form. But today behavior is not a crime until or unless the legislature passes a statute precisely describing the forbidden behavior and setting a maximum punishment for violators. There is a Latin phrase, *nullum crimen, nullum poena, sans lege*, which means "no crime, no punishment, without legislation." And with the rise of each new social problem, some Americans respond by demanding "There ought to be a law!"—about drug use, abortion, gun possession, and a great deal more. Although nearly unanimous agreement exists as to whether some behaviors should be defined legally as criminal, there is much controversy regarding others.

Types of Crimes

Someone may ask, "How much crime occurs in the United States?" The proper response to this question may well be: "It depends on what you mean by crime." The sheer volume of laws make general use of the word "crime" too broad. Also, qualitative differences are lost between specific criminal acts, such as disorderly conduct and forcible rape, when they are lumped under a single heading.

So we attempt to distinguish between various types of crimes in the following ways. (See Table 1.1) **Crimes against persons** include murder, assault and battery, sexual battery (or rape), kidnapping, and extortion. **Crimes against property or habitation** include larceny (theft), burglary, robbery, and arson. **Crimes against public morality** include fornication and illicit cohabitation, adultery, incest, prostitution, obscenity, gambling, intoxication, drug offenses, profanity, indecent exposure, and pornography. **Crimes against public order** include disorderly conduct, breach of peace, and vagrancy.

These offenses are most commonly recognized as crimes and a large amount of criminal justice attention is given to them. And under each type the behaviors listed are only representative; other offenses could be included. But that is not all. Some offenses may be considered **crimes against justice and public administration**—for example, bribery, perjury, obstruction of justice, resisting arrest, escape, and criminal contempt. Also, some crimes committed by people in business, commerce, or government are referred to as **white collar crimes**. White collar crimes include tax evasion, insurance fraud, computer crimes, insider trading, bankruptcy fraud, and a great deal more. And then there is the so-called **victimless crime**, which generally refers to offenses for which the victim and the offender are the same person—for example, gambling, illegal sex acts between consenting adults, and substance abuse.

Finally, the distinction between criminals (the bad guys) and the representatives

TABLE 1.1

Crimes against persons	*Victimless crimes*
Murder	Gambling
Assault and battery	Illegal sex acts between consenting adults
Sexual battery	Drug abuse
Kidnapping	
Extortion	*Crimes against property and habitation*
	Larceny (theft)
Crimes against public morality	Burglary
Fornication and illicit cohabitation	Arson
Adultery	
Incest	*Crimes against public order*
Prostitution	Disorderly conduct
Obscenity	Breach of peace
Gambling	Vagrancy
Intoxication	
Drug abuse	*White collar crimes*
Profanity	Tax fraud
Indecent exposure	Bankruptcy fraud
Pornography	Insider trading
	Computer crimes
Crimes against justice and public administration	Insurance fraud
Bribery	*Crimes committed by government authorities*
Perjury	Civil rights violations
Obstruction of justice	Police brutality
Resisting arrest	Political bribe taking
Escape	Genocide
Criminal contempt	Torture

of the government (the good guys) is not always easily made. Sometimes people in positions of authority also violate the law. These **crimes committed by government authorities** include offenses such as civil rights violations, police brutality, political bribe taking, genocide, and torture. They are not usually included in the average person's understanding of crime, and they are not reported in official crime statistics.[1]

The Seriousness of Crime

The seriousness of any type of crime—the degree of its threat to our social order—can be debated endlessly, with the debate having different outcomes depending on the debaters' points of view. Thus whether murder is a worse crime than improper toxic waste disposal, or whether crimes against individual persons are more threatening to our social system than "crimes against the people," have been argued many times. Which is worse, to steal money from a person's wallet or to profit from all the residents of a community through illegal price fixing of a commodity? Such questions are unlikely to be resolved by debate, yet the controversy goes on. Proposals are made to "decriminalize" certain behaviors, such as possession and sale of marijuana, and to "criminalize" or more seriously punish other types of conduct, like pollution or abortion, which until recently have not been viewed as serious threats to our way of life.

Common Law and Modern Crime

The ranking of crimes by degree of seriousness is not simply a debater's exercise. Distinctions between classes of crimes have been recognized throughout history. Our present-day criminal codes and corresponding sentencing structures owe much of their content to origins in common law. We retain in our written criminal codes many of the ancient and very serious bans on forms of conduct "evil in themselves" *(mala in se)* such as murder. To these we have added crimes peculiar to different stages of our modern urban industrial development, crimes that have no exact counterparts in common law, such as drug abuse or illegal toxic waste disposal. These are offenses created by legislation rather than history *(mala prohibita)*. With few exceptions, *mala in se* offenses are considered by most people as more serious than *mala prohibita* offenses, and both categories contain finer distinctions of seriousness, including major differences between heavily penalized felonies and less severely treated misdemeanors.

Felonies and Misdemeanors

Written criminal codes in all jurisdictions make distinctions between felonies and misdemeanors and sometimes lesser offenses called "violations" or "infractions." A **felony** is a serious crime with correspondingly harsh penalties including such civil disabilities as loss of voting privileges after conviction as well as criminal punishment of more than 1 year in prison. A **misdemeanor** is a minor offense, less serious than a felony, subject to penalties such as a fine or a jail term of less than 1 year.

Both felonies and misdemeanors are graded by degrees of seriousness. Often this grading is expressed in **degrees of crime** or of an offense. For example, a criminal code provides different penalties for the felony of murder. Murder in the first degree is defined as an act that is carried out after premeditation and planning. An important exception to this general rule is a killing that is not specifically planned but occurs during the commission of a serious felony, such as armed robbery. This is called "felony murder." Second-degree murder is any other murder than first-degree or felony murder. That is, no premeditation or malice aforethought existed, but the offender acted in a dangerous way without regard for human life. For instance, a person may wish to beat someone else severely, "within an inch of his (or her) life," as the saying goes, but the victim dies as a result of the beating. Such a murder is substantially different from one in which the offender planned for weeks or months to carry out a cold-blooded killing. In practice, second-degree murder convictions sometimes result from first-degree prosecutions that the jury determines do not deserve the harsh penalty—often death—of a first-degree conviction.

Manslaughter is also a form of murder which is not accompanied by malice or premeditation, such as a sudden eruption of passion during the course of an argument, resulting in the killing of a person. The unintentional killing of a person during the commission of a minor crime, during a negligent auto accident, or through other forms of negligence may also be considered manslaughter.

So, we can see that even a specific crime, in this case murder, has various degrees of seriousness. Similar differences are found regarding virtually all crimes.

Some crimes may cross the felony—misdemeanor line as their contexts or consequences become more or less serious. Aggravated assault is often defined as assault with a weapon with intent to do great bodily harm. Simple assault, on the other hand, is a misdemeanor covering common fistfights. Sometimes the distinction between felony and misdemeanor involving the same criminal conduct is determined by consequences, such as the loss suffered by the victim. Grand larceny is a felony because of the amount of money or property stolen; petty larceny—stealing smaller amounts—is

usually a misdemeanor. In some instances, the degree of the crime is determined by the intent of the perpetrator, which, unless the person confesses, can only be inferred from his or her behavior. Thus whether a homicide is murder, killing by reckless conduct, negligent homicide, or some lesser degree of manslaughter, depends on proof of the mental state of the actor—that is, the extent to which the criminal consequences were intended and willful or careless and negligent.

There is no single classification of crimes or of penalties that is identical and uniform in all places. Only by reference to specific statutory provisions in each jurisdiction can it be determined whether an offense is a felony or misdemeanor.

Elements of a Crime

Modern law contains six basic elements, or principles in addition to common law classifications and felony-misdemeanor distinctions.[2] First, *nullen crimen, nulla poena, sine lege,* as has been previously stated, means that there can be no crime or punishment unless a specific law prohibits a behavior and provides a punishment for it. Also, the U.S. Constitution prohibits *ex post facto* laws, or laws which define crimes retroactively. In order to be a crime, an act must be illegal at the time it is committed.

Second, there is the principle of **actus reus**, or wrongful act. Crime requires more than evil thoughts, it requires an act, a specific act of commission or omission by a person.

Third, there is **mens rea**, or guilty mind. An act cannot generally be considered to be criminal unless the accused intended to commit the prohibited act. A person who was insane, therefore, at the time of the act cannot form the intent necessary for criminal responsibility.

Fourth, *actus reus* and *mens rea* must both be present—the act and the intent must be fused together before a person may be punished by society. A person cannot be punished for merely entertaining an evil intention, or for the commission of an unavoidable act.

Fifth, harm must be caused by an act. A person's person, property, or reputation must be harmed before an act can be considered a crime. Or the interests of society in order, safety, peace, morality, or health must be harmed.

Sixth, causation must be established. That is, the harm must be caused by an act. For instance, a death must be caused by the actions of an accused person before that person can be found guilty of murder.

When these principles exist, or these elements are demonstrated, then a crime has been committed.

MEASURING CRIME

It is generally accepted that the crime rate in the United States is among the highest, if not *the* highest, of all industrial, urbanized societies in the world. This applies not only to such traditional crimes as homicide, robbery, burglary, and common forms of theft, but also to corporate crimes and crimes by prominent and trusted government officials. However, accurate data to substantiate or dispute this view do not exist. Most countries do not make the same serious attempt to accurately measure crime as the United States does. And many other countries are not open to a free press which will report whatever data exist, good and bad, to the public. Likewise, no two countries define crime the same way, so comparisons between countries' crime rates is difficult.

Despite our sophisticated census measurements and our ability to produce impressive economic and marketing data, the unfortunate fact is that there is no reliable

Violent Crime Trends in Large and Midsized Cities

Despite all the problems of crime measurement, one strength of the *Uniform Crime Reports* (UCR) is that they can point out interesting trends in crime rates. One such trend, reported by the FBI, is that violent crime rates have skyrocketed in midsized cities while rates in the largest American cities have actually fallen.

The traditional view held by most Americans is that the greatest danger of becoming a crime victim resides with people living in New York City, Chicago, Los Angeles, and other megacities, and that smaller cities are safe. But the new data indicate a person has a higher statistical chance of being murdered in Jacksonville, Florida, Charlotte, North Carolina, Milwaukee, Wisconsin, or other cities of that size. The UCR data show that in 1990 the violent crime rate in cities with populations of 500,000 to 1,000,000 jumped 16 percent, double the rise recorded in the very largest American cities.

Police in smaller cities, too, have recognized the trend. In Redford Township, Michigan, which borders Detroit's west side, Detective Lieutenant Wilson Bailey has seen armed robberies go from one or two a year to over two hundred, all in 11¼ square miles. Bailey credits the drug trade for the increase, and says it's a problem in small communities all over, that it's more than just spillover from Detroit. The connection between drugs and crime is supported by statistics. The percent of jail and prison inmates who have used drugs is about twice the percent of drug users in the general population.

The public perception in smaller cities that crime is a big-city issue may actually hurt police. In New Milford, New Jersey, population 15,990, when a state arbitrator sup-

Charlotte, North Carolina police officer Ben Davis on the scene where Marcus Grier, thirteen years old, was shot and killed. The event was the first high-school football game of the season. He was the victim of a random shooting.

ported a 27 percent pay increase for police, the municipal government solved its budget problems by threatening to lay off seven police officers. A compromise was reached. Despite serious financial trouble in New York City, the Police Department will expand from 26,000 to 31,351 by 1994.

Big crime is not just a big-city problem any more, according to the Uniform Crime Reports. And that's a statistic of concern to citizens of all communities.

SOURCES: John McCormick and Bill Turque, "Big Crimes, Small Cities," *Newsweek*, June 10, 1991, pp. 16–19; Alison Gardy, "Twenty-five Percent Pay Increase for Police Meets Approval and Disapproval," *New York Times*, November 10, 1991, p. 2NJ.

method of counting offenses or offenders. The criminal justice system is operating in a sea of law violations whose tides and depths are not fully known. Among other things, this means that no precise base exists from which to measure the effectiveness of different crime control techniques, especially when dealing with unreported crimes for which no currently available data are reliable. We can only speculate about the incidence of vice offenses like gambling or prostitution, and very little information is available about offenses known only to their perpetrators. There is no way of determining, for example, how many Americans carry concealed weapons, though the number surely is far greater than indicated by the number of persons arrested for this crime.

The two primary programs to measure crime in the United States are the ***Uniform Crime Reports***[3] (UCR) and the ***National Crime Survey*** (NCS). Each is sponsored by the U.S. government, and each has strengths and weaknesses.

Uniform Crime Reports

In 1927 the International Association of Chiefs of Police (IACP) began to develop a system to gather statistics on crimes known to the police. By 1929 the IACP had studied the state criminal codes and record-keeping practices in use. Seven offenses were chosen to serve as a Crime Index for measuring the fluctuations in the amount and rate of crime:

> Violent Crimes
>   Murder and nonnegligent manslaughter
>   Forcible rape
>   Robbery
>   Aggravated assault
>
> Property Crimes
>   Burglary
>   Larceny-theft
>   Motor vehicle theft
>   Arson (added in 1979)

These **index crimes** are referred to as **Part I offenses** by the UCR, but a number of additional crimes which the police routinely respond to have been added. These are called **Part II offenses**. See Table 1.2 for a list and definition of both Part I and Part II offenses.

In 1930 Congress enacted legislation authorizing the Attorney General of the United States to gather crime statistics, and the Attorney General in turn designated the Federal Bureau of Investigation (FBI) to administer the program, although none of the offenses measured is under FBI jurisdiction. Crime data are reported to the Federal Bureau of Investigation directly by police agencies or through state-level agencies which then report to the FBI. The FBI tabulates and publishes the data in a volume called *Crime in the United States* each year. It is this report that is more commonly referred to as the *Uniform Crime Reports,* or UCRs.

Data on Part I crimes include crimes known to the police and crimes "cleared by arrest or exceptional means." That is, police learn of some crimes either through their own investigations or by the reports of victims or others. Then, after they know about those specific crimes, the police clear by arrest a certain percent of them. (See Fig. 1.1.) If reported crimes are later discovered through investigation to be unfounded, or false, they are not included in the reports.

Crimes cleared by arrest are those for which one or more persons are arrested for the offense and then turned over to the prosecutor for further action. Crimes cleared by exceptional means include those cleared by the death of the offender through suicide, or justifiable killing by police, victims, or others. Additional exceptional means are defined as the victim's refusal to cooperate in the prosecution of the offender, or cases in which the charges are dropped because the offender is being prosecuted for other charges. Figure 1.2 shows the crimes cleared for Part I offenses (except arson) in 1990. The UCR also includes details about the person arrested, including age, race, and sex.

Part I offenses are used to compute the **crime rate**, the statistic which is used to demonstrate overall fluctuations in the incidence of crime. The crime rate is computed

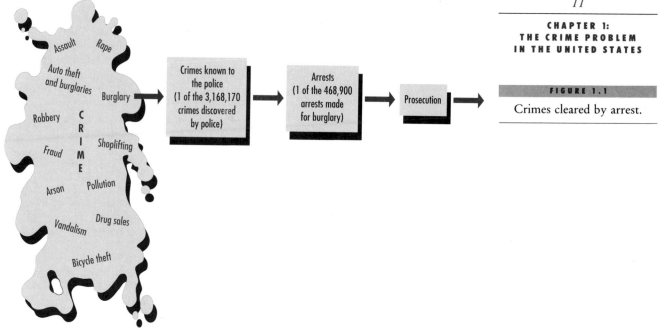

FIGURE 1.1

Crimes cleared by arrest.

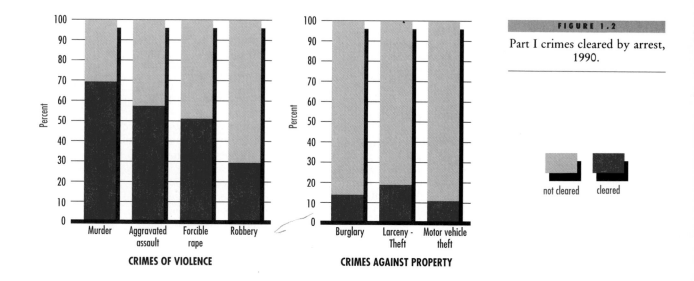

FIGURE 1.2

Part I crimes cleared by arrest, 1990.

by dividing the number of crimes reported to the police by the total population and then dividing by 100,000. The formula is:

$$\text{Crime rate} = \frac{\text{number of reported crimes}}{\text{total population}} \times 100,000$$

The crime rate per 100,000 has become a popular statistic to show crime trends over time and space in addition to the total number of crimes known to the police. (See Figure 1.3.) The crime rate is also used to show differences between neighborhoods, cities, states, and regions of the country. For instance, Fig. 1.4 shows the 1990 rates for

TABLE 1.2 *Part I and Part II Offenses in Uniform Crime Reporting*

Offenses in Uniform Crime Reporting are divided into two groupings, Part I and Part II. Information on the volume of Part I offenses known to law enforcement, those cleared by arrest or exceptional means, and the number of persons arrested is reported monthly. Only arrest data are reported for Part II offenses.

The Part I offenses are:

Criminal homicide—a. Murder and nonnegligent manslaughter: the willful (nonnegligent) killing of one human being by another. Deaths caused by negligence, attempts to kill, assaults to kill, suicides, accidental deaths, and justifiable homicides are excluded. Justifiable homicides are limited to: (1) the killing of a felon by a law enforcement officer in the line of duty; and (2) the killing of a felon by a private citizen. b. Manslaughter by negligence: the killing of another person through gross negligence. Traffic fatalities are excluded. While manslaughter by negligence is a Part I crime, it is not included in the Crime Index.

Forcible rape—The carnal knowledge of a female forcibly and against her will. Included are rapes by force and attempts or assaults to rape. Statutory offenses (no force used—victim under age of consent) are excluded.

Robbery—The taking or attempting to take anything of value from the care, custody, or control of a person or persons by force or threat of force or violence and/or by putting the victim in fear.

Aggravated assault—An unlawful attack by one person upon another for the purpose of inflicting severe or aggravated bodily injury. This type of assault usually is accompanied by the use of a weapon or by means likely to produce death or great bodily harm. Simple assaults are excluded.

Burglary—breaking or entering—The unlawful entry of a structure to commit a felon or a theft. Attempted forcible entry is included.

Larceny—theft (except motor vehicle theft)—The unlawful taking, carrying, leading, or riding away of property from the possession or constructive possession of another. Examples are thefts of bicycles or automobile accessories, shoplifting, pocket-picking, or the stealing of any property or article which is not taken by force and violence or by fraud. Attempted larcenies are included. Embezzlement, "con" games, forgery, worthless checks, etc., are excluded.

Motor vehicle theft—The theft or attempted theft of a motor vehicle. A motor vehicle is self-propelled and runs on the surface and not on rails. Specifically excluded from this category are motorboats, construction equipment, airplanes, and farming equipment.

Arson—Any willful or malicious burning or attempt to burn, with or without intent to defraud, a dwelling house, public building, motor vehicle or aircraft, personal property of another, etc.

The Part II offenses are:

Other assaults (simple)—Assaults and attempted assaults where no weapon is used and which do not result in serious or aggravated injury to the victim.

Forgery and counterfeiting—Making, altering, uttering, or possessing, with intent to defraud, anything false in the semblance of that which is true. Attempts are included.

Fraud—Fraudulent conversion and obtaining money or property by false pretenses. Included are confidence games and bad checks, except forgeries and counterfeiting.

Embezzlement—Misappropriation or misapplication of money or property entrusted to one's care, custody, or control.

Stolen property; buying, receiving, possessing—Buying, receiving, and possessing stolen property, including attempts.

Vandalism—Willful or malicious destruction, injury, disfigurement, or defacement of any public or private property, real or personal, without consent of the owner or persons having custody or control.

Weapons; carrying, possessing, etc.—All violations of regulations or statutes controlling the carrying, using, possessing, furnishing, and manufacturing of deadly weapons or silencers. Included are attempts.

Prostitution and commercialized vice—Sex offenses of a commercialized nature, such as prostitution, keeping a bawdy house, procuring, or transporting women for immoral purposes. Attempts are included.

Sex offenses (except forcible rape, prostitution, and commercialized vice)—Statutory rape and offenses against chastity, common decency, morals, and the like. Attempts are included.

Drug abuse violations—State and local offenses relating to the unlawful possession, sale, use, growing, and manufacturing of narcotic drugs.

Gambling—Promoting, permitting, or engaging in illegal gambling.

Offenses against the family and children—Nonsupport, neglect, desertion, or abuse of family and children.

Driving under the influence—Driving or operating any vehicle or common carrier while drunk or under the influence of liquor or narcotics.

Liquor laws—State or local liquor law violations, except "drunkenness" and "driving under the influence." Federal violations are excluded.

Drunkenness—Offenses relating to drunkenness or intoxication. Excluded is "driving under the influence."

Disorderly conduct—Breach of the peace.

Vagrancy—Vagabondage, begging, loitering, etc.

All other offenses—All violations of state or local laws, except those listed above and traffic offenses.

Suspicion—No specific offense; suspect released without formal charges being placed.

Curfew and loitering laws (persons under age 18)—Offenses relating to violations of local curfew or loitering ordinances where such laws exist.

Runaways—(persons under age 18)—Limited to juveniles taken into protective custody under provisions of local statutes.

SOURCE: *Uniform Crime Reports: Crime in the United States, 1989* (Washington, DC: U.S. Department of Justice, 1990), pp. 324–325.

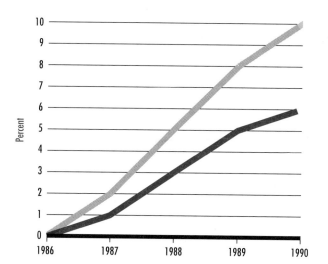

FIGURE 1.3

Crime index total (percent change from 1986).

number of offenses known—up 10%   rate per 100,000 inhabitants—up 6%

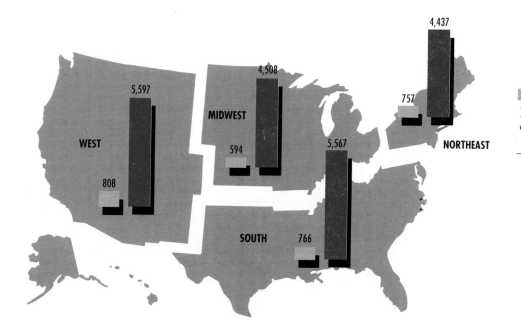

4,437

4,508

5,597

757

MIDWEST

WEST

594

5,567

NORTHEAST

808

766

SOUTH

FIGURE 1.4

Regional violent and property crime rates, 1990 (per 100,000 inhabitants).

violent crime rate   property crime rate

Part I violent crimes and Part I property crimes in the four regions of the United States.

In addition to providing details about crimes known to the police in the various regions of the country, the UCRs also provide analyses of crimes by month, urban and rural comparisons, types of weapons used if any, type and value of property stolen and recovered, crime on college and university campuses, and more. Data are also collected about law enforcement personnel, including the number of officers killed in the line of duty.

Only arrest data are compiled for Part II offenses, but as with Part I offenders, details are tabulated by age, race, sex, and suburban or rural setting. And the rates for states and cities are included.

Weaknesses of the Uniform Crime Reports

The UCR is a major source of crime statistics in the United States and are used widely by scholars, policy makers, and criminal justice administrators. The press and politicians often quote them as gospel truth. The scope of crime data gathering in the United States is indeed impressive, but these data do not tell the whole story about the extent of crime. The UCR exhibits several weaknesses.

First, UCR data tell more about police activity than criminal activity since they measure the amount of crime police know about and the number of arrests police make. Local police are not always involved in crime investigations. For instance, police may not know about major arsons if the fire department does not refer such cases to the police. Also, local police agencies do not typically investigate federal offenses, Securities and Exchange Commission violations, or offenses handled by the Federal Trade Commission. It is also important to note that the FBI index does not include such crimes as extortion, kidnaping, racketeering, airplane hijacking, or many white collar crimes. Of course, even crimes for which local police have responsibility are not always known to the police.

Also, contrary to fact, it is widely assumed that victims more or less routinely report crimes, especially Part I crimes, to the police. Of course, this is not necessarily so. Studies have indicated forcible rape, for example, to be one of the most under-reported of serious felonies. Other crimes are grossly underreported as well.

In addition, the FBI index counts only the most serious crime in cases involving multiple offenses. Thus, for example, if an offender steals an automobile to make an escape after robbing a bank and then kills a person while escaping, the robbery and auto theft are ignored and only the homicide is counted in the index.[4]

Finally, police are *not required* to report to any central source the numbers and types of crimes that come to their attention. Citizens, as victims of crime, are likewise not required to report their own victimization. However, the FBI regularly receives,

Measuring crime begins with crime reported to the police. Reporting a crime sometimes takes courage on the part of the victim. It is impossible to measure all crime.

on a voluntary basis, crime data from about 16,000 police departments. These 16,000 are not *all* the police agencies in the United States, but they do account for the large state and local agencies that serve over 96 percent of the U.S. population.[5]

National Crime Survey

Despite incomplete coverage, the FBI reports probably are still the best available source of crime data covering the nation as a whole. Crimes known to the police, of course, provide a very important category of baseline data. But what of crimes *not* reported? Everyone in the field of criminal justice, including the police, know there are a large but murky number of unreported crimes. The "dark side of crime" it has been called: offenses known only to perpetrators and victims.

In 1973, in an attempt to learn more about crimes, unreported crimes, and crime victims the *National Crime Survey* (NCS) was established by Congress. The NCS is conducted by U.S. Census Bureau personnel, who interviewed about 97,000 people in 1990 (interviewees must be over 12 years old). This nationally representative sample covered approximately 48,000 households. The data are collected annually and published by the Bureau of Justice Statistics (BJS).[6]

The NCS asks about crimes suffered by individuals and households, whether or not they were reported to the police. It specifically surveys all the index crimes except murder and arson, collecting data about the victims (age, race, sex, marital status, income, and educational level), the offenders (age, race, sex, victim-offender relationship), and the crimes (time, place, use of weapons, injury, loss). Also, the NCS asks for reasons why victims did not report their victimization to the police, their experiences with criminal justice agencies, possible substance abuse by the offenders, and the nature of any defensive measures taken by the victims. Table 1.3 shows the reasons victims of violent crime give for not reporting the events to the police.

The *National Crime Survey* has demonstrated that the actual incidence of crime considerably exceeds the incidence reported in the UCR. Based on the survey data, roughly 6 million crimes of violence occurred in the United States in 1990, only about 40 percent of which were reported to the police. More than 13 million thefts occurred, and the police knew nothing about almost 70 percent of them. In the aggregate, only

TABLE 1.3 *Reasons for not reporting crimes of violence to the police, 1985 (total: 3,497,760 crimes of violence)*

Reason	Percentage of nonreported giving this reason
Offender unsuccessful	4.6
Not important enough	19.4
Private matter	25.2
Reported to other agency	11.2
Lack of proof	6.4
Police would not want to be bothered	6.3
Police would be inefficient, insensitive	4.0
Fear of reprisal	4.7
Too time consuming	2.9
Miscellaneous or no answer	15.3

SOURCE: U.S. Department of Justice, Bureau of Justice Statistics, *Criminal Victimization in the United States, 1985* (Washington, DC: U.S. Government Printing Office, 1987).

TABLE 1.4 *The amount of crimes of violence, 1990*—National Crime Survey *("victim's survey responses") versus* Uniform Crime Reports *("crimes known to the police")*

	National Crime Survey			Uniform Crime Reports	
Crime	Number	Rate*		Number	Rate*
Rape	110,660	500		102,555	80*
Robbery	1,115,440	5600		639,271	257
Aggravated assault	1,582,620	7800		1,054,863	424.1

*The NCS rate per 100,000 is based on the population age 12 and over. The UCR rate is for the total population, except rape, which is computed only for 100,000 females in the country.

38 percent of all victimizations were reported to the police, including only about half of the violent crimes against persons.[7] Table 1.4 compares the *National Crime Survey* and the *Uniform Crime Reports* data for violent crimes in 1990.

Why Victims Do Not Report Crimes to the Police

A large number of crime victims choose not to involve the police. This is particularly true for property crimes, since many people who have things stolen prefer merely to take the loss rather than participate in a time-consuming police process unless they have theft insurance covering stolen items and are therefore required by their insurance companies to verify any loss prior to submitting a claim. But people also choose not to report their victimization for a variety of other reasons. Sometimes victims consider the events to be private in nature; other times they do not believe the police will be successful in finding the stolen property or the thieves; or perhaps they do not wish to involve the police because they fear reprisals from the criminals, or do not wish to have the police investigating anything or anybody close to them.

In addition, crimes against persons, violent crimes, are frequently not reported to the police.[8] Perhaps the most publicized underreported crime of violence is rape, for according to victimization studies a large number of rape victims do not report what happened to the police. Date rape and rape within families are generally known to be underreported. The same is true for assault. Table 1.3 shows the percentage of crimes of violence which were not reported to the police in 1985 and the reasons given for not reporting them.

Counting Criminals

Statistical measures of crime in our society, whether from police reports or victim studies, indicate the number of criminal *offenders* only in a very general way. The frequency of homicides may come closest to revealing the number of murderers, since, except for comparatively rare mass killings, murder is usually a single perpetrator—single victim crime. In contrast, one thief may be responsible for dozens of robberies, burglaries, or larcenies. A crime cleared by arrest in the FBI reports is just this, a crime for which an arrest was made, not the number of crimes committed by the criminal or the number of criminals arrested. One burglary arrest may clear a large number of crimes. Even in these FBI data a large discrepancy exists between crimes reported and crimes cleared. In fact, because so few property crimes are solved by arrest, the major message of these data is that most crimes are unsolved—that, on the basis of *probability* of arrest, crime *does* pay.

There have been attempts to measure the number of criminals by self-report surveys. Just as victim surveys ask people if they have been victims of crime, self-report surveys ask respondents if they have committed crimes. Obviously, the truthfulness of responses to self-incriminating questions is always suspect, even with promises of confidentiality or with anonymous data-retrieval methods. Yet a surprisingly high percentage of respondents anonymously admit to committing undetected crimes, some of which are quite serious. For example, in a survey of 1608 persons in metropolitan New York, 91 percent of the respondents stated that they had committed one or more crimes after the age of 16. If true, 64 percent of the male respondents and 29 percent of the females could have been convicted of felonies. The admitted felonious acts ranged from auto theft to robbery.[9] Even if, as some claim, people sometimes say on self-report surveys they have done things that they have not in fact done (as in some surveys of high school students' use of marijuana), the fact remains that a very sizable portion of the population has admitted committing crimes that did not result in arrest.

Statistics on crimes or criminals are normally based on measurement over a period of time, usually a year. It is no doubt useful to tabulate crimes in this way, but the number of criminals *accumulates.* Last year's murderers are joined by those who kill this year, and to these will be added successive future killers. The year 1991 produced over 23,000 murders ("nonnegligent" homicides). But even assuming all the perpetrators were caught and sent to prison, since few murderers are executed and regular hours, proper nutrition, and state-provided medical care make it possible for homicide offenders to live out full lifespans, the cumulative number of murderers is just that much greater.

Crimes other than murder and sentences shorter than life cause *criminal populations* to accumulate, both in prison and on the street, posing a perplexing question: Is a person who once committed a crime always a criminal? Despite some legislative attempts to expunge criminal records of former offenders who have completed their sentences and have remained law-abiding for a number of years, police intelligence units often keep track of known former criminals.[10] Roundup investigations are not uncommon, particularly when serious or heinous crimes have been committed. And even those few prisoners who receive pardons may be known as "ex-cons" for the rest of their lives.

There is no accurate census of the number of current and former criminals in our society. Various states and the federal government have extensive fingerprint banks, but these contain prints of suspects released without prosecution, including those arrested by mistake, and prints of others not caught up in the criminal justice system. Retrieval or expungement of fingerprints and other arrest records of those totally innocent or improperly accused is nearly impossible, even upon court order and with a willing police agency. Thus no one knows how many persons convicted of serious crimes—felonies—currently and in the past are alive in our society right now.

Cohort Measurement

Even if every criminal justice agency could develop adequate ways of counting the criminals it handles and accurate reporting procedures, they would be of value only for administrative purposes such as personnel allocation, budgeting, and other intra-agency coordination. Tracking cases across agencies through major decision points is not possible with summary statistics, yet the current demand for total system evaluation cannot be met without such measurement.

Full computerization of criminal justice processing of persons at all stages in the system is increasingly viewed as the only satisfactory solution to the need for complete and accurate data. The tracking of specific persons across the entire criminal process is sometimes known as **cohort analysis**. ("Cohort" here means all persons arrested on a given day or during a given week.) This technique begins with a sample of perhaps 10,000 persons arrested for felonies in a specific time period and follows their paths and branchings as they are processed deeper into the system or diverted out of it.[11] The technique requires data flow (i.e., data on individuals A, B, and C from one decision point to another, not just arrest or charging summaries) and can answer questions in ways not possible with only summarized tabulations. But most criminal justice systems currently lack the facilities required for cohort analysis.

During the large-scale research efforts of the 1960s and 1970s, the deplorable state of criminal justice statistics was fully revealed. Since then, high priority has been given to the development of criminal justice reporting systems, but despite strong federal pressure and significant amounts of federal funds granted to the states, data-reporting systems in most jurisdictions are still primitive.

Implications for Criminal Justice

The Need for Accurate Crime Data

If crime control efforts are to be accurately evaluated, there is a need for good, easily retrievable data covering the entire spectrum of the criminal justice process, not just crimes reported to the police. Important questions are being asked today about such postcrime matters as bail-or-jail determinations, indictments, acquittals or convictions, probation and probation revocation decisions, prison and prisoners, and parole and parolees.

Adequate statistics are needed by all criminal justice agencies to support sensible budget forecasts and to accurately assess the current achievements or failures of these agencies. Furthermore, such statistics are essential for planning innovative projects and assessing experimental programs. Most criminal justice agencies keep some form of **summary data** on persons processed. Summary data are kept by a simple tabulation, known as **gatekeeping**, similar to the tabulation used by a prison when counting the number of prisoners who come in and go out. By tabulating the number of people handled routinely by a criminal justice agency, an accurate picture of agency practice is established.

It is probable that accurate gatekeeping is found only in correctional agencies, where it is both a matter of legal accountability and a necessity for feeding and housing inmates. Reports of the arrest activities of police are required as a part of the booking procedure, but prearrest contact with citizens and suspects is rarely a matter of record. The largest gap in gatekeeping data may be found in prosecutors' offices and trial courts. In most cases, statistical reports from district attorneys or trial judges are not required annually, and even summary statistics can be retrieved only with great difficulty. This problem may be changing. Aided by federal funds, many prosecutors today are using computer techniques to screen serious cases for high-priority prosecution decisions.

Obstacles to Collection of Accurate Crime Data

There are many obstacles to collecting even rudimentary crime statistics. The criminal justice system is composed of relatively independent agencies, each with its own reporting forms, data needs, and traditional ways of doing things. Some agencies are municipal, some are county, others are statewide. Our criminal justice agencies rely on different budgets and many are indifferent to gathering information for other than immediate and local use.[12]

The entire criminal justice system is not only public, it is politically volatile as well. The result is that most criminal statistics are potentially embarrassing to past claims of effectiveness. Most crimes are *not* solved by arrest; prosecutors often accept guilty pleas to lesser offenses than are really committed; judges too often show disparity in their sentences; and few offenders are rehabilitated in correctional programs. Inevitably, some agencies, when offered elaborate computer devices that could provide full and accurate statistics, but which would also open their records to public accounting, show little enthusiasm for new reporting systems.

In addition to the application of data flow techniques to entire criminal justice jurisdictions, there is also a trend toward standardization of reporting systems so that cross-jurisdictional comparisons can be made. A major computer program, SEARCH, funded by the federal government, is aimed at integrating the reporting systems of all states. This requires a variety of technical modifications ranging from shared definitions of crimes, decision steps, and common terms (e.g., "frisk," "arrest," "initial appearance") to the adoption of common points and techniques of data retrieval.[13]

Increasing pressures for more accurate crime data along with the creation of large, secure, available data banks may indicate that a much clearer picture of our crime problem is developing. As with many technological revolutions, there is a danger that too much will be promised by, and too much expected from, electronic techniques. However elaborate, these devices will simply measure crime and evaluate programs; it is unlikely that they will do much to relieve the crime problem. Computers may be valuable aids in quickly identifying suspects, in suggesting ways to reduce delays in the courts, or, in their most sophisticated form, in providing data about associational patterns from which criminal conspiracies can be inferred. But it is unlikely that they will be able to identify specific causal factors in criminality, for our knowledge of the origins of criminal behavior is so fragmentary that we are unable to formulate many basic questions. Computers can respond only to precise questions; they cannot theorize or conceptualize on their own.

Also, the uncertainty of crime data makes it difficult for criminal justice agencies to sensibly anticipate trends and future needs. In this regard criminal justice is unlike other bureaucratic endeavors. Educational systems, for instance, can anticipate with some accuracy the numbers of students to be enrolled from one year to the next. And private corporations go to great effort to control their supplies of raw materials, labor, transportation, and support. But criminal justice agencies operate in relative darkness in terms of available data.

Difficulties in gathering data also point up another set of questions regarding criminal justice. What do we expect the agencies of criminal justice to accomplish? If we have difficulty determining how much crime exists from one time to another, or from one jurisdiction to another, how then can we place realistic expectations on the agents of justice?

THE MANY PURPOSES OF CRIME CONTROL

In the contemporary world statistical data is sought, valued, published, and explained in virtually every social context. Corporate profits and losses, market share, ratings, batting averages, yards per carry, the stock market, body counts, military or social welfare budgets—all revolve around numbers and statistical data. Computer technology has developed more rapidly than our ability to comprehend and apply data in many cases.

The current emphasis on crime data, as politicians and news commentators monitor the fluctuations of crime rates, arrests, prison populations, and other factors, has produced an increasing impatience with our failure to lower crime rates or increase arrests or lessen prison populations. People accustomed to looking to the bottom line, to the charts and graphs of industrial or economic progress, sometimes expect criminal justice agencies to demonstrate an ability to progress, to improve, to *win the war against crime*. If corporations were no more successful at improving statistical performance than criminal justice agencies are, it seems, they would go bankrupt.

One of the reasons comparisons of the criminal justice system with other large complex organizations, such as the armed forces or giant industrial corporations, are inappropriate is that the basic purposes of the criminal justice system are many and varied, and conflicts within and between the various agencies of criminal justice are not unusual. In corporate endeavors there usually is some agreement about objectives such as profits, growth, and perhaps public service. No such consensus exists about the specific purposes of the criminal justice system. Varied purposes are expressed, and there is often incongruity between both long-range and short-range objectives. For instance, police agencies want to lock offenders up; parole boards want to turn them loose. Police want to catch lawbreakers easily and quickly; courts demand the police carry out their duties in accordance with the cumbersome requirements of search warrants, warnings, and other due process procedures.

These multiple purposes compound the complexity of criminal justice processing. Although its principal objectives are to control crime and to maintain public order, the system rests on a set of multiple and occasionally conflicting beliefs and expectations as to how crime control and public order are best achieved. Some of these expectations, such as control through the punishment of violators, are ancient in origin, dating from the earliest conceptions of ordered society and drawing their philosophic justifications from ideas about human nature, sin, and repentance. Others, such as the rehabilitation of offenders, are latter-day products of social science, stemming from more modern concepts of behavior, personality, and change. Still others, such as the accurate and fair separation of the guilty from the innocent, come from our democratic political ideology, which stresses individual liberty, curbs on state power, and proper and humane treatment of even the worst among us.

In short, a variety of expectations about crime control affect the process of the criminal justice system. These expectations ebb and flow in their relative importance as times and philosophies change. All exist simultaneously, coloring every decision from the drafting and enacting of statutes to parole revocation. Several of these expectations are discussed below.

To Control and Prevent Crime

Whether short-range or long-range, the overall objectives of criminal justice fall into two general sets of purposes: the **control of crime** by solving crimes, arresting suspects, and processing and imprisoning offenders, and the **prevention of crime** through this processing or by other means. The crime control objective deals with the immediate situation and rests on the discovery of *past* criminal behavior, whereas crime prevention is *forward-looking,* forecasting and forestalling future crimes by present interventions. It is necessary to be aware of both control and prevention purposes, for only by such awareness can we explain certain legislative, court, and administrative agency activity.

It can be argued, of course, that control and prevention are so closely related as to be indistinguishable. For example, the purpose of the arrest, conviction, and correctional processing of an offender may be rehabilitation, with the aim of preventing future crimes. Or using marked police cars in high-crime neighborhoods may be designed to deter and therefore prevent criminal acts. Obviously, the two purposes become intertwined, though one or the other is usually given priority. The *use of force* by the police is primarily a control issue, but the *show of force* by police is future-directed and, in this respect, preventive in nature.

To Detect, Arrest, Convict, and Incarcerate Offenders

This is the most immediate, direct, and traditional purpose of criminal justice processing. The question of how best to do it, and to know when it has been done, is the source of many conflicts about criminal justice. In this respect, two major models can be applied, the crime control model and the due process model. Each generates disagreements about its worth and creates problems about how to achieve and measure success.[14] The crime control model holds that the criminal justice process should be invoked often, vigorously, and fully against criminals in our society. Measures of effectiveness of this position include high arrest rates, the charging of the most serious crimes possible, the convicting of offenders as charged, and the sentencing of violators to maximum terms.

The due process model stance is that a better and more effective criminal justice system can be achieved when the system acts reluctantly and when its purpose is to divert as many suspects as possible from criminal justice processing or, if arrest and conviction must occur, to remove offenders from the system as rapidly as possible; when processing defendants to charge only according to what seems best for the individual; and after conviction to put the offender on probation or in a community correctional facility for a short period of time.

Which approach is better or more effective is open to debate and generates some strong conflicts about the basic nature of crime control in our society. For example, there is the question of whether a "good" police department is one that makes many arrests or is one that keeps the streets "cool" by adjusting conflicts, using arrest only as a last resort. There is also the question of whether the presumption under which the sentencing judge operates following conviction should be to imprison the offender unless he or she has a good record or to consider probation first, incarcerating only if the offender has a bad record.

To Punish Criminals

There is little doubt that punishment of violators is an important purpose of the criminal justice process. The **punitive ideal**, though among the most ancient approaches to crime control, is still a force of major significance. To some punishment is an end in itself, consistent with our moral support for an eye-for-an-eye concept of justice. But the punishment aspects of our crime control system are also designed to compel conformity by hurting violators, much as a dog is conditioned to obey or naughty children are spanked to teach them to be good. And punishment has a related though separate purpose: It is intended to *deter potential violators*; to frighten them off, by demonstrating that crime does not pay (see the next section).

The application of punishment to law violators *in proportion to the seriousness of their offenses* is the cornerstone of criminal codes and sentencing structures. Beyond this, however, the punitive theme runs through all the determinations of the criminal process, coloring the perceptions of all participants, including suspects and defendants as well as agency personnel, its influence reflected even in uniforms, accouterments, and physical settings. At a minimum, the criminal justice process is designed to be stern and unpleasant; at its extreme, it is frankly punitive and indeed can put lawbreakers in cages for life or impose the death penalty on those who have wrongfully killed other people.

Though punitiveness may be muted by competing objectives, there is no pretense, official or otherwise, that the system is designed to further the best interests of those processed. This contrasts sharply with the underlying philosophies of other systems where state power is employed to compel conformity, as in public schooling, hospital commitment of the mentally ill, or the juvenile justice system. From start to finish, the criminal process is "the state *versus* John Doe," not as in delinquency processing, "the state *in the interest of* Johnny Doe."

Punishment is an aura pervasive throughout the process. It accounts in part for police behavior, which is typically far from friendly, even when correct, once the process starts. It is reflected in the prosecutor's need for convictions to maintain community support. It is visible in emotionally cool, stern, and formal court proceedings. It is epitomized by prisons. The punitive function of the criminal justice system not only has a long tradition, but even today it is never far from the surface at any decision point or in any program. Attempts to change criminal processing inevitably confront punishment requirements.

Early advocates of probation and parole achieved their objectives by demonstrating lower cost and greater effectiveness, but they also had to argue strongly that community sentences were indeed punishment. And modern correctional facilities, unwalled and without bars or cells, have been accepted slowly and grudgingly for fear they would diminish the punitive purposes of walled and turreted maximum-security prisons.

To Deter Criminals

Another goal of the criminal justice system is to effectively deter crime by stopping or frightening off potential lawbreakers. It is widely believed that permanent prevention of crime, if attainable at all, will require a basic modification of cultural values, the revision of opportunity structures, the reorganization of social class structures, and the elimination of economic imbalance. Personnel in criminal justice agencies generally see their preventive task in more modest terms. For the most part, *prevention* in the crime control context means short-range **deterrence** of potential violators.

Whether deterrence is actually possible is debatable, for inference about its effectiveness is essentially negative. How many people would commit crimes if they were not deterred is not known. There have been limited studies of certain offenses where a deterrent function has been observed. These tend to be planned, rational offenses where the chances of getting caught are immediate and certain. For example, in regard to more rational offenses like stealing, posting a police officer near an apple barrel is likely to reduce the number of apples stolen. But emotional crimes and crimes of passion, such as murder or child molestation, are difficult, perhaps impossible, to deter.

Two major approaches to deterrence are employed in the criminal justice system, and both generate controversies about their effectiveness and their appropriateness in our society. The first is based on creating a belief in the certainty of criminal justice processing and the hope that the severity of official reactions when offenders are caught will deter other people from initiating criminal activities. To this end there is a desire to make the criminal justice system appear *omnipresent*, its agents *visible*, arrest *certain*, and justice *swift*. At the police agency level, this involves such issues as the use of clearly marked prowl cars, uniformed officers with sidearms, techniques of frequent, random patrolling, and so on. It is expected that courts will be somber and dignified, with the raised bench and the black robes of the judges indicating seriousness of purpose in court proceedings—a posture critics feel is diminished by the more casual, juvenile court form of processing. It is expected that prisons too should look like prisons to those on the outside as well as to those incarcerated. The wall and the gun turrets of the maximum-security prison have dual functions: to control the inmates within and to demonstrate the severe price of crime to potential offenders on the outside.

A variation on this approach, though also designed to create an aura of certain arrest and stern punishment, maintains that the *system should be nearly invisible* while nurturing the belief that it is operating efficiently. Police should be primarily under-cover, like narcotics officers who infiltrate the drug subculture to make arrests. Statistics on the effectiveness of law enforcement efforts should be kept confidential, and a sort of "crime does not pay" posture should be maintained.

The second approach to deterrence involves taking actions that *prevent opportunities for crime* to occur or that *assure quick discovery* of violators. Devices used range from television cameras in banks to exact-fare requirements on public transportation. In New York City a public announcement that many off-duty police officers were driving cabs markedly reduced the incidence of taxi holdups for a period of time. Airplane hijacking was once a serious problem that elicited a strong demand for prevention. In addition to using a constructed "profile" of a skyjacker to screen passengers, airlines are required by federal law to subject passengers to luggage search and metal detection screening before boarding aircraft.

Experiments with other deterrence techniques range from the relatively simple and noncontroversial placing of "ghost" (unmanned) police cars distantly visible along superhighways to control traffic to the use of police dogs in surveillance and park patrol. But one problem with all deterrence techniques is the extent of the noncriminal population's willingness to tolerate such inconveniences as exact-change rules, searches upon entering public transportation, or the saturation of neighborhoods with armed police.

The common desire to use the crime control system to deter potential wrong-doers from committing crimes is closely related to the punitive ideal. As might be expected, making examples of those caught and proved guilty is widely believed to be effective in achieving this purpose. This is the basic argument of those favoring severe sentences, including the death penalty.

However, deterrence has a broader base. The *show of force* may accomplish conformity as well as or better than the *use of force*. Consequently, many practices in all agencies are influenced in some degree by deterrent objectives. The omnipresence of police on patrol, the secrecy of grand juries, the public nature of trials and sentencings by judges, and the visibility of prisons and other correctional agencies not only display the punitive nature of the system, but demonstrate its readiness to act.

While some attempts are made in practice to individualize justice by fitting the punishment to the characteristics and circumstances of the individual being processed, the action taken in a particular case is more routinely determined in part by its probable effect on others or, more abstractly, by how it may affect a general "respect for the law." An unobserved police officer may release a suspect with a reprimand; in similar situations but faced with an observing crowd, the officer may feel compelled to make an arrest. Sentences meted out in high-publicity cases tend to be more severe than otherwise. Wherever and whenever decisions about a suspect, defendant, or offender are partly based on considerations of the likely effects on others, including the "public," the deterrent function is being served.

To Protect the Community

There is a general expectation that the criminal justice process will protect the community from continued depredations of criminals. To accomplish this, authorities are permitted to take physical custody of suspects as well as of offenders and to restrain

them, subject to legislative and court limitations and controls. The ultimate power of restraint is symbolized by the maximum security incarceration of convicted felons. In fact, a primary purpose of imprisonment is the **restraint** and **incapacitation** of offenders to protect the community, an objective that most prisons achieve very well indeed. This is often overlooked when prisons are labeled as failures because they do not successfully rehabilitate many prisoners.

Restraint for community protection is not limited to imprisonment and other postconviction processes. It is an important function from the very outset of the process. Police may arrest one suspect at gunpoint, handcuff him or her, and hold the individual in close detention until a bail hearing. Another suspect may be arrested without the use of any force or hardware, and experience little physical inhibition. Often high bail and always preventive detention reflect the community protection function. It may also be seen at the charging decision; certainly community protection is a consideration in plea negotiation. Sentencing alternatives directly reflect this function, and it is a major factor in determining probation conditions, prison program and housing assignments, selection for parole, and parole revocation. The entire correctional process rests always on a balance between the needs and desires of the offender and concerns for community protection, even in systems giving high priority to rehabilitative programs.

To Correct, or Rehabilitate, Criminals

It is geneally expected that the criminal justice process will somehow reform or rehabilitate those caught up in it, or at least will not make them worse. It is recognized that virtually all persons who are processed, even those convicted and sentenced to life imprisonment, will eventually return to the community. Thus it behooves participants and agencies to take actions designed to enable their charges to live law-abiding lives once they are discharged from the process. Some argue that this may be accomplished by conditioning individuals through punishment to avoid the unpleasant consequences of criminal activity, much as animals can be conditioned to avoid painful stimuli. But more commonly today, agencies attempt to provide positive programs designed to rehabilitate prison inmates by changing their attitudes and teaching them new vocational skills; they also work to reintegrate offenders by assisting them to adjust to normal community living.

24

Although the corrective function has traditionally been assigned to postconviction agencies like prisons and probation and parole services, there is an increasing awareness that all stages of criminal justice have relevance to the corrective function. In this respect the police are seen as an intake agency, making a wide range of decisions within their discretion that have long-range effects on the fate of the persons with whom they have contact. The way an arrest is made, the amount of force used, the police behavior toward the suspect, and so on may influence the detainee's self-conception so as to harden his or her criminal attitudes or to have the opposite and more desirable effect of creating respect for the police and, more generally, for the legal process. Police diversion of suspects to community treatment resources rather than incarceration is seen as a corrective decision by many observers. The police rarely think of themselves as social workers, but the basic nature of their operations is increasingly seen—by the police as well as by others—to be critical to the overall objective of rehabilitation.

In the same manner, the discretion of the prosecutor to select among charges or to divert and not charge at all may be exercised with corrective purposes in mind. A basic motivation in plea negotiation is to individualize the consequences of conviction, rather than simply to avoid trial. And a trial itself may have corrective relevance. An opportunity to be heard, a day in court, a fair hearing have purposes beyond fact finding, perhaps acting to dispel cynicism and the belief in "railroading" not uncommonly expressed by offenders hurried through a guilty plea at a brief arraignment. Sentencing discretion is often delegated to courts in the expectation that the judge's choice will not only satisfy the punitive ideal but serve a corrective function as well.

The corrective function perhaps more than any other purpose of the criminal justice system ties together the discrete stages of the criminal justice process. From the perspective of this function it can be seen that decisions made at one point have relevance elsewhere, and that any overall function is ultimately served by the degree of congruence of all decisions.

Creation of an Ordered Society

It has been said that if criminals did not exist, they would have to be created, for they provide a necessary common enemy, a group of scapegoats, against whom we can measure our own righteousness.[15] The efficiency and the vengeance elements of the criminal justice system are reinforced by other elements that are more symbolic and ceremonial.

The pomp and rituals of the criminal court, the starkness of prisons, and the presence of the police with sidearms are all visible embodiments of "justice" that serve to assure order and protection from disorder in our daily lives. Tradition and symbolism are not only important parts of the system, but occasionally they may be impediments to what appear to be rational and sensible reforms. There is a tendency, particularly among professional people within the criminal justice system, to attribute to the system a high degree of rationality and to assume that logic and research will bring about desired and needed changes. This is rarely the case. It can be demonstrated, for example, that small, modern prisons—rooms instead of cells, only a fence for perimeter security, inmates dressed in civilian clothing, free to move about the institution and eligible for work release and furloughs—are not only more effective but are much cheaper than warehousing inmates in walled maximum-security prisons. But whenever such correctional facilities have been proposed, there has been great opposition based on the widely held belief that prisons are not supposed to be this way, that such quarters are too pleasant to be prisons, and that they would weaken the deterrent function of imprisonment. Most of us have deeply ingrained opinions about the way prisons should be, the way police officers should dress, and the way judges should act when on the bench. The proponent of change may be frustrated by what appear to be illogical components of the criminal justice system if he or she fails to take into account the important symbolic value of those components.

The desire for an *ordered* and *safe society* implies more than the visible presence of agencies of justice, giving an appearance of law and order. There is also a demand that the system be effective, and that somehow the police, courts, and other agencies make our streets and neighborhoods safe and create an environment where both the business and the pleasure of our people can take place freely and safely. If, indeed, this is expected of our criminal justice system, it has failed ruefully in its task, particularly in the heart of our metropolitan areas. Despite a federally declared "war on crime," the Safe Streets and Omnibus Crime Control Act, the extensive use of experimental crime control programs, and the pouring of federal money into law enforcement efforts from 1968 to 1981, many of our streets, neighborhoods, parks, and schools are neither safe nor orderly. It has been both easy and popular to blame these failures of crime control efforts on liberal court decisions, which over the past few decades have greatly expanded the rights of defendants at virtually all stages of criminal processing. In fact, this argument was a major issue in the Presidential election campaign of 1968 (a year that saw street rioting, looting, and burning in over a hundred different cities) and has influenced Presidential appointments in the Supreme Court in the years since.

The problem, however, is much more difficult and will not be ameliorated by merely establishing a liberal-conservative balance on the Supreme Court. An exceedingly complex set of forces have joined to create what the French sociologist Émile Durkheim long ago termed "anomie,"[16] a state of normlessness, of uncertainty of goals, purposes, identities, roles, procedures, and norms necessary for an ordered society to function. During the late 1960s, the frustration, rage, and increased political awareness of the poor, combined with youth protesting the Vietnam War, culminated in the resurgence of a revolutionary ethic manifested by the widespread outbreak of demonstrations and riots. Law enforcement was viewed as the enemy; the constable of yesterday became the "pig" of the war years. While the ardor and some of the rhetoric of those years cooled with the ending of the Vietnam War, anti-Establishment attitudes have persisted in the form of cynicism and suspicion during the revelations of illegal activities by officials close to every President since then. Disillusionment with the system continues today as we face a series of world crises, budget problems at home, high unemployment (particularly among minorities), racial discrimination, and all our other woes. All this means that our attempts to build and maintain an ordered society are much more complex and controversial today than in the past. In recent years roving and predatory youth gangs have elicited curfews, riot control measures, and all of the other facets of the show-of-force stance of the Vietnam War years. With an increasing population, an unstable economy, and a general feeling of hopelessness among many of our youth, the maintenance of an ordered society is perhaps the major challenge of our time and one of the most pressing and difficult tasks facing the criminal justice system. And undoubtedly such a task is beyond the limited abilities of the police, the courts, and correction facilities. This is especially true when the total budgets of criminal justice agencies are taken into account.

SUMMARY

We have introduced the definition and measurement of crime in the United States. Crime is a legal concept, of course, and in this chapter we have made distinctions between old common law crimes, acts evil in themselves, and newer offenses defined by legislatures in our modern, industrial society. We have drawn an important distinction between serious crimes—felonies—and lesser offenses—misdemeanors and violations. We have also distinguished between violent crimes against persons and property offenses.

We have discussed many of the difficult problems of accurate crime measurement. The *Uniform Crime Reports*, issued annually by the FBI, detail the number of serious crimes reported to or discovered by police agencies ("crimes known to the police") and also those crimes "solved," to police satisfaction anyway, by the arrest of suspects ("crimes cleared by arrest").

Methods of crime measurement other than police reports have also been described. These include surveys designed to discover the number of crime victims (or at least persons who claim to have been victimized in the past year) and self-report studies where individuals, in a confidential survey, indicate whether they have *committed* crimes and, if so, what kinds and how often.

The need for better crime data is obvious. But the difficulties of developing sophisticated computer methods of tracking cases through the system ("cohort analysis") are immense and not yet solved. Finally, there is some resistance to gathering better crime data on the part of the crime control agencies themselves. It may be that agency reluctance to develop better measurement techniques is as important an obstacle to collecting more accurate data as the absence of the technological means to measure crime control processing.

Through various charts and graphs we have summarized what is known about the extent of ordinary crime in our society. And it is a sad fact that our crime rate is among the highest of any nation in the world.

It was also noted that measuring crime is quite different from, though clearly related to, counting the number of criminals who are in our society. Not only may one criminal commit many crimes, but criminals accumulate from year to year as new lawbreakers are added to the residue of those convicted earlier. Generally the number of crimes is counted yearly, but the number of criminals, in or out of prison, continues to build up.

The need for better and newer types of crime measurement was discussed. And it was noted that there are reasons, on the part of some criminal justice agencies, for not wanting more accurate crime data.

With all the types of crimes and problems associated with crime measurement, the logical questions are: What do we expect the agencies of criminal justice to accomplish? How can we place realistic expectations on criminal justice if we are unable to accurately measure crime, and thereby assess the effectiveness of criminal justice?

With these questions in mind, we have described the various purposes of the criminal justice network as espoused by Americans at various times and places.

Notes

1. John M. Scheb and John M. Scheb, II, *Criminal Law and Procedure* (St. Paul, MN: West, 1989), pp. 6–7.
2. President's Commission on Law Enforcement and Administration of Justice, *The Challenge of Crime in a Free Society* (Washington, DC: U.S. Government Printing Office, 1967), p. 1.
3. *Uniform Crime Reports, 1990,* U.S. Department of Justice, Federal Bureau of Investigation, Crime in the United States (Washington, DC: U.S. Government Printing Office, 1991).
4. An excellent critical analysis of the limitations and use of the FBI index is available. See Robert M. O'Brien, *Crime and Victimization Data* (Beverly Hills, CA: Sage, 1986);

see also Michael J. Hindelang, "The Uniform Crime Reports Revisited," *Journal of Criminal Justice* 2, no. 1 (Spring 1974): 1.

5. *Uniform Crime Reports, 1990,* U.S. Department of Justice, Federal Bureau of Investigation, Crime in the United States, 1990 (Washington, DC: U.S. Government Printing Office, 1991).

6. U.S. Department of Justice, Bureau of Justice Statistics, *Criminal Victimization in the United States, 1990* (Washington, DC: U.S. Government Printing Office, 1991).

7. Ibid.

8. Ibid.

9. James S. Wallerstein and Clement J. Wyle, "Our Law-Abiding Law-Breakers," *National Probation* 25 (1947): 107. For more recent and similar findings see Delbert S. Elliott, David Haizinga, and Suzanne Ageton, *Explaining Delinquency and Drug Use* (Beverly Hills, CA: Sage, 1985).

10. The most common categories of known or suspected criminals compiled by the police include the names of alleged gamblers, prostitutes, narcotics pushers, and sex deviates, particularly rapists and child molesters. Specialized police units also frequently maintain lists of reputed organized crime members and alleged political extremists.

11. See Marvin E. Wolfgang, Robert M. Figlio, and Thorsten Sellin, *Delinquency in a Birth Cohort* (Chicago: University of Chicago Press, 1972), where those boys who were born in Philadelphia in 1945 and who resided there from their tenth to their fourteenth birthdays were defined as the cohort; for a more recent publication see Marvin E. Wolfgang, Terence P. Thornberry, and Robert M. Figlio, *From Boy to Man—Delinquency to Crime* (Chicago: University of Chicago Press, 1987).

12. Carl E. Pope, *Offender-Based Transaction Statistics: New Directions in Data Collection and Reporting,* U.S. Department of Justice, Law Enforcement Assistance Administration (Washington, DC: U.S. Department of Justice, 1975). See also, generally, R. McCleary, B.C. Nienstedt, and J.M. Erven, "Uniform Crime Reports on Organizational Outcomes: Three Time Series Quasi-Experiments," *Social Problems* 29 (1982): 361.

13. The System for Electronic Analysis and Retrieval of Criminal Histories (SEARCH) was launched in 1969. It was designed to explore the potentialities and feasibility of an on-line system that would permit interstate exchange of offender history files, as maintained by state and local criminal justice agencies. Funded by the federal Law Enforcement Assistance Administration (LEAA), Project SEARCH has already entered its implementation stage. See publications of SEARCH Group, Inc., now covering such topics as computerized criminal histories, criminal justice, offender-based transaction statistics, correctional resource management, and attribute-based crime reporting (Washington, DC: U.S. Government Printing Office, 1972–1980).

14. Herbert L. Packer, "Two Models of the Criminal Process," *University of Pennsylvania Law Review* 113 (1964).

15. The great sociologist Émile Durkheim once offered this example: "Imagine a society of saints, a perfect cloister of exemplary individuals. Crimes properly so called, will there be unknown; but faults which appear venal to the layman will create there the same scandal that the ordinary offense does in ordinary consciousness. If, then, this society has the power to judge and punish, it will define these acts as criminal and will treat them as such." From Durkheim's *The Rules of the Sociological Method* (New York: Free Press, 1956), pp. 68–69.

16. Durkheim expounded this theory of anomie in several of his major works, including *On the Division of Labor in Society* (Glencoe, IL: Free Press, 1949), and *Suicide* (Glencoe, IL: Free Press, 1958). The term was elaborated on by Robert K. Merton in a famous article, "Social Structure and Anomie," *American Sociological Review* 3 (October 1938): 672–682.

SUGGESTED READINGS

Bureau of Justice Statistics, *Report to the Nation on Crime and Justice*, 3rd ed. (Washington, DC: U.S. Government Printing Office, 1992).

Gary S. Green, *Occupational Crime* (Chicago: Nelson-Hall, 1990).

Robert F. Meier (ed.), *Major Forms of Crime* (Beverly Hills, CA: Sage, 1984).

Robert M. O'Brien, *Crime and Victimization Data* (Beverly Hills, CA: Sage, 1985).

DISCUSSION QUESTIONS

1. How do you rank the seriousness of the various types of crimes described in the chapter? Discuss.

2. Discuss the relative strengths and weaknesses of the UCR and the NCS. Which provides the most useful data in understanding the amount of crime in the United States?

3. Why do victims not report their crimes to the police? Have you ever been a victim of crime and chosen not to report it? Why not?

4. What obstacles or impediments to accurate crime statistics are produced by criminal justice personnel?

5. Why is crime data important? Or is it?

6. Describe the various purposes of crime control.

2

Ideological Framework and Models of Crime Control

In Timisoara, Romania, Josif Dorulescu was asleep in his home with his wife and four children, unaware that in the street outside their house the police were preparing to arrest him. They had kept Josif under close surveillance for weeks. They had installed an electronic listening device in his home months ago, and now, after an informant had given them new information, the police were prepared to question him extensively. His crime was that he had entertained a group of friends in his home and had been overheard criticizing the dictator, Nicolae Ceausescu. In Romania one could never be sure who to trust, or could not know which friend or neighbor was an informant for the secret police.

At 3:00 a.m. in the morning, the police stormed through the front door without warning. Mary Dorulescu heard them first as she slept next to her husband, and her shout of alarm was heard throughout the house. The four children and Mary were roughly pushed against the wall of their kitchen and held at gunpoint by seven officers armed with automatic weapons. Then Josif was struck in the face by one of the officers who used his weapon as a club, and the semiconscious husband and father was dragged outside to a waiting police car and taken away.

No warrant had been served, no information was given to the family. Josif was not informed of the charges against him, nor was he allowed to confront his accusers. For 6 days Josif was kept by the police, who questioned him around the clock, denying him sleep. He was beaten repeatedly while his interrogators attempted to make him sign a confession stating he was a traitor. They insisted that he tell them names of other "subversives." He was unable to wash himself, change clothes, or use the toilet.

Josif refused to sign the confession or to give names. Finally, the police dragged him out of the jail and placed him in the back seat of a patrol car in the middle of the night. He thought they were taking him away to shoot him. Instead, they pushed him out of the police car on the street in front of his house, and released him without any further word.

Such was the justice system in Romania in the 1980s. No constitution existed to guarantee individual rights; the power of a despotic dictator was the only law of the land. The police were hand-chosen by the dictator, and special privileges were given to them to assure their total loyalty. The regime was totalitarian, and what occurred to Josif was not uncommon.

Events such as these could not happen in the United States. We see ourselves as a people of law, we value individual rights. Don't we? Yet after an official visit to Romania in 1987, at the very time Josif was in custody, an American businessman praised Romanian society for its very low crime rate. He commented, "I could walk around in downtown Bucharest, the capital city, late at night without fear of being mugged. That sure is not the case in Washington, DC." Indeed, no one at all was allowed to move freely about the streets of Bucharest at night. Constant police patrols and secret police surveillance kept people in their homes for fear of immediate arrest on "suspicion." Thus Romania could claim to have very little crime.

All of us can easily see the differences between the justice system in a totalitarian regime and that in the United States. Sometimes people complain about the slowness associated with due process of law, or wonder aloud why heinous criminals should be allowed any rights at all. "Why don't we just take them out and shoot them?" someone may ask. But the ideological framework and purposes of crime control in the United States prohibit the imposition of law and order at any cost. This chapter explores that ideology and some of the models used to implement it.

About this chapter

All large industrial societies have complex systems of internal crime control. Third World countries and more primitive cultures also have methods to ensure conformity to laws and to punish lawbreakers, but these systems are often simple, direct, uniform, and sometimes brutal. Major countries—the United States, Germany, England, France, Japan, China, Canada, Australia, the Scandinavian countries, for example— have much more complex systems, though unfortunately sometimes they use methods no less brutal than those of more primitive systems.

All societies have about the same types of criminal justice agencies. In Russia, England, or Israel, you will find both city and state police. Courts exist in all countries, as do prosecutors in one form or another. Jails and prisons are found in all countries for the control of domestic lawbreakers. In short, these various crime control systems look very much alike on the surface. One can ask directions from a traffic cop in Paris or Kampala. One can visit prisons on the moors in Scotland or in the Tokyo suburb of Fuchu. Tel Aviv police have both vice and homicide units.

Yet systems of criminal justice differ in significant ways. The major difference lies in the political soil in which each system is planted. This soil is composed partly of the history unique to the country, and partly of the ideals and values underlying the country's form of government. Therefore, the evaluation of any criminal justice system is influenced both by the history of the country and by its political ideology. Crime control in a communist society may superficially look like crime control in a monarchy or a democracy or a fascist state, but it is significantly different.

In this book we are concerned with crime control in a democratic society, our own. Our perceptions of police, prosecutors, courts, and prisons reflect the context of our own history. Our crime control efforts must be evaluated in terms of the personal freedoms guaranteed by our Constitution, in reference to our fundamental political ideology, and in light of all the cherished values of our way of life. Neither arrest nor punishment of offenders can be viewed in a vacuum. No matter that we have a serious crime problem. What we do about it must be measured not only in terms of effectiveness, but by the way our procedures conform to our beliefs in liberty and personal freedom.

This chapter focuses on these beliefs and values. And, in order to provide a context for examining the ways American beliefs and values sometimes conflict with the practical world of criminal justice, we present two models of criminal justice: the crime control (conservative) model and the due process (liberal) model. For not only does our criminal justice system come from the political soil of our country—it also engages Americans in political debate. No issues are more political than those related to criminal justice practice and philosophy.

CRIME CONTROL IN A DEMOCRACY

Observers inside and outside the criminal justice network have often found reason to denounce American criminal justice as ineffective, unjust, or corrupt. It is easy to point to a high and increasing crime rate to show that, despite slogans to the contrary, crime *does* pay, and to ridicule the clumsiness and inefficiency of many of our crime control agencies. Examples of cruelty, indifference, incompetence, and corruption abound. This kind of criticism becomes especially intense when a so-called crime wave occurs or when particularly bad crimes are not solved.

Demands for quicker arrests, for swifter and surer trials and punishments, rest on the assumption that effectiveness—catching criminals and punishing them—is the *only* purpose of our crime control efforts. This is superficial, for American crime control philosophy is much more complex. If the sole objective of crime control, subject to no checks or balances, was arrest followed by severe punishment, this could be accomplished easily. Widespread use of electronic eavesdropping could provide

The public was outraged when Milwaukee police officers made a fatal error in judgment and left Konerak Sinthasomphone in Jeffrey Dahmer's home (see the introduction to Chap. 7). Despite the ideals of our crime control system, mistakes are made.

police with a much longer list of suspects. Mandatory use of lie detectors or truth serum would convict many more criminals and eliminate the need for jury trials. Experiments with chemotherapy or psychosurgery might be more effective than the present methods of probation, jail, and prison in restraining criminals.

However, even the strongest advocate of "law and order" is likely to retreat in the face of the full implications of unrestrained wiretapping, sweep searches, widespread preventive detention, long sentences, chemical or surgical manipulation of offenders, and dungeonlike prisons. Most of us will accept the fact that there are certain techniques, procedures, and devices more repugnant to our national ideals than inefficiency in law enforcement. Cruel enforcement devices in totalitarian regimes such as Ceausescu's Romania horrify most Americans.

Even in our own system we can find, upon close examination, some awful practices that, as Justice Frankfurter put it, "shock the conscience."[1] To control the misuse of state power, we have a series of complex checks and balances in our criminal justice system. The complexity is not accidental, nor does it result from mere historical drift. Rather, the taproots of our criminal justice system are deep in an ideology based on personal freedom and the fundamental worth and dignity of people.

IDEOLOGICAL FRAMEWORK OF CRIME CONTROL

The origins of our political order, expressed in the Declaration of Independence, the Bill of Rights, the Constitution, and the other great documents of our history, rest mainly on the desire to build safeguards that limit the power of the state to intervene in the lives of its citizens. Almost any statement in the Bill of Rights, and several amendments to the Constitution, relate directly to our criminal justice process. Historically, a relatively high proportion of Supreme Court decisions apply Constitutional restraints to uncontrolled crime control efforts.

It is thus fundamental to our ideals and to our system of government that a higher allegiance to principles of individual liberty, fairness, and due process of law must check and control law enforcement efforts, trial court procedures, and correctional treatment. Improper methods of catching criminals, no matter how effective, must not threaten the freedom of society at large.[2]

Constitutional Amendments 4, 5, 6, 8, and 14 set specific standards for criminal justice administration. (See Table 2.1) The Fourth Amendment prohibits illegal searches; the Fifth Amendment protects citizens from self-incrimination; the Sixth Amendment guarantees the right to trial by jury; the Eighth Amendment prohibits cruel and unusual punishment; and the Fourteenth Amendment forbids us to deprive anyone of life, liberty, or property without due process of law. The Supreme Court interprets each of these amendments so as to apply Constitutional protections to day-by-day situations. These foundation blocks of our democratic society are directly applicable to crime control and express our ideological principles.

"A fair trial" is fine as a general value, but it requires careful interpretation as to the kinds of evidence allowed, the permissible techniques of gathering evidence, the acceptable composition of juries, and a great many other issues. The continuous honing of the law, the sifting and winnowing of standards, shapes criminal justice. This process sometimes curbs law enforcement, as in the series of Supreme Court decisions which limited the methods police may use to secure confessions from suspects.[3] And sometimes this process gives impetus to new programs and proposals, as in the series of Supreme Court decisions during the 1960s and 1970s expanding the rights of poor defendants to the assistance of lawyers.[4]

It is not possible to provide here an exhaustive list of all our ideological principles, but it is important to note some of the most basic of these, for they are applied in one way or another at every step in the decision network of the American criminal justice process. Most expressions of our basic values are phrased in broad terms, often vague in language but firm in intent. Each requires careful judicial interpretation as to how it applies to situations arising in the daily activities of the police, prosecutors, courts, and correctional agencies.

The principles that are fundamental to our criminal justice system and that act to curb efficiency in crime control are legion. It should be clear from those listed that our process of criminal justice exists within a complex set of values, expectations, and

Freedom for the individual is a fundamental ideal in our system of government and our criminal justice system.

The Supreme Court: Tilting toward a Conservative Majority

The decisions and actions in the criminal justice system are influenced by the way the U.S. Supreme Court interprets the Constitution and the Bill of Rights. The nine members of the Supreme Court make up the supreme authority on crime control policies and decisions. And the nine justices are nominated by the President for lifetime terms, thereby making them free from political influences.

But are they truly free from politics? Probably not. Indeed, perhaps they should not be. A long time ago a famous Supreme Court Chief Justice, Oliver Wendell Holmes, stated that the Supreme Court responds to "the felt necessities of the time." It is that response to immediate needs that has enabled the Constitution to survive more than 200 years. And those changing needs constantly challenge the wisdom and fairness of the justices.

Immediate needs also make the Supreme Court subject to the political interests of the President, who must nominate justices to sit on it when vacancies occur through death or resignations. Sometimes the political interests of the President lead to attempts to "stack" the Court in order to further a particular political agenda.

For instance, in his election campaign of 1936, Franklin Roosevelt felt he had received a mandate from the people and set out to do something about what he termed the "nine old men" on the Supreme Court who had repeatedly thwarted his New Deal legislation. None of those men evidently intended to resign any time soon, so Roosevelt introduced legislation to add more justices to the Court. He would use those new openings to nominate justices having views which more closely agreed with his own. Members of the Supreme Court saw this move as a serious threat and a dangerous precedent. Two moderate justices on the Court joined with the progressive members and voted to uphold some key New Deal proposals which were dear to President Roosevelt's heart—the minimum wage and Social Security, among others. Roosevelt's arguments for expanding the Court were thereby weakened. And in the months that followed, Roosevelt was given the privilege of nominating new justices as some of the older ones retired.

Three decades later, Richard Nixon, in his acceptance speech at the 1968 Republican National Convention, claimed to speak for another mandate from the people, one arising out of different circumstances. At that time the Supreme Court was headed by Chief Justice Earl Warren, who had served in that position since 1959. Under his leadership the Court had supported civil liberties for persons accused of crimes, and many Americans associated the Court's decisions with a rise in crime and perceived moral decay. Nixon hoped to change the direction of the Court by appointing conservatives to it. He was presented with three opportunities in the course of his Presidency, and nominated three men who were confirmed to the Court by the Senate. However, President Nixon's conservative views were not followed as Harry Blackmun, Lewis F. Powell, Jr., and William Rehnquist still championed civil rights and social causes under the leadership of new Chief Justice Warren Burger after they joined the Court. For instance, death penalty statutes were declared unconstitutional in *Furman v. Georgia* (1972) and a woman's right to abortion was determined in *Roe v. Wade* (1972). Nonetheless, on the whole, a more moderate balance was achieved on the Court, even though conservatives had hoped for more.

Today, the Supreme Court is headed by Chief Justice William Rehnquist, and the present Court has moved past desires that preclude simplistic solutions to crime control problems. Merely to demand greater police efficiency, to call for a "get-tough" policy of enforcement, or to suggest that technological innovations turned loose will reduce crime is to ignore the complexity of the problems. Demands for greater effectiveness of police, prosecutors, courts, and correctional agencies are appropriate, but it must be clearly understood that there are other demands for fairness, propriety, and equal protection that also must be met if we are to retain our identity as a free and humane society.

The Warren Court: Key Decisions

Mapp v. Ohio (1961)
Freedom from unreasonable searches

Miranda v. Arizona (1966)
Individual protection from coerced confessions

Bandy v. United States (1961)
The purpose of bail is to permit pretrial release; persons should be released on personal recognizance if they are poor and cannot afford bail.

The Rehnquist Court: Key Decisions

California v. Acevedo (1991)
Warrantless searches of containers in automobiles is allowed if probable cause exists.

Arizona v. Fulminante (1991)
A coerced confession used at trial can be a harmless error as long as other evidence supports the verdict.

United States v. Salerno (1987)
Pretrial detention is allowed when the defendant is perceived to be a threat to an individual or a community.

the moderate days of the Burger Court. Only one remaining justice was appointed by a Democratic president, Byron White. And the Court has taken a decided turn toward conservatism. The Warren Court was criticized for making unprecedented decisions without legitimate precedents, while the Rehnquist Court is criticized for exhibiting too little respect for prior decisions of the Court as it has overturned them.

The Warren Court and the Rehnquist Court represent opposite ends of the ideological spectrum. The Warren Court upheld the liberal viewpoint of expanding the rights of individuals. The Rehnquist Court espouses the conservative

view of giving government more authority. But the differences in philosophy of the nine justices often result in close votes. In such cases of four-to-four split votes, it is the decision of the ninth justice which determines the direction of the entire Court.

The political swing of the Court, whatever it may be, is thus determined by the viewpoints of the majority of its members. And as all those members are nominated by Presidents who change from time to time and hold different political views, a final word on serious and difficult issues by the Court is perhaps not possible.

Due Process of Law

This general principle, expressed in the Fourteenth Amendment to the Constitution, states that no person shall be deprived of liberty, life, or property without **due process of law**. The scope of due process is broad and necessarily continuously interpreted and refined by appellate court decisions. Currently, though its boundaries are not fixed, it means that the state cannot intervene *arbitrarily or capriciously* in the

TABLE 2.1 *The U.S. Constitution and criminal justice*

We the People of the United States, in Order to form a more perfect Union, establish Justice, insure domestic Tranquillity, provide for the common defence, promote the general Welfare, and secure the Blessings of Liberty to ourselves and our Posterity, do ordain and establish this Constitution for the United States of America.

Article I
Sec. 8: To provide for the punishment of counterfeiting . . . to constitute tribunals inferior to the Supreme Court . . . to define and punish piracies and felonies. . . .
Sec. 9: The privilege of the writ of *habeus corpus* . . . No bill of attainer or *ex post facto* law shall be passed.

Article II
Sec. 2: The President . . . shall have the power to grant reprieves and pardons . . . except in cases of impeachment.

Article III
Sec. 2: The trial of all crimes . . . shall be by jury; and such trials shall be held in the state where the said crimes shall have been committed. . . .

Article IV
Sec. 2: A person charged in any state with treason, felony, or other crime, who shall flee from justice, and be found in another state, shall on demand of the executive authority of the state from which he fled, be delivered up, to be removed to the state having jurisdiction of the crime.

Amendments to the U.S. Constitution
I. Congress shall make no law respecting an establishment of religion, or prohibiting the free exercise thereof; or abridging the freedom of speech, or of the press; or the right of the people peaceably to assemble, and to petition the government for a redress of grievances.

IV. The right of people to be secure in their persons, houses, papers, and effects, against unreasonable searches and seizures, shall not be violated, and no warrants shall be issued, but upon probable cause supported by oath or affirmation, and particularly describing the place to be searched, and the persons or things to be seized.

V. No person shall be held to answer for a capital, or otherwise infamous crime, unless on a presentment or indictment of a grand jury . . . nor shall any person be subject for the same offense to be twice in jeopardy of life or limbs; nor shall he be compelled in any criminal case to be a witness against himself, nor be deprived of life, liberty, or property, without due process of law. . . .

VI. In all criminal prosecutions, the accused shall enjoy the right to expedient public trial, by an impartial jury of the state and district wherein the crime shall have been committed . . . to be confronted with the witnesses against him, to have compulsory process for obtaining witnesses in his favor, and to have the assistance of Counsel for his defence.

VIII. Excessive bail shall not be required, nor excessive fines imposed, nor cruel and unusual punishment inflicted.

XIII. Sec. 1: Neither slavery nor involuntary servitude, except as punishment for crime if the party shall have been duly convicted, shall exist within the United States. . . .

XIV. Sec. 1: . . . No state shall . . . deprive any person of life, liberty, or property, without due process of law; nor deny to any person within this jurisdiction equal protection of laws.

---

lives of its citizens, even those convicted of and sentenced for crimes.[5] Officials must have some appropriate amount and proper kind of *evidence* before a suspect can be arrested, charged with a crime, convicted, sentenced, and punished or rehabilitated.

More rigid procedural requirements are generally required *before* conviction than after. The fullest measure of due process is required and given at trial. A citizen accused of a crime is accorded rights that include notice of specific charges and, at the apex, a trial by a jury of peers. Due process also includes the rights of a defendant to confront accusers, to rebut evidence, to be taken before judicial authority for consideration of bail, to be publicly tried, and to be treated fairly and humanely. The dimensions of due process continue to be litigated, and the trend in the 1960s and 1970s to expand the number of decision points in the criminal procedure where full due process applies has been challenged in the 1980s and 1990s.

Fundamental Fairness

In general, our society holds a strong belief that crime control efforts must be fair even if enforcement efficiency is impaired or guilty people are freed. The concept of **fundamental fairness** is defined by statute or Constitution, and its application is reviewed on a case-by-case basis by appellate courts. Though the limits to fairness are not fixed with finality, the principle is clear. Accused persons are entitled not only to a trial, but specifically to a *fair trial*; confessions may be used to convict an individual by the person's own words, but these *confessions must be obtained in a fair manner*. A suspect may be placed in a police lineup, but must be exhibited fairly; for example, the suspect cannot be the only one handcuffed.

The **balance of advantage** between the state and the accused is also a part of fairness that has become increasingly important. It is clear that both the police and the prosecutor have tremendous resources for investigation and the accumulation of evidence, resources that are not available to most suspects and defendants. One major trend has been toward balancing this difference by providing more resources for defendants, particularly for those who are poor, friendless, and powerless. Various court decisions have extended to the poor the right to have a defense counsel, paid at state expense. Other decisions have allowed the accused greater access to the state's evidence before trial, and have provided trial transcripts to assist poor defendants in appeals.

Whether full equal balance between the accused and the state will ever be achieved is doubtful. It is unlikely, for example, that any defendant will be given the full investigatory power of a police department. But various programs, from legal aid for the poor to pretrial release on recognizance (word of honor) rather than monetary bail, have been developed to make the system fairer for the accused, and to achieve equity between wealthy and powerful defendants and their impoverished counterparts. All these issues will be discussed more fully in the chapters that follow.

Our society believes that Walter Leroy Moody, Jr., indicted for mail bombings in Alabama and Georgia that killed a federal judge and a lawyer, has a right to a fair trial, as do all accused persons. Moody is pictured here with his defense counsel, Bruce Harvey.

Propriety

Not only must the criminal justice system exhibit fairness in its functioning, but proper enforcement of the law also requires that evidence be obtained by the state in a proper fashion. The quantity of evidence alone is not enough for arrest or conviction—the quality of evidence is also important. This is known as **propriety**. In our society, we place restrictions on the way crimes can be solved, the way evidence can be gathered, and the manner in which offenders can be treated. We cannot entrap (trick) innocent persons; wiretaps must be judicially approved; searches must be properly conducted. Our belief in the need for a proper criminal justice system is reflected in the **exclusionary rule**.[6] This rule prohibits the use at trial of improperly obtained evidence, whether that evidence was obtained from an improper search or an improperly conducted interrogation.

Freedom from Cruel and Unusual Punishment

The Eighth Amendment to the Constitution guarantees **freedom from cruel and unusual punishment** and places a limitation on the way we treat even the worst among us. The authors of this amendment were aware of the brutal methods used to punish people in European countries: dismemberment, flogging, burning at the stake, among others practices. We have practically eliminated corporal punishment in criminal justice, at least officially. We no longer beat, brand, maim, or publicly ridicule offenders.

The outer boundaries of cruel and unusual punishment remain highly controversial. In 1972 the U.S. Supreme Court placed a moratorium on capital punishment.[7] Many people believe the death penalty is cruel and unusual punishment: cruel, in that it is cruel to put persons to death, and unusual in that it is rarely imposed at all, and then usually imposed disproportionately against the poor and minorities. But freedom from cruel and unusual punishment is not only an issue in regard to capital punishment. Prison authorities were free through much of our history to set prison punishment policy as they deemed necessary. Sweat boxes, isolation, bread and water diets, flogging, and other cruel practices were allowed, or at least tolerated. The courts turned a deaf ear and a blind eye to such abuses under what has been called the "hands-off" policy of the courts.

Current death penalty statutes and prison procedures include provisions which attempt to avoid the Eighth Amendment prohibitions against cruel and unusual punishments. Likewise, appellate courts no longer refrain from deciding prison issues on the grounds that wardens have been delegated full power to set prison rules and conditions by legislation. It is acknowledged that certain fundamental rights are retained by prisoners, and their effective demand for these rights has become one of the most important and most controversial issues in criminal justice administration. Chief among those rights is the Eighth Amendment right to be free from cruel and unusual punishment.

Equal Protection

It is a Constitutional principle that the law be applied equally and impartially to everyone—rich and poor, black and white, the powerful and the helpless. The idea has often been violated in the past (the monetary basis of bail is a clear example of economic discrimination), and it has been the subject of a great many challenges. This principle of **equal protection** has been affirmed often in recent years by legislatures and appellate courts in issues ranging from representative and fair jury selection to racial disparity in prison populations.

The **rule of law** principle means our system is supposed to be one ruled by the written law, not by the whims of individuals; this principle is closely related to the principle of equal protection. In theory, statutes forbid criminal conduct, courts interpret and apply these laws, and criminal justice agencies—the police, prosecutors, judges, and correctional personnel—carry out the legislative requirements without further interpretation. In fact, however, the criminal justice system does not, and probably cannot, work in such an automatic fashion.

All criminal justice personnel exercise **discretion** in applying the law.[8] Often, as with prosecutors and correctional authorities, such discretion—the authority to choose among alternative actions or not to act at all—is recognized by tradition or by legislative delegation. In other instances, as with the police, no formal discretionary authority exists. Nevertheless, no police agency has sufficient resources to investigate all crimes or to detect and arrest all violators of laws. Nor is this actually desired in daily operation. Police have literally thousands of citizen contacts in which arrests could be made but where, for a variety of reasons, the arrests are not carried out. Likewise, prosecutors often choose among different but possible charges to level against defendants or decide in certain cases not to charge at all. Also, not all people who are actually guilty are so found by judges or juries, and, in sentencing, a judge usually has a number of alternative punishments from fines to imprisonment among which to choose.

In actual operation, criminal justice is *individualized*, that is, choices are made in each case, within limits; laws are not automatically applied. Given the nature of the crime problem, the resources available for crime control, and the often conflicting purposes of criminal justice administration, discretion in the application of criminal law is inevitable.

Perhaps it is also desirable. Full enforcement of all laws would, in the words of Judge Charles Breitel, be "ordered but intolerable."[9] Currently there are various proposals to curb and to control discretion and in some cases, as with mandatory sentences, to eliminate it altogether. The effective control of discretion and attempts to monitor its proper use are other issues of great importance today in criminal justice administration.

Presumption of Innocence

If a number of ordinary citizens were asked to express in a single phrase the basic underlying philosophy of our criminal justice system, a common response would no doubt be the **presumption of innocence**: that a person is presumed innocent until proven guilty. There is little question that this is a very strongly held value. Yet in actual operation, it presents the system with a paradox. The criminal justice process begins and proceeds on an *increasing belief in a person's guilt.*[10] When the police arrest a suspect, they may indeed have in mind the fundamental principle of ultimate legal, "technical" innocence, but their function in the arrest depends on a reasonable belief that the suspect has committed a crime. Similarly, as the arrested person proceeds through the system, evidence of guilt is accumulated and tested by the grand jury or by a judge at a preliminary hearing.

The fullest adherence to the principle of presumption of innocence, perhaps the only place it exists at all, occurs during trial, when strict rules place the burden of proof of guilt on the state. Procedural law requirements, such as that requiring the *Miranda* **warning**[11] to be given in most cases immediately after arrest (notifying the suspect of the rights to remain silent and to have the assistance of counsel), reinforce the presumption of innocence until a trial can be held. Nevertheless, the presumption is primarily an ideal that applies most strictly at the trial. Initial steps in the process necessarily rely not on assumption of innocence, but on a belief in guilt.

MODELS OF CRIMINAL JUSTICE

We can see that our criminal justice decision network must not only be efficient in catching, trying, and locking up criminals but it must act properly, with strict attention to due process of law. Our justice system rests on principles of fairness, equal treatment of all persons under the law, a presumption of innocence at trial, and a ban against using cruel and unusual punishment. With so many competing goals, and considering the complexity of American values, how do we want the criminal justice agencies to operate? No doubt you have heard the debates, even participated in them, regarding how crime control should be accomplished.

In dealing with a mass of information, the social scientist, like the physical scientist, attempts to order the material so that general statements about it may be made. The same is true for criminal justice. We need to provide overviews of criminal justice without becoming lost in the details of its parts.

One such technique applies various "models" of processing to an entire system, with the effect of highlighting different issues. Models embody, or give an operational context to, the values we have discussed above, although the various actors in the criminal justice decision network (lawmakers, police, prosecutors, judges, defense attorneys, corrections professionals, etc.) do not consistently and consciously identify all of those values as being central to their actions. Rather, components of the underlying values dominate particular stages in the process, as we shall see.

Herbert L. Packer has described two models for criminal justice decision-making which are recognized by practitioners and scholars of criminal justice: the **crime control model** and the **due process model** (see Table 2.2).[12] Samuel Walker describes two "theologies" of criminal justice, **conservative theology** and **liberal theology**, which in some ways parallel Packer's models.[13] Walker claims conservatives and liberals have ideas about crime based on faith rather than fact. Conservatives believe, for instance, that the death penalty deters crime despite a lack of conclusive evidence to support their belief. Liberals, on the other hand, support rehabilitation programs for offenders despite the evidence that such programs do not work. According to Walker, such blind belief in the absence of factual evidence is similar to religious belief, and hence his use of the term "theology."

Other models exist, but for the purposes of this text we will focus on the ones suggested by Packer and Walker. We caution, however, that although the application of models to the criminal process has the advantage of a broad, sweeping view of the total system, there is a danger of overgeneralization, of distorting reality into simple yes or no, good or bad views. It is well to keep in mind that the purpose of the models discussed below is to attempt to clarify the assumptions that underlie criminal justice actions (policies) and to examine the conclusions which those assumptions lead us to if they are fully accepted.[14]

The Conservative Crime Control Model

According to Samuel Walker, conservative crime control theology is expressed in the dual slogans, "Get tough on crime" and "Lock 'em up." In this view criminal law makes up an important set of boundaries which mark the limits of behavior. Crime can be controlled by reshaping individuals. Walker writes:

TABLE 2.2 *Conservative versus liberal models of criminal justice*

Conservative crime control model

"Get tough on crime"
"Lock 'em up"
"Unleash the police and prosecutors"
Criminal sanctions resemble parental discipline
Abolish "loopholes" in criminal justice
Punishment-deterrence
Quick, efficient processing of guilty persons
Most important functions of criminal justice include:
- Repression of criminal conduct
- High rate of apprehension and conviction
- Speed and finality of criminal justice processing

Assembly-line conveyer belt justice
Presumption of guilt
Factual guilt

Liberal due process model

Criminal justice resembles a classroom
Emphasis on causes of crime
Due process of law
Criminal justice should be an obstacle course
Quality, not quantity, of arrests and convictions
Control the police and prosecutors
Individual rights
Legal guilt

The world of conservative crime control is modeled on an idealized image of the patriarchal family. Criminal sanctions resemble parental discipline. Minor misbehavior is greeted with a gentle warning; a second misstep earns a sterner reprimand. More serious wrongdoing is answered with severe punishment. The point is to teach the wisdom of correct behavior by handing out progressively harsher sanctions and threatening even more unpleasant punishment if the behavior continues. Communication of this message is the essence of deterrence theory. Many people were raised in this way and raise their own children in the same manner. Their personal experience tells them it works, and they assume that society should work the same way. Conservative thinking about crime is closely related to conservative ideas about the problem of permissiveness. [15]

Such an idealized world is not accurately reflected in either the real world of families or of criminal justice, according to Walker. Incorrigible children do not get the message, they do not accept the authority of parents or criminal justice, and punishment fails to deter.

Conservatives explain this by claiming that the structure of discipline has broken down because of loopholes in the justice system, such as the exclusionary rule, the insanity defense, the *Miranda* warning, and plea bargaining. Also, they claim, if the certainty of punishment were assured, people would get the message and would be deterred from committing crimes. And if punishment were made stronger through mandatory sentences, use of the death penalty, and longer prison terms, punishments would provide a strong deterrence. [16]

The conservative approach is described by Herbert L. Packer in his crime control model. This model pictures the system as essentially geared to quick, efficient processing of guilty persons. When the administrative fact-finders (police and prosecutors, primarily) are allowed to exercise *discretion* within the boundaries of good will and reason, then criminals can be discovered, apprehended, convicted, and incarcerated.

This model is based on the proposition that the most important function of criminal justice is the *repression of criminal conduct*. In order to operate successfully, this model must produce a *high rate of apprehension and conviction*, and do so with maximum speed and finality.

Speed of processing criminals is created through informality and uniformity, a process which seeks to be "swift and sure." Any delay in criminal justice processing is seen as contributing to the public's lack of respect for the criminal justice system. The administrative fact-finders must be unfettered to exercise their discretion and to respond to the huge number of criminal events that come to their attention as efficiently as possible.

Finality is created by minimizing the occasions for challenging or derailing the process. The criminal event must be repressed, disposed of, closed. The volume of cases requiring administrative fact-finding dictates the need to finalize cases in as efficient a manner as possible. Because of the limited resources available to the criminal justice network, and the enormous number of criminal events, it is necessary for decision-makers to assure high rates of arrest, quickly eliminate the innocent, and then convict as many offenders as possible, preferably by guilty pleas. In order to accomplish these goals, administrative fact-finders must utilize discretion (informality), treat all cases and offenders the same (uniformity), and be unencumbered by unnecessary rules and restrictions.

In the crime control model, criminal justice is seen as a factory, taking the raw materials (the criminals) and processing them along in such a way that they, and hence their crimes, are *controlled*. This **assembly-line conveyor belt image of justice** shows an endless stream of cases moving constantly to workers who stand at fixed stations and process the cases one step closer to being closed files. Each successive stage of this screening procedure—prearrest investigation, arrest, postarrest investigation, preparation for trial, trial or entry of plea, conviction, disposition—involves a series of routine operations. Cases must be passed along to a successful conclusion.[17]

Efficiency in processing the large numbers of cases ingested by the criminal justice network is the primary concern of the crime control model. If errors happen— and the crime control model optimistically points to the improbability of error— then such deviation is normal in the same way that a factory expects some standard deviation in its products. Whereas the factory builds in a quality control mechanism and expects a tolerable level of deviation, however, the primary concern of criminal justice as the crime control model sees it is the efficient functioning of the process. If efficiency demands that certain short-cuts be made that may result in less reliability in the fact-finding process, or put another way, if occasionally a truly innocent person is caught up in the "justice production line" and is thereby wrongly processed as criminal, well . . . although an unfortunate set of circumstances, the crime control model would be tolerant of such an error up to the point that the probability of mistakes would interfere with its goal of crime control.

Packer points out that this model rests on a **presumption of guilt**, not as a judicial norm, but as an operational prediction of outcome.[18] That is, cases in which it appears that the persons apprehended are *not* likely the offenders are thrown away, discarded as quickly as possible. The probably innocent are thereby screened out. Then the probably guilty are processed along the "justice conveyer belt." This model places confidence in the administrative fact-finding stages, believing that police and prosecutors have adequate screening abilities to guarantee reliable fact-finding and thereby to accurately identify the guilty individuals. According to the model this fact-finding can best be accomplished through *informal* actions by the agents of the criminal justice system.

It is important to this model, therefore, to place as few restrictions as possible on the police and prosecutors, except where the reliability of their conclusions might be enhanced. If they do their work properly and efficiently, the final stop on the "justice assembly line" will be a negotiated plea and a sanction that is agreed to by both the state and the offender. The crime control model, therefore, offers "two possibilities: an administrative fact-finding process leading (1) to exoneration of the suspect or (2) to the entry of a plea of guilty."[19]

The Liberal Due Process Model

Liberal crime control theology also has an idealized view of the world, according to Walker. This view sees crime as resulting from bad influences from the peer groups or neighborhoods, and from social factors such as discrimination and lack of economic opportunity. If conservatives view the world as a large family, Walker says, liberals view it as a big classroom:

> Rehabilitation, the core liberal policy, involves instructing the criminal offender in the ways of correct behavior. . . . A fundamental article of faith in liberal crime control theology is the belief that people can be reshaped. Much liberal thinking in this area is directed toward a search for an effective rehabilitation program. The history of prison and correctional reform is the story of a continuing search for the Holy Grail of rehabilitation. . . . Faith continues to survive in the face of repeated failure.[20]

Although liberals reject the conservatives' emphasis on individual choice and responsibility in criminal behavior, rehabilitation programs are designed to assist individuals make better choices, that is, noncriminal choices of behavior.[21]

The liberal approach is described by Packer in his due process model. Paradoxically, the criminal justice system can be viewed simultaneously from a due process perspective *and* a crime control perspective. Although the due process model appears to be at the opposite extreme from the crime control model, this does not necessarily follow. Indeed, the ideology of the due process model does not reject the need to control crime, but instead places more emphasis on the formal structure of law than on the ability of police and prosecutors to be able to accurately determine exactly what took place in an alleged criminal event. According to Packer, the due process model resembles a factory that places greater emphasis on quality control than on efficiency. The result, both for the factory and the criminal justice system, may be reduced quantitative output, but the quality of the goods improves.[22]

Whereas the crime control model places great confidence in the administrative fact-finding process, and particularly in the abilities of the police and prosecutors to determine the facts, the due process model sees those administrative fact-finders as needing to be regulated and controlled lest they infringe on the rights of the individual citizen.

The due process model places a higher value on individual rights, on controlling and limiting the power of the state *vis á vis* the individual citizen. Therefore, if the crime control model resembles an assembly line, the due process model looks very much like an **obstacle course**. Rather than allowing for unrestrained actions on the part of the representatives of the state, it places constitutional rules and prohibitions on the process that obstruct the power the state can exercise in regard to its citizens.

Packer explains that in the due process model the successive stages of criminal justice are designed to present formidable impediments to processing an accused person, that the accused person has a full opportunity to discredit the case against him or her, and that only then is the factual case heard publicly by an impartial tribunal. [23]

This obstacle course perception of the criminal process is based on realities just as valid as the assembly line analogy, although it is less frequently encountered in practice since most people have developed a great confidence in police and prosecutors to determine the facts in a case. But the due process model rejects the premise of criminal justice administrative fact-finding skill; it stresses the fallibility of the system and the possibility of error. Packer himself considers people to be notoriously poor observers of disturbing events. Indeed, the more emotion-arousing the context, the greater the possibility that recollection will be incorrect. Packer points out that confessions and admissions by persons in police custody may not be completely voluntary and witnesses may be biased. With these considerations in mind, therefore, the due process model rejects informal fact-finding as too unreliable.

The due process model views maximum efficiency on the part of the criminal justice system as leading to increased tyranny. The effective work of criminal justice means stigma and loss of liberty for the person found guilty, and this represents the most significant power the state can exert against an individual. That makes it imperative that the criminal justice process be subjected to controls, safeguards which prevent it from operating at absolute efficiency. In the due process model, efficiency is sacrificed in order to prevent the official repression of the individual by the oppressive, coercive power of the state. From its perspective, it is better that a hundred guilty persons be set free because of the effective exercise of procedural safeguards than for a single innocent person to be wrongly convicted.

Whereas the crime control model rests on the presumption of guilt, the due process model considers guilt to be the matter in question. Not only must an accused person be determined guilty factually, by sufficient evidence, but he or she must be found guilty according to proper procedures, by properly competent authorities, and in accordance with the various rules designed to protect citizens in the arms of the law and to safeguard the integrity of the process. Packer states:

> . . . the tribunal that convicts him must have the power to deal with his kind of case ("jurisdiction") and must be geographically appropriate ("venue"); too long a time must not have elapsed since the offense was committed ("statute of limitations"); he must not have been previously convicted or acquitted of the same or a substantially similar offense ("double jeopardy"); he must not fall within a category of persons, such as children or the insane, who are legally immune to conviction ("criminal responsibility"); and so on. None of these requirements has anything to do with the factual question of whether the person did or did not engage in the conduct that is charged as the offense against him; yet favorable answers to any of them will mean that he is legally innocent. [24]

Thus **legal guilt**, as opposed to **factual guilt**, must be determined by an impartial tribunal, quite separate from the police and prosecutors who clearly are unable or unwilling to apply these guilt-defeating doctrines. This impartial tribunal is normally understood to be the trial judge and jury. There, in that context, the "innocent until proven guilty" doctrine reigns. There the administrative fact-finders must present their evidence, subject their case to the standards of legal guilt as well as of factual guilt. And it is not uncommon that the adjudicative fact-finders will see a person who is clearly, factually guilty set free by the impartial tribunal due to a failure in one or more of the legal guilt tests.

This latter consequence is the source of great consternation to the police or prosecutors, or both, who have worked the cases. But the larger consequence of the due process model has been that illegally obtained evidence does not make its way into court, and that convictions may be reversed where procedural safeguards have been violated. Therefore, not only criminal offenders are held accountable before the law, but so also are the administrative fact-finders.

THE SEARCH FOR JUSTICE AND FOR LESS CRIME

Needless to say, no crime control effort receives the full consensus of *any* group, whether of participants in the process, those affected by it, or informed observers on the outside. And frustration with new methods of controlling crime sometimes spawns renewed calls for failed methods of the past. For example, today there are proponents of corporal punishment—long thought to have been abandoned as barbarous—as an alternative sanction for what is perceived to be the more brutalizing use of long periods of incarceration.[25] And in many cities officially recognized and supported vigilante law enforcement groups exist, a phenomenon commonly thought passé with the closing of the American Western frontier. What American would bet against the possibility of penal colonies on distant planets if we eventually perfect space travel?

Most of the problems faced by our criminal justice system are as old as humanity. Moreover, the same basic problems that faced our forebears are likely to be confronted by our children. Obviously, we have not effectively prevented, controlled, or diminished crime. We have made no breakthroughs in crime control or prevention comparable to those in medicine or in physical science, where advances have become so common as to be almost routine.

Such comparisons may be unfair, however, for crime is not a disease, nor is crime control a science in the same sense as physics or biochemistry. Given the values espoused in regard to and the conflicted debates over the causes of crime, given our political philosophy, and given the fact that crime encompasses a wide range of types of conduct and is subject to shifts in definition, perhaps it is not surprising that breakthroughs have not occurred.

Nonetheless, and quite naturally, most people would like to live in a crime-free society. Most of us recognize that the total elimination of crime in our society is not possible, so we are left to hope for a crime control system that protects law abiders from the predators, one that prevents or controls crime as much as possible. But in the United States, a free society built on principles of justice and freedom, we expect even more from a crime control system. Prevention and effective law enforcement, although important, are not the sole determinants of appropriate criminal justice efforts. Whatever preventive or control measures are taken must be consistent with our sense of justice. And this term—justice—is as elusive of definition, as difficult to measure or evaluate, as any concept in our language.

The search for justice is an age-old quest. Undoubtedly it will remain unresolved as long as humanity lives in ordered societies. At times in the past we thought it solved, or at least better defined. An eye for an eye, the wisdom of Solomon, the Declaration of Independence, the teachings of Freud, and the early claims of social science—all promised new insights into justice and solutions to the crime problem. Yet for every variation in definition, for each new solution, significant questions and challenges were raised, and justice still somehow has failed to be caught in a word formula and to be achieved in a simple way.

After Anita Hill's charges of sexual harassment against Supreme Court nominee Clarence Thomas were made public in 1991, these Congresswomen marched to the Senate to make known their opinion that the confirmation vote should be delayed until a fair hearing of the charges had taken place. Though the televised hearings that ensued were criticized as being poorly handled and painful to all the participants, their essential goal was truth and justice.

From our origins as a colonial people to the present day, American history can be characterized as a search for justice. We have slowly and often painfully constructed a Constitution, a government, and a highly intricate set of administrative machinery intended to maximize liberty, afford wide opportunities for the pursuit of happiness, and protect the civil liberties of all our citizens. But we have not yet fully achieved these goals.

We have at times supported repressive institutions, like slavery, that in hindsight seem unbelievable and that took a civil war to change. Rejecting aristocracy, we still developed a class-entrenched society. Our treatment of all minorities, racial, political, sexual, and economic, has been less than consistent with our ideals. Our history is littered with examples of injustice and only too frequently with cases of corruption in our own institutions. Yet the search for justice continues.

Some observers see our elaborate efforts to ferret out crime and catch criminals as endless and futile, so long as we fail to overhaul our entire society in the direction of a more just, egalitarian order.[26] In this view, crime is merely a symptom of underlying conflicts in our massive industrial society and is inevitable as long as we continue to stress competition and capitalism while creating social barriers to equal opportunities by our class structure, or by racial discrimination.

Other observers regard our failure as primarily the result of the ineffectiveness and inefficiency of present law-enforcement techniques. They believe that crime control can be achieved by increasing the certainty of detection and arrest and more effectively processing those who are caught and convicted. The failure of past efforts is a common assumption of both positions; there are few, if any, serious observers of the system who think we are doing a fine job.

It may well be that a significant reduction in the amount of crime will require basic modifications in our society and a shift in many present-day values. However, it seems clear that such changes will not come about overnight, and indeed may never come about, not only because of human reluctance and resistance to change, but also because no one is really sure which changes will lead to crime reduction. Nor do we know the other costs of change, even if certain modifications could be agreed upon.

The problem of crime is immediate and constant. Even if we accept the necessity of long-range change and recognize the limits of traditional approaches to crime control, the hard fact is that we must take action currently to at least curb and contain criminal behavior, for unless we do, we face very real threats to the safety and security of everyone. We are saddled with the present crime situation, and, though we may have doubts about its ultimate effectiveness, we do have an ongoing criminal justice system that most persons want to be more effective and just. Although improvement of approaches to crime control methods may not ultimately lead to a crime-free society, we can and should demand greater effectiveness in the criminal justice system and closer adherence to standards of justice.

Few will deny that we have progressed from the days of the Salem witchcraft trials or the frontier justice of Judge Roy Bean. We have introduced higher standards of propriety in processing suspects and defendants, we have become more humane in the treatment of most offenders. Progress has admittedly been snail-slow and neither linear nor uniform. Nowhere have we fully achieved our ideals of equal protection under the law, due process, and effective and humane treatment of violators. But progress has been made and is ongoing.

One certainty about our criminal justice decision network is that it is never static. Not only are all parts of the system continually changing, but the nature of the crime problem changes as well. Variations in types of crime and frequency of occurrence require the constant adjustment of resources at all levels. In most communities the number of burglaries that will be committed in any given year, how many homicides there will be, and the extent of other crimes can be approximated in advance. Police, courts, and correctional facilities are built and staffed in anticipation of these rates.

Aside from these necessary but routine adjustments, the criminal justice system is continuously called on to respond to crises. Some crises are very real—new forms of crime, an outbreak of particularly heinous offenses, or some part of the system grossly overburdened and out of whack, as is currently the case with prison overcrowding. Other crises, perceived for a while as real and threatening, like civil disobedience during the Vietnam War, tend to disappear or seem less significant than once thought.

The study of criminal justice, therefore, presents a complex challenge to us all. The fact that university courses on criminal justice have expanded to virtually every campus in the United States during the past 25 years is an indication of the seriousness with which the subject is considered in academia. In addition to courses taught in departments of criminal justice or criminology, several academic disciplines within the university structure offer their own insights into the subject: sociology, political science, psychology. This multidisciplinary interest reflects the variety of approaches available for the study of criminal justice.

The many parts of our criminal justice network pose tough problems which make it difficult to understand the network, to be able to ask sensible questions about it, and to suggest feasible changes or reforms for better crime control. The study of only a single agency such as the police or a single decision point like sentencing provides at best only fragmentary information about criminal justice; at worst, it may distort the overall aims and objectives of crime control. At the same time, it is obvious that a broad, total system overview cannot be completed quickly or easily. After all, there are 51 separate jurisdictions in the country (the states and the federal system), and although they are more alike than different, there are variations in practices and policies from place to place. Since all these variations cannot be discussed in detail, we concentrate on the common decision points, common agencies, and common ways of controlling crime while remaining fully aware that local practices may vary.

Such a generalized approach is not without shortcomings, however. We are unable to provide, in a single volume, a detailed analysis of every part and every issue relevant to criminal justice; thus we will focus on the mainstream, normal, daily (almost mundane) decision stages in the process of solving crimes and dealing with suspects, defendants, and convicted offenders. We recognize that other approaches exist and that each has merit. Where possible, we include the valuable contributions of those approaches and supply the reader with any insights to be learned from them.

Notes

1. *Rochin v. California*, 342 U.S. 165 (1952).
2. "When society acts to deprive one of its members of life, liberty, or property," wrote former Chief Justice Earl Warren, "it takes its most awesome steps. No general respect for, nor adherence to, the law as a whole can well be expected without judicial recognition of the paramount need for prompt, eminently fair, and sober criminal law procedures. The methods we employ in the enforcement of our criminal law have aptly been called the measures by which the quality of our civilization may be judged." *Coppedge v. United States*, 369 U.S. 438, 449 (1962).
3. *Miranda v. Arizona*, 384 U.S. 436 (1966).
4. *Gideon v. Wainwright*, 372 U.S. 335 (1963), held that the states have a duty in all serious criminal cases to provide counsel for those indigent defendants who have not

knowingly and intelligently waived their right to counsel. The Court extended the duty to indigent defendants accused of minor crimes in *Argersinger v. Hamlin*, 407 U.S. 25 (1972).

5. *Wolff v. McDonnell*, 94 S.Ct. 2963 (1974).

6. In 1914 the Supreme Court held in *Weeks v. United States*, 232 U.S. 383 (1914), that the Fourth Amendment required the application of the exclusionary rule in federal prosecutions. In *Wolf v. Colorado*, 338 U.S. 25 (1949), however, the Court was divided on the issue of whether the rule had to be used in state courts where evidence had been obtained by unconstitutional search and seizure methods. The exclusionary rule was finally extended to state courts in *Mapp v. Ohio*, 367 U.S. 643 (1961), holding that evidence leading to the conviction of a defendant charged with possession of lewd and obscene material had been obtained illegally, and thus that it must be excluded as evidence. In 1984 the Supreme Court allowed a limited "good faith" exception to the exclusionary rule.

7. *Furman v. Georgia*, 408 U.S. 238 (1972).

8. An excellent treatise on the operation of this recurrent discretionary power is found in Kenneth C. Davis, *Discretionary Justice: A Preliminary Inquiry* (Baton Rouge: Louisiana State University Press, 1969).

9. Charles D. Breitel, "Controls in Criminal Law Enforcement," *University of Chicago Law Review* 27 (Spring 1960): 427.

10. Herbert L. Packer, *The Limits of the Criminal Sanction* (Palo Alto, Ca: Stanford University Press, 1968), esp. pp. 160–161.

11. *Miranda v. Arizona*, 384 U.S. 436 (1966).

12. Packer, op. cit.

13. Samuel Walker, *Sense and Nonsense about Crime: A Policy Guide*, 2nd ed. (Pacific Grove, CA: Brooks/Cole, 1989), pp. 10–11.

14. Packer warns: "There is a risk in an enterprise of this sort that is latent in any attempt to polarize. It is, simply, that values are too various to be pinned down to yes-or-no answers. The models are distortions of reality. And, since they are normative in character, there is a danger of seeing one or the other as Good or Bad. . . . The attempt . . . is primarily to clarify the terms of discussion by isolating the assumptions that underlie competing policy claims and examining the conclusions that those claims, if fully accepted, would lead to demand consistently polarized answers to the range of questions posed in the criminal process. The weighty questions of public policy that inhere in any attempt to discern where on the spectrum of normative choice the 'right' answer lies are beyond the scope of the present inquiry. The attempt here is primarily to clarify the terms of discussion by isolating the assumptions that underlie competing policy claims and examining the conclusions that those claims, if fully accepted, would lead to." (pp. 154–155)

15. Walker, op. cit., p. 13.

16. Ibid., p. 13.

17. Ibid., pp. 159–160.

18. Ibid., pp. 160–162.

19. Ibid., pp. 162–163.

20. Walker, op. cit., p. 16.

21. Ibid., pp. 199–234.

22. Packer, op. cit., pp. 164–165.

23. Ibid., pp. 163–164.

24. Ibid., p. 166.

25. See Graeme R. Newman, *The Punishment Response* (Cambridge, MA: Pallinger, 1978), and Ernest van den Haag, *Punishing Criminals: Concerning a Very Old and Painful Question* (New York: Basic Books, 1975).

26. See, for example, Michael J. Lynch and W. Byron Groves, *A Primer in Radical Criminology* (New York: Harrow and Heston, 1986); David Greenberg, *Crime and Capitalism* (Palo Alto, CA: Mayfield, 1981); and Edwin Schur, *Our Criminal Society: The Social and Legal Sources of Crime in America* (Englewood Cliffs, NJ: Prentice-Hall, 1969).

Suggested readings

Archibald Cox, *The Court and the Constitution* (Boston: Houghton Mifflin, 1987).

Elliott Currie, *Confronting Crime* (New York: Pantheon, 1985).

Fred P. Graham, *The Self-Inflicted Wound* (New York: Macmillan, 1970).

Anthony Lewis, *Gideon's Trumpet* (New York: Vintage Books, 1964).

Herbert L. Packer, *The Limits of the Criminal Sanction* (Stanford, CA: Stanford University Press, 1968).

Jeffrey H. Reinman, *The Rich Get Richer and the Poor Get Prison: Ideology, Class and Criminal Justice*, 2nd ed. (New York, John Wiley & Sons, 1984).

Samuel Walker, *Sense and Nonsense About Crime: A Policy Guide*, 2nd ed. (Pacific Grove, CA: Brooks/Cole, 1989).

Discussion questions

1. How does due process of law affect police? prosecutors? trials?

2. How does fundamental fairness affect police? prosecutors? trials?

3. What controls are placed on the criminal justice system by the value of propriety?

4. Why is the rule of law difficult to follow in criminal justice?

5. Does the presumption of innocence apply equally at every stage of the criminal justice system?

6. Describe the crime control model.

7. Describe the due process model.

8. Compare and contrast the conservative crime control model and the liberal due process model.

9. Discuss the search for justice in a democratic society. What are the impediments to the creation of a crime-free society? Is a high crime rate the price we must pay to live in a democratic society? Explain.

3

Explaining Crime

Fear struck Gainesville, the hometown of the University of Florida, during the late summer of 1990 when the brutally murdered bodies of three young college women were found in their apartments just as thousands of students were moving into apartments, fraternity and sorority houses, and dormitories for the new school year. First, late Sunday afternoon, 17-year-old Christine Powell and 18-year-old Sonya Larson, both University of Florida students, were found by a janitor inside the townhouse the girls had rented 2 weeks earlier. Their nude, partially decomposed bodies had been mutilated approximately 72 hours earlier, police said. Then the body of Christa Leigh Hoyt, a part-time employee of the sheriff's office and a student at Santa Fe Community College, was found in her apartment about 2 miles away at about 1:00 a.m. Her supervisor had become concerned because she had not reported for work at midnight and so had asked the police to check her apartment. Her body had also been mutilated. It was later reported that one of the girls had been decapitated.

Newspapers and television stations sent reporters to the scene immediately, news of the events spread like wildfire, rumors and suspicion grew with each passing hour. And, as is always the case when such a notorious crime is committed, talk of crime permeated every conversation. Virtually everyone in the college community made changes regarding their personal habits and took additional precautions. Crime, and the talk of crime, had captured everyone's attention. Psychologists, psychics, sociologists, and criminologists rendered learned opinions about why such crimes had been committed and what kind of person could do such things. Barbers and beauticians, radio and television personalities, ministers and bartenders—virtually everyone—formed opinions about these issues.

ABOUT THIS CHAPTER

The local newspapers in virtually every community, as well as local television news programs, daily describe a variety of crimes. Burglaries, rape, robberies, murder, as well as white collar crimes, drug busts, drunk driving—every kind of crime is brought

In Gainesville, a body is removed from a crime scene.

to our attention every day. And even without such notorious and tragic events many of us speculate about why people commit crimes. It seems everyone has an opinion.

Specifically, two types of questions are raised: What causes people to commit crimes? What can be done about crime? Indeed, are not these two questions central to the subject of criminal justice? Why *do* people commit crimes? Can you conceive of a set of circumstances which would prompt you to enter a store with a gun, order the clerk to hand over the cash, and threaten everyone there with death? The *Uniform Crime Reports* reported 639,271 robberies in 1990, with an average "take" of $364 in those involving convenience stores. What motivates a person to commit such relatively unprofitable crimes, knowing the risks to life, limb and liberty?

The companion question, "What can be done about crime?" also confronts us each day. Because news reporting focuses on the dramatic, and crime is among the more "newsworthy" events of the day, most of us have a strong sense that crime is *increasing*, that something must be *done* about it. People feel a sense of urgency about crime, even a fear of crime. During election seasons, which come like clockwork every 2 years, proposals are made by incumbent and aspiring office-holders to curb crime. Political aspirants are expected to propose solutions, congressional representatives and Senators must express their positions, Presidents and governors must establish crime policies, mayors and sheriffs must tell us how they intend to reduce crime. Even city council, county commission, and school board candidates must demonstrate superior qualifications to deal with the crime problem. But even though most people express with conviction preconceived solutions to the problem of crime, how to deal with it is no easier to answer than why people commit criminal acts.

Questions about the causes of and solutions to crime are often addressed in a context of fear, hysteria, political opportunism, and sensationalism. This chapter, on the other hand, provides a broad overview of criminological theory, explaining how scholars have explained crime and its control. First we discuss the impact of theory on the criminal justice system.

IMPLICATIONS OF CRIMINOLOGICAL THEORY FOR CRIMINAL JUSTICE

Throughout history theorists have attempted to determine the causes and solutions to crime, in an effort to reduce or eliminate it. Yet, criminal justice policy and practice is established seemingly without regard to criminological theory because theories contradict each other, and no one theory has been proven right. Some crime policies deal with individual offenders, seeking to apprehend, restrain, incarcerate, deter, or to rehabilitate them by locking them up. Other approaches may attempt to address the social causes and the social environment of crime, and may attempt to change society. Advocates of some crime policies may attempt to change the laws by decriminalizing certain offenses so as to remove them from the jurisdiction of the criminal justice system, while advocates of other policies may attempt to criminalize additional behaviors in order to bring about a desired improvement in the overall social environment.

Police practice is based on a belief that criminals choose to commit crimes and will choose not to commit further crimes if the proper punishments are imposed. However, most police officers and officials acknowledge the harmful effects of living in crime-laden communities. Indeed, many police officers are themselves products of those same areas, and understand the pressures inherent in lower-class environments. But the law and police practice leave little room for social engineering.

Prosecutors are often influenced by theoretical aspects of criminal behavior in making the charging decisions. An offender who clearly needs alcohol rehabilitation, psychological counseling, or some other treatment may find the prosecutor willing to defer prosecution, or even to drop charges completely when the offender agrees to seek help for the problems which have caused the criminal acts. But, especially in serious crimes such as murder, regardless of the presumed causes of the crime, free-will choices on the part of the offender are usually assumed and the prosecution seeks to punish the behavior, not rehabilitate the offender, to deter other such potential crimes in the society at large.

American law, as established in the U.S. Constitution, emphasizes punishment for crimes. Punishments are provided to deter potential criminals without regard to the biological or social causes of crime. Nowhere in the Constitution does the word "rehabilitation" appear, nor does it address the causes of crime.

Prisons, probation and parole agencies, and other so-called correctional agencies are perhaps suited to respond to the presumed theoretical causes of criminal behavior. Prisons have group counseling, drug and alcohol rehabilitation, vocational training, and a host of other programs designed to assist a person overcome the adverse social conditions which led to the life of crime. But little evidence exists to demonstrate that such programs provide effective solutions—recidivism rates remain high despite such well-meaning programs.

The juvenile justice system is perhaps better suited to apply solutions to the causes of delinquency. Juvenile offenders are still young, impressionable, change-able—perhaps that is the time to exert a maximum effort to identify the causes of delinquency and treat them.

The difficulty is that little consensus exists as to the causes of crime and delin-quency. And where consensus may exist, crime policies responding adequately to the perceived causes are difficult to establish if they are at odds with the established order of criminal justice practice. The political context of criminal justice today places an emphasis on punishment as deterrence; anything less is rejected as being "soft on crime." However, crime policies can be responsive to the findings of criminological theory. Modern police, courts, and correctional administrators can develop programs and policies which are both consistent with scientific findings and effective in satisfy-ing the loud insistence that a war on crime be waged.

Table 3.1 summarizes the major criminological theories presented in this chap-ter.

CLASSICAL CRIMINOLOGY

Conservative Crime Control

Any criminology theory finds its relevance in what it proposes ought to be done about crime. Conservative theory, as expressed by the phrase "Lock 'em up and throw away the key," recommends preventive detention for dangerous or multiple-offense criminals awaiting trial rather than pretrial release on bail. This view holds that crimi-nals should be incapacitated, and locked in prisons away from society so as to prevent them from preying on law-abiding citizens. And conservatives believe judges should be required to hand down hard, mandatory sentences rather than "slaps on the wrist." Conservative crime control theorists believe such practices will constitute a deterrence to crime.

The fullest expression of deterrence is capital punishment, but the system should also "crack down" on other lesser offenses such as drunk driving so that the message will be clear to potential criminals that crime does not pay.

Also, conservative theory calls for "unleashing the cops," by removing pro-cedural restraints. Police are seen as "handcuffed" by such unnecessary restraints as

TABLE 3.1 *Criminological theories and theorists*

Classical criminology

Conservative crime control theory: People choose to commit (or not) crime of their own free will.

Historical:
  Cesare Beccaria (1738–1794): Law and government should serve the goals of society. Law can be moral.

Contemporary:
  Criminals are responsible for their crimes. Consistent and vigorous punishment will deter further crimes.

Positive criminology

Liberal crime control theory: Environmental, biological, or genetic factors contribute to criminal behavior.

Biological determinism	Sociological determinism

Historical:
  Cesare Lombroso (1835–1909): Introduced scientific method to criminological study. His study of human physique led him to believe that criminal behavior is the result of biological conditions.
 	
  Francis Gall (1758–1828): Espoused phrenology.
 	
  William Sheldon (1898–1977): Body types determine behavior, temperament, and personality.
 	
  Alfred Binet (1857–1911): Developed IQ levels used to determine mental age. Links between IQ and criminal behavior are controversial.
 	
XYY chromosomes:
  Erroneous assumptions that an extra Y chromosome leads to increased tendencies to violence opened the door to the study of genetic influences.
 	
Contemporary biological research:
  C. Ray Jeffrey: Focus is on the brain and central nervous system, and on hormones. Behavior is seen as the result of complex interactions between genetics and the environment.
	Clifford Shaw/Henry McKay—*The Chicago school and social disorganization:* Using a mapping system, studied the characteristics of neighborhoods classified as high and low in delinquency.
	Conclusions: Delinquency rate is influenced by a socially disorganized environment and the conditions of poverty.
	
	Edwin H. Sutherland—*Differential association:* Techniques, motives, and rationalizations for crime are learned behaviors.
	
	Ronald Akers—*Social learning theory:* Crime is learned, depending on the rewards and punishments attached to it by reference groups.
	
	Albert K. Cohen—*Middle-class measuring rod:* Delinquency is a product of collective consensus among lower-class boys against middle-class values. Delinquency is a means to develop positive self-concepts through antisocial values.
	
	Walter Miller—*Lower-class focal concerns:* Delinquent boys are competent youngsters whose needs are not met through socially accepted channels, who seek status and a sense of belonging among their peers.
	
	Robert K. Merton—*Social structure and anomie:* People substitute unacceptable goals and means when they are unable to achieve society's institutional goals.
	
	Robert A. Cloward/Lloyd E. Ohlin—*Differential opportunity theory:* Blocked opportunity causes delinquency, expanded opportunity should lower delinquency.
	
	Travis Hirschi—*Control theory:* People with strong social bonds are less prone to criminal activity.
	
	Edwin Lemert—*Labeling theory:* Two types of deviance: *primary* behavior caused by biological or social conditions; *secondary* behavior which comes from a person having a self-image as a deviant.
	
	George Vold/Austin Turk—*Conflict theory:* Members of society who are the most powerful influence the law and the criminal justice system; members of the lowest classes are powerless and are most often legislated against, and hence are most often labeled as criminal.
	
	Radical/Marxist criminology: Crime is a product of the struggle between the classes within society.

the exclusionary rule and *Miranda* warnings. More police should be hired, detective work should be improved, and career criminals should be targeted by the revitalized police.

Conservative theory also seeks to close the "loopholes" which get in the way of punishing criminals. Such loopholes include the insanity defense, plea bargaining, and lengthy appeals. If these measures are taken, conservatives believe victims will be protected and crime will diminish.

Samuel Walker summarizes this conservative agenda and expresses the assumptions of this **conservative crime control model** as follows:

> Criminals lack self-control. Their passions get the better of them and they break the rules. They kill because they cannot curb their anger. They steal because they cannot control their desire to possess what they do not have or they cannot defer gratification until they have earned the right to possess something legitimately. Poverty is no excuse. If they are poor, it is only because they refuse to exercise enough self-discipline to get an education and a job that will lift them out of poverty.[1]

Individual free will and responsibility requires that rule breakers must be punished. Criminals can thereby learn to obey the rules and any potential criminal, upon learning of the punishment, will be taught that crime does not pay and therefore will be deterred from violating the law. At any given moment, a person can choose between committing a crime and not committing it.[2] This conservative crime control approach is an expression of the school of **classical criminology**.

Free Will: The Choice to Commit Crimes

An agent of the Federal Bureau of Investigation (FBI) was addressing a criminal justice class in a state university when a student asked about a series of recent bank robberies. The FBI had reported that each of the several bank robberies had been committed by the dean of a neighboring college, a man with no prior arrest record, a man who friends and colleagues described as a good, law-abiding citizen. The student asked the FBI agent, "Can you tell us why a man would do such crimes? What would cause a well-educated, professional, family man to do such a thing?" The agent replied, "That's easy, greed. He wanted more money, so he stole it." That explanation, although surely oversimplistic, expresses a major theory about crime, the classical approach. The classical school of criminology understands criminal behavior, as all behavior, to be the product of a person's **free will**, a product of choice.

Classical criminology, as it is commonly understood, has its roots in the eighteenth century writings of Cesare **Beccaria** (1738–1794).[3] Beccaria's treatise, *On Crimes and Punishments* (1764) (see Box 3.1), is perhaps the best known among contemporary students of criminology of any publication from that era. And the influence of the philosophy found in that work, as well as in other works of that genre, had a profound influence on the language of both the Declaration of Independence and the United States' Constitution.

Beccaria's writings represent the intellectual history of his age, often referred to as the Age of Enlightenment. Following the Protestant Reformation of the preceding centuries, and the Church Age which had dominated Europe for several centuries prior to that, the intellectual climate in the Europe of the eighteenth century encouraged revolutionary ideas. New social structures emerged which obliterated the ancient domination of the European monarchies. The French Revolution, and the American Revolution, brought about new governments, new types of governments. Much of what was written by Beccaria, therefore, was a reaction against the legal and social abuses of the Church Age, abuses which included torture, arbitrary sentencings by

BOX 3.1

Cesare Beccaria (1738–1794)
On Crimes and Punishments
(1764)

A GENERAL THEOREM In order for punishment not to be, in every instance, an act of violence of one or of many against a private citizen, it must be essentially public, prompt, necessary, the least possible in the given circumstances, proportionate to the crimes, dictated by the laws. (p. 99)

private tribunals following secret accusations, and inefficient methods of enforcing laws and imposing social control.

Dramatic historical changes, and the new intellectual openness, spawned a philosophical critique of government. Great European philosophers, including Hobbes, Locke, and Hume—the "Social Contract Writers"[4]—espoused the idea that people should be served by government rather than government served by people. The social contract between people and their governments meant that individuals were required to relinquish only the amount of freedom necessary to protect the rights of other people, the aim of such an arrangement being to produce the greatest happiness for the greatest number of people.

According to that philosophy, laws should be written in such a way that people would willingly accept and obey them. The power of the government should be restrained and limited so as to eliminate the possibility of a recurrence of the excesses of the Church Age. Under previous systems of government, a person could be tortured, drawn and quartered, burned at the stake, dismembered, or branded, among other terrible punishments, for such minor offenses as blasphemy. Beccaria argued against that kind of cruelty. During the Church Age confessions were extracted from people through torture, and the belief was that God would intervene on behalf of truly innocent individuals to rescue them from the fate of false confessions forced from their lips through those methods. Beccaria argued that such a system of "justice" was irrational.

Under such an austere and cruel system, the privileged classes, at least, including the clergy, had developed ways to circumvent the law and the harsh consequences of unlawful behavior. For example, church and legal authorities were immune from legal punishment for their crimes. Among the common people, respect for the law diminished, and even disappeared.

Beccaria sought to eliminate torture as an interrogation tool, to limit the amount of punishment the state could impose, and to "let the punishment fit the crime." Thus he aimed at creating a legal structure that would have the support of everyone and would result in peace and security for the greatest possible number of people.

The Age of Enlightenment writers in general espoused the belief that in order to have a meaningful legal system, the people being governed must be in agreement with and in control of their government—this is known as government by the consent of the governed. In such a system the law would be established by the people and the power of the government would be restrained by the same system of law that defined illegal behavior.

Also, in this view, law and government should serve utilitarian purposes. That is, laws should be designed to promote the general welfare, to benefit the greatest number of people, to lead toward the greatest good and happiness possible. Beccaria believed the law could accomplish these goals, that it could be both moral *and* utilitarian. Society could be made to accommodate people's needs and desires, with the social contract as the avenue through which these advantages for human beings could be realized.

Therefore classical criminology, as derived from these roots, views human beings as willful, free, hedonistic, rational, and responsive to the principles of pleasure and pain. Crime is committed purposively by persons who have chosen to do so after considering the consequences in terms of pleasure and pain. Therefore, a person will choose not to commit an act if the pain it produces will be greater than the pleasure to be derived from it. Punishments should be designed to entice potential law breakers toward the decision to remain law abiding. People are assumed to be prone to violating laws and must be held in check by the vigilance of a legal system which deters potential criminals by a combination of commanding their assent to its demands and threatening them with apprehension and punishment should they transgress it.

Cesare Beccaria: The Father of Modern Criminology

Cesare Bonesana, Marquis of Beccaria (1738–1794), son of an aristocratic Italian family, was a member of a small, somewhat radical, reading group called the Academy of Fists, so named because their frequent debates sometimes led to violent disagreements.

He published his famous essay, *On Crimes and Punishments* (or *Dei delitti e delle pene*) in 1764 after he, along with the rest of the Academy of Fists, had studied the writings of contemporary French and English scholars, including Voltaire, Montesquieu, Rousseau, Hume, and Locke. Beccaria and his friends were impressed with the social contract theory espoused by those thinkers, which reasoned that government should serve the interests of the majority, that all people should have equal rights under the law, and that state-administered punishment should not be cruel, excessive, or capricious. The same writers challenged the rule of the Church of Rome, and the insistence on the divine right of kings, both of which positions further attracted the young members of the Academy of Fists.

Beccaria applied the reasoning behind social contract theory to criminal justice practices of his day. In *On Crimes and Punishments*, he presented a tightly reasoned attack on the prevailing system of criminal justice in Europe. That system was characterized by corruption, secrecy, and cruelty. The concept of "due process of law" did not exist. Secret accusations were brought against people who were then imprisoned on little or no evidence, horrible methods of torture were designed to gain "confessions," death sentences were carried out for hundreds of crimes often after the condemned person was mutilated, and judges had unlimited

Cesare Beccaria

discretion to inflict whatever punishments they could dream up. Poor and powerless people were subjected to the same horrors of incarceration whether they were convicted of crimes or merely accused of them. Well-connected churchmen or rich and powerful citizens avoided any criminal sanctions whatsoever, and widespread dissatisfaction with the process was beginning to contribute to social unrest in much of Europe in the eighteenth century.

Beccaria's essay aroused resistance and hostility from the churchmen and others with vested interests in Europe. It joined Montesquieu's *On the Spirit of New Laws* on the

Contemporary Classical Criminology

The emphasis on free will and responsibility has resurfaced with the recent general conservative resurgence in American society. Several criminologists advocated a "justice model" for the corrections system during the 1970s in which prisoners would be coerced into reforming their behavior through flat-time, definite sentences.[5] Similarly, Ernst Van den Haag's book titled *Punishing Criminals* (1975)[6] renewed popular discussions about the proper role of punishment in criminal justice.

Vatican's Index of Prohibited Books, where it stayed until 1962. Beccaria was charged with sedition and irreligion. In Paris, however, only a few short years before the French Revolution, he was welcomed as a hero by a society poised to overthrow the system he criticized.

Also, Catherine the Great invited him to come to St. Petersburg to overhaul the laws of Russia. He refused to go because of the cold weather in Russia, but Catherine instructed Russian scholars to translate Beccaria's essay, and Russian government officials to implement his ideas. Frederick the Great of Prussia and Emperor Joseph II of Austria both relied heavily on Beccaria's essay to draft new criminal codes. And the framers of the Constitution for the newly emerging United States of America were intrigued by it. John Adams, Thomas Jefferson, and James Madison quoted Beccaria and were influenced by his argument that work on public projects by criminals was a proper substitute for the punishment of death. Scholars and reformers throughout Europe and the New World are thus indebted to Beccaria's essay, and Beccaria can rightly be called "the father of modern criminology."

Beccaria's view of human nature was that people are self-centered and self-seeking, motivated to gain all they can from one another, but that nevertheless they must live together in society. In order to keep their behavior within boundaries in that society, punishment inflicted against wrong-doers is needed. That punishment, Beccaria maintained, should be in proportion to the extent to which an individual's actions threaten the existence of society. Beccaria argued that government should exercise its right to punish only sparingly, when necessary to defend the rights and freedom of all the people. Beccaria saw severe punishment as useless in preventing crime and as contrary to enlightened reason and justice.

Beccaria believed that severe or cruel punishment deterred crime less than the certainty of prompt punishment. He believed severity of punishment could even produce more crime since it could lead people to commit further crimes to escape punishment. He urged that offenders be tried speedily so as to enhance the connection between committing criminal acts and the resulting punishment.

Beccaria argued that the death penalty is neither legitimate nor necessary. If humans live within a social contract, he wrote, it is inconceivable that one person would grant another the authority to take his or her life, for life is the greatest human good of all. Execution is an act of barbarism and cruelty, and therefore causes more ferocious behavior rather than less. Beccaria argued that the effects of execution are only momentary, while the effects of punishment which is continuous are more lasting.

Beccaria wrote that it is better to prevent crimes than to punish them. Good legislation, therefore, encourages people to strive for the greatest happiness and the least misery. Since the discomfort caused by the punishment of a crime always exceeds any pleasure derived from committing the crime, he believed crime is best prevented if society rewards virtue and educates people regarding the benefits of proper behavior and the penalties for crimes.

Beccaria ended his essay with the following words: "So that any punishment be not an act of violence of one or of many against another, it is essential that it be public, prompt, necessary, minimal in severity as possible under given circumstances, proportional to the crime, and prescribed by the laws."

SOURCES: Cesare Beccaria, *On Crimes and Punishments*, (Indianapolis: Bobbs-Merrill, 1963); Elio Monchesi, "Cesare Beccaria, 1738–1794," in Herman Mannheim, *Pioneers in Criminology* (Montclair, NJ: Patterson Smith, 1973); Graeme Newman and Pietro Marongui, "Penological Reform and the Myth of Beccaria," *Criminology*, 28 (1990): 325–346.

Contemporary classical criminologists find Beccaria's premise that everyone is equally responsible to be untenable in the light of scientific studies of human behavior. Not all people are equally responsible for their acts—some are too young, others insane, still others incapacitated in other ways. For those, since they are less guilty than the "free-will" decision-making criminal, treatment rather than punishment may be appropriate. But for the criminal who acts out of his or her free will, contemporary classical criminology believes more punishment, quickly and justly administered, will either deter or incapacitate potential future criminals.

Wilson and Herrnstein, in their book *Crime and Human Nature: The Definitive Study of the Causes of Crime*, maintain that criminals *choose* to commit crimes. Exceptions to this include people who are psychologically or biologically impaired.[7] The contemporary view, therefore, is that criminals should be held directly responsible for their crimes, and that by consistently and vigorously implementing penalties for crimes, those criminals as well as potential ones will in future decline to commit crimes.

Positive criminology

A talk show host asked a guest, a social worker from an agency located in the poorest area of a large city, "Why do so many young men from that area of town commit crimes of violence, why do they threaten the safety of anyone who passes through the neighborhood?" The social worker replied, "The constant presence of poverty, hopelessness, joblessness, and despair that those young men experience causes them to act in antisocial ways. They want to do better, to be law abiding citizens, to succeed just like you and I do, but they just do not have the opportunity." The talk show guest expressed a view identified with the school of **positive criminology**, the view that human beings are basically social, desiring to conform, and are impelled into criminality by conditions beyond their control. Positive criminology looks to the individual and to the environment for explanations of crime.

Positive criminology is usually understood to represent the systematic empirical study of crime and criminals, the search for causes and cures for crime, and, ultimately, the control of crime and the preservation of social order. Its proponents understand conformity to the social order to be normal and deviance from social conformity to be abnormal, or pathological. The individual criminal is assumed to be fundamentally different from noncriminals in detectable, and thus curable, ways.

Liberal Crime Control

Liberal crime control, a form of positive criminology, disagrees sharply with the conservative model's explanation of crime. Samuel Walker expresses the liberal approach:

> People do wrong because of bad influences in the family, the peer group, or the neighborhood, or because of broader social factors, such as discrimination and lack of economic opportunity. This assumption points in two directions with respect to policy: reshaping individuals and reforming society. . . . Rehabilitation, the core of liberal policy, involves instructing the criminal offender in the ways of correct behavior. Parole, for example, was invented to teach prisoners that they could earn early release by behaving properly. Supervision under probation or parole is designed to guide the offender in the proper direction. . . . Whereas conservatives emphasize individual responsibility, liberals stress the impact of unemployment and racial discrimination. Liberals argue not only that government has a responsibility to reduce these problems but that properly designed programs can work.[8]

In addition to the environmental factors which cause people to become criminals, the liberal crime control approach recognizes biological, genetic factors which contribute to such behavior. The liberal approach is summed up by the notion that criminals cannot help being criminal because they are influenced by factors beyond their control, factors which need to be addressed before criminal behavior can be inhibited.

The school of positive criminology owes much of its heritage to **Cesare Lombroso** (1835–1909), Enrico Ferri (1856–1929), and Raffaele Garofalo (1852–1934).[9] However, perhaps no name in the history of criminology is as familiar as Lombroso. Indeed, when one discusses the positivist tradition in crime-related studies, immediate reference is made to Lombroso, even to the point of calling him the "father of modern criminology."

For Lombroso, a surgeon, the study of the criminal entailed a physiological examination of the human body. As the excerpt in Box 3.2 details, Lombroso was aroused by his study of the physiques of criminals, and especially of their skulls. His studies of insanity, as well as his studies of Italian soldiers, led him to conclude that criminals were fundamentally different from noncriminals in observable, physiological ways. This view was influenced by the evolutionary theories of Charles Darwin who, more than any other thinker of his age, had a profound impact on scientific views of human nature and the scientific study of people. In Lombroso's view, criminals were not as evolved as noncriminals. Criminals were characterized by animalistic, amoral behavior. They did not choose to commit crimes, as Beccaria stated, but their criminal behavior was innate—a result of biological conditions beyond their control. Lombroso believed that criminals were **atavistic** throwbacks to a more primitive stage of human development.

Although among contemporary criminologists virtually none of Lombroso's conclusions about criminals are still accepted, he is largely responsible for introducing the **scientific method** to the study of crime. He changed the focus of crime studies from the classical school's philosophical emphasis on the law to a scientific emphasis on criminal behavior. And, of course, Lombroso is a patriarch of the view that human behavior is biologically determined.

The scientific study of the physiology of criminals began early in the nineteenth century. Lombroso's studies emerged from an intellectual context in which scientists studied humans in the same way they studied other animal species. Human beings, as part of the animal kingdom, were studied and their physical characteristics documented by scientists in the same ways a biologist or botanist would study and document animals and plants.

In such a context, humans were not seen as willful creatures capable of doing whatever they choose; instead they were viewed like other animals, their behavior determined by pre-existing conditions, breeding, and natural selection. Therefore, humans were understood to vary as individuals according to the physiological evolution of their ancestors, which up until the time of Darwin and Lombroso had not yet been studied. Scientists schooled in the biological sciences believed that differences in human behavior, including the propensity to commit crime, would be explained by the scientific study of people's bodies. This school of thought is called **biological determinism**.

Biological determinism theories have focused on studies of physical stigmata, or body types, genes, and chromosomes, as well as of differences in the brain and central nervous system. Such studies have differed in the parts of the human body thought to contain the key to understanding human behavior, but all of them take as their starting points the idea that behavior has its genesis in conditions caused by the biological makeup of the individual, conditions which are inherited.

Phrenology
Among the earliest approaches to biological determinism was **phrenology**, often referred to as the "lumps on the head" theory, which was first publicly espoused by Francis Gall (1758–1828). As a young medical student, Gall noticed that some of his

---

BOX 3.2

Cesare Lombroso (1835–1909)
L'Uomo Delinquente
1876

This was not merely an idea, but a revelation. At the sight of that skull, I seemed to see all of a sudden, lighted up as a vast plain under a flaming sky, the problem of the nature of the criminal—an atavistic being who reproduces in his person the ferocious instincts of primitive humanity and the inferior animals. Thus were explained anatomically the enormous jaws, high cheekbones, prominent superciliary arches, solitary lines in the palms, extreme size of the orbits, handle-shaped or sessile ears found in criminals, savages, and apes, insensibility to pain, extremely acute sight, tattooing, excessive idleness, love of orgies, and the irresistible craving for evil for its own sake, the desire not only to extinguish life in the victim, but to mutilate the corpse, tear its flesh, and drink its blood.

fellow students had distinctive head shapes. He began to examine every skull he could in an attempt to discover why some people seemed to have "such different faces and such different natures; why one was deceitful, another frank, a third virtuous."[10] He studied heads in medical laboratories, prisons, and lunatic asylums. Gall concluded that differences in head shapes and bumps on the head demonstrate corresponding parts of the brain which were housed in those compartments of the skull. He developed a system to show the relationship between head shapes, or knobs, and behavior and character traits.

Galls' studies were widely publicized in Europe and his theories became extremely popular. The American phrenologist Charles Caldwell published *Elements of Phrenology* in 1824, which reported three compartments of the brain, "one the seat of the active propensities, another of moral sentiment, and the third of the intellectual faculties."[11]

Body Types

Body types, the early focus of Lombroso's attention, were also seen as determinants of criminal behavior by William H. Sheldon. In the 1940s, Sheldon conducted physical studies of delinquent boys in a small institution for delinquents in Boston. He observed three basic body types among males and concluded each had corresponding behavior and temperament characteristics, or personalities.[12]

Sheldon classified the body types as **endomorph, mesomorph,** and **ectomorph**: people with *endomorph* body types being rotund and heavy with jovial and outgoing personalities; people with *mesomorph* body types being muscular and well proportioned, with competitive, aggressive, and driven personalities; and people with *ectomorph* body types tending to be slender and frail, with introverted, aloof, and withdrawn behaviors. Sheldon classified individuals according to a 10-point endomorph-mesomorph-ectomorph scale. No one was completely, perfectly any one of the body types, but had various qualities of each. Sheldon concluded that criminals tended to be mesomorphic in body build.

Later studies of the relationship between body build and delinquency have to a certain degree supported the general hypothesis of Sheldon's theory.[13] However, a direct link between body build and criminality has not been proven. The sample sizes in Sheldon's research were quite small. Also, the extent to which delinquency is due to social factors, not body build, is not adequately explained. And not only criminals tend to have mesomorphic body types, but police do as well. These and other flaws have been pointed out, but among the theory's proponents the focus on biological factors in behavior persists.

Intelligence

The relationship between intelligence quotient (IQ) and crime has been explored throughout this century, for as long as measures for intelligence have existed. One of the first such measures was developed by the French psychologist Alfred Binet (1857–1911), who used task-related skills to measure intelligence. The tasks were devised to test reasoning ability and arranged in a series where each task required a higher level of ability. The individual was assigned a *mental age* based on the tasks he or she was able to complete successfully. The IQ score was determined by dividing the mental age by the chronological age and then multiplying by 100. In such a manner, a 9-year-old child who performed the tasks up to the mental age of 9 would receive a score of 100, smarter children would have a higher score, and less smart ones a lower score. Later, Stanford University scholars expanded the number of tasks on what was known as the Binet-Simon scale from 54 to 90 and arranged them so as to cover mental ages from 3 years to what was called "superior adult." This, which has become the most widely used form of intelligence testing, is today known as the Stanford-Binet scale.

Although Binet himself rejected the idea that intelligence is completely hereditary and fixed at birth, his IQ test was used by others to categorize people according to their "potential." People with IQs over 115 were considered suitable for the professions, those with a somewhat lower score were suitable for semi-skilled labor, and so forth. The primary concern was to identify the "subnormals" and "feebleminded" so as to isolate them and keep them from breeding additional offspring considered undesirable.

The link between **feeblemindedness** and crime was popularized by H. H. Goddard,[14] who earlier in this century administered the Binet tests to all inmates at the New Jersey Training School for the Feeble Minded at Vineland. He found no inmate with an IQ over 75, so that figure was set as the upper limit for feeblemindedness. Psychologists also administered the tests to a great number of other people in prisons, jails, and other public institutions. The results, showing that about 70 percent of the criminals were feebleminded, seemed to support the notion of a feeblemindedness-crime link. But later, during World War I, Goddard administered the same tests to draftees and discovered approximately the same proportion of feebleminded individuals in that population also, a finding he could not adequately explain. He then changed his mind about his conclusions and the proposals to incarcerate all feebleminded persons and prevent them from reproducing.[15]

That was not the last word on the issue, however. In 1977, Travis Hirschi and Michael Hindelang supported the IQ-delinquency link anew in a review of scientific research on the subject in which they reported an average gap of 8 points in the IQs of delinquents and nondelinquents.[16] They reported that low IQ is at least as relevant to official delinquency reports as social class or race. They also concluded that IQ is directly related to self-reported delinquency rates, and that lower-class delinquents are more likely to have low IQs than lower-class nondelinquents. They were less certain about IQ and adult criminality, and they suggested that low IQ might be connected to school failure, which in turn might lead to truancy, vandalism, and other forms of juvenile delinquency which in turn could lead to more serious forms of criminality. Adult criminal acts often require more thought and planning; therefore a low-IQ connection to adult crime is less evident.

Considerable controversy still surrounds claims of an IQ-crime link. Research which measures the IQs of prisoners is suspect since low IQ may be a better explanation of why a person was caught rather than why he or she committed a crime. For instance, Ted Bundy had an above average IQ, as evidenced by his education and the fact that he served as his own defense attorney at trial. Indeed, his intelligence enabled him to evade capture for a long period of time.

Convicted criminals and delinquents probably do not constitute a representative sample of the overall offender population; the best and brightest may not get caught, prosecuted, and convicted. However, some crimes—stock fraud, embezzlement, complex white-collar crimes, swindles, or fraud, for instance—probably require a higher-than-average IQ. So we may ask: To what extent does IQ reflect biological-genetic factors in the human organism at or before birth, or social conditions present after birth? And how is a person's IQ related to delinquent or criminal behavior, if at all? It is not strange that questions persist about the IQ-crime link.

XYY Chromosomes

Abnormalities in sex chromosome associations introduced genetic research to the study of crime.[17] The normal female has XX sex chromosomes, the normal male XY. Studies of prisoners revealed that a statistically significant number of prisoners had an XYY chromosome abnormality. Since the Y chromosome determines maleness, the idea developed that the extra Y chromosome constituted a "supermale," a person more aggressive and therefore potentially criminal.

The **XYY male** was said to be about 6 inches taller, at 6 feet 1 inch, than the average male. The early view was that the extra Y chromosome meant more testosterone and therefore more violence and aggression. Also, the extra Y chromosome was considered to be related to lower IQ. However, as research continued, these findings were largely refuted. XYY males have been shown to be less aggressive, not more, to have lower criminal rates, not higher, and to be less likely to commit crimes against persons than the XY male.

But research always points the way toward gaining new knowledge and insights. The existence of chromosomal abnormalities among prisoners has opened the window of exploration into genetic influences on criminal behavior beyond that of chromosomes themselves.

Contemporary Biological Research

Because much of the early research into biological influences on criminal behavior was disproven, this approach was largely rejected by criminologists through much of the twentieth century. However, with the recent advances in medical science, and with the remarkable growth of technological approaches to curing disease, biological theories concerning behavior have re-emerged stronger than ever. Today it is generally accepted that heredity is a significant causative factor in diseases as diverse as alcoholism, cancer, and heart disease, as well as in violent behavior, including crime. Studies show that nutrition and early childhood care affect behavior patterns for years after their actual occurrence.

Today the focus of the biological determinism approach is on the brain and central nervous system, and on hormones. C. Ray Jeffery is a leading proponent of that focus:

> Genes influence behavior through pathway mechanisms such as the brain, brain chemistry, and hormonal systems, all in interaction with one another and with the environment. . . .
>
> The brain has major centers for sensory input and motor output. The brain also contains centers for the control of emotional and motivational behavior, as well as for the control of rational behavior and decision making. Behavior is a product of the interaction of the millions of neurons in the brain.
>
> The brain functions primarily as a bioelectrochemical system, which in turn produces electrical and neurochemical activity in the neurons. These neurochemical activities in the neurotransmitter systems and hormonal systems are subject to the influence of diet and nutrition, as well as environmental pollution. The most important new development in the behavioral sciences has been in the brain sciences, and the joining of psychology, biochemistry, neurology, and psychiatry into an interdisciplinary approach to a theory of human behavior.[18]

The brain, then, stands between the environment and behavior. In this view, human behavior is not a simple response to free-will, rational decisions. Behavior is the product of extremely complex interactions between genetics and the environment.

Jeffery points out that there is no crime gene lurking in the human body which springs into action causing a person to pounce on another to rape or pillage. Genes do not cause crime. Rather, genes influence biological traits. Those traits may be recessive, that is, they may remain in the background, invisible and inactive, until or unless they are triggered. For instance, a person with a schizophrenic parent is not necessarily going to become schizophrenic. Schizophrenia might be the product of a recessive gene. But, if the person with the recessive schizophrenia gene is subjected to great stress, that stress may trigger the schizophrenia gene into action. The same stress exerted on a person without the schizophrenia gene would not produce schizophrenia. This same principle may be true of other physical systems as well. Susceptibility to cancer and heart disease are related to genetic factors more than to any other variables. Behavior, even criminal behavior, may be similarly attributable to genetics.

Your family may tell you that your appearance or behavior reminds them of a great grandparent or some other ancestor. All of us share certain traits with our family members. We can recognize the familiar appearance or mannerisms of famous families, the Kennedy family for instance. When a newborn baby arrives, the first statements from family members include comments about who the baby looks like. If genetic influences are so readily seen in the visible appearance of people, they must also exist in the nonvisible area of behavior traits.

Sociological Determinism

Sociology is concerned with the social environment in its search for explanations for crime. It does not ignore the individual, but its primary focus is the environment, the social context of crime. This approach identifies factors in the social environment which are believed to contribute to a person's behavior—the family, peer group, economic conditions, success opportunities, school, and all the other myriad influences into which a person is born. These factors are outside the individual and are seen to exert powerful influences on the individual, influences beyond a person's will which cause delinquency and crime. This approach is known as **sociological determinism**.

The Chicago School and Social Disorganization

The environmental approach had its genesis in the studies conducted by a group of University of Chicago sociologists on behalf of the Institute for Juvenile Research in Chicago in the late 1920s and is sometimes referred to as the **Chicago School of criminology**. It is most commonly associated with the work of Clifford Shaw and Henry McKay, among others.[19]

Using official data, these researchers mapped delinquency by plotting police reports and juvenile court referrals on a map of Chicago (see Fig. 3.1). They then drew concentric circles from the center of the city on the map. The clusters of crime were identified as the areas of the city which appeared to have the highest rates of delinquency. This technique is referred to as a "mapping system." Shaw and McKay, along with their associates, next studied Chicago neighborhoods to discover what characteristics distinguished high- and low-delinquency areas. And by intensively studying the people in those neighborhoods, by virtually living with them, the researchers were able to observe the everyday lives of individuals in their natural environments, much like botanists study flora and fauna in *their* natural habitats. For this reason the technique is sometimes called the "ecological approach."

Juvenile referrals were discovered to be highest in neighborhoods of rapid change, poor housing, poverty, tuberculosis, adult crime, and mental disorders. These neighborhoods were closest to the center of the city, and delinquency tended to decline with distance from that core. Over time, the maps and charts of delinquency in the Chicago area showed a consistent pattern of crime and other social problems in inner-city areas despite rapid changes in the ethnic populations living there.

The first zone, called the "central business district," had few residences but many businesses and factories. The next zone, called the "zone of transition," was an area of deteriorating homes and encroaching factories and businesses. Immigrants to Chicago tended to settle there first because of the cheap housing and close proximity to factories where employment could be found. Then, as they were able, these immi-

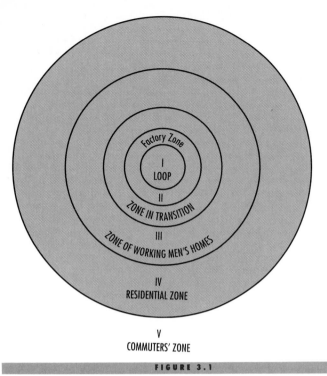

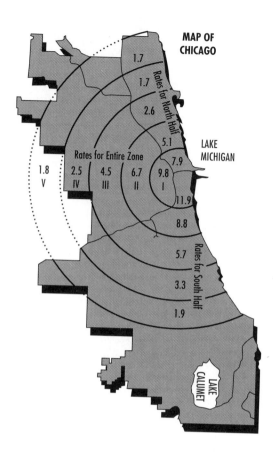

MAP OF CHICAGO

LAKE MICHIGAN

LAKE CALUMET

Zone rates of male juvenile delinquents, Chicago, 1927–1933. (*Source:* Clifford R. Shaw and Henry D. McKay, *Juvenile Delinquency and Urban Areas,* University of Chicago Press, Chicago, 1969, pp. 51 and 69.)

grants moved into the next zone, called the "workingmen's neighborhood," and as affluence allowed, later moved into more stable, wealthy, and crime-free, neighborhoods. As already noted, the further out from the core, inner-city area, the less delinquency, crime, and other social problems the researchers discovered. And each group of immigrants moving out of the core city was replaced by new immigrants moving in for the same reasons as their predecessors and facing the same problems.

Shaw and McKay concluded from their studies that delinquents were essentially normal adolescents who were adversely influenced by the criminogenic influences of their socially disorganized environments. Chief among those influences were youth gangs, which flourished in the neighborhoods into which new immigrants moved. Those gangs were the result of the difficulty immigrants experienced in maintaining primary family relationships in their new cultural setting: Young people would become detached from social institutions such as school and church and from normal family controls, and thus alienated would drift into association with other adolescents like them; together, then, they would engage in delinquent acts.

This concept of **social disorganization** greatly influenced the study of crime and delinquency. But with the coming of the Great Depression of the 1930s and the subsequent decline in immigration, Shaw and McKay had to revise their theory to account for the continuing high rates of delinquency in inner-city neighborhoods despite the lack of mobility. They directed greater attention to poverty and unemployment as contributing causes of delinquency, as well as other social strains which people experience in economically deprived areas. Indeed, perhaps the foremost contribution the Chicago school made to criminology was to relate crime to lower-class issues and connect causally the conditions of poverty which contribute to delinquency and crime.

Official data (police reports) continually reinforce the relationship between social class and crime, that is, they show that crime is largely a lower-class phenomenon. This may be because crimes known to the police and arrest data appear to cluster in poverty areas, areas that the police patrol more intensively than middle- or upper-class neighborhoods. And lower-class crimes are more likely to result in arrest since they include such high-visibility activities as muggings, assaults, public drunkenness, and other so-called "street crimes" that are readily discovered and punished. If the scientist uses official data as a starting point to study crime, therefore, the conclusion that crime is a lower-class activity is inescapable, and this view has dominated much of sociological theory about crime.

Differential Association

One of the more famous scholars to emerge from the Chicago school was Edwin H. Sutherland.[20] Sutherland used the Chicago school methods—statistical data analysis and the case history (or life story)—and expanded his data base to include the newly introduced *Uniform Crime Reports* (UCRs), which the FBI began publishing on a yearly basis in the early 1930s (see Chap. 1).

In 1937, he published *The Professional Thief*,[21] a book written in collaboration with Chic Conwell, himself a professional thief. Based on lengthy interviews with, and written answers to questions by, thieves, the book explored the professional world of theft, stealing as a business, crime mobs, the "fix," and criminal rackets, as well as attitudes of thieves toward the law and society. Sutherland stated in the book: "The essential characteristics of the profession of theft . . . are technical skill, status, consensus, differential association, and organization."[22]

Sutherland developed this concept of **differential association** into a theory which he discussed in his 1939 book *Criminology*,[23] and which he subsequently revised in 1947. The theory, briefly stated, is as follows:

The Chicago school connected the conditions of poverty to delinquency and crime.

1. Criminal behavior is learned; it is not inherited, nor is it invented, but is acquired through training.
2. Criminal behavior is learned in interaction with other persons in a process of communication; that communication may be either verbal or "the communication of gestures."
3. The principal part of the learning of criminal behavior occurs within intimate personal groups; secondary sources such as movies, books, or newspapers are relatively unimportant.
4. When criminal behavior is learned, the learning includes (a) techniques of committing the crime, which are sometimes very complicated and other times very simple, and (b) the specific motives, drives, rationalizations, and attitudes that cause people to commit crimes.
5. People are surrounded by other people who view the legal code either as rules to be obeyed or rules to be violated. The individual's own orientation toward obeying or breaking the law results from the favorable or unfavorable view he or she has toward the legal code.
6. A person becomes delinquent because he or she defines the law as something to be violated rather than to be obeyed; that way of defining the law comes from the type of culture and the personal associations which have influenced the person most heavily.
7. Different personal associations may vary in frequency, duration, priority, and intensity; but criminal behaviors which begin in childhood through the influence of associations with significant others persist throughout life.
8. The process of learning criminal behavior or rejecting it by association with those who exhibit criminal or anticriminal patterns of behavior involves the same mechanisms as any other type of learning; it is not merely imitation, but becomes internalized in much the same way a person learns how to lay bricks.
9. While criminal behavior is an expression of general human needs and values, it is not explained by them since noncriminal behavior is an expression of those same needs and values; that is, both thieves *and* honest laborers attempt to secure money to meet their personal needs. The sources of criminal and noncriminal behaviors lie in a different area.

Social Learning Theory

In a significant restructuring of differential association theory, Ronald Akers combined it with the psychological theory of operant conditioning.[24] Akers contended that behavior is shaped by behavioral reinforcers, either positive (rewards) or negative (punishment). These reinforcers can come from direct nonsocial sources such as the physiological effects of alcohol or drugs; but usually they come from social sources such as family and peer groups from which most behavior is learned. Akers stated that both conforming and nonconforming behavior is acquired through the process of learning definitions of behaviors as good or bad, justified or not justified. And, as with all learning as understood by operant conditioning theory, criminal behavior is learned depending on the rewards and punishments attached to it by the significant groups with which people interact. This is known as **social learning theory**.

Middle-Class Measuring Rod

Albert K. Cohen's book *Delinquent Boys* (1955)[25] advanced the notion that lower-class values and lifestyles differ significantly from those of the middle class. It claimed that much juvenile delinquency is the result of the frustration experienced by lower-class boys who are measured against the **middle-class measuring rod**.

Cohen listed the middle-class values as (1) drive and ambition; (2) individual responsibility; (3) achievement and success in every area of endeavor; (4) deferred gratification; (5) long-range planning and budgeting; (6) courtesy and self-control, especially with strangers; (7) control of verbal or physical violence and aggression; (8) "wholesome" recreation, such as a hobby; (9) respect for the property of others. According to Cohen, the failure to adhere to those values, and the failure to perform well in the middle-class dominated school system, leads lower-class boys to reject those values and the school system and to act out against them. In that sense, delinquency is a product of a collective consensus among lower-class boys.

Cohen assumed that lower-class males tend to do poorly in school, that poor school performance is related to delinquency, that poor school performance results from the conflict between the middle-class values of the school system and the values of the lower class, and that delinquency in a gang context is a means of developing more positive self-concepts and expressing antisocial values. Cohen believed that all people seek status, and that the failure to achieve personal status in accepted, legitimate ways leads one to seek status in collective ways—hence the delinquent gang.

The delinquent gang, for Cohen, was characterized by behavior he considered to be nonutilitarian and malicious, apparently senseless acts by mean boys. But he also considered acts such as vandalism, terrorism on the playground, and defecating on the teacher's desk to be expressions of hostility to bolster the poor self-image of the "street corner" boys who committed them. And he saw much delinquent gang behavior as negativistic, direct attacks on middle-class values.

Lower-Class Focal Concerns

Walter Miller's work among lower-class people in Boston led to a different set of conclusions.[26] Although he also considered lower-class delinquent gang behavior as anti-middle-class, he saw it as normal and useful in the lower-class context. He identified categories of attributes, or roles, it promoted for the male gang member: the ability to handle trouble, being tough, being smart, finding life exciting, finding it fateful, and being autonomous.

Being able to handle trouble for lower-class males means being able to handle run-ins with police and other authorities, as well as being able to fight, drink, and engage in sexual activity. Being tough, or engaging in masculine bravado, means showing strength, sexual skills, tatoos, the lack of emotion. Being smart means to have street savvy, including the ability to outwit someone, to hustle unsuspecting "johns," or to "play the game." An exciting life means the heightened adventure, the thrill found in alcohol, sex, gambling, and other behaviors which come before and after prolonged periods of inactivity, called "hanging out." Fate refers to the belief that one is unable to control events, that strong forces of destiny or magic take one's future out of one's hands. And being autonomous is the very desirable ability to be independent of controls, especially those of a spouse or a boss.

These **lower-class focal concerns**, according to Miller, flourish in the female-based households which predominate in such families. Boys need to belong, to have status among their peers. These needs are met in the street-corner gang. The delinquent boys, therefore, are not emotionally disturbed or inferior, but represent competent youngsters whose needs are not met in middle-class ways, who do not have proper male role models to help them succeed in mainstream society.

Social Structure and Anomie

Robert K. Merton's 1938 article "Social Structure and Anomie" was published in the *American Sociological Review* during the Great Depression. It is the most frequently cited article in sociological or criminological textbooks.[27] Merton observed

Albert K. Cohen saw delinquent behavior as one way to achieve status for those unable to achieve status in legitimate ways.

the collapsing social conditions brought about by severe economic conditions, and rejecting the notion that crime is an intrinsic and individual behavior, looked beyond the immediate personal environment of criminals to the broader context of **social structure** and **anomie** for explanations.

Merton borrowed the term **anomie** from Émile Durkheim, a French sociologist who introduced it in his book *The Division of Labor in Society* (1893) and later used it in his book *Suicide* (1897).[28] Durkheim had studied the French and American cultures after the Industrial Revolution and had noted that economic crises and a general breakdown of normal societal conditions created a "deregulation" of social and moral rules. This deregulation, which he called "anomie," could lead to all sorts of social deviance including suicide and crime.

Anomie is understood to be the condition which exists when norms no longer control people's behavior. When people no longer have clear rules, when norm-lessness exists, then controls on behaviors and aspirations cease to exist. Merton maintained that anomie is especially likely to exist in a society such as the United States, where there is unequal opportunity and an emphasis on material success, and claimed it can explain a broad range of socially deviant behavior. In Merton's view, American society has established institutionalized goals, usually understood to be financial success, which society emphasizes and reinforces. Then, socially structured avenues to achieve those goals exist, called "means." When such goals are over-emphasized and extolled to the population at large, but the means to achieve them are unavailable to a considerable part of that same population, then anomie is likely. That is, when people whose paths to what is commonly regarded as success are blocked, those individuals experience strain, and must either adjust their aspirations downward or devise alternative routes to achieve the goals. In such an environment, deviant behavior is widespread.

Merton described five **modes of adaptation** to achieve goals: conformity, innovation, ritualism, retreatism, and rebellion (see Table 3.2) *Conformity* is the path taken by most people, according to Merton, even if they realize that the means to achieve their goals are restricted. However, the remaining four modes present alternatives to conformity which may lead to various forms of deviance, including crime.

Innovation occurs when a person accepts a goal, but rejects the accepted, legitimate means to achieve the goal. For instance, if a child wants a new bicycle, legitimate means to obtain it exist: asking grandparents for a bicycle at Christmas, saving money from one's allowance or part-time jobs, etc. If those means are not available, or if the child is not sufficiently committed to them, then alternative—innovative—means may be chosen, such as theft.

TABLE 3.2 *Robert Merton's five modes of adaptation*

Modes of adaptation	Cultural goals	Institutionalized means
Conformity	+	+
Innovation	+	−
Ritualism	−	+
Retreatism	−	−
Rebellion	±	±

SOURCE: Robert Merton, "Social Structure and Anomie," in *Social Theory and Social Structure* (Glencoe, IL: Free Press, 1957).

Ritualism refers to the person who continues to follow the institutionalized means of achieving goals, hard work and thrift, but who has lost sight of the goals, or has rejected them. This may describe the so-called rat race, in which people work diligently in socially approved ways but have no hope of success in achieving their goals, or no longer identify with long-term goals.

The third mode is *retreatism*, in which both goals and means are rejected. The retreatist response to an inability to reach goals is to drop out, to quit trying. This may lead to extreme retreatist behavior such as alcoholism, drug addiction, or vagrancy.

Rebellion is an option for people who reject the approved goals and means to achieve them for new goals and means. Rebels and revolutionaries are disgruntled individuals who view accepted goals as unattainable or undesirable and socially approved means of reaching them as demeaning or unworkable. Therefore, these persons substitute new, socially unacceptable goals and means, such as the redistribution of wealth through a socialist political structure.

Merton's theory has gained great popularity, as evidenced by the frequent references to it in sociological literature. This was largely due to its focus on issues larger than personal environment—to its focus on the overarching social structure which influences behavior, and which especially serves to disenfranchise large numbers of poor people. Among the many theorists who were influenced by the notions of social structure and anomie were Richard A. Cloward and Lloyd E. Ohlin, to whom we now turn.

Differential Opportunity Theory

Cloward and Ohlin took Merton's concept of illegitimate means, and Sutherland's theory of differential association, as the background of what they called **differential opportunity theory**, which they proposed in *Delinquency and Opportunity: A Theory of Delinquent Gangs* (1960).[29] Essentially, this theory states that blocked opportunities to achieve economic goals cause feelings of frustration and poor self-images, and those feelings in turn lead to delinquent gangs of juveniles.

Cloward and Ohlin contended that opportunities to commit illegal acts are distributed unevenly throughout society, just as opportunities to participate in conformist behavior are. They identified three types of lower-class gangs: criminal, conflict, and drug-oriented or retreatist.

According to differential opportunity theory, *criminal gangs* emerge in neighborhoods where adult, organized, long-term criminal behavior exists. Adult criminals are the tutors and role models for adolescent gang members. Gang behavior is stable and theft-oriented; crime is supposed to be businesslike and disciplined, not violent and irrational. Adult criminals, such as fences, and local business leaders and political officials integrate conventional and unconventional behavior to accommodate personal gain and neighborhood stability.

Conflict gangs emerge where no such adult criminal role models exist, where conditions of poverty are greater, and where neighborhoods are less stable and more transient. Blocked opportunities lead to frustration and then to violence. Conflict gangs seek to obtain through violence that which they cannot obtain legitimately and which they do not have the opportunity to achieve through nonviolent, theft-oriented ways. These gangs lack the stable system of social control evident in criminal gangs. And Cloward and Ohlin point out that when a social street worker attaches to a conflict gang, gang violence diminishes due to the recognition by gang members that they are no longer rejected, that they can begin to gain access to legitimate success opportunities.

Some gangs are dominated by drug use. These Cloward and Ohlin labeled *retreatist*, or *drug-oriented, gangs*. Sometimes members of criminal gangs or conflict gangs gravitate toward retreatist gangs, making those youths "double failures" who are unable to achieve success either by legitimate means *or* illegitimate means. These gangs are characterized by "street-corner boys" who have scaled down their aspirations and have dropped out of active involvement in any goal-directed behavior.

Cloward and Ohlin advocated the expansion of opportunity structures in American society. And many of the social programs which emerged at the national level in the 1960s were spawned by the widespread reading of *Delinquency and Opportunity.* If blocked opportunities cause delinquency, then many of those concerned about juvenile delinquency believed that expanded opportunities should lower delinquency rates.

Control Theory

A **control theory** about crime and delinquency was developed by Travis Hirschi in his book *Causes of Delinquency* (1969).[30] Hirschi stated that people's tendency to commit deviant acts is controlled by social bonds, bonds consisting of attachment, commitment, involvement, and belief.

Attachment means strong ties to parents and friends, including a good peer group, as well as to teachers and others in school. Strong attachments to significant people like family members, friends, and teachers (or a significant person from some other area of one's life) can help one resist criminal tendencies.

Commitment to conventional lines of action helps a person resist unconventional, or criminal, lines of action. For instance, a conventional way to obtain wanted merchandise is to work to earn money with which to purchase goods. To the extent to

Strong attachments to family members, friends, teachers, or others help a person resist criminal tendencies.

which a person is committed to following conventional lines of action he or she is able to resist the temptation to take a "short cut," or the "easy way," to obtaining goods through crime.

Involvement in conventional activities keeps a person busy so that no time is available for mischief. "The idle mind is the devil's workshop," the old saying goes, and when a person is involved in school, church, hobbies, clubs, teams, or work activities, then temptations stemming from idleness do not survive.

Belief, for Hirschi, involves not only religious belief, but also the acceptance of commonly held values. Among those values is respect for the feelings and property of others, and belief in obeying the law and social norms.

Control theory demonstrates the qualities of life that help bond a person to his or her society, and therefore control his or her behavior. People with strong bonds are less likely to commit criminal acts than those with weak bonds. And Hirschi has not only demonstrated the value of the family, school, and other kinds of social groupings in the formation of conventional or criminal behavior; he has provided some direction for corrective and preventive efforts to help control behavior.

Labeling Theory

Labeling theory looks beyond the criminal act to the process of defining the act criminal. It examines the process by which persons become labeled as criminals, delinquents, or deviants. And it attempts to explain how labeling influences a person who has been labeled.

Edwin Lemert is the recognized proponent of this view,[31] although Howard Becker and John Kitsuse are also identified with the theory.[32] Lemert asserted that two types of deviant acts occur, **primary and secondary deviance**. *Primary deviance* is that behavior which may be caused by biological or social conditions, or may be minor violations of the law such as childhood pranks. *Secondary deviance* is that behavior which comes after a person has developed a self-image as deviant, when crime or delinquency becomes incorporated into his or her identity or lifestyle.

Labeling theory assumes that no act is inherently criminal, that the label placed on the behavior and on the actor by the **social audience** determines whether or not an act or actor is criminal. Labeling theory has two aspects. First, labeling affects the person(s) labeled, and second, it affects the person(s) assigning the label. The first effect involves the process of "self-fulfilling prophecy," the process by which a person acts according to his or her self-perceptions. A person is given the status of criminal, or delinquent, a stigmatizing label which results in degradation, incarceration, and isolation. The person is subjected to treatment which causes him or her to *become* the thing he or she is described as being. In short, if you see yourself as a criminal, you will behave as a criminal, and finally you will become a criminal. And then you will join with others who have been labeled similarly and develop a criminal subculture. For the labeling theorist, the self-image is a product of assigned labels, and people tend to act out, or fulfill, the labels assigned to them, especially if those labels are internalized, made part of the persona. And the label is more important than the act the label describes. The harmful effect of labeling a person criminal occurs whether or not that person actually committed a crime.

The second effect involves the social audience, or those in a position to assign labels. The social audience includes family, peer, schools, psychologists, neighbors, and the criminal justice system. Consider the negative labels that can be assigned by parents and school officials: unwanted child, slow learner, disruptive child, behavior problem, unruly, disobedient, disrespectful, etc. Or consider negative labels that can be assigned by psychologists: emotionally disturbed, mentally retarded, passive-aggressive, etc. These labels, and their positive counterparts, can affect not just the person labeled if the labels are accepted, believed, and internalized, but also the social audience. People behave differently toward a labeled person; they respond to the label rather than to the person.

Labels assigned by the criminal justice system are uniformly negative, and can be circular, making it difficult to escape them: suspect→defendant→convicted felon→probationer→inmate→parolee→ex-offender→suspect. None of these improves a person's self-image, and none is considered desirable by the social audience—which in this case would be everyone *not* so labeled who hears the term. What would happen if a young woman said: "Mother, please say hello to my new boyfriend, Sam. He is a convicted felon." Mother would undoubtedly respond to the label before she did to Sam. The same principle applies to employers, police, school officials, and others in the social audience.

Labeling theory claims that labeling is especially powerful in regard to children and adolescents, and among those who are wrestling with their own self-concepts. And labeling is more likely to be applied to lower-class persons. Labels may impel an individual into delinquency; the labeling process can actually help create delinquency and criminality by harshly and publicly degrading a person, forcing him or her to retreat from the mainstream of society.

Proponents of labeling theory demonstrate that labelers tend to be white, middle-class, authority figures. Labeled criminals and delinquents tend to be poor, minority ethnics, and powerless. Labeling theory has focused attention on the social audience as well as on the offender. And it has contributed to the view that social class is related to perceived criminality, whether or not the people so labeled are actually criminals, and to an understanding of the process by which individuals become criminals.

Conflict Theory

Conflict theory is related to labeling theory in that it looks beyond the simple identification of criminals in society to the processes by which laws are made and certain lawbreakers are identified as criminals. But where labeling theory emphasizes the social audience as a causative factor in criminality, conflict theory shifts the focus even further from the individual offender to the established social order, to the power structure which writes into the criminal law its own interests, its own values. George Vold and Austin Turk are major spokespersons for this approach.[33]

Conflict theory concludes that criminal laws and criminal justice agency policies are established and influenced by political pressures. Those pressures are based in economics and comprise the predominant influence on the making of laws and the practices of the police, the courts, and corrections agencies. According to conflict theory, those members of society who are higher up the ladder of social class are the most powerful, exert the greatest influence on social policies, and impose their values on the rest of society. Those members of society who are lowest on the ladder of social class are powerless, find themselves the targets of the criminal justice system, and are unable to influence the law or that system; therefore they are most often legislated against, and their behavior is most often labeled as criminal.

Turk maintains that two methods are used by the powerful to control the less powerful. The first is coercion, or the use of force to control the population and make it conform to the requirements of the law. The more this type of control is used by the authorities, the more difficult it is to control a society, and the greater the likelihood of higher crime rates among the less powerful.

The second form of control is found in the law itself. The law may assume a great deal of importance, even more importance than the people whose behavior it regulates. In Turk's view, the law consists of lists of undesirable behaviors, along with their corresponding punishments, as well as procedures for the criminal justice system to follow. Turk also introduced the concept of "living time," which refers to generational transitions or the process by which older generations of people die out, leaving younger generations made up of people who have experienced only the existing legal order and therefore have less reason to resist the law or to question existing social structures. Turk believed that during such "living times" the relationship between the powerful and the less powerful is less conflict-oriented, thus leading to less crime.

Turk claimed that crime is higher among the less powerful when the power of the controlling groups is greatest. He also thought that if the less powerful were to become organized, conflict with the authorities would become greater, and the likelihood of higher crime rates would increase as well.

Radical/Marxist Criminology

Radical/Marxist criminology focuses attention on the people who have the political and economic power to define crime for the rest of society. Labeling and conflict theory both focus criminological inquiry away from the individual offender toward the impact of the criminal justice system itself, and away from individual deviant behavior toward the wider quest of the social origins of crime. Radical-Marxist theory explains crime and delinquency as a product of a struggle between the classes within society, between the "haves" and the "have nots," and especially between those who own the means of production (the bourgeoisie) and those who do not (the proletariat). The language is borrowed from the writings of Karl Marx, as is the critique of capitalist social and legal structures, although Marx himself did not write specifically about crime in capitalist society.

This view explains crime, therefore, as a product of the economic system of capitalism and the social class system it establishes. The criminal justice system is seen as a tool of the capitalist class—the rich and powerful people who own industry and have money—to control the lower classes. Since most crime, according to official data, is committed by members of the poor, working classes against other poor people, and as pointed out earlier this type of crime is very visible, the attention of the poor is drawn away from the less visible exploitation they experience at the hands of the rich.

Radical/Marxist criminology also discusses crime from another point of view. For example, William Chambliss[34] stated that crime is a rational reaction to the life conditions of a person's social class, and that the criminal law expands as the gap between the bourgeoisie and the proletariat widens so as to coerce the proletariat into submission. Richard Quinney[35] expanded on this to identify two broad categories of criminality: crimes of domination and repression, and crimes of accommodation and resistance. Crimes of the first type are committed by the agents of the capitalist class in order to maintain capitalist supremacy. Crime control policies are used by the capitalist class to suppress the lower classes, and crime control agencies may even break the law in order to maintain order. Quinney also argued that crimes of economic domination are committed by the powerful to preserve the capitalist system. These would include white collar crimes, environmental pollution, and organized crime.

Crimes of accommodation and resistance, on the other hand, are committed by the working classes in order to survive in the oppressive capitalist system. These would include burglary, robbery, and drug dealing, committed by poor people to provide the goods and services they are unable to provide for themselves through legitimate, legal means. Crimes such as murder, assault, and rape arise out of the frustration and rage resulting from the inequality in capitalist society.

Summary

As we said early on in this chapter, criminal justice policy and practice are seemingly established without regard to criminological theory. To some extent the gap between theory and practice may be due to the lack of consensus among criminologists as to the causes of crime. But the poor state of criminological theory itself is no doubt due to the minimal priority given to criminological research. Legislators, bureaucrats, and criminal justice agents appear to operate on and be satisfied by the same "commonsense" understanding of criminal motivation. Why did that person rob a bank? The answer is simple: greed. And so the search for reasons ends and the ineffective and inefficient practice of criminal justice proceeds on its way, based on the unfounded myths that punishment is an adequate deterrence and that rational theories of criminal behavior explain why crime occurs.

Likewise, in regard to the classical and positive approaches to criminology, there is also a gap between practice and theory. Most of the scientific evidence points to the correctness of the assumptions of positive criminology. Yet in American criminal justice the classical view prevails. Especially in serious crimes such as murder, regardless of the presumed causes of the crime, free-will choices on the part of the offender are assumed and the police, prosecutors, and correctional workers all seek to punish the offender in such a way as to deter other potential offenders in the society at large. In other words, despite the fact that most of the scientific evidence points to positivistic causes of crime, the law represents the values of the classical approach.

More research into the causes of crime is needed. It has been argued that such research is hampered in large part because of legislation which prohibits physiological research on criminals. C. Ray Jeffery has written, "We can put criminals in hell-holes called prisons, and we can execute them, but we cannot do research as to the causes of criminal behavior."[36] Legislation has indeed prohibited some of the more intrusive forms of physiological research on criminals. But it is an overstatement to claim that research is not possible. Important research has been and is being conducted into the causes of crime, as criminological journals regularly report, but much more interesting and provocative research into the causes of crime does need to be conducted.

Notes

1. Samuel Walker, *Sense and Nonsense about Crime: A Policy Guide* 2nd ed. (Pacific Grove, CA: Brooks/Cole, 1989), p. 11.
2. Ibid., p. 11; also see James Q. Wilson and Richard Herrnstein, *Crime and Human Nature: The Definitive Study of the Causes of Crime* (New York: Simon & Schuster, 1985), p. 44.
3. Beccaria, Cesare, *On Crimes and Punishments*, trans. Henry Paolucci (Indianapolis: Bobbs-Merrill, 1963).
4. For a summary of Beccaria's writings as well as a description of the influence of the social contract writers, see George B. Vold, *Theoretical Criminology* (New York: Oxford University Press, 1958), pp. 14–26. Also see George B. Vold and Thomas

J. Bernard, *Theoretical Criminology*, 3rd ed. (New York: Oxford University Press, 1986), pp. 18–35.

5. See David Fogel, *We Are the Living Proof* (Cincinnati: Anderson, 1979).

6. Ernest van den Haag, *Punishing Criminals* (New York: Basic Books, 1975).

7. Wilson and Herrnstein, op. cit., p. 44.

8. Walker, op. cit., p. 16.

9. Ibid., pp. 27–40; also see John Lewis Gillin, *Criminology and Phrenology* (New York: Appleton-Century, 1935), pp. 195–241.

10. Quoted in Harry Elmer Barnes and Negley K. Teeters, *New Horizons in Criminology* (New York: Prentice-Hall, 1943), p. 159.

11. Ibid., p. 161.

12. William H. Sheldon, *Varieties of Delinquent Youth: An Introduction to Constitutional Psychiatry* (New York: Harper and Row, 1949).

13. See, for example, J. B. Cortes and F. M. Gatti, *Delinquency and Crime: A Biopsychological Approach* (New York: Seminar Press, 1972); also see Sheldon Glueck and Eleanor T. Glueck, *Physique and Delinquency* (New York: Harper, 1956).

14. H. H. Goddard, *Feeblemindedness: Its Causes and Consequences* (New York: Macmillan, 1914); also see H. H. Goddard, "Feeblemindedness and Delinquency," *Journal of Psycho-Asthenics* 25 (1921): 168.

15. Vold and Bernard, op. cit., p. 73

16. Travis Hirschi and Michael Hindelang, "Intelligence and Delinquency: A Revisionist Review," *American Sociological Review* 42 (August 1977):571.

17. Herman A. Witkin et al., "Criminality in XYY and XXY Men," *Science* 193 (August 13, 1976): 547. See also Jan Volavka et al., "EEGs of XYY and XXY Men Found in a Large Birth Cohort," in Sarnoff A. Mednick and Karl O. Christiansen, eds., *Biosocial Bases of Criminal Behavior* (New York: Fardner Press, 1977), pp. 189–198.

18. C. Ray Jeffery, *Biology and Crime* (Beverly Hills, CA: Sage, 1979), p. 184. See also C. Ray Jeffery, *Criminology: An Interdisciplinary Approach* (Englewood Cliffs, NJ: Prentice-Hall, 1990), pp. 166–210.

19. Clifford R. Shaw and Henry D. McKay, *Social Factors in Juvenile Delinquency* (Washington, DC: Government Printing Office, 1931). Others identified with the Chicago School include Robert E. Parks and Ernest Burgess, *Introduction to the Scientific Study of Sociology* (Chicago: University of Chicago Press, 1924); also, William F. Whyte, *Street Corner Society: The Social Structure of the Italian Slum* (Chicago: University of Chicago Press, 1943).

20. Edwin H. Sutherland, *Principles of Criminology* (Philadelphia: Lippincott, 1922).

21. Edwin H. Sutherland, *The Professional Thief: By a Professional Thief* (Chicago: University of Chicago Press, 1937).

22. *Ibid.*, p. 197.

23. Edwin H. Sutherland, *Criminology*, (Philadelphia: Lippincott, 1939).

24. Robert L. Burgess and Ronald L. Akers, "A Differential Association-Reinforcement Theory of Criminal Behavior," *Social Problems* 14 (Fall 1966): 128. Also see Ronald L. Akers, *Deviant Behavior: A Social Learning Approach*, 3rd ed. (Belmont, CA: Wadsworth, 1985).

25. Albert K. Cohen, *Delinquent Boys* (New York: Free Press, 1955).

26. Walter B. Miller, *Juvenile Gangs in Context* (Englewood Cliffs, NJ: Prentice-Hall, 1967).

27. Robert K. Merton, "Social Structure and Anomie," *American Sociological Review* 3 (1938):672.

28. Émile Durkheim, *Suicide: A Study in Sociology* (1897) trans. George Simpson (New York: Free Press, 1951); *The Division of Labor in Society* (1893) trans. G. Simpson (New York: Free Press, 1933).

29. Richard A. Cloward and Lloyd E. Ohlin, *Delinquency and Opportunity* (New York: Free Press, 1960).
30. Travis Hirschi, *Causes of Delinquency* (Berkeley: University of California Press, 1969).
31. Edwin M. Lemert, *Human Deviance, Social Problems, and Social Control* (Englewood Cliffs, NJ: Prentice-Hall, 1967).
32. Howard S. Becker, *Outsiders—Studies in the Sociology of Deviance* (New York: Free Press, 1963); John Kitsuse, "Societal Reaction to Deviance: Problems of Theory and Method," *Social Problems* 11 (Winter 1962):131. See also Kai T. Erikson, "Notes on the Sociology of Deviance," *Social Problems* 9 (1962): 307.
33. Austin T. Turk, "Conflict and Criminality," *American Sociological Review* 31(1966): 338; also see Austin T. Turk, *Criminality and the Legal Order* (Chicago: Rand-McNally, 1969).
34. William B. Chambliss, "Toward a Political Economy of Crime," *Theory and Society* 2:152; also see William B. Chambliss and Robert B. Seidman, *Law, Order, and Power* (Reading, MA: Addison-Wesley, 1971).
35. Richard Quinney, *Critique of Legal Order* (Boston: Little, Brown, 1973).
36. C. Ray Jeffery, *Criminology: An Interdisciplinary Approach* (Englewood Cliffs, NJ: Prentice-Hall, 1990), p. 184.

SUGGESTED READINGS

Cesare Beccaria, *On Crimes and Punishments* (Indianapolis: Bobbs-Merrill, 1963).

Francis T. Cullen, *Rethinking Crime and Deviance Theory* (Totowa, NJ: Rowman & Allanheld, 1983).

C. Ray Jeffery, *Criminology: An Interdisciplinary Approach* (Englewood Cliffs, NJ: Prentice-Hall, 1990).

Jack Katz, *Seductions of Crime: Moral and Sensual Attractions of Doing Evil* (New York: Basic Books, 1988).

Hermann Mannheim (ed.), *Pioneers in Criminology*, 2nd ed. (Montclair, NJ: Patterson Smith, 1973).

Edwin H. Sutherland, *The Professional Thief* (Chicago: University of Chicago Press, 1937).

George B. Vold and Thomas J. Bernard, *Theoretical Criminology* (New York: Oxford University Press, 1986).

James Q. Wilson and Richard J. Herrnstein, *Crime and Human Nature* (New York: Simon and Schuster, 1986).

DISCUSSION QUESTIONS

1. How do theories about the causes of crime influence criminal justice practice, especially in regard to the punishment or treatment of offenders?

2. Compare and contrast the conservative crime control model and the liberal crime control model from a crime theory perspective.

3. What are the major tenets of the conservative and liberal approaches to crime?

4. Discuss the IQ-crime link.

5. How did the Age of Enlightenment influence the development of the conservative crime control model?

6. Describe the research methods of the Chicago school.

7. Explain the concept of differential association.

8. Explain the major components of social learning theory.

9. Describe the various types of delinquent gangs.

10. Describe Hirschi's control theory of delinquency.

4

The Criminal Justice Decision Network

Seven elderly men, all of them retired, enjoyed playing pinochle together. They would meet at a favorite table under a shade tree in the public park at approximately 3:00 p.m. every afternoon, unless it rained, in which case they would meet at the band shelter. The men laughed at each other's funny stories, talked about current events, and otherwise passed the time in harmless fun. However, this harmless pastime was interrupted one warm day when a local police officer, as part of his walking patrol in the park, observed them gambling. The men customarily wagered 20¢ on each game of pinochle, and the coins were in plain view when the officer approached.

The law was clear on the matter of gambling. Gambling was a crime. So the officer placed the seven under arrest, called for a paddy wagon, and transported the men to jail. They were "booked" and released on their own recognizance. After the arresting officer finished his investigation, the cases were referred to the state's attorney for prosecution. The men's wives were horrified and embarrassed, but the seven friends took some pleasure in their newly acquired status as criminals.

The case became widely known; it was the talk of the town. And almost everyone agreed that the officer was not acting properly when he arrested these "harmless old men," even if gambling is a crime. After a local television station featured the men and their case on the 6:00 p.m. news, and the local newspaper published a full description of the crime, many people began to contact the police department and the state's attorney to protest. Letters to the editor complained about the waste of criminal justice resources on such a trivial matter when the city was plagued by serious crime. Pressure began to build on the prosecutor, and finally the formal announcement was made that no charges would be brought against the seven men. Soon the seven were back at their familiar table, playing pinochle for 20¢ a game, and enjoying their new notoriety.

About this Chapter

The many purposes of crime control in our democratic society, pursued within the ideological framework inherent in that democratic society, are addressed through a complex network of decisions made by people who work in criminal justice agencies. That network is organized to include decisions made by the legislature, appellate courts, chief executives, and the on-line actors in the police, prosecution, court, and corrections agencies. Criminal justice is a large package, a forest with many trees. All parts are related so that what the police do or do not do affects the courts, and what the courts do or do not do affects the prisons *and* the police, and what the prisons do or do not do affects both the police and the courts in a complex, interrelated whole.

The trees in that forest are the major decision points in the network: the investigation of crimes and the arrest of suspects, pretrial release, charging, conviction, sentencing, probation, imprisonment, release, revocation, and even capital punishment. The individual regarding whom those decisions are made unifies the decisions into a network. Otherwise, each decision is made by a separate agency whose goals are often separate and sometimes conflicting.

Every tree in the forest is fascinating in its own right. Numerous books have been written about each decision point. Police work is endlessly fascinating, the drama of the courtroom is standard media fare, the heavy clang of prison gates heralds a world of captives that sometimes would shock Dante. But each step in the process, each set of ponderous laws or exciting field practices is but a part of the whole. That whole is so finely tuned that no tree can be cut or trimmed or pruned without affecting the forest itself.

All the participants in the criminal justice decision network act with the authority of the law. Police, prosecutors, judges, juries, wardens, parole officers—everyone connected with the system, whatever their roles—are representatives of our government. None is a mere robot, of course, simply and automatically doing whatever state legislatures, Congress, or the Supreme Court orders. All can act with a certain amount of discretion, and have the ability to choose among alternative actions in carrying out their jobs; but this discretion is controlled by Constitutional restraints, appellate court decisions, and, in many cases, by statute as well.

The agencies of our criminal justice decision network are created by legislation and funded by legislative grants from tax revenues. The laws they enforce are in the form of written statutes enacted by state and federal legislative bodies. The procedures they follow are authorized by law, and limited by law as well.

But all legislation is subject to interpretation by appeals courts and above all, in our political system, laws, whether they define crimes or police procedure, must be consistent with the provisions of our federal and state constitutions. Indeed, the provisions of the Bill of Rights and other amendments to the Constitution of the United States are the highest laws of the land.

The sources of authority in the criminal justice decision network derive from the complex relationships among the Constitution, the Supreme Court, the legislatures, the elected chief executives of the nation and of each state, and the criminal justice agencies themselves. These complex relationships give the police, courts, and prisons power to act. This chapter describes these sources and deals with relationships among them.

STEPS IN THE CRIMINAL JUSTICE PROCESS

The complexity of the criminal justice process does not make for a clear picture of a well-defined and manageable system. The system appears even more disorganized when viewed with its multiple objectives, but it becomes more clearly a system when its actual operation is traced. For the glue which holds it together is the **decision network** which transforms individuals from free citizens into suspects, then into defendants, into convicted offenders, into probationers, and into inmates or parolees, leading, in most instances to their eventual discharge from sentence and their return to society. The full-scale network includes a number of major decision steps made about crime, and about suspects and offenders, which, though made at different times, by people in different agencies, are linked and flow into one another. See Fig. 4.1 for a flow chart of the system.

Another way to depict the criminal justice process is as an ever-narrowing funnel which screens offenders. See Fig. 4.2. Out of the large, unknown mass of crimes, some are brought to police attention either through police initiative or, more likely, through citizen reports and complaints. Then, of those crimes known to the police, a lesser number result in an arrest. Following that, fewer still are prosecuted, an even lesser number are convicted, and finally a yet smaller number are incarcerated.

Each step in the criminal justice system will be discussed in detail in later chapters. In this section, we provide a broad overview.

Investigation, Arrest, and Bail

The criminal process normally begins when the police set out to **investigate crime**, either because they have received a report that a crime was committed or

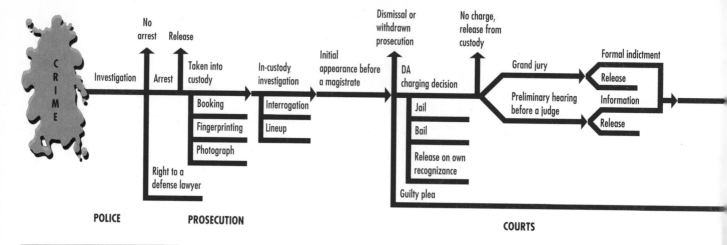

FIGURE 4.1

Criminal Justice
Decision Network.

because, as a result of indirect evidence, they believe that a criminal act has taken place. If they discover a crime *has* occurred, their next action is to determine who the violator was and apprehend the individual. This, of course, is the **arrest decision**. After arrest the individual (now a suspect) is taken into **custody** and "booked," that is, the arrest is registered in a precinct house and the suspect fingerprinted and photographed. The next step is **in-custody investigation** which, among other things, involves interrogation and may require the suspect to appear in a "line-up," that is, appear on a stage with persons of roughly similar appearance for viewing by victims or witnesses to the crime.

After in-custody investigation, the suspect is taken to a court for what is called the "**initial appearance** before a magistrate." A major purpose of this appearance is for the judge to decide "at first glance" whether it appears that the alleged crime was committed and that the accused committed it. Many cases are resolved at this point as a result of guilty pleas, dismissals, or withdrawals of charges. If the judge is satisfied regarding the probability of the crime and the accused's role in it, the question of release pending trial is faced. The judge can set a certain amount of bail or free the person on his or her word of honor to appear for later proceedings ("release on the accused's own recognizance"). If the suspect posts bond or is released on his or her own recognizance, he or she is then free to return home until summoned for later proceedings.

At each of these early decision points from arrest onward, the suspect has a right to a defense lawyer, provided at state expense if he or she cannot afford to pay for counsel.

The Charging Decision

While the suspect is free on bail or waiting in jail, the police reports are passed on to the prosecutor (also known as the district attorney or DA) for a decision on whether to charge the suspect with criminal activity and a determination of the specific crime or crimes involved; this latter also involves how many charges to bring, since not infrequently an individual has been arrested for more than one offense. Sometimes a prosecutor decides not to charge any crime, perhaps because the evidence does not seem sufficient to result in conviction, or because the evidence obtained by the police was wrongfully seized and would likely be held inadmissible at trial, or, more rarely, simply because the DA does not wish to prosecute a particular kind of crime; then the suspect is released from custody. But more commonly the district attorney decides to

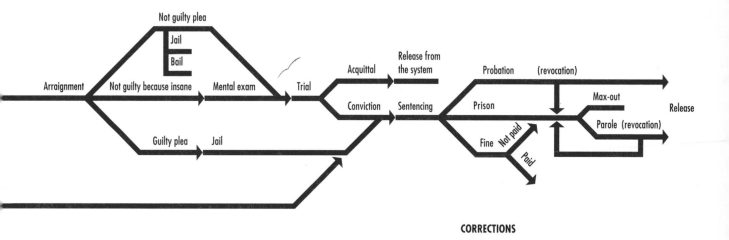

CORRECTIONS

proceed with the prosecution and, depending upon the provisions in the jurisdiction, may bring a formal charge against the suspect (now a defendant) in one of two ways. Where the grand jury system is used, the prosecutor (without the defendant or the defendant's lawyer present) appears before a grand jury, presenting some (but not all) of the evidence and asking the grand jury to issue an **indictment**, which is a formal charging document describing in legal language the crime or crimes of which the defendant stands accused. In those jurisdictions where the grand jury system is not used, the prosecutor goes before a judge at a preliminary hearing (here the defendant and his lawyer may attend). Again the DA introduces some evidence and requests the judge to issue an **information**, which is also a formal charging document almost identical to the grand jury indictment. It is rare for either a grand jury or a preliminary hearing judge to turn down a prosecutor's request since only the state's evidence is presented; defense rebuttal is reserved for trial.

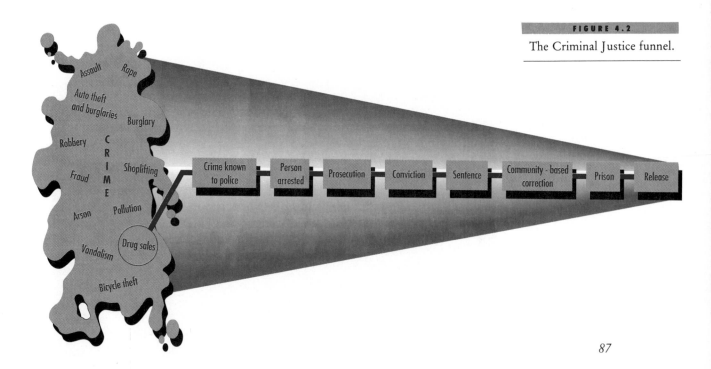

FIGURE 4.2

The Criminal Justice funnel.

Pleading and Trial

The next step is **pleading**: Once formally charged with a crime the defendant, with a lawyer, is brought before a court for arraignment, which is the point where the charges are read and the defendant is asked to plead to them. If the plea is not guilty, a time is set for the trial and once again bail is reconsidered or the defendant is returned to jail to await trial. If the plea is guilty and the court accepts it, the defendant is usually sent to jail to await sentencing, which occurs sometime after a presentence investigation is conducted by probation officers attached to the court. Sometimes special pleas, such as "not guilty because insane," are allowed and the defendant is sent for a mental examination before being returned to the court for trial or sentencing or, if found insane, for commitment to a mental hospital.

Sentencing

If the defendant is acquitted at trial he, or she, is freed. If convicted, by trial or plea, the defendant (now an offender) is returned to court after the judge has received the presentence report, which contains a great deal of social and psychological information about the offender to assist in making a sentencing decision. At sentencing the judge listens to whatever the offender or the offender's counsel wishes to say, ordinarily requests a sentence recommendation from the district attorney, and reads the presentence report. The judge then imposes sentence on the convicted person.

While sentencing choices vary from one place to another, and from one crime to another, in general the judge may fine the offender a set amount of money, order the offender to perform a specified number of community service hours, order probation (that is, a sentence served in the community under supervision of a probation officer and subject to rules and conditions imposed by the court), order the offender incarcerated in a local **jail** (usually for a definite amount of time—30, 60, 90 days, 6 months, or any time up to 1 year), or impose incarceration in a **prison** for a term defined by both a minimum and a maximum number of years. The minimum prison sentence is the length of time the offender (now an inmate) must serve before becoming eligible for **parole** (release from prison under supervision of a parole officer until the max-

Trial judges listen to both the prosecutor and defense attorney alone. But appellate court judges sometimes listen to oral arguments as a group (en banc), as pictured here.

imum term expires). However, having served the minimum sentence by no means guarantees the inmate will be automatically released on parole; he, or she, is simply eligible for such release and, in fact, few inmates (except first offenders sentenced for minor crimes) are usually released at their first appearance before a parole board.

Prison, Parole, and "Good Time"

The maximum sentence, usually set by a judge at some point within a permissible outer limit fixed by legislation, is the date at which the inmate *must* be released from confinement, not on parole but as discharged from sentence. Inmates who serve their full term are said to "max-out," but except for short prison terms of 1 or 2 years, this is rare. Most inmates are paroled at least once between their minimum date of eligibility and the expiration of the maximum sentence. Additionally, in almost all states, inmates can earn time off the maximum sentence for good behavior while serving sentence. "**Good time**" provisions vary considerably from one state to another but, in general, these laws can substantially reduce the maximum sentence (and sometimes the minimum period for parole eligibility) of inmates who serve their sentences without causing disruptions in the prison or trouble by fighting, smuggling contraband, or otherwise violating prison regulations.

As can be seen, the actual time served in prison by any inmate is determined through a complex series of decisions. An example might help to clarify this complexity. Assume that a statute provides a sentence of not more than 20 years in prison for an offender convicted of armed robbery. The same, or a related statute, allows the sentencing judge to set a court-imposed maximum at any point up to 20 years, but not beyond this limit. Simultaneously, the law provides that a minimum term may be fixed by the judge, usually at not more than one-third the imposed maximum. In a particular case a sentence of 3 to 10 years would appropriately fall within this penalty structure, which is the term the judge imposes. The sentenced robber could be paroled in 3 years or any time after that up to 10 years. He, or she, could also max-out at 10 years, having completed the full sentence. Good time statutes, however, may reduce the actual maximum by as much as 6 or 7 years so that if the inmate accumulates all possible good time credits, and is not paroled, release will be in 3 or 4 years. Thus the maximum legal sentence of 20 years is reduced by the judge to 10 years and further reduced by good time provisions to 3 or 4 years.

While this example may seem complicated, it is actually simple compared to what *could* happen. If parole were granted and later revoked or if some good time credits were disallowed because of misbehavior by the inmate, the calculation of time actually served would be considerably more complicated. And it could be still further tangled by the imposition of consecutive sentences for multiple crimes or a new sentence imposed upon the offender for a crime committed while on parole.

Probation Conditions and Revocation

Offenders can also be sentenced to **probation** outside jail or prison. Probation rules and conditions are fixed by the court. These are generally standard requirements that the probationer keep a curfew, avoid excessive drinking, not associate with known criminals, keep his or her whereabouts known to the probation officer, and otherwise behave in a law-abiding manner. Sometimes special conditions are imposed, such as requiring the offender to seek psychological help, to make restitution to victims, or to carry out other tasks relevant to the particular case. Should the probationer violate any of these conditions (and, in many places, should he or she fail to "cooperate" with probation authorities), probationary status can be **revoked** by the court and incarceration imposed. Interestingly, in most places time served on probation prior to a revocation does not count toward sentence completion; the sentence starts anew once the offender is incarcerated.

Prison Conditions

Convicted offenders sentenced to prison are classified according to their estimated escape risk, as well as according to whatever educational, vocational, or counseling needs they may have which can be delivered by in-prison services. Generally, both prisons and prisoners are classified in terms of maximum, medium, or minimum security and many of the conditions of serving time are determined by these classifications: decisions in regard to which type of prison (maximum security, etc.) inmates will be sent to, what kinds of cells and jobs prisoners will be assigned to, and who will be allowed to visit them or send them mail. Some inmates may find themselves housed in minimum-security forestry camps or farms, others in fenced, medium-security institutions involved in vocational training, while still others (the majority, in actual fact) in walled, gun-turreted fortress-like maximum-security prisons, working in such state-use industries as furniture manufacturing or the making of road signs.

Release from Prison and Discharge from Sentence

The next major step in the criminal justice process is release from incarceration or successful completion of a designated period of probation supervision. As mentioned earlier, prison inmates are released in one of three ways: on parole (subject to rules, conditions, and supervision very similar to those imposed on probationers), upon completion of their maximum sentences, or upon completion of their maximum sentences less time off for good behavior. Probationers who successfully complete their terms of supervision and prisoners who max-out are **discharged from sentence** but, of course, still retain their criminal records, which will last all their lives.

Parole terms can be revoked and parolees returned to prison to complete their maximum sentences; in a number of states, supervision is also required of good time releasees, whose releases also may be revoked and the offenders returned to complete their maximum sentences.

Though the criminal justice process ends for a particular offender when he or she is released from state control, a record of conviction and sentence remains, and the effects of that record may continue to be felt by the ex-offender throughout his or her life. In most jurisdictions persons convicted of a felony lose a number of rights, ranging from the eligibility to vote to the ability to obtain a driving license and enter certain occupations and professions. Today some jurisdictions have procedures for **restoration of rights**. The ex-offender may apply to a court for such restoration, usually no sooner than 5 years after discharge from sentence. In some places, there are procedures for "**expunging**," or erasing or wiping out, records of youthful offenders who have successfully completed sentences and remain law-abiding for a period of time. Restoration or expungement procedures vary and their success has been limited. Some negative aspects of having been convicted of a crime and having served a sentence may be diminished, but the record of having been a prisoner persists.

SOURCES OF AUTHORITY

Criminal justice decisions are not made in a vacuum—they do not reflect merely the whims of the decision maker. All crime control decisions, and all programs for crime

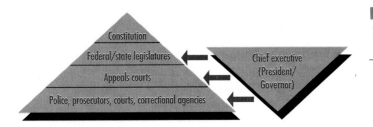

FIGURE 4.3

Hierarchy of the Criminal Justice System's Authority.

control, rest on government authority. Above all else, the criminal justice system is a *legal* system. Its *sources of authority* may be found in the U.S. Constitution and in each of the major branches of our government: executive, legislative, judicial.

The executive branch (the President, state governors, or city mayors) functions primarily to initiate legislation, appoint administrators, and propose budgets. Sometimes it has a more direct role in the criminal justice system, such as when it pardons prisoners or commutes sentences (that is, lessens them so inmates can be paroled). The legislative branch defines crimes, and the judicial branch decides how the law should be applied.

Various agencies in the criminal justice system—police, prosecutors, trial courts, probation offices, prisons, and parole authorities—administer this authority by enforcing the laws; they are in charge of the overall criminal justice process on a daily basis, and in that role are given some rule-making authority.

Traditionally the criminal justice system's authority structure has been seen as a hierarchy. (See Figure 4.3.) At the very top is the U.S. Constitution. Next is the legislature, which defines crimes, subject to judicial review on Constitutional grounds. Appeals courts come next, with the power to interpret and apply statutes to specific criminal cases brought by the operating (or "on-line") agencies. At the bottom of the hierarchy are the police, prosecutors, courts, and correctional agencies, which are expected to do no more than carry out what the legislature and the higher courts demand. In brief, power flows downward from the U.S. Constitution to the legislature which makes the laws, to the judicial branch which interprets them, and finally to the police and other agencies, which, in theory, have no discretion to ignore or modify written laws or court orders. In this model the chief executive stands somewhere outside the system, feeding ideas, programs, and appointive personnel into it, but chiefly acting indirectly as an influential political leader.

While this sort of hierarchical authority structure does exist, the criminal justice system actually operates in a more complex, less automatic way. The complete system of criminal law cannot be found simply by looking at statute books. Other parts— appeals courts and enforcement agencies—have *lawmaking* functions as well. To understand how our criminal justice system works, it is necessary to know the role and functions of all actors in the network. The major sources of authority—U.S. Constitution, legislatures, courts, and agencies—are *mutual and simultaneous partners*, although not always equal partners, in crime control efforts.

The usefulness of this mixed-power approach rests on the need to apply legislative language to actual street crime situations. All statutes are necessarily broad and general, whether defining a crime or permitting such procedures as search and trial. It is virtually impossible to provide written laws that cover all the variations of situations that arise. It is equally impossible to specify all the proper (or improper) actions of a police officer, who is constantly confronted with diverse and unpredictable street situations.

THE U.S. CONSTITUTION

The U.S. Constitution is the basic document that gives authority to criminal justice agencies. It also sets the outer limits to their efforts, making sure that our system of crime control fits our form of government. All of the provisions of the Constitution apply to crime control, though a number of amendments are system-specific. For instance, the Fourth Amendment prohibits illegal searches and seizures of evidence; the Fifth prevents self-incrimination during questioning; the Sixth guarantees a right to jury trial; the Eighth provides for reasonable bail and prohibits cruel and unusual punishment; and the Fourteenth prevents us from depriving anyone of liberty without due process of law. It is surprising, perhaps, that so many Constitutional provisions, drafted two centuries ago, dealt *specifically* with crime control decisions. If nothing else, it demonstrates how eager we, as a new nation, were to escape the unfairness and brutality of many of the criminal justice systems in our ancestral lands.

However important the other authority pillars of our criminal justice network are, its bedrock is the U.S. Constitution—and, it should be noted, the constitutions of each of the fifty states. In a showdown, the U.S. Constitution takes precedence but states have constitutions too, and most are consistent with the U.S. Constitution (although not always in each particular). Part of the history of our constitutional democracy has involved the long, painful process of conforming state constitutions to the federal document. Indeed, we fought a very bloody War between the States over this very issue: the dominance of the federal Constitution over those enacted by each state.

In a very real sense, our criminal justice system starts with the Constitution and, as we shall see in some of the important Supreme Court cases, it ends there as well. Various practices of law enforcement, trial court behavior, and prison treatment can be developed by the on-line criminal justice agencies, but ultimately these practices are tested for **Constitutional conformity**. If they do not conform, they must be changed: the U.S. Constitution, as interpreted by the U.S. Supreme Court, is the last word.

LEGISLATIVE FUNCTIONS

Legislatures exist at all levels of government, from the federal Congress to city councils. Defining crime is limited to Congress, which enacts federal criminal laws, and to state legislatures, responsible for statewide criminal codes. County and city councils have limited authority to enact local **ordinances**, which are civil violations, not crimes, although violators can be fined. City councils cannot define felonies or misdemeanors. Crimes must be illegal acts defined at least statewide. Therefore, in criminal justice terminology, **legislature** refers to Congress or to the state legislatures having crime-defining powers.

Definition of Criminal Conduct

Crime is what the legislature defines as crime. The primary legislative function is to define criminal conduct and some defenses to criminal charges such as insanity or entrapment. These crimes and defenses are written into laws called **statutes**. Statutes typically specify elements that distinguish different degrees of a crime. For instance, the amount of money stolen is used to distinguish grand from petit larceny. However, even the most specific statute must be interpreted as it applies, or does not apply, to

Birth of a Bill

3/30/81 John W. Hinckley, Jr., attempts to assassinate Ronald Reagan. Reagan and Timothy J. McCarthy, a Secret Service agent, are wounded, but recover sufficiently to return to work. Thomas K. Delahanty retires on disability from the police force after the shooting. James S. Brady, Reagan's press secretary, is left permanently disabled from taking a shot in the head.

6/30/88 In the House of Representatives, an amendment is added to a drug enforcement bill that calls for a 7-day waiting period in the sale of pistols before a purchaser would be given the gun, to allow time for police officers to check the purchaser's background. The amendment, introduced by Representative Edward F. Feighan of Ohio, is named the Brady Amendment, for James Brady, in the House Judiciary Committee.

7/6/88 President Ronald Reagan, a long time opponent of gun controls and a member of the National Rifle Association, comes out in favor of the 7-day waiting period. The Law Enforcement Steering Committee, a national police organization, takes President Reagan's words to Congress and lends its support to the call for a waiting period.

9/15/88 The House strikes the Brady Amendment from the major drug legislation. In what gun control supporters call a sham, a substitute for the amendment directs the Attorney General to come up with a plan to give gun dealers immediate access to criminal records to screen purchasers.

Representative Feighan says, "We were outgunned by the N.R.A."

Eleven professional police organizations lobby for the amendment, already law in twenty-two states.

Presidential candidate Vice President George Bush opposes the amendment.

James and Sara Brady with members of the Senate on June 29, 1991, after the Brady Bill was passed in the Senate.

5/8/91 The Brady Bill is once again before the House. The influence wielded by the National Rifle Association in opposing it is seen by some gun control advocates as having weakened. The N.R.A. has been in the throes of internal struggles. However, the bill is in danger of being defeated by passage of the competing Staggers Bill.

The Brady Bill would:

- Establish a 7-day waiting period before the purchase of a handgun could be completed.
- Require the gun dealer to give the name of the purchaser to the police, who would have the option of checking the buyer's background for criminal and mental health records.
- Allow the sale to take place after 7 days, unless blocked by the police.

The Staggers Bill would:

- Mandate point-of-purchase checks on the criminal records of gun purchasers, using a computer network that would take 5 to 10 years to establish.
- Establish fines or penalties for gun dealers failing to use the network.

Money and time costs in setting up a national computer network system make the Staggers Bill unrealistic. Representative Charles E. Schumer, Democrat of Brooklyn and chair of the House Judiciary Committee's crime panel, calls the Staggers Bill a ruse of the National Rifle Association.

Any gun control bill that passes the House must go to the Senate, and if passed there, then go to the White House. Marlin Fitzwater, spokesperson for President Bush, states that the President will veto any gun control bill unless it is part of the comprehensive anticrime legislation he has proposed.

5/9/91   The Brady Bill passes the House by 239 to 186. The door to its approval is opened when the Staggers Bill is defeated by a surprising margin.

Mr. Brady talks to Ronald Reagan on the phone and comments afterward, "I told President Reagan in the end, truth wins out. Truth did win out. This time the little guys won."

Representative Shumer says, "The stranglehold of the N.R.A. on Congress has been broken."

Representative Mike Andrews, Democrat of Texas, votes for the Brady Bill this time, after voting against it in 1988. "Gun ownership has a long and proud tradition in Texas," he says. "So does law and order."

Wayne La Pierre, executive vice president of the N.R.A., launches a media campaign against the bill.

6/29/91   The Senate passes the Brady Bill, although it changes the waiting period to 5 days and makes police checks mandatory. The waiting period would be lifted after two and a half years, by which time a nationwide computer system should be in place, allowing for instant checks of prospective buyers.

Brady says his advice to President Bush is, "It's a good bill and you're a good man. Sign it."

President Bush indicates he will accept the Brady Bill if it is part of an overall crime bill. Overall legislation on an anticrime package is delayed until after the July 4 holiday.

7/12/91   A broad anticrime bill passes in the Senate that includes the Brady Bill. The bill is deliberately tough on crime, in a political move to make it more in line with President Bush's anticrime

individual cases. Even what seem to be precise definitions can prove to be inadequate in practical situations. For instance, statutes forbid carrying a concealed weapon. What is a weapon? Is a starter pistol a gun? The issue becomes much more complex with statutory definitions of the mental-state elements of crimes, such as "willful intent," "negligence," and "reckless disregard for life."

In spite of these difficulties, our criminal laws must be specific, and terms need to be **strictly construed** (that is, read just as written) by courts. Statutes that are not specific may, upon judicial review, be held unconstitutional on grounds of vagueness. It is an important principle in our society that all definitions of criminal conduct be clear so that everyone may know the limits of criminal law. Yet in many criminal codes there are offenses that are not precisely defined; these often include public-order misdemeanors such as vagrancy, loitering, and unlawful assembly. These are rarely challenged in court because they typically involve the poor and the homeless and because the penalties are less severe than the jail time those charged serve while awaiting trial. Such vague offenses pose tough enforcement problems, and many proposals, and hence to make its veto less likely. The bill includes:

- Limits on federal court review of prison inmate petitions
- Fifty-one additional felonies to be punishable by the death penalty
- Broadened standards on the admissibility of evidence seized by the police
- The right for federal prosecutors to try certain state crimes involving guns
- Mandatory prison sentences for violent crimes against the elderly

Senator Strom Thurmond, Republican of South Carolina, supports an anticrime bill sponsored by the Administration, but says "the heart of the President's bill" is included in the one that the Senate has passed.

The complete anticrime bill now moves back to the House.

10/18/91 Members of the House of Representatives, in the process of deliberating a broad anticrime bill, react with different points of view to a recent massacre at a Luby's cafeteria in Killeen, Texas. In the end, the provision that would ban certain semiautomatic firearms and multiple-bullet gun clips like those used by George Hennard to murder 22 people in Killeen is rejected 247 to 177.

11/27/91 The anticrime bill, including the Brady Bill, passes in the House, but debate is reopened in the Senate and it is voted down. The bill has become entangled in a political struggle between Democrats and Republicans. President Bush has threatened to veto the bill if it passes Congress and comes to him. The President has not come out directly against the Brady Bill, but objects to other parts of the anticrime bill that he perceives as too soft on criminals.

House Democrats may reintroduce the Brady Bill next year.

SOURCES: Barbara Gamarekian, "Reagan Statement Buoys Opponents of Rifle Group," *The New York Times*, July 6, 1988, p. A20; Charles Mohr, "Gun Control Plan Rejected in House," *The New York Times*, September 16, 1988; Gwen Ifill, "House Passes Bill to Set 7-Day Wait to Buy Handguns," *The New York Times*, May 9, 1991, p. A1; Alex Prud'homme, "A Blow to the N.R.A.," *Time*, May 20, 1991, p. 26. "Senate Strengthens Provisions of 'Brady Bill,'" *The Star-Ledger*, June 29, 1991, p. OE5; Gwen Ifill, "Broad, Tough Anti-Crime Measure Is Easily Approved by the Senate," *The New York Times*, July 12, 1991, p. A1; Gwen Ifill, "Congress Still Torn on Gun Control by Complex Regional Divisions," *The New York Times*, October 20, 1991, p. 19. Clifford Krauss, "After Senate Backs Bush and Blocks Anti-Crime Bill, Congress Goes Home," *The New York Times*, November 28, 1991, p. D22.

probably are unconstitutional on the grounds of vagueness. In recent years these and other "victimless" crimes have been frequent targets for legislative repeal.

Legislative attention to crime matters is not frequent, except in rare periods of total penal code revision. And since the 1960s about half our states have revised their criminal laws. However, even after revision, most jurisdictions every year see some new crimes added to the penal code or old crimes modified in some way. There are numerous reasons for this. In some cases, the legislature is attempting to resolve conflicting court interpretations of crimes or defenses. In others, a new or overlooked or controversial form of misconduct may be brought to legislative attention, thus creating a new crime. This occurred in the mid-1960s in the case of glue sniffing, which was felt to be a serious matter by both police and health officials, although most states at the time did not legally prohibit the behavior.

In some cases, legislatures are redefining punishment or sentencing procedures to make them conform to the U.S. Constitution after appellate courts have held earlier provisions to be unconstitutional. For instance, following the Supreme Court's decision on capital punishment in the *Furman* case decided in 1972,[1] several state legislatures rewrote capital punishment codes to comply with the newly interpreted Constitutional standards. By 1990, thirty-eight states had enacted death penalty provisions along these lines.

Determination of Appropriate Sentences

Legislatures react to particularly serious crimes, or perhaps to a so-called crime wave, by creating new statutes, increasing penalties for particular offenses, or both. For example, in recent years a number of state legislatures have increased penalties for drug-related crimes, and others have increased penalties for driving while intoxicated.

An important legislative function is to determine the appropriate sentences for crimes. Many recent code revisions have been undertaken because of the need to modify sentencing provisions, reconciling what often were clearly inequitable penalties.

The lawmaking function of legislatures is not always the rational procedure it is widely assumed to be. Legislators are first and foremost politicians who represent a wide variety of interests. They are often pressured by various political groups, lobbyists, and mail campaigns, and sometimes by public demonstrations. Although most legislative activity has little to do with crime and public interest in the revision of an insignificant statute may be minimal, the crime-defining (or -repealing) function occasionally becomes a hot political issue. Continued controversies regarding overturning the 1973 Supreme Court ruling legalizing abortion illustrate the intensity of public feeling and the political implications of each legislator's actions in connection with this question.

Expression of Public Morality

Many legislators feel duty-bound to express standards of public morality, though they realize that laws which attempt to legislate morality are impossible to fully enforce. Many criminal codes contain proscriptions against adultery, fornication, and other consensual sexual conduct, public drunkenness, gambling, and other behavior deemed immoral. At best these laws can be enforced only loosely. In some cases, there may be no serious legislative intent that they be enforced at all. Why have these laws at all then? Many legislators evidently feel a political need to publicly take a vigorous stance now and then against what many pressure groups feel to be rampant immoral conduct. Also, despite the impossibility of full enforcement and the tacit understanding that full enforcement is not intended, these laws have a suppressant effect on behaviors that are not necessarily seen as criminal but are nonetheless discouraged by society. That is, the law makes a statement of moral standards and for many people it encourages (rewards) moral conformity.

Repeal of Laws

It is comparatively easy for a legislator to win passage of a statute establishing a new "crime" on the basis of high principle; it is very difficult to **repeal** such a law. A number of so-called **blue laws**—ancient legislation making it a crime to work on the Sabbath, to graze cattle on the public green, and so on—still exist in many states, sometimes because their repeal has been overlooked, but also because motions to repeal them may be politically damaging. Few legislators wish to be identified as supporters of adultery or consensual homosexual behavior. It is true that a number of victimless crimes, primarily sexual misconduct statutes, have disappeared from legislation in recent years. But usually this was achieved by omission during total code revision, when the responsibility for repeal did not attach to any single legislator.

For instance, David W. Neubauer points out that several of the gray areas of the criminal law were decriminalized in Illinois during the redrafting of the Illinois criminal code in the 1960s. These included homosexuality between consenting adults in private, Sunday blue laws, and public drunkenness. At the same time statutory rape was reduced from a felony to a misdemeanor.[2] Such changes in the content of criminal law codes is not unusual during code revision, for in that process potentially damaging floor debates over any particular activity is avoided.

There are, however, reasons other than fear of political retaliation for not repealing criminal laws, even ancient blue laws. The proliferation of criminal statutes can be advantageous to the state in providing the technical means for "getting" certain dangerous or notorious offenders who cannot be arrested for the worst of their crimes. This has been called the "**Al Capone theory of lawmaking**,"[3] because the famous mobster was successfully prosecuted for tax law violations when he could not be charged with more serious crimes, such as murder. Several decades ago Thurman W. Arnold wrote: "Substantive criminal law for the most part consists not in a set of rules to be enforced, but in an arsenal of weapons to be used against such persons as the police or prosecutors may deem to be a menace to public safety."[4]

It is generally desirable for criminal laws to be worded precisely, not only to avoid a constitutional challenge on grounds of vagueness, but also to minimize uncertainty regarding arrest, charging, and adjudication decisions. Occasionally, however, legislation is drafted in *deliberately* ambiguous terms. One reason for this is the difficulty in specifying all possible varieties of conduct in certain crime categories. For example, few legislators doubt that sexual molestation of children is and must be considered a serious crime. The difficulty, however, arises in wording statutes to fully cover the range of conduct to be outlawed. Making "carnal knowledge and abuse of a minor" a felony leaves a great deal of interpretation to enforcement agencies and courts.

Renowned for his life as a gangster, Al Capone is now also renowned for the "Al Capone theory of lawmaking."

Another reason for occasional ambiguity is to prevent the introduction of technicalities, or "loopholes," by which serious or professional criminals can avoid prosecution. Gambling statutes in some jurisdictions are examples of this. Most often the legislature's purpose in outlawing gambling is to curb professional gambling or the bookmaking activities of organized criminals rather than to hinder neighborhood poker games or church bingo. To avoid the difficulty of distinguishing professional from amateur and friendly gambling, the statute may be written to forbid *all* gambling, with a tacit expectation that the law will be enforced sensibly—implying that enforcement officials will concentrate on bookies, numbers games, and other forms of professional gambling rather than poker games in the locker room of the country club.

Definition of Procedural Law

In addition to defining crimes and fixing penalties, legislatures also establish some criminal justice procedures. In most jurisdictions, statutes delimit the conditions under which arrests can be made with or without warrants, standards for the amount of force that may be used in making arrests, and requirements for using search warrants or wiretaps. Legislatures have been less precise in defining such procedures than in drafting substantive criminal laws. The basic reason is the nearly impossible task of spelling out in specific detail all the conditions necessary to cover the variety of enforcement situations confronted in the criminal justice system's daily operations. In most cases, no attempt is made to legislate specific conditions for arrest. Rather, the effort goes toward stating in general terms that the officers making the arrest must have probable cause or a reasonable belief that a felony has been committed and that the person being arrested is responsible for the act. Or, if the offense is a misdemeanor, the law may require that the arresting officer have witnessed the offense for an arrest to take place. Similarly, only such force as is necessary may be used to effect an arrest, and warrants can be issued only on probable cause. The determination of probable cause or reasonableness is determined first by the police officer at the scene, then by litigation at the trial court level, and finally, if necessary, by appellate review.

Generally, legislative procedural laws have been limited to police activities and the trial court stages of the criminal justice process up to and including sentencing. Legislatures have done little about postsentencing procedures, preferring instead to create correctional agencies and to delegate almost complete authority to them, subject only to U.S. Constitutional restrictions against cruel and unusual punishment.

There are some indications that legislatures now are taking a more active interest in all procedural matters, including those for processing inmates, probationers, and parolees. In some states, such as New York, legislatures have passed "stop-and-frisk" laws that attempt a codification of the conditions under which police officers may pat down suspects for weapons. Similarly, there are statutes spelling out criteria for wiretaps, for preventive detention, for procedures to be followed in parole revocation, and for other operational decisions.

Budgetary Appropriations

Authorizing budgets for crime control efforts is a very important legislative function. Not only is this a power where legislative authority is supreme but, by granting or withholding funds, legislatures can limit the exercise of agency discretion. The director of a correctional system, for example, will find the ability to make changes in the agency largely a function of the budget for the agency approved by the legislature. The director may be powerless to make any modifications that cost money when funds are not allocated and, indeed, may be forced to cut existing programs when budgets are reduced.

Although legislatures have become more liberal with funds as the crime problem has assumed greater political significance, few agencies are adequately staffed and supported. One of the complex problems of budgeting is that some criminal justice agencies are locally autonomous, whereas others are statewide in their jurisdiction, and still others are federal. Local expenditures are primarily for police, county budgets support jails and courts, and state monies fund prison systems. Discrepancies in funding may exist within the criminal justice system because different legislative bodies with different tax bases are responsible for the monetary support of the different parts of the system.

Other Powers of the Legislature

Thus it is obvious that legislatures play an important part in the criminal justice system; the system starts here, with legislatures setting the limits of criminal justice intervention and providing the monetary support.

But legislatures also have additional powers that impact on criminal justice. For example, the investigatory power of legislative committees is a function that occasionally assumes major significance.[5] And legislatures have impeachment power over certain criminal justice participants, including prosecuting attorneys, although impeachment is a cumbersome and rarely used procedure.

Finally, the functions of legislatures vary from one place to another, and in some instances unique powers exist. For example, in Vermont the legislature *elects* district court judges for the state. Or legislatures may have the authority to approve or reject executive appointments to courts and agencies.[6]

EXECUTIVE AUTHORITY

The chief executive of any jurisdiction (the President of the United States, the governor of a state, and to a lesser extent the mayor of a city) has a number of important functions in the criminal justice system. Some executives become directly involved; others act in a subtle or indirect fashion, perhaps with equal effect. Though there are variations among jurisdictions, executive functions fall into four major categories:

1. The *appointment of personnel*, including judges, boards and commissions, and directors of major criminal justice agencies.
2. The *introduction of legislation*, requests for new programs, and submission of executive budgets.
3. *Direct intervention* into the criminal justice process through powers of pardon or commutation, the creation of investigatory commissions, the appointment of special prosecutors, and the removal of incompetent officeholders.
4. Use of the power and prestige of office to *give direction* to crime control efforts by proposal, persuasion, and skillful application of political pressure.

The effectiveness of the executive in shaping the criminal justice system depends in part on individual style and the extent of interest a particular individual holding the executive office shows in crime control matters. Some executives have strong opinions about certain issues, such as the death penalty, and may push vigorously to exert a personal influence on the legislature, the courts, and the agencies. This type of executive may propose sweeping legislative reforms to fulfill campaign promises, or may do so simply out of personal conviction. Another executive may exhibit a quite different

Naming Clarence Thomas as a nominee for the Supreme Court is one example of President George Bush's executive authority.

style, allowing maximum legislative autonomy and waiting to react to legislation as it reaches his or her desk.

The function of the executive also varies according to the opportunities available, particularly with respect to the appointment of personnel. In some jurisdictions, the executive has no authority to appoint judges or prosecutors except on an interim basis because these are elective offices. In others, the chief executive may be able to appoint judges at all court levels as vacancies occur. And in some states, prosecuting attorneys and public defenders serve at the pleasure of the governor. Similarly, the executive may be able to appoint parole board members, a police commissioner, a director of corrections, and perhaps even wardens and some lower-echelon personnel. In some states, however, agency heads or parole board members have civil service tenure or overlapping term appointments that can be filled by the executive only when vacancies occur by retirement or resignation or when terms expire.[7]

The governor may use pardon and commutation powers frequently in some jurisdictions, particularly where long sentences are commonly imposed. In others, the use of pardons may be rare, limited to a few "Christmas commutations" and exceptionally meritorious cases.[8]

One important function of executive power is the **veto**, an example of the checks and balances built into our system of government. Even if rarely used, the veto tends to restrain legislative excesses. The executive may veto any legislation, whether it deals with definitions of crime or fund allocations. Though the veto ultimately may be overridden (usually a two-thirds vote of the legislative bodies is required to do so), this is a difficult and cumbersome process, particularly if there is no single-party domination of the legislature. Vetoes have been overridden by legislative coalitions, but the threat of executive veto remains a potent force for influencing legislative deliberation. Its power is more than an inconvenient obstruction to easy passage of laws. The exercise of veto power usually attracts widespread publicity, crystallizing public support for or against the measure under consideration and thereby focusing political attention on individual legislators, who may find themselves pitting their own popularity against that of the President, a governor, or a mayor.

Appellate Court Authority

The relationship between appellate courts and legislatures has been long, stormy, and controversial. An important form of check and balance in our system of government is the power, derived from the **supremacy clause**[9] of the U.S. Constitution, of judicial review to revoke legislation found to be unconstitutional.

The principle of judicial review is an important—indeed vital—appellate court function. Though all laws duly enacted are presumed to be Constitutional, the law-making power of legislatures is by no means uncontrolled, and our history is full of examples of the Supreme Court nullification of statutes. This power of appellate courts illustrates the complexity of the basic authority underlying our criminal justice system—that the court function is not simply one of the interpretation and application of statutes and that, in Constitutional matters, the Supreme Court is the highest authority in the land.

Appellate courts do not conduct trials. They act only on appeals of lower-court decisions. The appellate process relies on the records of lower-court proceedings, responding to briefs submitted by petitioners and government lawyers. Higher courts normally do not deal directly with defendants, nor do they (except in very unusual cases) review the factual evidence brought out at trials. Instead, they decide points of law, determine the applicability of statutes to the particular cases in question, examine transcripts for prejudicial errors, re-examine denials of motions to suppress evidence, and so on. Appellate courts have the authority to reverse convictions or to remand cases back to the lower courts for retrial or other action.

All jurisdictions have levels of courts, topped by the supreme court of each state.[10] At the top of the nation's judicial system is the U.S. Supreme Court. A jurisdiction may have intermediate appellate courts (most commonly found in large states and in the federal system) that hear appeals arising from trial courts within a particular region of the state, encompassing a number of counties, or, in the federal system, appeals from district courts in one of eleven federal circuits. The decisions of these intermediate courts can in turn be appealed to the supreme court of the jurisdiction and in some state cases even beyond this, rising eventually to review by the U.S. Supreme Court.

Power to Select Cases for Review

The appellate process is complex and costly, particularly when a case appealed through state channels moves into the federal appellate process.[11] The right to appellate review of a lower-court holding is by no means automatic; sufficient arguments must be made to convince the appellate court that the appeal is "meritorious," i.e., that it is not based on frivolous claims. The U.S. Supreme Court (and the supreme courts of some states) has the power to select among the petitions it receives to determine those it will act on—it may decide not to consider a case at all. Once arrived at this level, a case is presented to the Supreme Court by a **writ of *certiorari***—a request for review—and the Court may deny this review without giving reasons. Denial of *certiorari* may not mean the justices find the case lacks merit, but rather that they do not think its implications are broad enough to affect the law of the land; or denial may indicate that the Court does not wish to consider such matters at this time. There have been long periods of inactivity in the Supreme court review of criminal cases, but during the past 30 years, both that court and the state supreme courts have been more willing to consider significant criminal law and procedural matters.[12]

Role in Law Reform

The controversy between legislatures and appellate courts is not limited to the judicial review of the constitutionality of statutes. Another important issue is whether legislatures or courts should dominate in law reform. The intensity of this issue varies from state to state. In some places appellate courts tend to be passive and conservative, interpreting laws as cases arise, holding to the judicial principle of *stare decisis* (consistently following precedent from former cases), and being unwilling to take the lead in shaping laws or defining legal procedures.

There have been several opposing trends recently in the relations between executive, legislative, and judicial involvement in the criminal justice system. One has been an *increasing legislative involvement* in criminal law policy. Another has been a move by chief executives, especially U.S. Presidents, to attempt to curb the judicial activism of the higher courts so evident in recent decades. Then again, each opening on the U.S. Supreme Court, either as a result of the retirement or the death of a member, has met with vigorous debate and political maneuvering by liberal and conservative forces to place a new member there who would, presumably, espouse the philosophy of law espoused by those doing the maneuvering. Also, one of the powers of the executive is to appoint members to the lower appellate courts for life terms. This tends to make those courts a source of authority for the criminal justice system that is relatively independent of political pressure from both the general public and other branches of government.

AGENCY AUTHORITY

Each of the on-line criminal justice agencies (i.e., those agencies engaged in day-to-day criminal justice operations) has rule-making powers and a good deal of independence in decision making too. The outer limits of police, prosecution, judicial, and correctional authority are set by legislation and modified by appellate courts, but within these boundaries the range of decision alternatives—the discretional power left to the agencies—is great indeed. In fact, such discretional power may be even more important than the impact of legislatures or appellate courts in determining what our criminal justice system is like in daily operation. To view on-line agencies as automatically carrying out legislative purposes or following court dictates would be to oversimplify their role.

Sources of agency discretion vary. Legislative delegation is the most familiar source of discretionary authority. For example, it is usual for prison systems and parole boards to have broadly delegated authority over their functions. Often there is little legislative direction beyond the creation and funding for a department of corrections for the "care and treatment" of prisoners, and perhaps providing for a parole board given the power to "make rules and specify procedures for the release of inmates prior to the expiration of their terms."

Police Authority

Police comprise the largest component of the criminal justice network. In terms of both citizen and suspect contact, they are more directly involved than any other agency. And in most cases the criminal justice process begins with the police.

Cases of traditional crime processed through the system may originate in a number of ways:

1. A complaint or call for help made to the police.
2. Routine police patrols, other forms of surveillance, and the stopping and questioning of suspicious people.
3. Police searches for violations, as in placing wiretaps on the phones of suspected gangsters or the use of undercover cops to investigate the drug subculture.

Yet with minor exceptions, police agencies have *no formally delegated or traditional discretion* with respect to enforcing criminal laws. In theory, the police have a mandate to enforce equally and impartially every criminal law, to keep the peace, to search out crime, and, when evidence warrants, to take all violators into custody. But as every observer of police activity has pointed out, and as most citizens know, full enforcement is a myth. Selective enforcement is the rule: **Police discretion** (judgment as to alternatives in enforcement) is exercised by the police agencies as a whole and by each individual police officer. Reasons for police discretion range from community expectations of "sensible" enforcement to police efforts to achieve desired purposes without using the entire justice process—for example, handling drunks by helping them home or warning rather than arresting those violating minor laws.

The specters of corruption and discrimination are present whenever discretion exists, but this potential misuse of authority is characteristic of the entire system of criminal justice. Why does the myth of full police enforcement of laws continue to persist although the police themselves, courts, prosecutors, researchers, legal scholars, and many other people are aware of the discretion any way they use their power? The primary reason is that legislatures and courts have refused to sanction police discretion, which in turn puts police officials in a defensive position. Without an

express delegation of authority, the police official who admits to discretionary practices is put in the untenable position of appearing to overrule the legislature and courts. Admitting to such practices also requires the police to confront the most complex and difficult task of all in criminal justice administration: defining, defending, and monitoring criteria for discretion.

Officially recognized or not, there is little doubt that the discretionary practices of police are critical to the criminal justice system. In recent years large departments have attempted to develop policy guidelines for the exercise of discretion. In some instances, methods of monitoring officer discretion have been tested, for example, by requiring written reports of all citizen contacts whether or not they result in arrest. In general, however, without firm guidelines, the criteria for the actual exercise of police discretion remain obscure, resulting in what Professor Joseph Goldstein many years ago labeled a complex of "low-visibility" decisions.[13]

Prosecutor's Authority

The discretion of the prosecutor is probably as broad as that of any participant in the criminal justice system. It is noteworthy that this discretion is more often "recognized" than delegated by the legislature. The origin of the prosecutor's broad powers is in common law antecedents in both English and French legal history. Regardless of its origins or antecedents, however, such discretion is intrinsic to the task of screening the hundreds of cases brought to prosecutorial attention each year.

Prosecutorial discretion is clearly broad in scope, ranging from the power of **nolle prosequi** (a decision *not* to initiate prosecution even with sufficient evidence to do so, sometimes abbreviated to *nol pros*) to the selection of specific charges to be leveled against any defendant. In some jurisdictions there are legislative attempts to develop appropriate checks on the DA's authority. This may be done by requiring written reasons for *nol pros* decisions or by requiring the district attorney to continue to prosecute once an indictment is issued. In general, however, checks on the wide discretionary authority of the prosecutor have been ineffective. In some states the attorney general may have some "supervisory" authority over local prosecutors or may have concurrent jurisdiction to prosecute, but this power to intervene is rarely used.

The prosecutorial process is really a series of decisions, ranging from deciding whether to prosecute at all to determining the number of and specific charges to be presented to a grand jury or a judge at a preliminary hearing. Decisions not to prosecute are virtually uncontrollable, short of evidence of corruption or other forms of malfeasance on the part of the district attorney. Decisions to proceed to prosecution, however, are subject to screening by grand juries or judges at preliminary hearings. In about half the states, the grand jury system can be used, although it is seldom used as the exclusive way of charging serious crimes; in the other states a preliminary hearing is held. Both procedures are designed to test whether there is probable cause to hold the defendant for trial on the crimes charged. Distinctions between these screening processes are detailed in Chap. 9, but it should be noted here that they serve as a check on the prosecutor's discretion.

There is little doubt that the district attorney establishes broad enforcement and prosecutorial policies in addition to functioning as a decision maker in each individual case. For example, the police may notice that the prosecutor almost never charges assaults growing out of family disputes, or may consistently dismiss bad check cases whenever restitution is made to the victim. In this manner, without directly saying so, the prosecutor establishes enforcement policies regarding such offenses. Why should the police bother to arrest anyone in domestic dispute cases when it is known the prosecutor will refuse to charge? And the police may decide that proper police procedures need not be followed in certain cases if it is known the DA will overlook the use of improper procedures.

Prosecutors' policies may be stated explicitly, either in oral directives to chiefs of subdivisions or by memoranda distributed to all assistants. Policies issued in these ways may state standards for determining whether evidence is admissible at trial, the appropriate charges to be leveled in certain kinds of cases, or even procedures and guidelines for plea bargaining. Such discretion is justified and generally supported. Just because a crime has been committed, it does not follow that there must necessarily be a prosecution. The district attorney determines whether acts fall within the literal letter of the law and whether they should as a matter of public policy be prosecuted or not.

Trial Court as an On-Line Agency

Although it has the title "court," in operational terms the trial court, presided over by a judge, is an on-line agency for the processing of accused offenders and the sentencing of those convicted of criminal activities. The police and the prosecutor move cases along the assembly line of justice and the court stamps individuals "convicted" and moves them along to the correctional agencies.

In addition to formal duties at trial and sentencing, a judge is responsible for court personnel, from clerks to probation officers. Not only is the judge given *discretion by statute*, but he or she may also have the authority to *delegate discretion* to particular members of the court staff such as probation officers who conduct presentence investigations.

The legislative delegation of sentencing discretion to trial judges is normally quite specific. Except in those cases where statutes fix **mandatory sentences** for certain crime (life imprisonment for first-degree murder, for example), judges are usually granted the authority to choose among several sentencing alternatives. Generally, judges are delegated discretion to choose *types of sentences* (fines, probation, or imprisonment), to set some *conditions of sentences* (particularly rules of probation), and to fix minimum or maximum *lengths of prison sentences* within the outer limits set by statute.

In making a finding of guilt or innocence at trial, the discretion of the judge is less liberal than at sentencing. At trial it is assumed judges will rely on the impartial analyses of evidence and will arrive at their decisions on a purely professional basis using their skills as lawyers and jurists. Dismissals or acquittals on other than evidentiary grounds are not part of a judge's delegated powers, although in practice such things occasionally occur. Conviction on insufficient evidence is, of course, improper and subject to appellate reversal.

Relationships among on-line criminal justice agencies

Social scientists interested in studying complex organizations have argued that the criminal justice system is not a "system" at all because it has no core organization. Rather it is a series of processes by which people are passed through a series of separate agencies that, though related through the process, are structurally independent. In a traditional sense of "system," this is accurate. The on-line agencies of crime control are indeed separate and distinct from one another, without the common organization chart usually found in industrial, military, and other large bureaucracies. Yet the term "criminal justice system" has come into general usage with a full awareness that it is different in a variety of ways from more traditional systems, complex organizations, or even administrative agencies.

The organization of on-line criminal justice agencies differs from more traditional, "monolithic" complex organizations in at least six major dimensions:

1. Noninterchangeable personnel and absence of central authority
2. Separate, unrelated budgets
3. Differing jurisdictional boundaries
4. Separate labor pools, with personnel in each agency recruited from different professions or occupations
5. Differing patterns of personnel selection from one agency to another (and sometimes between the same type of agency in different jurisdictions)
6. Variations in the amount of citizen involvement in agency decision making

Some of the major conflicts in crime control can be attributed to these variations in the way agencies are organized, funded, and staffed. And rooted in this structure, or lack of it, are a number of problems that tend to obstruct easy changes or improvements. But this, it should be noted, is not the whole story.

Social Values Served by Variations in Criminal Justice Organization

There is little doubt that the hodgepodge structure and diverse staffing patterns of the on-line criminal justice agencies compound inefficiency, create stresses and tensions in and between those agencies, and make it difficult to suggest workable reforms. From the standpoint of efficiency, it would be more businesslike to merge all the agencies and offices into a unified whole, perhaps even to "federalize" all police, prosecutors, judges, and correctional services, and to set common personnel standards and requirements.

Yet it must be remembered that efficiency is only one goal of our criminal justice system. Just as the governmental separation of the powers of the legislative, judicial, and executive branches supports our political philosophy of pluralism and freedom, so the mixture of agency organizations and personnel standards serves certain other values that we espouse as well.

At best, we give reluctant support to crime control efforts because we must. We want safety and domestic order, but we also fear the enforcement power of the state and wish to maintain a degree of community control over the way the law is administered. As attractive as a federally controlled criminal justice system may appear from an efficiency viewpoint, any proposals in this direction tend to conflict with preferences for home rule and local autonomy in the staffing and funding of agencies. Likewise, the professionalization of criminal justice roles and the removal of some jobs from patronage (whereby newly elected or appointed agency administrators replace personnel with their own close associates or supporters) to the neutrality of civil service protection, while desirable from many perspectives, tend to prevent the involvement of ordinary citizens in criminal justice decisions. Thus all the differences in jurisdictions, budgets, methods of role selection, and degrees of lay involvement in on-line agencies serve multiple purposes. The principle of home rule is maintained by the local staffing patterns used in the selection of most police officers, prosecutors, and judges, while centralism exists in prison systems, where problems are beyond the coping capacity of local jurisdictions. Most prosecutors, judges, and chief executives are chosen by ballot. But educational prerequisites and competitive examinations remove incumbents from direct political whim or threat. Juries continue to function and lay police volunteers are assuming new importance, but the trend toward professionalism goes on. The result is a mixture of lay and expert decision makers across the criminal justice process, or in some instances working side by side in a single agency.

A careful analysis of the criminal justice system clearly shows that its basic structure, cumbersome and inefficient though it may be, nevertheless serves values that are central to a democratic society. A more uniform, better organized system would probably be achieved only by diminishing citizen control and forfeiting local autonomy. We are evidently unwilling to pay this price, in part because there is no assurance that a single, national criminal justice system would be more effective, nor that it would necessarily be more honest and just. As all of us who have lived through recent governmental exposés are fully aware, corruption and unfairness exist not just locally but on state and national levels, where they can be even larger and more pervasive in scale. We view with deep suspicion centralized police power—by which we mean the authority of all criminal justice agencies to compel conformity. And while we recognize the need for police, courts, and prisons, we have too many historical and contemporary examples of totalitarian police states to relinquish altogether the checks and balances that exist on that power in this country. The complex relationships among on-line agencies and the separation of sources of power may not be perfect from any single perspective, but these arrangements serve many different ideals, each in its own way fitting notions of a proper form of justice for our society.

Summary

Each major branch of our government contributes to the crime control effort. The U.S. Constitution is our most fundamental source of criminal justice authority. Federal and state legislatures create substantive and procedural criminal law and approve budgetary appropriations for the fight against crime. Occasionally legislators are called upon to investigate, impeach, and try public officials accused of crimes while in office. The executive branch (headed by the U.S. President, state governors, or city mayors) contributes to crime control by nominating officials or groups to positions in the criminal justice decision network, by introducing proposals for new legislation to deal with crime and criminal justice, and by exercising the power to commute sentences or to pardon prisoners. The judicial branch accepts pleas, conducts trials, and decides disputed points of law and the constitutionality of statutes. The judiciary also sentences criminals within legislative limits. The administrative agencies of the criminal justice system (police, prosecutors, trial courts, prisons, etc.) conduct the day-to-day operations of the criminal justice decision network and therefore have wide discretionary powers.

This chapter dealt with the relative independence each criminal justice agency has in regard to the others. There is no common hierarchical link or command among them so that, except indirectly, neither a judge, nor a prosecutor, nor a prison warden can tell the police what to do or not to do, and vice versa. In short, there is no operational boss of the criminal justice decision network as a whole—no person, office, or commission to oversee the entire process. Legislatures can commit or withhold criminal justice agency funds, appellate courts can overrule lower court decisions, trial judges can acquit suspects and bawl police out for not getting proper evidence. But the parts of the criminal justice decision network do *not* make up a unitary whole, like branches of a corporation or units in a military organization. It is important to realize that the criminal justice agencies are separate entities with separate budgets and distinct jurisdictional boundaries. In addition, each agency recruits, trains, and promotes its personnel differently, and the amount of citizen input or participation varies with different agencies and at different stages of the criminal justice process.

Finally, it should be noted that each official within the criminal justice system has a certain amount of discretionary power, that is, the power to decide between alternative courses of action. There is a growing awareness among those concerned with the operations of the criminal justice system that the control and regulation of discretionary practices is one of the most important problems in criminal justice administration.

NOTES

1. *Furman v. Georgia*, 408 U.S. 238 (1972).
2. David W. Neubauer, *Criminal Justice in Middle America* (Morristown, NJ: General Learning Press, 1974).
3. The Capone theory is discussed in Monroe Freedman, "The Professional Responsibility of the Prosecuting Attorney," *Georgetown Law Journal* 55 (1967): 1030. It should also be noted, however, that this approach is by no means limited to the prosecution of notorious gangsters. In 1972, for example, the IRS acknowledged that it had created special investigative units with the aim of building tax evasion cases against alleged political extremists and drug pushers.
4. Thurman W. Arnold, "Law Enforcement: An Attempt at Social Dissection," *Yale Law Journal* 42 (1932): 1 (esp. 17–18).
5. In 1988 the Iran-Contra Hearings before the U.S. Senate Judiciary Committee examined whether, and the extent to which, actions taken by officials in President Reagan's administration constituted violations of law. Much discussion throughout the country revolved around whether Oliver North was a criminal or a hero.
6. President Reagan withdrew his nomination of Douglas Ginsburg to the Supreme Court when it became obvious that the Senate Judiciary Committee would reject his nomination. Later, the Senate rejected Robert Bork as well, another Reagan nominee. On many occasions Presidential appointments of agency administrators have been

rejected, as in the case of President Carter's nomination of Norval Morris to the Law Enforcement Assistance Administration.

7. An example of this is the attempts made by Los Angeles Mayor Thomas Bradley to unseat Police Chief Gates after an incriminating video tape depicting Los Angeles police officers brutally beating a traffic violator who had led police on a chase was widely shown. Chief Gates, with civil service, refused to resign and could not be fired.

8. Presidential pardons occasionally are made. President Ford not only pardoned his predecessor but as one of his last acts in office also pardoned "Tokyo Rose" of World War II notoriety. One of the first acts of President Carter was the pardoning of draft evaders from the Vietnam War. For general discussions of executive clemency, see Winthrop Rockefeller, "Executive Clemency and the Death Penalty," *Catholic University Law Review* 21 (1971): 94; *Note*, "Governor Reagan and Executive Clemency," *California Law Review* 55 (1967): 407.

9. U.S. Constitution, Art. V, sec. 2. See also Robert A. Friedlander, "Judicial Supremacy: Some Bicentennial Reflections," *Rutgers Camden Law Journal* 8 (1976): 24.

10. The title of the highest state court is not always "supreme court." In New York, for instance, a supreme court is a trial court, with the highest appellate body known as the Court of Appeals.

11. For a description of this intricate appellate process, with special emphasis on a landmark U.S. Supreme Court decision, see Anthony Lewis, *Gideon's Trumpet* (New York: Random House, 1964).

12. The record of the "activist" Warren Court is assessed in Archibald Cox, *The Warren Court: Constitutional Decisions as an Instrument of Reform* (Cambridge, MA: Harvard University Press, 1968); Fred P. Graham, *The Self-Inflicted Wound* (New York: Macmillan, 1970). See also B. J. George, Jr., "From Warren, to Burger, to Chance: Future Trends in the Administration of Criminal Justice," *Criminal Law Bulletin* 12 (1976): 253. See also Bob Woodward and Scott Armstrong, *The Brethren* (New York: Simon and Schuster, 1979).

13. Joseph Goldstein, "Police Discretion Not to Invoke the Criminal Process: Low Visibility Decisions in the Administration of Justice," *Yale Law Journal* 69 (1960): 543.

SUGGESTED READINGS

Kenneth Culp Davis, *Discretionary Justice* (Baton Rouge, LA: Louisiana State University Press, 1969).

Harold DeWolf, *Crime and Justice in America: A Paradox of Conscience* (New York: Harper & Row, 1975).

Joan Petersilia, *The Influence of Criminal Justice Research* (Santa Monica, CA: Rand Corporation, 1987).

John M. Scheb and John M. Scheb, II, *Criminal Law and Procedure* (St. Paul, MN: West, 1989).

James Q. Wilson, *Thinking About Crime*, 2nd ed. (New York: Basic Books, 1983).

DISCUSSION QUESTIONS

1. Trace the decision network which moves individuals from being free citizens through the criminal justice system and back to society as ex-offenders.
2. What is the difference between indictment and information?
3. What are the sentencing options available to a judge?

4. What are the sources of authority for crime control decisions?
5. How does the U.S. Constitution impact on crime control decisions?
6. What power does the legislature exercise in criminal justice?
7. What functions do Presidents, governors, and mayors serve in the criminal justice process?
8. What is meant by "legislative delegation of discretion?"
9. How do prosecutors' decisions impact on the criminal justice decisions of the police and corrections agencies?
10. Describe the relationship between criminal justice agencies.

The Police

5

Policing in American Society

■ **KEY TERMS**

aggressive preventive patrol
call boxes
community-oriented policing
detective units
fee system
foot patrols
incident-driven policing
justice of the peace
Kansas City patrol experiment
National Advisory Commission on
Civil Disorders
patrol
Pinkerton's
pledge system
political era
preventive patrol
"Private Eye"
private police agencies
proactive policing
problem-oriented policing
reactive policing
reform era
shire reeve
slave patrols
"strike forces"
team policing
tithing, hundred, constable
watch system
Wells-Fargo
Wickersham Commission

■ **KEY NAMES**

Herman Goldstein
J. Edgar Hoover
George L. Kelling
Sir Robert Peel
Allan Pinkerton
August Vollmer
James Q. Wilson
Orlando W. Wilson

Competing drug dealers and prostitutes, some of them transvestites, hang out on the street corners in a run-down section of town, waiting for passing cars to stop and ask about prices and availability. Frequent complaints have been made by the few residents and business owners who remain in the area, and robberies are commonly reported by "johns" and others who have been ripped off by the street corner toughs.

Residents of a large apartment complex are victims of frequent burglaries committed by people who break into apartments through windows or sliding glass doors. Cash and easily fenced items such as stereos are usually stolen.

A large number of rowdy teenagers congregate around a convenience store parking lot on Friday and Saturday nights. The manager of the store reports shoplifting, underage drinking, and vandalism to the police each week, but the problems persist.

Neighbors report loud and abusive language coming from a house where a married couple have been known for years to engage in frequent fights. Police have been dispatched to the same address dozens of times during the past year, but on this Friday night when the police arrive, they find a man lying in a pool of blood on the kitchen floor, shot to death by his wife.

Residents in a quiet residential neighborhood complain to the police about cars cruising the streets with "boom boxes" blaring music which can be heard in every home throughout the day and night. Also, some neighbors complain about young boys who ride their dirt bikes through flower gardens and lawns, causing damage to carefully manicured plants.

ABOUT THIS CHAPTER

These problems, and a host of others, are the common fare of police. It seems Americans have developed great expectations of the police, and regardless of the time of day, the weather, or the inconvenience citizens expect them to respond to calls for assistance. A detailed listing of the expectations placed on the police is not possible here, but in general people want them to function in the following ways[1]:

To prevent and control "serious crime," that is, any conduct widely recognized as threatening our lives or property

To assist and protect victims of crime, especially those in danger of physical harm

To protect constitutional guarantees, including those of free speech and assembly

To facilitate the movement of people and vehicles

To assist the intoxicated, addicted, mentally ill, physically disabled, old, young, and others who cannot care for themselves

To resolve conflict between individuals, groups, and anyone in conflict with the government

To identify problems before they become more serious for individuals, police, or the government

To create and maintain a feeling of security in the community

If police did not exist to take complaints on a continual basis, 24 hours a day and 7 days a week, to whom would citizens turn? What techniques do police traditionally employ to handle citizen complaints? How did the police come to be, and what is the legacy of American policing? Can police departments be better organized so as to better serve the public and solve crime-related problems?

This chapter attempts to answer these questions. We describe the history of the American police, examine the most common function of policing (patrols), discuss police detectives, examine the way police respond to incidents in the community, and describe the current technique known as problem-oriented policing.

HISTORY OF THE POLICE

Many of our perceptions of how police functioned in the past have been created by novels, television, and the movies. Most of us recognize the Lone Ranger, the Keystone Cops, Dirty Harry, Batman, and the Untouchables as representing stereotypes of various stages of police development. Yet what the police actually do and what they are properly expected to accomplish in American society differ significantly from these popular representations. Most of us have had dealings with the police. We have called on them for assistance, or perhaps we have been arrested. And, depending on the nature of our personal experiences with them, each of us has formed opinions about the police. Although the cowboy sheriff, or the FBI "G-Man," or the big city TV cops color our understanding, we need to acknowledge the fictional nature of much of the popular depiction of American police. For starters, police do not originate in America.

English Antecedents

Like much of our common law tradition, many of our modern police practices had their origins in early English history. Before the Norman Conquest (in 1066) there were no police. Every citizen was held responsible for aiding neighbors who might be

Made-for-the-movies police action with actors Danny Glover and Mel Gibson in Lethal Weapon 2.

plagued by outlaws and thieves. This was known as the **pledge system**. People were pledged to help protect their neighbors, and in turn their neighbors were pledged to help protect *them*.[2]

In early England, ten families (called a **tithing**) were bound together by the pledge, each promising to cooperate in policing their own problems. Ten tithings were grouped into a **hundred**, directed by a **constable** (appointed by the local nobleman) who, in effect, became the first police officer, that is, the first official with law enforcement responsibility greater than simply helping neighbors.

Just as the tithings were grouped into hundreds, after nearly a century the hundreds were grouped into shires, which were similar to our counties. For each shire the king appointed a supervisor, whose duty was to ensure that order would be kept. The supervisor was known as a **shire reeve** and was the forerunner of our modern sheriff.

A century later (in the 1300s) a **watch system** was created to protect the larger cities and towns. Appointed night watchmen patrolled the cities at night to be on the lookout for thieves and disturbances and to act as fire watches. These watchmen reported to the constable, who became the central law enforcement officer. In the early 1300s the office of **justice of the peace** was created to assist the shire reeve in controlling his territory. The local constable and the shire reeve became assistants to the justice of the peace, supervised the night watchmen, served warrants, and took prisoners into custody for appearance before justice of the peace courts. This was the first formal relationship between the police and the judiciary and this system continues to the present day.[3]

Originally constables were appointed from the gentry, and the position was more or less honorary; since constables could not function solely on their own, they in turn hired assistants. These constables' assistants became the first paid police officers. By the seventeenth century a combination of night watchmen, constables and their assistants, and justices of the peace made up the first criminal justice system. The sheriff functioned then as now as the chief enforcement officer in rural areas and small towns.[4]

With the industrial revolution came the first large cities (built around the factories) throughout England. For the first time congested, urban populations required more sophisticated policing activities than could be provided by a constable and watchman. In 1829 **Sir Robert Peel**, the British Home Secretary, organized the first metropolitan police force in London. This force was composed of over a thousand men and was structured along semimilitary lines. For the first time, police officers in England wore uniforms but were not, and generally still are not, armed. These early police were directed by two judges who eventually came to be known as "commissioners." Police officers in England are still called "Bobbies" in honor of Sir Robert Peel. Peel's experiment in London was so successful that by 1856 every borough and county in England was required to form its own police force.[5]

The Legacy of American Police

The history of police in the United States is incoherent, nonlinear.[6] Every town, village, and hamlet has police, counties are policed by sheriffs and deputies, highways are patrolled by state troopers, and the Federal Bureau of Investigation (FBI) investigates federal crimes. Each level of policing has a different history, and in the various sections of the country the history varies greatly. Our Founding Fathers evidently feared a strong, centralized police apparatus more than they feared crime, for by leaving policing to local governments they guaranteed that police would be dispersed, unorganized . . . ineffective. With thousands of police agencies developing simultaneously in every sector of the country, with several layers of jurisdictions, and with

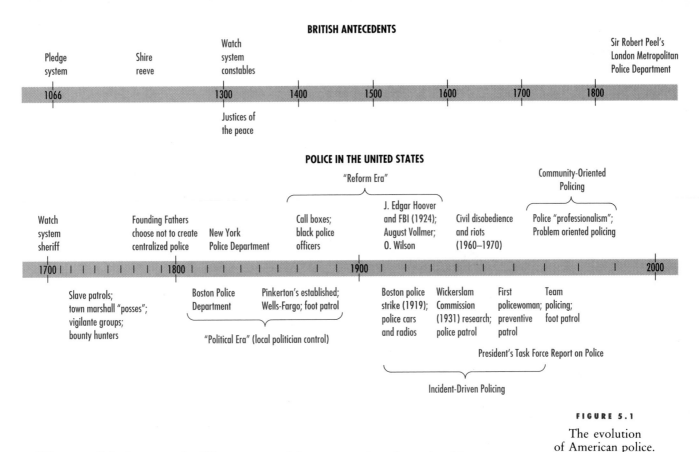

FIGURE 5.1

The evolution
of American police.

different political contexts in different parts of the country, it perhaps should come as no surprise that no consensus exists as to how police have evolved in the United States.[7]

To a great extent, colonial America's policing followed the British model. The county sheriff was the most important law enforcement agent as long as the colonies remained small and primarily rural. The sheriff had many duties other than apprehending criminals. In fact, at first he had no patrol function, but acted only upon complaints of citizens. Sheriffs were paid by a **fee system**, that is, they were given a fixed amount for every arrest made or subpoena served and for each court appearance. The primary function of sheriffs was tax collecting, rather than law enforcement, and since the sheriffs received higher fees based on the taxes they collected, law enforcement was not one of their primary concerns.

In the early American towns, the British-style constable was eventually replaced by a town marshal, who often called on vigilante groups (or "posses") to assist him in his law enforcement duties. But as cities grew, it became increasingly difficult for the marshal and posse system to enforce the law effectively.

Professors George Kelling and Mark Moore trace the history of American policing through three stages: the political era, the reform era, and the community problem-solving era.[8] This approach has been criticized by Hubert Williams and Patrick Murphy, who write that Kelling and Moore do not take account of the effects of race—especially slavery, segregation, and discrimination—in the American police legacy.[9] They argue that no history of the police can be useful in understanding the present state of American policing, nor help in objectively assessing the profession's future directions, without acknowledging its racist past.[10] With that warning in mind, we will trace the developmental stages of police work in the United States along the lines suggested by Kelling and Moore. (See Fig. 5.1.)

117

American police in the nineteenth century represented the local politicians who placed them in power and gave them their resources and authority. Those local politicians were uniformly male and white. In northern cities the local ward boss and the local political machine recruited police. As representatives of the local political powers, the police provided a variety of services to citizens such as collecting garbage, operating soup lines, and finding work and lodging for recent immigrants. And, importantly, the police helped the local politicians maintain their positions by encouraging citizens to vote for them, discouraging any opposition or any voting for opposition candidates, and occasionally even rigging elections. If new local politicians did happen to be elected, the police too were replaced. Cities were divided into precincts and each police precinct operated autonomously under the direction of the ward leaders. Precincts hired, fired, managed, and deployed personnel, usually on **foot patrols** (walking a beat), and in this decentralized fashion responded to the demands of local citizens.

This is not to say that the police in America's northern cities in the nineteenth century did not work to prevent crime and maintain order—they did both. While on foot patrol they handled disorderly conduct and other minor problems as well as responded to more major crimes. **Call boxes** were placed at strategic locations on an officer's beat to allow him to maintain contact with precinct headquarters. Unfortunately, although police worked at close quarters with the community and provided many useful services to its members, the lack of supervision sometimes led to corrupt practices such as taking bribes, and rather frequently to racial discrimination and violence. Night sticks were used to enforce "curbstone justice," while the image of the bungling Keystone Cops often fit the reality.[11]

Boston created the first "professional" police department in 1838, and New York City established its own in 1844, using Peel's London Metropolitan Police as a model. Philadelphia followed in 1854.[12] Slowly, night watchmen were replaced by police officers, and sheriffs were relegated largely to serving court orders and running local jails and lockups. The marshal system moved westward with the frontier, eventually disappearing, except in the federal system where marshals still play a law enforcement role, usually by serving federal arrest warrants and transporting and protecting prisoners and witnesses. In the mid-1800s, the Boston police set up the first detective bureau, replacing amateur bounty-hunters as the chief searchers for criminals.[13]

In the south the local political structure was different. There the institution of slavery existed. Indeed, some police historians contend that American policing began in the southern "**slave patrols**" of the 1740s.[14] The fear of slave revolts among plantation owners and the rest of the southern white populace led to the enactment of laws providing for the surveillance of all blacks, free and slave. The slave patrols had complete power to break open houses, punish runaway slaves, whip any slave who interfered with or resisted arrest, and arrest and take any slave suspected of any crime before the closest magistrate. These slave patrols enforced the southern laws that forbade blacks to move freely, keep guns, or strike a white person.

Southern states had no monopoly on racism, however, and the oppression of blacks was not limited to states or cities where slavery was legal. The major cities in the north experienced many large-scale race riots during the nineteenth century, and overt hostility and hatred toward blacks was common. The north also had its own version of slavery in the early nineteenth century, and the police were responsible for enforcing the slave laws.[15] Even later Illinois, Ohio, Indiana, Iowa, and California did not allow blacks to testify in court if whites were involved in the case, and Oregon forbade blacks to own real estate, file lawsuits, or make contracts. Massachusetts outlawed interracial marriage and enforced segregation in hotels, restaurants, public transportation, and theaters.[16] And freed slaves had to register and carry "freedom papers" which could be inspected in any city north or south or by any suspicious white.[17]

In such an environment, virtually no black police existed anywhere in the United States, little attention was given by police to the needs of areas populated by racial minorities, and no doubt a lingering effect of this system exists to this day for both whites and blacks.

After the War Between the States, change came very slowly. A few black police began to appear in Houston, Selma, and Raleigh in the 1870s. In predominantly black New Orleans by 1870 the five-member police board, with three black members, had appointed a police force which included 177 blacks.[18] The first black police officer in the north was appointed in Chicago in 1872, followed by Washington, DC (1874), Indianapolis (1876), Cleveland (1881), Philadelphia (1881), and Boston (1885).[19]

When blacks were appointed as police officers in Philadelphia, several white officers quit in protest. There, as elsewhere, the black officers were assigned in or near black neighborhoods and were restricted as to what they could do. In Miami black police were called "patrolmen" and whites were called "policemen," in St. Louis black officers worked "black beats," and in Los Angeles they were assigned to a special "black watch."[20] As late as 1961 many police departments throughout the United States restricted the power of black police to make arrests, generally forbidding them from arresting white suspects.[21]

The Reform Era

As noted earlier, police represented powerful political leaders during the "**political era**" of police history, and their duties included maintaining the segregated American social structure. Despite lingering racial imbalances and prejudices, however, dissatisfaction with abuses of power, corruption, and political favoritism on the part of the police led to pressures from inside and outside police departments for reform, and police work entered a **reform era**.

Not only was American policing inefficient in that it was disjointed, with little information passed from one jurisdiction to another, but critics pointed out that the decentralized nature of its authority contributed to a lack of leadership and discipline. They noted that the police were more the private servants and cronies of local political bosses than anything else, and that they spent much of their time running political errands and guarding private plants, docks, or railway stations; they charged that police chiefs were figurehead lackeys of local political machine bosses—lackeys who showed little policing know-how and had little authority.[22]

By the 1850s various technological improvements, such as call boxes, were being introduced into urban policing. Moreover, structural changes were introduced, such as police administrative boards, which were created in many cities in an effort to cut down on police corruption and to curb political influence.

At first such reforms met with little success. But the need for change became increasingly clear. For example, there was a long, bloody, and costly police strike in Boston in 1919. The police there, dissatisfied with their salaries, attempted to become affiliated with the American Federation of Labor (AFL). They were opposed by the city and they struck on September 9, 1919. Looting broke out and rioting occurred. Governor Calvin Coolidge called in the state militia to take over the city, the police received little public support, and the strike was broken. But the events stirred an interest in police reform.

Another important stimulus was **J. Edgar Hoover** becoming the director of a federal bureau of investigation in 1924 and transforming it from a discredited and corrupt agency into the prestigious Federal Bureau of Investigation, with a sterling reputation for honesty and integrity. Hoover raised eligibility standards for and implemented training of agents, and established the bureau's reputation for professionalism. He kept his agents out of narcotics investigations, which could have had a corrupting influence on them, and utilizing a powerful public relations approach, created the image of an incorruptible crime-fighting organization always presented by the media in the most favorable light.[23] Local police now had a role-model for professionalism.

In the aftermath of the Boston strike, various crime commissions, including some on the national level, began to investigate the extent of American crime and the ability of the police to deal with it. Probably the best known of these was the **Wickersham Commission**, created by President Herbert Hoover in 1931.[24] This commission pointed out that there was no intensive effort made to educate, train, or discipline police officers or to eliminate those who were incompetent. The commission also noted that with few exceptions police forces suffered from inadequate methods of communications and had poor equipment. While the Wickersham Commission received a great deal of attention, its report was issued at the beginning of the Great Depression, so that the local funds needed to implement its suggested reforms were generally not forthcoming.

The move toward modern police professionalism was also sparked by a number of early pioneers in policing, in particular **August Vollmer**. Vollmer was police chief in Berkeley, California, and he instituted university training as an important part of the development of the young officer cadre of his police. One of Vollmer's students, **Orlando W. Wilson**, pioneered in the use of advanced training for officers in Wichita, Kansas, and later in Chicago.[25]

The work of Vollmer, Wilson, and others did a great deal to upgrade the standards of American policing. With their innovations and the introduction of various technological advances (including the radio, the patrol car, the two-way radio, and new techniques in forensic science and criminalistics), major police agencies rapidly moved toward the scientific control of crime.

It should be noted, however, that reform efforts did not significantly address the residual effects of racism. Although police agencies began to raise their standards for police recruits, and improved police salaries and benefits, civil service examinations, which put people denied access to quality education at a disadvantage, often eliminated blacks from consideration. And background investigations of police applicants also put blacks at a disadvantage since many departments eliminated people with arrest records, those who had changed jobs too often, or those who had associated with known criminals. The net result was that minorities were largely excluded from police work throughout much of the twentieth century.[26]

During the 1960s, American cities faced racial tensions which erupted into riots, riots the police were not only not prepared to prevent or suppress, but which some observers claimed the police precipitated. President Johnson established the **National Advisory Commission on Civil Disorders** in 1967, which determined that in only 7 of the 26 cities studied did the numbers of nonwhite police match by even one-third the percentage of nonwhites in the cities' general populations.[27] The commission also found that many of the riots studied followed incidents of police brutality. An atmosphere of hostility between blacks and whites was reinforced by the widespread belief among blacks that the police used a double standard in dealing with minority communities, and that white society created the black ghetto, white police maintained it, and white institutions condoned its continued existence.[28]

Since the late 1960s, a number of reforms have been instituted designed to reduce the tensions between police and inner city blacks and other minorities. More black officers patrol the streets, and there are strict rules against police brutality, discourtesy, the use of weapons, and verbal harrassment. More needs to be done, to be sure, but police work today is finally becoming more representative of the heterogeneity of American society.

In addition to the changes already mentioned, the reform era produced several other effects.[29] Police departments were restructured in a quasimilitary fashion, so that they became hierarchical organizations with centralized authority which passed directives down through a chain of command. Officers were selected and promoted according to merit-oriented, civil service, competitive, impersonal procedures. Police work became routinized, impersonal, and "professional" crime fighting. Serious crimes were treated with a new importance, both by chiefs at the top of the organization, who used the focus on them to garner public support and respect, and by the officers at the bottom of the organization, who could achieve rapid advancement for "good busts," or serious crime arrests.

Private Police

A great deal of policing has historically been performed not by government-sponsored police departments but by **private police agencies**. Perhaps the best known of the private agencies is the earliest, **Pinkerton's**, which was founded in Chicago in 1850 by **Allan Pinkerton**, a Scottish immigrant and Chicago detective. Pinkerton's is still a major private police agency with over 100 offices in the United States and Canada. The company supplies private security guards, consultants, electronic surveillance equipment, and undertakes investigations. The term "**Private Eye**" can be traced back to a Pinkerton advertisement which shows an unblinking eye with the caption "We Never Sleep." Pinkerton agents worked with railroad companies and were credited with hunting and capturing famous outlaws of the Old West. They were also used in the late 1800s to help put down striking workers.

Another well known private agency is **Wells-Fargo**, a banking company begun by Henry Wells and William Fargo in 1852, whose stage coach line carried millions of dollars in gold dust from California to the East Coast during the nineteenth century. Because of the constant threat of bandits, Wells-Fargo structured its own security force which included treasure boxes ("safes") and armed guards for all shipments. When thefts occurred, specially trained "agents" hunted the bandits down ruthlessly.[30]

Both Pinkerton's and Wells-Fargo are still vibrant companies, and they are not the only private police agencies today. Many others have emerged which provide private security guards, alarm systems, armored vehicles with armed guards, protected delivery of valuables, vaults, and a great many other such services. Additionally, private corporations, retail stores, educational institutions, warehouses, shipyards, health care facilities, financial institutions, and a host of other private concerns hire their own private security personnel. And still additionally are the private investigators who advertise in the yellow pages of most telephone books and who conduct "confidential investigations." Significantly more money is spent in the United States on private than on public policing, and the growth of private police forces is exceeding the growth of those in the public sector.[31]

Serious problems have existed—and still exist—between public and private police. Today, well over a million people are employed by private police forces, or by private security agencies, and sometimes they are resented by or interfere with city or county police. Most public police officers refer to private agents as "Rent-a-Cops," a term usually intended to be derogatory. Although many states have recently passed legislation requiring the licensing of private police companies and the training of and background checks on private agents, there are still many private cops who are not trained or otherwise properly equipped to carry a gun and enforce law and order even on private property.[32]

INCIDENT-DRIVEN POLICING

The police patrol car and the telephone have revolutionized police work more than anything else. The telephone gave the public immediate access to the police, and the patrol car provided police with the ability to respond immediately to citizen calls. This led to **incident-driven policing**, a reactive response to citizen initiatives. Police became attached to the squad car, reluctant to leave it for any reason for fear of missing a call, or perhaps missing an opportunity to make a "good collar." Police administrators moved officers from foot patrols to cars, placing value on the "response times" of officers to citizen calls rather than on the knowledge of community problems which foot patrol officers had.

Incident-driven policing is described by John Eck and William Spelman as a series of actions taken by police officers who respond to dispatcher calls following a citizen call to the police station. The officer arrives at the address given to the dispatcher by the citizen caller, talks to the caller and others who may have information, and then tries to resolve the complaint. Often, especially in a domestic disturbance or a noise complaint, the officer tries to negotiate a resolution without creating an official record. If a criminal report must be made, the officer usually records the complaint on an official police report form and passes it on to detectives without making an arrest. But if the offender is present or if people at the site become hostile and unruly, the officer may invoke the criminal law and make an arrest. Indeed, just the threat of arrest

An example of proactive police work is the St. Louis Police Department's program to buy guns from the public, no questions asked. Their goal: to get guns off the street.

usually helps the officer reach a negotiated settlement. Then, once the call has been handled, the officer returns to patrolling the streets until the next call comes from dispatch.[33]

This is also called **reactive policing** in that incidents that have already happened make up the work loads of police officers and detectives. Of course, not all police work is of this nature. There is also **proactive policing**, in which vice and crime prevention officers actively seek out problems before, or without, specific citizen complaints. But proactive policing generally comprises a small percent of the overall police effort. (See Fig. 5.2.)

Incident-driven policing involves police officers and detectives gathering information from victims, witnesses, and other citizens that can help resolve the problem, or help make an arrest. Also, incident-driven policing relies heavily on the fact that officers and detectives have the criminal law power of arrest as their primary tool in resolving problems.

The effectiveness of this kind of policing is measured by statistics which group the incidents handled together in their aggregates. Clearance rates and arrest rates are two such measures. Figure 5.2 describes this process of policing.[34]

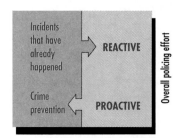

FIGURE 5.2

Police activities are usually reactive, a response to events that have already occurred. Sometimes they are proactive, an effort to solve problems before they occur.

Police Patrol

The cop on the beat has been and continues to be the mainstay of policing.[35] The patrol function is so fundamental to law enforcement that the need for it seems beyond dispute. As both a concept and a technique, **patrol** remains basic to all but the most specialized police agencies such as the FBI. Indeed, to many citizens, the ever-present force of officers dispersed throughout the community, in uniform and armed, on call 24 hours a day, *is* policing. All other police activities are service functions, seen by many people as necessary but as secondary in importance to working the beat.[36] This attitude is a bit extreme, yet there is some truth to it. The patrol officer is the *generalist* of law enforcement, the source of a vast amount of police discretion, and the most visible embodiment of authority, of law and order, in our communities. And there is little doubt that the success or failure of law enforcement, no matter what test is applied, depends in great part on the quality of patrol officers and the ways in which they are used by their commanders.[37]

Types of Patrol

In contrast to the village constable of yesteryear, who walked a beat and came to know the citizens of his small area, the typical patrol officer today covers a beat in a marked, radio-equipped patrol car. As the National Advisory Commission on Civil Disorders commented, "The patrolman comes to see the city through a windshield and hear about it over the police radio."[38] Thus **preventive patrol** became a popular policing technique—that is, police officers cruising in squad cars through the community as an omnipresent deterrence to potential criminals. Already by the 1950s preventive patrol was well entrenched.

Not all patrolling today is done in cars, however. Some techniques are still used going back to the time of the village constable. Foot patrols are used in certain areas of some cities and in recent years some new experiments have been done to measure the effectiveness of foot patrol.[39] Horse-mounted police officers are familiar sights in some of our larger cities and common in our most desolate outlands. And there are also newer techniques that do not involve car patrols. Occasionally officers use motorcycles or small motorbikes. In some communities, officers patrol waterfronts and parks with dogs (called K-9 squads), and large police agencies often have small air forces with both fixed-wing planes and helicopters on patrol. Depending on location and need, some police agencies have miniature navies for river and harbor patrol.

Patrol Functions

Patrol officers represent the full authority of police power and are expected to perform all the functions involved in general law enforcement as well as to achieve specific objectives set by their own departments. Patrol, in all forms, has three primary purposes: (1) the answering of calls for assistance; (2) the maintenance of a police presence in the community; and (3) the probing of suspicious circumstances.[40]

In precincts characterized by high crime rates and other social problems, patrolling officers may spend most of their on-duty time responding to calls. In smaller communities and less busy precincts—and even in high crime areas at certain times—calls for assistance may be infrequent, leaving much uncommitted time for officers to patrol the area.

The pattern followed during any particular police patrol depends on a variety of factors. In some cases the routes to be followed by prowl cars may be prescribed by patrol regulations and monitored by a supervising sergeant. In this way, police departments try to achieve the deterrent function of making the police presence known in the area being patrolled. (See Field Practice A:1.)

Although there may be regulations requiring a precinct to be "fully covered" during each tour of duty, the actual routes taken by cruising patrol cars are more commonly left to the discretion of individual officers. Indeed, it is expected that an experienced officer will vary the patterns of patrol, selecting areas of emphasis based on current conditions in the precinct, a knowledge of "trouble spots," and past experiences with incidents occurring at particular checkpoints. (See Field Practice A:2.)

Of course patrol patterns are broken when unusual circumstances are observed and must be investigated, when suspicious characters are stopped for questioning and when calls for assistance are received. The motorized beat officer is constantly within radio range of a police dispatcher and, in fact, the dispatcher-patrol officer relationship is central to policing.

Often the information communicated to patrol officers is brief to the point of being cryptic: "Investigate family trouble," "Prowler on the roof," "See the man at Broad and Tenth," "Investigate burglary," and so forth. Sometimes the calls are urgent and the dispatcher gives some indication of danger: "A man with a gun," "Shots fired," "Robbery in progress," or, the one most likely to elicit the most rapid response, "Officer in trouble" or "Officer down."

Officers on patrol spend a lot of time in their cars waiting for calls from the dispatcher.

Police Patrol

1: Sarge

A supervising patrol sergeant in a large center-city precinct earned the nickname "Stop Watch" after he issued an order that he wished to see a moving patrol car every 5 minutes as he traveled around the precinct. He was known to demand a report of positions if he failed to see a prowl car within a 6-minute period.

2: Crime Scenes

A police officer and her prowl car partner jointly worked out a series of major checkpoints on their patrol route which they were careful to visit at staggered, unpredictable times. These checkpoints included an alley containing rear doors to a number of warehouses, a schoolyard where youth gangs were known to congregate, a subway station where a homicide had occurred some 2 years earlier, an isolated bus stop, and a pawn shop that had often been burglarized in the past. When not responding to calls, their patrol duties were otherwise random within their precinct, but these checkpoints were always visited at least twice during each tour of duty. ■

The dispatcher-patrol officer relationship is an equation of discretion. The dispatcher uses discretion in deciding whether to send a car on a call at all and, if so, whether to assign to the call a degree of urgency. In turn the patrol officers who receive the call must decide whether to respond and, if so, in what manner. Based on a study of 4,371 dispatch situations, Professor Al Reiss reported that the police evaluated 18 percent as requiring an urgent response. In those cases they drove rapidly to the scene, often using the flasher or siren. They handled another 73 percent in a clearly routine manner, observing all the traffic rules and laws on the way to the scene, and even looking for a parking space. They considered 6 percent of the dispatches so unimportant that they deliberately wasted time responding, their attitude being: "It'll probably turn out to be nothing"; "No need to rush"; "We'll never catch him"; "If we go slow, that'll be over before we get there." Further, in 2 percent of the dispatches, the officers even stopped on the way to the scene to buy a pack of cigarettes, to pick up dry cleaning, or to sell tickets to a police officers' benefit.[41]

The Kansas City Patrol Experiment

Are crimes deterred merely by the visible presence of police in an area? If so, the aggressive presence of police who are known to be constantly checking, probing, and inquiring should have an even greater impact.[42] And it would seem that increasing the numbers of officers in any patrol area, to the point of saturating it with police, while increasing the vigor with which suspicious circumstances are investigated and suspicious persons are questioned, would reduce crime rates.

In 1972 the Kansas City Police Department in conjunction with the Police Foundation undertook the year-long **Kansas City patrol experiment** to study exactly these questions. Under controlled conditions, the impact of different levels of patrol on crime and perceptions relating to crime were compared. Precincts across the city were divided into three groups. One area received the same type and level of patrol it had received in the past; another received no routine patrol (cars from other precincts responded to distress calls in this district); the third area received two to three times its normal patrol assignment. The major conclusion of the study was that variations in level of patrol *produced no significant differences in the amount of reported crime* in the areas. Moreover, there were no differences in the amount of crime in the three areas measured by community surveys instead of official reports. Furthermore, there seemed to be no differences in the extent to which citizens in the different areas feared criminal attack.[43]

The Kansas City experiment has been both firmly supported and vigorously criticized. For example, the Kansas City police department found it difficult to maintain the experimental conditions, and some critics pointed out that a number of cities patrolled their streets more heavily than even the highest-level experimental zone in the study.[44] Nonetheless, the results of the experiment did cast considerable doubt on past claims of the effectiveness of preventive patrol practices, crystallizing into skepticism on the part of many police administrators. Other studies have shot further holes in the historic assumption that the best way to deploy police is through patrols.[45]

It seems reasonable that the visible presence of a police officer will deter some potential law violators. And as any motorist who spots a prowl car in the rear-view mirror can testify, such deterrence does in fact occur. However, it is also evident that the amount and kinds of crimes that can be so deterred are limited. Many of the crimes most feared by the public, like homicide and assault, are customarily committed indoors, out of sight of roving patrols. And even common street crimes, such as snatch-and-grab thefts and muggings, happen so quickly that effective deterrence would require police officers stationed every few yards along every street. Clever, experienced offenders are almost as familiar with police patrol practices as the officers themselves; when the marked prowl car passes an alley, it can simply indicate free time for thefts until the next patrol is due.

Research had thus demonstrated that patrol in general is at least a questionable use of police resources. And one form of patrol, to which we now turn, has proven to be not only ineffective, but counterproductive.

Aggressive Preventive Patrol

Sometimes police patrol is not performed in a reactive, wait-for-a-call manner. Officers occasionally are instructed to engage in **aggressive preventive patrol**—that is, to take the offensive against possible crime, to be more vigorous in probing, stopping, questioning, and frisking suspects, almost at random. Not all aggressive patrols are random or preventive. Sometimes officers are ordered to round up suspects aggressively in the wake of serious, high-publicity crimes. (See Field Practice B.)

The Zebra stops mentioned in Field Practice B:2 caused an uproar in the black community. For a while all young black males walking the streets of the city involved were stopped, told to "spread-eagle" their hands and feet and lean against a wall or across a car, and then frisked and questioned by teams of police.

In most instances of aggressive preventive patrol, the police have no specific probable cause, and the individuals stopped, questioned, and searched cannot "reasonably" be considered individual suspects. Consequently, any admissions or evidence obtained cannot be used in prosecutions. Further, and more importantly, stops in which the police have no reasonable suspicion or probable cause to believe a crime is being, has been, or is about to be committed are *illegal*. Why then do such practices persist?

Common street crimes—assaults, muggings, traffic in narcotics, rapes, and even many homicides—do not occur in equal distribution throughout a community. In metropolitan areas particularly, police can easily identify high-crime neighborhoods with such accuracy that incidents of various types of offenses can be predicted on a weekly or monthly basis, and sometimes even daily. Residents in these areas understandably demand protection and insist that the police do something to make their neighborhoods safe. The police are also subject to outside pressures—from political figures, citizen action groups, the press, and other sources—to "clean up" the city and to crack down on lawbreakers. In addition, it is often demanded that police *prevent*

Aggressive Preventive Patrol

1. Cowboys

The chief of patrol of a large metropolitan police department had available three special tactical units which he assigned nightly to unannounced and randomly selected high-crime areas with instructions to conduct widespread field interrogations, frisks, and searches to "get the weapons and junk off the street." All three tactical units, called "Cowboys" by regular patrolmen, operated every night, year-round. They would sweep into an area—some officers in uniform, some in civilian clothes, some in patrol cars, some in unmarked cars—and stop pedestrians, particularly groups of young males, and, usually at gunpoint, interrogate and search them.

2. Selected Stops

After a series of apparently random and motiveless murders, the police dispatcher used the code word "Zebra" to notify officers on patrol of other similar killings. Based on the testimony of some witnesses who noticed "suspicious circumstances" at the site of some of these murders, the police intelligence unit came to the conclusion that the Zebra killers were two or three young black males. The victims had all been white. Based on this information, the chief of patrol issued instructions to his officers to stop and question *all* youthful black males whenever they were encountered by patrols.

3. How to Make People Mad

In Detroit . . . after a series of rapes and murders of women, persons were stopped, searched, and in about 1,000 cases arrested. After two brothers killed one policeman and seriously wounded another, Baltimore police officers searched more than 300 homes, most belonging to Negroes, looking for the gunman. The searches were often made in the middle of the night and were based almost entirely on anonymous tips. The U.S. Court of Appeals for the Fourth Circuit stated: "Lack of respect for the police is conceded to be one of the factors generating violent outbursts in Negro communities. The invasions so graphically depicted in this case 'could' happen in prosperous suburban neighborhoods, but the innocent victims know only that wholesale raids do not happen elsewhere and did happen to them. Understandably they feel that such illegal treatment is reserved for those elements who the police believe cannot or will not challenge them. . . ." ∎

Source for B:3: President's Commission on Law Enforcement and Administration of Justice, Task Force Report: The Police (Washington, DC: U.S. Government Printing Office, 1967), pp. 184–185.

---

crimes as well as solve them. In these circumstances, the continued existence of high-crime pockets becomes frustrating. No matter that the root causes of such crimes may be well beyond the ability of the police to relieve—the urgency of the situation demands action, and aggressive patrol is the result. The police simply take techniques such as field interrogation, which have proven efficient in more orderly circumstances, and apply them intensively and at random.

Citizens have a constitutional right to be free from "unreasonable searches and seizures," and aggressive patrol tactics violate that right. Although the police do not deny the extralegal nature of aggressive patrolling, they often justify its use on the grounds that there are no alternatives. Brief stops to identify persons in the neighborhood fix those individuals in time and place and become "intelligence" information that may be used later if a crime is reported. Frisks and searches "get the weapons and drugs off the street," ostensibly preventing more serious crimes. Furthermore, the saturation of a neighborhood with officers, the police claim, acts to deter potential violators.

Whether aggressive patrol accomplishes all these things is debatable. It may lead to arrests for investigation. These arrests are not based on sufficient evidence at the time but are used to obtain it later, so that they serve as a kind of "fishing expedition" by the police. Sometimes such arrests are nothing more than harrassment. But whether they deter crime is questionable.

Moreover, one of the major difficulties caused by aggressive patrol is the negative effects its use have on police-community relationships, which may far outweigh any gains made by seizing contraband weapons. The community cost of aggressive patrol is detailed in the report of the President's Commission on Law Enforcement and Administration of Justice already cited in connection with Field Practice B:3.[46] And the final costs of unfettered aggressive patrol and widespread arrests for investigation may be greater even than simple feelings of community hostility toward police. Excesses in the patrol function may, in fact, *precipitate* riots and mass disorders. The National Advisory Commission on Civil Disorders mentioned earlier pointed to both aggressive patrol practices and the increasing "motorization" of police as contributing to ghetto tensions and the outbreak of civil disorder.[47]

Also, some evidence exists that police patrol efforts, whether they are aggressive or not, tend to *displace* crime rather than prevent it. As one *New York Times* reporter who was investigating the effectiveness of police patrol efforts to prevent crime wrote, the displacement effect of such efforts shows itself

> In the prostitutes whom the police have thrown off the north side of 86th Street but who parade, each night, along the south side; in the drug dealers and gamblers who renew their operations in one store or on one corner almost as quickly as they are shut down on another, and in the youths who, with their beer and their blaring radios, annoy residents of one block after they have been chased from the last.[48]

Detectives

If uniformed police officers are the frontline troops of law enforcement, civilian-clad police detectives are not far behind, and make up the second wave in crime control efforts. Most city police departments of any size have **detective units**, distinct from but in close working relationships with the patrol force. In specialized instances, like the FBI and similar governmental enforcement agencies that have no routine patrol functions, both frontline officers and most of their superiors are detectives.

In general, detectives occupy a higher status and enjoy more prestige than uniformed officers, both within and outside the police department.[49] This does not necessarily mean that a detective occupies a higher rank than a patrol officer; in fact, rank in the paramilitary structure of most police agencies has little to do with whether an officer is a member of the patrol force or a detective in a special investigating unit. Typically in large departments, patrol officers of different ranks from rookie through various "grades" to sergeant, lieutenant, captain, and so forth, are under the command of a chief of patrol. In terms of functions, working conditions, privileges, and prestige, becoming a detective at any rank is ordinarily considered a promotion. Detective status is normally earned after an officer has served on patrol or in some other uniformed capacity.

The real nature of police work on all levels is only dimly understood by most outsiders, but of all police activities, that of the detective has been the most romanticized, to the point where common notions about it have almost nothing to do with the reality. A detective "mystique" exists which consists of nonsense written and televised about detectives and which sometimes affects the detectives' own behavior and obscures their real role.[50]

It is hard to convince most people that crime investigation is not a very scientific enterprise, that the work of detectives is no more important than the work of patrolmen, that being a detective is not very exciting, and that not all crimes can be solved by detective work. The mystique persists, and yet detectives themselves report that most of their activities are routine and simple, involving a lot of paperwork, and are often less demanding and less challenging than situations handled by police officers on patrol. Most working detectives admit that their ability to solve crimes is grossly exaggerated and that luck rather than skill or training is often the most important element in solving cases.

In the wealth of research studies and extensive commentary on policing that has accumulated since the mid-1960s, the work of detectives has for some reason been neglected. Most police research concentrates on "basic" policing, which encompasses police practices, management, the issue of discretion in general, the selection of recruits and training patterns, the relationship of police administrators to line-and-staff departmental problems, and such important issues as the relationship of police authorities to political leaders in the community. The place and use of detectives, the entire matter of crime investigation beyond patrol, have only recently begun to attract the professional interest they deserve.

The results of one major study of detectives, conducted by staff members of the Rand Corporation, was published in 1975 in a three-volume report titled *The Criminal Investigation Process*; the study was based on observations of detective operations in 25 police agencies and a survey of detective practices in an additional 156 departments.[51] The complete list of the conclusions of this research is much too long to be discussed in detail here; only a few examples are given.

One result—no surprise to those familiar with police work—is that the research findings belie all the popular conceptions of detective work. For example, the Rand analysis showed that an investigator's time is largely consumed reviewing reports, documenting files, and attempting to locate and interview victims in cases that experience indicates will never be solved. Furthermore, even for cases which are solved, that is, where a suspect is identified, a detective spends much more time in *postclearance processing* than in actually determining the perpetrator.

The public in general and criminal juries in particular expect detectives to employ elaborate scientific investigative devices, like fingerprints, DNA prints, lie detectors, ballistics reports, and spectrographic analyses of physical evidence. Yet the Rand report showed that more than half of all serious reported crimes received only superficial attention from investigators. Latent fingerprints, voice patterns, bloodstain analysis, and the like rarely provided the basis for identifying a suspect. But the detective is caught in a bind. Juries are reluctant to convict in cases where there are no fingerprints or other bits of "hard" scientific evidence,[52] and crime victims often feel cheated if a detective fails to look for physical "clues."

The Rand study showed that the single most important determinant of whether a case is solved is the information given by the victim to the patrol officers responding to the complaint initially. If the needed information is not obtained at that point, the perpetrator will likely never be identified. Even in cases in which the officers responding to the call receive no on-scene identification of the offender, any subsequent arrest is usually the result of routine police procedures rather than the work of detectives.

Detective "**strike forces**," which are units of detectives assigned temporarily to contend with a specific problem (such as a rash of armed robberies), sometimes have significant potential to make arrests when concentrated on a few difficult target offenses which they are uniquely qualified to investigate.

The Rand report reached several controversial conclusions,[53] and it is not without its critics, particularly with respect to the researchers' methodology.[54] For many knowledgeable police administrators, however, the report's conclusions do not differ from their own experiences. Many observers accept the necessity of destroying the mystique surrounding detective work before realistic improvements can be expected, and studies more recent than the one by Rand Corporation agree on that point.[55]

Detectives are distributed within police organizations in a variety of ways, depending on the administrative preferences of top police officials. In some police departments, especially smaller ones, it is customary to have *generalist detectives* assigned to perform a wide range of investigative duties, primarily followup investigations of cases originated by patrol officers.

If a city is large enough and presents sufficiently complex enforcement problems, specialized detective units (intelligence, vice, burglary, homicide, robbery, and similar crime-specific squads) may be distributed throughout the detective divisions and housed in decentralized offices.

Detectives assigned to specialized units like vice squads or organized crime intelligence units may perform a good many duties similar to those of patrol officers. They may be assigned to stake out premises, street corners, hotel lobbies, or other suspicious sites, keeping them under surveillance for extensive periods of time. Or they may be required to tail suspects, to act as bodyguards for dignitaries, or to go out and look for crimes in the community like patrol officers do.

Detective work often entails visiting the scene of a crime to look for clues, interrogating victims and witnesses, and making a record of the nature of the loss and the harm done. Contrary to popular conceptions, there is ordinarily little a detective can do at the scene of a crime, for there is rarely much fresh information to be gathered at such a site after the initial visit by the patrol officers. With very serious crimes, such as murders, bombings, and safecrackings, detectives may call on crime laboratory experts to dust for fingerprints, analyze bloodstains, recover and analyze bomb fragments, or otherwise collect physical evidence that eventually may be used against the perpetrator. In more routine, less serious offenses, however, detectives normally can do little more than look around and make a record of the crime, often primarily to help victims fill out their insurance claims.

The greatest tool of detective work, and the technique most commonly employed, is *interrogation*. Usually detectives simply question crime victims and any witnesses to confirm information already gathered by the patrol officers who first arrived on the scene. But occasionally detectives also carry out postarrest interrogations of suspects—almost exclusively a detective function.[56]

COMMUNITY-ORIENTED POLICING

Much police work is reactive, whether it is patrol or detective. And a continuing debate regarding police practices, especially concerning motorized patrol, has done little to change their basics. Police administrators have increasingly experimented with new techniques and programs, many of which are designed to correct the schism between the community and the police which has occurred in recent decades. But the traditional staples, especially patrol, continue to characterize contemporary police work. Rather than eliminating patrol, ways to improve it, to make it more professional and responsive to community needs, have begun to surface.

Community Problem Solving: Team Policing, Foot Patrol, and Community Patrol Officer Programs

The Kansas City Study clearly set the stage for a decade of important research into police practices. Efforts were made to improve the efficiency (speed) of police response to calls, but research revealed that police do not *need* to respond rapidly to incident-driven patrol calls.[57] Indeed, citizens themselves do not report crimes immediately to the police.[58] Studies also revealed that no matter how soon detectives start their investigations they are usually unable to solve the crimes unless witnesses or victims tell them who the perpetrators were; and according to research, most crimes are unsolvable anyway because there are often no clues.[59]

Also, during the 1970s and 1980s police departments faced external pressures from communities to change their daily activities, and internal pressures from police officers to change management practices. Many communities, especially minority communities, demanded that police become more involved in the life of those communities in order to identify ways to serve them better. The use of unnecessary force by police was bitterly criticized. In response, police administrators first attempted to involve citizens in "review boards" and to create community relations units to deal with conflicts and violence. But officers resisted civilian review, and communities placed no confidence in the community relations units.

So some police administrators attempted to bring officers into the communities they served through **team policing**. This approach placed small groups of officers in storefront, neighborhood-centered stations. It encouraged contact between police and citizens, and helped develop relationships between police and neighborhood residents and merchants. Police team members were generalists who could investigate any crime, and participant management was the order of the day.

Team policing was not a widespread success, partly because of resistance to change on the part of entrenched police organizations,[60] but three tactics it implemented have survived; foot patrols, community watch programs, and storefront police stations. These placed police in the community at all times, giving them constant communication and contact with citizens.[61] This exposure in turn led to additional neighborhood demands to expand the scope of police work. Burglaries and robberies, very important to the police operating according to the incident-driven model, were less important to people in the community than broken windows, unruly youths, or public drunks.

A word should be added about the reintroduction of foot patrols. Foot patrols had been abandoned during the 1960s when the rush to motorized patrols was in full swing because they were considered too geographically limited. Officers on foot were clustered together in neighborhoods and could not be moved quickly in response to emergencies, and this was interpreted as a wasteful use of personnel. But foot patrols have advantages which were being overlooked. Two professors at Michigan State University, which has a National Neighborhood Foot Patrol Center, compared perceptions of safety between citizens protected by foot patrols and those protected by motorized patrols. They found that people felt much safer with foot patrols, although the actual impact of using such patrols on the incidence of crime was not as clearly demonstrated.[62]

Of course foot patrols are inappropriate in rural or suburban areas, and the motorized police presence will not be totally replaced by walking police officers in any area. But in densely populated inner cities, in established neighborhoods and housing projects, walking beat officers can accomplish much good by being close to the people they serve. In addition, a great number of services rendered by foot patrols are not directly crime-related.

A word also needs to be said about participant management. Police administrators have come to realize that the traditional, rigid organizational structure of police departments is not capable of meeting community demands. Despite that structure, police officers exercise a broad, unregulated discretionary power, which has always been tacitly accepted as necessary by police administrators. But when those administrators began attempting to define that discretionary power through policies and structured procedures, they found themselves at a loss to prescribe the proper responses to the varied situations police officers encounter. They were unable to write rules for appropriate, creative police responses. Moreover, police administrators have increasingly become aware that a new generation of police officers is less willing than its predecessors to submit to hierarchical authoritative organizational structures. They have found that incident-driven police work fails to motivate many officers because

Beat Cops Prove Their Worth

Homeless men and women, vagrants, and other street people crowd around commuters and tourists moving through the Port Authority Bus Terminal on 8th Avenue and 42nd Street in Manhattan. For some, getting off a bus can be a heart-pounding experience, and no doubt the haunting eyes of the street people produce memories of reports of many muggings in the area. On the avenue the stores for "adults only" and the X-rated marquees contribute to the seaminess of the dirty street. But if you pass through Port Authority these days, you cannot help but notice something else—a surprising number of police officers.

New York City Police Commissioner Lee P. Brown has long been a champion of cops on foot patrol and has initiated a community policing program for the city that began in Brooklyn in April 1991. But in Times Square before that, beat cops proved their worth in an area which many people considered to be the crime capital of the world. In July 1990 extra beat cops were assigned to the midtown area, and by April 1991 when the community policing program was started, the city reported a decline in robberies by 18 percent from the previous year.

Indeed, police statistics also show a decline in street crime in the subway stations, and most police officials believe the increased number of transit cops on patrol at Times Square and Pennsylvania Station are responsible. Robberies in those subway stations were down 32 percent from the previous year, and all felonies committed in the area fell 19 percent.

By March 1992, all felonies committed throughout the five boroughs had decreased 4.4 percent from the previous year. In Manhattan's Midtown North section, the decrease in all felonies was 14.5 percent. Officials are slow to credit

Midtown police officers on foot patrol.

any one factor for the trend. Demographics, economics, and coincidence are believed to play their part. But it is impossible to ignore that these positive statistics coincide with a 290 percent increase (from 786 in August 1990 to 3,000 in March 1992) in the number of city beat officers. And one thing is certain. The sight of police officers on the job nearby is reassuring to anyone considering a trip to midtown Manhattan.

SOURCE: George James, "In Every Category, Crime Reports Fell Last Year in New York City," *New York Times*, March 25, 1992, pp. A1, B4. George James, "On Foot and Twirling a Nightstick, via Madison Ave.," *New York Times*, October 9, 1991, pp. B1, B7. John Tierney, "As Crime Drops in Midtown, Even Criminals Credit Police," *New York Times*, April 24, 1991, p. B1.

the officers find the opportunities for meaningful work limited, they do not feel a sense of responsibility for the outcome of their work, and they do not receive feedback about how well they are doing their jobs. The police organizations have found they need to reform to meet these needs of modern police officers. As John Eck and William Spelman conclude in their book *Problem-Solving: Problem-Oriented Policing in Newport News*:

132

Incident-driven policing is obsolete. The police can no longer restrict their tactics to preventive patrol, fast response to calls, and reactive investigation; such tactics are incapable of preventing or solving most crimes. Such innovations as crime analysis, differential police response and investigative case management have helped police manage their time better, to implement these tactics more efficiently. But they have not helped to reduce crime. . . . In fact, crime itself can no longer be the sole concern of the police.[63]

The result is that, borrowing from business and psychological models, police departments have begun to move away from their traditional incident- driven methods and toward participant management, where officers have a say in structuring their own jobs and duties. A new world of police work is emerging, one that recognizes the police do much more than just fight crime. The police today face problems that no one else can solve, that are often not directly crime-related, and that require new methods. It is to a discussion of those new methods that we now turn.

Community-Oriented and Problem-Oriented Policing

Several innovations have surfaced very recently, foremost among them being **community-oriented policing** and **problem-oriented policing**. Both of these approaches center on removing the police from the isolation of patrol cars and placing them among the people in the community in intimate, continuous ways. Many police departments—including those in Boston, Houston, San Francisco, and New York—have begun Community Patrol Officer Programs (CPOP). A recent article in *Time* describes the experiences of one CPOP officer in Lansing, Michigan,[64] summarized in Field Practice C.

Community-oriented policing is advocated by Professors **James Q. Wilson** and **George L. Kelling**, who admit that the popularity among police chiefs that the concept enjoys "is as great as the ambiguity of the idea."[65] Indeed, the concept can encompass a variety of ideas and programs, but the significant contribution it has made

1700 newly graduated New York City police officers, trained intensively in community policing.

Sparrow Estates

One typical CPOP officer is Donald Christy, 36, of Lansing, Michigan. A little over a year ago, he was assigned to cover a nine-block area of the city. At first disheartened by the sight of crack houses and blighted streets, Christy took pains to get on a first-name basis with many of the area's 700 residents and learn what neighborhood problems concerned them most. Those conversations led him to recognize, he says, "that the good people far out-numbered the bad." Meanwhile, he organized a volunteer community cleanup, which filled 30 Dumpsters with litter; arranged federal funding for floral plantings; and even held a contest to choose a name for the neighborhood: Sparrow Estates.

His unconventional approach to policing paid big dividends in terms of crime control. Residents began to give Christy tips that helped him drive away criminals. Indoor dealers found themselves evicted by absentee landlords. "You can walk around the block now without fear of being attacked," says Ralph Casler, a retired mechanic who has lived in the area for 30 years. Says Christy, "I haven't made an arrest in eight months." ∎

is that it puts police officers in closer proximity to the people they serve, thereby changing the perceptions police often have about people in high-crime areas. This in turn can lead to a moderation of the "them vs. us" attitude so often felt by both sides in such areas, allowing community-oriented policing to be a success.

As with any innovative technique, the degree of success enjoyed by those introduced by police agencies varies. Jerome Skolnick and David Bayley studied innovative police practices in six American cities and concluded, in part, that the quality of leadership within a police department is critically important to the success or failure of innovative programs. With proper leadership the community support and the political environment needed to improve the chances of their successful implementation can be achieved.[66]

Professor **Herman Goldstein** is identified as the developer of the problem-oriented approach to policing. The two examples found in Field Practice D were offered by Goldstein as illustrations of the approach. And, like parables, they give us an insight into today's new world of policing.[67]

Problem-oriented policing in both cases involved a process of (1) identifying the problem, (2) analyzing the problem, and (3) developing an effective response to the problem. In the Gainesville case, top-level police management along with governmental leaders performed the three steps. In the Philadelphia case, a street-level police officer carried them out.

The first step, identifying the problem, requires the police to develop a series of questions regarding the actors involved in the problem. The actors include victims, offenders, and witnesses and other "third parties." Then, a series of inquiries about the incidents that make up the problem must be developed, for example, inquiries into the sequence of events, the physical context of the events, and the effects of the events. Finally, the police examine the responses to the problem by the police themselves and by other community institutions.

After the problem has been identified and the appropriate questions have been developed, an in-depth analysis is carried out. The sources of information for this step include relevant literature, police officers, official police reports and other data, other government agencies, the community at large, even the problem makers themselves, the suspected offenders. Also, the analysis can include inquiries outside the local region or state to see how other communities have dealt with similar problems. Analysis is a difficult and time-consuming process, and requires the best investigative

Problem-Oriented Policing

Example 1

During the spring of 1985 the city of Gainesville, Florida experienced a dramatic increase in the number of robberies in convenience stores. Gainesville police conducted a detailed analysis of the problem, searched the country for knowledge about the problem and strategies to deal with it. This analysis led them to focus attention on characteristics of the stores, especially whether they had one clerk or two on duty at the time of the robbery. They concluded that stores with only one clerk on duty at night were more vulnerable to robbery during the night hours. Although the store management did not agree with police findings, the police department was able to secure independent research which confirmed the police conclusion that the presence of two clerks was the primary factor in deterring convenience store robberies in Gainesville. The nationwide study of the problem also discovered several communities which had reached the same conclusion and had enacted ordinances which required convenience stores to have more than one clerk on duty at night. With these precedents and local data the police approached the city council with the proposal that a local regulation be established which requires two clerks on duty in convenience stores during certain hours. This was challenged in the courts, but the regulation was upheld, in large measure because of the careful analysis of the problem which the police documented. And, a follow-up study revealed that convenience store robberies dropped by 65 percent immediately after the new ordinance was adopted.

Example 2

A sergeant in the Philadelphia Police Department was introduced to the concept of problem-oriented policing. Shortly after being assigned to a new district, he observed that police officers were being dispatched to the same bar several times a day to answer a complaint of loud noise. He discovered that police had been dispatched to the address 505 times in six months. Police always categorized the complaint as "unfounded." The sergeant decided to respond to a dispatcher call to that bar with his officers, and found that there was no loud music and no disorderliness. He asked dispatch for the name of the complainant and was told that policy did not require recording the source of complaints in this type of call. At the sergeant's request the dispatcher took the name and address of the complainant the next time the call was made, a woman who had apparently made all of the calls. The sergeant approached the woman and offered to help her with her concerns. Studies with a decibel meter revealed the bar was operating within the noise control ordinance. He found that it was not the noise which was the source of irritation as much as it was the vibration created by jukebox speakers which were attached to a common wall. The sergeant made arrangements with the bar operators to move the speakers to another wall and for the woman and the bar operators to communicate with each other directly. The woman was pleased, the bar was pleased, and the calls to the police have stopped. ■

---

efforts the officer or department can put into it to ensure that it is sufficiently thorough.

Then, after the problem has been identified and analyzed, the final step is developing alternative strategies to cope with, or developing tailor-made responses to, the problem. This can challenge the ingenuity and creativity of the top-level and street-level police involved. In some cases proposed solutions may eliminate or significantly reduce the problem, or perhaps may minimize the harm it causes. In others they may lead to better police techniques for dealing with the problem, or maybe even to a decision to remove it from police consideration.[68]

SPECIAL POLICE RESPONSES TO CRITICAL PROBLEMS

In many ways police departments are bureaucratic, conservative, quasimilitary hierarchies which are slow to change. But in the modern era, the police must be flexible. They must be able to respond effectively to sudden crises and emergencies of a noncriminal nature while carrying out their routine crime control duties. A major fire makes demands on the police department as well as on the fire department; police must be able to assist other government agencies as well as keep public order during tornadoes, earthquakes, floods, and other natural disasters. Moreover, in many crisis situations like street riots, bombings, and acts of terrorism, the police are expected to do more than assist other agencies. They often have sole responsibility of dealing with the problem, and only rarely receive enforcement assistance from the National Guard or other police agencies. Responding to emergencies requires careful planning and the skillful deployment of staff, for while some units are responding to the riot or flood, others must be retained elsewhere in the community. Crises may involve some changes in routine and a reduction in the numbers and sizes of regular patrols as officers are assigned to the crisis site, but the entire force cannot be committed to a crisis site as that would leave the rest of the city unprotected.

In addition to planning effective crisis strategies, the police often are expected to invest imaginative enforcement techniques for routine and recurring problems not responsive to control by ordinary operations. For example, police are commonly called on to conduct intelligence operations focused on organized crime and vice in the community. And assaults growing out of family disputes and lovers' quarrels are recurring police problems of the first magnitude. An inordinate amount of police time is spent dealing with situations related to public intoxication, vagrancy, gang activity, drunk driving, prostitution, purse snatching, and similar behavior, some of them serious or potentially serious problems and others merely "nuisance" problems about which there is a good deal of public pressure to "do something."

Such routine problems are unending, and many, like family disputes and public intoxication, are chronic concerns that cannot be resolved by the usual revolving-door process of arrest, fine, and release.

It is interesting to note that for many years the police believed that the best way to handle family disputes, including wife beating, was by "settling" the case, that is, by cooling down the actors, and even counseling them.[69] A number of departments set up elaborate "family crisis intervention" units and the corresponding training programs for police officers. Arrest of family "sluggers" was generally thought to be futile and counterproductive unless homicide was imminent. Then a 1984 study conducted by Lawrence W. Sherman and Richard Berk, and sponsored by the Police Foundation, cast doubt on those notions, indicating that *arrest* of wife-beating husbands is more effective in preventing further violence than any other technique of family intervention. However, this so-called "arrest effect" cannot be considered to have been clearly shown.[70]

The types of crisis situations that occur change from time to time, some disappearing or diminishing for long periods then reappearing in new forms with new complexities. During the late 1960s and the early 1970s, police agencies were preoccupied with mass disorders, riots, firebombings, snipers, looting, and other street phenomena common to the Vietnam War era. Today these have diminished. Police now train and plan for hostage situations, either instigated by politically motivated terrorists or by desperate fugitives or deranged individuals. There seem to be fads in the nature of crises requiring police intervention, often sparked by a single incident. For example, the assassination of one public figure may be followed by others, one airplane hijacking can lead to another, or a terrorist-hostage situation can breed others. In each case, the police are expected to quickly develop the appropriate responses, even for situations that arise without forewarning or for which there are no precedents.

The range of special responses demanded of the police is almost infinite. And the ingenuity shown by many police agencies in developing special strategies and tactics is admirable. The development of responses, though, is sometimes slow and painful, since responses effective in one situation do not necessarily apply to others.

We have explored some of the history of the American system of policing, from its English antecedents to contemporary approaches to problem solving and crisis response. In a cursory way we have explored the evolution of American police through the political era, with its precinct ward bosses in the north and slave patrols in the south. We have discussed the racism and political patronage associated with much of the history of policing in the United States. We have also described the reform era, the role of police "patriarchs" like Peel, Vollmer, Wilson, Hoover, and the impact of the Wickersham Commission report. We have attempted to explain private policing, detectives, and community-oriented policing, among other specialized issues. And we have discussed the controversies and problems surrounding such traditional police activities as patrol.

Police, we have seen, do much more than merely enforce the law. In many ways, we can conclude, the police task is too large, too difficult, too complex for any single agency. Perhaps the emergence of private police with very narrow responsibilities— guarding a warehouse, delivering a valuable package, monitoring conversations, watching for shoplifters—has occurred for this very reason.

Likewise, we have seen that normal police practices seldom match the stereotypes promoted by television or the movies. Popular art seldom portrays real culture accurately and, as pointed out in this chapter, that is particularly true in the case of police detectives.

The advent and impact of contemporary police practices, especially of community-oriented policing and problem-oriented policing, provide the prospect of better days ahead for police. With new approaches that place officers among the citizens they serve, in personal and helpful contexts, perhaps a new era of effective police work is now beginning. But whatever the techniques employed, the police can expect to continue facing a variety of situations, for it is certain they will continue to be involved in handling whatever crises occur.

NOTES

1. Herman Goldstein, *Policing in a Free Society* (Cambridge, MA: Ballinger, 1977), p. 35.
2. Thomas A. Critchley, *A History of Police in England and Wales*, 2nd ed. (Montclair, NJ: Patterson Smith, 1985); Samuel Walker, *A Critical History of Police Reform: The Emergence of Professionalism* (Lexington, MA: Lexington Books, 1977).
3. See Samuel Walker, *Popular Justice* (New York: Oxford University Press, 1980), and Daniel Devlin, *Police Procedure, Administration and Organization* (London: Butterworth, 1966).
4. See Patrick Pringle, *The Thief-Takers* (London: Museum Press, 1958), and Bruce Smith, *Rural Crime Control* (New York: Columbia University Institute of Public Administration, 1933). Also, see Critchley, op. cit.
5. See Patrick Pringle, *Hue and Cry* (New York: William Morrow, 1965).
6. Samuel Walker, *A Critical History of Police Reform: The Emergence of Professionalism* (Lexington, MA: Lexington Books, 1977).
7. Francis X. Hartmann (ed.), *Debating the Evolution of American Policing* (Washington, DC: National Institute of Justice, 1988).
8. George L. Kelling and Mark H. Moore, *The Evolving Strategy of Policing* (Washington, DC: National Institute of Justice, 1988).

9. Hubert Williams and Patrick V. Murphy, *The Evolving Strategy of Police: A Minority View* (Washington, DC: National Institute of Justice, 1990).

10. Kelling and Moore provide an interpretive history of police strategies which Williams and Murphy criticize for not giving due attention to racism and slavery in the history of American policing. We have combined the historical analysis of each issue, and where possible, include perspectives given by both sets of authors.

11. Kelling and Moore, op. cit., pp. 2–4.

12. See Robert Fogelson, *Big City Police* (Cambridge, MA: Harvard University Press, 1977); Roger Lane, *Policing the City, Boston 1822–1885* (Cambridge, MA: Harvard University Press, 1967); and Thomas A. Reppetto, *The Blue Parade* (New York: Free Press, 1978). For an analysis of innovative police techniques, see Jerome H. Skolnick and David H. Bagley, *This New Blue Line: Police Innovation in Six American Cities* (New York: Free Press, 1986).

13. See Bruce Smith, *Police Systems in the United States* (New York: Harper and Bros., 1949).

14. Ibid. Williams and Murphy cite P. L. Reichel, "Southern Slave Patrols as a Transitional Police Type," *American Journal of Policing*, 7(2):51–77, and T. Cooper (ed.), *Statutes at Large of South Carolina*, vol. 3, part 3 (Columbia, SC: A. S. Johnston, 1838), p. 568.

15. Williams and Murphy, op. cit., pp. 4–5.

16. Williams and Murphy, op. cit., p. 5. Also cited therein, Roger Lane, *Policing the City: Boston: 1822–1885* (Cambridge, MA: Harvard University Press, 1967), and E. A. Savage, *A Chronological History of the Boston Watch and Police, from 1631–1865*, available on Library of American Civilization microfiche 13523. (Original published in 1865.)

17. See P. S. Foner, *History of Black Americans: From Africa to the Emergence of the Cotton Kingdom* (Westport, CT: Greenwood, 1975), p. 206; also see I. Berlin, *Slaves without Masters: The Free Negro in the Antebellum South* (New York: Pantheon Books, 1974), pp. 316–317. Both are cited by Williams and Murphy.

18. Ibid., p. 7. Also see M. Delaney, *Colored Brigades, 'Negro Specials' and Colored Policemen: A History of Blacks in American Police Departments* (unpublished manuscript, no date), p. 12, and J. W. Blassingame, *Black New Orleans, 1860–1880* (Chicago, IL: University of Chicago Press, 1973), p. 244.

19. Ibid., p. 8. Also, Walker, op. cit., Note 6, p. 10; Delaney, op. cit., p. 20; and R. Lane, *Roots of Violence in Black Philadelphia: 1860–1900* (Cambridge, MA: Harvard University Press, 1986), pp. 60–67.

20. Ibid., p. 8.

21. Ibid. Also see Foner, op. cit., p. 342.

22. John E. Eck and William Spelman, *Problem-Solving: Problem-Oriented Policing in Newport News* (Washington, DC: National Institute of Justice, 1987), p. 11. Also cited, Eric Monkonnen, *Police in Urban America, 1860–1920* (Cambridge, England: Cambridge University Press, 1981); and see Walker, op. cit.

23. Hartmann, op. cit., p. 4; Kelling and Moore, op. cit., pp. 4–5. See also Richard G. Powers, *Secrecy and Power: The Life of J. Edgar Hoover* (New York: Free Press, 1987).

24. National Commission on Law Observance and Enforcement, *Report on Lawlessness in Law Enforcement*, no. 11 (Washington, DC: U.S. Government Printing Office, 1931).

25. August Vollmer, *The Police and Modern Society* (Berkeley: University of California Press, 1936). Also see O. W. Watson and Roy C. McLaren, *Police Administration*, 3rd ed. (New York: McGraw-Hill, 1972), and Gene E. Carte, *Police Reform in the United*

States: The Era of August Vollmer, 1905–1932 (Berkeley: University of California Press, 1986).

26. Williams and Murphy, op. cit., p. 10.

27. *Report of the National Advisory Commission on Civil Disorders* (New York: Bantam, 1968), p. 321, 304–305.

28. Ibid., pp. 1, 2, 299.

29. See Eck and Spelman for an analysis of the effects of the reform era.

30. Clifford D. Shearing and Philip C. Stenning, *Private Policing* (Beverly Hills, CA: Sage, 1987).

31. William C. Cunningham and Todd H. Taylor, *The Growing Role of Private Security* (Washington, DC: National Institute of Justice, May 1985).

32. Ibid., pp. 17–18; Also see Albert J. Reiss, Jr., *Policing a City's Central District—The Oakland Story* (Washington, DC: National Institute of Justice, 1985).

33. Eck and Spelman, op. cit., p. 1.

34. Ibid., p. 2.

35. Vern L. Folley, *Police Patrol Techniques and Tactics* (Springfield, IL: Charles C. Thomas, 1973), p. ix. See also Robert C. Trajanowicz and Denis W. Banas, *Perceptions of Safety: A Comparison of Foot Patrol versus Motor Patrol Officers* (East Lansing: National Neighborhood Foot Patrol Center, School of Criminal Justice, Michigan State University, 1985); Stephen Meagher, "Police Patrol Styles: How Pervasive Is Community Variations?" *Journal of Police Science and Administration* 13 (1985): 36–45; Margaret J. Levine, *Patrol Deployment* (Washington, DC: U.S. Department of Justice, 1985); Richard C. Larson, *Synthesizing and Extending the Results of Police Patrol Studies* (Washington, DC: U.S. Department of Justice, 1985).

36. But see William P. Brown, "Local Policing—A Three Dimensional Task Analysis," *Journal of Criminal Justice* 3 (1975): 1–15. In this article Professor Brown argues that the police function is one of community service and that crime control is only one part of that overall purpose. See also Timothy J. Flanagan, "Consumer Perspectives on Police Operational Strategy," *Journal of Police Science and Administration* 13(1)(1985): 10–21.

37. George M. Pugh, "The Good Police Officer: Qualities, Roles and Concepts," *Journal of Police Science and Administration* 14(1)(1986): 49–61; Paul M. Whisenand and R. Fred Ferguson, *The Managing of Police Organizations* (Englewood Cliffs, NJ: Prentice-Hall, 1973), pp. 199–201; Herman Goldstein, *Policing a Free Society* (Cambridge, MA: Ballinger, 1976), pp. 111–112. See also William K. Muir, *Police: Streetcorner Politicians* (Chicago: University of Chicago Press, 1977).

38. *Report of the National Advisory Commission on Civil Disorders*, pp. 304–305.

39. Trajanowicz and Banas, op. cit.

40. Goldstein, op. cit., p. 49.

41. Albert J. Reiss, Jr., *The Police and the Public* (New Haven, CT: Yale University Press, 1971), pp. 10–11.

42. Goldstein, op. cit., p. 49.

43. George L. Kelling, Tony Pate, D. Dieckman, and Charles E. Brown, *The Kansas City Preventive Patrol Experiment and Summary Report* (Washington, DC: Police Foundation, 1974).

44. Eck and Spelman, op. cit., pp. 13–14.

45. Ibid., p. 14.

46. President's Commission on Law Enforcement and Administration of Justice, *Task Force Report: The Police* (Washington, DC: U.S. Government Printing Office, 1967), pp. 184–185.

47. *Report of the National Advisory Commission on Civil Disorders* (see note 27 above),

p. 14. See also Raymond I. Parnas, "The Police Response to the Domestic Disturbance," *Wisconsin Law Review 1967* (Fall 1967): 914–960.

48. M. A. Farber, "Big Push on Crime Merely Pushes It Elsewhere, Many Officers Feel," *New York Times*, June 1, 1982, pp. B1, B6, cited in John E. Conklin, *Criminology* (New York: Macmillan, 1989), p. 441.

49. Peter B. Bloch and Donald R. Weidman, *Managing Criminal Investigations* (Washington, DC: U.S. Department of Justice, 1975), p. 17.

50. Goldstein, op. cit., p. 55. Goldstein writes: "Many of the techniques employed by detectives today are more heavily influenced by a desire to imitate stereotypes than by a rational plan for solving crimes. The myths and fantasies that pervade detective operations deter the police and the public from examining the utility of what it is that detectives in fact do."

51. Peter W. Greenwood and Joan Petersilia, *The Criminal Investigation Process*, vol. I; Jan M. Chaiken, *The Criminal Investigation Process*, vol. II; and Peter W. Greenwood, Jan M. Chaiken, Joan Petersilia, and Linda Prusoff, *The Criminal Investigation Process*, vol. III (Santa Monica, CA: Rand Corporation, 1975).

52. For an analysis of factors in jury decisions, see Harry Kalven and Hans Zeisel, *The American Jury* (Boston: Little, Brown, 1966).

53. Greenwood and Petersilia, *The Criminal Investigation Process*, vol. I.

54. Daryl F. Gates and Lyle Knowles, "An Examination of the Rand Corporation's Analysis of the Criminal Investigation Process," *Police Chief* 43 (July 1976): 20.

55. Bloch and Weidman, op. cit. The Rand report is not the only research on investigatory functions, nor is it the first call for the improvement of detective services. During the early 1970s, for example, the Police Foundation held a series of conferences on improving investigatory procedures through better management. And today there are various studies and reports outlining strategic and tactical alternatives that can be followed to make detective work more effective in solving crimes and apprehending suspects.

56. Rossiter C. Mulvaney, "Wanted! A New Look at Interrogation and Interview," *Police Chief* 43 (July 1976): 42.

57. Eck and Spelman, op. cit., p. 14.

58. Ibid.

59. Ibid. See also, John E. Eck, *Solving Crimes: The Investigation of Burglary and Robbery* (Washington, DC: Police Executive Research Forum, 1982).

60. Lawrence W. Sherman, Catherine H. Milton, and Thomas O. Kelly, *Team Policing: Seven Case Studies* (Washington, DC: The Police Foundation, 1973).

61. Eck and Spelman, op. cit., pp. 18–19.

62. See Robert Trajanowicz and P. R. Smith, *A Manual for the Establishment and Operation of a Foot Patrol Program* (East Lansing: National Neighborhood Foot Patrol Center, School of Criminal Justice, Michigan State University, 1985); also see K. E. Asbury, "Innovative Policing: Foot Patrol in 31 Divisions, Metropolitan Toronto," *Canadian Police College Journal* 17(1989): 165–181.

63. Eck and Spelman, op. cit., p. 31.

64. Richard Lacayo, "Back to the Beat," *Time*, April 1, 1991, pp. 22–24.

65. James Q. Wilson and George L. Kelling, "Making Neighborhoods Safe," *The Atlantic*, February 1989, pp. 46–52. Also see New York City police commissioner Lee P. Brown's article "Community Policing: A Practical Guide for Police Officials," in *Annual Editions: Criminal Justice 91/92*, (Guilford, CT: The Dushkin Publishing Group, 1991), pp. 89–98, reprinted from *Perspectives on Policing* (Washington, DC: U.S. Department of Justice, September 1989), pp. 1–11; George L. Kelling, *Police and Communities: The Quiet Revolution* (Washington, DC: The U.S. Department of

Justice, 1988); and George L. Kelling, *Neighborhoods and Police: The Maintenance of Civil Authority*, (Washington, DC: U.S. Department of Justice, 1989).

66. Jerome H. Skolnick and David H. Bayley, *The New Blue Line: Police Innovation in Six American Cities* (Washington, DC: National Institute of Justice, 1986). Also see George L. Kelling, *What Works—Research and the Police* (Washington, DC: U.S. Department of Justice, 1988).

67. Herman Goldstein, *Problem-Oriented Policing* (New York: McGraw-Hill, 1990).

68. Ibid., p. 49.

69. William Geller, "Deadly Force: What We Know," *Journal of Police Science and Administration* 10 (1982): 151–177.

70. Lawrence W. Sherman and Richard Berk, *The Minneapolis Domestic Violence Experiment*, vol. 1 (Washington, DC: Police Foundation Report, 1984), pp. 1–8.

SUGGESTED READINGS

Goldstein, Herman. *Problem-Oriented Policing.* New York: McGraw-Hill, 1990.

Goldstein, Herman. *Policing a Free Society.* Cambridge, MA: Ballinger, 1977.

Kelling, George L., and Mark Moore. *The Evolving Strategy of Policing.* Washington, D.C.: U.S. Department of Justice, November 1988.

Klockars, Carl B. *The Idea of Police.* Beverly Hills: Sage, 1985.

Klockars, Carl B. *Thinking About Police.* New York: McGraw-Hill, 1983.

Miller, Wilbur R. "Cops and Bobbies, 1830–1870." *Journal of Social History* (Winter 1975): 81–101.

Niederhoffer, Arthur. *Behind the Shield: The Police in Urban Society.* Garden City, NY: Doubleday, 1967.

Rubinstein, Jonathan. *City Police.* New York: Farrar, Straus and Giroux, 1973.

Skogan, Wesley G. *Disorder and Decline: Crime and the Spiral of Decay in American Neighborhoods.* New York: Free Press, 1990.

Skolnick, Jerome H., and David H. Bayley. *The New Blue Line: Police Innovation in Six American Cities.* New York: Free Press, 1986.

Tobias, John J. *Crime and Police in England, 1700–1900.* New York: St. Martin's Press, 1979.

Walker, Samuel. *A Critical History of Police Reform: The Emergence of Professionalism.* Lexington, MA: Lexington Books, 1977.

DISCUSSION QUESTIONS

1. Trace the development of the American police from their English antecedents to the present.

2. Describe the political era of American policing; describe the reform era.

3. How did private police develop in the United States?

4. Explain incident-driven policing.

5. What values and purposes are served by police patrols?

6. Describe the Kansas City patrol experiment and discuss its impact on American policing.

7. What benefits and what harmful effects are created by aggressive preventive patrol?

8. Describe the role of detectives in police work.

9. Describe the techniques of team policing, CPOP, and problem-oriented policing.

10. What critical problems confront police daily, on a recurring basis, in crisis situations, and due to the incidence of new community responses and police officers' needs? How do police respond?

6

Police Decisions: Detection, Arrest, and In-Custody Investigation

Officers Smythe and Helwys of the Metropolitan Police Department were working the 4 p.m. to midnight shift. The two men had been partners for over a year, and Smythe had graduated from the police academy about 18 months before Helwys. On this evening they had enjoyed a routine shift. They had worked a minor accident in the 5 p.m. traffic, responded to a domestic disturbance call in which neighbors had called police about a fight between a man and his live-in girlfriend, arrested a teenager for driving under the influence of alcohol, and otherwise responded to the sights and sounds of the city. In short, they were on routine patrol, "fighting crime" and "serving the community" as the needs and opportunities arose. The two men stopped at a favorite hamburger stand for their evening meal and talked about their families and mutual interests.

Unseen by the officers, the owner of the hamburger stand sold cocaine through the back door. If the officers had entered the kitchen and opened the cabinet door, they would have seen drugs and cash. Across the street a pawn shop owner was examining some stolen goods he had just purchased from a local thief. If the officers had entered the shop and searched the shelves in the backroom closet, they would have found stolen goods from a number of recent burglaries in a neighborhood on the other side of town. And, in the trunk of a passing automobile, a young woman was transporting a briefcase containing betting slips for the large illegal sports betting ring she worked for. If the officers had stopped the car, opened the trunk, and then opened the briefcase, they would have found evidence of the criminal betting ring.

However, the officers could not see the illegal activities occurring around them, and no one informed them of what was happening. So they ate in peace.

ABOUT THIS CHAPTER

In another society, or indeed another time in this country, the freedom of police to arbitrarily enter homes and businesses, stop and search automobiles at random, and otherwise interrupt citizens in the search for crime would go unquestioned. But in the United States today, police are prohibited from such interference without "reasonable suspicion" that a crime has been, is being, or is about to be committed.

This freedom from unreasonable search was established in 1791, over 200 years ago, when the **Fourth Amendment** to the United States Constitution was ratified (see Box 6.1). But the Fourth Amendment was largely ignored for many years, and many unreasonable searches and seizures were conducted by law enforcement authorities, producing evidence used in trials to gain convictions. Indeed, the Fourth Amendment prohibition in the United States was not taken seriously by police until 1914 when the U.S. Supreme Court decided *Weeks v. United States*, establishing the **exclusionary rule**. The exclusionary rule prohibits the use in trials of illegally obtained evidence, that is, evidence obtained through illegal searches and seizures. The Fourth Amendment protects citizens from such police misconduct, even if the evidence obtained by those means proves guilt.

Police work and police decisions are thus controlled by law, by the U.S. Constitution, by local, state, and national policies, and by the training police officers receive. Officers Smythe and Helwys no doubt are good, honest, effective police officers. And as such they must obey the law and follow the prescribed processes of law enforcement. This chapter addresses how the representatives of the law must themselves obey the law, and how their decisions must be in keeping with the law.

In the final analysis the whole criminal justice apparatus waits for and depends on decisions by police. In this chapter we also describe those basic, important deci-

---

BOX 6.1

The Fourth Amendment to
the U.S. Constitution
(1791)

The right of the people to be secure in their persons, houses, papers, and effects, against unreasonable searches and seizures, shall not be violated, and no Warrants shall issue, but upon probable cause, supported by Oath or affirmation, and particularly describing the place to be searched, and the persons or things to be seized.

sions, giving attention to the practical and legal influences that affect them. Why is it that some crimes are detected, investigated, and "solved" and others are not? How do police choose from the arsenal of investigative techniques available to them and who decides when, how, and against whom to direct those techniques? What limitations are placed on police power to intrude on personal freedom? How much has to be known by police *before* an arrest? What techniques are available for, and what limitations exist on, determining facts *after* an arrest? These questions and more are addressed in this chapter. But they are not easily dealt with, and are not simply a matter for casual discussion. Indeed, the decisions police make are among the most controversial in our society. Political campaigns often involve debate about the exclusionary rule, whether and to what extent police should be restrained, and how to control (or loosen control over) police actions. The conservative and liberal approaches to crime and justice are perhaps nowhere more different than on the subject of police decisions, as discussed at the conclusion of the chapter.

CRIME CONTROL DECISIONS

Enforcing the criminal law is a primary duty of all police agencies. Acting to investigate and solve crimes involves a series of police decisions, each of which is closely controlled by courts and legislative bodies. (See Fig. 6.1.) Every police enforcement decision is as complex and controversial as any in the criminal justice process, yet effective policing is clearly necessary to preserve our social order. In the front-line decisions made by the police, both our personal safety and our democratic principles as a nation are at stake.

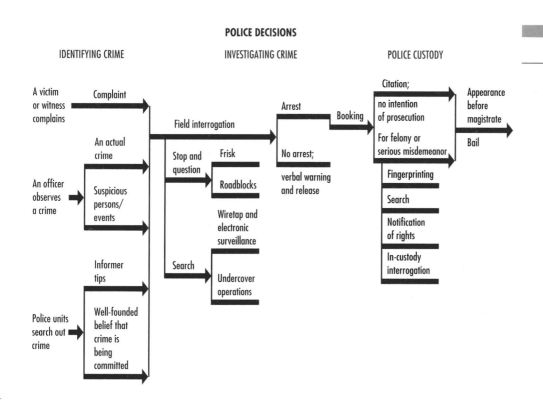

POLICE DECISIONS

IDENTIFYING CRIME   INVESTIGATING CRIME   POLICE CUSTODY

FIGURE 6.1

Police decisions.

Crime Reported

1: Burglary

The police received a call from a homeowner who stated his residence had been burglarized while he was on vacation. The desk officer dispatched a patrol car to the scene. Officers observed signs of forcible entry, interviewed the complainant and neighbors, and filed a report with the Burglary Division. Detectives from Burglary followed up by dusting the scene for fingerprints, making an inventory of the property stolen, and filing an MO report (method of operation of the burglar) with the Records and Intelligence (R&I) Division.

2: Pickpocket

At 1:30 a.m. a man appeared at a precinct station and reported that his wallet had been stolen while he was riding on a city bus. He was interviewed by a detective, who became suspicious of the complaint, for the man appeared intoxicated and the officer knew that late at night there were few riders on the particular bus where the crime allegedly occurred. Further questioning brought an admission that the complainant had lost all his money in a card game but was afraid to tell his wife. Consequently, he invented the pickpocket story. He was reprimanded for filing a false report of a crime and sent home.

3: Rape

A counsellor from a Rape Crisis Center called a precinct station and requested an officer be sent to the center to investigate a rape case. The desk sergeant dispatched a policewoman, who, at the center, interviewed a 19-year-old college student who claimed she had been attacked and raped on a path through a city park. The girl was bordering on hysteria but was able to give a description of her assailant. She was sent for a medical examination, which confirmed evidence of rape. The police officer requested an APB (all-points bulletin) to be broadcast by the radio dispatcher giving the description of the rapist and the location of the crime. ■

INVESTIGATING CRIMES AND IDENTIFYING SUSPECTS

The criminal justice process usually begins when the police suspect that a crime has been committed, is being committed, or is about to be committed and when the situation is investigated to verify or dispel this suspicion. There are three major ways in which police suspicion is aroused: (1) A victim or other witness *complains*; (2) an officer on patrol *observes* a crime; or (3) police units actively *search out* crime.

The first occurs when the police receive an *initial complaint* that a crime has taken place. Normally all complaints trigger investigations which vary in intensity depending on the type of crime reported, the apparent credibility of the complainant, and other specifics of each situation. (See Field Practice A.)

The second way in which police suspicion is aroused is by *observation* of street behavior while on *routine patrol*. An officer working a beat, in a prowl car, or occasionally at a fixed post, may observe some occurrence—a person running from a warehouse in the early hours of the morning, a clean automobile with dirty license plates, or a similar unusual situation—that in his or her experience may indicate the commission of a crime and justify further investigation. Or the officer on patrol may witness an actual crime or what appears to be a crime being committed. Many jurisdictions state that warrantless arrests for misdemeanors can be made only if the offense is committed "in view" of the police officer.[1] Thus a driver cannot be arrested for speeding on the complaint of another driver; the infraction must be witnessed by the arresting officer. (See Field Practice B.)

Field Interrogation

Observation of suspicious persons or unusual activity generally leads officers to investigate further. This often means they stop and question the individuals whose

Police Observation

1: Wobbly Driving

A foot patrolman on traffic duty saw a car moving slowly but erratically toward him. Before the car reached the officer's intersection it hit the curb and bounced into a parking meter. The officer ran to the auto and discovered the driver slumped over the steering wheel. Not knowing whether the operator was injured, sick, drunk, or all three, the traffic cop summoned a prowl car and an ambulance.

2: Burn, Baby

Two officers in a patrol car turned a corner and encountered a serious fire in an apartment house directly in front of them. Apparently it had just started; no fire trucks were at the scene. One officer radioed for fire department help; the driver turned on his flasher and siren and rushed toward the house. A crowd was beginning to gather and the sound of fire trucks on the way could be heard when one of the officers saw a young man running *from* the direction of the blaze. The officer and his partner took off in pursuit of the young man.

3: Did You Win a Prize?

Two patrol officers, parked on a side street, glanced at a new Lincoln Continental passing them. The car was well within the speed limit but the driver and rider—teenage boys with leather vests, headbands, one earring apiece—looked incongruous. The officers, without saying anything to each other, turned on their flashing lights and siren and pulled the Continental over to question the young men. ■

---

actions aroused their suspicions and/or others in the area. This is known as **field interrogation**. The police ask those they have stopped for identification and briefly question them about their actions. Such field interrogation may confirm police suspicions, so that an arrest results, or it may simply produce a satisfactory explanation by the person, so that he or she is allowed to move on. (See Field Practice C.)

The legality of field interrogation is cloudy. Normally the police rely on the cooperation of those they stop. But what if someone refuses to stop or to answer any questions? Should the officers drop the interrogation, or does the refusal to cooperate coupled with the original suspicious circumstances constitute sufficient evidence to proceed with an arrest?

There has been little legislative or appellate court authorization of field interrogation practices, and such authority as does exist is unclear in just what it allows. Statutes in many jurisdictions permit police to stop automobiles to check vehicular registration, but the law is often silent concerning police authority to stop pedestrians in the absence of evidence sufficient for arrest.

In general, the authority of the police to stop people briefly for questioning is covered by the notion of *reasonable suspicion*: If the officers have reasonable grounds to suspect that a person has committed, is committing, or is about to commit a crime, or that the individual is a wanted criminal, they may stop the suspect for questioning. In addition, police have the authority to stop and question (1) persons in suspicious circumstances, (2) witnesses near the scenes of certain crimes, and (3) suspects sought for previously committed felonies.[3]

But such authority is cloudy, and even the Constitutionality of laws that *do* permit the police to stop suspicious-looking individuals is not always clear. In 1983 the U.S. Supreme Court considered the California case of "The Walker," a man who had been arrested and detained 15 times over a 2-year period for violating a statute that required persons who "wander or loiter" on the streets to provide "credible and reliable" identification to a police officer when asked to do so. The man, Edward Lawson, was stopped by police frequently because he "looked suspicious" and "out-

A pat-down search, or frisk, is used to discover weapons when the officer has reason to believe he or she is in danger.

Field Interrogation

1: School Days

Police received several reports of child molestation occurring near a particular school. Even though there was no good description of the alleged molester, officers made it a patrol practice to cruise near the school both in the morning when children were arriving and in the afternoon when school was dismissed. On one occasion they noticed a man in a car parked near the school. After watching him for a few minutes, the officers approached the car and asked him to get out. They asked for his identification and his reasons for parking near the school. His identification was in order and he gave a satisfactory explanation for parking in the area. The officers thanked him and continued on patrol.

2: Weight Lifters

Early in the morning, in a high-crime area, officers on patrol saw two men coming out of an alley carrying what appeared to be a heavy trunk. The officers stopped them and asked permission to see what was in the trunk. One of the men opened it and convinced the officers that it was filled with his own clothing and other personal belongings. He explained that he was sneaking out of his apartment to avoid his landlord because he was overdue with the rent. The officer told him that this was the wrong way to solve his problem but allowed the men to continue carrying away the trunk.

3: Panel Truck

Police on patrol in a residential area observed an unmarked but battered panel truck driving slowly through the streets. They stopped the vehicle and asked the driver for his identification and an explanation of his presence in the neighborhood. The driver had no license or truck registration and his explanation of his actions was vague. The officers arrested him for driving without a license and upon examining the truck discovered a number of bicycles stolen from garages and carports in the area. ∎

of-place." He was black, wore a dreadlock hairstyle, and often walked through all-white neighborhoods. When stopped, he either could not or would not provide appropriate identification. There were no allegations that Lawson committed any crime other than failing to provide identification. He brought legal action against the arresting police officers, and sought an injunction to restrain enforcement of the statute, asking, in fact, that the statute be declared unconstitutional. The Supreme Court agreed with Lawson. Justice Sandra Day O'Connor, writing for the majority, held the statute to be unconstitutionally vague, since it gave virtually unlimited discretion to the police to determine in any given case whether the statutory requirements were being met.[4]

Obviously, this is an area of continuing controversy.

Frisk

The right of police officers to frisk people who are stopped for questioning is authorized by statute in some jurisdictions. **Frisk** involves a "pat-down" search of the suspect *only* to discover weapons, not to recover contraband. The scope of a frisk is much more limited than a full-scale search, and a frisk can occur only under specified conditions where the officer has reason to believe he or she is "in danger of life or limb."

A police officer's decision to question, and perhaps frisk, a suspect is often the result of the officer using his or her "street smarts," that is, the perception of suspicious and possibly dangerous situations based on years of patrol experience. Like trained hunters, experienced officers may find their suspicions aroused by circumstances that would not give pause to the ordinary citizen. But this use of street smarts often has a dubious legal status. Police, in contrast to other participants in the criminal justice process such as prosecuting attorneys and judges, often use abilities not generally recognized or justified on the basis of formal education, training, or state certification, so that their actions based on those abilities can be called into question.

One such instance arose in a case known as *Terry v. Ohio*. A detective McFadden, acting on his street smarts, stopped and frisked three men he observed engaging in suspicious behavior, and found concealed weapons (see Box 6.2 for details). Later his right to stop and frisk on the basis of suspicion alone was called into question. The case made it to the Supreme Court, and in this instance, the Court found in favor of Detective McFadden, declaring that the behavior of the three men *did* warrant further investigation. The Court wrote: "It would have been poor police work indeed for an officer with 39 years experience in the detection of thievery from stores in this same neighborhood to have failed to investigate this behavior further."[5]

In the more important aspects of the case as to whether the officer was justified in invading the suspects' persons by searching them for weapons, again the Court answered in the affirmative, declaring that a police officer is justified in making certain "that the person with whom he is dealing is not armed with a weapon that could unexpectedly and fatally be used against him." The sole justification of such a search is the protection of the police officer, and in this particular case the search was limited to the outer clothing; McFadden did not place his hands inside pockets, or under the suspects' outer garments, until he felt the weapons. The search had been carefully limited.[5]

Another legal problem with frisking arises when evidence of a crime other than possession of a concealed weapon is discovered. Court decisions in these cases usually depend on just how the pat-down was conducted. A companion case to *Terry v. Ohio*, known as *Sibron v. New York* (the two were even decided the same day) involved a New York policeman finding glassine envelopes containing heroin while frisking a known narcotics dealer. The Supreme Court allowed the exclusion of this evidence in the trial based on the following considerations: the suspect was not under arrest at the time of the frisk (police can carry out a thorough search of suspects under arrest), nor did the policeman have a warrant to carry out a proper search; the policeman placed his hand inside one of the suspect's pockets instead of merely patting down his clothing; and the material found was not a weapon that could endanger the officer's life.[6]

Searches of Vehicles and Luggage

Searches of stopped automobiles and of the luggage of airline passengers who fit drug courier "profiles" have presented special legal problems when evidence of a crime, usually possession of narcotics, is discovered. Carrying out a search based on no probable cause or reasonable suspicion to believe that a suspect possesses narcotics has been the basis for invoking the exclusionary rule, that is, for excluding any wrongfully seized evidence (in this case narcotics) from admission into a trial. Usually, for prosecution to proceed, the use of the evidence must be justified by the **"plain-view" doctrine**, in which evidence of another crime is in plain view and "immediately apparent"—as, for instance, when an automobile is stopped for speeding—or be the result of a justified search, such as in *Terry v. Ohio*, where experienced officers observe suspicious behavior.[7]

In 1991, however, the U.S. Supreme Court ruled in *Florida v. Bostick* that evidence seized in a drug sweep of a public bus was admissible. Two police officers boarded a bus heading from Ft. Lauderdale to Miami, clearly identified themselves as police officers, said they were searching for possible drugs, and asked passengers to

BOX 6.2

The *Terry v. Ohio* Case

Detective McFadden, a policeman for 39 years, was on afternoon patrol in a city when he observed two men standing at a corner. One would walk past a store, look in the window, go a short distance, and then return to the window for another look. The other man would then repeat the same pattern. After this took place a dozen times the men walked off together. Officer McFadden came to the conclusion that the men were "casing" the store for a possible robbery. He followed them, and when they stopped to confer with another man, he approached and asked all of them their names. When they mumbled in response, he turned one of the men around, patted him down, and found a .38 caliber revolver in his overcoat pocket. Frisking the other two, the officer found another gun. He took the men with the guns into custody and they were charged with carrying concealed weapons.

show identification and submit to a search of their luggage. The officers had no reasonable suspicion that anyone on the bus carried drugs. When a passenger named Bostick was approached, he voluntarily surrendered his ticket and identification, which raised no suspicion. The officers then asked to search his luggage and explained that he had the right to refuse. Bostick consented (he later disputed this), and the officers found cocaine. They arrested Bostick, and charged him with possession of a controlled substance with intent to distribute. He pled guilty, but retained the right to appeal the search. In a split decision, the U.S. Supreme Court ruled that Bostick was not "detained" in the bus and therefore could have freely refused the search, and that such warrantless searches without probable cause are justified in the effort to fight the war on drugs.[8]

On the other hand, in roadblock situations where the police do not have enough evidence to arrest each driver, courts have disallowed searches of automobiles without warrants. According to the courts, such searches cannot be justified on the basis of arrest, nor can the automobile occupants be said to freely consent to search since the stops are forcible and required. Some roadblock searches have been upheld, but only when very serious crimes were involved, a dangerous offender was sought, or the purpose of the roadblock was to save the life of a kidnap victim.[9]

Occasionally roadblocks have been declared legally justified. In 1991, in *Michigan Department of State Police v. Sitz*, the U.S. Supreme Court ruled that such temporary roadblocks are a reasonable tool in the law enforcement arsenal to deal with drunk driving. The court concluded that since roadblocks had discovered that 1.5 percent of the stopped drivers were legally intoxicated, the intrusion into the lives of and inconvenience experienced by the remaining 98.5 percent of sober drivers was justified.[10]

Sometimes the problem with roadblocks is less legal than social. One such example occurred in the Florida Keys several years ago when the State Highway Patrol set up a roadblock on the only highway to and from Key West in a search for illegal aliens. The public uproar about the resultant traffic jam, overheated cars, and other inconveniences caused the policy to be discontinued.

Temporary roadblocks can discover drunken drivers.

Searching Out Crime

1: Peephole

Police received a call from a store owner who reported numerous customer complaints about homosexual solicitation in the store's restrooms. Vice squad officers went to the store and set up "peephole" observation stations to attempt to gather evidence of criminal solicitation.

2: Rumble

Police received information from a number of informants that a "rumble" between rival motorcycle clubs was scheduled to take place in a local park. Members of the Tactical Unit were dispatched to the park with instructions to stake out the scene, remain hidden, but keep the area under surveillance.

3: Sheets

A police intelligence unit received word from an undercover officer that the Ku Klux Klan (KKK), long under investigation, was planning to burn a cross on the property of a prominent Jewish businessman. On the night in question, some police officers in plainclothes concealed themselves in the businessman's house, others hid in a police decoy panel truck (ironically marked "Roger's Laundry" because of the Klan sheets) parked nearby, and additional uniformed officers in patrol cars cruised within radio distance of the panel truck. Since the KKK is on the U.S. Attorney General's criminal conspiracy list, the FBI was notified and two FBI agents were in the panel truck with the local police. When the Klansmen arrived, set up the cross, and lit the fire, police burst out and made eleven arrests on state charges ranging from harassment to arson. Federal charges of violation of civil rights statutes were also made. ■

SEARCHING OUT CRIME

Police investigations sometimes are triggered even when there are no complaints of crimes by witnesses or observations of suspicious activities while on routine patrol. Instead, the police may decide to go out and look for specific criminal activity. This form of investigation originates in the belief, sometimes supported by informer tips but more frequently based simply on knowledge of local conditions, that certain types of crimes are occurring or will occur in the community. These investigations are usually directed toward so-called victimless crimes such as organized gambling, prostitution, the sale of narcotics, and other vice offenses, but they may include looking for criminal conspiracies ranging from robbery plots by professional criminals to meetings of "political revolutionaries." Large police agencies often have specialized detective units—vice squads, organized crime intelligence units, and the like—for the investigation of these types of offenses and the observation and tailing of persons believed to be involved in vice, rackets, or conspiracies.

Calling these offenses victimless is misleading. Many of them are very serious in nature, and there are many actual victims of narcotics pushers, terrorists, and others engaged in criminal conspiracies. More accurately, these are crimes without specific complainants, rather than without victims, and are crimes that are ordinarily not discovered on routine patrol. The conspiracies themselves often have to be searched out, as do the conspirators, particularly the higher-ups in narcotics manufacturing and distribution rings, in gangs of professional bank or jewelry store robbers, in terrorists groups, or the like. It is the uncovering of these crimes and the arrest of these criminals that pose the biggest challenge to police enforcement efforts. And the methods used by the police to discover such crimes and to make arrests connected with them are all controversial. Such "proactive" rather than "reactive" policing poses the greatest threat to many of our democratic values. Yet proactive policing is often the only way

151

we have any chance to uncover and control some types of very serious crimes and to catch some types of very dangerous criminals in our society. (See Field Practice D.)

The techniques used by police to seek out possible criminal activities are varied, depending on the quality of their information, the extent of community pressure for enforcement of particular laws, and the kinds of offenses toward which investigation is directed. Investigations may involve searches, electronic eavesdropping, and other kinds of surveillance in addition to undercover infiltration of ongoing criminal activities.

Search

Search is an investigatory technique that can be used at any time, before or after the arrest of a suspect. Following a lawful arrest a suspect may be searched without a warrant. Search prior to arrest normally requires the consent of the person searched or a **search warrant**, a court order instructing police to search for and return to the court specific items to be used in the prosecution of a person.[11] Freedom from unreasonable searches is guaranteed by the Fourth Amendment to the Constitution, and the U.S. Supreme Court has held that evidence improperly seized cannot be admitted at trial. Prior to this decision, each state could make its own determination of whether improperly seized evidence could be used, and twenty-two states did allow it to be introduced. Today, the exclusionary rule has been applied as a Constitutional requirement in all states as well as in federal jurisdictions. The court decision expanding the exclusionary rule was *Mapp v. Ohio*. (See Box 6.3.)

At the time of the Mapp search and arrest, Ohio did not require that evidence improperly seized be excluded at trial. But in its final decision, the Supreme Court stated, "*We hold that all evidence obtained by searches and seizures in violation of the Constitution is, by that same authority, inadmissible in a state court.*" If a criminal goes free because "the constable has blundered," then, the Court wrote, "The criminal goes free, if he must, but it is the law that sets him free. Nothing can destroy a government more quickly than its failure to observe its own laws."[12]

In general police and prosecutors strongly criticized the exclusionary rule as acting to "handcuff" the police in their law enforcement objectives. Under the *Mapp* decision, evidence wrongly seized by police, even if the officers believed they were acting properly, would be excluded from trial. Various law enforcement interest groups succeeded in gaining a "good-faith exception" to the rule. They argued that the results of a search conducted by police who in good faith believed they acted properly should be admissible, thereby limiting trial exclusion of evidence seized only when the police *knowingly* acted improperly in obtaining it. Thus officers believed, in good faith, that their actions were authorized by warrants which turned out to be defective, the evidence could still be used.[13]

Search of persons, premises, and vehicles is an extremely complex and controversial investigatory technique, yet one considered essential by most police agencies. Where the scene of an arrest is a suspect's home, searches undertaken without warrants must be limited to those areas immediately adjacent to where the arrest occurred. The reasoning behind this is that police must be allowed to search *places within the suspect's reach* in order to prevent him or her from grabbing a weapon or destroying evidence. Searching the rest of the home requires a warrant.[14]

In recent years the searching of automobiles has been treated somewhat differently from the searching of premises, giving a wider scope to warrantless motor vehicle searches.[15] However, not even automobiles may be searched beyond the reach of the driver or occupants *unless* an arrest has been made or the car has been impounded for an "inventory search" (of property inside the car) in a police car park.

BOX 6.3

The *Mapp v. Ohio* Case (1961)

Three Cleveland police officers arrived at the home of a woman named Mapp, acting on information that a person was hiding there who was wanted for questioning in connection with a bombing and also that the home contained gambling paraphernalia. Mapp, after conferring by phone with her attorney, refused to admit them. The three officers placed the house under surveillance until joined some 3 hours later by four additional officers. They approached the house and forcibly entered it. In the meantime Mapp's attorney arrived, but the police would not allow him to enter the house or confer with Mapp. When Mapp demanded to see a search warrant, the officers held out a paper they claimed was a warrant and Mapp seized it and placed it in her blouse. After a struggle the police recovered the paper, which apparently was not really a warrant, and handcuffed Mapp because she had resisted their recovery efforts. She was forcibly taken upstairs to her bedroom and restrained while police searched the entire house. In the basement they discovered and confiscated obscene materials, possession of which later became the basis of the charge for which Mapp was convicted.

In 1991 in *California v. Acevedo* the U.S. Supreme Court upheld the search of a man's car without a warrant. In this case police had been informed that marijuana was being shipped via Federal Express and staked out the Federal Express office. They observed the addressee claim the package, followed him to his apartment, and then observed another man enter the apartment. When the second man came out of the apartment, he was carrying a brown paper bag containing what the officers considered to be a package about the size of one of the marijuana bundles in the Federal Express shipment. The officers did not have time to obtain a search warrant, and were afraid the man would leave the scene and dispose of the package, so they stopped him, searched the car, opened the trunk and the bag, and discovered the marijuana. The court ruled that such a search was permissible.[16] Box 6.4 summarizes the key cases involving frisk and search.

Wiretap and Electronic Surveillance

Modern police have many techniques to investigate, watch, and eavesdrop on suspects. For instance, they use dogs to detect drugs by their odor. And there is **electronic surveillance**: Parabolic listening cones can be used outdoors to pick up conversations hundreds of feet away, tiny microphones can fit into and broadcast from a Martini olive, scopes give vision in the dark, heat sensors follow suspects at midnight, and tiny camouflaged television cameras can be strategically placed in various locations from banks to park pathways.

One of the older but still widely used eavesdropping techniques is **wiretapping**. After securing a search warrant, the police arrange with the local telephone company to implant electronic recording devices ("bugs") in the telephone lines of suspects. In this way they can listen to and record all incoming and outgoing phone conversations. Similar bugs, again used with judicial approval, are sometimes concealed, often quite cleverly, directly in the houses of suspects to pick up and record non-telephone conversations in their homes.

The use of surveillance in general raises two questions: Is the evidence it yields legally admissible in court, and, if so, when and under what conditions? The answers to these issues ultimately depend on whether a Constitutionally protected right to privacy exists,[17] and how far that right extends. In 1984 the U.S. Supreme Court considered a case in which police officers, acting on a tip that someone was growing marijuana, went to his farm, followed a path around a locked gate posted with a "No Trespassing" sign, and found a field of marijuana about a mile from the farmhouse. The suspect was arrested, but at trial moved to have the case dismissed, arguing that the method of gathering the evidence against him constituted an illegal invasion of his privacy. The lower appellate courts agreed with his position, but the U.S. Supreme Court held the evidence to be admissible under an "open-fields" doctrine, that is, that the Fourth Amendment protects only reasonable expectations of privacy.[18]

Sometimes simple surveillance ("tailing" an individual or "staking out" a residence) or electronic surveillance is used not to gather evidence specifically to be used in court but to accumulate "intelligence" information, which, in its entirety, might be used to determine the extent of, or in future, to prove a criminal conspiracy. Occasionally surveillance, whether conducted on an informer's tip or not, pays off with the observation of a crime being committed. And now and then surveillance is carried out by means of unusual assistance rendered to the police. (See Field Practice E.)

Surveillance techniques, like search techniques, are controversial, and as electronic eavesdropping techniques have become more sophisticated, they have been heavily litigated. Covert, unobtrusive observation of suspects or premises is difficult to control but creates few problems if the officers undertaking it remain hidden. In

Surveillance

1: Boring Duty

Convinced that a particular businessman was a local kingpin of organized crime, police assigned two unmarked cars and six plainclothes detectives to follow him as he went about his daily activities. The officers recorded the time he left his home in the morning, followed him to his office, noted all callers, logged his visits to various restaurants, and so on, until he retired each night. Surveillance was continuous, 7 days a week, 24 hours a day. Information was forwarded to an Organized Crime Strike Force once every 24 hours.

2: White Powder

Acting on an informer's tip, police staked out an apartment that was believed to be a heroin "factory." They obtained permission from a neighbor to set up an observation post in a house 150 feet away, and by watching through binoculars eventually observed suspects pouring white powder into envelopes. At this point the officers radioed for a police raid to be made on the apartment.

3: "Man's Best Friend"

Police suspected that drugs were being smuggled into a city in the hand luggage carried by certain airline passengers. They brought a dog, trained to recognize the odor of illicit drugs, to the airport. The dog sniffed the carry-on luggage of passengers leaving certain flights. Before long the dog came to an "alert" position after sniffing a particular briefcase. The officers arrested the owner, seized the briefcase, searched it, and discovered cocaine. ■

1983 the U.S. Supreme Court considered a case in which the police placed an electronic beeper (a radio transmitter) in a container holding a chemical commonly used in the illegal manufacture of amphetamines. When a suspect purchased this container, police followed the beeper signals and by this means alone discovered a laboratory for illicit drug production hidden in a remote cabin owned by the suspect. After observing the cabin and obtaining a search warrant, officers conducted a raid and seized drugs and manufacturing equipment. At trial the suspect moved to have the evidence excluded because the beeper was placed in the container before the police had sufficient evidence for a warrant. The Supreme Court, however, held the police technique in this instance to be proper, neither a wrongful invasion of any legitimate expectation of privacy on the part of the suspect nor, in itself, an instance of search or seizure.[19] However, when stakeouts or tailing becomes obvious, they may be construed as harassment, allowing suspects to seek and obtain injunctions against their use.

Police surveillance is of major concern to everyone in our democratic society for the uncontrolled rise of eavesdropping and other surveillance techniques would threaten us all. In general, courts and legislatures have tried to set reasonable limits on surveillance practices, as they have on search practices, limits intended to control police *misuse* of their power while allowing them to effectively gather evidence of crimes. Simple observation and tailing of suspects, and staking out of locations, are usually left to police discretion, subject to court restraints only if the practices border on harassment. The use of electronic surveillance, however, is more stringently regulated, and both appellate courts and legislatures (including Congress) agree that prior judicial approval must be obtained before wiretapping and other mechanical forms of eavesdropping can be employed. Courts enforce this by invoking the exclusionary rule, forbidding any evidence obtained without prior approval to be used in legal cases. Legislatures set time limits on wiretapping and require police to clearly identify targets of investigation before proceeding.

Congress has passed legislation providing stricter judicial control over electronic eavesdropping and specifying conditions and criteria limiting both the legitimate purposes and the scope of oral interceptions.[20] The American Bar Association has published model standards relating to electronic surveillance,[21] and there has also been much scholarly comment on these techniques.[22] One of the best known cases of electronic eavesdropping involved the Watergate scandals of the 1970s. Starting with the discovery of the covert bugging of the Democratic National Headquarters, the Watergate drama moved on to the disclosure of high-level governmental misconduct as revealed by the White House tapes, leading eventually to the resignation of President Nixon.

Virtually all of the police techniques used in domestic surveillance are also employed by major governmental powers in international relations. In 1987 it was revealed that a newly constructed U.S. embassy building in Moscow was so full of listening devices placed in its basic construction that it could not be occupied by American diplomats.

Undercover Operations

A major police investigatory technique is **undercover** work, in which officers whose identity and profession are concealed join criminal gangs and suspected criminal conspiracies.[23] They pretend to be criminals themselves, in all sorts of settings from drug-dealing to terrorism, and pass along the information they gain to their police colleagues, who then "make the bust," that is, arrest the suspects identified by the undercover cops.

Usually the undercover officers act merely as informants, telling the "visible" police who to look for and where and why to look for them (and unlike citizen informants, who are usually participants in the crimes they are reporting on, the undercover police officers only *pretend* to be criminals). But sometimes an undercover officer makes the bust himself or herself (it is not uncommon for women to work undercover) by "flashing the badge" and arresting his or her former "colleagues" in crime. It should be noted that from the point of view of police administrators, however, an undercover officer is more valuable if he or she maintains the undercover status and continues to pass along incriminating information. Once the identity of an

Sometimes it is hard to tell who is a police officer by their appearance. Here, at Tompkins Square Park in New York City, undercover police try to enforce a 1 a.m. curfew.

Undercover Cops Stop Chop Shops

A Brooklyn "chop shop" was raided by almost 40 cops in March 1992 after undercover police officers posed as car thieves to infiltrate the crime operation which specialized in stealing cars to fill customer orders for specific car parts. The shop dismantled an average of five cars daily and displayed the parts in a large warehouse.

The various parts of an automobile, sold separately, have far greater value than the intact automobile. And, stolen car parts are virtually impossible to trace. Organized car thieves have for many years operated chop shops, places where stolen cars are dismantled and the various parts sold to salvage dealers who in turn sell them to automobile body shops which specialize in the use of used parts for repairing wrecked or otherwise damged cars.

Police are faced with an overwhelming problem of car theft from up-scale city neighborhoods such as Miami, Los Angeles, and New York, where expensive cars are common, and where they are frequently parked on the street, since garages are scarce. The rate of car thefts from those neighborhoods has been escalating each year, largely because of the market for expensive cars and parts. And, it is very difficult to catch professional car thieves in the act.

A large chop shop car theft ring which shipped stolen car parts all over the United States was prosecuted in Florida in 1991. The shop was located in a remote orange grove in central Florida, but the cars were stolen in the wealthy neighborhoods of Miami, Ft. Lauderdale, and Palm Beach. Informants helped close the Florida chop shop, but in most instances the only way to combat chop shops is through undercover techniques.

A successful undercover operation resulted in the arrest of car thieves.

New York City police began a stepped-up effort against car theft in 1991 by establishing "Operation Buy-Back," a sting operation. A police detective was assigned to the undercover operation and quickly established himself as a fence for stolen cars. A telephone number began circulating in May of 1991 to car thieves, and during the next four months more than two dozen people called and 50 stolen cars were bought by the undercover detective. Arrests were made in October and charges were made against 26 people.

SOURCES: Interview with Sgt. Peter Sweeney, New York City Police Information Office; Joseph P. Fried, "Police 'Chop Shop' Fools Car Thieves in Queens," *The New York Times*, October 17, 1991, p. B3.

officer becomes known (in police terms, when the officer's "cover is blown"), as it inevitably does when he or she makes an arrest, the usefulness of the no longer hidden agent is lost.

The extent to which an undercover police officer must become personally involved, or participate, in illegal activity in order to maintain credibility while gathering sufficient evidence to arrest others is a major problem in such operations. Police officers sometimes blend in with the criminal gangs they have infiltrated not only by wearing the appropriate disguises, but by emulating criminal behavior. But should police officers commit crimes in order to enforce the law? See Field Practice F for an illustration of this difficult issue.

Undercover Operations

Hooked

A police officer who had infiltrated an alleged drug conspiracy smoked marijuana, took some LSD, and otherwise participated fully in the drug subculture to lend credibility to his cover. He also acted as a courier in carrying narcotics from one city to another for the major actors in the conspiracy. His participation in the use and transportation of drugs were justified by his superior officers as activities necessary to obtain evidence against higher-ups in the narcotics organization. ∎

Related to the matter of the personal involvement of police officers in crime is the question of the extent to which undercover officers may "encourage" others to commit offenses in order to make arrests. "Encouragement" involves crimes committed privately with "victims" who are willing participants—usually "vice crimes" such as solicitation by a prostitute, gambling, and the illegal sales of liquor, narcotics, or pornography.[24]

"**Encouragement**" is a word used to describe the activity of the police or a police agent who (1) acts as a victim; (2) intends, by his or her actions, to encourage a suspect to commit a crime; (3) actually communicates this encouragement to the suspect; and (4) thereby has some influence on the commission of the crime. It does not usually consist of a single act but a series of acts, part of the normal interplay between "victim" and "criminal."[25]

Although encouragement is an important practice, used by national, state, and local law enforcement agencies throughout the country, it has no generally accepted name. At times it is loosely or mistakenly refered to as **entrapment**, a label properly reserved for outright illegal forms of encouragement. The term "encouragement," although imperfect and perhaps connoting impropriety to some, is intended only to be descriptive, a neutral word neither critical nor complimentary of the practice. But the ambiguousness of the term points to our uneasiness over the propriety of police encouragement of criminal activity.[26]

One of the most elaborate, and publicized, undercover encouragement operations was conducted by the FBI in 1980 under the code name ABSCAM. ("Scam" is slang for a confidence game in which the participants, law enforcement agents or their employees, act as if they are criminals.[27] The term "ABSCAM" is commonly thought to have been derived from the words "Arab Scam," but actually was derived from the name of a phony Arab "sheikh" code-named Abdul.) In this operation, the FBI persuaded a convicted swindler named Weinberg to pose as a Middle East sheikh called Abdul, who, with an equally false colleague named Habib, expressed a willingness to handsomely reward certain Congressmen and other political figures if they would sponsor private legislation to allow these two "sheikhs" to obtain asylum in the United States, bypassing normal immigration procedures. Several prominent politicians were secretly recorded and photographed while accepting bribe money from the "sheikhs." One U.S. Senator, seven U.S. Congressional representatives, and several local officials in New Jersey and Pennsylvania were implicated, based on the videotapes. Some of these officials were convicted of accepting bribes and were sent to prison. Most lost their political positions.

In 1990, Mayor Marion Barry of Washington, DC, was arrested by the police in a hotel room and charged with the possession and use of cocaine. Police officers had conspired with a woman, a sometime girlfriend of the mayor, to invite (entice) him to her hotel room for sex. When he arrived, the woman offered him cocaine, he accepted, and the police sprang in to arrest him. At his trial, Mayor Barry asserted that he had been entrapped. The jury found him not guilty.

One of the major issues raised by ABSCAM and Mayor Barry's arrest is whether the offenders were entrapped into their criminal behavior. Entrapment is allowed as a defense against a criminal charge, but there is some disagreement as to what constitutes entrapment. Generally, if a person is a known criminal (i.e., a person with a record of prior convictions), the defense of entrapment is not available even though he or she was fooled by a police officer in undercover disguise. A common saying is that it is impossible to entrap a practicing prostitute or a known drug peddler. In general, entrapment can be used as a defense when an undercover officer induces an otherwise innocent person to commit a crime.[28]

ARREST

The first step in the criminal justice system is police investigation of a crime and the identification of suspects, that is, identification of the persons believed to have committed the crime, either through victim report, observation on the part of police officers, or the various investigative methods discussed above. Once there are suspects, and the police have "reasonable grounds" to believe the individuals did indeed commit the crime, arrests can be made.

For a suspect, involvement with the criminal justice system really begins with arrest, no matter how long the police may have spent investigating that individual's criminal activities. Arrest is the point of "intake" for the criminal justice process—the point at which governmental power actually touches the arrested person and compels

Police immobilize a suspect as they wait for a police van to arrive and transport him to jail for booking.

Arrest

1: Stranger

Prowl car officers observed a man walking in a residential area in the early morning hours. This particular neighborhood had experienced a recent wave of burglaries. The officers stopped the man, but he could not satisfactorily explain his presence and gave as his home address a location in another part of the city. He was placed under arrest.

2: Victim's Eyes

Police responded to a call about a robbery at a liquor store. Upon arrival they were met by the owner, who reported that two young men had taken money from him at gunpoint. The robbers had fled, but the owner said he thought he recognized one of them as a youth who lived nearby. The police went to the young man's home and placed him under arrest. ■

---

him or her to conform to its practices. Arrest is also the point where criminal records are born, for this is the stage where suspects are "booked".

In some instances—say where a suspect has been named by a complainant—police may apprehend the individual through the authority of an arrest warrant. But more commonly, felony arrests are made without warrants. Such arrests are proper if, at the time they are carried out, the arresting officers have *probable cause* to believe that a felony has been committed (or is being committed) and that the person arrested is the one who committed the crime.

Arrest, properly speaking, involves taking a person into police custody, meaning that the individual is no longer free to go his or her own way, and transporting the person to a police station where **booking** takes place, that is, where the arrest is registered. There are some variations in this procedure and in the requirements for arrest. In some situations, primarily involving minor offenses, the suspect may be issued a **citation**, an order to appear at a later date, rather than being taken physically into custody. In regard to misdemeanors, as already mentioned, statutory laws, with some exceptions, require officers to actually witness the crime being committed—probable or reasonable cause to believe the person committed the crime does not in itself provide sufficient grounds for carrying out a warrantless arrest. And in making felony arrests, police officers may use such force as is necessary to take and maintain custody of suspects.[29] (See Field Practice G.)

The issue of reasonable or probable cause is always a problem in regard to arrest. For example, in the case described in Field Practice G:2, subsequent investigation revealed that the suspect arrested was totally innocent of the crime. If the police could not prove they had reasonable grounds for their arrest, they could be held liable for damages in any legal action brought by the person they arrested. Civil juries determine the propriety of police behavior in arrests based on probable cause, *not* on the guilt or innocence of the suspects involved.[30]

It is commonly assumed that when police arrest a suspect they will accumulate evidence and move the case along to the prosecutor for a charging decision. However, Wayne R. LaFave has identified a number of circumstances under which police *arrest with no intention of prosecution*. These include arrests of drunks, who are taken into custody for their own protection; street-walking prostitutes detained to "control and contain" the problem; certain sex offenders who are public nuisances; and petty gamblers and liquor law violators where the penalties are small and the inconvenience of arrest is considered sufficient punishment.[31] Where no prosecution is intended, the police need not exercise special care to obtain evidence in ways that would make it admissible at trial.

In-Custody Interrogation

A suspect arrested for a felony (and for serious misdemeanors) is fingerprinted and photographed during the booking procedure. The prisoner is searched and, after appropriate notification of a right to remain silent and to have a lawyer present, an **in-custody interrogation** is carried out, during which the suspect is questioned regarding the offense for which he or she was arrested. The prisoner may also be questioned in regard to other offenses. The suspect has the right to refuse to answer questions, as guaranteed by the Fifth Amendment to the U.S. Constitution. (See Box 6.5). Also, if the suspect requests legal assistance, interrogation cannot proceed until he or she has conferred with counsel.

It should be noted that the implementation of such rights has not always been standard. Uniform nationwide requirements for notification of rights prior to in-custody interrogation were only established by the U.S. Supreme Court in 1966, in **Miranda v. Arizona**[32] (see Box 6.6). That case had to do with Ernesto Miranda, who was arrested in Phoenix, Arizona, and charged with kidnaping and rape. He was taken to police headquarters, where he was identified by the complainant. He was interrogated for 2 hours by detectives who admitted at trial that he was not advised of any right to have counsel present at the interrogation. Miranda signed a written confession and was subsequently convicted, but appealed; nevertheless, his conviction was upheld by the Arizona Supreme Court. The U.S. Supreme Court, however, reversed the decision, declaring that such confessions are coerced and that interrogations carried out in the course of police investigations without notification of rights or the offer of legal assistance place suspects under "the will of the examiner."

The Supreme Court based its decision on the possibility that coerced confessions may be untrue. Certainly such confessions violate the Fifth Amendment prohibition against self-incrimination. Moreover, interrogations of suspects held in police custody

---

BOX 6.5

The Fifth Amendment to the
U.S. Constitution (1791)

No person shall be held to answer for a capital, or otherwise infamous crime . . . nor shall be compelled in any criminal case to be a witness against himself, nor be deprived of life, liberty, or property, without due process of law. . . .

BOX 6.6

Interrogation:
Miranda v. Arizona
(1966)

Before interrogating suspects who are in custody, police must warn them of their right to remain silent, their right to have a lawyer present during questioning, and their right to terminate the interrogation at any time; they must also be warned that anything they say can and will be used against them.

Police officers can interrogate a suspect who makes an informed decision to waive the Constitutional right to remain silent or to have the assistance of an attorney.

are inherently coercive, so that suspects should (must) be informed of their legal and Constitutional rights, and, even more, those rights should (must) be honored by the police. Thus *Miranda* served primarily to protect unsophisticated, uneducated, and disadvantaged suspects from the intimidating practices of police interrogations, since sophisticated criminals have always known and exercised their Fifth Amendment rights and refused to answer any questions without their attorneys' presence.

By the time of the *Miranda* case, police use of confessions to gain convictions of criminals had become a primary tactic in investigations, even to the extent of ignoring more productive avenues of evidence gathering. The Court stated:

> Although confessions may play an important role in some convictions, the cases before us present graphic examples of the overstatement of the "need" for confessions. In each case authorities conducted interrogations ranging up to five days in duration despite the presence, through standard investigation practices, of considerable evidence against each defendant.[32]

The *Miranda* decision has dramatically impacted American police techniques, but from the day it was decided, it was extremely controversial, and bitterly opposed by many law enforcement officials. For one thing, it marked a departure from usual Supreme Court opinions in that it listed *specific steps* that must be followed by the police prior to in-custody interrogations. Most Court decisions that define the limits of search, arrest, interrogation, or other police procedures are essentially negative in that they *forbid* particular practices but do not specifically tell the police how to proceed properly. The Court normally prefers to leave the determination of proper practices to the police. For example, it might decide that a search took place under certain conditions that made it illegal under the Fourth Amendment, but, except by inference, not specify the conditions that would have made it legal. In *Miranda*, however, the court not only held the particular conditions of the interrogation to be improper but provided specific steps, the so-called *Miranda* warning (Box 6.7), that officers must follow if they wish any confessions by suspects to be accepted as admissible evidence at a trial.

BOX 6.7

The *Miranda* Warning

You have the right to remain silent. Anything you say can and will be used against you in a court of law. You have the right to talk to a lawyer and have him present with you when you are being questioned. If you cannot afford to hire a lawyer, one will be appointed to represent you before any questioning, if you wish. You can decide at any time to exercise these rights and not answer any questions or make any statements. Do you understand each of these rights I have explained to you? Having these rights in mind, do you wish to talk to us now?

A number of police supporters criticized the *Miranda* decision as "going too far," as "handcuffing the police" in their enforcement efforts, claiming that such a rule would make confessions virtually impossible to obtain.[33] Some police departments developed practices designed to get around the *Miranda* warning, mainly by inducing suspects to waive their rights. Peter Lewis and Harry E. Allen reported a technique called **"participating *Miranda*" warning** used by the homicide squad in a large police department. It works as follows. The suspect is arrested and driven in silence to the station house. There he or she is met by a "friendly cop" who begins a long dialogue in which parts of the *Miranda* warning are mentioned, but in odd ways. For example, the officer might say, "You have the right to remain silent, but the police often arrest the wrong person"; or "I can understand why anyone would want to carry a gun to protect himself, and besides, the victim probably had it coming"; or "You have the right to an attorney, but obviously an innocent person shouldn't have to pay for a lawyer. Of course, if you can't afford it, the state will provide one of their lawyers"; and so forth. Eventually all the steps in the *Miranda* warning are covered, and when the suspect is finally prepared to talk, the police ask for a signed waiver of *Miranda* rights, which now are more formally stated in order to reinforce police claims that the confession was properly obtained.[34]

Studies of police practices in the years following the *Miranda* decision show that these requirements do not seem to affect the success of interrogation, recovery of stolen property, police clearance rates, or percentage of offenders convicted for serious crimes.[35] Nonetheless, over the years there have been a number of proposals to abolish or otherwise nullify *Miranda*, including suggestions for federal legislation allowing some interrogations to be carried out without the full warning.

The Court considered a case (***Brewer v. Williams***) in which a defendant accused of murdering a 10-year-old girl was denied effective assistance of counsel when, while being transported from the point of arrest to the jurisdiction of the crime, he revealed to the officers the location of the girl's body. He had been given *Miranda* warnings and the officers, though they did not allow his lawyer to accompany him on the trip, promised not to interrogate him during the ride. However, they did talk to him about the crime, playing on his feelings of guilt and inducing him to reveal the location of the body. The Supreme Court held this evidence to be inadmissible. In a strongly worded dissent which shows the emotions evoked by any restraints that prevent police from solving crimes, Chief Justice Burger stated that this decision was:

> . . . intolerable in any society which purports to call itself an organized society . . . it mechanically and blindly keeps reliable evidence from juries whether the claim of constitutional violation involves gross police misconduct or honest human error. Williams is guilty of the savage murder of a small child; no member of the Court contends he is not. While in custody, and after no fewer than five warnings of his rights to silence and to counsel, he led police to the place where he had buried the body of his victim. The Court now holds the jury must not be told how the police found the body. . . . I cannot possibly agree with the Court.[36]

Williams was given another trial at which the incriminating statements were not admitted but which resulted in his reconviction anyway. Williams again appealed and in 1984 the Supreme Court reconsidered the case in the light of the second conviction. With Justice Burger delivering the majority opinion, the conviction was upheld this time, primarily because in the Court's opinion search parties would have discovered the victim's body even without Williams' incriminating statements.[37]

In 1980 the Supreme Court reviewed ***Rhode Island v. Innis***, a case in which the definition of interrogation was the issue. The suspect, a man named Innis and believed to have murdered a cab driver with a shotgun, was transported to police headquarters by three police officers after having been notified of his *Miranda* rights and after the officers were instructed not to interrogate him during the trip. While in transit, two of the officers, talking to each other and not directly to the suspect (although he could overhear them), discussed the fact that the murder had taken place near a school for handicapped children and expressed fear that one of these children might find the shotgun and injure someone. At this point, Innis offered to lead the officers to where the shotgun was hidden, thereby incriminating himself. The U.S. Supreme Court, upholding the conviction of Innis, ruled that the conversation was not an interrogation and that the suspect's rights had not been violated by the police.[38]

Release from Police Custody

A short time after arrest, suspects must be taken before a magistrate for consideration of bail. How short the interval must be between arrest and this initial appearance depends on the law and court decisions in each state. Most jurisdictions require a bail hearing, also called a **probable cause hearing**, be held within a "reasonable time" after arrest, "promptly," or on the first occasion the court is open for business, while in some places, including cases under federal jurisdiction, the initial appearance must be "immediate."

However, in 1991 the U.S. Supreme Court upheld the practice used by the police in Riverside, California, of holding people arrested without a warrant for up to

48 hours without seeing a judge. In *McLaughlin v. County of Riverside* the Court ruled that even though California law requires a probable cause hearing within 36 hours of arrest, excluding Sundays and holidays, the practice in Riverside and other communities of detaining people for longer periods is not a violation of their rights.[39] (See Box 6.8.)

As with most criminal procedures, this time interval is a controversial matter, for the sooner bail is fixed (assuming the suspect can post bond or is otherwise released by the magistrate) the shorter the opportunity for the police to carry out an in-custody interrogation. Bail will be discussed fully in Chapter 8.

TWO COMPETING VIEWS OF POLICING

Police and the Conservative Crime Control Model[40]

The conservative crime control model believes that the courts, especially the U.S. Supreme Court, have "handcuffed" the police and saddled them with unnecessary "technicalities" which allow known criminals to go free and frustrate the honest efforts of police to protect society. It claims these technicalities place unwanted and unnecessary parameters on police conduct, especially regarding searches, seizures, interrogation, and the use of force. These parameters are enforced by the exclusionary rule, the rule that prohibits improperly obtained evidence from being used against a person at trial. The solution to this problem, according to conservative precepts, is not only to eliminate the exclusionary rule, but to change the rules of police work so as to unleash the police to go after criminals. If, as occasionally happens, the police err in their methods, the solution is not to turn the criminals loose, but rather to correct, or change, police procedures. In addition, conservatives believe the streets are not safe because criminals go free, which happens because the police are unable to obtain confessions usable in court. The conservative crime control model would solve this by eliminating the Supreme Court-mandated *Miranda* warning.

Conservatives also believe more police officers should be hired to enhance the ability of police departments to prevent crime and arrest criminals. The more police, they believe, the less crime. Since so many crimes go unsolved and do not result in arrest, the addition of more officers would make detection and arrest more of a certainty and thereby deter crime. And since the public seems to want more police protection, more police would contribute to the feeling of community protection.

This call for more police officers extends to a call for more and better trained detectives. Since the crime caseload is so large, and detective bureaus are so small, the argument goes, the addition of detectives would improve clearance rates and career criminals would be taken off the streets. Moreover, since a small number of career criminals are responsible for a large percentage of the crimes committed in this country, a larger number of detectives would mean the activities of those career criminals could be targeted by special units of detectives.

Police and The Liberal Crime Control Model

According to the liberal crime control model, the conservative wish list, even if granted fully, would not reduce crime. The exclusionary rule is rarely invoked, liberals argue, and has had a minuscule impact on the ability of prosecutors to gain convictions. Plus, in a free society the police above all others should operate within the law and according to the U.S. Constitution, the sources of those "technicalities" the conservatives are ready to trash.

Liberals believe the *Miranda* ruling is a clear manifestation of Constitutional principles—it represents the *right* and *just* approach to interrogation. Also, they believe *Miranda* has had virtually no impact on confessions. They point out that, even with full knowledge of the right to remain silent, a large percentage of criminals confess. This, they claim, is due to the improved professionalism of the police in recent years, who generally arrest suspects after gathering significant evidence so that, when arrested, guilty people are prone to confess, especially if they believe concessions may be forthcoming. Therefore, liberals argue, due process restrictions, like the exclusionary rule, have very little effect on run-of-the-mill felony case prosecutions.

As for more police, liberals contend that adding officers will not reduce crime. It is a more creative use of existing police—implementing problem-oriented policing practices, for example—that would impact on crime rates. According to liberals, the Kansas City experiment showed that just hiring more officers and throwing them at the problem of crime is not going to make that much of a difference.

The liberal crime control model also believes that detectives are highly overrated, and that more, improved, better trained, and better equipped detectives would have little impact on crime. Most crimes, liberals point out, are solved by victims or witnesses identifying the criminals. Crimes tend to solve themselves.

The liberal crime control model looks to innovations in the police task to control crime. It believes police should represent the due process ideals of the law, and should be involved in a proactive way to address the *causes* of crime rather than just reacting to criminal incidents.

It should be pointed out that the problems addressed in this chapter, among others related to police work, often tend to polarize people's opinions. Those espousing a particular view often grasp for data, especially statistical data, to bolster that view. But the fact remains that the effectiveness of police performance, whether it is modeled after the conservative or the liberal approach, is often very difficult to assess.

SUMMARY

Several important Supreme Court decisions have influenced greatly the manner in which police carry out their duties. Prior to the 1960s the police enjoyed almost total autonomy from appellate court interference. But, as we have seen, a succession of major decisions rendered by the Supreme Court have brought about a greater degree of professionalism and more careful actions by police.

In light of these Court decisions, this chapter examined the major decisions made by police in the course of carrying out their duties of criminal law enforcement. It started with techniques of investigating crime and the problems involved in stopping and questioning suspects, surveillance, and undercover operations. It described the conditions under which a police officer can stop and frisk a suspect as set forth in the Supreme Court decision on *Terry v. Ohio*. It also described several more recent Supreme Court decisions affecting police search and frisk practices.

The chapter discussed the limits on police power to search people and premises and to obtain evidence by means of electronic eavesdropping equipment. The exclusionary rule was explained and its Constitutional basis illustrated in terms of the case *Mapp v. Ohio*.

Police arrest decisions were discussed, as well as limits on in-custody interrogation imposed by the U.S. Supreme Court in its *Miranda v. Arizona* decision. Entrapment used as a defense against a criminal charge was explained. Finally, the chapter discussed release from police custody by a magistrate within a reasonable period of time, the point at which the flow of police decisions ends.

NOTES

1. See Wayne R. LaFave, *Arrest: The Decision to Take a Suspect into Custody* (Boston: Little, Brown, 1965), pp. 232–243.
2. See Lawrence P. Tiffany, Donald M McIntyre, Jr., and Daniel Rotenberg, *Detection of Crime: Stopping and Questioning, Search and Seizure, Encouragement and Entrapment* (Boston: Little, Brown, 1967), Chap. 1.
3. American Law Institute, *A Model Code of Pre-Arraignment Procedure*, Official Draft No. 1 (Philadelphia: American Law Institute, 15 July 1972), Sec. 110.2.
4. *Kolender v. Lawson*, 103 S. Ct. 1855 (1983).
5. *Terry v. Ohio*, 392 U.S. 1 (1968).
6. See *Sibron v. New York*, 392 U.S. 40 (1968).
7. For the "plain-view" doctrine see *Coolidge v. New Hampshire*, 403 U.S. 443 (1971). See also *Texas v. Brown*, 103 S. Ct. 1535 (1983). For an extension of a Terry Search see *Michigan v. Long*, S. Ct. 3469 (1983) and for the "drug courier profile" see *Florida v. Royer* 460 U.S. 491 (1983).
8. *Florida v. Bostick*, 115 L. Ed. 2d 389 (1991).
9. See *Brinegar v. United States*, 338 U.S. 160 (1960).
10. *Michigan Department of State Police v. Sitz*, 429 N.W. 2d 180 (1991). For a discussion of this case see Geoffrey P. Alpert, "Establishing Roadblocks to Control the Drunk Driver—*Michigan Department of State Police v. Sitz*," Criminal Law Bulletin 27(1) (January-February 1991): 51–58.
11. See Thomas J. Hickey and Rolando del Carmen, "The Evolution of Standing in Search and Seizure Cases," *Criminal Law Bulletin* 27(2)(March-April 1991). Also, see *Schneckloth v. Bustamonte*, 412 U.S. 218 (1973), and Peter W. Lewis and Henry W. Mannle, "Warrantless Searches and the 'Plain-View' Doctrine: Current Perspective," *Criminal Law Bulletin* 12 (1976): 5–25.
12. *Mapp v. Ohio*, 367 U.S. 643, 81 S. Ct. 1684, 6 L. Ed. 2d 1081 (1961).
13. *United States v. Leon*, 468 U.S. 897 (1984), and *Massachusetts v. Sheppard*, 468 U.S. 981, (1984).
14. *Chimel v. California*, 395 U.S. 752 (1969); *Delaware v. Prouse*, 440 U.S. 648 (1979).
15. *Stone v. Powell*, 428 U.S. 465 (1976). See also *Illinois v. Gates*, 462 U.S. 213 (1983).
16. *California v. Acevedo*, 500 U.S. xxx, 114 L. Ed. 2d 619 (1991).
17. *Katz v. United States*, 389 U.S. 347 (1967).
18. *Oliver v. United States*, 466 U.S. 170 (1984).
19. *United States v. Knotts*, 103 S. Ct. 1081 (1983).
20. See Omnibus Crime Control and Safe Streets Act of 1968, P.L. 90–351.
21. American Bar Association, *Standards Relating to Electronic Surveillance* (New York: Institute of Judicial Administration, 1968).
22. Gary T. Marx, *Undercover: Police Surveillance in America* (Berkeley: University of California Press, 1988); G. Flannery, "Eavesdropping Left and Right," *The Nation*, April 17, 1989, vol. 248, pp. 516–518. Also see Samuel Dash, Richard F. Schwartz, and Robert G. Knowlton, *The Eavesdroppers* (New York: DaCapo, 1959), and Alan F. Westin, *Privacy and Freedom* (New York: Atheneum, 1967).
23. See Gary T. Marx, "Thoughts on a Neglected Category of Social Movement Participant: The Agent Provocateur and the Informant," *American Journal of Sociology* 80

(1974): 402–442; and George E. Dix, "Undercover Investigations and Police Rulemaking," *Texas Law Review* 53 (1975): 294.

24. See Tiffany, McIntyre, and Rotenberg, op. cit., p. 277.

25. Ibid., pp. 308–311.

26. Ibid.; see also *Sherman v. United States*, 356 U.S. 369 (1958). See also Richard C. Donnelly, "Judicial Control of Informants, Spies, Stool Pigeons and Agent Provocateurs," *Yale Law Journal* 60 (1951): 1091; and Roger Park, "The Entrapment Controversy," *Minnesota Law Review* 60 (1976): 163–274.

27. See Steven Gillers, "In Defense of ABSCAM: Entrapment, Where Is Thy Sting?" *The Nation*, February 23, 1980, p. 203; and Paul Chevigny, "A Rejoinder," *The Nation*, February 23, 1980, p. 205. See also *Williamson vs. United States*, 311 F. 2d 441 (5th Cir. 1962), where an informer was promised money for incriminating a defendant, and *People v. McIntire*, 23 Cal. 3d 742 (1979), where an older sister was cajoled into buying narcotics (from an unsuspected undercover agent) by her teenage brother.

28. American Law Institute, *Model Penal Code*, Proposed Official Draft (Philadelphia: American Law Institute, 1962), Sec. 2.13.

29. Floyd R. Finch, Jr., "Comment—Deadly Force to Arrest: Triggering Constitutional Review," *Harvard Civil Rights—Civil Liberties Law Review* 11 (1976): 361.

30. Citizens may sue police officers for damages if they are improperly arrested. In common parlance, the citizen's claim is called "false arrest," but technically suit is brought under the tort of "false imprisonment," meaning that the person's freedom of movement was wrongfully curtailed, even for a brief period of time. The police officer's defense against an allegation of false imprisonment is that the arrest was lawful. Whether in fact the officer had "probable cause" to arrest is determined by the civil jury. In general, civil actions by citizens against police are not an effective means of curbing abuses of police power. See Herman Goldstein, "Administrative Problems in Controlling the Exercise of Police Authority," *Journal of Criminal Law, Criminology and Political Science* 58 (1967): 160.

31. LaFave, op. cit., pp. 437–489.

32. *Miranda v. Arizona*, 384 U.S. 436 (1966).

33. "Whether these restrictions on traditional police practices have actually reduced police effectiveness is a matter of some controversy, even among police and prosecutors; but a significant consensus among police officers of all ranks in every part of the country interprets these decisions as favoring the criminal and as deliberately and perversely hampering, indeed punishing, the police." David P. Stang, "The Police and Their Problems," in James T. Curran, Austin Fowler, and Richard H. Ward (eds.), *Police and Law Enforcement 1972* (New York: AMS Press, 1973), p. 36. Also see, for a related discussion of Supreme Court restraints on the police, "A Symposium on the Supreme Court and the Police: 1966," *Journal of Criminal Law, Crimonology and Political Science* 57 (1966); and Fred E. Inbau, "Playing God: 5 to 4," *Journal of Criminal Law, Criminology and Political Science* 57 (1966): 377. However, for a contrary view, see Witt below.

34. Peter W. Lewis and Harry E. Allen, "Participating Miranda: An Attempt to Subvert Certain Constitutional Safeguards," *Crime and Delinquency* 23 (1977): 75–80.

35. James W. Witt, "Non-Coercive Interrogation and the Administration of Criminal Justice: The Impact of Miranda on Police Effectuality," *Journal of Criminal Law, Criminology and Political Science* 64 (1973): 320–332.

36. *Brewer v. Williams*, 430 U.S. 387 (1977).

37. *Nix v. Williams*, 467 U.S. 431 (1984).

38. *Rhode Island v. Innis*, 446 U.S. 291 (1980).

39. *McLaughlin v. County of Riverside*, 888 F. 2d 1276 (1991).

40. The descriptions of the conservative and liberal crime control models here depend largely on Samuel Walker, *Sense and Nonsense about Crime: A Policy Guide* 2nd ed. (Pacific Grove, CA: Brooks/Cole, 1989).

SUGGESTED READINGS

Brown, Michael K. *Working the Street*. New York: Russell Sage Foundation, 1981.

Geller, William A. (ed.). *Police Leadership in America*. New York: Praeger, 1985.

Greene, Jack R., and Steven Mastrofski (eds.). *Community Policing: Rhetoric or Reality?* New York: Praeger, 1988.

Muir, William K., Jr. *Police: Streetcorner Politicians*. Chicago: University of Chicago Press, 1979.

Skolnick, Jerome H. *Justice without Trial: Law Enforcement in a Democratic Society*. New York: Wiley, 1966.

Wilson, James Q. *Varieties of Police Behavior*. Cambridge, MA: Harvard University Press, 1968.

DISCUSSION QUESTIONS

1. Trace and discuss the crime control decisions made by the police.

2. Describe the impact of *Terry v. Ohio* on police practice.

3. How have Supreme Court decisions in 1991 changed police practices?

4. Discuss the difference between entrapment and encouragement.

5. What are the weapons in the police arsenal to search out crime? What controls exist on their use?

6. Discuss the role of the exclusionary rule in police decisions.

7. Compare and contrast the conservative crime control model and the liberal crime control model regarding police decisions.

7

Issues in Modern Policing

Dateline Milwaukee: Police Decide Not to Arrest Dahmer; Later Found to be a Serial Killer. *This is the kind of newspaper headline that spells trouble for police.*

Milwaukee Police Chief Philip Arreola was confronted in 1991 with public protest over the decisions of his officers in the case of Konerak Sinthasomphone, a 14-year-old Laotian boy, whose murder occurred apparently as soon as officers left him alone with Jeffrey Dahmer. Dahmer, a young white man, was reported by two black women neighbors to Milwaukee police after they had seen the boy naked, bleeding, and incoherent in the street near Dahmer's apartment. Police investigated, questioned Dahmer in his apartment, and dismissed the incident as a domestic dispute between two consenting homosexuals.

The three officers involved in the case say they acted with sensitivity. They claim they responded to a report of "a naked man down," inspected Sinthasomphone in the street and in Dahmer's apartment, and observed no bleeding from the anus as was later claimed. They said the youth seemed calm and his only wound was a scruffed knee. The officers saw pictures inside Dahmer's apartment of the boy in underwear, but believed he had posed willingly for his friend. They concluded that a caring relationship existed between Dahmer and the boy. Police tapes recorded one officer saying amid laughter after the three left Dahmer's apartment, "Intoxicated Asian, naked male, was returned to his sober boyfriend."

The tapes also revealed that when one of the neighbor women called 911 after the boy had been returned to Dahmer's apartment by the police, the following conversation took place:

Woman: My daughter and my niece witnessed what was going on. Do you need information or anything from them?

Officer: No, not at all.

Woman: You don't?

Officer: Nope. It's uh, an intoxicated boyfriend of another boyfriend.

Woman: Well, how old was this child?

Officer: It wasn't a child. It was an adult.

Woman: Are you positive? This child doesn't even speak English.

Officer: It's all taken care of ma'am.

Woman: Are you sure?

Officer: Ma'am, I can't make it any more clear. It's all taken care of. He's with his boyfriend at his boyfriend's apartment, where he's got his belongings.

Woman: I mean, are you positive this is an adult?

Officer: Ma'am. Like I explained to you. It's all taken care of. It's as positive as I can be. I can't do anything about somebody's sexual preferences in life.

Woman: I'm not saying anything about that, but it appeared to have been a child.

Officer: No, he's not. OK?

Apparently, by the time of this conversation, Dahmer had killed the boy and dismembered his body. Later, at least 17 murdered and dismembered bodies were traced to Dahmer, who quickly became one of the best known serial killers of recent times.

The controversy, however, did not focus on the actions of Dahmer, but on those of the Milwaukee police officers. Black citizens complained bitterly that these police actions were further evidence of racism, that had Dahmer been black and the women reporting the crime white, the police would have treated the events with greater seriousness. They pointed out that a routine computer check was not run on Dahmer, something that would likely have been done for a black male, and which would have revealed the fact that Dahmer was currently serving a probation sentence for sexual molestation for which he had served 10 months in jail in 1988 and 1989. Likewise, members of the local gay community charged that the callous attitude of the police was consistent with their homophobic biases.

Chief Arreola suspended the three officers pending an investigation.[1]

ABOUT THIS CHAPTER

Decisions made by police are among the most important and difficult in all of criminal justice. They can have life or death results, as in the case of Konerak Sinthasomphone. Very little about the police role is automatic or spelled out in tightly worded directives or instructions. Police agencies as well as individual police officers make conscious decisions about daily activities—investigation, arrest, use of force, or even use of deadly force. As "crime fighters" police are expected to control or reduce crime, protect citizens, provide service to the public, and be representatives of the public order.

Chapter 6 examined police decisions from the point of view of the criminal justice process as a whole. This chapter examines the constraints on the many decisions left to police discretion, and the issues that surround and influence police behavior. Perhaps no other segment of society is charged with as complex a task as the police. The power they wield is sometimes frightening, as in the case of deadly force. Police techniques and their effectiveness remain largely unknown to most people. Instead, the cops-and-robbers myth spawned by television and movies distorts the public's understanding of the role of police.

Policing in modern society is difficult, complex, and frequently controversial. Given the extent and variability of our crime problems, the old truism that the consta-

Jeffrey Dahmer in a Milwaukee courtroom with his attorneys.

ble's lot is not a happy one is often vividly experienced by police officers, who must balance their concern to meet community demands for vigorous and effective crime control against the legal restraints on their authority. Any action taken by a police officer—and their actions are often based on split-second decisions—is subject to criticism and reprimand. Officially, police have a mandate to fully enforce all criminal laws; in practice, laws are vague, staffs and resources are limited, and full, literal enforcement may be unnecessary or undesirable in many situations. Police are often disliked for what they do and blamed for what people think they should do but have not done.

Most of us reluctantly accept the need for police but expect that police interference with our lives will be minimal and police power will not be misused. We want effective crime control tempered by restraint, fairness, and sensible patterns of enforcement. A long list of problems associated with policing could be made up, ranging from serious matters such as police corruption to more trivial issues such as the proper dress for police officers. A complete list is not possible here, but we do examine some of the more relevant contemporary problems.

These problems do not exist in a vacuum, nor do they spring from thin air. What makes them problems, even difficult dilemmas, is the fact that honest, often heated debate over them exists—debate rooted in the political and ideological conflicts of our democratic society. This conflict is perhaps best described in a general way in terms of the conservative vs. liberal attitudes toward police work discussed in Chap. 6. But in this chapter we discuss the ways in which the police enforce criminal law in terms of the discretionary choices they make on a day-to-day basis in their work.

THE EFFECTIVENESS OF THE POLICE

It has already been noted that the police have many duties in addition to solving crimes and chasing suspects. They are responsible for traffic control, answering emergency calls, guarding dignitaries, settling disputes between neighbor, and many other functions—some far removed from the TV image of cops and robbers. The police have these other duties in good part by default; there is simply no other organization or agency, staffed 24 hours a day, which patrols the streets and is ready to be called on. Often the police are not only the last resort, but the *only* resort. Missing children, treed cats, vandalized schools, suspicious lurkers, family fights, gutter drunks—all become police problems and, it should be added, take a lot of time and staff to handle.

The diverse demands society makes on the police in turn make it difficult to define the limits of the police role or to establish agreed-upon measures of police effectiveness. Of course the police are expected to solve crimes and arrest the guilty. But is this the major way they should be tested and evaluated? Suppose the police force of a certain city solves (by arrest of thieves and recovery of stolen property) a very high percentage of burglaries, but finds itself unable to handle the city's traffic flow, which is constantly fouled up, and results in a high rate of auto accidents with correspondingly higher-than-average automobile insurance rates for local residents. Is this a good, effective police force? Suppose most murders, robberies, and even rapes are solved but vandalism in the schools is rampant. Suppose the police make many mugging arrests but most citizens are still afraid to walk the streets. Or, conversely, suppose foot patrols saturate a community and the constant police presence makes citizens *feel* safer while, in fact, muggings continue to increase. How, in these and similar situations, is police effectiveness to be measured?

This is perhaps one of the most subtle, difficult, and, when examined closely, controversial issues in policing. Good police are not simply officers who are neither corrupt nor brutal, but officers who accomplish their tasks efficiently (at reasonable costs) and effectively. The difficulty of determining what effective policing is lies in the nature of the police tasks measured and the methodology employed to measure effectiveness.

Police departments often use the *number of arrests* officers make as the indicator of their effectiveness. Indeed, some police officials set internal departmental arrest quotas for different units to show that the force is working hard and performing effectively. But quiet and safe streets may be a better measure of real police effectiveness—although, unlike arrest quotas, quiet and safe streets may be difficult to measure objectively. In a recent article titled "**Broken Windows,**" James Wilson and George Kelling argue that a major purpose of policing is to prevent neighborhood deterioration.[2] There have also been various "foot patrol" experiments as described in Chap. 5 in which uniformed police officers walk neighborhood beats. These foot patrols are designed to diminish citizens' fear of crime and encourage people to use the streets. It is hoped that because there are more people around, street crime will diminish.[3] But whether the measure is the solving of actual crimes, the reduction of fear of crime, the way officers handle emergency responses, or the steps the police can take to prevent community deterioration, there is no common basis for assessing police effectiveness.

It may be that our expectations of effective policing are unrealistic. The police can and do solve many of the "big" crimes—homicides, kidnappings, bank robberies—but *most other crimes are not solved*. Police agencies monitor car traffic, inspect automobiles, and license drivers, but automobile accidents still occur. Police presence, even in saturation force, has a limited deterrent effect on crimes and may, in fact, serve to escalate the commission of certain kinds of crimes such as riots. The constable's lot is indeed an unhappy one, and a confusing one as well. For we have diverted so many tasks and assigned so many functions to our police that they cannot ever be as effective, on all levels, as we expect them to be. The truth is, the best, most hardworking, highly educated, strongly motivated, honest police force in the world cannot achieve all that is expected of it.

Police discretion

The Myth of Full Enforcement of the Law

Police activity in criminal law enforcement is a crucial function, not only with respect to those who are processed through the criminal justice system, but in terms of the most basic values of our social order. Yet that crucial function is carried out by individual police officers who must make frequent decisions about whether or how to investigate suspicious circumstances, whether to arrest, when and to what extent to use force, and a great deal more. The decisions which a police officer faces are known primarily only to the police. Solidarity among police officers, along with a corresponding social isolation from others in the community, is a well-known characteristic of police work.[4]

Police decisions are not made in a vacuum. Policing is often a thankless task; many police officers are disliked for doing their job effectively, for few people like to be questioned or given traffic citations even when such actions are reasonable and warranted. Although national polls generally show that most citizens have a high opinion of the work of police, members of racial, ethnic, and economic minorities, who have the most contact with police, tend to view them with a high degree of hostility and a lack of confidence.[5]

Policing is a dangerous business, and police officers believe that they face potential violence in all confrontational situations, even when called on to provide emergency assistance or to perform apparently uncomplicated peace-keeping functions. A speeding car is usually nothing more than a traffic violation, but now and then it holds an armed felon fleeing the scene of a crime or wanted by police elsewhere. All experienced police officers know, and continually repeat to colleagues, stories of other officers hurt or killed in what appeared to be routine, nonthreatening calls, stops, or other investigations. This constant awareness of potential violence leads officers to act with what often appears to citizens as undue suspicion and unnecessary caution in situations in which there seems to be no reason for such protective action.[6]

Furthermore, over time a police officer becomes accustomed to crimes and other emergency situations, handling them as routine matters, often to the dismay of victims and witnesses. When the police arrive at a scene to respond to a call or to stop a fight, the victims and suspects are all agitated, fearful, and tense. But the police have seen it all before. Instead of offering sympathy and immediately taking the victim's side, they may seem cool, suspicious, or disinterested.[7]

Faced with these factors, and others, perhaps it is too much to expect police officers to be completely dispassionate at the many points in the criminal process at which they have the opportunity to exercise discretion. No doubt much of the misunderstanding about police work stems from a failure to recognize the discretionary nature of the police role in criminal justice. That failure results in unrealistic expectations placed on the police to enforce all laws without fear or favor, and to always vigorously and rigidly enforce them.

Effectiveness on all levels of the broad police task may be too much to ask, but what about the vigorous enforcement of criminal laws? Traffic control is one thing, but "real" police work, defined this way by many police officers, as well as citizens, is catching crooks, protecting the community from the "criminal element." And in doing so, should not the police *enforce all criminal laws*, evenly and uniformly?

In theory, and indeed according to the laws of most jurisdictions, the police have no authority to choose to enforce some laws and ignore others. Nor can they arrest only some among the individuals they reasonably believe to be guilty of committing crimes while letting others go. To suggest otherwise seems wrong somehow, even when bribery or police corruption are not at issue. Yet police **discretion**—that is, the choice by police to enforce some laws vigorously and others reluctantly, if at all, and to take into custody only some suspects but to release others—is a reality everywhere in our land.

Discretion Not to Arrest

Police have the clear authority to investigate crimes and arrest suspects when there is sufficient evidence to do so. However, there is a question of whether they *must* act—must investigate or arrest—or instead whether they may properly decide, despite adequate evidence, not to follow through. The issue arises from the expectation of full enforcement conflicting with the desire for reasonable use of the criminal process. Is intake into the criminal process mechanical, with police officers mere automatons? Or is their expertise sufficient not merely to justify suspicions, as in Officer McFadden's actions in *Terry v. Ohio*[8] (see Chap. 6), but also to decide when and under what conditions the criminal process should *not* be used? Consider the cases described in Field Practice A. Do you consider the decisions described there to be proper police work?

Laws authorizing police discretion *not* to arrest when they have evidence sufficient to do so are rare. In many states the laws are silent on the issue or grant such discretion only in special circumstances. Studies of actual police practices, however, show that nonarrest is common, indicating an important dimension of the police job

Police Discretion Not to Make Arrests

1: Blinkers

An officer on patrol observed an automobile parked in a No Standing zone and obstructing traffic. The car was empty but its blinker lights were flashing. As the officer investigated, a woman approached the car and explained to the officer that she had parked there temporarily while delivering some baked goods to a church. The officer reprimanded her but did not issue a citation.

2: Klepto

Police were called to a department store by the owner, who had apprehended a shoplifter. Upon arrival at the store the officers found the shoplifter to be a respectable businessman, who admitted the theft, saying he stole the items on a sudden impulse. Because the store owner did not wish to press charges and the suspect had no prior record, the officers merely reprimanded the violator and did not make an arrest.

3: Weed

Officers on patrol came upon a youth gang in a schoolyard who were engaged in a noisy and vigorous snowball fight. They stopped to investigate and observed two young men discard what appeared to be marijuana cigarettes. Officers retrieved the discarded cigarettes convinced they were indeed marijuana. Since this was not a troublesome gang and neither of the two smokers were known to have been in trouble with the law before, they merely ordered the gang to disperse and warned them of serious trouble should marijuana be discovered again.

4: Uncle Charlie

In an unusual ceremony, a 60-year-old police officer in a small town was given an award by the Chamber of Commerce for not having arrested any local resident for a period of 10 years. In accepting his award, the officer said, "There's no need to arrest people you know real well. These things can be handled in other ways and better, too. Most problems can be solved without throwing people in jail. Strangers, now that's another matter. People coming from out of town to commit crimes here will find themselves arrested, and quickly too. But my job is to keep our town a good place to live and when our people get a little wild or silly, why there's plenty of ways they can be straightened out without being put in jail. ∎

---

not revealed by arrest statistics. Based on field observations, Wayne R. LaFave has described a number of circumstances in which the police do not use their full authority, identifying the reasons for this exercise of discretion.[9] In some of the situations decisions not to arrest are based on police *belief that the legislature did not intend full enforcement*, even though the conduct is outlawed. This is illustrated by decisions not to arrest when:

1. The law is vague, as in complaints regarding obscene materials.
2. The statute appears to have been designed as a device to deal with "nuisance" behavior rather than to call for full criminal processing, as with vagrancy and loitering.
3. Broad statutes have been enacted to cover professional criminal activity but the situation encountered involves no criminal intent, as when legislation prohibits *all* gambling but the police come upon a friendly poker game.
4. The intent of law is merely to express a moral standard without a real expectation of its full enforcement, such as the prohibition of "normal" adult consensual sexual misconduct.
5. The legislation is out of date, as when "blue laws" remain on the books because of legislative oversight or traditional reluctance to repeal.[10]

In other circumstances the police may not act because to do so would *strain limited resources*, as when arresting an offender would take up too much police time in filling out reports, clog already overcrowded jails, and overburden prosecutors and courts. Included in these types of situations are:

1. Trivial offenses
2. Conduct that is felt to be common, even normative, among a particular subgroup of the community although generally prohibited, as in cases of fistfights and family assaults in lower-class neighborhoods
3. Instances where the victims do not desire prosecution and refuse to sign complaints or testify at trial
4. Instances where the victims are parties to the offenses, as when the client of a prostitute complains of having been "rolled"[11]

LaFave identified still other circumstances, unrelated to the interpretation of legislative intent or to limited resources, in which the police may decide *not* to arrest even though arrest would be technically correct. These include situations in which:

1. Arrest would be ineffective, as in continuous arrests of skid-row drunks
2. Arrest would cause loss of public support, as in sudden crackdowns on public gambling or other technically illegal activities that have long been tolerated in a community
3. Informants or persons who may become states' witnesses to assist long-range enforcement goals are involved
4. Arrest would cause harm to the offender outweighing any risk from inaction, as when young first offenders or others with good reputations are involved in minor violations.[12]

Obviously, reasons for police inactivity are not all alike or of the same dimensions. Some are self-serving, like rewarding informants. Others rest on an awareness that long-range objectives of crime control may be achieved in ways other than arrest and prosecution, like releasing a first offender with a reprimand rather than giving him or her an arrest record. Some are matters of convenience, such as overlooking trivial offenses. Others rest on police attitudes toward differences in morality and lifestyles exhibited by various social classes and minority groups in the community. Whether these patterns of police discretion are good or bad is open to controversy. They are often what Professor Joseph Goldstein calls "low-visibility" decisions.[13] The range of these decisions is impossible to describe; only illustrations can be given. (See Field Practice A.)

Discretion to Make *an Arrest*

The reverse of the type of discretion just discussed involves officers *making* arrests in situations where common practice normally would be simply to warn or reprimand the suspects. Here the characteristics or behavior of the suspect when stopped, or other circumstances of the incident, including an affront to the officer's dignity or a challenge to his or her authority, or characteristics of the neighborhood may lead to arrest instead of routine dismissal.[14]

The cases in Field Practice B demonstrate how police can often act on their own prejudices or perhaps take out their own frustrations on a person. The arrest, or ticket, or cuffing is an overt way in which a police officer can demonstrate authority. And that authority is within the officer's power to use.

Police Discretion to Make an Arrest

1: Call My Lawyer

On a routine registration check, a police officer stopped an automobile and asked the driver for his license and registration. The officer noticed a shotgun on the back seat; investigation revealed it was fully loaded. The driver's registration and license were in order, and it was hunting season, a time when this officer customarily merely warned drivers that they must not carry loaded guns in their automobiles and that all shotguns must be displayed and "broken," that is, opened to show that they are unloaded. However, in this case the driver was surly and arrogant. Before the officer took any action, the driver demanded to see a lawyer, whereupon the officer arrested him for carrying a loaded shotgun in his car.

2: The Black Hand

An officer summoned to the scene of an automobile accident noted that one of the drivers involved in the crash was a reputed organized crime figure in the community. Although the accident was minor, this driver was apparently at fault. The officer arrested him for reckless driving, later explaining to his partner that normally he would not have made an arrest, but that it was his private policy to arrest "hoodlums" wherever and whenever possible.

3: Late Bloomer

An officer on patrol observed a group of young men running from a school building which was closed for the weekend. He ordered the youths to stop, and an investigation revealed some minor vandalism in the school in the form of obscene remarks written on blackboards and papers strewn around a teacher's office. The officer ordered the young men to erase the blackboards and replace the papers. When this was done he released all but one with a severe reprimand. The persons released were all students in the school, but the remaining suspect was 28 years old and in no sense a student. The officer charged him with illegal entry and property damage, later explaining, "There's got to be something weird about a 28-year-old man who trashes a high school." ∎

The major issue is not whether police discretion exists, but how it can be controlled. There is a fine line between prudent **selective enforcement** and **discriminatory enforcement**, which is clearly harmful to our social order. The first step in the control of police discretion is the frank recognition of its existence. The second step is to develop internal police department policies and review procedures and to forbid certain forms of discretionary practice altogether. Recognition and control of discretion are important steps on the road to police professionalism. For until the police themselves come out from behind the mask of full enforcement, until they abandon the pretense of being simple gatekeepers of the law, mere robots carrying out policies made by others, professional recognition will be withheld.

Legislatures sometimes respond to demands from the public to do something dramatic about a certain type of crime by passing laws intended to solve the problem by restricting police discretion. An example of this is legislation regarding domestic violence, which in some jurisdictions requires the police to arrest one party or the other in such cases. Police do not like this, and no doubt legislation limiting police discretion is usually a poor method to fight crime; indeed, even where police misconduct is at issue, legislation may be a counterproductive way of controlling the misuse of police discretion.

Discretion is a vital element of policing, but until the police administrators themselves recognize its dimensions, and prepare officers properly, and until the issue is frankly addressed by legislatures and courts, the true nature of police work cannot be fully understood. Having said this, it must be admitted that controlling discretion is an extremely difficult task that may never be completely realized.

Individual Discretion

At the primary level, discretion involves the choice of alternative actions by individual police officers, including taking *no* action. This is **individual discretion**. Every situation confronted by a patrol officer on a beat and a detective in the course of his or her investigations requires the use of judgment. This is simply another way of saying that discretion is always exercised. Every day, on each tour of duty, police officers must decide where to patrol, what to look for, which suspicious circumstances or persons to investigate, and, having done this, what to do about situations that arise, including those that involve possible criminal behavior. As for detectives, they must decide what priorities to give to investigations (for rarely do detectives work only on a single case), the steps to be followed, the vigor of the pursuit, and, at the end, how to deal with those cases in which criminal guilt is evident. Situations calling for the exercise of police discretion may be established by police commanders or by state statutes, but the precise codification or proper and improper discretionary choices covering all possible situations is virtually impossible.

Command Discretion

A second level of police discretion involves decisions made by the police command staff regarding departmental objectives, enforcement policies, the deployment of officers and resources, the size of staff for and budget allocated to special units, and the like. **Command discretion** is a critical part of the entire police discretion issue, for it offers a major point for structuring and controlling first-level discretionary practices.[15]

Command discretion is implicit in the very structure and organization of a police force. Decisions concerning the training of patrol officers and the development of detective and special units are made by police officials, often with no outside guidance or controls. Determinations must be made about how many officers are to be assigned to the traffic division, to patrol, to the detective unit, to the homicide unit, about the use of a vice squad, the size and purposes of a police intelligence unit, internal security policies, and so on. Normally the size and deployment of different units reflect insofar as possible the nature of the local crime problem and the service needs of the community. Yet exceptions to this rule are not unusual, as when a new commissioner or chief alters organizational patterns even though community problems remain unchanged.

In addition to the organizational pattern of a department, command discretion may be seen in policy manuals, written orders, and operational memoranda from the command staff to on-line units. Such manuals, orders, and memoranda are intended to establish departmental objectives and standard operating procedures. When these documents are well researched, carefully reasoned, and comprehensive, they provide direction and valuable guidelines for the sensible and effective use of on-the-street discretion. They also provide an appropriate basis for the evaluation of police operations and, as noted earlier, lend credence to police claims of professionalism.

Not all command discretion is the product of careful staff work and systematic review. Police commanders are continuously called on to make discretionary decisions quickly, not unlike the patrol officer on the beat. But unlike the on-the-beat decisions, command decisions are often more visible to members of the press and the public and occasionally have far-reaching consequences for law enforcement in the

Command Discretion

1: Blue Laws

Several businessmen complained to the police commissioner that the Sunday closing laws were not being enforced against major discount houses and that this was adversely affecting their sales and profits. Members of this same group had earlier approached the district attorney, who told them that enforcement was a police matter and that if cases were brought to him by the police, he would prosecute. The commissioner, however, told the businessmen that his officers had more important things to do than to enforce blue laws. He pointed to the rate of serious crimes in the community and said he would not waste valuable resources enforcing obsolete laws.

2: Moving Chess Pieces

Faced with a flat budget and the refusal of the city council to allocate funds for increased personnel, yet confronting adverse newspaper commentaries on the failure of police to solve three serious murders in the community, a police commissioner decided to reorganize his department. He doubled the size of the homicide unit by reducing some positions in traffic control, transferring a number of detectives from vice to homicide, and eliminating two neighborhood police units.

3: Hiding in the Weeds

A police command staff developed a plan for the selective enforcement of traffic laws designed to apprehend drunken drivers. The plan involved assigning special patrol units to stake out certain bars and roadhouses on Friday and Saturday nights with instructions to tail cars leaving these taverns, stopping any "erratic" or "uneven" drivers. These special enforcement units would be moved to new locations weekly. The plan was considered top secret in the department and no advance knowledge of enforcement locations was given to the police themselves or the public. ∎

community and for the career of the commissioner or chief making them. (See Field Practice C.)

Control of Police Discretion

Controlling discretion does not mean that it must be eliminated. Police work probably cannot be properly done without officers exercising substantial discretion at the operating level. However, detailed policies covering particular aspects of police functioning, such as the manner in which officers should handle street gatherings or domestic disputes, are impossible to provide since an infinite number of possible circumstances could occur in such instances. Recognizing this difficulty, it would seem desirable that discretion be structured in such a way that *all officers in the same agency are operating on the same wavelength*.

Limits on discretion, therefore, should embody and convey the objectives, priorities, and operating philosophy of the agency. They should be sufficiently specific to enable an officer to make judgments in a wide variety of unpredictable circumstances in a manner that will win the approval of top police administrators, that will be free of personal prejudices and biases, and that will achieve a reasonable degree of uniformity in handling similar incidences in the community.[16]

THE PROPRIETY OF POLICE TECHNIQUES

The methods used by police to detect crime and gather evidence against suspects are often controversial. Techniques that violate Constitutional rights are clearly improper

Unusual Techniques

1: Fuzz Buster

A traffic control unit of a state police agency used not only unmarked cars but "souped-up" unmarked panel trucks with out-of-state license tags in the detection of speeders on interstate highways and for high-speed chases and the apprehension of speeders.

2: Taxpayer's Money

The vice unit of a major metropolitan police force, instructed to "cleanup" street prostitution before a major political convention was held in the city, convinced the mayor to purchase two Lincoln Continentals and two Mercedes automobiles for use in "trolling for prostitutes." ■

and, as discussed in Chap. 6, have been condemned by the Supreme Court and limited by the exclusionary rule. Wrongful searches, excessive interrogations, "third-degree," entrapment procedures, and other practices are now beyond the bounds of proper policing. As Justice Felix Frankfurter once put it, such techniques "shock the conscience" and must be condemned.

But there are many policing methods that fall short of clear violations of Constitutional provisions yet offend common values. Sometimes it may appear that the techniques routinely employed by the police are as devious as those used by the offenders they are trying to catch—or even more so. However, these techniques are often justified by police officers who feel that they must "stay one step ahead of the criminals" and that "all's fair" in the detection and apprehension of law violators and in the perpetuation of the image of police effectiveness.

Unusual Techniques

This eagerness to be, or at least to appear to be, effective is displayed by local police, especially those charged primarily with traffic control responsibilities, who have to continually develop new law enforcement techniques. Many citizens view avoiding the police while speeding as a kind of a cat-and-mouse game, and enjoy using "fuzz busters," CB radios, and other gadgets to foil police radar. So the police counter this behavior with their own increasingly ingenious (and sneaky) techniques. (See Field Practice D:1.)

Vice control officers sometimes put themselves in a position to be solicited by street-walking or car-hopping prostitutes and, when approached, make an arrest. Normally, the officers sit in bars known to be frequented by prostitutes, walk slowly through suspected red-light districts, or drive unmarked cars slowly past street-corner girls in an attempt to lure and catch them. In some cities similar techniques are used to apprehend male hustlers.

Sometimes police departments, which have a constant need for new undercover police, recruit them directly from the police academies (see Field Practice E). Officers who go undercover to infiltrate criminal conspiracies, ranging from drug dealing to terrorism, must be "clean," that is, clearly not known as police. The danger in undercover work is clear: An officer whose cover is blown is useless, even if the officer manages to stay alive.

Recruitment for Undercover Work

Welcome to the Team

A selection committee from a chief of detectives' staff was assigned the duty of choosing new detectives for undercover work. Known as the "Talent Scouts," this committee interviewed and observed new recruits, particularly those from identifiable racial and ethnic minorities, selecting some for immediate transfer to the Detective Division before they entered recruit training. These recruits were secretly sworn in as law enforcement officers and immediately placed on assignments throughout the city. Some had not received even a day's training as a police officer. ■

To the victim of a house burglary, the crime is horrendous. His or her personal sanctuary has been invaded and looted! But to the police, burglary is commonplace, old hat, not really very serious on their scale of atrocious crimes. Furthermore, the police know only too well that most burglaries are never solved, most loot never recovered. But should they share this information with a victim? Should they downplay the crime and the likelihood of its being solved? Sometimes police detectives go through the motions of crime scene investigation more for the benefit of the victim than with any realistic expectation that uncovered evidence will result in subsequent arrest and successful prosecution. (See Field Practice F.)

Police sometimes use **decoys** to catch criminals. An officer acts like a vulnerable victim and, when the crime is about to occur, arrests the perpetrator. Sometimes officers act alone in this role; more often they are electronically transmitting their conversations to other officers hiding nearby, who at the appropriate time jump out and catch the mugger, rapist, or whatever type of criminal is involved. Being a decoy victim, like going undercover as a decoy criminal, is dangerous. Yet in many situations

Burglary Investigation

Rest Easy

As a followup to a call reporting a burglary, two detectives visited an apartment in an expensive housing development. After being admitted by the owner-victim and looking around, they wrote down the nature of the loss and gave the apartment owner some information on obtaining better locks for his front door. As they prepared to leave, the victim demanded to know why the detectives had not taken fingerprints. One officer responded, "Don't need them. We have plenty to go on." The other detective said, "These guys always wear gloves anyway." On the way out one of the detectives said, "Don't worry. We'll get the guys. Remember, they'll never come back so you can rest easy." ■

Decoy

Down and Out

A police officer, acting like a chronic drunk, set himself up as a decoy in a subway station. Unshaven, disheveled, wearing torn clothing, with holes in his shoes and the reek of whiskey on his person, he lay on the floor of the subway exit, apparently unconscious or in a deep alcoholic sleep. From the hip pocket of his soiled jeans, the edges of a $10 bill could be seen, along with a $1 bill. When a train disgorged its passengers, most stepped over the drunk but two teen-age boys stopped, stared at him, looked around—and one grabbed the money. The officer sprang into action, seized the boy, and, at pistol point, frisked and handcuffed him. The other boy got away. ■

it seems to police authorities that this is the only way to catch persistent criminals in the act. Sometimes it may seem that a realistic decoy is *too attractive* to potential offenders, that the officer looks so vulnerable that he or she might induce an otherwise honest person to commit a crime. (See Field Practice G.)

Successful police work, particularly the work of detectives, depends very much on information received from **informers**. And most detectives work hard to build an informant network so that when serious crimes occur they can pass the word to their informers to be on the lookout for leads. Many informers, most in fact, are themselves criminals who are given a break (not arrested) by police in return for future underworld information. Indeed, if informants did *not* have criminal contacts, they would be of little use to the police. Some informants play the role to avoid their own arrest; others are paid, usually from police department funds for this purpose. How much and how often they are paid depend on the importance of the information they pass on and the past reliability of their information.

In general, the police do not like to publicly admit how much of their success is

Informer by Blackmail

Peek-a-Boo

Vice squad officers, by using a hidden peephole, discovered a college student purchasing cocaine from a known drug dealer in the restroom of a bus station. Instead of arresting the student for possession of a controlled substance, the police offered a deal. They would not charge him with any offense or notify university authorities if the student would act as a "narc" (a narcotics informer) in his dormitory and on the campus generally. He agreed and was given a 24-hour phone number to report any "major" sales of crack or other forms of cocaine. The police promised to protect his identity, saying, "Unless a case goes to trial, but most don't— they plead out—you really have nothing to worry about." If the student failed to perform satisfactorily, the police threatened to expose him to university authorities and to his parents. ■

Roundup

A Discouraging Word

Following the rape-murder of a small child, a crime that received extensive newspaper coverage, detectives were sent to interview all "known sex deviates" residing in the community regarding their whereabouts at the time of the crime. There were 117 active records on known sex deviates in police files. Some of those interviewed were on parole for sex crimes, others had completed sex crime sentences years earlier, and about thirty had never been convicted or sentenced although they had been arrested for sex offenses in the past. Following the interrogation of these individuals, the police focused their suspicions on three of them, one of whom eventually confessed to the crime. He was one of the thirty who had been previously arrested but never convicted of a sex offense or any other crime. ∎

due to informants, paid or otherwise. It is better public relations to maintain an air of mystery about how leads are developed or cases are solved. Yet among themselves, police officers recognize the importance of informants. Indeed, there is a common courtesy displayed by most police agencies: "We lay off informers for other police [the FBI, for example] and they are expected to lay off ours."

Sometimes the police are too vigorous, too ruthless, in developing informers. Young first-offenders arrested for drug-related crimes who are often very concerned about keeping their arrest secret from parents or others have been recruited by police to lead them to "higher-ups" in the drug trade. Many police informers in the major cities are known addicts and ex-cons. Sometimes police informant activities may lead to injury or death. (See Field Practice H.)

Once a person has a police record it becomes easier for that person to be arrested. Persons on probation or parole are "known to the police" and generally become primary suspects when new crimes are reported. Police sometimes use what is called a **roundup**, a technique whereby all former offenders known to the police are brought in for questioning even if the police have no direct evidence or information to implicate them in the crime being investigated. The use of this technique may hamper the readjustment efforts of a person who is making every attempt to lead a law-abiding life, or, when the roundup arrest occurs at the person's place of employment, it may result in humiliation or loss of a job. (See Field Practice I.)

Police are generally aware that disproportionate numbers of crimes in any community are committed by a comparatively small number of persistent repeat offenders, or **chronic criminals** (often called "chronics" by police). With this in mind police departments sometimes set up a "chronic criminal" bureau to focus on this problem. (See Field Practice J.)

Whether any or all of the above-described police techniques are appropriate to use or not is largely a matter of judgment. The judgment used by individual police officers may or may not reflect the values of the community he or she serves. As the police become more open to community involvement through innovative practices such as community-based policing and problem-oriented policing, perhaps the perceived need for questionable practices will disappear. But as long as police work behind a cloak of secrecy, behind the "blue curtain," their controversial practices will continue to exist, often known only to the people directly involved.

Chronic Offenders

We're behind You

Officers in the chronic criminal unit of a police department identified twenty-four male residents of the city who had been arrested for (but not necessarily convicted of) at least three felonies in the past 7 years. Ten of the chronics were in prison and parole dates were obtained for each. A surveillance team providing 24-hour coverage was assigned to each of the free fourteen chronics and a team would be assigned to each imprisoned chronic on the day of his parole. The teams tailed and watched each chronic around the clock. The officers were not particularly concerned if the chronic discovered he was under observation. "Our job is to prevent as well as bust," one plainclothes officer explained. ■

High-Speed Pursuit

Police movies and television shows have for years included scenes of **high-speed pursuit** or police car chases, often as the exciting finish to the story. Viewers have become accustomed to police chase scenes in San Francisco (the hills always provide camera angles that maximize the excitement of cars flying over bumps), Chicago (racing through the supports of an elevated train lend an obstacle course element), and Miami (the avenues along Biscayne Bay in *Miami Vice* add color and beauty). Indeed, such scenes are almost obligatory. But seldom do those scenes include the more common, and often tragic, elements of actual chases. Viewers do not see the pursuits initiated by traffic offenses, nor do they see the tragic consequences of innocent bystanders placed in danger by them or visit the courtrooms where lawsuits are heard alleging negligence by the police when an innocent person is seriously injured or killed as the result of a chase.

Not much is known about police chases—how they begin, under what conditions they are continued or broken off, how they are terminated. The few studies which have been published are limited in their scope and methodology, but some things are known.[17] Geoffrey Alpert and Patrick Anderson describe seven possible endings to police high-speed pursuits:

1. The offender stops the car and surrenders.
2. The pursued vehicle crashes into a structure and the offenders are apprehended, escape, or are injured or killed.
3. The pursued vehicle crashes into another vehicle without injuries or death to passengers or bystanders.
4. The pursued vehicle crashes into another vehicle with injuries or death to passengers or bystanders.
5. The pursued vehicle hits a pedestrian (with or without injuries or death).
6. The police use some level of force to stop the pursued vehicle, including firearms, roadblocks, ramming, bumping, boxing, etc.
7. The police car crashes (with or without injuries to officers or civilians).[18]

Of course, the fleeing driver may also escape capture, thereby ending the chase. But if the chase results in anyone's injury or death, one party or the other often brings legal action against the police.

Police are empowered to violate traffic laws in the performance of their duty. This usually means they are exempt from laws related to speed, traffic signs and lights, right-of-way, and so forth. On the other hand, the law and public expectation require police to drive in such a way as to protect the public and to make the roads safe for all persons, and to operate their vehicles in a nonnegligent manner.

Why do the police chase suspects? The police mission is to apprehend criminals, so chases are expected. And many officers feel that any law violator must be apprehended. Moreover, it is often impossible to find an offender who has fled successfully, even if an accurate description of the car and license number is given, so officers choose to pursue immediately. On the other hand, if an officer chooses not to chase, is that a violation of the duty to enforce the law and apprehend criminals? And if the public becomes aware the police do not pursue traffic violators, will that knowledge result in more offenders fleeing? What about the officers' self images and reputations if they allow law violators to escape? All of these factors and others lead the police to act intuitively, and sometimes to try to catch the offender at all costs.

As noted above, however, the costs of high-speed pursuit can be high. The consequences of aggressive police pursuits without policy guidelines and training can be the needless loss of property and life. Some police departments have issued guidelines forbidding prolonged pursuit of traffic violators, and have established policies for when to initiate chases and when to break them off. Such policies and practices take into account the individual officer's training and preparation, the conditions of the road and neighborhood, and the events leading up to the chase.[19]

Most chases start after police observe a traffic violation, usually by a male driver under 20 years old, at night, and continue for only a minute or two for less than 5 miles. Most suspects are apprehended without an accident. When known felons are pursued, about half result in accidents.[20] Field Practice K describes some real police chases.

Police chase scenes in movies rarely conform to the reality of police pursuits.

Police High-Speed Pursuit

1: Motorbike

A police officer frequently observed a teenage boy riding through his residential neighborhood on a small motorbike without wearing a helmet as required by law. The officer had previously given the boy a verbal warning, a written warning, and finally two tickets for operating a motorbike without wearing a helmet. The boy was belligerent and seemed to take delight in riding past the police car and waving at the officer. On one such occasion, the officer attempted to stop the boy by following him and turning on his car's flashing lights. Instead, the boy fled. The officer pursued, reaching speeds over 60 miles per hour in the residential neighborhood, and running through stop signs with lights flashing and siren blaring. The boy finally crashed the motorbike into a parked car and received serious head injuries.

2: Green Card

A police officer riding a downtown beat in a major city at 2 a.m. observed a car roll through a stop sign without stopping. The officer turned on his flashing lights and followed the car to make a routine traffic stop. The driver fled. The officer began to pursue, notified dispatch, and ultimately was joined in the chase by three other patrol officers, the supervising sergeant, and a helicopter. The chase was at very high speeds, several parked cars were side-swiped, and garbage cans were scattered in the wake of the speeding cars. The other officers, including the sergeant, shouted encouragement into their radios: "Get him!" "Don't let the bastard get away!" Finally, the fleeing car entered the ramp to a freeway, but going the wrong way, and crashed headlong into a car occupied by a vacationing family of four. The mother and father were killed instantly, along with the fleeing offender, and both children, who were asleep in the back seat, were seriously injured. Subsequent investigation revealed that the suspect was an illegal immigrant who did not have a "green card" which would allow him to stay in the United States and was evidently attempting to avoid being apprehended and sent back to his native land. The estate of the deceased filed a lawsuit against the police alleging negligence.

3: Bank Robbers

Two bank robbery suspects were pursued by city police after a report and description was given to dispatch. The fleeing suspects were said to be armed. The chase led through the city streets during the middle of the day, and finally the fleeing car entered a freeway and began to drive at speeds exceeding 100 miles per hour. A road block was set up several miles ahead of the fleeing car by highway patrol officers. Other traffic was slowed, some stopped. The driver of the fleeing car attempted to avoid the stopped traffic, lost control, and crashed into the rear of a car which was stopped in traffic. The occupant of the stopped car was burned to death in the resulting explosion, and the bank robbers were both killed. ∎

POLICE MISCONDUCT

The considerable exent to which police discretion exists contributes to a climate in which police misconduct can occur. Police have been known throughout history to engage in wrongful acts, to abuse their power, and to violate the trust placed in them by society. "Without fear or favor" is the motto many police officers recite, but too often they intimidate people for their own profit and overstep their lawful power to use force. Police use their power to give favorable treatment to certain people for profit. This is a conclusion that even police recruits accept when they enter police training academies.[21]

The fact that police often work in an environment of poverty, frustration, and crime in the inner city contributes to a "them vs. us" attitude. The psychological impact of daily confrontations often cause officers to turn inward, to surround themselves socially with fellow police officers, to become part of the "blue code" which prohibits one officer from informing on another. This social world of police, and the secrecy which surrounds much of what police do, coupled with the frustration which

Kansas City Police Go After Own 'Bad Boys'

KANSAS CITY, Mo.—Lightning slashed across the sky over this city known for its hot barbecue, cool jazz and tough police officers. One officer, Jim Pott, sat in a patrol car watching the storm and talked about his place on what he and colleagues bitterly call "the bad boys list."

The list, a computer printout of 25 officers who have an unusually large number of citizen complaints against them, is part of the Kansas City Police Department's new "early warning system." The program is intended to prevent officers from using the kind of excessive force that provoked public outrage last spring when a videotape of Los Angeles police officers beating a motorist was made public.

"We want to latch on to the officer who has problems dealing with the public as soon as possible, before they get into bad habits that can cause a lot of problems," said Capt. Dean Kelly, the commander of the internal affairs unit.

He said the first group of bad boys was sent to a special eight-hour class that used role playing and other methods to help the officers improve their communications skills.

Jim Pott was among the first to be reeled in.

"Sometimes I get carried away with the macho image; a lot of us do," Officer Pott said, blowing a cloud of cigarette smoke out the window. "I consider myself an aggressive officer; you have to be. I like messing with the real bad guys. Not too long ago, the unwritten rule was if somebody ran on you and you caught 'em, you'd smack 'em one."

"To be honest," he said with a smile, "in the past we got away with quite a bit. But everything is post-L.A. now."

Experts say that in any city a comparatively small group of officers provoke most complaints of excessive force. That was borne out here in a recent study that was ordered by Chief Steven C. Bishop after an alarming string of excessive-force allegations, including the striking of two black clergymen and the televised beating of a suspect after a car chase.

Problems of a Few

The study found that over a three-year-period the 25 officers on the list were responsible for more than half of the

Police—citizen encounters create problems for police as well as citizens.

600 complaints filed every year against the 1,200-officer department.

Similarly, in Los Angeles, a commission established to investigate the Police Department shortly after the beating last March of the motorist, Rodney G. King, also found a minority but still "significant number of officers who repetitively misuse force."

Even before the Los Angeles incident, the Kansas City Police Department had acted to prevent rough tactics. In his first 14 months on the job, Chief Bishop has forced out 24 officers for bad conduct, a previously unheard-of action. "And I have two more hanging in the wings," he said with a sad, slow sigh.

But the Chief's policies have met with resistance from the rank-and-file. Last year, he handed out the stiffest suspension in department history, 120 days without pay when an officer hit a Baptist minister in the back of the head with the butt of a shotgun during a robbery investigation.

The officer's colleagues held a monthlong work slowdown to protest the action and raised thousands of dollars for the officer by auctioning off the same kind of shotgun he used to strike the minister.

"We as officers felt the Chief had gone way over the line with discipline," Officer Pott said.

Nevertheless, Lawrence W. Sherman, president of the Crime Control Institute in Washington, called the Kansas City department "a model of preventative action to control police use of excessive force."

'On the Right Track'

And Hubert Williams of the Police Foundation, a research group in Washington, said Chief Bishop "was on the right track" by dismissing problem officers.

"Excessive use of force by police officers creates such a cleavage within the community that police departments can almost become dysfunctional in certain areas of a city," Mr. Williams said. "It's critical that police managers send a strong, clear message that this kind of behavior is not tolerable. You have to draw a line and say: 'If you want to be a cop, you have to be one of the good guys, you can't be a bad guy, busting heads.'"

Still, only a handful of departments go as far as Kansas City has, Mr. Sherman said.

The New York City Police Department has identified and provided counseling for more than 8,200 officers since 1973. Officers receive help through the department's early intervention program for a variety of reasons, including gambling, financial troubles, alcohol abuse and marital problems.

Here in Kansas City, the department's main objective is to correct questionable behavior on the street. A secondary goal is even harder to achieve: changing attitudes.

"We've learned we cannot necessarily change people," Captain Kelly said. "There is prejudice that people carry with them that we cannot change. But what we can do is make them aware that they have these attitudes and that they have to put them at the back of their minds and carry on business as if they didn't exist or else they can start looking for a new job."

The 25 officers on the first list were sent to the special class in April. They used role playing, lectures, videotapes and group discussions to demonstrate ways to communicate better on the street and at home.

The class also teaches the officers to avoid using what Captain Kelly calls "blockers" to communication.

He said many officers on the list wear mirrored sunglasses and other trappings of authority. Out on the street, they are humorless and approach the increasingly complex job like 1950's cardboard television characters: just the facts ma'am and no backtalk. Some wear two or three pairs of handcuffs and rest their hands on their guns during even the most routine traffic stops.

"We talk about eye contact, facial expressions, stance," Captain Kelly said. "You rest your hand on your gun; cops don't realize that it offends and even scares people. I don't know how many times I have heard people complain, 'I thought he was going to shoot me for running a red light.'"

The Kansas City plan is part public relations. Months before the Los Angeles incident, police officials here grap-

accompanies the knowledge that many of those they arrest will "get off" with little or no official sanctions, sometimes lead to police misconduct. "Street justice" may be administered with the nightstick, more than necessary force may be used, and trouble may be sought out by misfit officers who are predisposed to brutality. Some officers may also choose to benefit financially in the police world, and many opportunities exist for unscrupulous police.

Police Brutality

Television viewers not long ago were shocked at the repeated showing of a videotape of Los Angeles police officers kicking, clubbing, and beating Rodney King in March 1991.[22] The fact that King is black and the officers involved were white led to public accusations of racism among Los Angeles police. But most police observers know that **police brutality**, and racial abuse, are not isolated events occurring only in pled with how to handle "our own Rodney King incident," Chief Bishop said.

Last September, after chasing a van through the streets of the city, several officers yanked the driver, a white man, through the window and began kicking him and beating him with a blackjack-like weapon.

The incident was filmed by a television cameraman who had been following the chase in his own van.

"I think our officers realize now we had a problem with the way we were treating people," the Chief said. "But that was a very small minority of our officers."

Although the Chief's words and actions have encouraged many, there is still a deep sense of caution, a sense that the changes are only temporary. The president of the Kansas City branch of the National Association for the Advancement of Colored People, Herman Johnson, said the department's reputation has been "terrible for years and years and years."

"It's better now," he said, "But there's been trouble before. They clean it up, change some policies but as soon as it quiets down, they go right back to what they were doing."

In Kansas City as in other cities, most complaints filed against an officer are never substantiated. And filing a complaint is not an uncommon tactic of some suspects, who hope to derail aggressive but legitimate police work.

But Chief Bishop said a pattern of complaints against an officer, whether substantiated or not, is a good sign that trouble could be developing.

He said that he was pleased with the program and that in tracking the first group of "bad boys" to go through it, not one had received a complaint. He said that over all,

complaints of all kinds against officers were down this year by 22 percent, the first decrease in 10 years.

Complaint records are now checked every month to update the list and commanders are notified anytime an officer has received three or more complaints in a six-month period.

Out on the street where the action is, Officer Pott lit another cigarette, and talked about how he had moved from his hometown of Grand Rapids, Mich., to pursue his life-long dream of becoming a policeman.

"I just like the possible excitement of it all," he said. "But I had a real problem with communicating. I think I was a bad listener. I could always talk though. I could always tell people what to do out here or at home."

He said initially he was angry and embarrassed about being on the list but was now happy that he had taken the class. He said he was more tolerant and open minded "and my marriage is 100 percent better."

He said he was fourth on the list after receiving 13 complaints in two years but none of those complaints, he said, has been substantiated.

The dispatcher's voice broke in "Man with a gun in his shorts."

Flicking his cigarette out the window, Officer Pott made a U-turn.

And then, heading his cruiser toward the stranger with the gun, he smiled and said, "I love this job."

SOURCE: "Kansas City Police Go After Own 'Bad Boys,'" Don Terry, *The New York Times*, September 10, 1991. Copyright © 1991 by The New York Times Company. Reprinted by permission.

Los Angeles. Other cases became well known after the King tape was shown. (See Field Practice L.)[23]

Most police officers in the United States are honorable, naturally decent men and women who sincerely wish to protect and serve the public. But the work they do can sometimes brutalize them, making them hard and insensitive. And sometimes people who already have authoritarian, hostile, suspicious, and prejudiced attitudes are attracted to police work.[24] For those, the working world of police can exacerbate those characteristics and lead to brutality.

Whatever its causes, police brutality must be controlled. Many observers blamed Los Angeles Police Chief Daryl Gates for the actions of the L.A. cops in the King beating. The Los Angeles Police Department paid approximately $10.5 million to plaintiffs who won police misconduct lawsuits in 1990, and critics charged that Chief Gates had taken little or no disciplinary action against the officers involved.[25] Indeed, civil lawsuits have been a major factor in reforming police practices. Police admin-

Police Brutality

1: Hog-Tied

Five New York City police officers were accused of hitting, kicking, and choking a 21-year-old Hispanic man suspected of car theft. The police cuffed his hands behind his back, using a second set of handcuffs binding his hands to one ankle and kept him face down on the ground during the attack. The man died and the five officers were indicted on murder charges.

2: These Boots Were Made for Walking

A black county sheriff in Memphis was convicted of violating the civil rights of a black drug suspect who was choked to death. The suspect's body was covered with bruises in the shape of shoe prints.

3: No Place for Toys

People demonstrated in Plainfield, New Jersey, over reports that a police officer had beat a 14-year-old black youth on a sidewalk near his home. The boy had been playing with a remote-control toy car and a motorist had stopped where he was playing. A police car ran into the rear of the stopped motorist's car; the officer then allegedly jumped out of his own car and accused the teen-ager of obstructing traffic, choked and injured him, and then arrested his parents when they interfered.

---

istrators have created new policies or revised existing ones to discourage police misuse of force. In-service training and improved recruit screening and training increasingly address the proper use of force, especially in the face of civil litigation against police departments.

Police Corruption

Relatively low salaries, high stress, and the perpetual risk of personal harm have all been cited as causes of the continuing problem of **police corruption**. These factors coupled with the extensive training required for police, and the low esteem many police believe the public holds them in, have contributed to the attitude among some police officers that one way to compensate for these and other debts owed to them by the public is to accept favors and personal rewards.

Favors have historically been offered to police officers. A free cup of coffee, cut-rate dry cleaning, half-price or free meals at restaurants, and discount apartment rents have all been part of police officers' unofficial compensation for decades. Businesses have benefited from such payments by having a police presence. That is, business owners perceive police cars in their parking lots as a deterrent to crime, so as far as they are concerned, if giving a discount or a "freebie" can assure greater police presence, all the better. The implication is clear: Would business owners have *less* police protection if they did not entice police to frequent their businesses? Police administrators have learned that such "enticements" can lead to corruption, to officers enforcing the law with favor, or even to their soliciting gifts, or "shaking down" citizens for gifts. See Field Practice M.

During the 1970s, in response to wide-spread allegations of police corruption in New York City, the **Knapp Commission** was established to investigate the charges. When the commission's report was published in 1972[26] it concluded that corruption

Los Angeles Police Chief Darryl Gates reading the Christopher Report, an independent commission's study of LAPD practices, which found racism, brutality, and supervisors who tolerate both in the LAPD.

Police Corruption

1: We're Having a Party

Police officers planning a "policeman's ball" visited liquor stores while riding their beats and told store owners, "We're having a policeman's ball and would like you to donate some liquor. We know you would like to support police morale in this way. Other liquor stores and bars in the area have already donated." When one store owner refused, and complained to the chief of police, the chief issued a new directive stating that such solicitations were against department policy. He also suspended the officers involved for 3 days without pay.

2: Motel Heaven

Dispatch received a call from a motel cleaning woman who said she had observed a drug deal taking place in a motel room. The two officers who responded found two men with a large amount of cocaine and a large amount of cash. While one of the officers placed the two suspects in the back of the patrol car, and radioed for assistance, the other returned to the room alone and stuffed several thousand dollars into his clothing. The two officers split the money evenly, and justified the act by saying, "No one will ever miss the money. It would have just gone into the police vault, and besides we put our lives on the line every day and deserve some benefits from our thankless job." ■

did exist, mostly in the form of accepting bribes. The commission classified corrupt police officers into two categories: "**meat eaters**" and "**grass eaters**." Meat eaters were those officers who aggressively demanded bribes or payoffs and threatened legal action if the favors were not received. Grass eaters were those who merely accepted what came their way without overtly asking or demanding anything.

Others have also identified corrupt police practices and categorized them. Ellwyn Stoddard has described police officer corruption, or "blue-coat crime," in terms of "mooching" (receiving gifts or discounts), "chiseling" (demanding gifts or discounts), "shopping" (taking items from store shelves without paying), "shakedown" (taking expensive items from burglary scenes and reporting it as stolen in the burglary), and "favoritism" (not enforcing the law for friends or relatives, especially in regard to traffic violations).[27] Lawrence Sherman has categorized police departments as "rotten apples" and "rotten pockets" (departments with a few rotten apples who, when they get together and cooperate, become rotton pockets of corruption), "pervasive unorganized corruption" (departments with many corrupt officers who act as individuals, not as groups), and "pervasive organized corruption" (departments in which almost all of the officers are involved in systematic, organized corruption).[28]

Much police corruption exists in the area of vice crimes—gambling, prostitution, and drugs. A great deal of money is available in vice, along with opportunities for police officers to take payoffs and bribes, or to actively participate in the crimes. The cases described in Field Practice M describe only two common types of corrupt police practices among the many that exist. Some police officers believe that corruption exists in every department, and that it is inevitable.[29] But police corruption can be controlled. Some critics advocate removing the vice crimes from police jurisdiction by decriminalizing those behaviors. Other observers say that the "blue curtain" of secrecy must be eliminated by the creation of citizen oversight committees and more public accountability. But rather than relying on outside forces to address the issue of corruption, police administrators themselves can help control it through the careful screening of police applicants, the thorough training of police recruits, and the active promotion of an atmosphere of police professionalism within their departments.

POLICE USE OF DEADLY FORCE

In the United States all official police agency officers are armed. In addition to a shield, or badge, identifying a person as a sworn police officer, each individual officer carries a gun—sometimes, when the officer is in uniform, in the open; at other times, when in plainclothes, concealed. But firepower is omnipresent, and it is not limited to pistols and other handguns. Prowl cars often have shotguns, either kept for easy access in the front seat or stored away in the trunk. All types of modern weaponry, from tear gas launchers to rockets, are available to municipal, state, and federal police. Even bombs are not unheard of. A few years ago the Philadelphia police, attempting to drive members of a cult called MOVE from a dwelling, dropped a bomb from an airplane on the building. The bomb killed a number of the dwelling's residents and the resulting fire burned 60 homes in the immediate area. The MOVE attack was originally motivated by a charge of "trespass," a misdemeanor. The charge was eventually upgraded to "resisting arrest," but even that hardly justified the level of force used, according to many observers as well as the subsequent investigating commission.

An 11-year-old boy was caught in police crossfire and seriously wounded.

Not only are the police armed, but they have the authority, under law, to use force, including **deadly force**, to maintain compliance with our criminal laws. *Most* police officers in most jurisdictions complete their entire careers, in uniform or in plainclothes, *without shooting* or attempting to shoot at any suspects. On the other hand, officers assigned to certain high-crime precincts, usually urban ghettos, often carry their sidearms out of holsters and at the ready, though shooting even in those circumstances is still comparatively rare. There are no accurate national statistics on the annual number of civilians killed by police; the best *official* estimate is about 250, with another 1000 to 2000 civilians wounded. Unofficial estimates place the number much higher, perhaps twice as many. Even so, this is a small number, considering all the police departments, all the shifts, and all the days of the year the statistics cover. There were 10,110 police *departments* reporting to the FBI's *Uniform Crime Reports* in 1990 and police make over *14,195,100 arrests* annually. Some estimates of the total number of police agencies go as high as 40,000. So, the numbers of civilians wounded or killed seems low in comparison.[30]

Much has been written in recent years about police shootings. A number of factors have been associated with police use of deadly force: individual factors such as age of the officer, his or her educational attainment, and race; situational factors such as the physical setting or location of the shooting, events precipitating the incident, the opponent's weapon, and more; organizational factors such as the restrictiveness of department policies and administrative philosophies regarding firearm discharges; and, community-level factors such as population size and violent crime rate. Some of the research focuses on police killings as "justifiable homicides," or fatal shooting rates. These studies exclude information on shots fired which either miss their intended targets or wound, rather than kill them, which one would assume should still fall under the heading of use of deadly force. Professor Lorie Fridell has analyzed the research into police shootings and its inadequacies and inconsistencies.[31]

Nevertheless, the problems associated with deadly force and the variety of circumstances relating to police shootings, especially as they involve minority citizens and officers make this subject a very special issue in modern policing. In an interesting study of shootings by New York City police officers over a 5-year period, James J. Fyfe found that minority police officers were responsible for a disproportionate number of them. (Perhaps not as surprisingly, the study found that civilian minorities, particularly blacks and Hispanics, were more likely to be *targets* of police shootings as well.) The minority police officers, in Fyfe's study, were also much more likely to be

Deadly Force

1: Beer Cooler

In a medium-sized city, police administrators responded to a rash of convenience store armed robberies by placing officers armed with shotguns behind the glass refrigerators to watch for the robbers. On one such occasion, a man was observed to enter the store and walk around looking at various items on shelves. After other customers had left, he drew a gun, pointed it at the clerk, and demanded money from the cash register. While the clerk was taking the money out, the officer stepped from behind the cooler, "racked" the shotgun, and ordered the armed robber to drop the weapon. The robber, startled, turned suddenly toward the officer, who immediately fired two blasts, killing the robber instantly.

2: Give It Up!

Police received a call from a citizen reporting an armed robbery in progress at a liquor store. Patrol officers arrived at the scene, without sirens, parked opposite the front door of the store, and, using the patrol car as a shield, waited for the armed robbers to exit. When the robbers, two men wearing stocking masks and with pistols in their hands, came out, an officer who had a shotgun pointed it at them from behind the patrol car and shouted, "Police! Give it up! Throw down your weapons!" The robbers turned suddenly and pointed their guns toward the police, who immediately fired, killing both robbers.

3: Merry Christmas

A man wanted by the police for the murders of three motorists, including a young child and a highway patrolman who had attempted to apprehend him, was arrested with much publicity. He was being held in a small county jail awaiting transfer to a larger city jail. On Christmas Eve, sheriff's deputies later stated the man, acting as if full of remorse, offered to take the officers to a place where he had buried the bodies of other persons he had killed. The deputies took the man out of the jail, his hands cuffed behind his back, and drove him to a lonely rural area. When they stopped the car at a location the prisoner identified as the burial place, he bolted from the officers' grasp in an escape attempt. The deputies fired their weapons at the man as he ran, killing him.

4: Shoot—Don't Shoot

Officers answered a call to the scene of a reported "crazy man" who was threatening passers-by with a butcher knife. Three officers arrived at the scene first, surrounded the man, and began to talk to him in an attempt to have him peacefully put down the weapon. A fourth officer arrived, rushed toward the man and the officers, and forcefully told the man to "Put the knife down before we have to hurt you!" The man lunged toward the fourth officer, who drew his revolver and shot the man, killing him instantly. ∎

---

assigned to high-crime ghetto precincts than their white counterparts, which undoubtedly helps to explain the disparity in rates.[32] Field Practice N indicates the range of incidents that can spark the use of deadly force.

Variations in shooting rates by precinct, by day or night, and by other measures correlated with occurrences of violence and violent crimes can explain in a general way squad and shift differences in shooting incidents. Variations in shooting rates by city, however, are harder to explain. Why should cities with comparable crime rates and comparable sizes of police forces show marked variations in police killings? Perhaps, in the past, part of this difference was the result of variations in laws and rules governing police use of deadly force. Until 1985 about half the states, following English common law traditions, allowed police to shoot and kill any or all felons who were running away to escape arrest, although most *large departments* had policies restricting such use of police force. The other half of the states outlawed the so-called **fleeing-felon rule**[33] and in 1985 the United States Supreme Court invalidated the rule for *all* states as a matter of federal Constitutional law and established deadly force law for police formally.

The Supreme Court case that made that ruling, *Tennessee v. Garner*, involved an unarmed 15-year-old boy killed by a Memphis police officer. The officer was investigating a prowler report, saw the boy running, and ordered him to halt. When the boy did not stop but began climbing a fence, the policeman shot and killed him. The officer testified that he did not believe the boy to be armed but shot him to prevent his "getting away." The Supreme Court held:

> The use of deadly force to prevent the escape of all felony suspects, whatever the circumstances, is constitutionally unreasonable. It is not better that all felony suspects die than that they escape. Where the suspect poses no immediate threat to the officer and no threat to others, the harm resulting from failing to apprehend him does not justify the use of deadly force to do so.[34]

Police use of deadly force is controlled by state statutes, by Supreme Court decisions like *Garner*, and by police department rules. Now that the fleeing-felon rule is no longer allowed, in general police can use deadly force in arresting a suspect only (1) when a felony involving the use or threat of deadly force has occurred, (2) when the officer reasonably believes that there is a substantial imminent risk that the person to be arrested will cause death or serious bodily harm to the officer or to another person, or (3) when such force must be used to prevent the escape of a prisoner from detention, jail, or prison. Deadly force can also be used to suppress a riot after sufficient warning has been given.

The most stringent requirements governing police use of their firearms comes from departmental regulations, which are tuned more finely than legislation or court decisions can be. For example, the New York City Police Department not only has a written policy on the subject (see Box 7.1) but a Firearms Discharge Review Board as well to examine and evaluate *all* incidents of police use of firearms.

Much more research and much better national statistics are needed regarding this important aspect of policing. The use of force, including but not limited to deadly force, is the real heart of police authority. It is here that the greatest threat to democratic rights exists; all the rest is shadow and smoke. It is extremely important that we devise ways to control police use of force, for it threatens us all. Yet we must allow force, including deadly force, to be used reasonably, sparingly, reluctantly to protect us from the predators among us, from the dangerous and deranged.

BOX 7.1

NYPD Firearms Policy

A. In all cases, only the minimum amount of force will be used which is consistent with the accomplishment of a mission. Every other reasonable means will be utilized for arresting, preventing or terminating a felony or for the defense of oneself or another before a police officer resorts to the use of his firearm.

B. A firearm shall not be discharged under circumstances where lives of innocent persons may be endangered.

C. The firing of a warning shot is prohibited.

D. The discharging of a firearm to summon assistance is prohibited, except where the police officer's safety is endangered.

E. Discharging a firearm at or from a moving vehicle is prohibited unless the occupants of the other vehicle are using deadly physical force against the officer or another, by means other than the vehicle.

WOMEN IN POLICING

Perhaps the question arises why women in policing should be included in this chapter as an issue in policing. The truth is that, for much of our history, police work has been the domain of men. Prior to the 1970s women who entered police work were selected by different criteria than men, and after they were hired they were assigned to specialized jobs such as juvenile and children's crimes, certain women's crimes, and of course clerical duties. With the passage of the 1972 Amendments to the Civil Rights Act, however, women were guaranteed under law equal employment opportunities in policing.[35]

Initially, some police officials expressed concern that women would not be emotionally and physically equipped to perform traditional police tasks. Indeed, the height and weight requirements for officers put forward by most police departments originally greatly limited the access of women to policing careers,[36] until in recent years physical fitness and proportional height–weight ratios have become the standard physical requirements.[37] Yet for some of those in police work, the police world remains a bastion of male dominance. Sometimes women police are referred to as "dickless tracys," and more than one macho male cop has said, "When I have to

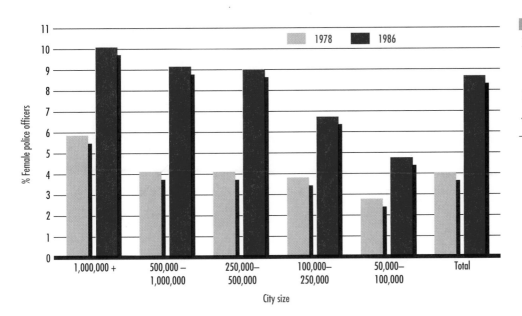

FIGURE 7.1

Percentage increases in female police officers for U.S. cities of different sizes, 1978 vs. 1986. (Source: Susan E. Martin, *Women on the Move*, The Police Foundation, Washington, DC, May 1989.)

wrestle with a big, drunk perp, or when I am attacked by several at one time, the last thing I need to see is a cop in a skirt coming to help me."

But research has demonstrated that women have performed admirably in traditional police roles.[38] And with that successful job performance has come an increasing rate of promotions within police departments. Susan Martin reports that the rate of women in supervisory roles has steadily increased since 1978, especially in large police departments serving populations over 250,000.[39] Figure 7.1 shows the percentage increases in female police officers between 1978 and 1986 for U.S. cities of different sizes. As the amount of time women serve in traditional police roles increases, no doubt the percentage of women in supervisory positions will also increase, for police departments usually promote largely on the basis of length of career, or seniority.

Not all women remain in police work after they have been hired. Women have a slighly higher rate of job turnover in policing than men.[40] One possible reason for this

Officer Wendy Rae of the Oakland Police Department arresting two suspects who had fled a crack sale location during a police raid.

is that for some women police work continues to be a hostile and unpleasant environment.[41] Also, men and women alike often find that changing shift duties (as is expected in many police departments) causes hardships on family life, and this is especially true for women who are single parents or pregnant.

Yet as women continue to climb the ladder of success in the police hierarchy, and as they assume high-profile supervisory positions, female role models will be increasingly available to encourage more women to enter the police profession. As anyone who has been approached by a female police officer for a traffic offense or any other official action can testify, women have definitely become comfortable in the police role.

Summary

For most citizens direct contact with the criminal justice system is through their local police. Few of us are actually arrested for crimes, put on trial, or serve sentences. Eventually, however, we all have some experiences with the police, even if they are limited to routine traffic control. Many civilians fear police and resent even slight intrusions into their privacy. Such resentment may be healthy in a democratic society where liberty and the right to be left alone are prized. Yet we need competent, efficient, and effective policing, for without it there would be anarchy. To be effective, policing must occur in a context of citizen cooperation and support; lack of such support creates a dangerous division between police and the public. Because the need for proper policing exists everywhere, and because the work of police departments more than that of any other governmental agency directly touches our lives, an understanding of and positive response to the police function are critical to its being successfully carried out. Most observers of the criminal justice process agree that policing encompasses many of its most complex and central issues. Issues of both freedom and control are involved, so that the quality of policing is of major concern to all students of criminal justice.

This chapter discussed the quality of policing from several different perspectives. First, it addressed the difficulty of measuring the effectiveness of police responses because of the many expectations assigned to police. Some observers evaluate police work in terms of arrest rates, others in terms of diminishing the fear that crimes will occur, and still others in terms of police response to emergencies. There are no clear-cut criteria because the police role itself is complex and not simple to define.

Second, the chapter described some of the major discretionary decisions police routinely make, especially in regard to arrest. Nothing is more central to policing than the discretionary powers officers exercise, and the discussion includes administrative discretion as well as that of line officers.

Several techniques used by police are controversial, and perhaps the student has until now been unaware of some of them. This chapter described some unusual techniques, such as the use of undercover agents and informants, and roundup efforts. And it introduced the issues surrounding police high-speed chases. None of these techniques are easily understood, or judged.

Police brutality and corruption continuously command the attention of us all. Television images of police officers mercilessly beating handcuffed suspects, and the specter of cops on the take, disturb us all. The chapter discussed some types of police corruption and brutality and realistically gave the reader issues to ponder.

All police are armed and, under the proper conditions, as when the lives of the police officers themselves or of other people are imminently threatened, are authorized to use deadly force, that is, to shoot to kill the criminals. However, because of a recent Supreme Court decision, police may no longer shoot a nonviolent fleeing felon.

Finally, the introduction of female police officers has been discussed. The role of women has expanded greatly in recent years and few barriers currently exist for women to advance in whatever areas of police work they choose.

In conclusion, modern policing is indeed characterized by difficult issues. We have not been able in a single chapter to offer complete solutions to the issues, but we have discussed some of the more prominent ones and, we hope, have raised the awareness of the student regarding the dilemmas facing the police during the last decade of the twentieth century.

NOTES

1. Sources for the Dahmer story: "The Secrets of Apt. 213," *Newsweek*, August 5, 1991; Annetta Miller with Patrick Rogers and Lynn Haessly, "Serial-Murder Aftershocks," *Newsweek*, August 12, 1991.

2. James Q. Wilson and George L. Kelling, "Broken Windows," *The Atlantic* 249 (3) (March 1982):29–38.

3. Robert C. Trajanowicz and Denis W. Banas, *Perceptions of Safety: A Comparison of Foot Patrol versus Motor Patrol Officers* (East Lansing, MI: National Neighborhood Foot Patrol Center, School of Criminal Justice, Michigan State University, 1985). See also Lawrence W. Sherman, "Patrol Strategies for Police," in James Q. Wilson (ed.), *Crime and Public Policy* (San Francisco: ICS Press, 1983). And see M. Hough, "Thinking About Effectiveness," *British Journal of Criminology* 27(1987):1.

4. See Jerome S. Skolnick, *Justice without Trial: Law Enforcement in Democratic Society* (New York: John Wiley and Sons, 1966), esp. pp. 42–70. See also William A. Westley, *Violence and the Police* (Cambridge, MA: M.I.T. Press, 1970).

5. President's Commission on Law Enforcement and the Administration of Justice, *Task Force Report: Police* (Washington, DC: U. S. Government Printing Office, 1967) pp. 145–156. See also Geoffrey P. Alpert, *Policing Multi-ethnic Neighborhoods: The Miami Study and Findings for Law Enforcement in the United States* (New York: Greenwood Press, 1988).

6. For an excellent analysis of police/citizen encounters and the perceptions of the police regarding danger, real or imagined, see David H. Bayley and James Garofalo, "The Management of Violence by Police Patrol Officers," *Criminology* 27(19)(1989):1–25(1989).

7. James Q. Wilson, *Varieties of Police Behavior* (Cambridge, MA: Harvard University Press, 1968), pp. 25–26. Also see Jeffrey S. Slovak, *Styles of Urban Policing* (New York: New York University Press, 1986).

8. *Terry v. Ohio*, 392 U.S. 1 (1968).

9. Wayne R. LaFave, *Arrest: The Decision to Take a Suspect into Custody* (Boston: Little, Brown, 1965), pp. 61–226.

10. Ibid., pp. 83–101.

11. Ibid., pp. 102–124.

12. Ibid., pp. 125–143.

13. Joseph Goldstein, "Police Discretion Not to Invoke the Criminal Process: Low Visibility Decisions in the Administration of Justice," *Yale Law Journal* 69 (1960):143.

14. See Westley, op. cit., pp. 118–119. Also see Herman Goldstein, "Toward Community-Oriented Policing: Potential, Basic Requirements, and Threshold Questions," *Crime and Delinquency* 33 (1)(1987):6–30; S. L. Johnson, "Race and the Decision to

Detain a Suspect," *Yale Law Journal* 93 (2) (1983): 214–258; Donald Black, *The Manners and Customs of the Police* (New York: Academic Press, 1980); and D. Smith, "The Neighborhood Context of Police Behavior," in Albert Reiss and M. Tonry (eds.), *Communities and Crime* (Chicago: University of Chicago Press, 1986), pp. 351–387.

15. Paul M. Whisenand and R. Fred Ferguson, *The Managing of Police Organizations* (Englewood Cliffs, NJ: Prentice-Hall, 1973), pp. 199–201. See also Kenneth J. Matulia, *A Balance of Forces*, 2nd ed. (Gaithersburg, MD: International Association of Chiefs of Police, 1982); Gary Cordner, "Open and Closed Models of Police Organizations: Traditions, Dilemmas, and Practical Considerations," *Journal of Police Science and Administration* 6 (1978): 22–34; and Robert Langworthy, *The Structure of Police Organizations* (New York: Praeger, 1986).

16. Herman Goldstein, *Policing a Free Society* (Cambridge, MA: Ballinger, 1976), pp. 111–112. See also William K. Muir, *Police: Streetcorner Politicians* (Chicago: University of Chicago Press, 1977).

17. Geoffrey P. Alpert and Patrick R. Anderson, "The Most Deadly Force: Police Pursuits," *Justice Quarterly* 3 (1) (March, 1986): 1–14.

18. Ibid., p. 3.

19. California Highway Patrol, *California Highway Patrol Pursuit Study* (Sacramento: Department of the California Highway Patrol, 1983).

20. Alpert and Anderson, op. cit., p. 6.

21. Thomas Barker, "Rookie Police Officers' Perceptions of Police Occupational Deviance," *Police Studies* 6(1983): 30–38.

22. See *Time*, April 1, 1991, cover story and related stories, "Law and Disorder: Why Cops Turn Violent."

23. These cases are described in Richard Lacayo, "Law and Disorder," *Time*, April 1, 1991, pp. 19–20.

24. See for example Thomas Barker and David L. Carter, *Police Deviance* (Cincinnati, OH: Anderson, 1986), and Michael Brown, *Working the Street: Police Discretion and the Dilemmas of Reform* (New York: Russell Sage Foundation, 1981).

25. *Time*, April 1, 1991, p. 21.

26. *The Knapp Commission Report on Police Corruption* (New York: Braziller, 1972).

27. Ellwyn Stoddard, "Blue Coat Crime," in Carl Klockars (ed.), *Thinking About Police* (New York: McGraw-Hill, 1983), pp. 338–347.

28. Lawrence J. Sherman, *Police Corruption: A Sociological Perspective* (Garden City, NY: Doubleday, 1974).

29. See Barker, op. cit., pp. 30–38.

30. See Samuel G. Chapman, *Cops, Killers, and Staying Alive: The Murder of Police Officers in America* (Springfield, IL: Charles Thomas, 1986).

31. Lorie Fridell, "Justifiable Use of Measures in Research on Deadly Force," *Journal of Criminal Justice* 17(3)(1989): 157–165.

32. James J. Fyfe, "Who Shoots? A Look at Officer Race and Police Shooting," *Journal of Police Science and Administration* 9(1981): 367–382.

33. See James J. Fyfe, "Fleeing Felons and the Fourth Amendment," *Criminal Law Bulletin* 19(6)(1983): 525–528.

34. *Tennessee v. Garner*, 471 U.S. 1 (1985).

35. Susan E. Martin, "Women on the Move? A Report on the Status of Women in Policing," *Police Foundation Reports* (May 1989):1–8.

36. C. Sulton and R. Townsey, *A Progress Report of Women in Policing* (Washington, DC: Police Foundation, 1981).

37. James J. Fyfe, *Police Personnel Practices* (Washington, DC: International City Management Association, 1986).

38. See, for instance, Lawrence J. Sherman, "Evaluation of Policewomen on Patrol in a Suburban Police Department," *Journal of Police Science and Administration* 3(1975): 434–438. For a critique of research on women in policing see M. Morash and J. Greene, "Evaluating Women on Patrol: A Critique of Contemporary Wisdom," *Evaluation Review* 10(1986): 230–255.

39. Martin, op. cit., pp. 74–75.

40. Ibid., pp. 78–79.

41. Susan E. Martin, *Breaking and Entering: Policewomen on Patrol* (Berkeley: University of California Press, 1980).

SUGGESTED READINGS

Abrecht, M. E., and B. L. Stern. *Making of a Woman Cop.* New York: Morrow, 1976.

Chalken, Maroia, and Jan Chaiken. *Public Policing—Privately Provided.* Washington, DC: National Institute of Justice, 1987.

Finn, Peter. *Police Response to Special Populations.* Washington, DC: U.S. Department of Justice, 1987.

Fyfe, James J. *Readings on Police Use of Deadly Force.* Washington, DC: The Police Foundation, 1982.

Hartmann, Francis X. (ed.). *Debating the Evolution of American Policing.* Washington, DC: U.S. Department of Justice, November 1988.

Murano, Vincent. *Cop Hunter.* New York: Simon & Schuster, 1990.

Porter, Bruce, and Marvin Dunn. *The Miami Riot of 1980: Crossing the Bounds.* Lexington, MA: Lexington Books, 1984.

Shearing, Clifford, and Philip C. Stenning (eds.). *Private Policing.* Newbury Park, CA: Sage, 1987.

DISCUSSION QUESTIONS

1. How should police effectiveness be evaluated?

2. Explain what is meant by "the myth of full enforcement of the law."

3. How can police discretion be controlled?

4. Describe some unusual techniques used by police. Explain how they may be abused by police or may enhance police performance.

5. Describe various types of police misconduct and explain how it may be controlled.

6. Explain how police brutality can be curbed.

7. Describe various types of police corruption.

8. Discuss the emergence of women in policing.

The Courts

8

Jail, Pretrial Release, and Defense Lawyers

In 1990, Mayor Marion Barry of Washington, DC, was arrested in a police "sting" operation and charged with several offenses, including possession and use of narcotics. Undercover police had videotaped Mayor Barry and a former girlfriend using cocaine in a hotel room. Unlike many other people charged with the same offenses, Mayor Barry spent very little time in police custody or jail. His attorney gained release for him pending further actions.

The videotape was shown to the American public on network news programs. The mayor had apparently been caught in the act. For 8 weeks trial testimony and other evidence, including the damning videotape, alleging the Mayor's history of drug abuse was presented to a jury. But despite the widely held view that Barry was clearly guilty of the alleged crimes, the jury found him guilty of only one misdemeanor charge of drug possession, acquitted him of another misdemeanor drug count, and failed to reach a verdict on the remaining twelve counts, including the most serious charges. The judge declared a mistrial on those twelve counts.

The mayor's chief lawyer, R. Kenneth Mundy, said after the verdict, "We feel very lucky." Lucky or not, most legal observers agree that the mayor received extremely capable defense from Mundy and his associates.

Can a defense lawyer make the difference between a guilty and not guilty verdict? Sometimes. The recent novel and popular movie Presumed Innocent *dramatizes the charisma and ability of a successful defense lawyer. If you were arrested and charged with a crime, would you hire the best defense lawyer available? Could you? How would you pay the attorney? What would you do if you had no money, or property, or any other resources needed to secure the services of a high-powered defense attorney?*

ABOUT THIS CHAPTER

For the person arrested and brought into the criminal justice network, especially for the first time, entrance into the world of police lockups, court arraignment, and jail detention is frightening. The intimidating surroundings are alien to most of us. No comfort can be found by knowing other people in the same circumstances, nor in a growing familiarity with the routines of life behind bars or with the faces and attitudes of police officers, guards, fellow arrestees, judges, or bailiffs. Most people caught up in the criminal justice process are eager to get out of jail or prison and return home to family and friends. A phone call is a welcome opportunity to say to someone, "Get me out of here!"

Likewise, the person now in the arms of the law typically needs help—help to obtain release, help to cope with the police investigation, help in the process of bringing the event to a close. "I want a lawyer." That simple statement reveals the prisoner's feelings of fear and anxiety, and his or her need to lean on someone, to find comfort, advice, and solace from a knowledgeable professional. If you were brought before the criminal justice system, you too would want a lawyer.

This chapter explains how a person moves through the early stages of court processing after arrest, and covers the important decisions involving detention in jail, release, and the assistance of counsel.

Former Washington, DC,

Mayor, Marion Barry.

JAILS AND LOCKUPS

The jail may be the most misunderstood institution in the criminal justice system. "Jail" and "prison" are often thought of as synonymous terms by citizens who use them interchangeably (e.g., "He was sentenced to 5 years in jail"). Even those who should know better—newspaper columnists and politicians, for instance—confuse the terms. **Prisons** are state or federal institutions for the confinement of sentenced felons who have at least 1 year to serve; **jails** are local county or city institutions for the temporary detention of persons awaiting indictment, arraignment, trial, or sentencing, and for persons serving short-term misdemeanant sentences (less than 1 year). In some cases jails also hold material witnesses—that is, witnesses to a crime who might flee or move away before the trial if they are not detained—as well as parole violators awaiting return to prison. Also, especially in states where prison overcrowding is acute, persons sentenced to prison terms are sometimes held in local jails pending transfer to the prison system.

Jails are pervasive in our society. Virtually every city, county, and town in the United States has a facility for the confinement of arrested persons and the incarceration of misdemeanants. According to the *National Jail Census*, approximately 3500 jails exist in the United States. Most are small. Village and town jails often consist of no more than a few cells for locking up six to eight persons. On the other hand, major city jails have hundreds of large group cells (called bullpens) as well as individual cells. For instance, the Cook County jail in Chicago houses more than 5000 persons, more than all but one or two prisons in the United States. The 508 jails throughout the nation which house 100 or more inmates hold about 81 percent of all jail inmates in the United States.

Police stations have **lockups**, small holding cells, for the temporary detention of persons under investigation or being processed for their initial appearance before a magistrate. The holding cell seen on the popular television program *Barney Miller* is a typical example of a lockup in a police station. However, police lockups are usually separated from police offices, out of sight and sound of the police officers. Persons placed in lockup cells must be screened for medical or psychological problems which may threaten their own safety, and once locked up they should be visually monitored so as to prevent self-inflicted harm.

Jails, in the pure sense, are not correctional facilities, although nearly half the jail population in the United States is serving sentence rather than awaiting trial. Typically jails have little if any correctional capability in terms of counseling, recreation, libraries, vocational training, educational programs, and the like. Jails maximize secure confinement of the greatest number of inmates with the fewest possible detention personnel (guards). Because most jail inmates are awaiting trial, and are therefore presumed "innocent," correctional programs are inappropriate.

In most urban jurisdictions persons who are sentenced for misdemeanors are housed in separate local correctional facilities rather than in city of county jails. Often the only sentenced persons housed in the large "holding" jails are those "trusties," that is, privileged convicts, who are assigned to do various operational chores such as laundry, cleaning, and cooking.

The population in America's jails in recent years has grown to about 420,000 persons on any given day.[1] The national jail census reported the population on June 29, 1990, to be 405,320. But note that over *10 million* people are booked in and out of jail annually. (See Table 8.1.) This makes jail by far the most utilized incarceration facility of the criminal justice system. In comparison, there are about 800,000 prison inmates in the United States, slightly fewer than half of whom are released and replaced every year.

The average length of stay in jail is 11 days, but many persons will be confined for not much more than 24 hours, or until friends or relatives raise bail or make other release arrangements. This is especially true of police lockups, where release is often arranged prior to arraignment or transfer to jail.

A mixture of persons charged with violent and nonviolent crimes, or not charged at all, are housed in the jail or lockup. Table 8.2 demonstrates that mixture of people in

TABLE 8.1 *One-day count and average daily population of jail inmates for 1978, 1983, 1988, 1989, and 1990*

| | Number of jail inmates | | | | |
| | National jail census | | | Annual survey of jails | |
	1978	1983	1988	1989	1990
One-day count*					
All inmates	158,394	223,551	343,569	395,553	405,320
Adults	156,783	221,815	341,893	393,303	403,019
Male	147,506	206,163	311,594	356,050	365,821
Female	9,277	15,652	30,299	37,253	37,198
Juveniles†	1,611	1,736	1,676	2,250	2,301
Average daily population					
All inmates	157,930	227,541	336,017	386,845	408,075
Adults	156,190	225,781	334,566	384,954	405,935
Male	146,312	210,451	306,379	349,180	368,091
Female	9,878	15,330	28,187	35,774	37,844
Juveniles†	1,740	1,760	1,451	1,891	2,140

* Note: Data for 1-day counts are for February 15, 1978; June 30, 1983, 1988, and 1989; and June 29, 1990.
† Juveniles are persons defined by State statute as being under a certain age, usually 18, and subject initially to juvenile court authority even if tried as adults in criminal court. Because less than 1 percent of the jail population were juveniles, caution must be used in interpreting any changes over time.
SOURCE: Bureau of Justice Statistics, *Jail Inmates, 1990* (Washington, DC: U.S. Department of Justice, June 1991).

jail—those already convicted as well as those awaiting various stages in criminal justice processing. Although all the prisoners reside in the same facility, it is very important that a classification procedure be used to separate them so that predators cannot prey on victims.

Unfortunately, down through the years jails have been used as dumping grounds for every conceivable human problem. Drunks, vagrants, the homeless, the mentally ill, and prostitutes, as well as persons arrested for all types of felony offenses and for every type of misdemeanor as well, have found their ways to local jails. In virtually any large jail in the United States, especially on a weekend night, the booking area displays an intriguing variety of humanity. Jailers like to say that sooner or later everyone comes to the jail—lawyers, doctors, judges, ministers, teachers, students, laborers, young and old, rich and poor, members of every race, color, and creed. However, poor people generally contend that jails are built for them, and indeed most people in jail are poor, black, and young.

In the past police often used jailing as the ultimate exercise of their power. And even though most people taken to the jail are released on bail or their own recognizance almost immediately, for the police officer, placing a person in jail can serve as a kind of closure to an arrest ("Book'im, Dan-O!"), satisfying the officer's desire to "do something" about the offense in question. (See Field Practice A.)

Jails are typically operated under the authority of law enforcement officials, the chief of police for the city jail and the sheriff for the county jail. This has been the traditional arrangement, but in recent years some jails have been reorganized under a separate department of corrections. Sheriffs and police have been hesitant to relinquish control of jails because they generally do not relish having a separate governmental

TABLE 8.2 *The mix of jail populations*

	1989	1990
*Conviction status of adult jail inmates, by sex, 1989–1990**		
Total number of adults	393,303	403,019
Convicted	189,012	195,661
Male	171,181	177,619
Female	17,831	18,042
Unconvicted	204,291	207,358
Male	184,869	188,202
Female	19,422	19,156
Annual jail admissions and releases, by legal status and sex, 1989–1990†		
Total admissions	9,774,096	10,064,927
Adults	9,720,102	10,005,138
Male	8,606,700	8,894,706
Female	1,113,402	1,110,432
Juveniles[a]	53,994	59,789
Male	45,294	51,226
Female	8,700	8,563
Total releases	9,494,814	9,870,546
Adults	9,442,773	9,811,198
Male	8,367,519	8,723,872
Female	1,075,254	1,087,326
Juveniles[a]	52,041	59,348
Male	43,559	50,913
Female	8,482	8,435

* Note: Based on *Annual Survey of Jails*. Data are for June 30, 1989, and June 29, 1990. *Annual Survey of Jails* data may underestimate the number of convicted inmates and overestimate the number of unconvicted inmates. Some facility records do not distinguish inmates awaiting sentence (or other convicted persons) from unconvicted inmates. The 1989 *Survey of Inmates of Local Jails* figures indicate that 43 percent of the inmates were unconvicted and 57 percent were convicted.

† Note: Based on *Annual Survey of Jails*. Data are for years ending June 30, 1989, and June 29,1990.

[a] Juveniles are persons defined by State statute as being under a certain age, usually 18, and subject initially to juvenile court authority even if tried as adults in criminal court.

SOURCE: Bureau of Justice Statistics, *Jail Inmates, 1990* (Washington, DC: U.S. Department of Justice, June 1991).

agency controlling access to detention. Moreover, jails have been a source of revenue for law enforcement agencies, particularly for sheriff departments that operate their jails on a fee-per-inmate basis. In some jurisdictions a significant portion of a sheriff's budget is derived from jail operations. Jail inspectors are usually representatives of the state department of corrections; they attempt to "persuade" counties and cities to adopt minimum standards of care and staffing, but by and large jails operate in an autonomous fashion.

Jail

1: "Gotcha!"

At 2 a.m. in a small city police officers on routine patrol observed two young males passing items through a ground floor window of an apartment complex. When the officers approached, the two men dropped a television set and ran. The officers caught the two after a brief foot chase, determined that the apartment had been broken into illegally, and after the field investigation and notification of the detective division, took the two men to the jail and booked them.

2: Big Mouth

Police officers on routine patrol observed a car swerving erratically and conducted a routine traffic stop. The driver was asked to step out of the car and show identification and car registration, which he did. A passenger began to talk loudly to the officers, questioning their motives and the marital relationship of their parents, and generally harrassing them. The officers repeatedly instructed the passenger to be quiet and not to interfere with the performance of their duties. Finally, one officer threatened to take the passenger to jail if he did not stop interfering, and when he continued with his belligerence, the officer took him to jail and booked him for obstruction of justice.

3: Hooker Parade

The prosecuting attorney and chief of police in a city, under increasing pressure from downtown businesses to "do something" about street-walking prostitutes working in the vicinity of various stores and shops, agreed to a "street sweep" of prostitutes. A large contingent of police, complete with paddy wagons, arrested 30 young ladies and men dressed as ladies as they walked in the downtown area speaking to men on the sidewalk and in passing automobiles. They were taken to the jail and booked for soliciting for prostitution.

4: Passing Through

Police in a small rural town adjacent to a major highway observed a young male and female standing on the side of the road hitchhiking at 9 p.m. on a Friday night. The officers stopped to ask them where they were going and where they had come from. The couple stated that they were "just passing through" on their way to California. The officers asked for identification and the female could not produce any. The officers suspected that they were underage runaways, so they picked the pair up. After questioning, both young people admitted they had run away from home in a neighboring state. The officers notified their parents and the juvenile authorities in their home community and took them to jail to await transportation back.

5: Passing Out

Police responded to a call regarding a drunk and disorderly woman at a downtown tavern late in the afternoon. When they arrived, the officers found a woman who appeared to be approximately 60 years old arguing loudly with the barkeeper. When the officers asked about the nature of the disturbance, the barkeeper said the woman came into the bar a short time earlier, drank a couple of beers, and then began arguing with anyone in sight. The woman then cursed the officers and began to walk toward the door saying, "I'm going home." The officers stopped her and asked for identification. She refused. They then called for backup, finally subdued her, and transported her to the police lockup in a paddy wagon. Upon arrival at the lockup, the woman could not walk without assistance. She was carried to a cell and locked in. Two hours later, while on a periodic cell check, the guard found her hanging from the cell bars by panty hose she had tied around her neck. ∎

Most veteran prisoners will agree that jail time is much more difficult to serve than a prison sentence. While jail terms are usually shorter, typically the jails themselves are not equipped with outside recreation facilities, adequate activities to break the boredom, or adequate sanitary facilities. Jails are crowded, dirty, unsafe, and populated by an unstable mixture of felons, misdemeanants, drunks—often those considered the "dregs of society." By and large, jail inmates are unclassified by category and housed together, whereas prisons attempt to separate the aggressive from the weak prisoners, the "crazies" from the sane. And in comparison to jails, most prison facilities provide a great deal of stimulation in the form of hobby and craft activities, vocational training, educational opportunities, outdoor activities, movies, religious programs, and a great deal more. Visitor facilities in jails typically are dismal, crowded, and without privacy. In many jails visitors must talk though little speaker boxes in cellblock doors and peer through small, thick Plexiglas windows at the inmates they are visiting. By comparison to jails, spending time in a medium- or minimum-security prison is like spending a day at the beach.

Jails and lockups have alarmingly high rates of suicide. Whereas deaths by other causes are not as high among the jail population as they are among the general population, suicides in jail occur at a rate considerably higher than that of the general population.[2] Attempts to develop prediction scales and profiles of suicide-prone inmates have had limited utility.[3] The sad fact remains that conditions in detention facilities such as jails and lockups are poor and persons confined in them are unhappy indeed.

Violence and homosexual assaults are well-known problems in jails and lockups, although accurate statistics about them do not exist. Classification by prisoner types and constant surveillance by trained guards provide the best protection for people locked in group cells.

Holding a person in custody implies a responsibility to provide care for that person who, by virtue of being incarcerated, is no longer able to fully provide for his or her own needs. When the police agency arrests someone, even for the individual's own protection, the responsibility for that person's safety and health lies with the police. Therefore, in properly managed jails and lockups, medical screening is provided. Guards are trained to recognize threatening behavioral characteristics, policies require routine standards of care, and officers are trained and equipped to render aid quickly and expertly in any emergency.

For all these reasons, various national organizations have attempted to upgrade jail conditions by instituting accreditation procedures and by publishing minimum desirable standards. For decades, organizations such as the National Sheriffs' Association, the American Correctional Association, and the American Medical Association have published standards for the safe operation of jails that meet constitutional criteria. Still, jails remain the "poorhouse of the twentieth century,"[4] "brutal, cesspools of crime—institutions which serve to brutalize and embitter men to prevent them from returning to a useful role in society," "crucibles of crime."[5] Perhaps today they are

Newly appointed Essex County Jail Warden Geraldine Foushee with Newark Mayor Sharpe James and county Executive Thomas J. D'Alessio. Foushee is the first woman warden in New Jersey history.

better than they were during Colonial days or even earlier in this century. But in 1923 Joseph Fishman was still able to write the following imaginary statement made by a judge to a person he is sentencing to jail:

> I not only sentence you to confinement for thirty days in a bare, narrow cell in a gloomy building, during which time you will be deprived of your family, friends, occupation, earning power, and all other human liberties and privileges; but in addition I sentence you to wallow in a putrid mire demoralizing to body, mind and soul, where every rule of civilization is violated, where you are given every opportunity to deteriorate, but none to improve, and where your tendency to wrong-doing cannot be corrected, but only aggravated.[6]

PRETRIAL RELEASE OR DETENTION

When the police bring a person they have arrested to jail, for booking, the suspect is taken before a magistrate for an **initial appearance**, usually within 24 hours of arrest. This is the first time the suspect appears in court. Sometime during this same 24-hour period the case materials are turned over to the prosecutor for the consideration of formal charges. At this point in the criminal justice process, the police task is done. Of course the officers may be required to testify later at a trial, if the case goes that far, but in the majority of instances the police role is over after this initial appearance before a magistrate.

At the initial appearance several matters are resolved. First, the defendant is informed of the arrest charges, often by the reading of the complaint, although he or she is not asked to plead to them. Second, the defendant is again informed of his or her Constitutional rights, including those that pertain to self-incrimination and legal representation. Third, an attorney is assigned to indigent defendants, if they desired one, or the public defender's office is officially notified that the case will proceed to trial.

But the fourth issue resolved, and the one that most immediately affects the person in police custody and charged with a crime, is decided by the judge—that is, whether to release the individual pending further processing, or to detain the individual in jail pending further processing. This step is often called, in shorthand, "bail or jail," and the judge's decision depends on many factors. Police have arrested the person on evidence of criminal behavior. The person may even have been caught in the act of committing the crime. And the prosecutor has stated the intention to prosecute, to secure a conviction either through a guilty plea or a trial. Is it safe to allow the accused to remain in the community at large? What was the nature of the crime? What is in the best interests of the accused? If the judge allows the individual to go free pending further processing, it is known as **pretrial release**. If the judge does *not* allow it, pretrial release has been denied. The following sections discuss in more detail pretrial release and the occasional reasons for denying it.

Pretrial Release: Alternative Methods

Several pretrial release options are used by the courts today making most defendants, regardless of economic status, eligible for release pending trial. (See Fig. 8.1.) Of course, the most commonly known method for pretrial release is **bail**, an amount of money the posting of which a judge deems necessary for pretrial release. The bail money is posted to assure the defendant's later appearance at trial.

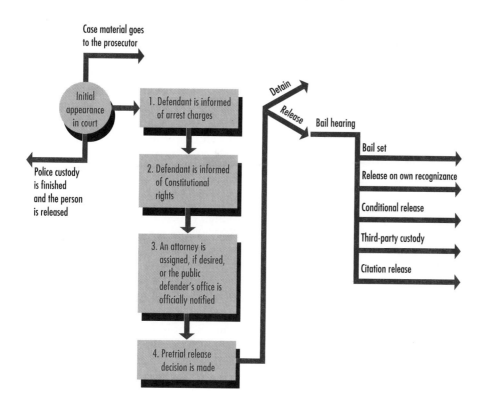

FIGURE 8.1

Pretrial release or detention.

Four different types of money bail (or bond, as it is sometimes called) are used: (1) **fully secured bail**, in which the defendant must post the full amount of bail with the court; (2) **privately secured bail**, in which a bail bondsman signs a promissory note for the full amount for the defendant in exchange for a fee of 10 percent of the full amount and some collateral in addition; (3) **deposit bail**, in which the court allows the defendant to post 10 percent of the full amount with the court, which is usually refunded when the defendant appears for trial (the full amount is due if the defendant does not show); and (4) **unsecured bail**, in which the defendant pays no money to the court but is liable for the full amount of bail if he or she fails to appear for trial.

In addition to financial bail, alternative release options exist including (1) **release on recognizance (ROR)**, in which the defendant is released on the promise to appear for trial; (2) **conditional release**, in which the court releases the defendant with specific requirements, such as that he or she attend a drug rehabilitation program or meet some other special condition; (3) **third-party custody**, in which the defendant is released into the custody of another individual or agency on the promise that his or her later appearance will be assured; and (4) **citation release**, in which the arresting officer grants the defendant a release through a written order, or citation, for his or her first court appearance.[7]

Pretrial Release: Bail

Where did pretrial release originate? Bail has roots in the British tradition of **surety**, whereby accused persons were required to place some real property as collateral against their failure to appear at a future trial. In the American experience, the drafters of the U.S. Constitution retained the concept of bail, reacting only against the European practice of setting extreme bail on poor defendants, stating that "excessive

211

bail shall not be required" (see the discussion of the Eighth Amendment in the section Right to Bail later on in this chapter). Prior to the modern era, such a system of placing a surety to guarantee later appearance had greater importance, since defendants could easily "disappear" by departing the jurisdiction involved. Today, however, the ability of the agencies of the criminal justice system to track down and reapprehend offenders, has diminished the possibilities of such successful absconding.

The imposition of money bail in this century has resulted in a burgeoning private business operated by **bail bondsmen**, who for a fee (about 10 percent of the amount of the bail, as noted earlier) will secure and post the surety bond that allows the suspect to be released. The bondsman assumes responsibility for the person's later appearance at court and keeps the 10 percent fee.

All forms of discrimination, racial and otherwise, can be and have been practiced by bondsmen, who have total discretion as to their choice of clients. Greedy practices of bail bondsmen have been the focus of much of the criticism directed at the bail system, resulting in much of the reform in the bail system that has occurred. A bondsman, for instance, is not required to post bond even if the defendant can pay the 10 percent. Furthermore, bail bondsmen have literally unchecked power to pursue and apprehend bail jumpers, and can disregard all the Constitutional protections that criminal justice agency personnel must honor, including those disallowing the kidnapping and transportation of individuals without extradition. While our courts have imposed strict rules about how evidence can be obtained, there are no questions asked about how bail-jumpers are found. Former Supreme Court Justice Arthur Goldberg stated that the bail system "at best . . . is a system of checkbook justice; at worst, a highly commercialized racket."[8]

The traditional purpose of bail has been to assure the later appearance of defendants at trial, that is, to prevent or discourage flight. This implies that bail should only

Bail bondsmen are available anytime day or night to help people in jail get out on bail, for a fee.

be set at an amount necessary to achieve this purpose. In **Stack v. Boyle** (1951), a landmark Supreme Court decision that reaffirmed the traditional right to freedom before conviction, the Court considered the case of several defendants charged with offenses which carried maximum penalties of not more than a $10,000 fine or more than 5 years in prison. Their bail had been set at $50,000 each. The government argued that previous defendants, charged with similar offenses, had jumped bail set at lower amounts, so that the higher bail in *Stack* was needed to assure the defendants would remain around—in jail—until trial. The Supreme Court disagreed. Justice Felix Frankfurter, joining in the majority decision, stated:

> The practice of admission to bail, as it has evolved in Anglo-American law, is *not a device for keeping persons in jail* upon mere accusation until it is found convenient to give them trial. On the contrary, the spirit of the procedure is *to enable them to stay out of jail until a trial* has found them guilty. Without this conditional privilege, even those wrongly accused are punished by a period of imprisonment while awaiting trial. . . . Thus, the amount is said to have been fixed not as a reasonable assurance of their presence at the trial, but also as an assurance they would remain in jail . . . it is contrary to the whole policy and philosophy of bail.[9] [emphasis added]

Although the primary purpose of bail is to prevent flight by setting the amount so high that it would be excessively costly to abscond, there is another motivation, particularly in setting bail so high as to block release: that is, to protect the community from further crimes by defendants while they are awaiting trial. At best, however, this is a secondary purpose of bail. Constitutional purists continually reiterate that the traditional reason for bail is the only one—to assure later court appearances. Crime prevention or witness intimidation is not within the scope of bail objectives.

Some magistrates use the bail decision itself as punishment. Judges sometimes set very high bail for alleged drug dealers, knowing full well that upon release the suspect will travel directly to the closest international airport and leave for a foreign country, never to be seen or heard from again; nevertheless, the offender has been "punished" since the government keeps the bail money. And, of couse, setting bail high enough so that a defendant cannot meet it means the accused does jail time *even before trial.* In this way, accused persons whom a magistrate is convinced are guilty but perhaps not convictable by trial standards can be punished before their guilt or innocence is formally determined.

Economic Discrimination and Bail

Whenever and wherever money becomes a factor in criminal justice processing, as it does in the determination of bail and the assessment of fines, the result is obvious discrimination against the poor. And in our system of criminal justice, dealing as it does with ordinary street crime, the fact is that most suspects and defendants are poor. Many, if not most, suspects cannot even afford to pay a bail bondsman a hundred dollars. Lacking access to this amount, or any dollar figure over it, thus means pretrial detention is the fate of perhaps 85 percent of all accused felons and a high proportion of misdemeanants, too.[10] Table 8.3 demonstrates the variations in the probability of posting bail based on the defendant's bail amount, income, stability, race, sex, and age.

Money bail has been criticized for being contradictory to the "equal protection" clause of the Constitution and a violation of the principle of fundamental fairness. Reforms affecting defendants charged in federal courts were made in the Bail Reform Act of 1966 and the District of Columbia Bail Agency Act. Also, changes in Rule 46

Running Box: Bail and the Public's Right to Safety

In cases where public safety is at risk, a high bail may be set to ensure a defendant will be jailed before trial. This appears to have been the situation for Roger A. Koney, who was held on a $100,000 bail. Koney, a 27-year-old electrical engineer, was held in the Essex County House of Correction in Massachusetts, awaiting trail on vehicular homicide charges stemming from the death of Salvatore Reale, Jr., on September 15, 1991. Reale was killed stepping out of his pickup truck as Koney sped down the wrong side of the street. Koney was drunk at the time, the police said. But the police also learned that he had eight previous convictions for drunken driving and nineteen other serious vehicular offenses.

Bail was set at $3 million for Edward Savitz, nicknamed "Uncle Ed," when he was arraigned in 1992 in Philadelphia on charges of sexual abuse, including sexual abuse of children. Savitz was an AIDS patient who allegedly had sex with a large number of young boys. He was released when his brother posted $300,000 cash bond, but shortly thereafter, he was arrested again on seven new charges involving sex with boys. This time bail was set at $20 million, a figure too high for Savitz to arrange release.

On March 26, 1992, after heavyweight boxer Mike Tyson was convicted of rape and his lawyers announced their intention to appeal the conviction, Judge Patricia Gifford refused to release Tyson on any amount of bail pending his appeal. Judge Gifford based her decision on her belief that Tyson did not understand the seriousness of his crime and was capable of committing it again. She stated, "As to whether you are capable of committing this crime again, quite honestly I am of the opinion that you are." At sentencing, Tyson had pled for leniency, saying, "I haven't hurt nobody. Nobody has a black eye or broken ribs. When I'm in the ring I break jaws. To me, that's hurting someone."

These three cases demonstrate how judges sometimes require very high bail, or refuse bail altogether, when the public safety is threatened by a person's release. The pure

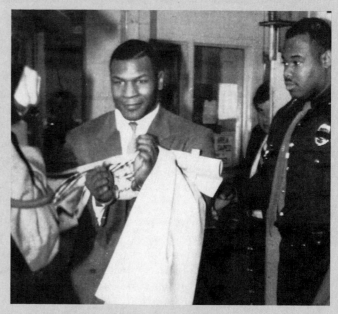

Boxer Mike Tyson on his way to prison in Indianapolis after Judge Patricia Gifford rejected his lawyer's request for his release on bail pending appeal. Tyson was sentenced to begin serving six years in prison for rape and deviate conduct.

function of bail, to make sure a person appears for later court hearings, would be accomplished by granting release on bail in these three cases, no doubt. But, the apparent inability of the court to keep Koney off of the road and Savitz away from boys, as well as to protect other women from Tyson's failure to appreciate the physical harm of rape, evidently led the judges to use high bail, or the refusal of bail altogether, as a means of keeping them off of the streets.

SOURCES: Fox Butterfield, "Drunks Who Drive and Kill: A Problem Personified," *New York Times,* October 29, 1991; Philly Sex Abuse Suspect Held on $20 Million Bail," *The Star-Ledger,* March 30, 1992, p. 2; "Tyson Draws 6-year Term, Ordered Jailed," *The Star-Ledger,* March 27, 1992.

TABLE 8.3 *Felony defendants released before or detained until case disposition, by original bail amount set and the most serious arrest charge, 1988**

Original bail amount set and most serious arrest charge	Felony defendants in the 75 largest counties with an original bail amount set					
	Number of defendants	Total, %	Percent detained until case disposition	Percent released before case disposition		
				Total released, %	Financial release	Nonfinancial release
$20,000 or more						
All offenses	8415	100	68	32	28	3
Violent offenses	1197	100	74	26	23	3
Property offenses	3678	100	76	24	22	2
Drug offenses	2738	100	53	47	42	5
Public-order offenses	802	100	68	32	32	0
$10,000 to $19,999						
All offenses	5057	100	61	39	32	7
Violent offenses	767	100	63	37	34	3
Property offenses	1707	100	73	27	21	6
Drug offenses	2248	100	50	50	41	9
Public-order offenses	335	100	43	57	53	4
$5,000 to $9,999						
All offenses	6166	100	45	55	43	12
Violent offenses	1175	100	40	60	56	4
Property offenses	2072	100	53	47	33	14
Drug offenses	2486	100	41	59	45	14
Public-order offenses	433	100	43	57	49	8
$2,500 to $4,999						
All offenses	3849	100	28	72	54	18
Violent offenses	1069	100	19	81	70	11
Property offenses	1206	100	40	60	41	19
Drug offenses	1388	100	23	77	57	20
Public-order offenses	186	100	25	75	54	21
Under $2,500						
All offenses	3417	100	22	78	65	13
Violent offenses	1522	100	15	85	77	8
Property offenses	806	100	29	71	58	13
Drug offenses	906	100	15	85	70	15
Public-order offenses	184	100	25	75	67	8

* Note: Data on both original bail amount set and detention-release outcome were available for 92 percent of all cases. Table includes only released defendants for whom a bail amount was originally set. The actual amount required to secure release was usually 10 percent of the original bail amount if release was on surety or deposit bond and 100 percent of the original bail amount if release was on full cash bond. Detail may not add to total because of rounding.
Source: Bureau of Justice Statistics, *Pretrial Release of Felony Defendants, 1988* (Washington, DC: U.S. Department of Justice, February 1991).

("Release on Bail") of the Federal Rules of Criminal Procedure promoted the position that *pretrial release is preferred*, that alternatives to money bail must be developed, and that pretrial detention is to be reserved for uncommon cases.

The primary inequity in the money bail process is that poor people are detained for failing to have money or property to put up as collateral and that rich people are easily and routinely released without hardship. This inequity was addressed in 1961 in *Bandy v. Chambers*, in which Justice William O. Douglas considered the question of whether an indigent person should be denied freedom in cases in which a wealthy person would be allowed to go free, simply because the poor person lacks property or money. Justice Douglas concluded that no person should be denied release purely because of indigence and that people should be released on personal recognizance if other considerations support the likelihood that they will return for trial.[11]

Release on Own Recognizance

Most persons released prior to trial are not arrested for new crimes while awaiting trial. And the adverse effects of pretrial detention on the outcomes of defendants' trials have been frequently noted in research. Between the years of 1954 and 1957, the **Vera Institute** (a privately financed nonprofit foundation for the improvement of criminal justice) conducted studies of bail practices in Philadelphia.[12] These studies showed that only 18 percent of persons jailed pending trial because they could not afford bail were acquitted, whereas 48 percent of persons released on bail were acquitted. Further, detained persons received prison sentences two and a half times as frequently as released persons, and released defendants received suspended sentences four times as frequently as jailed defendants.

As a followup to the Philadelphia studies, the Vera Institute created an experimental pretrial release program in New York City in the 1960s, known as the **Manhattan Bail Project**.[13] Vera staff investigated indigent arrested persons in regard to their ties to the community (such as length of residence and employment, and family relationships) as indicators of who would not abscond if released after their initial appearances. Based on that information, Vera personnel then convinced magistrates to consider releasing accused persons on their own promise to return for later proceedings if they could not meet monetary bail. The project was remarkably successful in that the rate of return for ROR releasees was consistently equal to or better than the return rate for those on monetary bail.

ROR programs based on the Vera model spread across the nation, and are now found not only in most large jurisdictions in the United States but around the world wherever bail procedures are used. Recognizance release is one of the most widespread modern reforms in criminal justice. It is remarkable that it was instigated from outside the system by a private foundation rather than by agencies within the criminal justice system itself. (For examples of ROR, see Field Practice B.)

The success of the Manhattan Bail Project also led to the introduction of other types of pretrial release. For instance, the New York City Police Department (and many other police departments since this began) instituted a process called **stationhouse release**, in which some suspects are issued citations (something like traffic tickets) to appear in court at a later date, thereby bypassing both formal, in-custody release and the need for an initial appearance. This too has worked well as a way of allowing more suspects to remain in the community until court determinations can be made about their guilt or innocence.

After the results of the Manhattan Bail Project were published, the prevailing view became that release of defendants prior to trial should be available, regardless of financial circumstances, unless overwhelming factors preclude it, and legislation has been passed on both state and federal levels implementing the practice.

ROR

1: Down and Out

An 18-year-old girl arrested for shoplifting requested release on recognizance, claiming to be indigent. A field investigation showed that she lived with an unemployed boyfriend, had no steady employment, had dropped out of school in the eleventh grade, and was indeed indigent. She had one prior arrest for shoplifting but the charges had been dismissed for reasons not known. On her prior arrest she had posted a bail of $200 and this was returned when the charges were dropped. The ROR investigator recommended pretrial release but the judge remanded her to the municipal jail to await arraignment.

2: Con Artist

A 40-year-old male was arrested for fraud and forgery. He was accused of posing as a representative of a roofing company, talking some homeowners into ordering new roofing from a fictitious firm and forging a false name to endorse their initial deposit checks. Actually, he was employed half-time as a car salesman, lived in his own home with his wife and three young children, and had one prior conviction for drunk and disorderly behavior, resulting in a fine of $75, which he had paid. An ROR investigation showed him to be unable to post bail without undue hardship to his family. He was a lifelong resident of the city and was well thought of by the car dealer for whom he worked. The magistrate granted pretrial release on recognizance.

3: Slugger

A 20-year-old male accused of mugging an elderly man (robbery in the third degree) requested ROR. An investigation showed that he was employed full time as a movie usher, that he lived with his parents rent-free, and that he had no prior record as an adult. He had been judged delinquent because of chronic truancy when he was 13 years old and had spent one school year in a foster home. Based on residence, employment, and community ties, the field investigator recommended ROR. The magistrate, however, set bail at $5,000, which the defendant could not provide. He was sent to jail to await indictment and arraignment. ∎

Pretrial Release, the Presumption of Innocence, and Community Safety

Pretrial release does not rest on a presumption of innocence. The obviously guilty as well as those who insist on their innocence both have access to it. But the effect of it—whether achieved by bail or other means—may well be to preserve that presumption, even though such a result is neither the formal purpose of release nor the intent of most judges in making their release decisions.

The majority of defendants released on monetary bail or on ROR return for later proceedings without further incident. However, some arrested persons who are dangerous professional criminals might indeed commit additional crimes while on pretrial release. This presents the system with a dilemma: should a greater emphasis be placed on crime control (community protection) or on individual rights (due process)?

This issue, not surprisingly, finds the conservative crime control model and the liberal due process model of criminal justice on opposite sides of the argument. It is those views we will now describe.[14]

The Conservative Crime Control View

Although the importance of pretrial release to the defendant is clear, according to conservatives, the need for community protection from possible depraved behavior by bailed offenders is a very real concern. Herman Goldstein has presented the problem in the case described in Field Practice C.[15] Frank Wallace's case is exactly the kind of example that has stirred community demands for stricter pretrial release procedures.

The Frank Wallace Case

Frank Wallace was, at the age of 19, convicted of rape and sentenced to the Illinois State Penitentiary for 3 years. Approximately 1 year after his release, he became the prime suspect in a wave of robberies of pensioners. The police learned that a number of old men had been robbed and threatened with bodily harm if they filed complaints. Detectives identified one of the victims and obtained sufficient information from him to identify Wallace as the perpetrator of these crimes. A warrant was signed and Wallace was arrested and charged with robbery. Shortly after his initial appearance when he was released on bail, Wallace broke into the apartment of the 71-year-old man, beat him

about his head, kicked him numerous times, and left him unconscious. He then ransacked the apartment, taking approximately $3000 and a .38 caliber revolver. The victim required seven stitches in his head and suffered a concussion.

Wallace was identified by the victim and quickly apprehended. He acted arrogantly toward the arresting officers, threatening to shoot them on sight after his release, and boasting that he would be back on the street immediately after his appearance in court. Most of the money and the revolver were found on his person. While in custody, he was identified by another pensioner as having robbed him also and threatening him

with bodily harm if he complained to the police. He was indicted on two counts of robbery and released on bail of $1500. Upon his release, Wallace returned to the home of the first victim and again assaulted him in an effort to dissuade him from testifying. He was again apprehended and charged with aggravated battery. Bail of $50,000 was set at the initial appearance and the case scheduled for the grand jury within 12 days. On the scheduled date, a request for continuance was granted and the amount of bail was reduced to $5,000—enabling Wallace once more to be released. ■

Studies have shown that 16 percent of all suspects released prior to trial are rearrested, and that 30 percent of those rearrested are rearrested more than once. About half of those rearrested defendants are later convicted.[16] Conservatives argue that these statistics, along with well-publicized crimes committed by defendants released on bail,[17] show the need for changes in pretrial release practices to better protect communities from offenders.

Concern over these problems has generated a number of new **preventive detention** programs aimed at keeping suspects in custody who might commit crimes while on pretrial release. Probably the best-known preventive detention program was developed in Washington, DC, in 1971 and revised in 1973.[18] The DC Code, in common with all similar preventive detention legislation, provides for a special hearing to determine whether the individual fits the criteria specified in the Code for implementing preventive detention. At this hearing, the defendant can be represented by counsel.

In general, preventive detention criteria specify that the individual must be indicted for a violent or "dangerous crime" and have at least one prior conviction (usually within a specified period of time, such as 10 years) for a similar crime, and that the current crime must have been committed while the individual was on bail or some other form of community release, such as probation or parole. Since the criteria invoked for preventive detention include factors other than just the likelihood of reappearance at trial, there has always been some question about the Constitutionality of laws. In a 1974 case in the District of Columbia, the Court of Appeals upheld the use of preventive detention in a case involving a defendant indicted for assault with a deadly weapon who was on parole for an earlier robbery and had an extensive record of dangerous and violent crimes extending over a 22-year period. Furthermore, while on bail the defendant had several times threatened the complainant in the current assault case. Under these conditions the Court of Appeals held that the appellant was lawfully detained under the preventive detention provision of the DC Code.[19]

At the very least, according to conservatives, preventive detention appears to offer a partial solution to the crime problem by keeping known offenders off the streets by refusing to grant them release on bail.

The Liberal Due Process View

According to liberals, pretrial detention is a dismal failure. The truth is that we are unable to predict with any certainty who is likely to commit crimes while on pretrial release and who is not. And additionally, they argue, there are major purposes served by pretrial release: allowing the accused to continue with his or her normal activities, including work and family support, as well as allowing the defendant to help prepare a defense to the charges. Irving J. Klein[20] provides the following illustration of the importance of pretrial release to defendants (who, it should be remembered, are always presumed innocent until their guilt has been established through legal proceedings):

> The reader should imagine him/herself as being arrested for a robbery committed several days before the arrest. Let us further imagine that the reader is innocent and at the time of the robbery was in a crowded bar located on the other side of town from the robbery location, imbibing in some spirits with some newfound acquaintances of the night. The reader is processed in the usual police procedure and comes before a magistrate who is determined that no robbers will be tolerated in his/her town. Bail is fixed at $25,000 and you do not have more than $50 to your name and on your person; you have no friends or relatives who have any assets that can be used as

TABLE 8.4 *Sentencing outcome for convicted defendants, by whether released or detained and the most serious original felony arrest charge, 1988**

Detention-release outcome and most serious original felony arrest charge	Defendants convicted in the 75 largest counties					
	Number of defendants	Total, %	Percent sentenced to incarceration			Percent not sentenced to incarceration
			Total	Prison	Jail†	
Released defendants						
All offenses	13,703	100	50	21	29	50
Violent offenses	1,991	100	61	28	33	39
Property offenses	5,204	100	44	18	26	56
Drug offenses	5,019	100	53	23	29	47
Public-order offenses	1,488	100	47	19	28	53
Detained defendants						
All offenses	10,729	100	83	46	37	17
Violent offenses	2,388	100	89	59	30	11
Property offenses	4,550	100	80	44	36	20
Drug offenses	3,031	100	84	40	44	16
Public-order offenses	760	100	84	42	42	16

* Note: Information on sentencing outcomes was available for 88 percent of all cases that had been adjudicated at the end of 1 year. Details may not add to total because of rounding.
† Includes sentences that also involved probation.
SOURCE: Bureau of Justice Statistics, *Pretrial Release of Felony Defendants, 1988* (Washington, DC: U.S. Department of Justice, February 1991).

BOX 8.1

Pretrial Release

THE CONSERVATIVE CRIME CONTROL VIEW Conservatives believe that:

Community protection from people released on bail is most important.

Keep known offenders off the streets by denying them release on bail.

Preventive detention is an important factor in helping to control crime.

THE LIBERAL CRIME CONTROL VIEW Liberals believe that:

A person is presumed innocent prior to being found guilty in court.

We cannot predict with any accuracy who is likely to commit crimes while on pretrial release and who is not.

Pretrial detention costs too much, adversely affects the defendant's family, makes it difficult for defendants to participate in the preparation of their defense, and often results in more severe sentences than pretrial release.

collateral for your bail. A lawyer is assigned to defend you and you protest that you are innocent. The lawyer asks you if you have any witnesses and you answer that if you could only get out of jail, you could locate some of the people who were at the bar on the night of the robbery who would testify that you were at the bar with them when the robbery took place.[20]

In addition to the fact that pretrial detention makes it difficult for the accused to contribute to a defense, or to continue with important aspects of his or her personal life, liberals point to other clear disadvantages of pretrial detention: the financial burden on society to maintain jails for this purpose; all the costs of the loss of liberty, including the appalling conditions in many jails, which threaten the life and limb of the detainee; and the impact on the family of the detained person.

And as mentioned earlier, yet another important consequence of pretrial detention is the fact that the outcomes of trials appear to be affected adversely by it. Detained suspects are found guilty more often than those released, and their sentences are harsher and for longer periods of time. Table 8.4 demonstrates how sentences vary according to whether a defendant has been held in jail under pretrial detention, or allowed to go home under pretrial release. Clearly defendants brought directly from jail receive longer sentences, on average, than releasees, although it is unclear to what extent the factor of pretrial release or detention was the direct cause of the discrepancies in sentencing.

The conservative and liberal positions are summarized in Box 8.1.

RIGHT TO BAIL

Do we have a Constitutional right to pretrial release? To make bail if we can? Although the Constitution does not guarantee the *right* to bail, the **Eighth Amendment** to the United States Constitution states that "Excessive bail shall not be required. . . ." What is excessive? Is the $2 million bail excessive in the "wise guy" case described in Field Practice D:1? For most of us a $1000 bail would be possible to raise, we could call family or friends for help if the amount was beyond our own means. But what about extremely poor, unemployed, friendless defendants?

Although the U.S. Supreme Court has never held that the Fourteenth Amendment requirements of "due process of law" and "equal protection of the laws" make the "excessive bail" clause applicable to the states, inclusion of the key word "excessive" has had the practical effect of establishing a right to pretrial release on *reasonable* bail that has been generally acknowledged.[21] On the other hand, over the years, the Supreme Court has allowed states to define certain crimes, usually capital offenses such as murder and treason, as "nonbailable" at the discretion of the magistrate, so that most states have developed a list of nonbailable charges. And in 1987 the U.S. Supreme Court ruled in **United States v. Salerno** that no absolute right to bail exists under the Eighth Amendment.[22]

Then, in 1984 the Bail Reform Act was signed into law. This dramatically changed the process of granting pretrial release, so that it must be considered in more detail.

The Bail Reform Act of 1984

After considerable consternation over the perceived problem of crimes committed by persons free on bail, the U.S. Congress in 1984 passed legislation supported by the Reagan Administration allowing broad preventive detention of persons perceived

Bail

1: Wise Guy

A defendant, reputed to be a "leader of organized crime," was arrested on a charge of conspiracy to "fix" a state lottery. At the initial appearance the magistrate set bail at $2 million, noting as he did so the gangster reputation of the defendant. Most conspiracy charges of crimes less than homicide elicited bail amounts ranging from $500 to $10,000. The defendant appealed and subsequently a higher court held the bail to be excessive and reduced it to $50,000, still higher than average. The defendant deposited the full amount in cash and left the courtroom.

2: Daddy's Home

A defendant accused of incestuous relations with his 9-year-old daughter, upon the complaint of his wife, had his bail set at $10,000. Through a bail bondsman he provided the appropriate collateral and was released pending further proceedings.

3: Nobody's Home

An 18-year-old male accused of murdering his entire family (both parents and two sisters) with a .22 caliber rifle was denied bail at the initial appearance. He was remanded to jail and later moved to a hospital for the criminally insane for psychiatric evaluation at the request of the prosecutor. ∎

to "pose a threat to individuals or to the community."[23] The **Bail Reform Act of 1984** established that at the federal level a detention hearing must be held before a judge to determine whether an arrested person is to be released or detained pending trial (likewise a hearing must be held to determine whether a person awaiting the imposition of a sentence pending appeal of conviction or sentence is to be released or detained; for a discussion of this topic, see the next section). The defendant awaiting trial may be released on personal recognizance (ROR), also referred to as an "unsecured appearance bond," or on "condition or combination of conditions," unless the judicial officer in charge decides the release will pose a threat to an individual or the community.

The Bail Reform Act of 1984 is a major departure from the traditionally held view that the purpose of bail is to permit pretrial release. The act provides for an adversarial hearing in which the attorney for the government petitions for pretrial detention. The accused has the right to counsel, the opportunity to present evidence and testify, and the right to cross-examine hostile witnesses. A decision to detain requires "clear and convincing evidence" that an accused person will fail to appear at future trial. A decision to grant pretrial release must be based on several considerations, including the seriousness of the crime, the weight of evidence, the personal background and characteristics of the defendant, and, importantly, the nature and seriousness of the dangers to other individuals or the community that release might entail.

The Bail Reform Act of 1984 has had the effect of institutionalizing a practice utilized in some jurisdictions for some time. It involves defendants being detained for perceived "dangerousness" by setting unattainable bail levels or by denying bail altogether. The Constitutionality of the act was upheld in 1987 in the case mentioned earlier, *United States v. Salerno*, in which defendants reputed to be high-ranking organized crime figures were detained pending trial by a judge who held that their release would result in the defendants continuing "business as usual," including murder and other acts of violence. The defendants argued that such a law "authorizes punishment before trial," but Chief Justice Rehnquist, speaking for the Supreme Court majority, noted that the Congressional intent of the legislation was regulatory, not punitive, and that the pretrial detention provision was sufficiently narrow and demanding in regard to procedural safeguards. Rehnquist wrote:

When the government, proves by clear and convincing evidence that an arrestee presents an identified and articulable threat to an individual or the community, we believe that, consistent with the Due Process Clause, a court may disable the arrestee from executing that threat.[24]

In upholding the act against an Eighth Amendment challenge, Rehnquist further wrote:

When Congress has mandated detention on the basis of a compelling interest other than prevention of flight, as it does here, the Eighth Amendment does not require release on bail.[25]

Justices Marshall and Brennan, in their dissenting opinion, called the statute "an abhorrent limitation of the presumption of innocence."[26]

Although the Bail Reform Act of 1984 and the *Salerno* decision deal with pretrial detention decisions in federal jurisdictions, they also affect the Constitutional validity of state legislation relating to the topic. The evolution of law in this regard is clear. Under the Bail Reform Act of 1966, a defendant in federal court was *entitled to bail* "unless the court or judge has reason to believe that no one or more conditions of release will reasonably assure that the person will not flee, or pose a danger to any other person or any other community." The Bail Reform Act of 1984 *reversed* that presumption of entitlement. Now the defendant has the burden of proving an entitlement to release on bail based on the criteria of the Act.

Release Pending Appeal

After conviction, if defense counsel files notice of appeal of the conviction, the question arises once again as to whether or not the defendant should be granted

General Manuel Noriega was held in jail without bail prior to and during his trial on drug trafficking charges in Miami.

freedom pending the outcome of the appeal. The same types of release already discussed are generally available to persons so situated, but before granting bail the Bail Reform Act of 1984 mandates that the court must determine the following:

1. The defendant is not likely to flee or pose a danger to the safety of any other person or the community if released.
2. The appeal is not merely for the purpose of delay in serving sentence.
3. The appeal raises a substantial question of law or fact.
4. If that substantial question is determined favorable to the defendant on appeal, that decision is likely to result in reversal or an order for a new trial on all counts for which imprisonment has been imposed.[27]

See Box 8.2 for a summary of the important court decisions relating to bail.

DEFENSE LAWYERS

The **Sixth Amendment** to the United States Constitution states in part, "In all criminal prosecutions, the accused shall enjoy the right . . . to have the Assistance of Counsel for his defence." Lawyers have always been available for those defendants who have the money and resources to employ them, but for much of the history of the United States, lawyers have not been available to poor people. Today, due to U.S. Supreme Court decisions in the 1960s, that has changed. Everyone, rich or poor, is entitled to be defended by a defense attorney when charges are brought against him or her, and if the individual cannot pay to hire an attorney, the state must provide one free of charge.

The Role of the Defense Lawyer

As soon as a person is arrested he or she needs a defense attorney. As a matter of fact, even the most seasoned offender, accustomed to the maze of decisions about to be made and familiar with the language of criminal justice, turns to a defense attorney as quickly as possible. If such a need does not immediately come to mind, the police routinely remind the suspect that "you have a right to an attorney. . . ." And the role of the defense attorney begins almost as soon as an arrest occurs, for the accused needs the assistance of counsel to make sure interrogation and other pretrial procedures are conducted in a Constitutional manner.

After that point, the defense counsel role is to review the documents and other evidence the police have accumulated against the accused, and to interview or question the arresting officers and others involved in the case. The defense attorney may interview witnesses to the crime, and may even conduct an independent investigation.

Important work of the defense attorney is done in conversations with the prosecutor. Defense attorneys usually have dealt previously with the prosecutors assigned to their particular cases. Thus defense and prosecuting attorneys know each other, and can feel each other out for impressions about the strengths of cases.

At bail hearings and in plea negotiations defense attorneys represent the accused. They prepare pretrial motions and often argue them in pretrial conferences and hearings. Then, if all else fails and the cases go to trial, the defense attorneys prepare the defense material for trial, all the while maintaining open ears for any possible opportunities for advantageous plea negotiations with the prosecutors.

At trial defense attorneys question prospective jurors, cross examine prosecution witnesses, call defense witnesses, and generally represent the accused. If cases

BOX 8.2

Key Court Decisions: Bail and Pretrial Release

Stack v. Boyle (1951) A person arrested for a noncapital offense is entitled to bail. The purpose of bail is not punishment, but to insure the appearance of the accused person in court. Bail set at an amount higher than reasonably necessary to accomplish this goal is "excessive," and therefore unconstitutional.

Bandy v. United States (1961) No person should be held in jail prior to trial purely because of poverty. If other considerations support the likelihood the person will appear for trial, then release on "personal recognizance" should be made.

United States v. Salerno (1984) No Constitutional right to bail exists under the Eighth Amendment when the basis of detention is other than prevention of flight. Persons accused of violent crimes, especially those with histories of committing violent crimes, may be held without bail pending trial.

result in conviction, the defense attorneys help those convicted gain the best possible sentences. Then, sometimes appeals may be pursued, which can entail written documents arguing for reversal of the decisions or sentences.

Defense attorneys are involved, intimately, in every stage of the criminal justice system beginning with the arrest. And throughout all of the stages of criminal justice decisions they are responsible for protecting the accused's Constitutional rights, to be sure their clients are not treated unfairly or improperly. Everyone accused of a crime needs a good defense attorney.

Right to a Free Defense Lawyer

From the very beginning of our system of justice, defendants who were financially able could hire lawyers to represent them at trial. Poor defendants, however, had to rely on whatever provisions regarding state-paid attorneys existed in each jurisdiction. In some states there were provisions to assign counsel to any defendant unable to afford a lawyer; in others the assistance of state-paid counsel was limited to very serious cases, usually those involving capital offenses. For many years, the U.S. Supreme Court took the position that this was a "states' rights" issue, that there was no federal Constitutional requirement that states must provide counsel.

Then in 1932 the U.S. Supreme Court considered the appeal of an Alabama court decision known as the "Scottsboro Rape Case," in which nine young black men had been convicted of raping two white women and were subsequently sentenced to death. In **Powell v. Alabama** the court held that the advice of counsel was essential as a Constitutional matter in such capital cases.[28] Thus, for the first time, in state trials involving a possible death sentence, defense lawyers were required, if requested by defendants, and at state expense if the defendants were too poor to pay an attorney's fees.

Powell was an important, but obviously limited, decision. Most felonies were not capital crimes while most criminal defendants are poor. This meant that, even after *Powell*, states could decide whether they wished to provide lawyers for most poor defendants or not. And many did not.

Ten years later, in 1942, in **Betts v. Brady** the Supreme Court *again* held that states, as a matter of federal Constitutional rights, did not need to appoint lawyers for the poor in noncapital cases.[29] It was only in 1963, 31 years after *Powell*, that the Supreme Court again confronted a case concerning the right to counsel. That case, **Gideon v. Wainwright**, proved a landmark decision, probably having a greater impact on the criminal court process than any other single Supreme Court decision.[30]

Clarence Earl Gideon was charged in a Florida state court with having broken and entered a poolroom with intent to commit a misdemeanor. That offense was a felony under Florida law. Appearing in court without funds and without counsel, Gideon asked the court to appoint a lawyer to represent him.

The judge said, "Mr. Gideon, I am sorry but I cannot appoint Counsel to represent you in this case. Under the laws of the State of Florida, the only time the Court can appoint Counsel to represent a defendant is when that person is charged with a capital offense. I am sorry, but I will have to deny your request to appoint Counsel to defend you in this case."

Mr. Gideon responded, "The United States Supreme Court says I am entitled to be represented by Counsel."

Gideon was referring to the Sixth Amendment to the U.S. Constitution, which states in part, "In all criminal prosecutions, the accused shall enjoy the right . . . to have the Assistance of Counsel for his defence."

Put on trial before a jury, Gideon conducted his defense about as well as could be expected by a nonlawyer. He made an opening statement to the jury, cross-examined the state's witnesses, presented witnesses in his own defense, declined to testify himself, and made a short argument "emphasizing his innocence to the charge contained in the information filed in this case."

The jury returned a verdict of guilty, and the judge sentenced him to serve 5 years in the state prison. Later, Gideon filed a petition in the Florida Supreme Court attacking his conviction and sentence on the ground that the trial court's refusal to appoint counsel for him denied him rights "guaranteed by the Constitution and the Bill of Rights by the U.S."

However, the conviction was upheld under the Florida law which specified appointed counsel only in capital cases. Gideon then filed a handwritten petition to the U.S. Supreme Court, and prominent attorney Abe Fortas was appointed to represent him. Attorney Bruce Jacob prepared and presented the case on behalf of the State of Florida.

The U.S. Supreme Court agreed with Gideon and ordered a new trial. It also required that the Sixth Amendment be applied to the states through the Fourteenth Amendment's requirements of "due process of law" and "equal protection of the laws," and even held the *Gideon* ruling to apply *retroactively* to the states, which resulted in new trials for or the outright releases of thousands of inmates around the country. In addition, the decision increased the rules of criminal procedure that govern the trial process in terms of size and complexity markedly.

Gideon has resulted in a dramatic expansion of the presence of attorneys at virtually every "critical stage" of judicial decision making regarding an accused person. Today free defense counsel is provided to indigent defendants either through public defender programs, assigned counsel, or contracts between courts and law firms or other legal entities. And although *Gideon* did not assure the presence of *effective* counsel, a vast amount of law on that topic has since emerged.[31] In addition, persons charged with serious misdemeanors are now included in the right-to-counsel rulings, expanding the right to counsel to any defendant who seriously faces the possibility of incarceration.[32]

For a summary of the key court cases relating to the right to a free attorney, see Box 8.3. A word should be said about the rather rare instances where a defendant refuses the assistance of court-appointed lawyers, or public defenders, and asks the judge for permission to act as his or her own defense lawyer. This is permitted, since the state cannot force an attorney on a defendant who *intelligently waives the right to representation of counsel.*[33] The Supreme Court requires trial judges to thoroughly examine defendants in such instances, to encourage them to accept the help of effective counsel, and to make sure the waiver of counsel is intelligently and knowingly made. The test for the validity of such a waiver is not necessarily the legal skill or knowledge of the defendant but rather his or her understanding of the advantages of counsel. The judge must let the defendant know that it is better to have counsel, that the prosecutor is a lawyer and will have a great advantage over a defendant who does not have a lawyer, and that if technical legal matters arise during the course of the trial the judge may rule against the defendant with no obligation to explain the technicalities to the defendant. If the trial judge feels that a defendant should be allowed to refuse the assistance of counsel, yet the judge does not feel that a fair trial will result without the defendant having some legal assistance, the judge may appoint a "Standby Counsel" for the defendant. This counsel will sit with the defendant and be available in the event the defendant may wish to confer and obtain legal advice during the course of the trial.[34]

BOX 8.3

Key Court Decisions: Right to Free Attorney

Powell v. Alabama (1932) In a capital case where the defendant cannot defend himself on herself because of ignorance, feeble-mindedness, illiteracy, or the like, and where he or she is unable to employ a lawyer, the court should assign counsel for defense. Fundamental fairness and the due process of law require that indigent defendants have free court-appointed lawyers if they cannot otherwise provide for counsel.

Betts v. Brady (1942) In cases involving the death penalty, where "special circumstances" such as ignorant defendants or indigent defendants exist, the Sixth Amendment requires court-appointed counsel.

Gideon v. Wainwright (1963) The right to counsel is extended beyond the special circumstances already enumerated and death penalty issues. The Sixth Amendment requires court-appointed counsel for indigent defendants in *all* criminal prosecutions.

Public defenders offer free legal defense to defendants who cannot afford to hire private attorneys.

Who Defends the Poor?

States have developed three primary models for providing legal help for poor defendants. Those are public defender programs, assigned counsel systems, and contract systems.[35]

Public defender programs serve 68 percent of the nation's defendants and are the dominant form of legal defense in 43 of the 50 largest counties in the United States.[36] The public defender may be attached to either a statewide agency or a local agency. Fifteen states have public defenders systems headed by a person who is responsible for providing defense in the various counties in that state. Thirty-two states have local systems which are autonomous. The public defender, much like the assistant state attorney, is usually a government employee.

Assigned counsel systems involve private attorneys who are appointed by a judge to provide legal defense on a case-by-case basis. A minimum fee is usually paid by the state for the legal services. In some jurisdictions a court administrator oversees the appointment of lawyers and develops standards and guidelines for the program. Assigned counsel systems operate primarily in small counties with fewer than 50,000 residents, which amount to about two-thirds of the counties in America.

Contract systems involve the government contracting with individual attorneys, bar associations, or private law firms to provide services for a specified dollar amount. Contract systems are relatively new and are found in both small counties and very large ones. Contract laywers sometimes handle the overflow cases public defenders do not have the time for and also represent codefendants in cases of conflict of interest.

SUMMARY

"Go directly to jail. Do not pass GO. Do not collect $200." That famous line from the board game *Monopoly* does not reflect the bitter truth about jails, nor the people

226

locked in them. Jails, and police lockups, serve the single purpose of holding individuals caught in the arms of the law, confining them securely so they cannot freely move about the community. We have attempted to describe the reality and the purposes of jails in the criminal justice network, and we have explained the typical composition of the jail population. Perhaps no part of criminal justice is more misunderstood than jails.

Likewise, perhaps nothing in criminal justice is more controversial than the matter of releasing persons after their arrest for a crime but before their trial. Sometimes a police officer complains: "That crook beat me back to the neighborhood after I arrested him. The paperwork I had to complete took me longer than it took for him to get out of jail!"

This chapter explained the conflicting justifications for pretrial detention and release. This legal area is governed by statutes and Supreme Court decisions, but a certain amount of discretion still exists. The issues it raises are difficult to solve.

This chapter also discussed the issue of bail. The primary purpose of bail is to prevent the flight of defendants between their release from police custody and their arraignment or trial. However, most defendants are poor, and many are indigent, with no financial resources at all to secure bail. So the chapter also describes a program for releasing poor defendants on their own promise to return for trial (release on recognizance) that was developed in Manhattan and has now spread widely across the nation. It explained how ROR programs rest on the brief investigations of defendants to see if they have community ties, families, employment, and the like, so as to determine whether they are likely to abscond before trial.

Defendants who cannot post monetary bail or make ROR are held in jail to wait for later court proceedings. Conditions in most jails are very bad and a jailed defendant has greater difficulty in preparing a defense than does one on pretrial release. However, releasing suspects on bail or their own recognizance can present problems since some bailed defendants commit crimes while on pretrial release. The chapter discussed this issue, explaining how some communities have developed preventive detention procedures for denial of bail (even if it can be paid) when it can be shown there is a high probability the defendant will commit additional serious crimes if he or she is released before trial. Recently the Supreme Court has recognized the propriety of such preventive procedures in some instances.

"You are entitled to have an attorney. . . . If you cannot afford an attorney, one will be appointed to represent you." These are *Miranda* warning words on the right to legal counsel which police must provide to all arrested suspects prior to their interrogation. They are perhaps better known than the words of the Sixth Amendment right which they express: "In all criminal prosecutions, the accused shall . . . have the Assistance of Counsel for his defence." This chapter explained that right to counsel, and how defense lawyers are provided to poor defendants.

Notes

1. U.S. Department of Justice, Bureau of Justice Statistics, *Jail Inmates, 1990* (Washington, DC: U.S. Government Printing Office, June 1991).
2. See L. Thomas Winfree, "Toward Understanding State-Level Jail Mortality: Correlates of Death by Suicide and by Natural Causes, 1977 and 1982," *Justice Quarterly* 4 (1) (1987): 51–71.
3. See Daniel B. Kennedy and Robert J. Homant, "Predicting Custodial Suicide: Problems with the Use of Profiles," *Justice Quarterly* 5 (3) (1988).

4. Ronald Goldfarb, *Jails: The Ultimate Ghetto* (Garden City, NY: Anchor Books, 1975), pp. 29, 53–57.

5. See Clemens Bartollas, *Introduction to Corrections* (New York: Harper & Row, 1981), p. 210.

6. J. F. Fishman, *Crucibles of Crime: The Shocking Story of the American Jail* (Cosmopolis Press, 1923).

7. U.S. Department of Justice Bureau of Justice Statistics, *Report to the Nation on Crime and Justice* (Washington, DC: U.S. Government Printing Office, 1988).

8. Ronald Goldfarb, *Ransom* (New York: Harper & Row, 1965), p. ix.

9. *Stack v. Boyle*, 342 U.S. 1 (1951).

10. See Herbert Sturz, "Experiments in the Criminal Justice System," *Legal Aid Briefcase* 25 (1967): 111; John S. Goldkamp, *Two Classes of Accused: A Study of Bail and Detention in American Justice* (Cambridge, MA: Ballinger, 1979).

11. *Bandy v. Chambers*, 82 S. Ct. 11, 13 (1961).

12. U.S. Department of Justice, Bureau of Justice Statistics, *Pretrial Release and Misconduct* (Washington, DC: U.S. Government Printing Office, 1985).

13. Vera Institute of Justice, *Programs in Criminal Justice Reform, Ten-Year Report, 1961–1971* (New York: Vera Institute of Justice, 1972).

14. Again, we acknowledge our indebtedness to Samuel Walker, *Sense and Nonsense about Crime*, 2nd ed. (Pacific Grove, CA: Brooks/Cole, 1989), pp. 63–68, and to Herbert L. Packer, *The Limits of the Criminal Sanction* (Stanford, CA: Stanford University Press, 1968), pp. 210–221.

15. Herman Goldstein, Address before the National Conference on Bail and Criminal Justice, 27–29 May 1964, *National Conference on Bail and Criminal Justice, Proceedings* (Washington, DC: U.S. Government Printing Office, 1965), pp. 153–154.

16. *Pretrial Release and Misconduct*, cited in Note 12.

17. *Report to the Nation on Crime and Justice*, cited in Note 7.

18. DC Code 1973, Secs. 23–1322.

19. *Blunt v. United States*, 322 A. 2d 579 (App. DC 1974).

20. Irving J. Klein, *Constitutional Law for Criminal Justice Professionals* (Miami: Coral Gables Publishing Co., 1986), p. 442.

21. *Stack v. Boyle* (see Note 9 above).

22. *United States v. Salerno*, 481 U.S. 739 (1987).

23. Bail Reform Act of 1984, PL98-473, Title II; see *United States v. Miller*, 753 F. 2d 19 (3d Cir. 1985).

24. *United States v. Salerno*, cited in Note 22.

25. Ibid.

26. Ibid.

27. John M. Scheb and John M. Scheb, III, *Criminal Law and Procedure* (St. Paul, MN: West, 1989).

28. *Powell v. Alabama*, 287 U.S. 45 (1932).

29. *Betts v. Brady*, 316 U.S. 455 (1942).

30. *Gideon v. Wainwright*, 372 U.S. 335 (1963). The reason for the decision in Gideon's favor is summed up by the Court: "Lawyers to prosecute are everywhere deemed essential to protect the public's interest in an orderly society. Similarly, there are few defendants charged with crime, few indeed, who fail to hire the best lawyers they can get to prepare and present their defenses. That government hires lawyers to prosecute and defendants who have the money hire lawyers to defend are the strongest indications of the widespread belief that lawyers in criminal courts are necessities, not luxuries. The right of one charged with crime to counsel may not be deemed fundamental and essential to fair trials in some countries, but it is in ours. From the very

beginning, our state and national constitutions and laws have laid great emphasis on procedural and substantive safeguards designed to assure fair trials before impartial tribunals in which every defendant stands equal before the law. This noble ideal cannot be realized if the poor man charged with crime has to face his accusers without a lawyer to assist him. . . ."

31. See *Strictland v. Washington*, 466 U.S. 688 (1984).

32. *Argersinger v. Hamlin*, 407 U.S. 25 (1972). The *Gideon* decision, while a landmark case on the right to counsel, left unsettled the question of whether states must provide lawyers for indigent defendants charged with *any* crime. *Powell* limited the right to capital cases; *Gideon* involved a felony conviction. What about defendants charged with misdemeanors? Nine years after *Gideon* and 40 years after *Powell*, the Supreme Court again considered the right to counsel at trial this time in a case in which the defendant, convicted of carrying a concealed weapon, a misdemeanor, was sentenced to 90 days in jail. In *Argersinger v. Hamlin* the Court held that states must provide counsel at trial for poor defendants charged with *any* crime, whether it is called a petty offense, a violation, a misdemeanor, or a felony, if the offense involves a possible sentence of incarceration in a jail or prison. In effect, *Argersinger* expanded the right to a trial lawyer to *all* criminal cases where the real possibility of incarceration exists. Sometimes indigent defendants are required to reimburse the state for the costs of appointed counsel under the "Standards of Indigency."

33. *Faretta v. California*, 422 U.S. 806 (1975).

34. See *Mayberry v. Pennsylvania*, 400 U.S. 455 (1971); also see *Illinois v. Allen*, 397 U.S. 337 (1970).

35. For a discussion of these methods of indigent defense, see Robert L. Spangenberg et al., *National Criminal Defense Systems Study* (Washington, DC: Bureau of Justice Statistics, 1986), updated by the Spangenberg Group in March 1987. See also *Report to the Nation on Crime and Justice*, cited in Note 7.

36. Ibid.

SUGGESTED READINGS

Eskridge, Chris W. *Pretrial Release Programming*. New York: Clark Boardman, 1983.

Flemming, Roy B. *Punishment before Trial*. New York: Longman, 1982.

Lewis, Anthony. *Gideon's Trumpet*. New York: Vintage, 1966.

McIntyre, Lisa J. *The Public Defender: The Practice of Law in the Shadow of Repute*. University of Chicago Press, 1987.

Wice, Paul. *Freedom for Sale*. Lexington, MA: Lexington Books, 1974.

DISCUSSION QUESTIONS

1. Describe the types of people commonly found in jail.

2. Discuss the importance of the initial appearance and describe the matters decided there.

3. Describe the pretrial release options and the types of pretrial release. What is the Constitutional purpose of pretrial release?

4. What is the role of bail bondsmen? What criticisms are made of bail bondsmen?

5. Compare and contrast the views on pretrial release presented by the conservative crime control model and the liberal due process model.

6. Discuss the right to bail.

7. Describe the Bail Reform Act of 1984 and discuss its implications.

8. Discuss the role of defense attorneys in criminal justice.

9. Describe the evolution of law which culminated in the *Gideon* decision and discuss the implications.

10. Describe the various ways poor people obtain free defense lawyers.

9

The Prosecutor's Decisions and Plea Bargaining

Brian Watkins was stabbed to death while being robbed in a New York City subway station on September 2, 1990. He was on vacation with his family from Utah at the time, and the culprits apparently were after money to go dancing. Eight young men were later arrested for the crime, and Assistant District Attorney Thomas Schiels charged the eight with felony murder, although only one, Yull Gary Morales, was actually accused of the stabbing.

New York State penal law holds that anyone involved in a robbery which results in the death of the victim is guilty, under felony law, of second degree murder. A defense can be made if the accused had no knowledge that one of the group carried a weapon.

In seeking murder convictions, the district attorney showed confidence in the credibility of the evidence against the defendants, believing it would stand up in court. Guilt must be proven beyond a reasonable doubt in a trial, and with so many defendants involved in a single act of murder, the prosecutor was faced with the challenge of proving each defendant had knowledge of the weapon. The prosecutor relied on videotaped confessions when the first four defendants went on trial, and again in a second trial for three more of the defendants. An eighth defendant, who had not made a videotaped statement, was to be tried later. The videotapes were made after police, acting on eyewitness information, picked up the defendants shortly after the stabbing. Defense lawyers put forth to the jury that the defendants had been tricked by police into making incriminating statements.

In the end, neither jury deliberated long before delivering its verdict: All seven defendants were found guilty of murder and robbery.[1]

ABOUT THIS CHAPTER

The police have concluded, based on their investigation and the evidence obtained that an individual is guilty of a crime. Now, after arresting and booking that person, various decisions must be made by someone else as to what should be done next. The prosecutor is that decision-maker, and the decisions involve whether or not to move the case forward through formal charges, seeking an indictment or filing an information, and then on to the pretrial motions and other stages of prosecution.

Even after a person has been apprehended by the police for a crime, and has been taken before a magistrate for the bail or jail decision, a trial does not necessarily follow. As a matter of fact, a large percentage of arrests do *not* result in prosecution. The prosecutor, or district attorney, can for any number of reasons—or for no obvious reason—decide not to prosecute. And if the defendant has been arrested for more than one offense, the prosecutor decides which offense to charge once the decision to prosecute has been made. (In the case of Brian Watkins, for example, the prosecutor charged the first four defendants with three offenses: second-degree murder, first-degree robbery, and second-degree robbery.) Briefly stated, the prosecutor has considerable discretion as to how to proceed against a person caught in the arms of the law. The prosecutor's decisions, discussed throughout this chapter, are outlined in Fig. 9.1.

Defense attorneys and judges also influence prosecutors' decisions. The most obvious way this influence is seen is in plea bargaining. Perhaps no part of the criminal justice decision network is more controversial, or more misunderstood, than bargained justice. Yet plea bargaining results in unmistakable advantages both to the accused and to society, and without plea bargaining it is doubtful the wheels of justice

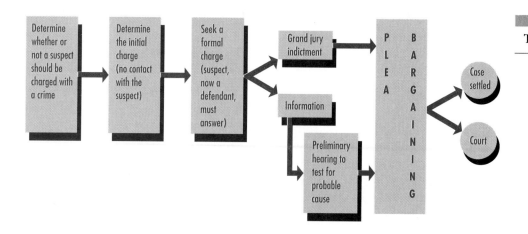

FIGURE 9.1

The prosecutor's decisions.

could continue to roll. The actors in the plea bargains, and the collective decisions they make, provide a main focus of this chapter.

THE PROSECUTOR'S DISCRETION

The first formal duty of the prosecutor involves determining whether a defendant *should* be charged with a crime. Even if the evidence clearly indicates the guilt of a suspect, the prosecutor is free to choose whether to prosecute and, if so, what charge to press. In some cases the criminal process begins with a complaint made directly to the prosecutor's office. If the alleged criminal is named by the complainant, the prosecutor may seek an arrest warrant from a judge and direct the police to take the suspect into custody. In cases in which the complainant accuses a specific suspect directly to the police, the police may obtain an arrest warrant by showing probable cause to a judge for taking the suspect into custody.[2] In such cases the **initial charge** is determined by the warrant, but the final, formal charge may differ as evidence accumulates or dissipates. Arrests without warrants, however, are common, and in such instances the actual point of determination of the initial charge is less precise. The decision to charge, therefore, results from a series of other, earlier, decisions. Usually, the suspect is in custody when the decision is made.[3]

In a routine case the suspect, having been arrested by the police, is in jail or out in the community on pretrial release after a bail hearing. The police have records of all the evidence they have accumulated, including the names of witnesses and the identity of the victim or complainant if there is one. They pass this information on to the prosecutor along with a written report of their investigation of the crime and reasons to believe the defendant committed it. The prosecutor receives this written information from the police, and in routine cases does not interview or otherwise confront defendants at this point. Instead, as a lawyer, he or she translates the factual situation given by the police into what appears from the record to be the illegal behavior involved. For instance, in considering all the elements of a theft, the prosecutor determines whether the defendant's conduct is appropriately labeled larceny, burglary, or robbery and then determines the **degree of the crime** (grand larceny, robbery in the second degree, etc.) that is likely and provable by the evidence in hand and any evidence that may be found later.

But the prosecutor is not a mere automaton, stamping criminal conduct with appropriate statutory labels and proceeding to trial. The prosecutor's discretion is

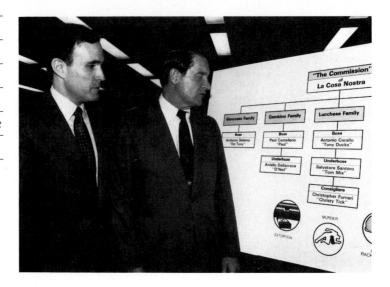

much broader and is based on many considerations beyond legal expertise in fitting charges to different factual situations. The prosecutor is a political figure as well as a lawyer and, like all politicians, is responsive to community pressures and sensitive to community norms.[4]

Many political leaders began their political careers as prosecutors. Executive and legislative leaders as well as many judges have served as prosecutors at some point in their careers. Experience as a prosecutor is a familiar stepping stone to higher office. The political emphasis of a prosecutor varies from one jurisdiction to another: For example, he or she may be required to run for office in partisan or nonpartisan elections. Also, the political powers of a prosecutor are formidable, making the prosecutor an important personage in the community. The prosecutor's job is considered glamorous. If he or she is not truly independent and professional, the powers of the office can be misused for political or other improper purposes. The prosecutor's activity is in large part open to public gaze through the press so that the least mistake as well as the most successful exploit is likely to be magnified.[5]

At the same time, the prosecutor is a member of the American Bar Association (ABA), bound by its code of ethics, and holding an office that has its own ethical traditions. (See Fig. 9.2.) It is generally agreed that the basic duty of the prosecutor is to "seek justice, not merely to convict,"[6] but beyond this, the American Bar Association's *Standards* posit the "duty to improve the law," to stimulate efforts to reform criminal justice.[7]

Sometimes the prosecutor is also referred to as the "chief law-enforcement official" of a district, and in this sense his or her role is seen as *proactive* (i.e., searching out criminal activity) as well as *reactive* (i.e., responding in the charging function to cases brought by the police). Normally the prosecutor relies on the police or other investigative agencies to uncover illegal acts, but the American Bar Association places a responsibility on prosecutors to "investigate suspected illegal activity when it is not adequately dealt with by other agencies."[8]

The scope of the prosecutor's duties—the community expectations commonly assigned to this role—coupled with broad discretionary authority make this office one of the most powerful and complex in the criminal justice system. Lawyer, politician, law-enforcement official, administrator, reform advocate, the "architect of fair trials," local "minister of justice"—all are parts of this job. Moreover, elements of the district attorney's role embody expectations expressed by both the philosophy of the

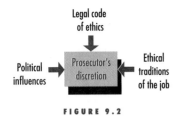

FIGURE 9.2

Influences on the prosecutor's discretion.

234

conservative crime control model and that of the liberal crime control model, which complicates any analysis of that role.[9] So first a few comments regarding those expectations.

The Prosecutor and the Conservative Crime Control Model

The prosecutor is expected to marshal society's resources against the threat of crime. The conservative crime control model emphasizes the law enforcement aspect of the prosecutor's role. But this aspect does not mean the prosecutor indiscriminantly prosecutes all the cases brought by the police. The prosecutor has no interest in prosecuting cases which have no chance of conviction. And the prosecutor is in the best position to study all the relevant facts in a case and decide if the evidence will support a conviction. The prosecutor's own reputation is at stake, since that reputation is based in large measure on the proportion of convictions obtained after charges are filed against a defendant. Thus, according to this model, the prosecutor should be in control of the **decision to charge**.

In addition, the prosecutor is a public figure who is expected to take a visible stand against crime and for justice and is called upon to make public statements, to propose legislative reforms, or to direct the energies of the law-enforcement machinery of the community. In this sense, the prosecutor is the chief law-enforcement person in the community, for without the prosecutor, police arrests would be meaningless.

The Prosecutor and the Liberal Crime Control Model

On the other hand, the office demands, and on sober thought the public expects, that *the prosecutor respect the rights of persons accused of crime*. The liberal crime control model maintains that the prosecutor cannot be trusted to screen cases any more than the police can. It is not realistic to believe the police bring only cases that have sufficient evidence to gain conviction at trial. The liberal crime control model emphasizes the view that our nation began with resistance to oppressive official conduct and that our traditions, embodied in the national and state Constitutions, demand that the prosecutor accord basic fairness to all persons. Because of the power the prosecutor wields, according to the liberal model, we impose a special duty on prosecutors to protect the innocent and to safeguard the rights guaranteed to all, including those who may be guilty. The public nature of his or her position should be used by the prosecutor to rally citizen support for the values which are evident in the U.S. and state Constitutions and to represent the interests of the accused as well as the interests of the state (police) when cases are presented by the community or the police.[10]

Deciding Not to Charge

Also in the prosecutor's control is the **decision *not* to charge**—that is, the prosecutor has a traditional power of ***nolle prosequi***, or the discretion *not* to charge a suspect even though there is sufficient evidence that the suspect has committed a crime.[11] Studies have shown that a significant number of felony arrests, once the cases have been forwarded to the prosecutors' offices, are rejected by prosecutors and dropped without further action. (Table 9.1 shows the results of one study of cases not prosecuted in seven different jurisdictions, and the reasons the cases were not pursued.) Also, even if a prosecutor chooses to proceed with a case and file charges against the arrested person, the prosecutor can later decide to dismiss the charges. (Table 9.2 shows the number of cases dismissed for sixteen jurisdictions, along with the reasons

TABLE 9.1 *Cases not prosecuted in seven jurisdictions, 1981 (Evidence problems are the most common reason for prosecutors to reject cases)*

Jurisdiction	Declined cases*	Percentage of felony arrests declined for prosecution because of—							
		Insufficient evidence, %	Witness problems, %	Due process problems, %	Interests of justice, %	Plea on another case, %	Referral to diversion, %	Referral for other prosecution, %	Other, %
Golden, CO	41	59	27	2	5	2	2	2	0
Greeley, CO	235	52	7	0	38	0	1	2	0
Manhattan, NY	995	61	23	5	4	0	—†	3	4
New Orleans, LA	4114	38	30	12	8	0	7	4	—†
Salt Lake City, UT	973	58	12	1	8	1	2	19	—†
San Diego, CA	4940	54	15	6	9	1	0	9	7
Washington, DC	1535	30	24	—†	13	0	—†	3	29

* Excludes cases for which reasons are unknown.
† Insufficient data to calculate.
SOURCE: Barbara Boland and Ronald Sones, INSLAW, Inc., *Prosecution of Felony Arrests, 1981* (Washington, DC: Bureau of Justice Statistics, 1986).

TABLE 9.2 *Cases dismissed in sixteen jurisdictions, 1981* (*Guilty pleas on other charges are a major cause of dismissals*)

Jurisdiction	Dismissed cases*	Percentage of cases dismissed because of—							
		Insufficient evidence, %	Witness problems, %	Due process problems, %	Interests of justice, %	Plea on another case, %	Referral to diversion, %	Referral for other prosecution, %	Other, %
Brighton, CO	443	16	7	1	10	43	21	2	0
Colorado Springs, CO	675	13	11	2	3	40	16	14	0
Fort Collins, CO	257	4	5	1	5	41	27	15	0
Golden, CO	709	14	14	1	7	38	17	9	0
Greeley, CO	207	12	25	1	4	18	20	20	0
Indianapolis, IN	639	27	15	1	33	21	—†	1	1
Los Angeles, CA	8,351	29	16	2	17	2	10	10	14
Louisville, KY	272	11	10	3	28	5	15	3	24
Manhattan, NY	10,233	26	24	1	17	4	0	1	26
New Orleans, LA	429	22	16	20	15	6	7	1	14
Portland, OR	906	15	22	—†	6	23	7	13	13
Pueblo, CO	146	16	11	2	7	43	14	6	0
St. Louis, MO	1,097	22	20	9	4	10	—†	1	32
Salt Lake City, UT	917	16	17	1	2	27	9	9	19
San Diego, CA	2,630	25	11	3	7	18	10	6	20
Washington, DC	3,656	21	16	1	4	9	7	1	41

* Excludes cases for which reasons are unknown; dismissed cases in this table include diversions.
† Insufficient data to calculate.
SOURCE: Barbara Boland and Ronald Sones, INSLAW, Inc., *Prosecution of Felony Arrests, 1981* (Washington, DC: Bureau of Justice Statistics, 1986).

A lawyer questions a young

witness in county court in

Rockville, Maryland.

Sometimes, children present

"witness problems" because

they may give unclear or

contradictory statements, or

become confused on the

witness stand.

why.) The most common reasons for deciding not to prosecute, or for dismissal of charges, are the following:

1. *Insufficient evidence*, which results from a failure to uncover enough evidence to link a suspect to the crime. Table 9.1 shows this to be the largest category of cases not prosecuted.
2. *Witness problems*, which arise when a witness fails to appear, gives unclear or contradictory statements, refuses to testify, or is unsure of the identity of the offender. Also, a major cause of witness problems is a prior relationship between the victim and the defendant, a factor which has been shown to dramatically reduce the number of prosecutions and convictions.[12]
3. *The interests of justice*, which lead the prosecutor to conclude that certain offenses violate the letter of the law but not the spirit, such as a case of elderly men betting a few cents in a pinochle game.
4. *Due process problems*, which involve violations of Constitutional requirements in the obtaining of evidence or in securing statements from the accused.
5. *A plea on another charge*, or guilty pleas, whereby the accused is charged in several cases or on several counts and the prosecutor agrees to dismiss, or drop, some charges in exchange for guilty pleas on others. Table 9.2 shows this to be the largest category of reasons for dismissals.
6. *Pretrial diversion*, in which the prosecutor and the court agree to drop charges when the accused complies with some condition, such as completion of a drug rehabilitation program.
7. *Referral for other prosecution*, such as when an accused person is charged with more serious crimes in another jurisdiction and the decision is made to transport him or her to that jurisdiction for processing.[13]

Several examples are given in Field Practice A.

The prosecutor's right *not* to prosecute, even with sufficient evidence, is one of the broadest, most powerful examples of discretionary authority in the entire criminal justice system. This traditional discretion, with its origins in early common law, always has been controversial. Many years ago Thurman W. Arnold wrote: "The idea that a prosecuting attorney should be permitted to use his discretion concerning the laws he will enforce and those which he will disregard appears to the ordinary citizen to border on anarchy."[14] The common argument that the *nolle prosequi* power of the prosecutor is one-directional, that is, it is discretion *not* to act and therefore is a form of leniency, has not gone unchallenged. For example, Professor Kenneth Culp Davis has commented about the frequency of using the discretion *not* to be lenient as well as the discretion to be lenient. He wrote, "The power to be lenient is the power to discriminate."[15]

Despite this and other criticisms, the discretion of the prosecutor to engage in selective enforcement of the law and to prosecute for less than the full extent possible has been repeatedly upheld by appellate courts.[16] The prosecutor still retains the "absolute power" to dismiss cases against defendants, even if a trial court disapproves.[17] The American Bar Association has issued standards for the exercise of prosecutorial charging discretion which require that the prosecutor only charge in cases which have sufficient evidence to support a conviction, that the prosecutor "should give no weight to the political advantages or disadvantages" in the decision whether to charge, that the prosecutor's decision not be influenced by a desire to enhance his or her record of convictions, and that the prosecutor should not be intimidated by the past failure of juries to convict persons accused of the criminal act in question.[18] In addition to these standards, or guidelines, for prosecutors, the ABA

No Charges

1: True Love

Police arrested a man on the complaint of his wife that he had cut her with a knife during a family argument. The husband was arrested for felonious assault, could not make bail, and was held in the police lockup overnight. The next morning his wife appeared at the prosecutor's office and requested that the charges against her husband be dropped. The assistant district attorney who interviewed her commented on the seriousness of the assault based on the number of bandages on the wife's arms and the deep scratches on her face. He told her he thought it was foolish for her not to press the complaint since she might be endangered in the future. Nevertheless, the wife insisted that she did not wish her husband charged with a crime. Finally the prosecutor agreed and the husband was released from custody.

2: Dry Out

A chronic drunk was arrested for stealing from a restaurant cloakroom three overcoats which he intended to pawn for wine. The police complaint forwarded to the prosecutor indicated that the arrest was based on violation of a petit larceny statute. The prosecutor, however, decided not to press the larceny charge. Instead he requested that the police refer the suspect to a local detoxification program as a "volunteer."

3: We had him first

Police arrested a 32-year-old man for breaking and entering a vending machine at 2 a.m. at the local bus station. He was transported to the jail and booked, and the case was referred to the state attorney's office for possible prosecution. Further investigation revealed the man had given a false address, and the name and other information he had given the police proved to be false as well. Upon checking with the National Crime Information Center (NCIC) and finger print files, the prosecutor learned the man was wanted in a neighboring state for violation of parole. When the parole officer was notified, she said "We had him first—send him home and we will proceed with revocation of parole and have him sent back to prison." The prosecutor agreed, decided not to prosecute on the breaking and entering charge, and arranged the man's return. ∎

---

recognizes that the following factors may influence a prosecutor's choice *not* to prosecute:

1. The prosecutor's doubt that the accused is in fact guilty
2. The extent of the harm caused by the offense
3. The disproportion of the authorized punishment in relation to the particular offense or the offender
4. Possible improper motives of a complainant
5. Reluctance of the victim to testify
6. Cooperation of the accused in the apprehension or conviction of others
7. Availability and likelihood of prosecution by another jurisdiction.[19]

Applying the Probable Cause Standard

A formal final charge may be brought against a defendant when the prosecutor has evidence sufficient to show probable cause that the defendant is guilty of the crime. This evidence test in many jurisdictions is phrased exactly like the standard required for a lawful arrest. But at arrest "probable cause" is essentially backward-looking; the officer must have had sufficient evidence in hand to establish probable cause at the time of the arrest of the suspect. If sufficient evidence was not present, the officer may be held liable for damages for what is commonly called "false arrest," but which is, more precisely labeled, a civil action for "false imprisonment" (detaining a person for even a short period of time without proper grounds to do so).

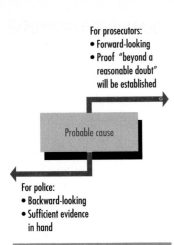

FIGURE 9.3

Probable cause has a different meaning for police and prosecutors.

The prosecutor, however, is not interested in justifying past actions but is looking ahead toward the trial at which the higher evidence standard of proof "beyond a reasonable doubt" is necessary for conviction. (See Fig. 9.3.) In this sense, the district attorney's application of probable cause is colored not only by the higher trial standard, but also by such tactical considerations as the credibility of witnesses, the likelihood of a successful defense or of motions to exclude evidence, the likely effect on the jury of the reputation of the suspect or the victim, and similar factors.

Determining the Initial Charge

If the district attorney decides to proceed to prosecution, the specific charge or charges to bring and how many counts to seek in a formal charge must be decided. If more than one offense is contained in the complaint, or if more than one defendant is involved in the crime, the prosecutor must decide whether to **join** offenses and offenders in a single prosecution or to **sever** them for separate charges and trials.[20] If the suspect's record makes it possible to do so, the prosecutor must decide whether to levy additional charges, such as being an "habitual offender." (See Field Practice B.)

In routine cases the district attorney's initial charging determination is made in the absence of the suspect, who at this point may be out on bail or held in jail awaiting further processing. The prosecutor may interview the arresting officer and perhaps the complainant or available witnesses. Upon request, the prosecutor may talk with the suspect's defense attorney if one has been hired or appointed at this time. In certain "hot" cases—generally those involving very serious crimes or famous or notorious suspects, or cases that otherwise have generated a good deal of publicity—the prosecutor may interrogate the suspect. These are comparatively rare occurrences; usually the initial determination to charge or not is made without contact with the suspect.

Like police officers, prosecutors should exert the fair use of authority to make just and sensible distinctions among cases without, of course, neglecting any duties. Although the district attorney has the authority to charge the highest crime supported by the available evidence, in practice he or she may charge a lesser crime or not charge at all, dismissing the case ("settling" it) or diverting the defendant to some other

A prosecutor discusses the case with the arresting officer, the victim, and a witness before making the initial charge.

Initial Charge

1: Bar Fight

Police arrested a suspect for homicide following a fatal knifing that occurred in a barroom. He was held without bail by the magistrate at initial appearance. The prosecutor reviewed police reports of interviews with witnesses, questioned the arresting officers, and finally decided to seek a charge of second-degree murder. She told the arresting officers that she did not think the evidence would support "premeditation" required in this jurisdiction for first-degree murder and that subsequent investigation might well reveal some mitigating circumstances that would preclude the higher charge.

2: Track of the Cat

Police arrested a suspect they believed to be a "cat burglar" who had plagued the city in recent months. After his arrest, the police, armed with a search warrant, recovered a good deal of stolen property hidden in an attic of a house owned by the suspect's uncle. The recovered property included loot from thirty-five reported burglaries. The prosecutor decided to charge three counts of burglary against him and rejected police requests that his uncle be charged either as an accessory or for the crime of receiving stolen property. ■

---

process. On the basis of an analysis of prosecutorial practices in three states, Professor Frank W. Miller has described situations in which prosecutors commonly decide to settle cases without prosecution, dismiss charges, and charge lesser crimes than possible with the available evidence. These situations involve a wide variety of considerations and circumstances including:

1. Decisions not to charge when there are more effective civil sanctions, such as license revocation
2. Decisions to drop charges because adequate alternatives exist, such as commitment to a mental hospital or revocation of parole on a prior sentence
3. Decisions to drop or reduce charges for informers or cooperating state's witnesses
4. Decisions to dismiss or reduce charges because full conviction would place an undue hardship on "deserving" defendants, as in technical violations by otherwise law–abiding citizens or youthful first offenders
5. Dismissal or reduction of charges because the victim either precipitated the offense by his or her own conduct or appears unwilling to cooperate fully in the prosecution
6. Dismissal or reduction of charges when the offender, otherwise not a serious or persistent violator, has made restitution or other amends and the victim is satisfied with the settlement
7. Charge reduction because maximum prosecution would be excessively costly and time-consuming and comparable sentencing results could be achieved by lesser charges
8. Charge reductions as part of overt plea bargaining to avoid trial[21]

BRINGING FORMAL CHARGES

Assuming the initial decision is to prosecute, the next step in the charging process is to seek a final **formal charge** that the defendant must answer. As mentioned earlier, this may be done in one of two ways, depending on the law in particular jurisdictions. One involves seeking an *indictment* from a grand jury; the other requires the prosecutor to draft the formal charge as an *information* and, in some instances, to test it for probable cause at a *preliminary hearing* before a judge.

The Grand Jury Indictment Process

A **grand jury** is commonly (but not in all places) composed of twenty-three members but may act with a quorum of sixteen present. An indictment is issued upon the vote of twelve members.[22] Members are usually drawn from voter registration rolls, although in some states drivers' license lists are used. And, unlike a trial jury which sits only as long as the trial lasts, usually only a few days, grand juries may be empaneled for extended periods, sometimes months or even a year or more.

Grand jury proceedings are secret, not only from the public and the press, but also from the defendant. Defense counsel is likewise excluded from these hearings. With the permission of the trial judge, the transcribed minutes of grand jury deliberations *may* be shown, in part or in whole, to the defense counsel immediately before or during the trial. However, transcripts are usually made available *only* if the defendant can show a "particularized need" to obtain the testimony or other evidence presented to the grand jury in order to prepare a defense for a later trial.[23]

After the American Revolution, the grand jury was incorporated into the Constitution as a key part of our system of criminal justice. The Fifth Amendment, normally remembered for its protection against self-incrimination, reads as follows:

> No person shall be held to answer for a capital, or otherwise infamous crime, unless on a presentment or indictment of a *Grand Jury*, except in cases arising in the land or naval forces, or in the Militia, when in actual service in time of war or public danger; nor shall any person be subject for the same offense to be twice put in jeopardy of life or limb; nor shall be compelled in any criminal case to be a witness against himself, nor be deprived of life, liberty, or property without due process of law; nor small private property be taken for public use, without just compensation. (emphasis added)

A grand jury meets in a room in the courthouse to make indictment decisions.

The federal government is required to prosecute by grand jury, then. But in the states today, the grand jury serves two purposes. The first is to screen cases brought by the prosecutor. The other is to conduct independent investigations of possible criminal conduct in the community even when no defendant is brought to the jury by the prosecutor. If the prosecutor brings a case and the grand jury finds probable cause to believe a crime was committed and that the defendant committed it, grand jury members issue an **indictment**, a formal charging document. If on their own investigation they find a probably guilty person, they issue a **presentment**, which is a charging document just like an indictment but which is generated by the grand jury itself.

How the Grand Jury Works

When a grand jury is assembled for the first purpose, to screen a case for possible formal charging, the district attorney appears before it and requests an indictment. The prosecutor need only show sufficient evidence to convince a majority of the jury's members that there is "probable cause" to hold the defendant for trial. There is no requirement at this stage to reveal all of the state's evidence or bring forth all the witnesses. Furthermore, in most places, evidence presented to the grand jury need not conform to trial standards of admissibility.

Because grand jurors hear only the state's evidence without any opportunity for defense or rebuttal or contradiction, it is to be expected that they will honor the prosecutor's request for an indictment in most cases. But it is a cumbersome charging process and is falling into disuse even in those states where it has been the traditional means of charging felonies.

The investigatory role of grand juries is perhaps a more important function: investigating possible crimes, corruption, and assorted wrongdoings of citizens, public officials, and agencies. Generally, **investigatory grand juries** are assembled for this purpose and are separate entities from **charging grand juries**, but this is not always the case. All grand juries can pursue almost unlimited investigations if they wish and may level charges on their own motions if they uncover crimes. The investigatory grand jury has traditionally played a particularly important role in organized crime investigations and official inquiries into such matters as police corruption and forceful state reactions to mass disorders, prison riots, and so on. While the charging function of grand juries may be waning, their investigatory functions are likely to remain important within the criminal justice system. Many jurisdictions that have abandoned the use of grand juries in charging retain them for investigatory purposes.

The Preliminary Hearing/Information Process

Today the major way by which felony charges are formally brought against defendants is by the prosecutor drafting an **information**, a formal document noting in statutory language the highest crime charged and the number of charges against the defendant. In some instances, the prosecutor tests the case for probable cause to support the charges at a preliminary hearing before a judge. The information is equivalent to an indictment for most purposes, although prepared and tested differently.

The **preliminary hearing** differs from grand jury proceedings in several significant ways:

1. The defendant has a right to be present at the preliminary hearing and currently, even if indigent, has a Constitutional right to a lawyer.
2. Unlike the grand jury indictment process, the preliminary hearing may be waived (refused) by the defendant.
3. The preliminary hearing is open to the public, and the testimony or evidence presented is available to the press and other media.
4. Hearsay evidence is not usually permitted over the defendant's objection at a preliminary hearing.

The first difference, the right to counsel, was established in *Coleman v. Alabama* (1970), in which the Supreme Court stated that the preliminary hearing is a "critical stage" in criminal justice decisions. The Court stated that a poor defendant needs "the guiding hand of counsel at the preliminary hearing" in order to be protected "against an erroneous or improper prosecution." Four reasons were given why a defendant should have a lawyer present at the preliminary hearing. First, a lawyer may expose fatal weaknesses in the case through the skillful questioning of witnesses, which may lead to dismissal. Second, even if the case is not dismissed, the skilled examination and cross examination of witnesses by an experienced lawyer can uncover vital information which can be used at trial to impeach an adverse witness, or to preserve helpful testimony from a witness who may not be able to appear at the trial. Third, a trained lawyer can learn the nature of the case against his or her client and can better fashion a defense for the trial. Fourth, counsel can also be helpful at the preliminary hearing by making effective arguments for the accused on such matters as the necessity for an early psychiatric examination or bail.[24]

At the preliminary hearing the defendant is not asked to plead to any charge and need do nothing but listen to the evidence presented by the prosecutor. However, independently or through counsel, the defendant may cross-examine state's witnesses

Preliminary Hearing

1: Self-Defense

In a preliminary hearing on a charge of second-degree murder, the prosecution produced three witnesses to a tavern fight which had led to the killing. Each testified that the defendant shot the deceased. The defendant did not personally testify but was allowed to place three defense witnesses on the stand, each of whom testified that the defendant shot the deceased only when the latter was lunging toward him with a knife, after the defendant had attempted to break up a fight between the deceased and another customer.

After the testimony of the third defense witness, the judge dismissed the case against the defendant.

2: Run for Daylight

At a preliminary hearing the prosecutor introduced only one witness, the arresting officer. The police officer testified that he saw the defendant with packages under each arm leaving the rear door of a department store which was closed for the night. The officer said he chased and caught the defendant about two blocks from the scene of the al-

leged burglary. The officer was subjected to vigorous cross examination as to the darkness of the night, how clearly he saw the defendant, whether the defendant was in his sight for the whole two-block chase, and the route taken in the alleged escape. Although the officer testified that it was very dark and he did not get a perfectly clear view of the defendant's features until he stopped him two blocks away, the judge decided to bind the defendant over for trial on the burglary charge.   ■

and otherwise challenge evidence introduced by the prosecutor. In some jurisdictions the defendant is allowed to introduce an affirmative defense—for example, an alibi purporting to show that he or she was elsewhere and otherwise engaged when the crime was committed.[25] Field Practice C gives examples of the outcomes of two preliminary hearings.

Because the defendant has a right to cross-examine state's witnesses even though he or she may choose not to do so, direct testimony presented at the preliminary hearing may be used at the trial, if for a valid reason the witness is unavailable later. This is *unlike* testimony given to a grand jury, where the defendant has no opportunity to confront and challenge his or her accusers.

Furthermore, unlike grand jury proceedings, the defendant may waive (choose not to have) the preliminary hearing, in effect accepting the information as drafted by the prosecutor, and have his or her case go directly to pleading.

A variety of reasons may exist for a defendant to waive the preliminary hearing, but there are two major ones: (1) an already firm decision to plead guilty, and (2) a desire to avoid the negative publicity that is likely to follow such a hearing.[26] Typically, only the state's case is presented at a preliminary hearing, whereas evidence in rebuttal is not revealed until the trial, perhaps months later. Even if a defendant is eventually acquitted, extensive damage to the defendant's reputation may flow from the reported testimony of preliminary hearing witnesses. Can you imagine being called a "mad-dog rapist" at a preliminary hearing only to be acquitted months later?

Though there are important differences between the grand jury and the preliminary hearing, their purposes are identical: the demonstration of probable cause sufficient to hold the defendant for trial. Both processes are referred to as *pretrial screens*, designed to act as curbs on police arrests for investigation and to reduce the possibility that the prosecutor will present the wrong charge. Actually, both tend to rubber-stamp the initial charging decision of the prosecutor, for like the grand jury, the preliminary hearing most often results in a finding of probable cause.

PLEA BARGAINING

245

CHAPTER 9:
THE PROSECUTOR'S
DECISIONS AND
PLEA BARGAINING

The result of the crowded court calendars, court delays, and clogged caseloads is that most cases do not go to trial at all. Most are "settled" through guilty pleas, pleas arranged between the prosecutor and the defense attorney. Guilty pleas are induced through negotiations between the prosecutor and defense counsel, and sometimes by the judge as well, whereby the defendant pleads guilty to reduced charges in exchange for a lenient sentence, that is, a lighter sentence than the judge would give after conviction at trial. This entire process is generally known as **plea bargaining** or plea negotiation. In recent years studies of plea bargaining practices have demonstrated that the technique is widespread, and that it is a very efficient way of reducing overcrowding in the middle stages of the criminal justice process. However, plea bargaining is the most controversial of all prosecution techniques.[27]

In all jurisdictions today, most defendants charged with either felonies or misdemeanors plead guilty to some crime, often a lesser offense than originally charged. There is no doubt that the guilty plea, not the trial, is the chief form of criminal conviction in our society.[28] A defendant who pleads guilty even to a very serious felony at an arraignment lasting only a few minutes stands convicted just as surely as if he or she had undergone a 3-month jury trial.

Guilty pleas are so common everywhere, in proportions occasionally exceeding 90 percent of all charged offenders, that court schedules, staffing, and other resources are planned in anticipation of a high rate of pleas. Though it is sometimes assumed that a high proportion of guilty pleas occur primarily in crowded, metropolitan courts, there is evidence to indicate that the proportion of guilty pleas is about the same in rural, less harried court systems.[29] For example, the percentage of guilty pleas in Vermont is about the same as in Manhattan.[30]

A guilty plea is, of course, a form of confession and in some cases may simply be the result of remorse. In part, confessions can be attributed to careful arrest practices and cautious charging. But a question remains: Why would even guilty defendants give up their rights to trial, thus foregoing the test of proof beyond a reasonable doubt? The answer, in short, is that there is an *implicit bargain* with the state in each guilty plea, and lighter sentences are given those who plead guilty in contrast to those who demand a trial and are later found guilty.

Leniency for Pleading Guilty

There has long been a question of whether leniency for a guilty plea is a proper practice in our system of justice. Notice that this is stated as leniency for a guilty plea, not harshness if convicted after trial. A more severe sentence given to a defendant solely because he or she had demanded a trial is clearly improper; judges who have threatened to "throw the book" at defendants unless they pleaded guilty have been reversed by appellate courts on the grounds that they have "coerced" pleas of guilty. So this fine distinction is made by those judges who wish to support the guilty plea process: leniency if the defendant has "copped out" (pleaded guilty) but no more severe sentence merely because a trial has been demanded. Sophistry, perhaps, but this is the way the issue is usually put. (See Field Practice D.)

Many judges feel it is proper to take a guilty plea into account in the sentencing decision. They point out that the costs of a trial are saved, guilty verdicts are assured without a chance of a jury acquittal, some defendants should be "given a break" because they have thrown themselves on the mercy of the court, and the guilty plea confession is the first step on the road to rehabilitation. In addition, some judges feel

Take It Or Leave It

Henry Lotsaluk was arrested by undercover police officers after he bought a $5 rock of crack cocaine. At arraignment Judge Takitorlevit offered Henry a sentence of 364 days in jail, plus placement in a drug treatment program in exchange for his guilty plea. Henry refused. After almost a year passed, during which time the case was continued on the court's docket, Henry went to trial. At trial the judge offered Henry, through his attorney, a 3½-year prison sentence for a plea of guilty. Henry responded by asking the judge to renew his previous offer of 364 days and drug treatment. The following exchange then took place:

JUDGE: He should have taken the offer when I made it. It is not available now.

ATTORNEY: Well, Your Honor, he would like for you to offer some type of probation with a mandatory drug rehabilitation program. . . .

JUDGE: No.

ATTORNEY: . . . due to the fact he may have a drug problem. . . .

JUDGE: No. He had the same drug problem the day of the arraignment.

ATTORNEY: But he would have been out of jail by now. . . .

JUDGE: Right. Next time he will know to take the offer when I make it. I only wish the guys that sit next to the ones at arraignment and give bad legal advice would be here at times like this.

After the state had presented its case, the judge renewed the offer of 3½ years in exchange for a guilty plea. Henry refused and asked for a shorter sentence in light of the drug problem. The judge responded, "Absolutely not. I offered him 3½ and he has about 15 seconds to take it or leave it." Henry refused. After the jury returned with a guilty verdict, the judge sentenced Henry to 9 years in prison, the maximum allowable under the sentence guidelines. The defense appealed, claiming judicial vindictiveness. ■

that the defendant who goes to trial and who takes the stand in his or her own behalf but is convicted anyway has added perjury to the original crime and therefore is not as deserving of leniency as one who has admitted guilt up front.

Purposes of Plea Bargaining

Plea bargaining is not new; in all probability it has gone on as long as there have been criminal courts. Out-of-court negotiations and arrangements customarily take place off the record, *sub rosa,* in the prosecutor's office or in the hallways of the courthouse. Defense lawyers and prosecutors rarely get into arguments about the guilt or innocence of a defendant today; justice is pursued behind the scenes by professionals who do their work and make their decisions within a closed, private system.[31]

The prosecutor is in a position not simply to apply statutes to facts, but also to apply the laws, including sentencing consequences, to individuals. Criminal laws are by their nature broad and encompassing, but cases are specific and almost infinitely varied. Furthermore, sentencing provisions are often severe because legislators usually have in mind the worst offenders—gangsters, and professional, hardened, or otherwise extremely vicious criminals. In the routine of the typical prosecutor's office, however, this type of violator is comparatively rare.

Most offenders, even those guilty of serious criminal conduct, are not in any sense professional criminals. For instance, in the day-to-day operations of the police and prosecutors, arrested narcotics sellers are rarely professional cocaine dealers, but more likely young people who sold marijuana or a few pills to acquaintances. Technically they are guilty of selling narcotics and face mandatory prison terms, often in the range of 20 years to life. Such harsh sentences have been established by legislatures

Plea Bargain

1: Is That the Man?

Upon the complaint of a woman and her young daughter, a suspect was arrested for child molestation (technically "carnal knowledge and abuse of a minor"), an offense carrying a prison sentence of 5 to 25 years. The defendant denied the allegation, and the only evidence against him was the testimony of the child, another young companion, and the hearsay complaint of the mother, who had not witnessed the alleged crime. The defendant had been charged with a similar offense 5 years earlier, but the charges had been dropped for unknown reasons. Defense counsel called on the prosecutor, first demanding that charges be dropped but later indicating that his client was willing to plead guilty to disorderly conduct or some other misdemeanor if he would be placed on probation. The prosecuting attorney, although "morally certain" that the defendant had indeed molested the child, came to the conclusion that the two children would be poor trial witnesses because there were some discrepancies in their stories. He offered to reduce the charge to "lewd and lascivious conduct," a misdemeanor, but would not recommend probation. The defendant accepted the offer of the lesser charge, pleaded guilty, and received a sentence of 90 days in jail.

2: Young at Heart

Two defendants, Roberts and Knapp, were arrested on a warrant charging them with armed robbery of a liquor store. The defendant Roberts, a 47-year-old man, was apparently the ringleader and mastermind of the crime. He had an extensive rap sheet, with one prior conviction for armed robbery, two for assault, one for reckless use of a firearm, one for a stolen auto, and numerous misdemeanors. On the other hand, Knapp, 18 years old, had a clean prior record with the exception of one disorderly conduct arrest when he was 17 years old. In the present instance, Knapp had evidently fallen under the influence of the older man and played a relatively minor part in the robbery. Though he was carrying a loaded .22 caliber pistol, his active participation was as lookout, standing on the street in front of the store while Roberts entered, pointed a gun at the clerk, and took the money. Both defendants were charged with robbery in the first degree, a crime carrying a mandatory prison term of 15 to 25 years. The prosecuting attorney decided to press the armed robbery charge against Roberts, but reduced the charge against Knapp to "larceny from a commercial building," an offense carrying a 2-year maximum sentence and probationable at the discretion of the trial judge. In exchange for Knapp's willingness to plead guilty to the lesser charge, the prosecutor also promised to recommend probation at the time of his sentencing.

3: What's in a Name?

A 24-year-old defendant accused of raping and sodomizing a 19-year-old college coed in a "date rape" episode was indicted for forcible rape, a felony carrying a possible prison sentence of $8\frac{1}{3}$ to 25 years. Through his attorney, he offered to plead guilty to a charge of aggravated assault ("assault with a deadly weapon evincing disregard for human life"), a felony carrying the exact same sentence. His attorney told the prosecutor his client did not want to be labeled a rapist, either in prison or afterward.

4: What Say You, Mr. District Attorney?

A defendant was charged with three counts of second-degree burglary (breaking and entering a dwelling at night, unarmed, with intent to steal). He had no prior record, either as an adult or as a juvenile. Through counsel, he offered to plead to one count of burglary if the prosecutor would promise to "recommend probation" at the time of sentencing. The prosecutor refused, offering instead to combine the three charges into one count and "not to oppose" defense requests for probation at sentencing, a somewhat weaker stance than an outright probation recommendation by the state. The defendant accepted the merged charge and the prosecutor's word of not opposing probation and entered a guilty plea. ∎

which seek to deter large-scale trafficking in drugs and to take professional pushers off the streets by sentencing them to long years in prison. Confronted with cases of amateurs charged with selling drugs, only a rare prosecutor or sentencing judge wishes to impose such long sentences. Yet the sentences are mandatory and the only way they can be avoided, assuming an unwillingness to dismiss the charges entirely, is to reduce the charge of selling drugs to some lesser offense—for example, "possession" of drugs—which normally involved a lighter sentence, often with an option for probation.

Usually the prosecutor's motive in plea bargaining is to arrive at a sentence appropriate to the actual harm done by the defendant. Also, concessions are often made in cases in which there are codefendants of unequal culpability. As described in Field Practice E:2, an older experienced robber may have a "lookout," a youthful accomplice with a clean record. Technically both are equally guilty of the crime, but the prosecutor may feel it serves justice to reduce the charges against the young accomplice while making no concession to the experienced robber.

Still another reason for charge reduction is that on-the-nose conviction might preclude some correctional alternative, such as probation, likely to be more effective in the long run than imprisonment. Also, prosecutors may agree to reduce charges in the cases of informers or cooperative state's witnesses in order to assist the police in making "big" cases.

Prosecutors also are amenable to plea bargains (actually charge bargains) in cases where conviction would carry mandatory prison terms which the prosecutors view as excessive punishment. For instance, a state law may require a mandatory prison term for conviction of any felony committed while armed. But sometimes, as in the case described in Field Practice F:1, where a prosecutor was faced with a woman charged with aggravated battery resulting from assaulting her drunken husband with a weapon, a reduction in charge may be desirable if the individual is not viewed as a "serious, violent" offender.

Advantages of Plea Bargaining for the State

The guilty plea obviously avoids the time, expense, and work of proving guilt at trial. But other important advantages accrue to the prosecutor, the court, and even the police as well. Most, if not all, complex corollary issues such as the admissibility of evidence or the propriety of police investigation and arrest practices are largely avoided. In most cases, assuming a competent (sane) defendant, the plea assures conviction, whereas the result of a trial, no matter how carefully conducted, is an uncertainty, given the vagaries of jury decisions. Furthermore, there is or may be a certain psychological satisfaction provided by an offender who admits guilt. A defendant who continues to protest his innocence even though found guilty "beyond a reasonable doubt" after a full and fair trial may nevertheless leave some doubts about his or her guilt and the propriety of the conviction. Furthermore, from the viewpoint of correctional authorities, rehabilitation can begin only after the person admits a problem. The probationer or inmate who steadfastly denies the crime presents a very real dilemma to treatment personnel.

Advantages of a guilty plea exist for victims as well, as they sometimes are reluctant to be exposed to the publicity and trauma of a trial. The guilty plea is quick and relatively anonymous. Not only are the details of the crime largely kept from public view, but there is ordinarily minimal interference with the daily routine of complainant and witnesses.

For judges the guilty plea, even if not preceded by charge reduction, offers both a rationalization for showing leniency to deserving defendants and an opportunity to do so in a setting ordinarily free from the publicity that attends a trial. Furthermore, law-enforcement agencies may benefit, directly and indirectly, from a guilty plea. They may escape the onerous duty of long court appearances and may avoid being challenged by the defense on their methods of arrest, investigation, or interrogation. Indirectly, a defendant pleading guilty may help them solve other crimes by admitting other offenses or may implicate other offenders in a crime. The police, of course, are under pressure to clear their books of unsolved crimes. A defendant who pleads guilty to one count of an offense is more likely to admit other counts and thereby "solve," to police satisfaction at any rate, a series of burglaries or whatever crimes are involved.

Charge Bargain

1: Reverse Assault

A 50-year-old woman who had been physically assaulted and emotionally abused by her alcoholic husband for over 20 years became frightened by him on one occasion as he became increasingly drunk and verbally abusive. After attempting to "scare him into leaving me alone" by pointing a .357 magnum pistol kept in the house at him, she struck him on the head with it as he tried to take it away from her. Police were called by rescue squad personnel who responded to the woman's call for assistance after she realized that her husband was seriously injured. Under state law where she lived, any conviction of a felony "with firearm" carried a mandatory 3-year term in prison. The assistant district attorney agreed to the defense counsel's request for a reduction in charge to simple assault in exchange for a guilty plea and court-ordered marriage counseling.

2: I Have News for You

An owner of a topless bar was arrested and charged with attempting to bribe a health inspector. Through his attorney he offered to serve as an informant against organized crime activities regarding food and service industry contracts in the city. The district attorney agreed to "set the charges aside" pending his cooperation in an on-going investigation of organized crime influence in the food industy. ■

Advantages of Plea Bargaining for the Defendant

Plea negotiation, like all bargaining, is a two-way street. While some guilty and remorseful defendants may plead guilty without any concessions being made to them, most defendants expect to receive clear advantages in waiving their right to trial. Apart from such matters as avoiding adverse publicity for themselves and their families in addition to whatever self-satisfaction confession brings, the defendant who pleads guilty is typically most concerned with what will happen following conviction. In pleading guilty, most defendants ordinarily expect a break.[32]

Throwing oneself on the mercy of the court is one thing; arranging for leniency *before* entering a guilty plea is a more controversial process. Sometimes bargaining occurs prior to filing an information, or after the defense lawyer has seen the evidence against the defendant through discovery or deposition of key witnesses scheduled to testify at trial. Sometimes plea bargaining occurs after the preliminary hearing and before the trial. The kinds and types of bargains also differ among jurisdictions, just as sentencing provisions vary from one state to another, for the major motivation in bargaining by any defendant is to achieve a lenient sentence. But other incentives to bargain also provide advantages for the defendant.

Depending on the crime or crimes charged and the sentencing provisions in the state, defendants seek one or more of the following concessions by plea bargaining:

1. *Charge reduction:* The defendant agrees to plead some lesser offense with a correspondingly shorter sentence.
2. *Dismissal of charges:* Sometimes called count bargaining, this involves the prosecution on only one or two charges with the other counts dismissed.
3. *Softer label:* This involves an alteration of charge from one carrying a particularly damaging label that implies depravity on the part of the defendant to one with less negative connotations, for example, rape to assault.
4. *Sentence promise:* The prosecutor promises to recommend probation or a shorter prison term at the time of sentencing.

There are other variations. For example, a defendant may express the willingness to "consent" to revocation of probation or parole on an earlier sentence if the current charges are dropped or reduced. There are also combinations of these concessions, but in each case the result is the same: The defendant is allowed to plead guilty to charges less serious than those warranted by his or her conduct and by state's evidence, or he or she receives a preconviction sentence promise in exchange for his or her willingness to waive trial, and thus receives a lesser punishment. As Albert W. Alschuler has written: "Virtually every aspect of today's system of criminal justice, in short, seems designed to influence defense attorneys to adopt the motto: when in doubt, cop him out."[33]

The Propriety of Plea Bargaining

Is plea bargaining a proper form of criminal justice in our society? This question has been raised by appellate courts and various commissions in the past few years. Some observers of plea bargaining condemn it as intrinsically improper to our idea of justice. One appeals court judge stated: "Justice and liberty are not the subjects of bargaining and barter." However, on a rehearing this same judge found that "proper" bargaining is appropriate and may be a necessity.[35] So, what is proper plea bargaining?

Is an *inducement-based* system any more proper than one which rests on *coercion*? Coercion is clearly contrary to our system of government. Is a promise by a prosecutor to "recommend" probation really any different from a threat to "throw the book" at a defendant who pleads not guilty? Is the dropping of a charge in an indictment to a lesser charge a proper practice when the prosecutor, court, and defendant know that the defendant committed a more serious crime and that the evidence in fact supports conviction on the higher offense? The major issue is whether plea negotiation with some control is justified on the grounds of expediency, or whether it is a distortion of our criminal justice ideology.

Although on the surface plea negotiations appear to be intrinsically improper, and therefore dangerous and corrupting, the administrative realities of current adjudication practices make bargaining—expressed or implicit—normative. The fact is that criminal justice has become so dependent on plea bargaining to keep the court calendar from becoming hopelessly clogged that it could not be instantly eliminated. The abolition of plea bargaining would inundate our already overtaxed prosecutorial and judicial facilities,[36] creating an even larger backlog of cases.

Nevertheless, several efforts have been made to eliminate, or at least seriously limit, the scope of plea bargaining. These efforts have not impacted sentencing practices noticeably, nor have they reduced crime, but they have shifted the burden of discretion downward to the arresting police officers.[37] Serious attempts to curb plea negotiation in already overcrowded big-city court systems would be disastrous. Furthermore, where bargaining has been reduced, sentence lengths have increased. This certainly would be unwelcome today in most of our states, which are already experiencing prison overcrowding.[38]

While the propriety controversy is still very strong, courts and commissions that condemn plea negotiation are in a minority today. The U.S. Supreme Court has generally supported the practice,[39] and former Chief Justice Burger has stated:

[plea bargaining] is an essential component of the administration of justice. Properly administered, it is to be encouraged. If every criminal charge were subjected to a full-scale trial, the States and the Federal Government would need to multiply by many times the number of judges and court facilities.

Disposition of charges after plea discussions is not only an essential part of the process but a highly desirable part for many reasons. It leads to prompt and largely

"I Didn't Mean to Have Her Killed"

Robert L. Ammidown was charged with first-degree murder and conspiracy to commit murder in the death of his wife. He admitted that a month prior to her killing he had arranged to have her murdered at a department store parking garage. At the last minute he changed his mind, because he did not want his son, who was to accompany his mother that day, to witness the murder. So, according to his confession, Ammidown and an associate, Richard Anthony Lee, devised a plan whereby Lee would abduct Mrs. Ammidown and by threat to her life extort a sum of money to be used by Ammidown and Lee to purchase a club in Maryland. According to the plan, Ammidown was to take his wife to a restaurant and after dinner Lee would halt Ammidown's car at a specified intersection near the restaurant and abduct Mrs. Ammidown.

At the prearranged spot Lee jumped into the car and directed Ammidown to drive to a certain location where Lee dragged Mrs. Ammidown from the car and raped her, as planned, to impress her with the "seriousness of the threat." However, at this point, Lee killed Mrs. Ammidown.

Ammidown denied complicity in the murder. Prior to the trial, the U.S. Attorney and Ammidown entered into an agreement that Ammidown would plead guilty to second-degree murder and the first-degree murder charge would be dismissed. In return Ammidown agreed to testify against Lee, who was believed by the prosecution to be involved in still another murder.

The trial judge, however, refused to accept the lesser plea on the basis that public interest required that the defendant be tried on the greater charge. Ammidown then pleaded not guilty to first-degree murder but at trial was convicted of first-degree murder and felony murder and sentenced to two consecutive terms of life imprisonment. He appealed.[33]

final disposition of most criminal cases; it avoids much of the corrosive impact of enforced idleness during pretrial confinement for those who are denied release pending trial; it protects the public from those accused persons who are prone to continue criminal conduct even while on pretrial release; and by shortening the time between charge and disposition, it enhances whatever may be the rehabilitative prospects of the guilty when they are ultimately imprisoned.[40]

The American Bar Association, as well as the American Law Institute, have accepted plea agreement procedures.[41] Furthermore, a revision of Rule 11 of the Federal Rules of Criminal Procedure (a part of the *Model Code of Pre-Arraignment Procedures* approved by the U.S. Supreme Court) contains detailed provisions for plea agreement procedures.[42]

Who Is in Charge of Plea Bargaining?

All current suggestions for controlling bargaining practices require that an *accurate record of any plea agreements* be made and submitted to the appropriate court for approval. This raises the issue of whether the prosecutor or the judge is the final arbiter of the bargaining decision.[43] Normally the prosecutor is understood to be in charge of the bargain. Only the prosecutor is in a position to know the work load of the office and the number of cases he or she is able to prosecute. But the issue goes beyond that. In their zeal to prosecute a particular defendant, the prosecutor and the police must undermine their case against at least one other codefendant. Is this decision a prerogative of the prosecutor and police alone? Should the trial court serve merely as a rubber stamp for the prosecutor's and police department's decision?

The answer is no, and as a result courts are given an oversight function in plea bargaining causes: A judge may withhold approval of a plea bargain if the prosecutor has failed to give consideration to the public interest or to the deterrent aspects of the criminal law. It should be noted that a trial judge is not free to withhold approval of a guilty plea merely because his or her conception of the public interest differs from that of the prosecuting attorney, but only if the judge can say that the action of the prosecuting attorney is an abuse of prosecutorial discretion.

Must Promises Be Kept?

If the prosecutor and the accused make a bargain and the deal is kept, usually there is no aggrieved party and no appeal. If, however, a prosecutor offers some concession and a defendant, relying on this, pleads guilty—and then for some reason the state reneges on its part of the bargain—the defendant naturally feels cheated. If he or she can show an unkept promise, the defendant can win one of two remedies: (1) withdrawal of the guilty plea and a chance to go to trial on the original charge (which, since the defendant bargained, he or she probably does not want) or (2) an order by an appellate court that the bargain be kept. The latter is simple enough and is becoming a more common practice than plea withdrawal. This works well if the bargain is within the traditional authority of the prosecutor or court. If, for example, a defendant was promised probation and instead was incarcerated, the appellate court, if convinced a worthwhile plea bargain agreement was not implemented, can simply order probation.

Equal Opportunity to Bargain

The American Bar Association's *Standards Relating to Pleas of Guilty* ends its discussion with the following proviso: "Similarly situated defendants should be afforded equal plea-agreement opportunities."[44] Which defendants could be more similarly situated than persons with equivalent prior records who are "rap partners" (codefendants in the same crime)?

This situation arose in a case from the District of Columbia involving two burglars named Newman and Anderson (not related, as far as we know, to the authors of this book) who were partners in housebreaking. After arrest they were both indicted for felonious burglary and larceny. Anderson, through counsel, negotiated with the prosecutor and obtained a bargain allowing him to plead guilty to the misdemeanors of *attempted* housebreaking and petty larceny. Newman requested the same bargain but the prosecutor declined to grant it.

Newman was convicted and appealed to the Federal Circuit Court (Washington, DC, is a federal jurisdiction) on the grounds that he was denied *equal protection* of the law (all persons must be treated equally under the Fourteenth Amendment), that is, he had been denied the plea bargain granted to his rap partner despite their similar backgrounds. The court, however, denied him relief, saying, in part, "Two persons may have committed what is precisely the same legal offense but the prosecutor is not compelled by law, duty or tradition to treat them the same as to charges. . . ."[45]

This whole problem of equal plea bargaining opportunities is complicated by the fact that bargaining, as well as the *types* of bargains offered and accepted, is generally informal, off the record, and neither written in statute nor posted on bulletin boards as common practice. A defendant, a local resident and familiar with the courts, and a criminal defense lawyer aware of the prosecutor's bargaining practices may indeed achieve the normal, routine leniency of the district attorney in exchange for a plea. But what about a stranger or a lawyer not really familiar with the "going rates" of bargains in a particular court system? For equal opportunity in bargaining to be achieved, must local practices and local norms of deals be posted somewhere? The equal protection issue is also raised in cases in which one rap partner agrees to testify against the other in exchange for charging or sentencing leniency.

Thus equal protection is one of the major unresolved issues of plea bargaining as a major form of adjudication in our criminal justice process. We try to control this somewhat today by making bargains part of the record at arraignment, but this neither provides adequate information for strangers to the system nor compels prosecutors to offer similar bargains to comparable defendants.

Other Issues in Plea Bargain Justice

There are many other unresolved issues in our system of plea bargaining, as well. Many of these spring from one peculiarity of its implementation: Not only is the bargaining process informal and hard to see and evaluate, as already noted, but it is rarely litigated because most bargains are kept and both the state and the defendant benefit. An appeal can be made only by parties directly interested in the outcome and, if everyone directly involved profits from the bargain, there is no one to appeal. Thus the appellate courts, including the U.S. Supreme Court, have not shaped law and practice here as they have in more commonly litigated decision points in the criminal justice process, from search to jury selection. Legislation and court decisions are totally silent about plea bargaining in many jurisdictions. There are court rules today making the process more visible, but there still remain many issues of controversy and uncertainty about bargaining. We describe some of them below.

Does Bargaining Convict the Innocent?

Can the guilty plea system be so seductive that innocent persons plead guilty? If a defendant, particularly one with prior convictions, is arrested for a crime he or she did not commit and, in spite of a prior record, is offered probation for a plea by the prosecutor, might the defendant plead guilty despite his or her innocence? The alternative is to face a jury at trial, always a problematic situation. Should the jury convict in spite of actual innocence, imprisonment could result. In these circumstances probation no doubt looks good.

This is the dilemma some defendants face and today, as mentioned, many judges are required to inquire into the *factual basis* of the plea before accepting it. This provision, first spelled out in Federal Rule 11 and now also included in many state court rules, is designed specifically to help prevent conviction of the innocent. Neither the scope of the inquiry required, however, nor the evidentiary test for the judge to be convinced of guilt is prescribed in detail. The evidence needed is clearly not "beyond a reasonable doubt" as at trial, though few judges would accept really doubtful pleas of guilty.

So the problem of the innocent pleading guilty remains, and no doubt will remain, with us. The fact is, myths notwithstanding, there is no firm assurance that even a full-scale jury trial will always accurately separate the guilty from the innocent. And there *is* evidence that innocent people have been convicted by trial after a full-scale adversary proceeding, although it is not common. Thus it is likely that some innocent offenders will continue to choose a lenient sentence rather than risk trial.

On the other hand, it *cannot* be said that the bargaining process is any more likely to be inaccurate than the trial system—at least no compelling evidence has been shown to support such an assumption. It may well be that the careful and proper exercise of discretion by prosecutors in our bargaining system works to standardize the law and to fit punishments to the fine gradations that occur in the behavior and backgrounds of the thousands of defendants who are processed in this manner every day.

Bargaining Nullifies Police Efforts and Ignores the Victim

By and large the police who arrest a defendant are not asked, indeed might not be informed of much less consulted, about leniency in exchange for a plea. Likewise, the victim of a crime has no opportunity to know that bargaining is being or has been conducted, let alone to be asked for his or her consent to the process. Unsatisfied with the outcome of a reduced-charge or lenient sentence, neither the police nor victims have any recourse. At the least perhaps there should be a requirement that police and victims be informed that bargaining is going on, so that their stories can be told to the prosecutors *before* the bargains are struck. Some state legislatures have considered legislation that would require the state to notify victims of any plea arrangement, and victims' rights advocates press for such legislation; but at present, this is not the practice. With the crowded court dockets and jealously guarded prerogatives of office enjoyed by most prosecutors, it is unlikely that police and victims will be involved actively on a wide scale in the process in the foreseeable future.

Plea Bargaining Circumvents Constitutional Protections

A defendant who pleads guilty, with or without striking a bargain, waives the necessity for the state to provide evidentiary proof of guilt and, in an overwhelming number of jurisdictions, waives all rights to challenge police arrest or search behavior. This means that not only is the test of the amount of evidence held by the state bypassed, but so is the legality of the manner in which this evidence was obtained. All the important Supreme Court cases on the early stages of the criminal justice process—*Mapp, Miranda,* even *Gideon*—are irrelevant in the case of a defendant who pleads guilty. Thus a guilty plea, no matter how obtained, not only does not sharpen and hone the law in regard to search, interrogation, force, or other important law-enforcement issues, it waives their examination altogether. The plea *avoids* many more legal issues than it answers.

Bargaining Lowers Respect for Justice

Plea bargaining is an unmistakable example of wheeling and dealing. Though it may be perfectly proper, it has the aura of a "fix" about it. A person charged with one crime bargains for conviction on a lesser one. Some observers argue that such arrangements breed disrespect for the law and our justice system. Indeed, the major lesson may be that everything can be "arranged" with the right lawyer and a willing prosecutor. Cynicism is the result—another crack in the foundation of justice in our society.

Only people sophisticated in the ways of the criminal justice system or a person caught in the web of arrest and prosecution can see the justice in a negotiation model. For most of us, something that is accepted practice in all sorts of civil legal disputes, from auto accident claims to labor relations, seems somehow inappropriate in criminal matters. How can a crime be negotiated or a compromise plea arranged? This, of course, is exactly what plea bargaining is. The settlement, negotiation, and compromise practices of civil disputes are carried over into the criminal sphere. But if settling "out of court" is desirable in most civil matters, somehow it is not quite as respectable in criminal cases.

Bargaining Conceals the Whole Truth

When a defendant is publicly tried, all the minute details of his or her conduct are made public, not only in the courtroom but in the media as well. A guilty plea, bargained or not, is less than revealing. There is a conviction, yes, but what about motives and other details of the crime? They are buried in the plea. The plea is so cryptic, so unrevealing, that this very avoidance of publicity may be one of the major factors leading to the frequency of convictions in this manner.

But to the public, hungry for news, the plea fails to reveal any of the gory details. In a routine, everyday case this makes little difference except to those acquainted with the offender or the victim. But when the defendant is prominent or notorious, when a political figure, movie star, professional athlete, or other well-known person is involved, a simple plea of guilty to the charge does not satisfy the public's need (some say "right") to know all the facts. Should Senator Edward Kennedy be allowed to plead guilty to a traffic violation after his female companion drowned when Kennedy drove off a bridge in Chappaquidick? Should James Earl Ray, the assassin of Martin Luther King, Jr., be allowed to say "guilty" and have it end there? In short, should the newsworthy be allowed to hide their conduct while admitting their guilt? This, like the rest of surrounding plea bargaining, remains controversial and has by no means been resolved.

SUMMARY

This chapter dealt with the charging decision, the middle stages of the criminal justice process, where the suspect, after being taken into police custody, is charged with a crime by the prosecuting attorney. At this point the suspect becomes a defendant.

The major official involved in these middle stages is the prosecutor, familiarly known as the district attorney, or D.A. He or she, a lawyer, has the job of translating the factual evidence brought by the police into a formal, legally correct criminal charge as defined in the jurisdiction's criminal statutes. The prosecutor must decide first whether to charge a crime or not and then, if so, which crime and how many counts of the offense to charge.

Plea bargaining is a major route to obtaining criminal convictions in our society; the method exists in all jurisdictions, large and small, and is used by every court no matter how crowded or leisurely its processing calendar may be. Most offenders, felons and misdemeanants alike, are convicted by their own admissions of guilt rather than by a jury trial. In some cases no overt bargain is made; the defendant simply pleads guilty and generally gets a more lenient sentence than do similar offenders convicted by trial.

In plea bargaining, however, a preplea deal is struck between the prosecutor and the accused so that in exchange for a guilty plea the charge is dropped to a lesser offense, a lenient sentence is promised, or both. In this way the prosecutor is assured of a conviction, which might not happen if the case were tried, and the offender gets a more lenient record and sentence than if convicted of the full charges at trial.

Naturally, plea bargaining is a controversial practice. Some people think it absolutely wrong to negotiate with criminals. Others, however, point out that compromise and settlement are common in noncriminal lawsuits, and see nothing wrong with their use in criminal cases.

There is a great deal of concern today over controlling plea bargaining since apparently it cannot be eliminated—and perhaps should not be eliminated. That concern centers on several issues: First, plea bargaining, since its outcome usually satisfies both the state and the defendant, is rarely litigated; this means there is no large body of legal decisions governing its use, as there is for other criminal justice practices. Second, the satisfactory outcome of plea bargaining may be so seductive from the suspect's point of view that in certain situations those who are *innocent* may opt to plead guilty; in such instances the criminal justice system's aim of determining guilt and innocence has been subverted. Third, only court officials can engage in bargaining, so that it is hard to ensure that victim and police rights are not overlooked in the process. Also, bargaining is generally carried out informally and off the record, so that it is not subject to close scrutiny; thus it is hard to ensure that the rights of offenders are enforced. And finally, plea bargaining by its very nature conceals some of the facts of a case and has about it the aura of a "fix"; thus public confidence in and respect for the law and the criminal justice system may be undermined.

Notes

1. Sources for the Brian Watkins case: "Utah Tourist Trial: How to Prove Murder If Someone Else Did It," *The New York Times,* November 8, 1991, p. 133; Ronald Sullivan, "4 Guilty of Murder and Robbery in Utah Tourist's Death in Subway," *The New York Times,* December 11, 1991, p. A1, B1; "Trio Guilty in Murder of Tourist," *The Star-Ledger,* April 24, 1992, (from the Associated Press).

2. Wayne R. LaFave and Frank J. Remington, "Controlling the Police: The Judge's Role in Making and Reviewing Law Enforcement Decisions," *Michigan Law Review* 63 (1965): 987.

3. Frank W. Miller, *Prosecution: The Decision to Charge a Suspect with a Crime* (Boston: Little, Brown, 1970), p. 11.

4. William F. McDonald, "Prosecutorial Decisions and Case Mortality and the Initial Screening." Paper presented at the American Society of Criminology, New York, November 5, 1973, mimeo, p. 6.

5. American Bar Association (ABA), *Standards Relating to the Prosecution Function and the Defense Function* (approved draft) (New York: Institute of Judicial Administration, 1971), pp. 18–19.

6. Ibid., p. 25.

7. Ibid., p. 47.

8. Ibid., p. 71.

9. See Samuel Walker, *Sense and Nonsense about Crime: A Policy Guide* (Pacific Grove, CA: Brooks/Cole, 1989), and Herbert L. Packer, *The Limits of the Criminal Sanction* (Stanford, CA: Stanford University Press, 1968).

10. ABA, op. cit., pp. 19–20. Also, see Packer, op. cit.

11. Joan E. Jacoby, *The Prosecutor's Charging Decision: A Policy Perspective* (Washington, DC: U.S. Department of Justice, 1977), p. 1.

12. K. M. Williams, *The Role of the Victim in the Prosecution of Violent Crimes* (Washington, DC: Institute for Law and Social Research, 1978); also see Brian Forst, *Arrest Convictability as a Measure of Police Performance* (final report) (Washington, DC: Institute for Law and Social Research, 1980).

13. These reasons for case dismissal are found in Barbara Boland and Ronald Sones, INSLAW, Inc., *Prosecution of Felony Arrests, 1981,* (Washington, DC: Bureau of Justice Statistics, 1986).

14. Thurman W. Arnold, "Law Enforcement—An Attempt at Social Dissection," *Yale Law Journal* 42, (1) (1932): 7.

15. Kenneth Culp Davis, *Discretionary Justice* (Baton Rouge: Louisiana State University Press, 1969), p. 170.

16. See, for example, *Oyler v. Boles,* 368 U.S. 448 (1962); *United States v. Cox,* 342 F. 2d 1967 (5th Cir. 1965); *Moses v. Kennedy,* 219 F. Suppl. 762 (D.D.C. 1963); *People v. Gray,* 254 Cal. App. 2d (1967).

17. *United States v. Cowan,* 524 F. 2d 785 (5th Cir. 1975).

18. ABA, op. cit., pp. 92–93.

19. Ibid., p. 4.

20. American Bar Association, *Standards Relating to the Joinder and Severance,* (approved draft) (New York: Institute of Judicial Administration, 1968).

21. Miller, op. cit., pp. 159, 161–162.

22. Marvin E. Frankel and Gary P. Naftalis, "The Grand Jury: An Institution on Trial," *The New Leader* 58 (10 November 1975): 7–9. Frankel and Naftalis note different sizes of grand juries in the various state jurisdictions. The number of votes required before an indictment is returned ranges from 4 to 12, depending on the size of the grand jury.

23. See *Pittsburgh Plate Glass Co. v. United States*, 360 U.S. 395, 79 S. Ct. 1237, 3 L. Ed. 2d 323 (1959), and *United States v. Procter and Gamble*, 356 U.S. 677, 78 S. Ct. 983, 2 L. Ed. 2d 1077 (1958); but also see *Dennis v. United States*, 384 U.S. 855, 86 S. Ct. 1840, 16 L. Ed. 2d 973 (1966), and, generally, Arthur Sherry, "Grand Jury Minutes: The Unreasonable Rules of Secrecy," *Virginia Law Review* 48 (1962): 668

24. *Coleman v. Alabama*, 399 U.S. 1 (1970).

25. Robert A. Weninger, "Criminal Discovery and Omnibus Procedure in a Federal Court: A Defense View," *Southern California Law Review* 49 (1976): 514. See also Note, *Georgia Law Journal* 56 (1967): 193; also see John M. Scheb and John M. Scheb II, *Criminal Law and Procedure* (St. Paul, MN: West, 1989), pp. 269–313.

26. Miller, op. cit., pp. 83–84.

27. Alissa Pollitz Worden, "Policymaking by Prosecutors: The Uses of Discretion in Regulating Plea Bargaining," *Judicature* 73:6 (April-May 1990): 335–340; also see Malvina Halberstam, "Toward Neutral Principles in the Administration of Criminal Justice: A Critique of Decisions Sanctioning the Plea Bargaining Process," *Journal of Criminal Law and Criminology* 73 (1) (1982): 1–49.

28. Donald J. Newman, *Conviction: The Determination of Guilt or Innocence without Trial* (Boston: Little, Brown, 1966); also, Albert W. Alschuler, "Plea Bargaining and Its History," *Law and Society Review* 13 (1979): 247.

29. See Frank Laurent, *The Business of a Trial Court: 100 Years of Cases* (Madison: University of Wisconsin Press, 1959).

30. See Donald J. Newman, "Reshape the Deal," *Trial* 9 (May-June 1973): 11.

31. For a readable analysis of the way plea bargaining works, see Arthur Rosett and Donald R. Cressey, *Justice by Consent* (Philadelphia: Lippincott, 1976), quote taken from p. 3. Also, for more on the culture of plea bargaining between prosecutors and defense attorneys, see Lisa McIntyre, *The Public Defender: The Practice of Law in the Shadows of Repute* (Chicago: University of Chicago Press, 1987).

32. See Newman, op. cit.; President's Commission on Law Enforcement and Administration of Justice, *Task Force Report: The Courts* (Washington, DC: U.S. Government Printing Officer, 1967), pp. 108–120; Note, "Guilty Plea Bargaining: Compromises by prosecutors to Secure Guilty Pleas," *University of Pennsylvania Law Review* 112 (1964): 865.

33. Albert W. Alschuler, "The Defense Attorney's Role in Plea Bargaining," *Yale Law Journal* 84 (1975): 1206.

34. *Shelton v. United States*, 246 F. 2d 571 (5th Cir. 1957).

35. Ibid., reversed on confession of error of Solicitor General, 356 U.S. 26, 78 S. Ct. 563, 2 L. Ed. 2d 579 (1958).

36. Donald J. Newman and Edgar C. NeMoyer, "Issues of Propriety in Negotiated Justice," *Denver Law Journal* 47 (1970): 374–376; and see William M. Landes, "An Economic Analysis of the Courts," *Journal of Law and Economy* 14 (1971): 61.

37. See Colin Loftin and David McDowall, " 'One with a Gun Gets You Two': Mandatory Sentencing and Firearms Violence in Detroit," *The Annals* 455 (May 1981): 150–167; U.S. Department of Justice, *The Nation's Toughest Drug Law: Evaluating the New York Experience* (Washington, DC: U.S. Government Printing Office, 1978); and Thomas W. Church, "Plea Bargains, Concessions, and the Courts: Analysis of a Quasi-Experiment," *Law and Society Review* 10 (Spring 1976): 377–401.

38. National Advisory Commission on Criminal Justice Standards and Goals, *Courts* (Washington, DC: U.S. Government Printing Office, 1973), Sec. 3.1, p. 46. This Nixon Crime Commission issued a report in 1973 calling for the abolition of all plea bargaining by 1978, which obviously did not happen. In New York a legislative limit was placed on the range of charge reduction that could be followed by prosecutors in bargaining for pleas in narcotics cases. In some places local prosecutors took it upon themselves to refuse to bargain, generally in small rural jurisdictions, but even in those few reported areas, backlogs of cases became a serious problem. The attorney general of Alaska ordered plea bargaining stopped in his state because "it gave the whole criminal justice system a black eye." The results of this expressed policy in Alaska and elsewhere is that it is possible to reduce plea bargaining in some small jurisdictions but only at the cost of increasing the number of trials. See N.Y. Crim. Proc. Law Sec. 220.30(3)(b)(i). And see, for example, "Crime Rate Down, Says 'No Deal' Prosecutor," *The Times Union* (Albany), 14 July 1975, p. 3. For a discussion, see Al Lawrence "With Liberty and Plea Bargaining for All," in *The Empire State Report*, June 1976. Also see D. C. Anderson, "You Can't Cop a Plea in Alaska Anymore," *Police Magazine* 2 (1) (1979): 4–12.

39. See, for example, *Brady v. United States*, 397 U.S. 742; 90 S. Ct. 1463, 25 L. Ed. 2d 747 (1970); *Parker v. North Carolina*, 397 U.S. 790, 90 S. Ct. 1458, 25 L. Ed. 2d 785 (1970); *North Carolina v. Alford*, 400 U.S. 25, 91 S. Ct. 160, 27 L. Ed. 2d 162 (1970). For a critique of Supreme Court decisions sanctioning the plea bargaining process, see Malvina Halberstam, "Toward Neutral Principles in the Administration of Criminal Justice: A Critique of Supreme Court Decisions Sanctioning the Plea Bargaining Process," *Journal of Criminal Law and Criminology* 73 (1) (1982): 1–49.

40. *Santobello v. New York* 404 U.S. 257, 92 S. Ct. 495, 30 L. Ed. 2d 162 (1970).

41. American Bar Association, *Standards Related to Pleas of Guilty* (New York: Institute of Judicial Administration, 1968), Sec. 3.1, p. 60; American Law Institute, *Model Code of Pre-Arraignment Procedures* (Philadelphia: American Law Institute, 1972), Art. 350.

42. Federal Rules of Criminal Procedure, Rule 11, Pleas, Sec. (e). Amended 1 July 1975.

43. For a discussion of the relationship between judge and prosecutor, see Abraham S. Goldstein, *The Passive Judiciary: Prosecutorial Discretion and the Guilty Plea* (Baton Rouge: Louisiana State University Press, 1981). For other factors in the decision process see Maynard, "The Structure of Discourse in Misdemeanor Plea Bargaining," *Law and Society Review* 18 (1984): 75; and P. F. Nardulli et al., "Criminal Courts and Bureaucratic Justice: Concessions and Consensus in the Guilty Plea Process," *Journal of Criminal Law and Criminology* 76 (1985): 1103.

44. American Bar Association, *Standards Relating to Pleas of Guilty*, Sec. 3.1(c), p. 60.

45. *Newman v. United States*, 382 F. 2d (D.C. Cir. 1967).

SUGGESTED READINGS

Bailey, F. Lee. *The Defense Never Rests*. New York: Stein & Day, 1971.

Fine, Ralph A. *Escape of the Guilty*. New York: Dodd, Mead, 1986.

Frankel, Marvin E., and Gary P. Naftalis. *The Grand Jury: An Institution on Trial*. New York: Hill and Wang, 1977.

Heilbroner, David. *Rough Justice: Days and Nights of a Young D.A.* New York: Pantheon, 1990.

Heumann, Milton. *Plea Bargaining*. Chicago: University of Chicago Press, 1978.

Maynard, Douglas W. *Inside Plea Bargaining*. New York: Plenum Press, 1984.

McIntyre, Lisa J. *The Public Defender: The Practice of Law in the Shadows of Repute.*

Chicago: University of Chicago Press, 1987.

Newman, Donald J. *Conviction: The Determination of Guilt or Innocence without Trial.* Boston: Little, Brown and Co., 1966.

Sanborn, Joseph B. "A Historical Sketch of Plea Bargaining." *Justice Quarterly* 3 (June 1986): 111–137.

Spence, Gerry. *With Justice for None.* New York: Penguin, 1989.

Discussion questions

1. Describe the decisions made by a prosecutor in a particular case.

2. What influences may affect a prosecutor's decisions?

3. Compare the conservative crime control model and the liberal crime control model in relation to the prosecutor's decisions.

4. What are the most common reasons not to prosecute? Discuss.

5. Is the *nolle prosequi* decision discriminatory? How?

6. Describe the grand jury indictment process.

7. Why would a defendant have an attorney present at the preliminary hearing?

8. What are the purposes of plea bargaining? How is the practice useful in criminal justice?

9. What are the advantages of plea bargaining for the state? For the defendant?

10. What concessions are sought by the defendant in plea bargaining?

11. What is the difference between inducement-based plea bargaining and coercive plea bargaining?

12. Who is in charge of plea bargaining?

13. Must promises made by the prosecutor in plea bargaining be kept?

14. Describe and discuss the issues surrounding the practice of plea bargaining.

15. What are the arguments against plea bargaining?

10

Arraignment and Trial

A *new act is about to open on Broadway. In the heart of Manhattan's Times Square district, the Longacre Theater is ready for a three-year run of real-life drama: community-based court.*

The proposal is to borrow the theater from its owner, the Shubert Organization, and to use it as a section of the New York City Criminal Court. The court would be transferred from downtown Manhattan. Only misdemeanor offenders caught in the act of committing their offenses within a 30-square-block area of midtown Manhattan would be arraigned at the theater. Felony cases and trials would continue to be handled at the downtown criminal court. Full attention would thus be given to "quality-of-life" crimes, such as vandalism, low-level drug possession, petty thievery, prostitution, subway-fare beating, and illegal peddling.

No final decision has yet been made by city officials on the proposal. Yet following on the heels of the success of community policing, the idea of a community court offers hope for improving the criminal justice system. Perhaps a judge in such a court would benefit from the knowledge he or she would acquire in the community environment, and sentences would therefore become relevant both to offender and community needs.

About this Chapter

Although few of us will ever be tried on Broadway, even the worst among us charged with the most unspeakable crimes, is entitled to a "day in court." A public and fair criminal trial is a hallmark of the American system of justice. The process by which persons are accused and convicted, the mechanism by which the state gains the right to intervene in a person's life by means of sanctions and punishments, is steeped in formality, ritual, and often drama. The courtroom scene in which a doggedly determined public-servant prosecutor engages a slick, professional defense attorney has long been a favorite subject of television and movies. Each of us is familiar with this contest, and we are equally familiar with the structure and arrangement of a courtroom. We are indebted to Judge Wapner, *L.A. Law*, Perry Mason, *Presumed Innocent*, and many other television shows, movies, and their characters for this familiarity.

This chapter details the procedures whereby a person progresses from being *accused* of a crime to being *convicted* of one, describing the various stopping-off places along the way (see Fig. 10.1 for a flow chart of these steps). Despite the central importance of the right to a fair and speedy trial to our system, a very small percentage of cases actually go all the way to trial; but for those cases several very important decisions must be made by the prosecutors, the accused, the defense attorneys, the judges, and the juries. Practical and legal influences on those decisions are described here in the sections that follow.

The Courts

"Order in the courtroom!" "Your honor, I object!" "The witness may be excused." "Do you swear to tell the truth, the whole truth, and nothing but the truth, so help you God?" "Has the jury reached a verdict?"

These quotes are well known to all of us, along with numerous others we identify with courtrooms. Anyone vaguely familiar with popular art and drama which have depicted courtroom scenes has heard these words, and sensed their importance. Indeed, the drama of the courtroom provides many of the best, and most interesting, aspects of the criminal justice system.

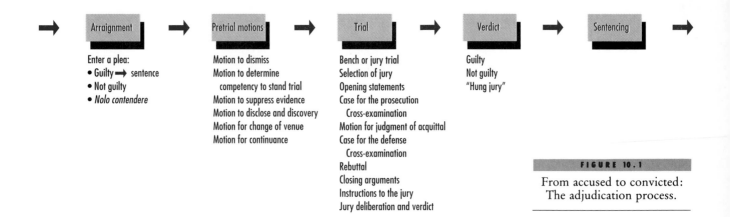

From accused to convicted:
The adjudication process.

In many ways the courtroom is a stage populated by people like the one Shakespeare described, "a poor player who struts and frets his hour upon the stage and then is heard no more." And yet other players are regulars who remain day after day as the parade of cases passes through. But actors or not, the people who appear in court, and those who play the leading court roles, are engaged in making decisions with enormous consequences, up to and including issues involving life and death. To better understand how these decisions are made, we first discuss the breakdown of the court system by jurisdiction: state, federal, trial, and appellate.

Federal and State Courts

The federal court system is made up of trial and appellate courts. The *federal district courts* are the trial courts for violations of federal law and crimes committed on federal property. Ninety-four federal district courts in the United States are presided over by federal judges who, like all federal judges, are appointed for life by the President of the United States with the advice and consent of the U.S. Senate. Federal district judges in turn sometimes appoint federal magistrates who hear pretrial motions and misdemeanor cases.

The *U.S. Courts of Appeals*, sometimes called the "Federal Circuit Courts of Appeals," are located in twelve geographic circuits, with one additional federal circuit court in Washington, DC. The circuit courts hear appeals from the district courts. Usually a three-judge panel in a circuit court votes either to affirm or reverse a lower-court decision. The U.S. Supreme Court is the highest court in the land. The nine justices can review the decisions of federal courts and many of the decisions of the highest state courts either on appeal or by writ of *certiorari*. The Supreme Court has the last word in applying the U.S. Constitution to criminal justice practices.

Each state has its own system of *state courts* that handle the overwhelming majority of the criminal prosecutions in the United States. Each state system includes both trial and appellate courts.

Trial Courts

The trial courts in the states conduct the day-to-day prosecutions of criminal defendants. They are presided over by judges who are elected and serve set terms of office.

However, the judge in any given court is not the only individual involved in the arraignment and trial processes. The following are also major players in the formal pleading and trial stages of the criminal justice process: the defendant, the prosecutor,

263

Federal and State Court Systems

"The judicial Power of the United States, shall be vested in one supreme Court, and in such inferior Courts as the Congress may from time to time ordain and establish" (U.S. Constitution, Art. III, Sec. 1). The federal court system is established under this authority by the Congress, and includes both trial and appellate courts. In addition, each state has its own independent court system, all of which also include (with some variation in detail) appellate and trial courts and which handle the vast majority of criminal cases in the United States.

Trial courts at both federal and state levels are presided over by a judge. The federal district courts are the principal trial courts in the federal system, and judges are appointed for life by the President with the consent of the U.S. Senate. In addition, in the federal system magistrates, who are appointed by the federal district judges, hear pretrial motions and misdemeanor cases. The majority of cases heard in federal district courts involve federal crimes, or crimes committed on U.S. government property.

State trial courts are referred to as county courts, superior courts, circuit courts, or district courts depending on which state one is in, and their judges are usually elected in nonpartisan elections. Trial courts hear misdemeanor and felony bench and jury trials. Convictions and sentences may be appealed to the courts of appeals, and death penalty appeals are generally heard in the state supreme courts.

Each state has an appellate court system, which usually includes a court of appeals, or district court of appeals, which hears the majority of the appeals filed from the lower trial courts. Cases are generally decided by a panel of judges who are appointed for life by the governor with the consent of the state legislature.

The state supreme court is the highest appellate court in any state, and usually consists of seven or nine judges who are appointed for life by the governor with the consent of the state legislature. This court may review some decisions made

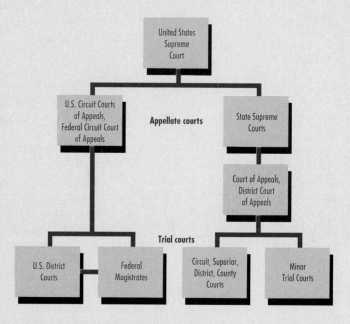

by the court of appeals, and generally hears appeals from trial courts where the death penalty has been imposed.

The U.S. Courts of Appeals, also known as the Federal Circuit Courts of Appeals, are divided into thirteen circuits. These courts hear both criminal and civil appeals from the district courts. Decisions are usually made by three-judge panels, who are appointed for life by the President with consent of the U.S. Senate.

The U.S. Supreme Court is the highest appellate court in the federal judicial system and has the jurisdiction to review decisions of the lower federal courts and many of the decisions of the state supreme courts. The Supreme Court can only review a small percentage of the cases decided by the lower courts, however, for it consists of only nine justices, also appointed for life terms by the President, with the consent of the U.S. Senate.

the defense lawyer, and the trial jury. Others involved include the bailiff, the court clerks, the court reporters, and the witnesses for the defense and for the prosecution, who offer testimony about the facts in the case. In some cases, "expert" testimony is given by expert witnesses who have established expertise about a particular issue involved in the trial.[2] For instance, a ballistics expert can testify whether a bullet

fragment was fired by a particular weapon, or fingerprint experts can testify as to the "match" between prints found at the crime scene and those of the defendant.

Also, since pleadings and trials are public (unlike grand jury proceedings), citizens uninvolved in the case may be present in the courtroom as observers. And press reporters, who, with some exceptions, are representatives of the print media, may be present. In recent years, as well, a number of states have allowed television cameras in courtrooms for news purposes.[3] Federal rules ban cameras from federal courts, however.

The formal pleading hearing, called an arraignment, and the trial are the most formal stages in the criminal justice process. None of the informality, even the friendliness, found in a juvenile court exists in the criminal court. Court proceedings require

decorum on the part of all the participants and observers. People who cause disruptions, including defendants, are forcefully and promptly removed from the courtroom and may be held in contempt of court, which frequently results in a fine, time in jail, or some other sanction. The judge is robed and is seated on an elevated bench; everyone in the courtroom rises when the judge enters or exits the courtroom; the jury sits to one side in a jury box; members of the press are seated at specially designated tables; onlookers are placed behind a rail, or bar, in front of which sit the defendant and defense attorneys; the district attorney is seated at a separate table. The courtroom setting is unmistakable to most Americans. We all know what it looks like from numerous photographs in the press and from television programs, even if we have never actually been in court. The setting no doubt embodies our concept of justice, just as police uniforms signify authority and force and a walled prison represents punishment.

Not only is the setting deliberately formal, but the procedures followed are rigidly circumscribed and controlled by law, tradition, and the gavel of the judge. Who may speak, when, and in what order are clearly predetermined and rigidly monitored by the judge. What can and cannot be said is also prescribed by the rules of evidence and pleading and by trial rules, and the rules are enforced by the court.

If one of the purposes of the pomp and circumstance surrounding court proceedings is to induce respect—perhaps even awe—for the law in people, the setting and the ritual used in arraignment and trial achieve that aim, except among the most cynical, radical, recalcitrant, or oblivious observers. It is through these proceedings that the criminal justice system separates the innocent from the guilty, releases the innocent, and prepares the guilty to move on to their just deserts. Defendants either become free citizens again or move on to the status of offender, of convicted criminal. All of the earlier decision steps in the criminal justice process—taking the suspect into custody, charging him or her with a crime—lead to these moments, these middle-stage decision points, where guilt is determined by full due process of law, and those found guilty enter into the final stages of the criminal justice process, sentence imposition and sentence execution.

ARRAIGNMENT: ENTERING A PLEA

At some date after the filing of the indictment or information—ordinarily ranging from a few days to a few weeks, depending on the court calendar—the defendant is brought before a court of *competent jurisdiction* (a court empowered to conduct felony trials, misdemeanor trials, etc.) where he or she is once more notified of the Constitutional right to trial, is presented with the formal charges, and is asked to plead to them. This is known as **arraignment**. In many instances the judge will accept a guilty plea and schedule the case for sentencing immediately, thereby ending the proceedings just as though a full jury trial had resulted in a finding of guilty. (See Field Practice A.)

Pleas available to a defendant at arraignment are (1) not guilty, (2) guilty and, in some places, (3) not guilty because insane, and (4) ***nolo contendere*** (no contest). This latter plea, available at the discretion of the trial judge in about half the states and in the federal jurisdiction, has the same *criminal* effect as a **guilty plea**—the defendant receives a criminal record and can be sentenced. But, unlike the guilty plea, a no contest plea may not be used in any subsequent civil action as proof that the defendant committed the act. *Nolo contendere* pleas are commonly entered in white-collar cases in which a corporate defendant is likely to be sued for damages and occasionally in cases involving traditional charges, such as assault in which the victim may also be bringing civil suit.[4]

If a defendant stands mute (does not respond) or otherwise refuses to answer the charges, a not guilty plea is entered. In a few states, a defendant is required to indicate an intention to use an *insanity defense* by entering a plea of not guilty because insane at

Smiling postal worker David Berkowitz is escorted by police officers to court, where he entered a plea of "not guilty because insane" in the Son of Sam murder cases.

Accepting a Guilty Plea at Arraignment

Speak Up!

JUDGE: You are Bernie Rogers?

DEFENDANT: Yes sir.

JUDGE: Mr. Schuffstal, how does your client wish to plead?

COUNSEL: Guilty of burglary, Your Honor.

JUDGE: Mr. Rogers, you have just heard your attorney say you wish to plead guilty to burglary. Is that how you wish to plead?

DEFENDANT: Yes sir.

JUDGE: Before I can accept your plea, I must ask you certain questions and tell you certain things. If you don't understand, stop me and I'll explain. If at any time you want to talk to your lawyer, let me know. I'll stop and you can talk with him privately for as long and as often as you want while we are doing this. You have been placed under oath and if you make any statements that are false, they can later be used against you in a prosecution for perjury. Do you understand what this means?

DEFENDANT: Yes sir.

JUDGE: How old are you?

DEFENDANT: 26.

JUDGE: Have you ever been treated for mental problems?

DEFENDANT: No sir.

JUDGE: Are you now under the influence of any alcohol, drugs, or medication of any kind?

DEFENDANT: No.

JUDGE: You do not have to plead guilty. You have the right to plead not guilty and have the following rights at trial: the rights to a jury, to see and hear witnesses testify and have your lawyer question them for you, to call witnesses and present evidence you want the jury to consider and to present any defense you might have to the jury; the right to testify yourself or not to testify; the right to require the prosecutor to prove your guilt by the evidence beyond a reasonable doubt before you can be found guilty. Do you understand these rights?

DEFENDANT: Yes sir.

JUDGE: Do you understand that if I accept your plea, you give up each of these rights, that there will be no trial and all I have to do is sentence you, and that you give up your right to an appeal?

DEFENDANT: Yes sir.

JUDGE: Mr. Schuffstal, have any agreements been made between the state and the defendant relative to any plea or any sentence?

COUNSEL: Yes, Your Honor. My client has agreed to plead guilty to a single charge of burglary in exchange for the prosecution's promise to drop additional charges and to recommend a guideline sentence.

JUDGE: Mrs. Prosecutor, is this correct?

PROSECUTOR: Yes, Your Honor.

JUDGE: Mr. Rogers, has anyone, including your lawyer, or the prosecuting attorney, or anyone else forced or pressured you into entering this plea?

DEFENDANT: No sir.

JUDGE: Are you pleading guilty because you are guilty?

DEFENDANT: Yes sir.

JUDGE: What actually did you do?

DEFENDANT: Well, I took these tires from the gas station.

JUDGE: Did you use forcible entry to break into the gas station?

DEFENDANT: Yes sir.

JUDGE: And how do you plead?

DEFENDANT: Guilty.

JUDGE: Do you realize that by pleading guilty you could be sent to prison for 3 years?

DEFENDANT: Yes sir.

JUDGE: And you still wish to so plead?

DEFENDANT: Yes, I do.

JUDGE: Very well, I accept your plea of guilty. I am ordering a Presentence Investigation Report and set the date for sentencing 3 weeks hence, that is, at 10 a.m. on August 15. ∎

---

the arraignment. More commonly, defense disclosure of the defenses of insanity or *alibi* ("I was elsewhere when the crime was committed") is required 5 to 10 days before trial rather than at arraignment, although in most places later entry of these defenses may be allowed with the consent of the court. The purpose of this disclosure of defense intentions is to allow the state the opportunity to submit the defendant to a psychiatric examination or to investigate the alibi.

If the defendant pleads not guilty, the arraignment ends by setting a date for the trial. Once again, release on bail or release on recognizance (ROR) is considered, with the judge having a choice to continue either, to raise or lower the amount of bail, or to deny release and send the defendant to jail to await trial. When a plea of not guilty because insane is entered, the defendant, upon the request of the prosecutor, is commonly sent to a mental hospital for psychiatric examination, with the trial time fixed for a date following this diagnostic interval. A psychiatric examination typically takes from 30 to 90 days.

Guilty Plea Procedures

Even if a defendant pleads guilty or *nolo contendere*, the judge need not accept the plea.[5] If, from the behavior, appearance, or words of the defendant during the brief arraignment process, the judge is led to believe that a defendant is mentally incompetent, or somehow does not seem to understand what is happening, or that the plea may be involuntary or greatly inaccurate in terms of what actually happened, the court may delay arraignment. This is often done to allow for psychiatric diagnosis or to enable the defendant to confer with counsel. However, the judge may simply reject the guilty plea without giving reasons and set a trial date just as if the defendant had pleaded not guilty.

In deciding whether to accept a plea of guilty, all judges, both federal and state, are required to *personally address* the defendant and make inquiries to establish the following:

1. The defendant knows of his or her right to a trial and that a guilty plea is a waiver of this right.
2. The defendant is "voluntarily" pleading guilty (i.e., was not forced or threatened into the plea).
3. The defendant understands the nature of the charges.
4. The defendant is aware of the possible *maximum* sentence that can be imposed if he or she pleads guilty.

Numerous appellate court decisions address the voluntariness of the plea, the defendant's understanding of the charge, and the defendant's awareness of the consequences of pleading guilty in light of judicial inquiry.[6] However, a more complex and unsettled matter is raised by a provision found in some state court rules or statutes and in the Federal Rules of Criminal Procedure, Rule 11, which requires the judge to inquire into the *factual basis* for the plea.[7] The factual basis requirement relates to the *accuracy* of the guilty plea, that is, whether there is adequate evidence to support the charge and therefore the plea. The extent of the inquiry needed to establish the factual basis of the plea, that is, whether the amount and type of evidence available is sufficient to support the charge, is left to the discretion of the judge, who, in the words of Rule 11, must be "satisfied that there is a factual basis for the plea."[8] To secure a reversal on appeal based on *inadequate* factual basis, an appellant must usually show that his or her conviction was unjust because the proof supporting the charges at the arraignment was *inadequate*. The standard of proof required to establish the factual basis of a guilty plea is less stringent than the test of "beyond a reasonable doubt" required for finding guilt at a trial. But it should be noted that many of the legal ramifications involved in the factual basis requirement are still unclear.

Withdrawal of a Guilty Plea

A defendant whose plea of guilty has been accepted by the court may later decide on a **withdrawal of the guilty plea** in order to go to trial. This change of heart may occur at any time after arraignment, and may rest on a variety of factors, ranging from hiring a new lawyer who advises a not guilty plea, to dissatisfaction with the sentence, to a belief that the state has somehow reneged on some preplea promise.

To withdraw a guilty plea, the defendant must petition the court with a *motion for withdrawal*. In most jurisdictions, the trial judge has discretion as to whether such a motion should be granted. In the past, some states allowed an absolute right to withdraw a plea up to the time of imposition of sentence, with postsentence withdrawal left to the discretion of the court. In other words, the only limitation placed on the defendant's right to withdraw a plea occurred *after* sentencing, when the defendant no longer could automatically withdraw a guilty plea just because he or she found the sentence imposed more severe than expected. Recently, though, the trend has been to give the judge discretion in this matter both before and after sentencing.

Often laws permitting withdrawal of pleas do not require any specific reasons be given for the request. However, a few states require the defendant to claim "total innocence" of the crime before allowing withdrawal. A more common test, however, is that withdrawal should be granted to correct any "manifest injustice." This is the test in the federal system[9] and is the suggested test in the American Bar Association's (ABA's) *Standards Relating to Pleas of Guilty*. Here certain situations are listed which might meet the manifest injustice test, including failure of the defendant to "receive the charge or sentence concessions contemplated by [a] plea agreement."[10]

Denial of a motion for plea withdrawal is appealable, and such appeals occur fairly frequently. If the trial court's denial is upheld on appeal, the guilty plea stands; if withdrawal is allowed, the defendant is scheduled for trial. An important issue which then arises is whether the fact that the defendant at one time pleaded guilty can be introduced at trial. The drafters of the ABA *Standards* suggest that a withdrawn plea "should not be received against the defendant in any criminal proceedings,"[12] but there are differing opinions about this in various jurisdictions.[11] For this reason, among others, defendants often enter a plea of *nolo contendere*, which also, in some jurisdictions, automatically allows them the right to a later appeal of the dispositive issue.

Presentence Investigations and Sentencing

If a defendant pleads guilty (or *nolo contendere*) and if, after examination in open court, the judge accepts the plea, the defendant stands convicted of a crime just as much as if he or she had been found guilty in a full-scale jury trial. After the plea is accepted by the court, the defendant is *bound over* for sentencing, that is, a date is set for the imposition of the sentence on the now convicted offender. Except in a few instances of very minor offenses (traffic violations where a fine is the maximum punishment) and more serious offenses that carry legislatively mandated prison terms (which give the judge no discretion as to sentence), that date is usually a few weeks or a month after the arraignment, which gives the probation officers attached to the court time to conduct a presentence investigation into the social and criminal background of the offender, his or her personal traits, employment, educational history, and so forth—information for the judge to use in making the sentencing decision.

Presentence investigations (PSIs), discussed in more detail in Chap. 11, are required by law in many states for all felony defendants except those subject to mandatory sentences. The judge must receive the report but is not required to base the sentencing decision on any information contained in it. The judge may, for instance, sentence solely on his or her attitude toward the offense at issue.

However, in guilty plea cases most judges rely on the PSI to help them impose a just sentence, taking into account not only the crime involved but the offender's past record, current status in the community, personality traits, and any other information that is deemed relevant not only to the past but to the future of the offender.

During the interval between conviction and sentencing, the offender may be referred to jail or sent to jail if he or she has been free on pretrial release. So, a bail or jail decision, just as described in Chap. 8, must be made again at this point.

Plea bargaining, which may begin very early—indeed, sometimes it starts before the defendant is in custody—may go on right through the trial if the judge chooses to allow it. Though it is not common, it is not altogether rare either for a defendant to move to withdraw a not guilty plea, changing it to guilty; this is often the result of a plea bargain negotiated right in the middle of the trial. The defense is allowed to negotiate for a reduction in the charge or leniency in a proposed sentence right up until a verdict is rendered by the jury or the judge accepts a plea, and this contributes to the fact that most prosecutions result in convictions.

PRETRIAL MOTIONS

Before the trial is conducted, several important decisions are made by the judge in response to written requests, called **pretrial motions**, on behalf of the prosecution or defense. Several motions are available to each side, the most common being the following:[13]

1. *Motion to dismiss.* A defendant may file a motion to dismiss the case based on the failure of the prosecution to allege a crime, or because the documents filed by the prosecution are inaccurate. Usually, if the court grants the motion to dismiss, the prosecution is granted time to refile the charges and correct the documents.
2. *Motion to determine the competency of the accused to stand trial.* Usually this motion is filed if the defense believes the defendant is mentally ill, or if a defense of insanity is planned.
3. *Motion to suppress evidence.* Three types of suppression motions are common. First, the defense can seek to exclude evidence obtained through search and seizure if it appears the search was carried out without a warrant or if the legality of the warrant was questionable. Second, the defense can move to exclude confessions, admissions, or other statements made to the police by the defendant if it appears they were not made voluntarily. Third, the defense may challenge the pretrial identification of the accused if it appears that police procedures violated due process standards.
4. *Motion to require the prosecution to disclose the identity of a confidential informant.* Here the court must balance the individual right of the accused to prepare a defense against the public's interest in protecting the free flow of information to the police. Trial judges have a great deal of discretion in these matters, and if the informant was an "active participant" in the offense, the prosecution may have to disclose the informant's identity.
5. *Motion for a change of venue.* This is filed if the defense believes that pretrial publicity makes it impossible to seat an impartial jury.
6. *Motion for a continuance.* This may be filed by either the prosecution or the defense to postpone a trial for any number of reasons including illness or emergency situations involving the defendant, the prosecutor, the defense counsel, or important witnesses which make it impossible for them to appear in court. Sometimes the motion is made when one side or the other has not had adequate time to prepare for the trial.

Pretrial motions are often argued in open court hearings. Often the decision of the judge about pretrial motions, especially regarding the suppression of evidence, can make or break the prosecution's case. These hearings determine to a great extent what evidence will be presented to the jury during the trial.

PRETRIAL DISCOVERY

Pretrial discovery of evidence means that both the prosecution and the defense seek to gain access to the evidence possessed by the opposing party before the trial begins. This can be done by filing the proper motions for discovery. Usually, the accused is entitled to know before the trial the names and addresses of witnesses the prosecution intends to call and any written statements they may have made, all statements made by codefendants and the name of anyone who heard such statements, a transcript of grand jury minutes, reports and statements by experts on issues relating to the case, the results of physical or mental tests, any physical evidence and the results of scientific tests relevant to the case, anything obtained from the accused the prosecutor intends to introduce as evidence, and any record of prior convictions of persons the prosecution intends to call as witnesses.[14]

The prosecution is usually entitled to require the accused to appear in a lineup; to speak so witnesses may make an identification of voice; to be fingerprinted; to pose for photographs not involving reinactments of the crime; to try on articles of clothing relevant to the case; to submit specimens of body fluids, material under the fingernails or in the hair, or any other materials from his or her body relevant to the case, to provide samples of handwriting; and to undergo tests the court deems reasonable and necessary. Also, the prosecution is entitled to know the defenses the defense intends to use, such as alibi, insanity, etc., along with the names and addresses of defense witnesses, written statements or anything else the defense intends to submit as evidence, any evidence in favor of the alibi to be used, and whatever other information the court in its discretion allows the prosecution to seek.

As you can see, pretrial discovery practically eliminates any surprises at trial. Each side knows what the other knows. This simplifies things, and the balance of information contributes to the plea bargaining process.

THE CRIMINAL TRIAL

The **Sixth Amendment** to the Constitution reads

> In all criminal prosecutions, the accused shall enjoy the right to a speedy and public trial, by an impartial jury of the State and district wherein the crime shall have been committed, which district shall have been previously ascertained by law, and to be informed of the *nature* and *cause* of the accusation; to be confronted with the witnesses against him; to have compulsory process for obtaining witnesses in his favor, and to have the assistance of counsel for his defense.

Each provision of this amendment, as with the provisions of most of the Constitutional amendments, has been litigated, interpreted, and refined over the years. And yet each provision remains controversial: For example, courts are still coping with such matters as what "speedy trial" means in practice, when and under what conditions the public (and the press) can be excluded from a trial, whether and why **venue** (location of the trial) can be changed, how witnesses may be compelled to testify and whether they must confront the accused in all cases, and how impartial juries can be found, among other issues. As with all Constitutional phraseology, the Sixth Amendment *sounds* simple but the complexity of situations that arise to test the meaning of each word is mind-boggling. And the changing members and changing philosophies of succeeding Supreme Courts have indeed made the Constitution a dynamic rather than a static document.

In most places, defendants who plead not guilty to felony charges can opt for either a jury or a bench trial, the latter meaning the judge acts alone as the fact finder. In general, jury trials in felony cases can be waived if both the defendant and the defense counsel agree. In some states, the prosecutor must consent to such a waiver.[15] In about one-third of state jurisdictions, the jury cannot be waived in *any* felony matter. And in still others, a waiver is permitted in all but *capital* cases.[16]

Bench Trials

In *most* cases, a defendant can choose to stand trial before a judge sitting alone. This is a **bench trial** for the word "bench" is commonly used as a synonym for "court" or "judge." Generally, jury trials are waived by defendants as a *tactical matter* in cases involving highly technical legal issues. The judge, being a lawyer, understands and is accustomed to considering fine and subtle points of law, whereas jurors are "civilians" and may not fully understand important legal matters in a technical defense. On the other hand, jury trials are eagerly sought in cases that have intense emotional overtones, where the outcome is more likely to rest on jury sympathies than on fine points of the law. For instance, a defendant accused of a complex fraud or charged with a conspiracy to commit a crime may choose a bench trial because of the legal complexities involved in proving such crimes. On the other hand, a defendant charged with the homicide of a fatally ill relative who wishes to enter a defense of "mercy killing" may perhaps prefer to be tried by a jury of peers.

The comparative tactical advantages and disadvantages of bench versus jury trials have generated a good deal of discussion.[17] Waiver of jury trial is often believed to be advantageous to a defendant when (1) the case has been the subject of a great deal of adverse publicity, (2) a highly technical defense will be utilized, or (3) it is believed that jurors are likely to be unsympathetic to the defense. Studies of jury behavior have demonstrated that while judges and juries agree on the outcome of cases about 75 percent of the time, juries are significantly more lenient—more likely to acquit—than judges in the remaining 25 percent of cases.[18]

Jury Trials

The right to a **jury trial** in felony cases is absolute, but in cases where a lesser offense is charged, jury trials are not always available. Constitutional provisions in many jurisdictions do not extend the right to jury trial to cases involving "petty offenses" unless the offense carries a potential punishment of more than 6 months in jail.[19] Petty offenses include the least severely punished misdemeanors and violations, such as public intoxication, disorderly conduct, other public-order crimes, and minor traffic violations. However, what falls under the specific designation of petty offense varies from one set of statutes and one jurisdiction to the next.[20]

The issue of when a state may refuse a defendant's request for a jury trial has been narrowed by a 1968 decision of the U.S. Supreme Court, which upheld the right to a jury trial in a state case where the defendant was charged with a misdemeanor.[21] In the context of a 1972 decision expanding the right to counsel for defendants on trial for even petty offenses,[22] this may mean that full-scale trials will become more common at the lower range of criminal charges. Some state constitutions provide for a jury trial on appeal from a nonjury conviction for petty offenses, and the American Bar Association suggests such a right of appeal as a desirable standard.[23] Interestingly, a defendant has no right to insist on a bench trial.[24]

In some states the trial judge is required to file a memorandum in support of the finding of guilt after a bench trial. In contrast, juries do *not* give reasons for their findings of guilt or innocence. A jury decision to convict, however, may be *set aside* by the trial judge if the judge believes trial evidence failed to meet the "beyond a reasonable doubt" test. Occasionally the judge may issue a **judgment of acquittal**, sometimes called a "JOA" or a "directed verdict," without waiting for a jury finding.[25] But it is more common for a judge who is convinced the evidence is insufficient to *convict* to wait for the jury decision and to overrule the conviction, if such is the decision, than to order an acquittal beforehand. After all, the jury might *not* convict, meaning no judicial action would be necessary. Both the directed verdict and the setting aside of a conviction put a judge at odds with the jury and, like the prosecution, judges are political figures who try to avoid conflict and criticism.

The judge's power to overrule the jury is one-directional only. No matter how convinced the judge is that a defendant is guilty, the judge *cannot* order a jury to convict, nor can the judge set aside an acquittal. The presumption of innocence is no longer *just* a presumption if either the jury or the judge so finds. And a finding of innocence cannot be overturned; only a conviction can be reversed by judicial action. The fact remains, however, that most jury trials result in the conviction of the accused for some offense, even if not the one charged.

Speedy Trial

The "time to trial" is the time that elapses between the arrest of a suspect and the commencement of the trial, which, in our system of justice, must be "speedy." The time does not begin to count until an arrest has been made. Thus a suspect who has fled and cannot be located can hardly claim denial of a **speedy trial** when caught later and eventually tried.

Speedy trial provisions, however, relate not to absconders but to defendants already under arrest. Today, with the courts in many jurisdictions crowded, the time between arrest and trial is often very long even when both sides, state and defense, wish to get on with it. The court calendar problem is such that trial justice is routine but slow. This remains a major problem for our criminal justice system, particularly in crowded metropolitan court districts.

Speedy trial provisions, found today in most state statutes, seek to prevent undue delay in bringing cases to court, to prevent persons from being held for extended periods of time in custody awaiting final judgment.

Delaying a trial has advantages and disadvantages for both sides in criminal litigation. The state can continue to accumulate evidence and, in cases in which the defendant is being held in jail, can in effect punish the accused before trial by extending pretrial custody. The defense, on the other hand, might want a delay so that publicity about the crime cools down and witnesses' memories fade. In general, the intensity of feeling a case generates diminishes by the time of sentencing. Indeed, defendants' requests for continuances pose a major problem not solved by speedy trial statutory provisions, which generally relate only to the state's readiness to proceed. But a clever defendant, reluctant to go to trial, and free on pretrial release, can extend the time to trial considerably by seeking adjournments, or by changing lawyers, or by introducing multiple pretrial motions to change venue, exclude evidence, and so on. Delay is often an important defense tactic and a difficult one to control, for the court faces problems if it forces to trial a defendant who claims not to be prepared to be tried for a serious crime. In such cases, justice delayed may be justice denied for the victim of the crime.

As mentioned above, the various court decisions and statutory speedy trial acts, now common in our states, are designed primarily to force the *state* not to delay trials without good reason. In a 1972 case, *Barker v. Wingo*,[26] the U.S. Supreme Court outlined a series of factors to assess in determining if a delay is unwarranted. These include the length of the delay, the reasons for it, the amount of prejudice to the defendant created by the delay, and the defendant's request for a speedy trial. In the particular case, Barker's trial was delayed for 5 years on various governmental requests for continuances before he was eventually tried, convicted, and given a life sentence. Interestingly, the Court held that Barker was *not* deprived of a speedy trial, thereby rejecting the doctrine of a "fixed-time rule" (i.e., "Trial must occur within 60 days"), stating instead that the speedy trial issue must be decided on a case-by-case basis.

In an effort to correct slow trial processes in the federal judicial system, Congress passed the **Speedy Trial Act of 1974**, which in federal cases requires an indictment or information within 30 days of arrest, arraignment within 10 days of formal charging, and trial within 60 days of arraignment. These strictures apply to government prosecutors, but the times can be extended, as mentioned, by defense requests for continuances and delays. Many states now have similar provisions.

Statutes of Limitations

One factor not yet mentioned that affects whether or not a trial takes place at all is **statutes of limitations** on the time allowed for the prosecution of certain crimes. That is, states place statutory limits on the length of time—generally 5 or 7 years—police have to arrest a suspect and prosecutors have to bring him or her to trial. After that time, the matter is closed. However, such provisions do not apply to *all* crimes. For very serious felonies—murder, for instance—there are *no* statutory limits, so that a killer who escapes detection for decades can still be tried when caught, no matter how old the evidence or how forgetful the witnesses.

Jury Selection

Historically trial juries have been composed of 12 members, but this is not a Constitutional requirement. In a case originating in Florida, the U.S. Supreme Court held it proper for states to use juries of as few as six persons in felony cases (six-member juries are common in misdemeanor trials) except in cases involving the death penalty.[27] Today only 14 states and the federal jurisdictions require 12-member juries in all felony cases; the remaining states allow smaller bodies.

Although a grand jury issues indictments based on a majority vote, it has been traditional for trial jury decisions to be unanimous. However, a unanimous decision is not required by either the Sixth or the Fourteenth (due process) Amendments to the Constitution. In 1972 the U.S. Supreme Court upheld in *Apodaca v. Oregon* an Oregon statute that allowed conviction on the vote of 10 out of 12 members of a trial jury; however, in 1979, in *Burch v. Louisiana*, the Supreme Court held that a six-person jury in a nonpetty offense must be unanimous.[28] How far nonunanimity may go (i.e., if only a simple majority vote is required) is still undecided.[29] Under the Uniform Code of Military Justice, for instance, a unanimous vote is not required for a conviction.

Jury members are ordinarily selected by lot or chance, from a master list of persons in the community where the trial will take place. Commonly today the master list is based on local voter registration rolls. Whether this really gives a representative cross section of the community is debatable since there is no law that all citizens must register to vote. Indeed, various studies have shown that perhaps as many as 40 percent of those eligible to vote do not register to do so, and it is believed that some people choose not to register to vote simply to avoid being called for jury duty. So some states now base their master lists for jury duty on drivers license lists, in the belief that a greater cross section of citizens will be represented.

No matter how the original polling list is established, there are always some exclusions. For example, literacy is usually required (as in American citizenship, which is automatic if the list is drawn up from registered voters). Minors are excluded, as are those with felony convictions, those hospitalized for mental illness or for serious medical conditions, and those who are members of essential occupations who cannot take the time to serve, such as firefighters, police officers, physicians, nurses, legislators, clergymen, and in many places attorneys, teachers, and professors. People who are called for jury duty may seek to be excused, usually for some cause such as illness or child care responsibilities. In general, the assembler of the eligible jury list (clerk of the court or jury commissioner) is lenient in excusing jurors unless there is a compelling need for a large jury panel.

An historic concern of jury selection has been the systematic exclusion of blacks and other minorities from jury duty. And in the civil rights efforts of recent decades, appellate courts have often attempted to eliminate patterned discrimination in jury composition. Indeed, one of the consequences of increased voter registration for blacks and other minority citizens has been that these groups have gained increased representation on jury selection lists. This, of course, is not the major purpose of voter registration—which is to give minorities a political voice—but it is an important side product.

Voir Dire

Once a panel of potential jurors willing and able to serve has been selected, some may still be excused from a particular case upon the request of the prosecutor or the defense counsel. These exclusions can take one of two forms: **peremptory challenge** and **for-cause removal**. A peremptory challenge is the informal dismissal of a potential juror upon the whim or trial sense of the prosecutor or defense lawyer; no explanation need be given or any cause demonstrated. Statutes or court rules usually limit the number of peremptories allowed, and once used up, potential jurors can only be removed for cause. That is, the prosecutor or defense attorney must prove to the judge that there is some factor in the potential juror's background or attitudes likely to bias his or her eventual decision in the case, upon which basis the judge then grants a dismissal.

Peremptory challenges and removals for cause are both normally based on potential jurors' responses to *voir dire* questioning. The ***voir dire*** ("to speak the truth") examination allows attorneys for both sides to question each potential juror in order to decide whether that person is suitable for the case from a prosecution or defense point of view. In general, *voir dire* focuses on the juror's previous familiarity with the case, his or her association with anyone involved in the case, his or her attitudes toward certain types of crimes, people, and punishments, any preconceived ideas about the guilt or innocence of the defendant, and any similar matters likely to affect the juror's eventual decision in the case.

In theory, the purpose of *voir dire* is to ascertain if a potential juror can render a fair and impartial verdict. In practice, neither peremptory nor for-cause jury exclusions based on the *voir dire* examinations are really designed to obtain an impartial jury. Both sides use both forms of exclusion tactically in attempts to build a *partial* jury, favorable to the sides of the case the attorneys represent. One side or the other may want more or fewer women on the jury, may wish to build the jury around some age span thought to be advantageous, or may try to equalize or slant the racial mix of jurors.

Unlike peremptory challenges, there is no limit to removals for cause. This is why jury selection may take so long and involve such a large pool of potential jurors in cases that have received a great deal of local publicity. If a crime has been heinous and the defendant is notorious, finding twelve local citizens who can be truly impartial in hearing the case may be difficult.

It remains a question whether the use of peremptory and for-cause challenges negates the formation of representative juries. There have been two interesting decisions on this point from the U.S. Supreme Court. In 1965 in *Swain v. Alabama* the court *upheld* the practice of using peremptory challenges to exclude jurors for reasons of race.[30] However, in 1986 the court in *Batson v. Kentucky* held that blacks may not be excluded from a jury because the prosecutor believes they *may* favor a defendant of their own race.[31] The Court held in *Batson* that:

1. The equal protection clause forbids a prosecutor to peremptorily challenge potential jurors solely on account of their race or on the assumption that black jurors as a group will be unable to impartially consider the prosecution's case against a black defendant.
2. A criminal defendant may establish a *prima facie* case of purposeful racial discrimination in the selection of the jury based solely on evidence concerning the prosecutor's exercise of peremptory challenges at the defendant's trial, without showing repeated instances of such discriminatory conduct over a number of cases.
3. Once a defendant makes such a *prima facie* showing, the burden shifts to the prosecution to come forward with a neutral explanation for challenging the jurors which relates to the particular case being tried.

Although this decision effectively overturned *Swain*, the Court did not hold that it should be applied retroactively.

Jury selection has always been a controversial problem. In the colonial period, for example, when the United States was a country of towns and villages, selecting a jury of peers, "equals" in the common meaning of this term, could not be achieved, for major segments of the population, including women and slaves, were excluded from jury duty. And even today, after black emancipation and in the era of "women's rights," there is a question of whether the "peer" ideal can be approximated, not only in metropolitan courts but in smaller jurisdictions. Moreover, the issue is by no means limited to the underrepresentation of blacks or women on juries.

Part of the problem is caused by jury selection practices, primarily certain exclusion provisions, which by law or custom keep those who do not own property or who do not have a permanent residence (often members of ethnic and racial minorities) off jury panels. Because criminal defendants are often poor, transient, and members of minority groups, such exclusions are felt to weaken the spirit, if not the letter, of the law regarding peer judgment. Although the law does not require juries to mirror all the economic, social, and personal characteristics of a defendant—in fact, a "peer" is generally held to be any other citizen—systematic exclusion practices have tended to weaken the philosophy of the jury trial.[32]

REASONABLE DOUBT AND THE PRESUMPTION OF INNOCENCE

The criminal trial, bench or jury, demands the highest level of evidence to convict; that is, conviction only if guilt has been proved "beyond a reasonable doubt"—not *any* doubt, but any "reasonable" doubt. This is a much higher standard than the "probable cause" needed to indict or the "preponderance of evidence" used in deciding civil lawsuits, or even the "clear and convincing" proof required in some civil proceedings.

Moreover, at trial our belief in the "presumption of innocence" reaches full flower. Indeed until the trial, from arrest through charging, the criminal justice process moves along on an increasing belief in the *guilt* of the suspect. Police do not arrest, nor do grand juries indict, on a presumption of innocence. True, we place great value on the presumption of innocence, but it does not really come into play until the trial stage of our justice system. For at trial the entire burden is on the state—the prosecutor—to demonstrate beyond a reasonable doubt all the elements required to prove the accused's guilt: the mental state (*mens rea*, such as premeditation), the act (*actus rea*, or act designed to be criminal, such as shooting to inflict death), and the consequences of the act (deprivation of property or life, for instance).

Defendants may do or say nothing at trial, but this is rare. At a minimum, through their attorneys, they usually challenge the state's evidence by cross-examining witnesses and questioning the reliability of physical evidence such as blood analysis or ballistics tests. Additionally, defendants may enter a defense, for instance, insanity, to negate the required mental state for the crime, or may plead entrapment or a number of other defenses to negate any or all the arguments of the prosecution. Witnesses for the defense, including expert witnesses, may take the stand and, under oath and subject to cross-examination by the prosecutor, rebut some or all of the evidence of the state. This defense or these rebuttal witnesses need not prove innocence; they need merely raise a reasonable doubt about the defendant's guilt.

STAGES IN THE CRIMINAL TRIAL

After a jury has been selected and seated, the trial begins with an **opening statement** by the prosecutor, which is an attempt to tell the jury what crime the defendant is charged with and how all the necessary elements proving guilt will be demonstrated. The defense may then make its own opening statement, and often does so if the defense attorney feels the opening statement of the prosecutor was particularly harmful to the defense case; however, the opening statement of the defense may be deferred until it presents its own evidence. Upon completion of the opening statement, the prosecutor presents his or her evidence—physical evidence such as fingerprints; testimonial evidence of witnesses or experts as to how, when, and where the physical evidence was obtained; eyewitness evidence; and any *circumstantial* evidence (i.e., any evidence from which a fact can be reasonably inferred—the defendant being seen with a gun near the scene of a shooting, for example). This is done through **direct examination** or questioning of states' witnesses.

A chemical expert explains

laboratory evidence of insulin

in the blood of Martha

"Sunny" von Bulow to the

jury in the Claus von Bulow

murder case.

After each witness for the prosecution has testified, defense counsel may carry out a **cross examination** in an attempt to cast some reasonable doubt on the evidence by questioning the manner in which the evidence was obtained or analyzed, or by questioning a witness's memory, or by showing inconsistencies in testimony, or perhaps by challenging the credibility or expertise of the witness. The prosecution then is allowed to question the witness again on **redirect examination** in order to give the witness an opportunity to clarify any issues raised in the cross examination. Then this may be followed by a *recross examination*, that is, the defense counsel may again put questions to the witness based on redirect testimony.

After all the prosecutor's witnesses have presented their evidence and been cross examined, and after the prosecution has presented all its other evidence, the state *rests its case*. At this point the defense frequently moves for a directed verdict of acquittal in order to give the trial judge an opportunity to dismiss the case for lack of sufficient evidence. This is primarily a tactical move, however, and the motion to acquit is routinely denied.

The defendant, through his or her attorney, then introduces witnesses or other evidence that favor the defendant's claim of being not guilty. The defense may begin with an opening statement by counsel, but is not required to do so. Normally, defense witnesses are sworn in and subjected to direct examination by the defense lawyers, then cross examination by the prosecutor. After all the defense witnesses have been examined, cross-examined, and examined again on redirect, the defense rests *its* case. There may be some further witnesses called by both sides, in order, and cross-examined in a process called **rebuttal.** Rebuttal witnesses dispute the testimony of the defendant's witnesses. Then the defendant's rebuttal witnesses may be called to dispute the testimony of the prosecution's rebuttal witnesses. After the final cross examination, the evidence phase of the trial is finally concluded.

Usually at this point a recess is taken in the proceedings to allow the judge to prepare **instructions to the jury**. A conference is often held in the judge's chambers and the attorneys for each side submit proposed instructions for the jury. The judge decides what the instructions will be and inform the attorneys of what they will be, after which the attorneys prepare their own closing remarks with an eye to the content of the judge's instructions.

Following this, first the defense and then the prosecution sum up by making closing statements. The defense tries to cast doubt on the prosecutor's evidence, or some of it, and the prosecutor—allowed the last word because the entire burden of proof is on the state—normally tries to show how the evidence introduced proves the defendant guilty "beyond a reasonable doubt."

After the closing statements, the judge charges the jury, instructing them in the applicable points of the law, in the nature and meaning of evidence they have seen or heard, and about the meaning of "reasonable doubt." The jury then retires to another location to deliberate the guilt or innocence of the accused. If agreement among jury members is reached, they return to the courtroom and notify the judge of their decision. The defendant then is asked to stand to hear the verdict of the jury. If the verdict is guilty, the judge sets a time for sentencing, usually some date in the future to allow time for a presentence investigation.

If unanimity is required for a verdict and, after an extended period of time for deliberation, jury members find they cannot achieve such a consensus, they report their dilemma to the court. The judge then may suggest strongly that the jury deliberate further or may instead conclude that they are a "**hung jury**," one that cannot reach a unanimous decision about guilt or innocence. If the jury cannot reach a verdict, the judge declares a mistrial. If this happens, the defendant may be tried for the same crime again before a different jury without the prohibition against double jeopardy applying.

Normally, after the verdict is announced, the judge dismisses the jury. Judges often use this occasion as an opportunity to thank the jurors for the important service they have rendered and to make a brief speech about the American system of justice. Remember, judges are politicians too.

APPEALS AND POSTCONVICTION REMEDIES

The **appeal** of criminal convictions in U.S. jurisdictions must be requested by the convicted defendant (now an offender) and granted at the discretion of the higher court. Exceptions include the military system of justice, which provides for automatic appeals, a few states where a first appeal is a matter of right, or death penalty verdicts, which automatically trigger appeals. Appeals by the defendant must be instituted within a specified time after conviction, although for good cause appellate courts in some jurisdictions may extend this period.

Generally there are two classes of appellate review sought by defendants. The first involves *appeal of conviction by trial*, including appeal of denial of pretrial motions to suppress certain evidence. Usually appeals of guilty plea convictions are not permitted because a guilty plea waives this right. The second class involves *challenge of the conditions of custody*; this follows conviction and is referred to as *postconviction relief*. Appeals of convictions proceed in various ways, with a few jurisdictions requiring approval by the trial court first. But more commonly they proceed by a **writ of error** (requiring the appellate court to review the trial court or arrest record for errors) or other writs submitted to the appropriate appellate court. Appeal of custody is commonly initiated by a **writ of *habeas corpus*** (literally "you have the body," that is, the person in custody who must be presented to the court).[33]

The appellate process may ultimately involve the entire range of state and federal courts, eventually reaching the U.S. Supreme Court.[34] Currently, before appeals move from state to federal review, state remedies must be exhausted. In the 1960s and early 1970s, however, many *habeas* actions involving state cases moved directly into the federal appellate process under claims of violations of the Civil Rights Act. But the Supreme Court has substantially curbed this route, now requiring that the state appellate process be exhausted if the remedy is likely to result in shorter incarceration and denying federal *habeas* relief if the petitioner has had a "full and fair litigation" of a claim in state courts.[35]

Appeals and other postconviction remedies are usually decided on the basis of relevant records and briefs, including written presentations of arguments. Frequently appellate arguments are presented orally before the appellate court by counsel with the petitioner not physically present. This is an expensive process, beyond the means of most petitioners. However, a series of U.S. Supreme Court cases has substantially expanded the right of poor petitioners to obtain court transcripts and the assistance of counsel at state expense, at least on first appeal.[36] In effect, under these decisions, if the state allows an appeal, then an indigent defendant has the right to free counsel for this purpose and the transcripts are provided without cost. In addition, public defenders frequently pursue appeals available to their clients as well.

Some states also allow appeals by the prosecution, under certain restricted conditions. The state cannot appeal a trial court finding of not guilty, because the defendant is protected from retrial by Constitutional prohibitions against double jeopardy. But a few states allow rather broad but "moot" prosecution appeals. These have the possible effect of settling a legal controversy raised by the case, but no consequences for the individual defendant.[37] Usually such appeals deal with (1) dismissal of charges, indictments, informations, or any count thereof; (2) suppression of evidence before trial including confessions, admissions, and evidence obtained by search and seizure; (3) an award of a new trial by the court; (4) an illegal sentence; or (5) discharge of the defendant on speedy trial grounds.

Summary

This chapter deals with the hearing at which a defendant is asked to plead to a formal charge, called the arraignment, and the trial if the plea is not guilty. At arraignment the indictment or information is read to the defendant, who is asked to plead. Pleas available are guilty, not guilty, or not guilty because of some defense like insanity.

If the plea is guilty, the judge must inquire if it has been freely and voluntarily entered and if the defendant understands the charge. The judge must inquire into the facts of the charge to find out if they fit the formal description of the statute and must warn the defendant of the maximum sentence that could be imposed if the guilty plea is accepted. At this point, too, the judge is informed of any plea agreements struck as a result of bargaining between prosecutor and defense and has an opportunity to reject them. If the guilty plea is accepted, the defendant stands convicted of the crime and after a presentence investigation is sentenced.

If the defendant pleads not guilty, a date for the trial is set on the court calendar. This may be a bench trial, where the judge sits alone, without a jury, to hear the case. Or the defendant may demand a jury trial. In this case jurors are selected by both the prosecution and the defense from a panel of potential jurors selected by the court clerk or jury commissioner. The lawyers for each side question potential jurors, dismissing those who have preformed opinions about the case revealing potential bias against their own side.

Once the proper number of jurors (usually twelve, but sometimes six) are chosen (as well as alternates, in case one or more jurors must be dismissed during the trial), the trial can begin. At trial the state must prove beyond a reasonable doubt all the statutory elements of the crime in order to convict the defendant. The defendant need only raise a reasonable doubt regarding the validity of the state's evidence. There is no requirement that the defendant prove innocence.

If convicted by trial, a defendant is held pending a presentence investigation and then brought before the court for a sentence hearing. Following conviction, certain avenues for appeal are available and postconviction relief may be pursued.

NOTES

1. Ralph Blumenthal, "Plan to Transform Theater into Courtroom Is Auditioned," *The New York Times*, November 15, 1991, p. B1.
2. See Patrick R. Anderson and L. Thomas Winfree, *Expert Witnesses: Criminologists in the Courtroom* (Albany: State University of New York Press, 1986).
3. Much public attention and debate were directed at the televised trial of Ronnie Zamora in Florida a few years ago. See *Zamora v. State*, 361 So. 2d 776 (Fla. Dist. Ct. App. 1978). Also, for a discussion of cameras in the courtroom, see John M. Scheb and John M. Scheb II, *Criminal Law and Procedure* (St. Paul, MN: West, 1989), p. 486; and S. L. Alexander, "Cameras in the Courtroom: A Case Study," *Judicature* 74(6) (April-May 1991): 307–313.
4. See "Comment," *Maryland Law Review* 25 (1965): 227. This plea was accepted in a case involving former Vice President Spiro T. Agnew as part of his plea bargain with the federal government. See Jack M. Kress, "The Agnew Case: Policy, Prosecution and Plea Bargaining," *Criminal Law Bulletin* 10 (January-February 1974): 80, and Donald J. Newman, "The Agnew Plea Bargain," *Criminal Law Bulletin* 10 (January-February 1974): 85.
5. For example, in the first prosecution for violation of the 200-mile fishing rights law, Federal District Judge Andrew Caffrey declined to accept the Russian trawler captain's *nolo contendere* plea. The captain then pled guilty, was placed on probation by the judge for 1 year, and was fined $10,000. In a civil suit, the Russians were ordered to pay an additional $240,000 as damages. See "Russian Pleads Guilty to Violating U.S. Fishing Laws; Is Fined $10,000," *New York Times*, May 3, 1977, p. 20, and "U.S. Frees Trawler after Russians Pay $240,000 for Illegal Fishing," *New York Times*, May

6, 1977, p. A14. But see *United States v. Ammidown*, 497 F. 2d 615 (D.C. Cir. 1973), reprinted in Chap. 7. The required scope of such judicial inquiry is still open to interpretation, but the Supreme Court has found a "silent record" of pleading to be insufficient in state as well as federal courts.

6. See Donald J. Newman, *Conviction: The Determination of Guilt or Innocence without Trial* (Boston: Little, Brown, 1966), Chap. 1–3. See *McCarthy v. United States*, 394 U.S. 459, 89 S. Ct. 1186, 22 L. Ed. 2d 418 (1969), and *Boykin v. Alabama*, 395 U.S. 238, 89 S. Ct. 1709, 23 L. Ed. 2d 274 (1969).

7. See Federal Rules of Criminal Procedure for the United States District Courts, Rule 11, Pleas. Amended 1 July 1968.

8. Ibid.

9. Ibid.

10. American Bar Association, *Standards Relating to Pleas of Guilty, Part II* (New York: Institute of Judicial Administration, 1968), Sec. 2.1(4).

11. See Annotations, 86 ALR 2d 326, 328–331 (1962).

12. American Bar Association, op cit., Sec. 2.2.

13. See John M. Scheb and John M. Scheb II, op. cit., pp. 443–446.

14. Ibid., pp. 448–450.

15. Article 3, Sec. 2, of the Constitution provides that "trial of all crimes . . . shall be by jury" but by and large court decisions have allowed waiver. See *Patton v. United States*, 281 U.S. 276 (1930). See also, generally, American Bar Association, *Standards Relating to Trial by Jury*, (approved draft) (New York: Institute of Judicial Administration, 1969), Commentary, Sec. 1.2.

16. See Note, *Cornell Law Quarterly* 51 (3) (1966): 342–343.

17. See June L. Tapp and S. J. Levine, eds., *Law, Justice and the Individual in Society: Psychological and Legal Issues* (New York: Holt, Rinehart & Winston, 1977).

18. Harry Kalven and Hans Zeisel, *The American Jury* (Boston: Little, Brown, 1966), p. 59.

19. *Codispoti v. Pennsylvania*, 418 U.S. 506, 94 S. Ct. 2687, 41 L. Ed. 2d 912 (1974). See American Bar Association, *Standards Relating to Trial by Jury*, Commentary, Sec. 1.1. See also Scheb and Scheb, op. cit., p. 480.

20. Title 18, Sec. 1(3) of the U.S. criminal code defines a "petty offense" as "any misdemeanor, the penalty for which does not exceed imprisonment for a period of six months or a fine of not more than 500 dollars or both."

21. *Duncan v. Louisiana*, 391 U.S. 145 (1968).

22. *Argersinger v. Hamlin*, 497 U.S. 25 (1972).

23. American Bar Association, *Standards Relating to Trial by Jury*, Sec. 1.1(b).

24. Scheb and Scheb, op. cit., p. 480.

25. See Federal Rules of Criminal Procedure, Rule 29(a); Richard H. Winningham, "The Dilemma of the Directed Acquittal," *Vanderbilt Law Review* 15 (1962): 699; and American Bar Association, *Standards Relating to Trial by Jury*, Sec. 4.5(a).61. In deciding the case of *In Re Winship*, 397 U.S. 358 (1970), the Supreme Court stated that the government must prove all elements of the offense beyond a reasonable doubt. This has created a great controversy as it could mean that certain legal presumptions, such as the presumption of sanity, are unconstitutional. See Ronald J. Allen, "*Mullaney v. Wilbur*, the Supreme Court, and the Substantive Criminal Law—An Examination of the Limits of Legitimate Intervention," *Texas Law Review* 55 (1977): 269–301; and Anthony M. Doniger, "Case Comment—Unburdening the Criminal Defendant: *Mullaney v. Wilbur* and the Reasonable Doubt Standard," *Harvard Civil Rights—Civil Liberties Law Review* 11 (1976): 390.

26. *Barker v. Wingo*, 407 U.S. 514 (1972).

27. *Williams v. Florida*, 399 U.S. 78 (1970).

28. *Apodaca v. Oregon*, 406 U.S. 404 (1972); *Burch v. Louisiana*, 441 U.S. 130 (1979).

29. See John V. Ryan, "Less Than Unanimous Verdicts in Criminal Trials," *Journal of Criminal Law, Criminology and Police Science* 58 (1967): 211, and Kalven and Zeisel, op. cit., Chaps. 36, 38.

30. *Swain v. Alabama*, 380 U.S. 202 (1965).

31. *Batson v. Kentucky*, 476 U.S. 79 (1986).

32. Some discriminatory practices in jury selection have been addressed in Supreme Court decisions. See *Swain v. Alabama*, 380 U.S. 202 (1965); *Glasser v. United States*, 315 U.S. 60 (1942); and *Ballard v. United States*, 329 U.S. 187 (1946).

33. See American Bar Association, *Standards Relating to Criminal Appeals* (approved draft) (New York: Institute of Judicial Administration, 1970); and American Bar Association, *Standards Relating to Post-Conviction Remedies* (approved draft) (New York: Institute of Judicial Administration, 1967).

34. For an example of this process, see Anthony Lewis, *Gideon's Trumpet* (New York: Random House, 1964), which follows the appellate process in the *Gideon v. Wainwright* case.

35. *Stone v. Powell*, 428 U.S. 465 (1976).

36. See *Griffin v. Illinois*, 351 U.S. 12 (1956), and *Douglas v. California*, 372 U.S. 353 (1963).

37. See American Bar Association, *Standards Relating to Criminal Appeals*, Sec. 1.4.

Suggested readings

Eisenstein, James, Roy Flemming, and Peter Nardulli. *The Contours of Justice: Communities and Their Courts.* Boston: Little, Brown and Co., 1988.

Hans, Valerie P., and Neil Vidmar. *Judging the Jury.* New York: Plenum Press, 1986.

Hastle, Reid, Steven Penrod, and Nancy Pennington. *Inside the Jury.* Cambridge, MA: Harvard University Press, 1983.

Israel, Jerold H., and Wayne R. LaFave. *Criminal Procedure in a Nutshell*, 4th ed. St. Paul, MN: West, 1988.

Posner, Richard A. *The Federal Courts: Crises and Reform.* Cambridge, MA, Harvard University Press, 1985.

Satter, Robert. *Doing Justice: A Trial Judge at Work.* New York: Simon & Schuster, 1990.

Scheb, John M., and John M. Scheb II. *Criminal Law and Procedure.* St. Paul, MN: West, 1989.

Turow, Scott. *Presumed Innocent.* New York: Farrar Straus & Giroux, 1987.

Wishman, Seymour. *Anatomy of a Jury.* New York: Times Books, 1986.

Zerman, Melvyn B. *Beyond a Reasonable Doubt: Inside the American Jury System.* New York: Crowell, 1981.

Discussion questions

1. Trace the arraignment and trial process.

2. Describe the pleas available to defendants at arraignment and discuss the consequences of each.

3. Describe and discuss pretrial motions.

4. Compare and contrast procedures for bench trials and jury trials.

5. Distinguish issues regarding speedy trial and statutes of limitations.

6. Discuss jury selection procedures and issues.

7. Discuss the *voir dire* process and its importance.

8. Describe and discuss the principles of reasonable doubt and the presumption of innocence as they apply to criminal trials.

9. Explain the stages in a criminal trial.

10. Describe and explain appeals and postconviction remedies.

11

Sentencing Criminals

The case of Regina v. Dudley and Stephens[1]*: The private yacht,* Mignonette, *sailed from Southampton, England, bound for Sydney, Australia, where it was to be delivered to its owner. Four men were on board, all crewmen. Dudley was the captain, Stephens the mate, Brooks a seaman, and Parker a 17-year-old cabin boy and apprentice seaman. Far out in the South Atlantic the yacht began to take on water and finally sank. The four men were left adrift in a small lifeboat without any food or water. After 20 days, the group had not yet sighted any other sailing vessels, and were without food or water except rain water, so Dudley killed the cabin boy for food. Stephens agreed to the deed; Brooks was not in favor. However, for the next 4 days all three men ate the boy's flesh and drank his blood. On the fifth day they were rescued.*

Dudley and Stephens were charged with murder. Brooks testified against them. The jury returned a special verdict based on the consideration that all four men would have died of starvation if they had not sacrificed one to save the other three. The jury left the question of whether or not the facts warranted guilt of murder to the court. Murder was a capital crime. The court ruled that Dudley and Stephens were guilty of capital murder, since no one is justified in taking the life of another innocent person to save his own. The sentence was later commuted to six months imprisonment.

About this chapter

The case of Dudley and Stephens is unusual, but it helps us focus on the sentencing decision. After the court has determined that the accused has done something wrong, that he or she has broken the law, a punishment must be meted out. Clearly Dudley and Stephens violated the law against murder, and even if we take the view that one dead body is better than four, that it is better that three men survive than none, we still cannot deny that the law has been broken. The more difficult question is, "What should be done about it?"

Perhaps one could take the position that these men must be punished to make other potential murderers think twice before they commit similar crimes, to say loudly and clearly, "It is wrong to kill a person even if the purpose is to prolong the life of others." But the fact is that this circumstance is not likely to occur with sufficient frequency to merit such a **deterrence** statement. And even if sailors in similar circumstances knew the serious punishments awaiting them, they might still choose to violate the law anyway to avoid their own deaths.

Some may wish to impose severe punishment on Dudley and Stephens for the sake of **retribution**, to say, "These men have done wrong and must suffer for it." Our sense of moral rightness demands punishment, we say. Perhaps someone else feels these men should be **rehabilitated,** given therapy, or job training, or some other form of behavior improving treatment. Others may say we must punish these men by isolating them from the rest of law-abiding society—that they are dangerous and should be removed from our midst.

Decisions regarding sentencing convicted offenders are perhaps the most difficult judges face. Judges make other important decisions, but most of them are pretty well constrained by law. In the area of sentencing, though, judges may exercise considerable discretion based on their own philosophy of sentencing and personal attitudes toward the offenders or the offenses. What are the myriad purposes, or goals, of sentencing? How is sentencing influenced by community attitudes, shifts in penal practice, formal recommendations by professional groups, and the law? What information is available to a judge to assist in the sentencing decision?

If you were a judge, charged with the responsibility of regularly deciding which offenders go to prison and which go home, who gets 6 years and who gets 15, what information would you seek to guide you about whether to be lenient or harsh? On what basis would you select sentence options? Criminal sentences can take a number of forms, including fines, probation, and incarceration in jail or prison. And, of course, the death penalty is available in most states. So for people who make the sentencing decisions, the manner in which sentences should be determined pose an important area of great interest. And again, the conflicting views of the conservative and liberal crime control models are evident.[2]

SENTENCING AND THE CONSERVATIVE CRIME CONTROL MODEL

The conservative crime control model starts with the premise that "bleeding-heart" liberal judges short-circuit the criminal justice ideals by handing down lenient sentences—that their decisions merely turn criminals loose on society again to commit more crimes. "**Get tough**" **laws** are seen as the answer to this problem, especially for crimes involving guns, drug dealing, and other illegal activities which are especially "hot" in the public eye.

The "get-tough" approach emphasizes punishment, incapacitation, and retribution and scoffs at the rehabilitation of criminals. It would require **mandatory sentences** and take the sentencing discretion away from judges. This can mean mandatory imprisonment for certain crimes, and the elimination of probation and suspended sentences as sentencing options. Or it can mean a mandatory minimum prison sentence, a certain number of years an offender must serve before being eligible for release. Of course, for mandatory sentences to work, plea bargaining must be abolished since that practice creates a loophole in the system, according to the conservative view of how criminal justice should work.

Another loophole, in the conservative view, is the use of "good-time" provisions, which allow inmates to gain extra credit for time served on good behavior. For instance, some states allow 45 days' credit for 30 days served on good behavior. The conservative crime control approach would abolish these good-time provisions and impose definite, flat-time sentences. Along with the use of presumptive sentencing (see section on Fair and Certain Punishment later in this chapter), such steps would serve to limit judges' sentencing decisions within narrow parameters.

SENTENCING AND THE LIBERAL CRIME CONTROL MODEL

The liberal crime control model argues that prison is a poor solution to crime, that the rehabilitation of offenders is unlikely to occur in a prison setting, and that the use of prison sentences to punish rarely makes people better, only worse. Also, to merely increase the amount of time offenders spend in prison is seen by the liberal crime control model as unrealistic, unworkable, and counterproductive to an effective criminal justice system. Liberals do not see the problem as weak judges, for serious offenders have always been sentenced harshly. They see the problem as the prison solution itself—that no evidence exists to demonstrate that any time spent in prison makes people turn away from criminal behaviors.

Rehabilitation is the cornerstone of the liberal crime control approach. Most criminals stop committing crimes sooner or later anyway, according to this view, and rehabilitation programs can help them stop sooner. And probation, properly administered, is the best correctional program to achieve this goal because it is the only one that seems to work. Probation serves desirable social goals, is much cheaper than prison, and offers a variety of rehabilitative services unavailable in prison. What is needed is for probation officers to have frequent face-to-face contact with offenders, regularly enforce drug and alcohol tests, provide jobs and educational programs, and offer couseling and therapy.

Therefore, in the liberal view, since probation is the most common sentence handed down to offenders, and since virtually every offender is sentenced to probation first and to prison only on subsequent offenses, if we can utilize it properly, and improve on its effectiveness, we can use it to reduce the amount of crime.

GOALS OF CRIMINAL SENTENCES

All sentences from the smallest fine to the longest prison term have a number of goals.[3] The basis for these goals lies deep in the philosophy underlying our criminal justice network. We want our criminal justice process to accomplish something, to achieve some social utility beyond merely solving crimes and catching criminals. We want to reduce the crime rate by stopping the criminal activities of apprehended offenders and deterring others from committing crimes. Sentencing is designed to achieve at least the following four major goals:

1. **Incapacitation**, which refers to preventing an individual from committing further criminal acts by restraining him or her. Sanctions imposed to incapacitate are not intended to reduce an offender's *inclinations* to future criminal acts, which would involve treatment to change the person's attitudes or personality, but to preclude *opportunities* for criminal behavior at least while the offender is under state control. The death penalty is obviously totally incapacitory. Long prison terms also illustrate the incapacitation goal, but so do lesser sanctions, including the rules and conditions of probation and the surveillance of persons serving sentences in the community.
2. **Deterrence**, which generally refers to the prevention of criminal acts in the population at large by making examples of persons convicted of crimes. Thus even if there is no need to restrain a particular offender by imprisonment, he or she still might receive a long prison term as a message to potential offenders, who might otherwise commit similar crimes. Two types of deterrence exist: *specific* deterrence, which is designed to deter an offender from committing a crime again, and *general* deterrence, which is designed to deter potential offenders by making an example of a captured one.
3. **Rehabilitation**, which involves a sentence designed to provide treatment for conditions in the offender's attitudes, personality, or general personal history that may have led to the criminal behavior. Sentencing a person to prison for rehabilitation is sometimes compared to sending a sick person to a hospital to receive treatment for an illness.
4. **Punishment**, which is a goal quite different from the other three, though a component of each. Incapacitation, deterrence, and rehabilitation are *future-oriented* in that they are designed to prevent additional crimes by an offender or others. Punishment, however, is *focused on the past criminal behavior* of the offender and is imposed to express condemnation of that behavior. Today the punishment goal is sometimes called "just deserts" or "commensurate deserts," implying that it is an appropriate goal of our criminal justice system to make a criminal pay for a crime in proportion to the harm done.

All of these goals coexist in any single sentence. However, one or another may predominate, so that a prison sentence may be primarily for treatment or primarily for incapacitation even though other goals, say deterrence and just desserts, are intended too. Which goal, if any, predominates varies from case to case, yet particular sentence goals tend to be the most important during different periods. Not long ago rehabilitation was the prominent though not exclusive goal of most criminal sentences, but today this has changed.[4]

IMPOSITION OF SENTENCE

Today in the United States offenders are subject to a variety of sentence options, depending on the offense charged and proven, the sentence guidelines which exist in the jurisdiction, and plea bargains and vagaries of the sentencing decision. See Table 11.1.

Except when an offender is convicted of a crime involving a mandatory sentence, the judge has discretion, usually within established guidelines, to select the type, the length, and sometimes certain other conditions of sentence. Depending on the offense and the law, the judge may be able to choose a fine, probation, or incarceration in a jail or prison. The latter alternative, jail or prison, ordinarily depends on whether the offense is a misdemeanor (jail) or felony (prison). Probation can be given in either category. Fines are more commonly imposed in misdemeanor cases, alone or com-

TABLE 11.1 *Types of criminal sentences*

Death penalty is available in most states today for the most serious crimes such as murder. The courts may sentence the convicted offender to death in the electric chair, by lethal injection, in a gas chamber, by hanging, or by firing squad depending on the provisions in a given state. Death sentences require a separate hearing, with jury deliberation and recommendation of life imprisonment or death for convicted capital offenders. Chapter 12 describes this in detail.

Incarceration is the confinement of a convicted criminal in a state or federal prison or in a local jail. Most sentenced prisoners serve their time in 1 of approximately 950 state prisons, usually called correctional institutions. Federal offenders are confined in 1 of the 47 federal facilities, and those sentenced to less than 1 year are locked in 1 of the 3500 or so local jails which are administered by county or city agencies. On any given day, approximately 1 million prisoners are locked up in prisons in the United States under sentence of a court. Daily jail populations amount to over 420,000.

Probation is a sentence to local community supervision by a probation agency. This is usually done by suspending a sentence to confinement, and the offender is subjected to rules and regulations stated by the court. Probation is the most widely used sentence. About 2 million adults are on probation in a given year, or 1 out of every 95 adults in the United States.

Split sentence, shock probation, and **intermittent confinement** are sentences that require the criminal to serve a brief term in jail, to "shock" him or her, or to get the offender's attention. Then, after the time in jail, the offender is required to serve a term on probation. Sometimes, in the intermittent sentence, the offender is required to follow probation rules during the week and then spend weekends or holidays in jail. This type of sentence is particularly popular in Idaho, New Jersey, Tennessee, Utah, and Vermont, where about one-third of those receiving probation sentences are sentenced to brief periods of confinement.

Restitution and victim compensation is a sentence that requires the offender to repay the victim either by financial payments or services rendered. Nearly all states plus the federal jurisdiction have restitution laws for the collection and disbursement of restitution funds.

Community service is a sentence which requires the offender to perform a specified amount of public service work, such as collecting trash or performing odd jobs around the courthouse or in public parks. Many states provide this sentence, and often community service requirements are made part of probation conditions.

Fines are levied most frequently in misdemeanor cases. They are an economic penalty which require the offender to pay a specified amount of money within a certain period of time. They are also used in relationship to probation requirements or in lieu of incarceration. Sometimes the law provides that money from the payment of fines be used to compensate victims, and in some jurisdictions the law provides for flexible fine amounts in relationship to the offender's earning power. The majority of criminal courts levy fines extensively.

Former Lincoln Savings and Loan officer, Charles H. Keating, Jr., was convicted of seventeen securities fraud charges on his sixty-eighth birthday. Then, on April 10, 1992, he was sentenced to 10 years in prison and a $250,000 fine.

bined with probation or incarceration, but they may also be imposed in some felony cases. Fines are commonly levied in white-collar violations such as embezzlement, income tax evasion, and corporate fraud. And of course the death penalty is available in most states today in certain circumstances.[5]

The *major* decision at sentencing involves the choice between probation (community supervision without going to jail or prison) and incarceration in jail or prison. And about thirty-five states and the federal jurisdiction allow split sentences. Usually, however, the basic concern to the offender at sentencing is whether he or she will remain in the community on probation or go to prison. If the decision is incarceration, there are the matters of where and how long. If the decision is probation, the issues are the rules and conditions of supervision.

Probation

It is often thought that probation is a lenient sentence, and it is when compared with any kind of imprisonment, but it is a sentence and not simply a dismissal of the case. The offender on probation must agree to a set of standard conditions—covering curfew, regular employment, restricted travel, restitution to the victim, and so on—and to supervision by a probation officer. When allowed by law, the judge may also set special conditions appropriate to the particular case but not required of all probationers. For example, a judge may order a defendant to submit to psychiatric counseling or join Alcoholics Anonymous as a condition of probation. Should the probationer violate any of the conditions (or commit a new crime) while on probation, he or she may, at the discretion of the probation staff, be returned to court for possible revocation and imprisonment. On successful completion of probation, the probationer is discharged from sentence.

A judge may sentence to probation in a number of ways: (1) by imposing a prison sentence (3 to 10 years, perhaps) but *suspending its execution* and placing the offender on probation; (2) by *suspending imposition* of any prison sentence and placing the offender on probation; (3) by placing the offender *directly on a sentence of probation*; (4) by *deferring judgment* and placing the offender on probation; or (5) by *adjourning judgment in anticipation of dismissal* and requiring the defendant to abide by probation conditions for a period of time. In the case where a judge has imposed a prison sentence but suspended its execution, the term of incarceration has already been set by the judicial imposition. However, if the judge has not set a specific prison term but has suspended its imposition and placed the defendant directly on probation, the length of incarceration, if any is needed, would be set at the time of revocation.

The length of probation can be set within whatever limits are allowed by statute, though this may not necessarily be equal to the length of imprisonment provided for the same crime. For instance, if a crime carries a possible sentence of 20 years in prison, the term of probation may be only 5 years. Conversely, if a 1-year prison term is authorized, a longer probationary period may be set by the court. In a number of jurisdictions conditions of probation can be changed from time to time by the court, and the length of the sentence can be reduced or extended.

Incarceration of Misdemeanants

Misdemeanants are sentenced to local jails, the same institutions that hold defendants awaiting indictments, preliminary hearings, arraignments, trials, or transfer to prison. Jail sentences are for specified times up to 1 year. Lesser sentences, up to a month, are commonly expressed in days—10 days, 30 days—and longer sentences in 3-month intervals—3 months, 6 months, 9 months, or 1 year. Some jails have work-release programs in which low-risk inmates go to work during the day and report to lockup at nights and on weekends. Though a few places have a form of jail "parole" that allows a prisoner to be released prior to serving the full sentence, in most cases jail time is "flat," that is, there is no minimum and maximum spread. Instead the inmate serves precisely the sentence imposed by the court.

Judicial Variations in Sentencing

Like all people, judges often have idiosyncrasies that may affect their sentencing practice. Certain judges may have deserved reputations for harsh or lenient sentencing in certain types of cases. One judge may abhor narcotics violations and impose long sentences in these cases. Another may view narcotics violations as minor, particularly if "soft" drugs are involved. There are "gun" judges who tend to impose long sentences on any offender who had a gun during the commission of a crime, whether or not the gun was used. But a gun judge may be lenient with sex offenders, believing they are sick rather than criminal. Defense lawyers who are aware of judicial likes and dislikes may spend considerable time "judge-shopping" to obtain sentence hearings for their clients in a sympathetic or at least nonhostile court. As Judge Marvin Frankel has written: "To underscore it by repetition, my first basic point is this: the almost wholly unchecked and sweeping powers we give to judges in the fashioning of sentences are terrifying and intolerable for a society that professes devotion to the rule of law."[6]

Robert O. Dawson has found a variety of factors beyond the nature of the offense itself which influence the judicial decision of long or short periods of imprisonment. Some of these he calls "administrative accommodations": showing more leniency to an offender who pleads guilty than to one who has had a full trial, or to an offender who is a police informer, or to one who has been a valuable state's witness, for example. Conversely, judges sometimes impose very long sentences, not to bury the offender in prison for many years, but to provide an extended parole supervision in the belief that the offender will need intensive assistance on his or her return to the community.[7]

Research has shown that male judges tend to sentence female offenders more leniently than male offenders convicted of comparable crimes.[8] Other studies have shown that judges affiliated with fundamentalist churches sentence black defendants more harshly than whites, and that democratic judges are less discriminatory than others.[9] Still other studies have investigated the factors involved in sentencing in rural courts, as well as various factors relating to the sex and race of both judges and offenders.[10] The social background of judges has also been shown to affect sentencing behavior.[11]

Most judges try to "individualize" sentences as much as possible—to fit the actual consequences of their sentences to the risk and reputation of both the offender and his or her family. It should be noted, however, that individualization is only one sentencing goal. Judges are lawyers, and in sentencing as in other matters they have strong allegiances to precedent. Over time it is not unusual for a judge to attempt to give comparable sentences for similar offenses and similar offenders.

Sentencing Leniency for Guilty Plea Offenders

Sentencing of those who plead guilty is so intertwined with plea bargaining that it is sometimes difficult to determine where and by whom the sentence decision is actually made in such cases. Overt plea bargaining generally affects the selection of probation, avoids mandatory sentences, and by reducing charges acts to lower the

Sentencing Discretion: The Case of Jim Bakker

In 1989, when the jury brought back a guilty verdict on every count charged by the federal prosecutors against television evangelist Jim Bakker, he immediately went before the horde of reporters, television cameras, and photographers waiting outside the courthouse and exclaimed: "I was innocent when I came into this court, and I am still innocent." One could almost hear the collective thought: "Oh yeah?"

Normally, the best strategy for people who have been convicted of but have not yet been sentenced for their crimes is to express remorse, to offer restitution, to act truly repentant. Yet Bakker still proclaimed his innocence. The rule of thumb for crooks before the bar of justice is to keep your mouth shut. If you must speak, try to show genuine remorse, humility, and abject submission to the authority of the court.

Bakker, then, should have begged forgiveness and offered to pay back the money to investors in his Heritage USA village. By doing so, he might have been able to hope for a light sentence, and at least hope the sentencing judge would use the available judicial discretion in the most favorable way. But Bakker's outburst was certainly no way to influence a judge to give a lenient sentence. Perhaps he thought his claims of continuing innocence would help keep his ardent supporters faithful. Or maybe his words were designed to bolster the anticipated appeal of his conviction, for surely it would be hard for Bakker to appeal the guilty verdict if he admitted his crimes to the world.

Bakker's statements on the courthouse steps were not the only violations of the informal rules of defendant behavior. The entire trial had been a soap opera, and he had used a poor strategy to gain favorable treatment by the criminal justice system. Early on, he would have been well-advised to plead guilty to something, *anything*, like former Vice President Spiro Agnew did when he was nailed by federal prosecutors in Maryland 20 years earlier. Agnew had quickly made a deal, copped a plea, and walked away.

When a defendant refuses to deal with a prosecutor, the risk is that charges will be "piled on," multiple charges filed. Bakker drew 24 separate charges, and the prosecutors chose to charge him under statutes which carried extreme sentence potential. Any time one goes to trial the likelihood of maximum charges and stiff sentences is great, and the risks one runs with a jury's verdict are great as well.

But Jim Bakker was a novice in the criminal justice system; he was a fish out of water. He failed to play the game properly with the prosecutor, the jury, and later, the judge. And both the prosecutor and the judge called him on it.

Bakker's first sentence was 45 years with no parole for 10 years. Judge Robert Potter arrived at that number by collapsing the 24 convictions into 9, then giving him the 5-year maximum sentence for each one. The judge also considered the risk of flight, the likelihood that Bakker and his wife Tammy Faye would catch a plane to Guyana or some other destination of cult leaders. Judge Potter said, "I'm concerned about the hundreds of letters I have here from people

limits of minimum and maximum sentences. Also, in some instances, a bargain includes the promise of a specific number of years in prison.

Trial judges generally support plea negotiations by honoring the bargains made between the defense and the prosecution. This, of course, is overt bargaining. But there is also the "implicit bargain" of offenders throwing themselves on the "mercy of the court" by pleading guilty. Very often they receive this mercy, for most judges, like most prosecutors, wish to encourage a high rate of guilty pleas. And most judges know that realistically there must be some break for pleading defendants to avoid the alternative—more demands for trials, even with frivolous defenses. For what would the defendant have to lose by making the state prove its case, if there were nothing to gain by copping a plea? And there might even be a chance, however remote, of acquittal by a jury.

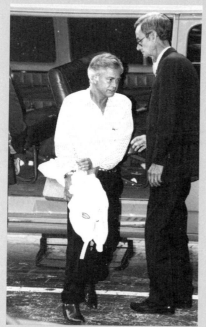

A federal marshall escorts PTL evangelist Jim Bakker, in leg irons and handcuffs, from a prison van to the federal courthouse in Charlotte, North Carolina. Bakker was resentenced 23 months after receiving a 45-year sentence for bilking millions of dollars from faithful followers of his ministry.

custody." And over the sobs of Bakker's daughter and the pleas of his lawyers, into custody he went.

Bakker was locked up immediately in a holding cell, his hands and feet chained, and then carried immediately in a government sedan to Talladega, the federal prison reception and classification center about 60 miles from Birmingham, Alabama. There was no chance for flight.

Bakker's attorneys appealed the sentence, claiming that Judge Potter had been prejudiced against their client. They claimed that the extreme sentence was under "old law," and that new sentencing statutes should be applied which would dramatically reduce the sentence. Finally, in the summer of 1991, Judge Potter recused himself from the case and a different judge, Graham Mullen, was assigned to hear resentencing arguments. In the meanwhile, Bakker remained in prison.

On August 23, 1991, almost 2 years after he first went to prison, Bakker stood with his attorneys before Judge Mullen. This time the 51-year-old prisoner spoke softly, apologized for his misdeeds, and pled for mercy from the court. He said, "Your honor, I am deeply and seriously remorseful for my moral failures and for the hurt I have caused so many people. I failed so many people that trusted me, my own church congregation, this community, my partners, the church world as a whole, myself and my God and my dear family."

Jim Bakker also spoke of his life in prison: "Prison is a sad world. It's the land of the living dead for me. It's not just strip searches. It's the separation from family and loved ones."

Judge Mullen reduced the original 45-year sentence to 14 years, making parole possible after he has served 4 years in prison.

who say they'd do anything for him that could include preventing Mr. Bakker from going to prison. I believe them. Because of that, I think we're going to have to put him into

Extended-Term Sentences

Sentences for young first offenders are usually shorter and more clearly directed to rehabilitative programs in reformatories than sentences for "ordinary" adult criminals. Often there are provisions for expunging records if these young offenders show treatment progress. It is believed that there is more hope for successful rehabilitation with the young. In many places the most modern facilities and most of the professional rehabilitation staff are found in youth programs. In general, this is noncontroversial; a majority of all the participants in the criminal justice system give high priority to leniency and high-quality correctional programs for youthful offenders.

Much more controversial are provisions for *extended sentences* for dangerous offenders, gangsters, and other persistent, professional criminals. Few would deny the

Charles Manson received the maximum possible sentences because he was considered to be a dangerous offender.

existence of some very dangerous offenders—persons who have committed violent, atrocious crimes—who kill, maim, rape, and otherwise seriously jeopardize the safety of us all. The existence of career criminals—professionals who make crime their lifelong occupation—as well as of gangsters and racketeers who traffic in heroin and who extort, intimidate, and corrupt others is an unpleasant reality. The problem of distinguishing these offenders with accuracy and by acceptable means from ordinary, limited-threat offenders is not easily solved. And the problem of what to do with them once they have been identified remains.

These issues generate very difficult legislative questions. Being a "dangerous person" is not in itself a crime. Nor is the appellation "gangster" constitutionally sufficient to warrant locking someone up. Code revisionists have sought ways to distinguish both dangerous criminal activities and dangerous offenders. For example, the *Model Sentencing Act*, which limits maximum sentences for ordinary crimes to 5 years, distinguishes these from "atrocious crimes," providing longer sentences for anyone convicted of several acts:

> If a defendant is convicted of one of the following felonies—murder, second degree; arson; forcible rape; robbery while armed with a deadly weapon; mayhem; bombing of an airplane, vehicle, vessel, building, or other structure—and is not committed under Section 5 [Dangerous Offenders], the court may commit him for a term of ten years or a lesser term or may sentence him under Section 9 [Ordinary Crimes, i.e., five years maximum].[12]

This is an attempt to classify some crimes as worse than others, making long sentences proper in cases where the crimes are intrinsically "atrocious."

Another approach focuses on the *criminal actor* rather than the act, providing longer sentences if the *person* is found to be "dangerous." Both the *Model Sentencing Act* and the *Model Penal Code*[12] have sections dealing with criteria for determining dangerous offenders, although the codes differ somewhat in their methods of determining dangerousness. In addition to the maximum 5-year term for ordinary offenders, 10 years for atrocious crimes, and life for first-degree murder, the *Model Sentencing Act* provides for extended-term sentences for a variety of other offenses. (See Box 11.1.)

In the past, the only provisions for extended periods of incarceration were for the "habitual criminal." In some places an offender became automatically eligible for a long habitual offender sentence upon a third or fourth conviction; in others, "being a habitual offender" was a separate charge, with a trial, if any, devoted primarily to proof of the offender's prior record. The real consequence of habitual offender laws was that many minor but "persistent" violators who were not really dangerous were engulfed in the process and spent long stretches of time in prison.

The federal jurisdiction, concerned with interstate organized crime, has criteria for including gangsters and racketeers under general provisions for extended sentences for dangerous criminals. The statutory framework is extremely complex and much too long and detailed to be reproduced in full here. In general, the approach is to deal with "patterns" of crime, "conspiracies," and offender income "acquired" but not earned.

Most participants in the criminal justice process, and for that matter most citizens, agree that there are some very dangerous people loose on our streets and in our prisons, but the problem of predicting *future* dangerousness is difficult, if indeed possible at all. If a person has killed once, will he or she kill again?

Atrocious crimes and dangerous persons are of major concern across the entire criminal justice system, not just at sentencing. Techniques designed to prevent or deter violent crimes range from sidearms carried by the police to the walls and gun turrets of maximum-security prisons. Prediction of dangerousness is a critical concern in all criminal justice procedures from stop-and-frisk practices to parole. At the preconviction stages, however, except for the limited and controversial practice of preventive detention, most assessments of dangerousness apply to *situations* rather than to persons. Every air traveler is subject to airport searches, and except for those fitting the hijacker "profile," dangerousness is not individually predicted. Under certain conditions in even routine investigations, police officers approach with drawn pistols without making individual assessments. But at *sentencing*, and in such postsentencing determinations as the granting or denial of parole, predicting future dangerousness involves decisions about individuals.

WHO REALLY MAKES THE SENTENCING DECISION?

After conviction by trial or guilty plea, the defendant is brought to court for imposition of sentence. The hearing at which the sentence is imposed is considered a "critical stage" of the criminal justice process, and convicted offenders, even those who are indigent, have a right to counsel at this time.[13]

Most sentences are imposed by a judge, but there are variations depending on the law in different jurisdictions. Seven states provide for **jury sentencing** in noncapital cases, and one additional state allows the offender to request jury sentencing. Twelve states have provisions for jury sentencing when a death penalty is involved and, consistent with recent Supreme Court decisions, this apparently will in future be the necessary structure in all death penalty jurisdictions.

Jury sentencing has existed since colonial times in some states. However, the practice has been questioned by a number of standard-setting commissions. The National Advisory Commission on Criminal Justice Standards and Goals called for the abolition of jury sentencing because it is "nonprofessional and is more likely than judge sentencing to be arbitrary and based on emotions rather than the needs of the offender or society."[14]

In some places, usually metropolitan areas where there are multijudge courts, there are **sentencing councils** of judges. This practice is still small and experimental, though the National Advisory Commission recommends its use whenever feasible.[15] Sentencing by council involves consultation between one judge who has the ultimate sentencing responsibility and two or more colleague judges in regard to what the sentence should be. The purpose of such consultation is to reduce sentence disparities among judges of the same court.

The question of who actually makes the sentencing determination, and when, is complicated by prevalent plea bargaining practices discussed earlier. Overt recognition of the propriety of plea agreements between prosecution and defense means that the sentence in a number of guilty plea cases is predetermined by the prosecutor. While the judge always has the option to reject such agreements, in practice this is uncommon.

A number of criminal codes require mandatory sentences upon conviction of certain crimes. In some jurisdictions certain offenses are defined as nonprobationable, thus preventing the judge from giving a suspended sentence. In others the probation alternative is left open, but if the judge imposes a prison sentence, the minimum or maximum length (or both) of incarceration is fixed by statute. In such cases it is not the court but rather the legislature that really performs the sentencing function.

Mandatory sentencing also usually means the sentence actually imposed, perhaps raised or lowered slightly from the presumed sentence, is *definite*, with no minimum or maximum spread. The offender does precisely the amount of time ordered by the court, and under this system there is no need for a parole board since

BOX 11.1

Model Sentencing Act, Sec. 5: Dangerous Offenders

Except for the crime of murder in the first degree, the court may sentence a defendant convicted of a felony to a term of commitment of thirty years, or to a lesser term, if it finds that because of the *dangerousness of the defendant*, such period of confined correctional treatment or custody is required for the protection of the public, and if it further finds, as provided in Section 6, that one or more of the following grounds exist:

a. . . . he inflicted or attempted to inflict *serious bodily harm*, and the court finds that he is suffering from a *severe personality disorder* indicating a propensity toward criminal activity.

b. The defendant is being sentenced for a crime which *seriously endangered the life or safety of another*, has been *previously convicted* of one or more felonies not related to the instant crime as a single criminal episode, and the court finds that he is suffering from a *severe personality disorder* indicating a propensity toward criminal activity.

c. . . . *extortion, compulsory prostitution, selling or knowingly and unlawfully transporting narcotics*, or other felony committed as part of a continuing criminal activity in concert with one or more persons.

[Emphasis added]

release is not discretionary. Prisoners can earn some time off the sentence for good behavior while in the institution, but this is not parole and does not depend on the offender being "treated."

Completely **indeterminate sentences**—1 day to life—are much less common today than they were some years ago. These zero to life sentences still exist, however, in some places, usually for sex crimes in which the offender is also diagnosed as a "sex deviate" or "sex psychopath." In these cases the actual sentence is left to the parole authorities who decide when, if ever, the offender will be released from prison.[16]

Three sources of decision making, therefore, determine the sentence an offender convicted of a particular crime will serve. These are the *legislature*, which sets sentencing parameters by statute; the *sentencing judge*, who actually imposes the sentence; and the *release authority*, which is usually a parole board.

The legislature may dominate the sentencing of certain offenders by fixing *mandatory prison terms* for conviction of a particular crime. For instance, statutes may provide that murder requires a life sentence. The sentencing judge has no other option.

More commonly, the legislature fixes the *range* of years in prison for certain crimes and offender history by setting a minimum and maximum term for each offense. For example, statutes might provide that armed robbery carries a minimum sentence of 3 years and a maximum of 10. They may also designate certain crimes as nonprobationable, foreclosing that option for both the judge at sentencing and the prosecutor at plea bargaining.

In some instances both the minimum and maximum terms provided by statute are mandatory, meaning that the judge must impose these exact years for the conviction of whatever crime is involved. More commonly, however, judges are given discretion to set a minimum and a maximum term within legislative outer limits. For instance, in the case of a 5- to 15-year term for armed robbery, the judge might set a minimum term no longer than 5 years. An appropriate sentence in a robbery case under this structure would be a judicially set term of 3 to 10 years. It falls within the legislative outer limits and the ratio of minimum to maximum is about the same. Although there are exceptions, in general, *minimum terms must not exceed one-third the maximum.*

Unless banned by statute, the judge might instead impose probation in this robbery case, in which case the length of probation would normally be *unrelated* to the possible prison sentence. In most states all felonies resulting in probation carry the same term of community supervision, 5 years.

The authority of the **parole board** comes into play between the minimum and maximum set either by statute or by the sentencing judge. The board has the authority to release any prisoner who has served the minimum sentence (or, in some places, after the minimum term minus time off for good behavior) and before the expiration of the maximum term.

Thus the time served in prison for any crime may be a combined function of the three sources of authority: the outer limits are set by statute, the judge may set a term less than the legislative limits, and actual time served may be a decision of the parole board within certain parameters set by the legislature and the court.

Of course, as discussed earlier, in all of this the prosecutor has an important role through plea bargaining. Often the issue is probation, or as some wise-cracking defendants say, "In or out—that's what it's all about." But *minima* and *maxima* can be influenced, too, by the common practice of charge reduction in bargaining sessions.

Actually, across our land, the sentencing structure picture is even more complicated than outlined here. There are various combinations of these mandatory and discretionary terms across and within states. There are no uniform sentences common to all jurisdictions. Sentencing provisions vary not only among the states and the federal jurisdiction but even within a single state for different kinds of crimes. Parsing this out, across the country we can identify at least seven major structures for imposing prison sentences, each with some variations:

1. *Flat* or *definite* prison sentences, with no minimum or maximum spread. The sentence is mandated by the legislature for each category of crime with only a small amount of variation in time allowed the judge based on aggravating or mitigating circumstances.
2. *Maximum* and *minimum* years of imprisonment set by a judge at any point within the legislatively designated outer limits.
3. Maximum terms for each crime *fixed by statute* and *imposed by the court*. However, the judge is given discretion to set a minimum term at any point up to the maximum.
4. Maximum and minimum *terms set by the judge*. In these cases the minimum term cannot exceed some fraction, usually one-third, of the maximum.
5. A minimum term of imprisonment *fixed by legislation* which *must* be imposed by the court but with the judge having discretion to set the maximum term.
6. Both maximum and minimum terms *fixed by statutory law* allowing the judge *no discretion* with offenders convicted of these crimes.
7. *Completely indeterminate sentences* (1 day to life), which must be imposed by the court and where the date of actual release is fixed by parole authorities.

This complex and somewhat confusing array of structures illustrates the conflicts between the major sources of authority in the criminal justice process. Mandatory sentences of any sort give sentencing power to the legislature and deny discretion to both judge and parole board. In systems where a judge can set a minimum sentence, this forecloses the possibility of parole until that minimum is served. On the other hand, systems that provide a large spread of time between minimum and maximum terms give to the parole board the power to determine the time that actually will be served.[17]

It is difficult to determine the most typical sentencing structure, for there are often different provisions within states from one offense to another. However, it can be said that in *most* jurisdictions for *most* crimes judges have some choice among alternative types and lengths of sentences. And today, even though some people think parole is on the decline, all but a few states have parole boards with some degree of discretion as to the release of *most* inmates.

In the past it was common for legislatures to fix specific sentences to each degree of crime. Thus the penalties for first-, second-, and third-degree burglary could be found within the laws defining these crimes. The same was true for robbery, larceny, homicide, and all other crimes. The result was an extremely large, diffuse, complex, and often inconsistent list of punishments in each criminal code. Furthermore, the number of statutes defining penalties increased over time as new offenses or variations on old ones were added at each legislative session, but few old statutes were repealed. The result was not only a disarray of sentencing provisions, but a hodgepodge of criminal laws. In some places, for example, one statute outlawed horse stealing, another was required to cover cow theft, and neither applied to dog stealing. Consequently, since the 1950s, most of the states have revised their criminal codes, with each paying particular attention to sentencing provisions.

Fair and Certain Punishment

Disillusionment with attempts to create effective offender rehabilitation programs has resulted in the drafting of new provisions stressing the *punitive* and *incapacitory* purposes of sentences rather than treatment. Death penalty provisions (hardly rehabilitative) have been rewritten in most states, and the impetus for this extreme punishment reflects that emphasis. In the new capital punishment laws, as well as in other new sentencing proposals, **fair and certain punishment** is the major thrust of the change. The operational consequences of this are a move away from the indeterminate sentence—prison terms containing a spread of time between a minimum and a maximum period of incarceration—and the abolition of parole. It was argued, by prisoners as well as a number of others, that indeterminate sentencing and the use of parole gave too much discretion to state authorities.[18] Indeterminacy meant not only that an offender was always uncertain of his or her actual sentence, but also that the parole system allowed correctional authorities to increase or decrease the amount of punishment based on factors unrelated to the offender's criminal act.

And thus, though parole and the indeterminate sentence were yesterday's reforms, there was a demand to return to a straight or definite sentencing system in felony cases much as is the current practice with misdemeanors.[19] It was argued that all sentences are really punitive and flat sentences could be devised to provide certain and definite punishments commensurate with the harm caused by the criminal acts being punished. The emphasis would be on how much punishment the offender deserved—"just deserts" directly related to conduct—rather than on treating the causes of the criminal behavior.[20]

Since the early 1970s there has also been a spreading movement toward instituting a **presumptive sentence** structure. In presumptive sentencing the legislature determines the number of years in prison that should be given by all judges to all offenders convicted of the same type of crime. In the case of robbery, for example, it is presumed that every judge in the state will impose the same definite number of years as provided by law.

In most presumptive sentencing proposals, the judge is given a small leeway to vary the sentence—a year in either direction is typical—if aggravating or mitigating circumstances were present. If the judge does deviate from the presumed sentence, written reasons for the decision must be given.

SENTENCING GUIDELINES

Sentencing guidelines have been developed in several states as well as the federal jurisdiction primarily as a means of combating sentence disparity, that is, the situation in which judges' sentence decisions have too great a discrepancy and offenders convicted of the same crimes, and with equivalent background characteristics, have been sentenced to unreasonably disparate sentences. That disparity has been believed to be exercised to the disadvantage of minority defendants. The purpose of guidelines is not to eliminate judges' discretion, but to channel it as much as possible within acceptable limits. Another goal of such guidelines is to make sentencing procedures neutral in terms of race, age, sex, and social and economic status.

Sentence guidelines categorize crimes and then establish sentence score sheets, or matrices, within each category for determining sentence ranges. For instance, the *Florida Rules of Criminal Procedure* set forth nine crime categories: (1) murder and manslaughter; (2) sexual offenses; (3) robbery; (4) violent personal crimes; (5) burglary; (6) thefts, forgery and fraud; (7) drugs; (8) weapons; and (9) all other felonies. Then, for each of these crime categories, five factors are scored. The factors are (1) primary offenses; (2) additional offenses at conviction; (3) prior record and prior convictions; (4) legal status at time of offense; and (5) injury to victim. Each factor is scored, a total score is tabulated, and the sentence range is computed by reference to the score sheet. The score sheet provides space for the "guideline sentence" and the

I. Primary Offense at Conviction

Degree	1	2	3	4	Points
Life	80	96	104	112	___
1st pbl	70	84	91	98	___
1st	60	72	78	84	___
2nd	(30)	36	39	42	**30**
3rd	20	24	26	28	___

Primary offense counts in excess of four:

- Add 8 for each additional life ___
- Add 7 for each additional 1st pbl ___
- Add 6 for each additional 1st ___
- Add 3 for each additional 2nd ___
- Add 2 for each additional 3rd ___
- Total **30**

II. Additional Offenses at Conviction

Degree	1	2	3	4	Points
Life	16	19	21	23	___
1st pbl	14	16	18	20	___
1st	12	14	16	17	___
2nd	6	7	8	9	___
3rd	4	5	6	7	___
MM	(1)	2	3	4	**1**

Additional offense counts in excess of four:

- Add 2 for each additional life ___
- Add 2 for each additional 1st pbl ___
- Add 1 for each additional 1st ___
- Add 1 for each additional 2nd ___
- Add 1 for each additional 3rd ___
- Add 1 for each additional MM ___
- Total **1**

III. A. Prior Record

Degree	1	2	3	4	Points
Life	60	130	210	307	___
1st pbl	48	104	168	246	___
1st	36	78	126	184	___
2nd	18	39	63	90	___
3rd	(6)	13	21	30	**6**
MM	1	2	(3)	4	**3**

Primary convictions in excess of four:

- Add 97 for each additional life ___
- Add 78 for each additional 1st pbl ___
- Add 58 for each additional 1st ___
- Add 67 for each additional 2nd ___
- Add 9 for each additional 3rd ___
- Add 1 for each additional MM ___
- Total **9**

III. B. Same Category Priors

Add 5 for each prior category 5 offense

3 Priors x 5 = **15** Total Points

IV. Legal Status at Time of Offense

Status	Points
No restrictions	0
Legal constraint	(10)
Total	**10**

V. Victim Injury (physical)

Degree of Injury	×	Number	= Points
None	(0)	___	0
Slight	5	___	
Moderate	10	___	
Death or severe	15	___	
		Total	**0**

Total = 65 points

GUIDELINE SENTENCE

Points	Recommended Range	Permitted Range
20 - 46	any nonstate prison sanction	any nonstate prison sanction
(47 - 71)	Community control or 12 - 30 months incarceration	any nonstate prison sanction or community control or 1 - 3 1/2 years incarceration
72 - 90	3 (2 1/2 - 3 1/2)	community control or 1 - 4 1/2 years incarceration
91 - 106	4 (3 1/2 - 4 1/2)	2 1/2 - 5 1/2
107 - 120	5 (4 1/2 - 5 1/2)	3 1/2 - 7
121 - 143	6 (5 1/2 - 7)	4 1/2 - 9
144 - 164	8 (7 - 8)	5 1/2 - 12
165 - 205	10 (9 - 12)	7 - 17
206 - 265	15 (12 - 17)	9 - 22
266 - 325	20 (17 - 22)	12 - 27
326 - 385	25 (22 - 27)	17 - 40
386 - 445	30 (27 - 40)	22 - Life
446	Life	27 - Life

INFORMATION FOR PREPARATION OF SENTENCING GUIDELINE SCORESHEET

George Defendant was convicted of *burglary of a dwelling*, a second degree felony, and *petty theft*, a second degree misdemeanor. He is scheduled to be sentenced for those crimes.

Defendant has a prior record: Three years ago he was convicted for *two petty theft offenses*, both misdemeanors. Two years ago he was also convicted of a third degree felony, *grand theft*. Then, only two months before his arrest for the burglary and theft charges for which he is now to be sentenced, he was placed on probation for a year following his conviction for *assault*, a misdemeanor.

His sentencing guideline scoresheet is completed as follows:

I. His primary offense, a 2nd degree felony is 30 points;
II. The additional misdemeanor is given a value of 1 point;
III. A. The prior record including one 3rd degree felony (6 points) and three misdemeanors (3 points);
    B. Three prior felony convictions are worth 15 points;
IV. He was on probation (legal restraint) when convicted, 10 points;
V. No victim jury.

TOTAL SENTENCING GUIDELINES POINTS: 65
GUIDELINE SENTENCING RECOMMENDED RANGE:
Community control (probation) or 12 to 30 month's incarceration.

BOX 11.2

Florida's Sentencing Guideline Scoresheet.

"sentence imposed." See Box 11.2 for an illustration using the Florida guideline score sheet for a category 5 crime, burglary.[21]

If a judge wishes to give a sentence which exceeds the guideline, he or she may do so but the sentence must survive appellate review, and an extraordinary reason must be shown to justify any sentence outside the guidelines. In such a way the government can show an evenhanded sentencing procedure. Although sentencing guidelines have not been met with universal acceptance by judges and others, the appellate courts have generally upheld the Constitutionality of their use.[22]

PRESENTENCE INVESTIGATION

As indicated, most sentences are imposed by judges who, with the exception of those few cases where conviction carries legislatively mandated sanctions, have a number of available alternatives. In the ordinary sentencing situation, however, the judge knows little about the defendant except for the formal conviction label. If a trial has been held, the judge may have formed some opinion about the character of the offender from testimony by witnesses or the defendant if he or she took the stand. But usually the judge faces a defendant who has pleaded guilty, which means contact between the two might have been limited to a few minutes and the exchange of only a few words.

To assist the court in imposing a fair and appropriate sentence, therefore, a **presentence investigation (PSI)** is normally conducted to gather relevant information about the offender. The judge sets a date for sentencing—commonly 10 days to 2 weeks or a month after conviction—and during that interval the probation staff attached to the court investigates the background of the offender and the crime. In some jurisdictions PSIs are mandated by statute or court rule; elsewhere they are left to the discretion of the judge. The American Bar Association recommends that such investigations be required in every instance where a sentence of incarceration for a year or longer is possible, where the offender is under 21 years of age, or where a first offense is involved.[23] In jurisdictions that use jury sentencing, PSIs may be superfluous, and in convictions for crimes where a mandatory sentence must follow, the judge does not need such an investigation, although in those instances the prison may conduct its own similar "admissions investigation."

Actually, the PSI often serves broader purposes than the primary one of aiding the sentencing decision. For instance, probation officers may use the PSI as a guide for establishing a casework plan. And prison intake officials often use it as a source of information to assist in classifying the newly arrived inmate. Later, the PSI surfaces again at the parole decision process. And PSIs are used as sources of data for systematic research into the nature of criminals and criminal behavior. More than any other document the PSI sticks with the offender on the journey through the correctional system.

Presentence investigations vary in scope and focus, depending on court resources and the needs of the sentencing judge. Generally, a probation officer is given the task of conducting an investigation into the background of the person to be sentenced, bringing together facts and opinions about the offender that may inform and otherwise assist the judge in determining an appropriate sentence. Sometimes a clinical "diagnosis" of the offender is desired or mandated by law, and the offender may be sent to a clinic, hospital, or in some places to a prison for psychiatric and psychological assessment. In routine cases, however, the probation officer collects the available records (the offender's police record, commonly called a "rap sheet," employment history, school reports, and so on), interviews people who know the offender (family, friends, teachers, employers, sometimes the victim or witnesses, and so on), solicits the offender's own story of the crime, and may, if desired by the court, offer a personal "diagnosis" of the violator and make specific recommendations for sentencing.[23]

Confidentiality of the Presentence Report

It is easy to see that the presentence report is an important aid to the sentencing judge. After all, he or she is dealing with years out of a person's free life and has the unwelcome task of balancing the effects of placing the offender in the brutal and brutalizing environment of a jail or prison against the prospect of that person's continuing to be a threat to society. Most judges welcome all the information they can get about the past behavior, present circumstances, and mental condition of the offenders who come before them for sentencing.

Offenders also have an interest in the content of the PSI because, if the information is false or misleading, the sentencing consequences may be devastating.

The history of presentence investigations is a stormy one, for traditionally they were considered confidential documents to be seen only by the judge and not to be disclosed to the defendant or defendant's counsel. But as the sentence hearing came to be defined as a critical stage in the criminal justice process, defendants, or defense counsel, came to argue that a hearing based on a secret, unshared document of such importance was merely a hollow exercise in justice, and that people have a right to know the basis of decisions affecting them, which in this instance amounts to the right to confront one's accusers. Probation staff countered with the claim that **confidentiality** must be promised to the persons interviewed if worthwhile information is to be obtained for the presentence report—that sources of accurate information would "dry up" if their identities could not be protected.[24]

Proponents of keeping the presentence report secret long rested their position on a 1949 U.S. Supreme Court decision, *Williams v. New York*.[25] In this case Williams was convicted of murder, but the jury recommended leniency, that is, life imprisonment rather than execution. The judge, however, imposed the death sentence based on a presentence investigation that he did not fully disclose to the defense. Williams demanded to cross-examine witnesses who gave testimony in the presentence investigation. The trial court denied this request and the U.S. Supreme Court upheld the lower court denial.

Actually this decision was much narrower than denying disclosure of the report.[26] The Supreme Court merely concurred with the trial judge that Williams could not confront and cross-examine persons who provided information in the presentence investigation. Nevertheless, for many years the *Williams* case was widely interpreted as justification for not sharing the presentence report or subjecting it to adversary testing at the sentence hearing.[27]

The situation is somewhat different today. In some places the entire presentence report, including psychiatric diagnoses, is available to both the defense and the state's attorney. More commonly the disclosure issue has resulted in a compromise. In a number of places, a sentencing judge may reveal *part* of the report, withholding the identity of antagonistic informants but "summarizing" their adverse statements.

Some courts distinguish the factual contents of the report (police records and so on) from the opinions of respondents, allowing disclosure of the first part, but not revealing sources of information in the second part. In capital cases state appellate courts have held that information contained in the PSI but not disclosed to the defendant cannot be used in the sentencing decision. The failure of the defendant to request to see the contents of the PSI does not constitute a waiver.

However the confidentiality issue is eventually resolved, the question of what constitutes appropriate and relevant information for a presentence report is still being

State of Madison
Presentence Report

Confidential: Date: July 21, 1992

P.O. John P. Orkis

District Court of Madison Unit 17: Jefferson, Magnolia County

Judge: Hon. William P. Patterson

Defendant: Thomas R. Burke

D.O.B.: May 1, 1972

Residence: 172 Quincy Street Jefferson, Madison 14589

Present Offense: Mad. Crim. Code Sec. 3.27: Robbery in the Second Degree (unarmed)

Date Convicted: June 20, 1992, by guilty plea. Two additional counts of Robbery (2nd Deg) were dismissed as a result of plea bargain.

District Attorney: Frank T. O'Neill, Jr.

Defense Counsel: Michael B. Gague

Arrest Summary

Patrolman Alan Trippi, Metro Precinct 20, Jefferson P.D.

On the night of May 29, 1992, at approximately 11:30 p.m., while on radio car patrol in Section 4, 20th Precinct, I was hailed by Mrs. Mary Wallace, 63, of 1417 Seventh Avenue. She was bleeding from a cut on her forehead and reported being mugged on the sidewalk in the 1200 block of Sixth Avenue. I drove her to the precinct station where she received medical aid. She was later examined at St. Luke's Hospital and released.

She reported that she was approached from the rear by a young man wearing a red tank top shirt and jeans who seized her shoulder-strap purse and wrestled it from her grasp. While she was struggling and shouting for help, the assailant hit Mrs. Wallace on the forehead with his clenched fist. Evidently he was wearing a ring that caused a cut. Mrs. Wallace did not see any type of club or weapon. She claimed she would recognize the assailant if she saw him again.

At approximately 12:07 a.m. the same night (May 30, 1992) Officer John Wilson found what was later determined to be Mrs. Wallace's purse, emptied, torn, and discarded in a doorway at 1306 Sixth Avenue. At approximately 1:06 a.m. on this same morning, this officer spotted a young man wearing a red tank top and jeans walking along Atlantic Avenue with two male friends. I stopped the trio, questioned them, and took red-tank-top into custody since he fit the description given earlier by Mrs. Wallace. He denied any involvement in the affair and his two companions said that all three had spent the previous 3 hours together in a movie further down Atlantic Avenue. I sent the other two on their way but took the suspect, who had identification as Thomas R. Burke, into the precinct house where he was booked and placed in lockup. The next morning, Mrs. Wallace and two other recent purse-snatching victims pulled Burke from a lineup. He subsequently confessed to his involvement in three street robberies, including that of Mrs. Wallace.

Family Situation

Thomas Burke lives with his mother and a younger sister (Ann, age 14) in half of a two-family house at 172 Quincy Street, Jefferson. His parents are divorced. His father, Daniel, is presently residing in Atlanta, Georgia, with a new wife and two stepchildren.

Prior Juvenile and Criminal Record

Age		Date	Charge	Disposition
14	(JD)	4/3/86	Larceny from a store	Adjudicated delinquent—probation
14	(JD)	5/16/86	Truancy	Reprimanded
15	(JD)	1/20/87	Larceny from a store	State training school 1/25/87–9/14/87
17	(YO)	2/15/89	Assault	30 days Jefferson Jail—2 years 11 months probation
18		3/14/90	Assault and robbery	Adult probation—5 years
18		6/1/90	Robbery	Dismissed
18		7/4/90	Public intoxication—possession marijuana	60 days Jefferson Jail—probation continued
19		7/16/91	Assault	Dismissed
19		9/14/91	Assault and robbery	Dismissed

Thomas's mother, Agnes, works as a bookkeeper and clerk at Redman's, Inc., a manufacturing firm on Locust Road. Mrs. Burke reports that she has had a "lot of trouble" with Thomas, not only because of his past involvement with the law but also because of his drinking. Mrs. Burke reports that Thomas is drunk "at least once a week" and often stays out all night. She blames his present and past troubles on "bad company" in the neighborhood and the fact that Thomas "did not have a father since he was 12 years old." Mrs. Burke receives no support from her ex-husband but earns enough to pay family expenses. She has had no trouble with the law nor has her daughter, Ann.

Mrs. Burke and Ann are religious, attending St. Paul's Lutheran Church regularly. Thomas does not attend church.

Educational Background

Thomas Burke graduated from Lincoln High School in Jefferson in 1990. According to four of his teachers he was a poor student, insolent in the classroom and often truant. He missed some school while in the State Training School at St. Alban's and once while in jail (his other jail term was during summer break). Nevertheless, Thomas managed to pass his courses and graduate with his class. He never failed a grade nor was he held back for any reason.

According to the school guidance counselor, Thomas recorded an IQ of 107 on a standardized test and scored well within the average, or normal, range on various attitude and personality inventories given, at his mother's request, to Thomas by the school psychologist.

Thomas did not participate in athletics or in clubs or other extracurricular activities in high school. He was disliked by most of his teachers and advisors and by many fellow students as well. Six of his ex-classmates, interviewed by this P.O. on July 12, 1992, agreed that Thomas associated with a "tough crowd" in high school. Not one of these six had anything good to say about him. He was

a "drunk," a "fighter," and was referred to as a "goobrock," a derogatory term used at Lincoln High.

Employment History

During high school Thomas worked summers for the Acme Home Construction Company of Jefferson. He was hired as a carpenter's helper but did many odd jobs. He was considered a good worker and his job was held for him the time he did 60 days in jail. In contrast to his high school friends most of the men he worked with found Thomas a "regular guy," a "hard worker," "willing to help out." After high school he was hired permanently by Acme and his supervisor, Mr. Ralph Thoreson, said while he was not too surprised by Thomas's arrest, he would still like to have Thomas work for him at Acme. He said "Bumper [Thomas's nickname] likes to drink a little and raise some hell. He was probably loaded when he slugged that woman. He's really not a bad kid."

Defendant's Story

I interviewed Thomas in the Jefferson Jail at 1:00 p.m. on July 7 and again on July 18, each time for about an hour. He admits robbing Mrs. Wallace. He said he had spent all his wages from work after he gave his mother $50 for household expenses. He says he was drunk, broke, and wanted to get in a card game with some friends. "So I saw this woman with a big purse walking along Sixth about midnight. I wondered what the hell she was doing out so late. Anyway, on the spur of the moment I charged her and grabbed her purse. I didn't mean to hit her but she clung onto her strap like it was her kid or something. So I rapped her skull and took the bag. She had only $28 and some change. I threw the cards and other stuff down a storm sewer on Atlantic but the purse wouldn't fit in the drain. So I tossed it in this building. Yeah, I'm sorry I hit her. I didn't really mean to cut her head. Women shouldn't go out alone at that time of night. That's a rough neighborhood over on Sixth, Seventh, and Eighth."

Sentence Alternatives

Madison Crim. Code Sec. 3.27, *Robbery in the Second Degree*, carries the following sentencing options:

Probation. 5 years, conditions standard plus others set by the court.

Split Sentence. Not more than 6 months in county jail followed by 4 years 6 months probation, conditions standard plus others set by court. Jail and probation must equal 5 years.

Prison. Minimum sentence not less than 1 year nor more than 3 years. Minimum cannot *exceed* one-third the maximum. *Maximum sentence* not less than 7 nor more than 15 years.

Plea Bargaining and Prosecutor's Recommendations

Two robbery charges were dropped for plea on the nose to Sec. 3.27. My recommendation is for incarceration for the maximum term allowed.

Victim Impact Statement

Mrs. Wallace has totally recovered from her head wound. Medical expenses were paid by her insurance. She is out the money stolen and has not recovered any of her credit cards, her driver's license, social security card, and other personal documents and items. She feels strongly that Burke should be "put away."

Probation Officer's Recommendation

Burke is not a suitable candidate for probation. He has had many chances in the past. His whole life has been disruptive. He simply takes what he wants and doesn't seem to care about consequences. He is not really remorseful; he blames Mrs. Wallace for being out too late.

I recommend incarceration in prison as this court may determine.

Respectfully Submitted, *John P. Orkis*, P.O.
Barry D. Martin, Supervisor. ∎

debated. For instance, can (or should) a presentence report include or make any references to or inferences about the criminality of the defendant that rely on evidence excluded at trial?

The general issue, clearly just emerging in the context of sentencing, is whether there are, should be, or will be, court-imposed limitations on the types of information included in presentence investigations. Probably there should be *some* restrictions. For instance, inaccurate or irrelevant information should not be allowed to serve as a basis for sentence determination.[28]

THE JUDGE'S SENTENCE DECISION

In the case of Thomas Burke, described in Field Practice A, if you were the judge, what sentence would you give? Assume all the options—probation, split sentence, prison—are open. On what information would you base your sentence? Why would you choose the *exact* sentence you did? If probation is involved, what conditions, if any, would you impose? If prison is your choice, why the particular number of years? What would you say is the underlying *purpose* of the sentence you chose? Evaluate the type and amount of information contained in the PSI. If you were the sentencing judge, what information would you want to have about the defendant?

Many criminal court judges consider sentencing to be their most difficult task. As lawyers, they are professionally capable of conducting trials, ruling on the admissibility of evidence, and dealing with all the other matters that normally characterize the procedural and substantive issues of courtroom law. But sentencing is a different matter: It is not taught in law school courses and only rarely discussed in meetings or seminars of judges.

Judges do not like to think of their sentencing patterns as disparate (different sentences for similar offenders convicted for the same offense) or arbitrary or capricious. Therefore, conscientious judges think a great deal about their own sentencing philosophies. In each case a judge must decide on priorities—whether sentencing should emphasize the deterrence of crime, restitution or victim compensation, the needs and feelings of the community at large, reducing the risk that the offender will commit further crimes, the impact of the sentence on the offender's family including children, the effects of prison life on the physical or mental health of the convicted, the punishment or rehabilitation of the offender, or any other of the many possible goals the sentencing decision can have.

Sentencing is a serious matter, not only for the offender but for the judge who passes the sentence and the correctional authorities who must receive the offender. Indeed, sentencing affects the entire justice system. Is the sentence just? Is it fair? Does it accomplish what is intended? Is it fitting to our time and place in history?

Some sentencing situations that appear to be simple can raise very complex and controversial issues. Based just on the *facts* given, without full PSIs and assuming *no limits* on your sentencing discretion, what would be *your* sentences in the examples described in Field Practice B?

The examples in Field Practice B demonstrate various issues, each of which is difficult to resolve. How should "respectable" offenders who commit white-collar crimes be sentenced? Should the age of the defendant or the reputation of the victim be a sentencing consideration? Should the likely effect of imprisonment on the offender be a relevant factor?

Sentencing judges deal with these matters every day. While there is no consensus on how important these variables are, there is agreement that sentencing is a hard decision to make if offender, victim, and community are to be treated fairly.

Sentencing

1: Hand in the Till

A 58-year-old business executive was convicted of six counts of embezzlement of funds from his firm over a 4-year period. The total amount embezzled was $74,625, of which $13,424 was recovered and returned to the firm. The offender offered to make full restitution by pledging his house, vacation cottage, and personal property in repayment. He has no prior criminal record. He is married and the father of four children, the oldest 19 and the youngest 8. Two children still live at home with the offender and his wife.

2: Hell No! I Won't Go!

A 20-year-old college student was convicted in federal court for failing to register for selective service during the Vietnam War. The crime involved failure to register, not failure to serve. The offender was offered the option of alternative service as a conscientious objector but refused. He argued, unsuccessfully, that registration itself violated his moral and religious principles by supporting war. He said he would take no step to support the war and refused to register even when he was assured he would have no combatant duties *if* drafted though it was uncertain he would be drafted because of factors other than his religious objections.

3: A Little High and to the Left

A 34-year-old offender was convicted of reckless endangerment and assault in the second degree, both felonies, for firing a shotgun at his estranged wife in the parking lot of a large shopping center. He claimed to have been intoxicated at the time and said he was merely trying to frighten his wife. Neither she nor anyone else was hit by the pellets, though there were a number of people nearby. Four unrelated automobile owners whose cars were in the lot at the time reported pellet damage to windows, paint, and metal in the total repair amount of $1,245. The offender paid the repair bills. The offender is a police sergeant on the Metro City Police Department. He has been on the police force for 14 years.

4: New Tricks

A 78-year-old woman was convicted of attempted bank robbery, both a federal and a state felony. She pointed a pistol (which was later determined to be a toy) at a teller in the First National Bank of Metropolis and demanded "all the money." The teller gave her $2416, of which $2000 was in marked bills called "bait money" by banks. The robbery took place at about 1 p.m. The woman left the bank and quickly disappeared. She was arrested 4 days later at a department store when she attempted to pass one of the bait bills. The police found and recovered most of the money ($1960) hidden in her house along with the toy pistol. She had no prior arrest record. The prosecutor, apparently concerned with jury sympathy for a woman her age, offered her the reduced charge of *attempted* bank robbery and the woman accepted the bargain.

5: The Pleasures of Sex

A 28-year-old accountant was convicted of the manslaughter of a 21-year-old woman who the police identified as a well-known prostitute with a street name of Cybil Rites. The offender, married and the father of two preschool-aged children, was a rather frequent "client" of Ms. Rites' for a period of about 2 years. He claimed Ms. Rites was attempting to blackmail him by threatening to send sexually incriminating photographs, which she had secretly taken, to the offender's wife and to his employer. In a struggle over the photos the offender struck Ms. Rites repeatedly in the face. They were in the alleyway behind a nightclub at the time of the beating. Ms. Rites, in attempting to flee, ran to the end of the alley with the offender in pursuit. Reaching her, he gave her a hard blow on the back of her head, causing her to stagger across the sidewalk into the road where she was struck by an automobile and killed instantly. The offender had one prior arrest for disorderly conduct when he was 21 years old. In that case he pleaded guilty and was assessed a fine of $150. ∎

SUMMARY

This chapter dealt with the difficult, complex, and controversial process of sentencing criminal offenders. All sentences have a number of objectives: punishment of offenders, deterrence of other crime, restraint of offenders, protection of the community, and—if possible—rehabilitation of lawbreakers. Rehabilitation in recent years has come under suspicion as not being effective and has been replaced by a "get-tough" philosophy on the part of both legislatures and judges.

The sentencing decision is primarily the responsibility of state lawmakers, who decide what kind of sentence—fines, probation, or incarceration—should be attached to each crime and, if in incarceration, for how long. Most prison sentences have minimum and maximum terms set by law; the judge may set terms *shorter* but not longer than those provided by statute. In turn, the parole board, which exists in most states, can, if it chooses, release a prisoner at the minimum sentence set by the court or at any time up to the maximum. Thus the time actually served by a prisoner depends on the maximum limit set by law, reduced by the judge if he or she so decides, but with release earlier by a parole board if the prisoner is a good risk. Various sentences are available to most courts for most offenses. They range from fines to the death penalty, depending on both the crime involved and the past criminal record of the offender. The most common sentence is probation, where the offender never goes to prison but serves time at home under the supervision of a probation office subject to rules and conditions fixed by the court. Should the probationer violate any of these rules or commit another crime, the probation can be revoked and the individual sent to prison.

Incarceration in jail for up to a year is a common sentence for misdemeanants, whereas felons are usually sent to state prisons for minimum and maximum terms of years up to life. There are variations. Some felons can be sentenced to split sentences involving a few months in jail (not prison) followed by a few years on probation (not parole). And some misdemeanants can serve intermittent sentences, for instance, a year of weekends and holidays in jail but weekdays at home and at a regular job.

The sentencing decision is typically made by a judge based on a presentence report conducted by the probation staff attached to the court. The presentence investigation is a compilation of background material on the offender, including his or her past criminal record, if any, school and employment history, family conditions, personal habits (particularly use of alcohol or drugs), leisure-time activities, and reputation in the neighborhood and among peers.

Today there are attempts to reduce sentence disparity (different sentences for similar offenders) by modifying laws so that all offenders convicted of the same crime get exactly the same punishment. This, however, does not eliminate the other form of disparity, where offenders who are different in background and criminal record get the same sentence for a similar crime.

Many states today have modified their sentencing structures to provide longer prison sentences (extended terms) for violent and dangerous criminals, that is, those guilty of "atrocious" crimes, as well as gangsters and racketeers.

Notes

1. See "In Warm Blood: Some Historical and Procedural Aspects of *Regina v. Dudley & Stephens, University of Chicago Law Review* 34 (1967): 387.
2. We are again indebted to Samuel Walker, *Sense and Nonsense about Crime: A Policy Guide* (Pacific Grove, CA: Brooks/Cole, 1989), and Herbert L. Packer, *The Limits of the Criminal Sanction* (Stanford, CA: Stanford University Press, 1968).
3. For a discussion of the goals of criminal sentencing and current sentencing proposals, see Vincent O'Leary, Michael Gottfredson, and Arthur Gelman, "Contemporary Sentencing Proposals," *Criminal Law Bulletin* 11 (1975): 555–586.
4. Andrew von Hirsch, *Doing Justice* (New York: Hill and Wang, 1976), esp. pp. 45–55.
5. See Bureau of Justice Statistics, *Jail Inmates, 1990* (Washington DC: U.S. Government Printing Office, 1991).
6. Marvin E. Frankel, *Criminal Sentences* (New York: Hill and Wang, 1972), p. 5.
7. See Robert O. Dawson, *Sentencing: The Decision as to Type, Length and Conditions of Sentence* (Boston: Little, Brown, 1969), pp. 79–80, 173–202.

8. John Gruhl, Cassia Spohn, and Susan Welch, "Women as Policymakers: The Case of Trial Judges," *American Journal of Political Science* 25 (1981): 308–322.

9. James L. Gibson, "Race as a Determinant of Criminal Sentences: A Methodological Critique and Case Study," *Law and Society Review* 72 (1978): 455–478.

10. Thomas L. Austin, *The Influence of Legal and Extra-legal Factors on Sentencing Dispositions in Rural, Semi-rural and Urban Counties* (Ann Arbor, MI: University Microfilms International, 1980); Cassia Spohn, John Gruhl, and Susan Welch, "The Effect of Race on Sentencing: A Re-examination of an Unsettled Question," *Law and Society Review* 16 (1) (1981–1982): 71–88; Darrell Steffensmeier and John H. Kramer, "Sex-based Differences in the Sentencing of Adult Criminal Defendants: An Empirical Test and Theoretical Overview," *Sociology and Social Research: An International Journal* 66 (3) (1982): 289–304.

11. Martha A. Myers, "Social Background and the Sentence Behavior of Judges," *Criminology* 26(4): (1988): 649–675.

12. See National Council on Crime and Delinquency, *Model Sentencing Act*, Sec. 8, 1963. American Law Institute, *Model Penal Code*, Philadelphia: 1961.

13. See *Mempa v. Rhay*, 88 S. Ct. 254, 389 U.S. 128, 19 L. Ed. 2d 2 (1967); Fred Cohen, "Sentencing Probation and the Rehabilitative Ideal: The View from *Mempa v. Rhay*," *Texas Law Review* 47 (1968): 1.

14. National Advisory Commission on Criminal Justice Standards and Goals, *Courts* (Washington, DC: U.S. Department of Justice, 1973), Standard 5.1 and Commentary, p. 110.

15. Ibid., Standard 5.13, pp. 182–183; see also Federal Judicial Center, *The Effects of Sentencing Councils on Sentencing Disparity* (Washington, DC: Federal Judicial Center, 1981); Charles D. Phillips, *Sentencing Councils in the Federal Courts: A Question of Justice* (Lexington, MA: Lexington Books, 1980).

16. See, for example, George E. Dix, "Differential Processing of Abnormal Sex Offenders: Utilization of California's Mentally Disordered Sex Offender Program," *Journal of Criminal Law and Criminology* 67 (1976): 233–243. See also Arthur D. Little, Inc., *Determinate and Indeterminate Sentence Law Comparison Study: Feasibility of Adapting Law to a Sentencing Commission-Guideline Approach* (San Francisco: Arthur D. Little, 1980).

17. For an analysis of sentencing discretion in state felony code provisions, see Caroline S. Cooper, Debra Kelley, and Sharon Larson, *Judicial and Executive Discretion in the Sentencing Process: Analysis of State Felony Code Provisions* (Washington, DC: American University, Washington College of Law, 1982).

18. American Friends Service Committee, *Struggle for Justice: A Report on Crime and Punishment in America* (New York: Hill and Wang, 1971), p. 84. Twentieth Century Fund, Task Force on Criminal Sentencing, *Fair and Certain Punishment* (New York: McGraw-Hill, 1976), pp. 96–100.

19. O'Leary, Gottfredson, and Gelman, op. cit., pp. 566–571.

20. Von Hirsch, op. cit., pp. 127–128.

21. *Florida Rules of Criminal Procedure* (1984); see also the federal sentencing guidelines in *Sentencing Reform Act of 1984*, 18 U.S.C.A. 3553 (a)(2) (St. Paul, MN: West, 1984).

22. *U.S. v. Brady*, CA 9, No. 89-50079, 1/30/90.

23. For a rather extensive literature about the appropriate contents of the presentence report as well as suggested standards in various model codes and commission reports, see "Standard 5.14 Requirements for Presentence Report and Content Specification," in National Advisory Commission on Criminal Justice Standards and Goals, *Corrections* (Washington, DC: Department of Justice, 1973), pp. 184–185; *Model Penal Code*, Secs. 7.01, 7.07, pp. 106–107, 117–120; Paul W. Keve, *The Probation Officer Investigates* (St. Paul: University of Minnesota Press, 1960); Victor H. Evjen, "Some

Guidelines in Preparing Presentence Reports," *Federal Rules Decisions* 37 (1964): 177; I. G. Campbell, "The Influence of Psychiatric Pre-sentence Reports," *International Journal of Law and Psychiatry* 4, (1/2) (1981): 89–106; Karen Lichtenstein, *Assessment of Variables Used in Presentence Recommendations and Court Decisions* (Olympia, WA: Social and Health Services Department, 1980).

24. For a collection of references to literature in which both sides of presentence disclosure are debated, see American Bar Association, *Standards Relating to Sentencing Alternatives and Procedures* (New York: Institute of Judicial Administration, 1968), pp. 214–215.

25. *Williams v. New York*, 337 U.S. 241 (1949).

26. For a discussion of the significance of *Williams*, see Sol Rubin, Henry Weihofen, George Edwards, and Simon Rosenzweig, *The Law of Criminal Correction* (St. Paul, MN: West, 1963).

27. Williams was not executed. His sentence was commuted to life imprisonment by the governor. Fourteen years later he obtained his release from prison by a *habeas corpus* action on the grounds that his confession, the principal evidence at his trial, was coerced. See *U.S. ex rel. Williams v. Fry*, 323 F. 2d 65 (2d Cir. 1963).

28. Donald J. Newman, "Perspectives of Probation: Legal Issues and Professional Trends," in *The Challenge of Change in the Correctional Process* (Hackensack, NJ: National Council on Crime and Delinquency, 1972), pp. 7–8.

SUGGESTED READINGS

Blumstein, Alfred, Jacqueline Cohen, and Daniel Nagin (eds.). *Deterrence and Incapacitation: Estimating the Effects of Criminal Sanctions on Crime Rates.* Washington, DC: National Academy of Sciences, 1978.

Goodstein, Lynne, and John Hepburn. *Determinate Sentencing and Imprisonment: A Failure of Reform.* Cincinnati: W. H. Anderson, 1985.

Hirsch, Andrew von. *Doing Justice.* New York: Hill & Wang, 1976.

Petersilia, Joan. *Expanding Options for Criminal Sentencing.* Santa Monica, CA: Rand, 1987.

Shane-Dubow, S., A. P. Brown, and E. Olsen. *Sentencing Reform in the United States.* Washington, DC: U.S. Department of Justice; National Institute of Justice, 1985.

Wheeler, Stanton, Kenneth Mann, and Austin Sarat. *Sitting in Judgment: The Sentencing of White-Collar Criminals.* New Haven, CT: Yale University Press, 1988.

Zimring, Franklin E., and Gordon J. Hawkins. *Deterrence.* Chicago: University of Chicago Press, 1973.

DISCUSSION QUESTIONS

1. Compare and contrast the conservative crime control model and the liberal crime control model regarding sentencing.

2. Describe the various sentences available to a judge. What are the various sentencing structures in the states?

3. Discuss the goals of criminal sentencing.

4. Who really makes the sentencing decision? Discuss.

5. How have sentencing guidelines affected the sentencing decision?

6. Discuss the importance of the presentence investigation and the issues regarding the confidentiality of the presentence report.

Corrections

12

Capital Punishment

Robert Wayne Williams and Ralph Holmes walked into a grocery store in Baton Rouge, Louisiana, on the night of January 5, 1979.[1] Both men wore ski masks and Williams was armed with a sawed-off shotgun. Willie Kelly, a 67-year-old security guard was bagging groceries when the two robbers approached him and attempted to remove his pistol from its holster. Williams pointed the shotgun directly at Kelly's face. The old man's hand moved toward his weapon, and as Williams yelled "Don't try it!" he pulled the trigger and the shotgun fired. Kelly was hit at point blank range in the face. He was dead before his body hit the floor.

The two robbers continued the robbery, collecting money from the cash registers and customers in the store. Holmes pistol-whipped one of the customers. As Williams placed the shotgun down to pick up some spilled money, it went off accidentaly, spraying pellets which struck several customers in the legs and feet. Cries of pain and terror remained in the store after Williams and Holmes were gone.

After several weeks of investigation, police finally received a phone call from an informant who told them that Williams and Holmes had committed the crime. After Williams' arrest, he gave a videotaped confession. On April 10, 1979, before an all-white jury, Williams, a black man, was put on trial. Prosecutors argued that he had planned the robbery, that he had borrowed the shotgun and bought magnum shells for it, and that he had deliberately cocked the gun, pointed it at Kelly, and blown Kelly's head off. They stated that Williams had joked about killing the guard later that night while in a card game in New Orleans.

Court-appointed defense lawyers argued that the shotgun was defective, that it had accidentally discharged, and that Williams had no intention of killing Kelly. A weapons expert testified that the gun could have accidentally fired. Williams did not testify on his own behalf. The jury found Williams guilty and mandated that he be put to death. Williams appealed.

Chronology of an Execution

April 7, 1980

Williams' conviction and sentence were affirmed by a 5 to 2 vote of the Louisiana Supreme Court.

May 19, 1980

A rehearing was denied, and an execution date was set for August 27, 1980. Attorney Richard Shipiro, a capital punishment opponent and civil rights activist entered the case. Williams was transferred to death row at Louisiana State Penitentiary.

August 19, 1980

The Louisiana Supreme Court stayed Williams' execution by a 6 to 1 vote in order to give newly retained counsel Shipiro time to prepare an appeal to the U.S. Supreme Court.

January 12, 1981

The U.S. Supreme Court denied certiorari by a 7 to 2 vote.

March 2, 1981

The U.S. Supreme Court denied a rehearing. A new execution date was set for March 31, 1981.

March 24, 1981

The trial court denied thirteen claims filed by Attorney Shipiro in a postconviction application.

March 25, 1981

The same thirteen claims were filed with the Louisiana Supreme Court in an attempt to stay the March 31 execution date.

March 26, 1981

The Louisiana Supreme Court denied relief by a 5 to 2 vote.

March 27, 1981

The same thirteen claims were denied by the U.S. District Court of Appeals.

March 28, 1981

The decision of the federal district court was appealed to the Fifth Circuit Court of Appeals, which issued a stay of execution and expedited appeal consideration of the district judge's denial.

November 3, 1981

The Fifth Circuit granted Williams' petition for an en banc rehearing.

June 21, 1982

Eleven judges considered six of the thirteen claims filed by Shipiro and rejected them in a 29-page decision by a 7 to 4 vote.

June 27, 1983

The U.S. Supreme Court denied certiorari by a 7 to 2 vote.

September 8, 1983

The U.S. Supreme Court denied an application for a rehearing by a 6 to 3 vote. Attorney Shipiro left the case because he had relocated to New Jersey. Attorney Samuel Dalton entered the case to mount another legal battle to save Williams' life.

October 4, 1983

An application for a stay and a writ of habeas corpus raising two new claims and two old ones was filed with the trial court and denied the same day.

October 14, 1983

Attorney Dalton presented the four claims to the Louisiana Supreme Court, asking for a stay of execution.

October 18, 1983

The Louisiana Supreme Court denied the claims.

October 20, 1983

The claims were submitted to the federal district court, again with the request for a stay of execution. The claims were summarily denied the next day.

October 22, 1983

Attorney Dalton applied to the Fifth Circuit Court of Appeals for a stay of execution, oral argument, and other petitions. The next day the court granted a stay but denied oral arguments.

November 7, 1983

The stay was lifted by the Louisiana Supreme Court by a 6 to 3 ruling.

November 14, 1983

Williams' execution date was moved to December 14.

December 5, 1983

The Louisiana Board of Pardons convened for the first time in 16 years to consider a reprieve or commutation of death sentence.

December 7, 1983

The Board rejected clemency by a 3 to 2 vote.

December 8, 1983

Security officers went to Williams' cell on death row and told him to prepare to be transferred to the disciplinary cell block which was emptied for use as a holding cell for prisoners awaiting execution. The officers inventoried all of Williams' personal property item by item, placed all the items on a blanket, and put the bundle in storage. Williams was transferred, with his legs shackled and handcuffs chained to his waist, in a prison patrol wagon, with two ranking security officers guarding him. A prison security car, with lights flashing, escorted the wagon to the outcamp on the edge of the prison compound where Williams was to be held.

December 9, 1983

Attorney Dalton delivered by special courier another appeal to the U.S. Supreme Court. Supreme Court Justice Byron White rejected the bid for a stay. Williams faced a long weekend in the holding cell. His mother, brothers, and pastor visited him during the next 3 days.

December 12, 1983

The U.S. Supreme Court denied certiorari *and a stay of execution by a 7 to 2 vote. Attorney Dalton met with Louisiana Governor Dave Treen to request the governor to intervene. Governor Treen refused.*

Execution Day: December 13 and 14, 1983

December 13 was the last full day of Robert Wayne Williams' life. There was a storm brewing outside, but blankets were placed over his cell windows and he could not see the thunder clouds gathering. The prison switchboard was busy with calls from state and national media representatives, most of whom were waiting until late in the day to send someone to the prison to cover the execution. Attorney Dalton spent the hours frantically moving from one court to another searching for a judge to stay the execution.

2:00 p.m.   *It became evident to most observers that Williams was going to be executed. Governor Treen issued a statement saying he would not intervene. Two ambulances were dispatched to the prison, one to carry Williams' body and the other to respond in case anyone else required medical assistance during the execution.*

3:00 p.m.   *All prisoners were surprised by an official order to return to their housing units. All inmate activity for the night was suspended and everyone was locked up except the prison newspaper (*The Angolite*) staff, which was confined to the paper's office. An additional 104 prison employees joined those on their regular shift. The prison's top secretarial staff remained at the prison after hours to assist with press releases and other matters.*

4:00 p.m.   *Security intensified. All visitors were thoroughly searched. Press people began to arrive. In all, 52 reporters were included in the press corps before the night was over.*

4:30 p.m. *The prison kitchen staff, without the help of inmate workers, prepared 450 sandwiches and placed them in refrigeration for the use of the media, extra security personnel, and the other people expected at the prison that night.*

6:30–9:00 p.m. *A delegation of Black lawmakers and civic and religious leaders met with Governor Treen appealing for him to stop the execution. He denied the request, and after the meeting was over, an aide said the governor wept.*

Heavy rains, strong winds, lightning, and thunder swept the area. Security officers set up road blocks and other security measures around the prison.

A group of about thirty people met outside the prison's main gate to protest the execution. Williams' mother stood at the gate in the rain after being denied admission. Warden Maggio refused her request to witness the execution.

8:00 p.m. *A career correctional officer who was known to have barbering skills, went to Williams' cell to shave Williams' head and a portion of his left leg.*

10:00 p.m. *The seven official witnesses were transported in a prison van to a building next to the death house, where they signed the necessary legal documents and began waiting for the execution.*

10:30 p.m. *The prison lights were turned out as the prison's 4600 inmates went to bed. Williams' pastor and the prison chaplain remained in front of his cell giving him religious comfort.*

10:45 p.m. *Warden Maggio arrived at the execution site. The generator which would provide the fatal electricity was turned on.*

11:30 p.m. *Maggio received a call from the Governor's office staying the execution for 1 hour while some last-minute legal efforts were being made. Williams was notified.*

12:05 a.m. *The U.S. Supreme Court denied the last-minute attempt.*

12:15 a.m. *Maggio was informed by the Governor's office that the execution would take place. He chose not to tell Williams.*

12:45 a.m. *Williams was given special pampers which he put on. Guards entered Williams' cell and placed the shackles and handcuffs on him. He began reciting the Lord's Prayer and the 23rd Psalm with the ministers. The witnesses were ushered into the witness room. They could see the electric chair through a large plate-glass window which separated them from the death assembly. No one could see the executioner, who was behind a screen and would be paid $400 for this duty.*

1:00 a.m. *Warden Maggio and two security officers entered the holding cell. Maggio said, "Robert, it is time for us to go." The group began to walk toward the death chamber, with Williams and the ministers continuing to recite the 23rd Psalm. When the group entered the chamber, Williams was led to a podium with a microphone where he spoke to the witnesses, looking each of them in the eye. When he finished, he turned, walked to the chair and sat down. The two officers began to fasten the straps which would hold him in the chair, two for each arm and leg and one for the chest. One electrode was attached to the top of Williams' head and another to his left leg. A leather hood was lowered over his head.*

1:06 a.m. *Warden Maggio nodded to the executioner, who pulled the switch sending a charge of 2000 volts of electricity into Williams, which he then lowered to 500 volts. This took 10 seconds. Then the procedure was repeated. The entire procedure took one minute and 10 seconds. An exhaust fan was turned on and the small amount of smoke coming from the leg and head was swept outside.*

1:11 a.m. *Warden Maggio nodded for the two medical examiners to enter the death chamber. They pronounced Williams dead at 1:15 a.m. The witnesses were escorted out of the witness room. Williams' body was removed and taken by ambulance to the funeral home his family had requested.*

ABOUT THIS CHAPTER

The Williams case demonstrates some of the historical, legal, and philosophical aspects of capital punishment in the United States. Few subjects arouse as much passion and interest as the death penalty. Execution is deeply ingrained in the minds of Americans as a historical reality and, according to many public opinion polls, most Americans believe that the execution of greater numbers of serious offenders would lead to less crime and violence in our society. On the other hand, many other people are opposed to capital punishment on moral, religious, or practical grounds. One is hard-pressed to find anyone not willing to express an opinion one way or the other about this subject.

Earlier in our history executions were public events and generated a great deal of interest. In the Massachusetts Bay Colony in the early 1600s, hundreds of people would travel at great inconvenience to observe a public hanging. In the nineteenth century crowds gathered in western towns to see outlaws executed, and photographs and historical records show that thousands of people have watched public executions in this century. Great interest—even fascination—in lawful death has existed throughout history.

However, in the criminal justice system, capital punishment is actually a minor contingency, an infrequent occurrence. Of the many hundreds of thousands of offenses committed, hundreds of thousands of offenders arrested, and tens of thousands of defendants tried and convicted, only a minuscule number of criminals are put to death. Although the subject is of critical importance to those affected by it, such as Robert Wayne Williams and his family and the family of Willie Kelly, for most of us it is a distant issue.

If in the day-to-day operations of the criminal justice process the death penalty plays a minor part, and if that process as we describe it in this book consists for the most part of interesting but routine events, decisions, and procedures, a legitimate question is why we devote an entire chapter to the subject of capital punishment. After all, although most states have death penalty laws, only a few use them. Fewer than 3500 persons are currently under the sentence of death, out of the more than 800,000 in adult prisons. Most communities confront capital cases only rarely.

But when a capital crime is committed, or a particularly heinous crime results in an arrest, or when a really bad criminal is on trial for vicious crimes, capital punishment becomes a matter of debate among criminal justice scholars and practitioners just as among the rest of the public. The press covers capital trials and interviews jurors and others involved in the cases. Casual conversation focuses on the issue; letters to the editor cry out for retributive, quick justice, or decry the most civilized of societies using the most primitive of punishments. Also, in recent years opinions about capital punishment have become rallying cries for political campaigns resulting in the death penalty becoming a centerpiece of national crime legislation. In 1991 President Bush's major crime bill, which Congress passed, called for the death penalty for fifteen crimes including the murder of poultry inspectors. And the 1992 Presidential campaign made capital punishment a central issue in the minds of many voters and news commentators.

In the chapters that follow we describe the postconviction stages of the criminal justice decision network, that is, the punishment and corrections processes in the criminal justice system. We detail and discuss community-based corrections, prisons, parole, and the decisions that result in a person's incarceration or freedom. To understand the "lesser," more common sanctions imposed against offenders, we think it helpful for you to consider issues surrounding the *ultimate punishment*, to consider what should be the appropriate role of government in the handling of the very worst among us.

The importance of capital punishment in our system of justice cannot be assessed solely by the relative infrequency of its use. The fact that it exists as an option at all, the fact that it is used today and that we are poised to use it more, says a great deal about our system of justice, and about our beliefs, expectations, and desires concerning crime and its control. For a period of time in the 1960s and 1970s executions ceased in the United States. Simultaneously a number of other civilized societies (e.g., England, Japan, Israel) banned capital punishment. But after a decade or more without executions, many states began attempting to pass death sentence legislation, and some *did* pass it. So executions began in America again, and though its use is still infrequent, capital punishment is back by popular demand.

Not only is capital punishment the ultimate sanction against crime, but it is irrevocable as well. Mistakes in this area, and there have been some, cannot be rectified. And although the death penalty serves some ends of justice—a life for a life, the ultimate incapacitation of the criminal—it apparently does not accomplish all that is hoped for it or all that is believed to accomplish. Most advocates of the death sentence hope, and indeed believe, that its use in one case of murder will deter others inclined to homicide. But evidence does not bear this out. Executing Robert Wayne Williams in 1984, and the other death row prisoners before and after him, has not stopped, or even lessened, the occurrence of capital crimes.

EXECUTIONS IN THE UNITED STATES

Death, the extreme punishment for crime, has been imposed throughout history in most cultures. In the United States, capital punishment has existed in one form or another throughout most of our history and in most jurisdictions. And except for a few years following the 1972 Supreme Court decision in **Furman v. Georgia**,[2] which ruled death penalty statutes in the states unconstitutional, executions have occurred with some regularity. In this century executions have been most common in southern and western states and still are. Since 1930, when data on executions were first collected by the federal government, and the end of 1990 there have been 4202 executions by civil authorities and 160 military executions. Georgia has used capital punishment the most times (380), followed by Texas (334), New York (329), California (292), and North Carolina (266).[3] (See Table 12.1.)

The Puritan settlers in the Massachusetts Bay Colony brought to this continent an acceptance of the death penalty based on European practices, especially those of England, as well as their own understanding of Old Testament biblical teachings. The resulting code allowed the death penalty for persons convicted of a curious mixture of behaviors. Some of these offenses were considered to be sins (blasphemy, idolatry, witchcraft, or sodomy, for example), which were not included in the British law but were allowed under the Old Testament Law of Moses. Others were traditional serious crimes (murder, for example), but their number did not approach the 350 or so capital offenses of English law. This mixture of Old Testament and English Common Law precursors resulted in a classification of crimes that were capital offenses in England but *not* in Massachusetts Bay (petty theft, for example), as well as crimes that were punished by death in Massachusetts but not in England (adultery, for example).

The number of offenses for which the death penalty applied in this country dwindled to 12 in the typical colony by the 1700s, but not before a large, but unknown, number of persons had been executed. In Boston alone we have records of executions by hanging condemned offenders on scaffolds erected in the city square, including men and women convicted of burglary, rape, murder, theft, and treason.[4] In

TABLE 12.1 *Number of persons executed, by jurisdiction in rank order, 1930–1990*

State	Number executed Since 1930	Since 1977	State	Number executed Since 1930	Since 1977
U.S. total	4002	143	Arizona	38	
Georgia	380	14	*Federal system*	33	
Texas	334	37	Nevada	34	5
New York	329		Massachusetts	27	
California	292		Connecticut	21	
North Carolina	266	3	Oregon	19	
Florida	195	25	Iowa	18	
Ohio	172		Utah	16	3
South Carolina	165	3	Kansas	15	
Mississippi	158	4	Delaware	12	
Pennsylvania	152		New Mexico	8	
Louisiana	152	19	Wyoming	7	
Alabama	143	8	Montana	6	
Arkansas	120	2	Vermont	4	
Kentucky	103		Nebraska	4	
Virginia	103	11	Idaho	3	
Tennessee	93		South Dakota	1	
Illinois	91	1	New Hampshire	1	
New Jersey	74		Wisconsin	0	
Maryland	68		Rhode Island	0	
Missouri	67	5	North Dakota	0	
Oklahoma	61	1	Minnesota	0	
Washington	47		Michigan	0	
Colorado	47		Maine	0	
Indiana	43	2	Hawaii	0	
West Virginia	40		Alaska	0	
District of Columbia	40				

SOURCE: Bureau of Justice Statistics, *Capital Punishment, 1990* (Washington, DC: U.S. Department of Justice, 1991), p. 3.

each of the colonies capital punishment was sufficiently accepted that the authors of the U.S. Constitution and the Bill of Rights acknowledged it in the Fifth Amendment:

> No person shall be held to answer for a *capital*, or otherwise infamous crime, unless . . . nor shall any person . . . be twice put in *jeopardy of life* or limb . . . nor shall he be . . . *deprived of life*, liberty, or property, without due process of law. [emphasis added]

Precise records do not exist regarding the imposition of death for crimes during the nineteenth century, but we are left to conclude, based on the records of plantation owners in the south prior to the Civil War, that a great number of blacks were executed. Many southern states developed *slave codes* prior to the Civil War, that is, a set of codes applying only to blacks. In the 1830s Virginia had seventy capital crimes for blacks and only five for whites; in 1848 Virginia enacted a law requiring death for blacks convicted of any crime punishable by 3 years or more in prison for whites. In 1816 Georgia required death for blacks who raped or attempted to rape whites, but imposed a 2-year sentence on whites convicted of rape.

During Reconstruction, despite the abolition of the slave codes, the race of the offender and that of the victim continued to be a major determinant of criminal penalties, including that of death. The law was a powerful tool of intimidation and was used to reinforce a caste system in which whites dominated and terrorized the black population, with impunity. Support for this conclusion is offered by the following actual incident:

> On April 6, 1866 in Micanopy, Florida a white man named John Denton shot and killed a black man for "insolence." Denton was arrested by U.S. Army troops, but a white mob met the soldiers in nearby Gainesville and freed the prisoner. Later, Denton was tried, convicted of manslaughter, ordered to pay court costs and to serve one minute in jail.[5]

Historians of the death penalty report that in addition to legal executions, a large number of **lynchings**, the process of "stringing up" a person by hanging him from a tree limb or other makeshift gallows, occurred. One study has claimed that over 5000 persons were lynched in the United States between 1888 and 1918.[6] Between 1900 and 1962, according to another, 1799 blacks and 196 whites were lynched, primarily in southern and border states.[7] Many of these lynchings were hasty executions of people recently convicted; some were expressions of mob anger after a black defendant was acquitted or his conviction was reversed. At times police participated in the lynchings, and sometimes the pressure from vengeance-minded mobs forced immediate "trials" and executions referred to as **"quick justice,"** so that the difference between a legal execution and a lynching was indistinguishable.

Sketchy records and tales from the west, like the stories about Judge Roy Bean, the "law west of the Pecos," lead us to conclude that hangings, lynchings, and other forms of execution were not uncommon outside the south either. And racial discrimination in the imposition of the death penalty against Native Americans, Chinese, blacks, and other ethnic groups occurred throughout the United States.

Historians agree that information exists about, in total, approximately 12,000 executions in our history. But the *total* number of persons *legally* executed since 1622 in the United States are estimated to be as high as 20,000.[8]

THE MOVEMENT TO ABOLISH THE DEATH PENALTY

From 1930, when data on executions were first collected by the federal government, until 1972, when the capital punishment statutes were declared unconstitutional by the U.S. Supreme Court, 3979 persons were executed in the United States (see Table 12.1). Figure 12.1 shows the number of executions by year since 1977 when capital punishment was reinstated. After the end of World War II, the United States experienced a steady decline in the number of executions. By 1968 executions had ceased to occur altogether, although persons were still sentenced to death. It was widely anticipated during the 1960s that the U.S. Supreme Court was about to make a landmark decision on the death penalty, the result of a sustained effort by the National Association for the Advancement of Colored People's (NAACP) **Legal Defense and Educational Fund** (commonly called the Legal Defense Fund) lawyers to prevent any further executions and to abolish capital punishment.[9] Persons arguing against the death penalty used this decline in the number of executions as evidence that widespread disenchantment with capital punishment existed, a claim that has not yet been documented.

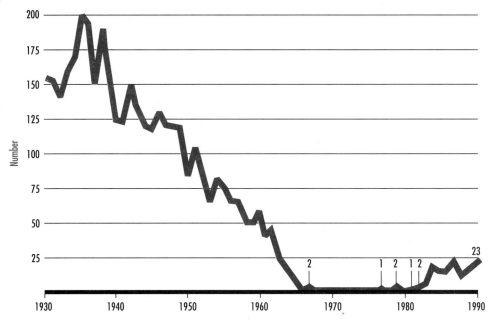

FIGURE 12.1

Persons executed, 1930–1990.
(*Source: Bureau of Justice Statistics,* "Capital Punishment, 1990," Washington, DC: U.S. Department of Justice. November 1991.)

Table 12.1 shows the number of death penalty executions by state since 1930 overall and from 1977 through 1990. As you can see, most of the executions occurred in about one-third of the states, most of those in the south. The Legal Defense Fund staff of lawyers has spent a great amount of time investigating, defending, and appealing convictions in selected cases. Many of these cases involved black defendants in the south accused of raping white women. Attorneys raised such civil rights issues as jury discrimination, forced or coerced confessions, and the right to counsel.

One such case occurred in Groveland, Florida, in 1950. Four black men were charged with the rape of a white woman after an all-white posse had located the four asleep in the woods. One was killed during the arrest. One of the remaining three was later given life imprisonment due either to his age (16) or to the jury's misgiving about his guilt. The other two were sentenced to death. Both death sentences were overturned by the U.S. Supreme Court. One of the two men was killed by the sheriff while being transported to court for a hearing.[10] The other was resentenced to death. After the prosecutor later asserted he had misgivings about the man's guilt and joined in an appeal to the governor for commutation, the sentence was reduced to life in prison. He was released on parole after serving 18 years of his sentence. The 16-year-old refused to join any appeals because he feared his life imprisonment sentence would be overturned and he would be given death.[11]

This case and others like it[12] received widespread notoriety. The Legal Defense Fund lawyers devised a strategy of appealing death penalty sentences based on the claim of widespread discrimination in their imposition.

The Statistical Argument Approach

To bolster its argument before state courts, the Legal Defense Fund developed the **statistical argument approach**: It secured the research services of an expert witness, Marvin Wolfgang, a prominent professor of criminology, to show statistically that the imposition of death in cases of rape was discriminatory against blacks.[13] Indeed, 405 of the 455 men executed for rape between 1930 and 1967 were black, and no white man had ever been executed for the rape of a black woman.[14] The drive to abolish the death penalty was therefore based on arguments about racial discrimination, which in turn were based on statistics gathered in southern states.

The strategy at first met with little success. For example, the use of statistics was misunderstood and rejected as late as 1968 in the *Maxwell v. Bishop* decision by the Arkansas Supreme Court.[15] The court stated:

> We are not yet ready to condemn and upset the result reached in every case of a negro rape defendant in the State of Arkansas on the basis of broad theories of social and statistical injustice. This is particularly so on a record so specific as this one. And we are not yet ready to nullify this petitioner's Garland County trial on the basis of results generally, but elsewhere, throughout the South.
>
> We do not say that there is no ground for suspicion that the death penalty for rape may have been discriminatorily applied over the decades in that large area of states whose statutes provide for it. There are recognizable indicators of this. But, as we have noted before, with respect to the issue of jury selection, *improper state practice of the past does not automatically invalidate a procedure of the present. . . .* [emphasis added]

The development and adaptation of statistical studies for the purposes of litigation posed formidable problems for defense attorneys, who did not find it easy to gain acceptance of their use by the courts. But even though rejected in *Maxwell*, these studies and the approach of gathering statistical evidence entered the court record as a legal tool.

The Class Action Approach

After *Maxwell*, Legal Defense Fund lawyers concentrated on other arguments against capital punishment. One was the **class action approach**. The early focus on southern rape cases was broadened to include all death row prisoners who sought to challenge their sentences on Constitutional grounds. The purpose of the lawsuits was to obtain a moratorium on all executions in the United States. A set of instructions, referred to as the **Last Aid Kit**, was developed to assist any attorney defending a capital case. Then, in 1967, the first class action suit with regard to the death penalty was filed in Florida, on grounds that the Constitutional rights of all those on Florida's death row had been violated. As a result the court granted a stay of execution for all of the fifty men under sentence of death in Florida so the suit could be litigated.

Later that year the same approach was used in California, where eleven executions in the gas chamber were scheduled for the summer months. Those eleven executions had been ordered by newly inaugurated Governor Ronald Reagan after Governor Pat Brown's reluctance to confirm executions had resulted in a backlog of seventy men on death row. The Supreme Court of California granted a class stay of executions similar to Florida's. With the arguments and approaches supplied by the Legal Defense Fund on behalf of virtually all of the approximately 500 persons on death row in various states in 1967, ample legal authority was established to effectively prevent any executions until the many legal issues had been resolved.[16]

Challenges to Due Process

Jurors' Preconceptions

A new set of challenges to the death penalty were presented in a 1968 Illinois case, *Witherspoon v. Illinois*. Witherspoon had been convicted of murder in Cook County, Illinois, in 1960 and the jury sentenced him to death. Under Illinois law at the

time, prospective jurors could be excluded from a case if they expressed *opposition* to the death penalty for religious, moral, or conscientious reasons. Attorneys for Witherspoon argued that a jury composed only of persons *in favor* of capital punishment would be unfairly predisposed toward the prosecution's case. The trial judge had stated early in the *voir dire*, "Let's get these conscientious objectors out of the way, without wasting any time on them." However, the U.S. Supreme Court rejected the argument that pro-death-penalty jurors would be biased toward conviction.[17]

A second argument raised in *Witherspoon* had to do not with the jury's determination of guilt or innocence, but with the sentencing stage of the trial. Although the Supreme Court rejected the argument that a preselected pro-death-penalty jury would be biased toward a verdict of guilt, the Court found that such a jury would be "uncommonly willing to condemn a man to die." The Court stated:

> Whatever else might be said of capital punishment, it is at least clear that its imposition by a hanging jury cannot be squared with the Constitution. *The State of Illinois has stacked the deck against the petitioner.* To execute this death sentence would deprive him of his life without due process of law. [emphasis added]

The *Witherspoon* decision also focused attention on the matter of public attitudes about capital punishment. The Court here relied on public opinion polls which indicated that less than 50 percent of Americans favored the death penalty, and that the trend in American society was for that percentage to diminish rather than increase. In their prediction that support for the death penalty would diminish further, the polls were wrong. But the Court expressed this view as follows:

> Culled of all who harbor doubts about the wisdom of capital punishment—of all who would be reluctant to pronounce the extreme penalty—such a jury can speak only *for a distinct and dwindling minority.* [emphasis added]

322

Risks of Trial

Also in 1968 the U.S. Supreme Court decided a capital case on a procedural point which, although affecting only a small number of persons under death sentences, further eroded the capital punishment statutes in the states. In this case, **United States v. Jackson**,[18] a defendant had been convicted under the Federal Kidnapping Act (the "Lindbergh Law") for a kidnapping that had involved bodily harm; the victim had suffered rope burns in escaping. This federal law permitted death sentences *only* in cases in which the defendant pled not guilty and proceeded to contest the charges at trial. If, on the other hand, a defendant pled guilty and waived the right to trial, the maximum penalty was life imprisonment. The Supreme Court ruled that such a procedure violated both a defendant's Fifth Amendment right to plead not guilty and the Sixth Amendment right to a trial by jury.

At the time of the *Jackson* decision, ten states besides the federal jurisdiction had such laws. Subsequent cases upheld the *Jackson* ruling that it is unconstitutional to subject a person to execution for asserting the Constitutional right to trial.

On June 28, 1971, the Supreme Court reversed thirty death sentences on *United States v. Jackson* and *Witherspoon v. Illinois* grounds. That left approximately 600 capital punishment cases, most of which would be affected critically by the resolution of an *Eighth Amendment issue*, that is, whether capital punishment is "cruel and unusual punishment." So the same day the Court announced that it would review four cases to settle the issue of the Eighth Amendment challenges to the death penalty.

Cruel and Unusual Punishment

The four cases which the Supreme Court considered in connection with the Eighth Amendment were **Aikens v. California**, *Furman v. Georgia*, **Jackson v. Georgia**, and **Branch v. Texas**.[19] Oral arguments were heard on January 17, 1972, before the Court sitting *en banc* (all justices present). In a wide-ranging and lengthy discussion between attorneys on both sides of the cases before the Court, and among the justices themselves, the various issues raised by Eighth and Fourteenth Amendment

February 18, 1972: After reading a newspaper account of the State Supreme Court decision to invalidate the death penalty, death penalty proponent Ronald Reagan gave a radio interview to express his opinions.

objections to the death penalty and the various meanings that could be assigned to the phrase "cruel and unusual punishment" were argued. This was an unusual occurrence; rarely has the U.S. Supreme Court entertained such a free-wheeling debate, and this time it even allowed professors to submit opinions and "findings."[20]

A month after these oral arguments were presented before the nation's highest court, the California Supreme Court heard and accepted virtually the same arguments against capital punishment. In *People v. Anderson* that court declared the death penalty in California to be "cruel and unusual punishment" in violation of the state constitution.[21] The *Anderson* decision had the result of rendering moot the *Aikens* case, besides reversing the death sentences of approximately 100 others on California's death row.[22]

The three remaining cases before the U.S. Supreme Court—*Furman*, *Jackson*, and *Branch*—were decided shortly after the California ruling. Furman had been sentenced to death for murder and Jackson for rape, both in Georgia, while Branch was under a Texas death sentence for rape; all three men were black. In brief, the anti-capital-punishment lawyers argued that the death penalty *as imposed* by the trial courts was *unusual* in that death was seldom imposed (note the steady decline in executions for a number of years prior to 1967 shown in Fig. 12.1) and, when it was, it was imposed disproportionately against blacks, other minorities, and poor people. The lawyers further argued that the death penalty was *cruel* in that the intentional taking of a prisoner's life after a sometimes lengthy period of incarceration cannot reasonably be characterized as anything other than cruel. Thus the lawyers claimed that death sentences violated the Eighth Amendment by being both cruel *and* unusual punishment.

The Supreme Court decision, collectively known as *Furman v. Georgia*, ended capital punishment as it was then practiced in the United States. But the final document was long, complicated, and itself unusual in that each of the nine justices wrote separate opinions. Five of them held that the death penalty in the cases before them was cruel and unusual, Justices Marshall and Brennan stating that it was totally impermissible under any circumstances. The remaining four dissented.

The variety of opinions expressed and the reservations stated about the death penalty by all nine justices reflected the confusion and disagreements expressed by most Americans about this issue. For example, as would be expected, the five majority opinions contain a plethora of arguments against capital punishment as administered by the states—expressing virtually all the standard reasons for opposition. However, three of the five majority justices did not state unequivocally that they would oppose the death penalty in *all* cases or in *all* circumstances. Most legal scholars agreed that the door was open for new death penalty statutes to be passed by state legislatures, which these justices would deem to pass Constitutional muster.

Moreover, the minority opinions by no means merely expressed pro-death-penalty views. Three of the four dissenting justices (Justice Rehnquist was the exception) expressed their own reservations about capital punishment and their opposition, at least in part, to the manner in which the sentence was typically imposed.

The dissenters' arguments against holding the death penalty unconstitutional under the Eighth Amendment involved two major points. First, they insisted that capital punishment did not violate the Eighth Amendment prohibition against cruel and unusual punishment. They argued that the death penalty had historically been considered an acceptable possible punishment for a state to include in its arsenal of criminal sanctions if the legislature so desired. Thus, they wrote, the arguments that capital punishment violated the intent of the framers of the U.S. Constitution were wrong, and current attitudes in American society did not warrant abolishing the "ultimate punishment." Second, the dissenters argued that the Supreme Court was overstepping its Constitutional bounds in outlawing capital punishment since it was interfering with the legitimate role of legislative bodies—in effect, it was itself legislating and therefore violating the Constitutional doctrine of separation of powers.

Each of the five majority opinions against capital punishment expressed different nuances, but the focus of all the objections was on four principles stated by Justice Brennan. First, Justice Brennan wrote, a punishment was cruel and unusual if it did not "comport with human dignity," that is, if it was "so severe as to be degrading to the dignity of human beings." Physical pain was but one measure of this degradation; the more important element, according to Brennan, had to do with treating people as "non-humans, as objects to be toyed with and discarded"; such treatment was unacceptable.

Justice Brennan's other three principles addressed the requirements that (1) a severe punishment not be inflicted *arbitrarily*; (2) *contemporary society find the penalty acceptable*; and (3) such a penalty *not be excessive*. He found a punishment to be excessive if it was unnecessary, a "pointless infliction of suffering" where a less severe punishment would accomplish the same ends.

For the majority on the Court, the crux of the problem was perhaps best summed up by Justice Stewart, who objected to how the legal systems in the jurisdictions that provided capital punishment permitted "this unique penalty to be so *wantonly and so freakishly imposed*."

CAPITAL PUNISHMENT AFTER *FURMAN*

Immediately after the *Furman* decision, Florida led the movement to reinstate capital punishment by calling a special session of its legislature. Similar efforts were made in other states where the majority of voters apparently favored imposition of the death penalty for certain crimes.

The new Florida statute attempted to resolve the objections to capital punishment as "arbitrary and capricious" in the manner in which it is imposed by listing nine *aggravating* and seven *mitigating circumstances* to guide judges and juries in making their decisions. Georgia and Texas passed similar legislation.

Meanwhile, the legislations in Louisiana and North Carolina, responding to the objections expressed in *Furman* to the "arbitrary" use of the death sentence, enacted laws *requiring* the death penalty for certain crimes, that is, **mandatory death sentences**. They apparently misread *Furman*, for in 1976 the U.S. Supreme Court ruled those statutes unconstitutional.[23]

There was also another unresolved issue from *Furman*. Could a state impose a sentence of death for a crime in which no life was lost? In 1977 the Court declared Georgia's death penalty for rape unconstitutional (**Coker v. Georgia**).[24] In a few states legislatures sought mandatory death sentences only for *some* murders, depending on the occupation of the victim or the prior conviction record of the perpetrator. New York, for example, enacted statutes providing capital punishment only for the intentional murder of an on-duty police officer or prison guard or the murder of any person (usually a prison inmate) by a criminal already serving a life sentence for murder. However, in 1987 the Supreme Court, in a case of a lifer killing another inmate, ruled that there can be *no mandatory death sentence* even in such clearly difficult-to-control circumstances.[25]

At the same time the Court ruled against the Louisiana and North Carolina mandatory death sentences, it upheld capital punishment statutes in Florida (**Proffitt v. Florida**), Georgia (**Gregg v. Georgia**), and Texas (**Jurek v. Texas**) where aggravating and mitigating circumstances were provided.[26] These new "approved" statutes were copied by several other states. Today thirty-seven jurisdictions in the United States

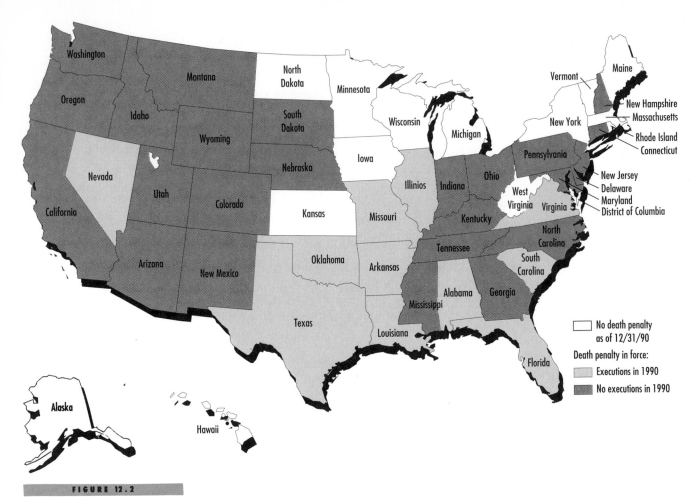

	No death penalty as of 12/31/90

Death penalty in force:

	Executions in 1990
	No executions in 1990

FIGURE 12.2

State death penalty executions in 1990. (*Source:* Bureau of Justice Statistics, *Capital Punishment, 1990,* Washington, DC: U.S. Department of Justice, 1991.)

(thirty-six states plus the federal jurisdiction) have enacted "Constitutional" capital punishment statutes; however, two of these—New Hampshire and North Dakota—have not sentenced anyone to die since pre-*Furman* days. Thirteen states and the District of Columbia still do not have capital punishment statutes. (See Fig. 12.2.)

The Two-Stage Trial

In those states adopting Constitutionally permissible death statutes, changes in sentencing procedures were found to be necessary. For the sentence of death to be imposed there must be bifurcated trial, or **two-stage trial**, in capital cases. The first trial stage, adjudication, involves the determination of *guilt, innocence,* or *guilt of a lesser charge*. After the determination of guilt of a capital offense, the jury begins the second stage of the process, a hearing to decide if the death penalty should be imposed. The prosecution is allowed to "make a case" for execution; defense "makes a case" for leniency (i.e., life imprisonment). The jury then deliberates and makes a *recommendation* of life imprisonment or death to the trial judge, and the judge renders the final decision. In most death penalty states, the trial judge does not have to follow the jury's recommendation (of either death or life in prison), but for political reasons, most do. However, this is a very controversial practice in that juries are required to participate in the difficult emotional process of agreeing to a life or death recommendation which the judge can then totally disregard.

What most legal scholars saw as the major objection to the death penalty expressed in the *Furman* decision was its arbitrary and capricious imposition rather than its "cruel" or "unusual" nature. In addition, the Supreme Court did not find mandatory death sentences for certain crimes to be any less capricious and arbitrary than the laws that preceded them. So new "Constitutional" statutes were enacted intended to address these problems by providing judges and juries with "guided discretion" in making their sentencing decisions. These statutes described a number of **aggravating circumstances**, the presence of any one of which would make a case "death-eligible," that is, the judge could impose the death penalty.

The list of aggravating circumstances varies slightly from state to state, but Georgia's law is representative. The death sentence can be imposed if any of the following conditions are involved:

1. The convicted person has also been convicted of a *prior capital felony*.
2. There is a *serious contemporaneous offense*.
3. The offender is a *grave risk to others*.
4. The crime was committed for *monetary gain*.
5. The victim was a *judicial officer*.
6. It was a *contract killing*.
7. It was a *vile killing*.
8. The victim was a *police officer*.
9. The *defendant was under sentence* for another crime.
10. The defendant *sought to avoid lawful arrest* during the commission of the crime.[27]

If any of these factors exist, then the prosecutor may seek the death penalty and normally argues before both judge and jury that they, too, should decide for death.

The statutes also describe a number of **mitigating circumstances**, the presence of which should normally guide the prosecutor to decide *not* to seek a death sentence, or should influence the judge or jury to decide that, even though guilt has been determined, death is not an appropriate sentence. The list of mitigating factors listed in the Georgia law are also representative of those found in other jurisdictions:

1. The *emotional state* of the defendant at the time of the crime must be considered (psychological problems but not insane).
2. The defendant has *no significant prior record*.
3. The defendant *cooperated with authorities* (e.g., employed life-saving techniques, called police, turned self in).
4. The defendant killed *under the influence of alcohol or drugs*.
5. The defendant acted in *good faith* or with *moral justification*.
6. The *defendant was underage* at the time of the offense.
7. The defendant does not appear to be a *continuing threat* to society.
8. The defendant was dealing with an *armed victim*.
9. The defendant killed in *self defense*.
10. The defendant killed *under provocation*.
11. There are concerns about the *strength of the evidence* that led to the conviction.[28]

In addition to including in these statutes aggravating and mitigating factors that the prosecutors, judges, and juries in trial courts must consider in *rational decisions* about whether to impose the death sentence, legislatures further attempted to ensure

You Be the Jury: Life in Prison or Death?

1: Return to the Scene of the Crime

A 22-year-old white male was convicted of murdering a 16-year-old high school girl who was an acquaintance but not a girlfriend. She evidently had a reputation as sexually promiscuous but when approached by this defendant refused his advances. Indeed, she taunted him, calling him, among other things, a "creep," a "wimp," and a "queer." In a fit of rage, the defendant struck the girl, rendering her unconscious. He placed her in his car, drove to a deserted area, and attempted to sexually assault her while she was in a comatose state. She revived, screamed, and continued to call the defendant derogatory names. He struck her repeatedly with a rock, killing her by crushing her skull. He then removed her clothing and all identification, later disposing of her clothing and purse by placing them in a weighted trash bag and throwing it into a river. He dug a shallow grave and placed the girl's nude body in it, covering her corpse with dirt, sticks, stones, brush, and leaves.

The girl was reported missing by her mother. The police questioned a number of friends and acquaintances, including the defendant, who, some days before the murder, had been overheard bragging about how he would "score" with the girl. He denied any knowledge of her whereabouts.

Three days after the murder, the defendant visited the scene, exhumed the body, and attempted (but failed) to have intercourse with the corpse. In frustration, he mutilated the body with a penknife before reburying it in its shallow grave.

A week later the girl's body was found and subsequent police investigation led back to the defendant. After he was questioned by detectives and could provide no alibi for the night of the murder, he confessed to the killing and to the subsequent mutilations. Appropriate procedural steps were followed—the defendant was provided counsel, was indicted, and later pleaded guilty to murder. No plea agreement was offered by the prosecutor.

A jury was assembled to hear the facts and decide the sentence. The prosecution claimed the murder was aggravated because of the brutal head wounds, the stripped corpse, the shallow grave, and the subsequent attempted intercourse with and mutilation of the corpse.

The defense offered in mitigation evidence of the previous and regular immoral behavior of the victim as well as her taunts and provocations. The defendant also had a clean record, not even traffic violations. He was a high school graduate, steadily employed, and generally enjoyed a good reputation with family, friends, employer, and colleagues at work. Also, though not a regular heavy drinker, on the night of the crime, according to evidence introduced by the defense, the defendant was drunk.

2: The American Dream

During the Christmas shopping season an 18-year-old black male attempted to hold up a store clerk in the process of making an after-hours deposit in the night deposit drawer of a branch bank in a downtown area. The clerk, carrying a canvas bag containing cash and checks in the amount of $2417, at first apparently thought the defendant was

that capital punishment resulted only from a process that was *even-handed* and *consistent*. This was accomplished by identifying the *decision points in capital cases*, the specific steps through which the determination of a death penalty must proceed. These steps are:

1. The prosecutor of the grand jury must decide either to keep the defendant eligible for the death penalty by charging a "death-eligible" offense or not to do so by charging a lesser offense (one that is not death-eligible).
2. The prosecutor may reduce the charge or waive the death penalty either in exchange for a guilty plea or unilaterally.
3. If the plea is not guilty, there must be a trial (usually by jury), where a defendant charged with a capital crime who pleads not guilty may be convicted of a noncapital crime or may be found not guilty.
4. In some states the prosecutor, even after a conviction of a defendant for a capital crime, may waive the sentencing hearing or waive the death penalty unilaterally. The court then imposes the noncapital penalty.

joking. Two witnesses who passed by at this time heard him laugh and ask, "Who in hell are you?" and "You're a card, Shorty." Shortly after this the witnesses heard a shot and saw the defendant running from the scene with a canvas bag. One called out, "Hey! Hey you! What are you doing?!" at which point the defendant paused, turned, and fired two shots in the witnesses' direction. Both shots missed. The victim, the store clerk, lay crumpled near the bank depository. The witnesses summoned police and an ambulance but the clerk was dead on arrival (DOA) at the local hospital. He had been shot once with a .22 caliber pistol and the bullet passed directly through his heart.

The defendant was arrested 2 blocks away within 20 minutes of the crime. He was stopped, frisked, given appropriate *Miranda* warnings, and taken to a police precinct where he was booked. A personal search revealed $724 in cash and some personal belongings. No gun was found on the suspect, nor were the canvas bag or any checks recovered at this time. Both the gun and the checks were found by the police later along a route taken by the fleeing suspect. The gun was unregistered and proved to be untraceable.

The defendant pleaded not guilty because insane. Evidence was introduced showing him to have been under medical care for "emotional instability" for 2 years. His IQ tested dull-normal. Psychiatric examiners for the state testified that he was "dull-witted, impulse-driven, and given to violent mood swings." He was not diagnosed as psychotic. At trial, the prosecution said that the defendant's fleeing from the scene and jettisoning the checks, canvas bag, and gun, showed he knew that the act was "wrong," the only proof needed to show "sanity" in this jurisdiction. He was convicted of murder in the first degree by a jury.

At sentencing the prosecution introduced the defendant's prior record, which included 13 juvenile arrests. As an adult (for less than 1 year) he had one prior felony conviction for grand larceny (shoplifting). He was on probation for that offense. Additionally, the prosecutor contended that the defendant's two shots at the witnesses aggravated the crime. He called for the death penalty, describing the defendant as a chronic, violent criminal who would present a danger to other prisoners if sent to prison, as well as to the public if eventually released.

In mitigation the defense lawyers presented evidence of the defendant's dismal life from very early childhood to the present. He was born to a 16-year-old single mother, was eventually placed in a state-run adoption agency, but was never adopted. He spent his early years in a series of foster homes and orphanages. He did poorly in school; a number of teachers thought him retarded. Acting-out behavioral problems began at about age 10. He fought other children, hit adult house parents and teachers, and had almost daily temper tantrums. At 12 he was adjudicated PINS (persons in need of supervision) for truancy, and that was followed by subsequent adjudications for running away and "incorrigibility." At 14 he was arrested for shoplifting; at 15 he was sent to a training school for breaking and entering a house and stealing money and a radio. He served 8 months, only to be returned for assault while on "aftercare" (parole).

His lawyers therefore argued that the defendant was "a poor unfortunate, neglected black youth who never really had a chance." He was "state-raised" since infancy and thus "understandably angry" most of the time. Discriminated against because of "race, poverty and powerlessness," according to the defense, the defendant sought to get the "good things" in our society "in the only way he could, by taking them." He had no intention to kill but was "surprised and suddenly angered" by the clerk's joking resistance. He fired "without thinking," for he was "unsocialized," a condition clearly not his fault. Thus, they argued, he "deserves to be punished but not to die." ∎

5. After the trial and conviction, there must be a sentencing hearing at which a jury or judge may spare the defendant's life and impose a sentence of life imprisonment.[29]

Post-*Furman* death penalty statutes, therefore, attempt to spell out the criteria and the process whereby persons are selected for capital punishment. As a final check on this process, the laws also require enhanced *oversight* (a speeded-up appeal) by the state supreme courts, often including *automatic appellate review*. In this review the state supreme court determines the following:

1. Whether any *legal error* occurred.
2. Whether the death sentence is *excessive* or *disproportionate* when compared to other similar cases.
3. Whether its imposition was the product of *passion* or *prejudice*.[30]

Field Practice A provides two examples where *you* can be the jury in capital punishment cases.

Despite heavy protests, Gary Gilmore was executed at 8 a.m. on January 17, 1977. Gilmore was condemned for the murder of a motel clerk in Provo, Utah. Norman Mailer's The Executioner's Song *is Gary Gilmore's story.*

CAPITAL PUNISHMENT IN THE UNITED STATES TODAY

As of December 31, 1990, the total number of death row inmates was 2350.[31] From the time of Gary Gilmore's execution by rifle firing squad in Utah in 1977 through December 1990 a total of 143 executions occurred (Fig. 12.3). In addition to executions, the Legal Defense Fund reports that twenty-one death row inmates committed suicide, forty-eight had their sentences commuted, and twenty-seven others were killed in prison or died of natural causes.

Race of Offenders and Their Victims

Between 1930 and 1991, 51 percent of those executed for murder in the United States were nonwhite. Of the 2350 persons on death row in December 1990, 48.45 percent were nonwhite.[32] Several studies have concluded that prosecutors are more likely to seek death sentences for minority racial offenders for crimes involving white victims[33] and that sentences of capital punishment are handed down disproportionately for persons whose victims are white.[34]

Velma Barfield, a 51-year-old grandmother, was condemned to die for poisoning members of her own family.

Females and Juveniles under Death Sentence

Of the 2350 persons on death row as of December 1990, thirty-two were female. Of the 143 persons executed since 1976, the only woman was Velma Barfield, who was executed in North Carolina in 1984.[35]

Three juveniles have been executed since 1976, two in Texas and one in South Carolina.[36] Most states specify a minimum age at which the death penalty can be imposed, the most frequently specified minimum age being 18, although in Indiana it is 10 and several other states cite ages under 18.[37] However, on June 29, 1988, the Supreme Court decided in *Thompson v. Oklahoma* that the execution of a person who was under the age of 16 at the time of the offense is an unconstitutional violation of the Eighth Amendment prohibition of cruel and unusual punishment. The Court with-

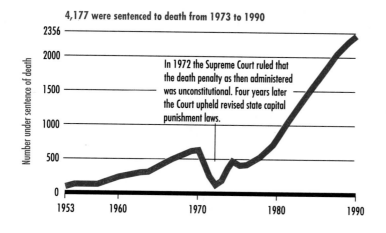

4,177 were sentenced to death from 1973 to 1990

In 1972 the Supreme Court ruled that the death penalty as then administered was unconstitutional. Four years later the Court upheld revised state capital punishment laws.

FIGURE 12.3

Number of executions and prisoners under sentence of death increase during 1990. (*Source: Bureau of Justice Statistics: Bulletin,* "Capital Punishment, 1990." Washington, DC: U.S. Department of Justice, September 1991.)

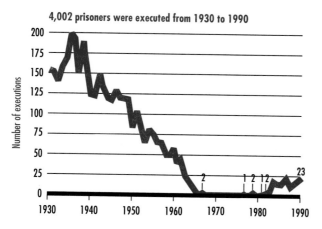

4,002 prisoners were executed from 1930 to 1990

held judgment as to whether the same would be true of 16- and 17-year-olds, but granted *certiorari* the next day on cases focusing on that question. (See Box 12.1 for a list of key capital punishment cases decided since 1968.)

The Demography of Death Row

In 1990 the median age of those under sentence of death was nearly 32 years, somewhat older than other typical felony prison inmates. The youngest offender under a death sentence was 16 and the oldest 74. One percent of the death row inmates were under 20 years of age; 2 percent were over 55.[38]

Almost all death row prisoners were men (98.9 percent). The median level of formal education was halfway through tenth grade; 9.1 percent of the condemned had some college education.

Two-thirds (66 percent) of death row prisoners had a history of felony convictions and 9 percent had a previous conviction for some degree of homicide. Of those with previous felony convictions about 40 percent were under sentence at the time of the more recent crime, 3 percent were escapees from prison, and 7 percent had charges pending when they committed the current murder for which death was decreed. Of those under sentence about half were on parole, 5 percent were on probation, and 3 percent were already in prison for other crimes. About a third of the condemned were married, 22 percent were divorced, and 2 percent were widowed. Nearly 44 percent had never been married.

BOX 12.1

Key Cases

The "statistical argument" approach was rejected by the Arkansas Supreme Court. Discriminatory application of the death penalty in past rape cases and in other jurisdictions does not automatically invalidate a present case.

WITHERSPOON V. ILLINOIS (1968) The U.S. Supreme Court ruled opponents of capital punishment could not be excluded from juries empaneled to hear cases in which the death penalty would be sought unless the prospective jurors stated they could not make impartial decisions on the issue of guilt or could never vote to impose the death penalty.

UNITED STATES V. JACKSON (1968) The U.S. Supreme Court ruled that laws which permitted the death penalty only in cases in which the defendant pleaded not guilty, but a maximum penalty of life imprisonment for defendants who pleaded guilty, are unconstitutional.

FURMAN V. GEORGIA (1972) The death penalty in Georgia was declared unconstitutional on the grounds that as it was administered it constituted cruel and unusual punishment. The discretionary manner in which judges and juries handled capital cases was held by the Supreme Court to result in arbitrary, capricious, and discriminatory decisions.

PROFITT V. FLORIDA, GREGG V. GEORGIA, JUREK V. TEXAS (1976) The death penalties in these cases were upheld by the U.S. Supreme Court due to aggravating and mitigating circumstances. The Court approved these cases as overcoming the ills described in the *Furman* decision.

COKER V. GEORGIA (1977) Georgia's death penalty for rape was held unconstitutional by the U.S. Supreme Court. The only crime for which the death penalty was held permissible is murder.

THOMPSON V. OKLAHOMA (1988) The execution of a person who was under the age of 16 at the time of the offense was held unconstitutional by the U.S. Supreme Court.

The Appeals Process

The average length of time spent on death row awaiting execution is somewhat under 7 years (actually 79 months). This delay is primarily the result of the time it takes to exhaust all legal appeals including sentence review by the state's supreme court as well as appeals on Constitutional and procedural grounds. There is so much national interest in the death penalty that appellate courts allow the filing of *amicus curiae* briefs ("friend of the court" briefs filed by uninvolved third parties) in capital cases. The American Civil Liberties Union, which opposes the death penalty in all cases, is active in filing such briefs.

Moreover, after all appeals have been exhausted, it is common for those still to be executed to ask for executive clemency from the state governor (or, in federal cases, the President of the United States). All governors and the President have the power to pardon prisoners or **commute** (change) their sentences. In the case of a death row prisoner, attorneys may seek a **reprieve** (a delay in carrying out the execution) and a commutation to life imprisonment. And appeals do **vacate** (set aside) many death sentences. According to the NAACP Legal Defense Fund, between 1973 (post-*Furman*) and 1991, 37 percent of the death sentences were vacated or reversed on Constitutional or other grounds.[39] So the 7-year (on average) delay in executions apparently does pay off for many on death row.

At the same time, the lengthy appeals process takes money. Not only must lawyers and judges be paid, but the prisoner must be housed, fed, and protected. Combined legal and correctional costs of capital punishment cases can be very high indeed. Some unsophisticated observers might think imposition of the death penalty is a cheap solution to serious crime. "How much can the electricity cost? What's the price of a few cyanide tablets?" they might ask. But while the actual final surge of current or gurgle of gas or poison may be inexpensive, the overall costs are much higher. Total costs of an execution have been computed to exceed $3 million.[40] For this amount three prisoners could be held in a maximum security prison for 40 years.

Legal costs relating to the appellate process can be justified as the price we pay for our wish as a society to avoid carrying out the ultimate sentence until every facet of the case has been examined for procedural errors or Constitutional shortcomings (although even this justification has been questioned by some individuals). But why the very expensive separate (and necessarily not equal) housing of condemned prisoners? Why a round-the-clock separate guard force for the death house? Why a death house at all? Are our regular prisons not secure enough to hold these murderers? They certainly hold prisoners doing life for the same types of crimes.

The answer is that only the state can legally kill the condemned. The separate death house does not exist to prevent the *escape* of these persons but to prevent the general prison population from killing them and, the other side of the coin, to prevent these killers from murdering any inmates among the general prison population. Would either of these happen if the condemned were mixed with other prisoners? Not in every case, of course, but death row killers bring enough heat to the prison system, and too often have committed brutal murders that disgust inmates as well as civilians on the outside, so that if the state is to reserve the execution prerogative for itself, chances cannot be taken.

The separate death house is not foolproof as protective custody. Inmates on death row do mingle with each other and occasionally commit murders. In 1985, for instance, two death row inmates were murdered by other inmates and one committed suicide, another form of death the "special housing unit" of the death house is supposed to prevent.[41]

It should also be noted that those death row inmates who through the appellate process or by gubernatorial clemency manage to win commutation to life imprison-

Death Penalty Appeals: Delay of Justice or Opportunity for Rehabilitation?

The U.S. Supreme Court has clamped down on multiple appeals by death row inmates. No one knows this better than condemned killer Warren McCleskey, who has twice been rebuffed in major decisions by the Court regarding his case. First, in 1987 the Court rejected the overwhelming statistical evidence presented by McCleskey's lawyers that the State of Georgia imposed the death penalty on killers of whites far more frequently than on killers of blacks. The Supreme Court decided that the evidence did not matter, by a 5 to 4 vote. McCleskey, or any other inmate, would have to prove that the jury in his specific case was biased against blacks (McCleskey is black) who kill whites (his victim was white).

Then, just before McCleskey was to be electrocuted, his lawyers learned that years earlier prosecutors had planted an informant in a cell adjoining his who questioned him about the crime and reported his statements to police investigators, a violation of the Sixth Amendment's right to counsel. But, when McCleskey looked to the Supreme Court for relief, the Court ruled that he should have raised the informant issue in his first round of appeals in 1981, despite the fact that his lawyers only learned of the issue in 1987.

McCleskey's case demonstrates what many observers interpret as evidence that the Supreme Court has become irritated with multiple appeals by death row inmates. In 1991, the U.S. Senate responded favorably to President George Bush's proposal to pass legislation which would sharply limit prisoners' legal maneuvers in federal court to challenge their conviction or sentence. Under that proposal, an appeal would not be considered if the federal judge who reviewed it concluded the convicted criminal received a "full and fair" hearing of his legal claims in state court. The Democratic alternative to Bush's proposal would place a 6-month deadline for death row inmates to file petitions in federal court after their state court appeals had been exhausted.

The frustration with the "endless appeals" by death row inmates is apparently complicated by the fact that former death row prisoners are more likely to stay straight, once released, than other ex-convicts. Of the 600 inmates released from death row after the *Furman* decision who later gained release from prison on parole, 80 percent have remained free. Fewer than 1 percent have been convicted of another homicide, and most live law-abiding lives.

For instance, Arthur Broussard was paroled from the Texas prison system in 1986. The 46-year-old Broussard had killed a Houston grocery store owner in 1970, and now he struggles to make a living renovating houses and hauling trash. Carl Harris, 44, shot his foster mother and a friend during an argument in 1967, and claims 24 years in prison changed his life. Everyone's life changes between the ages of 20 and 40, but prison changes a person dramatically.

But despite the data on convicted murders who are later successfully reintegrated into society, public sentiment often opposes any such release. Another Texas case illustrates this point. Leonardo Ramos Lopez and another man ambushed five Dallas County sheriff's deputies in 1971, bound their hands with wire, drove them to a desolate place on the banks of the Trinity River, and killed three of them. The other two escaped and later identified Lopez and his partner. A jury quickly sentenced them to death, but in 1972 *Furman* gained them a resentencing to life imprisonment. After sixteen unsuccessful legal efforts, Lopez was finally released on parole in 1991, much to the outrage of the two surviving police officers and many Texas politicians.

Practical reasons for releasing convicted murderers from prison many years after their conviction include the costs of incarceration. Texas, like many states, faces the high costs of maintaining aging prisoners, many of whom have developed chronic health problems in prison. Also, the aging process seems to diminish the antisocial impulses which initially led to the criminal violence of youthful convicted killers.

SOURCES: David A. Kaplan, "New Rules on Death Row," *Newsweek*, April 29, 1991, p. 68; "Senate Sides with Bush in Passing Curbs on Death Row Inmate Appeals," *The Star-Ledger*, June 27, 1991, p. 10; Ginny Carroll, "Staying Clean: Life after Death Row," *Newsweek*, May 6, 1991, pp. 56–57.

ment may *not* be treated exactly like other lifers. A number of states have enacted laws that severely restrict parole for death row inmates whose sentences have been commuted to life. In Connecticut, for example, commuted prisoners must serve life sentences without any possibility of parole.[42]

Methods of Capital Punishment

Today the most common methods of execution in the United States are lethal injection (sixteen states) and electrocution (fifteen states). Eight states use lethal gas, four states use hanging, and two states use the firing squad. (See Table 12.2.) Of the 143 executions carried out between 1977 and 1991, 54 were by lethal injection, 83 by electrocution, 5 by gas chamber, and 1 by firing squad. Eight states provide for more than one method of execution and grant the condemned person a choice, usually between lethal injection and another method.[43]

The use of lethal injection—the newest method of execution—has become increasingly widespread.[44] The major advantage of the method according to its proponents is that it is "painless." Federal offenders are executed by the method used in the state in which their execution takes place. The federal government, having no execution facilities of its own, rents them from the states. Thus, Julius and Ethel Rosenberg, executed for espionage in 1952, were held in the death house, then at Sing Sing in New York, and executed there. The federal government paid New York for the use of its death house and electric chair.

TABLE 12.2 *Methods of execution used in the United States*

Lethal injection	Electrocution	Lethal gas	Hanging	Firing squad
Arkansas*	Alabama	Arizona	Delaware	Idaho*
Idaho*	Arkansas*	California	Montana*	Utah*
Illinois	Connecticut	Colorado	New Hampshire	
Mississippi*,†	Florida	Maryland	Washington*	
Montana*	Georgia	Mississippi*,†		
Nevada	Indiana	Missouri		
New Jersey	Kentucky	North Carolina*		
New Mexico	Louisiana	Wyoming*		
North Carolina*	Nebraska			
Oklahoma‡	Ohio			
Oregon	Pennsylvania			
South Dakota	South Carolina			
Texas	Tennessee			
Utah*				
Washington*	Virginia			
Wyoming*				

* Authorizes two methods of execution.
† Mississippi authorizes lethal injection for persons convicted after July 1, 1984; executions of persons convicted before that date are to be carried out with lethal gas.
‡ Should lethal injection be found to be unconstitutional, Oklahoma authorizes use of electrocution or firing squad.
SOURCE: "Capital Punishment, 1985," *BJS Bulletin*, November 1986.

The Florida electric chair known as "Ol' Sparky." The chairs in front are for witnesses required at all electrocutions.

CONTINUING CONTROVERSIES ABOUT THE DEATH PENALTY

At present American juries and judges sentence murderers to death at the rate of about five or six a week, yet executions are currently being conducted at the rate of fewer than 20 each year. The result has been a dramatic increase in the number of people under sentence of death, causing, among other things, an overcrowded, expensive management problem for America's prison administrators.

Many offenders on death row believe that they will never be executed. They believe that a new challenge to the Constitutionality of the death penalty will result in mass commutations of death sentences. Or they think that through the work of anti-capital-punishment lawyers their own individual cases will win reversal with either a commutation to life imprisonment or (better for them, of course) outright release from confinement.

Many citizens express dissatisfaction with the slow rate of executions and the approximately 7-year gap between sentence and death. Letters to the editor in many local newspapers regularly express frustration regarding convicted offenders being held for so long on death row, the seemingly endless delays and appeals they are allowed, and the "lack of respect" for law and order perceived to result from this slow execution process.

Meanwhile, highly motivated and industrious attorneys who work to put an end to capital punishment in this country continue to oppose executions. They believe one reason so many death sentences are handed down by juries and judges is that actual executions occur only rarely, and that judges and juries know this and count on something or someone intervening after its imposition to prevent the execution from being carried out. Thus they feel they can be "tough" at sentencing, since they believe their decision will ultimately be nullified.

There may be some truth to this contention. If we began to execute people at the same rate as the sentences are handed down (or faster, since we are so far behind in actually executing those already condemned to death), it is likely the public would be appalled and outraged. Imagine daily executions, 5 days a week, 50 weeks a year, with extensive news coverage of each case. This rate would just keep up with current sentencing patterns. To eliminate the backlog of 1911 people already under sentence of death, we would need to execute about *eight persons a day*, 50 weeks out of the year, for some time to come. The prospect of our society ritualistically killing so many persons is mind-boggling.

The Case for Capital Punishment

Capital punishment is as controversial as any issue in criminal justice. In general the proponents of the death penalty argue that its use is justified in terms of *just desserts*—that taking the life of one who has taken another life is the only just retribution. This stance is supported by tradition going back to biblical prescriptions of an eye for an eye and a tooth for a tooth.

Proponents also argue that the death penalty is necessary to deter others from committing murder and other atrocious crimes and that without it there would be little reason for criminals to refrain from killing even more frequently. They see, for example, a kidnapper having "nothing to lose" in killing rather than freeing a hostage without the death penalty to serve as a restraint.

They also argue that execution is the only assurance a criminal will never again commit a murder or any other crime, an assurance that does not hold for life-term prisoners who may, and indeed sometimes do, commit crimes while in prison or upon release. (In fact, most lifers are eventually released.)

Proponents also hold that the death penalty is an essential social symbol, expressing the boundaries of our cultural standards of decency and humanity. All societies must set outer limits beyond which deviant behavior cannot be tolerated; the death penalty, according to its proponents, is a clear and firm statement of our outrage at and revulsion for murderous acts.[45]

Finally, advocates point out that 80 percent or more of Americans voice support for capital punishment.

The Case against Capital Punishment

Opponents of the death penalty point out that mistakes can and have been made in its imposition, that innocent persons have been executed, and, of course, that there is no remedy for any such mistake. Recently a new challenge to capital punishment has been made following the research of Hugo Adam Bedau, a long-time opponent of capital punishment, and Professor Michael Radelet. According to their findings, twenty-three persons have died wrongfully at the hands of the state since 1900, and another 300 were sentenced to death (many of them spent time on death row) before they were either given new trials by higher courts or exonerated. Bedau and Radelet state that in every year of this century one or more persons on death row have eventually been shown to be innocent.[46]

Opponents also maintain that the publicity surrounding an execution may *attract* unbalanced people to *commit* capital crimes rather than deter potential murderers, as they seek the attention given to the person being executed and therefore commit crimes in order to be on center stage themselves. Police agree that when well-publicized mass killers are being sought, for instance, a number of "crazies" attempt to surrender and confess to crimes they never committed.

Moreover, even if the deterrence effect of executions on rational persons is greater than the attraction they exert on potential murderers (as it probably is), opponents argue that the kinds of crimes for which we use capital punishment are essentially nondeterrable. Murder, torture, mayhem, and the like originate in deep-seated psychological and psychiatric personality factors just as terrorism and espionage rest on "true-believer" political values. Neither twisted personalities nor political martyrs are amenable to change by making examples of others. Capital punishment might deter rational and calculated offenses, like many white-collar crimes, but it is not used in these cases. Only murder elicits the death penalty today.

In addition, opponents point out that the long time lag between the commission of any crime and the actual imposition of the punishment (on the average nearly 7 years in capital cases) as well as the known probability of never getting caught or, if caught, of not being executed makes any simplistic stimulus–avoidance equation irrelevant in crime control.

And extensive historical evidence indicates that there is no diminution in capital crimes even when the death penalty is rapidly and publicly used. Capital punishment is one of our oldest methods of dealing with offenders, but the simple fact is that the frequency of application seems to bear no relevance to the crime rate. If the deterrence theory worked, theoretically there should be a decrease in serious crime where the death penalty is used and an increase where it is forbidden.[47] But in those states that had capital punishment and later abolished it, there was no increase in capital crimes. Conversely, in those states that did not have capital punishment but later adopted it, there was no decrease in capital crimes.

Opponents of capital punishment also point out that its use in the past clearly discriminated against the poor and against blacks and other minorities. They also feel that, given human nature and prejudice, no provisions in statutes or court rules can alter this in the future.[48]

And much less than being an essential symbol of our social values, opponents of the death penalty claim that its very existence as a possibility, the fact that it is in our codes even if not frequently used, is a *blight* on our claims to civility and humaneness. They argue that the state killing those who kill is descending to the level of the criminal—in effect compounding the felony. They see capital punishment as brutal and brutalizing and "deathwork" as not a proper occupation in a democratic society.

Opponents also argue against an issue raised by proponents of capital punishment in recent years (an issue arising perhaps out of the current economic turbulence of our society): the reputed cheapness of the death penalty. Why should the state spend all the money necessary to hold death row prisoners for life, proponents ask,

Death penalty protesters hold vigil outside a Georgia prison housing the electric chair. The vigil failed and the execution of Roosevelt Green took place within hours of this photo.

when only a few pennies worth of electricity, a few bullets, or a new rope is so much cheaper? But opponents are quick to note what was pointed out earlier in this chapter: The cost-effectiveness argument for the death sentence is both naive and inaccurate. There is quite a lot of evidence that life imprisonment is cheaper than execution.[49]

Finally, there is another argument against the death penalty used today that rests on pragmatism rather than philosophical values or a lack of evidence of its deterrence value. This is that the death rows of our nation should provide us with the opportunity to study murderers, our most serious and longest existing criminal type. Executing them prevents research into their histories, personalities, and even biological make-ups, research that might contribute to our knowledge of why people kill people. After all, we have nearly 2000 duly convicted murderers in cages on our death rows. Should we not use this as a research opportunity? Let all appeals be exhausted in whatever time that process takes—then, instead of executing these murderers, study them, in humane and proper ways, for the rest of their natural lives.

According to this argument, actual executions have provided us with an opportunity to see whether the death penalty deters, and we have done these studies. Now perhaps we should look into the emotional and maybe even chemical and physiological traits in the killers themselves. What we could possibly learn could be very valuable. Executing dangerous criminals might perhaps come as close as possible to punishing them according to their "just deserts." But we will never again have the opportunity to study those individuals alive, and perhaps we should.

It has been asked: Why not just study those on death row in the nearly 7-year interval before their execution? Well, during that time legal appeals and petitions are being filed and, quite properly, attorneys for the condemned forbid their cooperation in questioning or experimentation. And while we should pursue studies of lifers in those states without the death penalty, they are still a different class of prisoner than those who have sat long years on death row, unsure of their ultimate fate.

It may not be clear whether a case-by-case research into why Charlie murdered and Bill did not will be as fruitful as, say, the exploration of subcultures of violence.[50] But the fact remains that we know little about the actual persons who kill. Neither our knowledge in that area nor our ability to predict who will kill has grown much since the time of the first murder of Abel by his brother Cain.

Conclusion

Whatever the persuasiveness of the arguments and counterarguments regarding the death penalty, it is clear that a majority of Americans wish to have it kept on the books and used for murder and perhaps for other atrocious crimes. On the other hand, capital punishment will undoubtedly remain an issue of extreme controversy into the foreseeable future as legislatures adapt state laws to conform to Supreme Court guidelines and as state governors are confronted with the issue of whether they should or should not commute death sentences. The death penalty is not only a controversial political issue, but a controversial philosophic and moral issue as well. Unless and until the Supren.e Court totally outlaws all forms of execution under the Eighth Amendment, this controversy will continue to occupy center stage in American criminal justice debates.

SUMMARY

This chapter deals with perhaps the most controversial issue facing the American criminal justice system today: use of the death penalty. It seemed in 1972 that the

Supreme Court had, in effect, outlawed capital punishment, although the Court did not actually label it unconstitutional. For almost 10 years, there were no executions in our country. Since 1972, however, thirty-seven jurisdictions have revised their capital punishment statutes and procedures to comply with Supreme Court rulings on the topic, and once more our society is executing convicted criminals. Under these revised laws, murder is the only crime whose penalty can be death.

At the present time, we have a record number of prisoners on the death rows of states that allow capital punishment. Different states employ various means of carrying out executions. The most common are electrocution and lethal gas, although an increasing number of states also use lethal injections; more rarely, they employ hanging or rifle fire.

Evidence indicates that the death penalty is often used in a discriminatory manner against poor and racial and ethnic minority offenders in our society. Evidence also indicates that the use of the death penalty does not seem to deter others from committing murders.

The chapter concluded by considering the major arguments for and against the use of the death penalty.

NOTES

1. The source for this description is Wilbert Rideau and Billy Sinclair (eds.), *The Angolite: The Prison Newsmagazine* (Angola, LA: Louisiana State Penitentiary) 9(1) (January-February 1984): 21–70.
2. *Furman v. Georgia*, 409 U.S. 238 (1972).
3. Bureau of Justice Statistics, *Capital Punishment, 1990* (Washington, DC: U.S. Department of Justice, November 1991).
4. See Chapin Bradley, *Criminal Justice in Colonial America, 1606–1660* (Athens: University of Georgia Press, 1982).
5. Michael L. Radelet and Margaret Vandiver, "Race and Capital Punishment: An Overview of the Issues," *Crime and Social Justice*, 25 (1986): 94–113. The incident cited by Radelet and Vandiver is taken from Jerrell H. Shofner, *Nor Is It Over Yet* (Gainesville: The University Presses of Florida, 1974).
6. Walter White, *A Man Called White* (New York: Viking Press, 1948), cited in Radelet and Vandiver, op. cit.
7. See Radelet and Vandiver, op. cit.
8. Watt Espy, "The Historical Perspective," in Doug Magee (ed.), *Slow Coming Dark* (New York: Pilgrim Press, 1980).
9. Jack Greenberg, *Judicial Process and Social Change: Cases and Materials on Constitutional Litigation* (St. Paul, MN: West, 1977), p. 442.
10. Frank Trippett, "High and Mighty Sheriff," *Life Magazine*, November 17, 1972, pp. 83–94.
11. Greenberg, op. cit., p. 423.
12. Two of the most famous were the case of seven Black men electrocuted in Martinsville, Virginia, for raping a white woman, *Hampton v. Commonwealth*, 190 Va. 531, 58 S.E. 2d 288 (1950), *cert.* denied, 339 U.S. 989 (1950), and the Scottsboro case, *Powell v. Alabama*, 287 U.S. 45 (1932).
13. Wolfgang relates his experiences during *Maxwell* and other cases, and describes the difficulty in gaining acceptance for his testimony before the Arkansas Supreme Court. See Marvin E. Wolfgang, "The Social Scientist in Court," in Patrick R. Anderson and L. Thomas Winfree (eds.), *Expert Witnesses: Criminologists in the Courtroom* (Albany: State University of New York Press, 1987), pp. 20–35.

14. Bureau of Justice Statistics, *National Prisoner Statistics: Executions 1930–67*, No. 42 (Washington, DC: U.S. Department of Justice, June 1968), pp. 10–11.
15. *Maxwell v. Bishop*, 398 F. 2d 138 (1968).
16. Jack Greenberg and J. Himmelstein, "Varieties of Attack on the Death Penalty," *Crime and Delinquency* 15 (1969): 112–120.
17. *Witherspoon v. Illinois*, 391 U.S. 510 (1968).
18. *United States v. Jackson*, 390 U.S. 570 (1968).
19. *Aikens v. California*, 406 U.S. 813 (1972); *Furman v. Georgia*, 408 U.S. 238 (1972); *Jackson v. Georgia*, 408 U.S. 238 (1972); *Branch v. Texas*, 408 U.S. 238 (1972).
20. See *Criminal Law Reporter* 10 (1972): 4146.
21. *People v. Anderson*, 100 Cal. Rptr. 152, 493 P. 2d 880 (Cal. Sup. Ct. 1972) (*en banc*).
22. Greenburg, op. cit., pp. 496–497.
23. *Roberts v. Louisiana*, 428 U.S. 325 (1976); *Woodson v. North Carolina*, 428 U.S. 280 (1976).
24. *Coker v. Georgia*, 433 U.S. 584 (1977).
25. *Sumner v. Schuman*, 107 U.S. 2716 (1987).
26. *Profitt v. Florida*, 428 U.S. 242 (1976); *Gregg v. Georgia*, 428 U.S. 153 (1976); *Jurek v. Texas*, 428 U.S. 262 (1976).
27. Georgia Code 27-2534.1(b) (1978).
28. Ibid.
29. D. C. Baldus, C. A. Pulaski, and G. Woodworth, "Arbitrariness and Discrimination in the Administration of the Death Penalty: A Challenge to State Supreme Courts," *Stetson Law Review* 15 (1986): 133–261.
30. Ibid.
31. NAACP Legal Defense Fund, *Death Row, U.S.A.*, August 1991 (limited circulation update); see also Bureau of Justice Statistics, "*Capital Punishment, 1990*," already cited in Note 3.
32. Ibid.
33. See Michael L. Radelet, "Racial Characteristics and the Imposition of the Death Penalty," *American Sociological Review* 46 (December 1981): 918–927.
34. See Marvin E. Wolfgang and Marc Reidel, "Race, Judicial Discretion, and the Death Penalty," *Annals of the American Academy of Political and Social Science* 407 (1973): 119–133; also see Harold Garfinkle, "Research Note on Inter- and Intra-racial Homicides," *Social Forces* 27 (1949): 369–381.
35. See W. J. Bowers and G. L. Pierce, "Arbitrariness and Discrimination under Post-*Furman* Capital Statutes," *Crime and Delinquency* 26 (1980): 563–635; S. R. Gross and R. Mauro, "Patterns of Death: An Analysis of Racial Disparities and Homicide," *Stanford Law Review* 37 (1987): 27–153; also see Baldus et al., op. cit., who say that a person is 4.3 times more likely to be given a death penalty for the killing of a white than a nonwhite; see also *McCleskey v. Georgia*, 107 S. Ct. 1756 (1987); statement of Michael L. Radelet before the Subcommittee on Criminal Justice, Committee on the Judiciary, U.S. House of Representatives, July 16, 1987.
36. NAACP Legal Defense Fund, op. cit.
37. Bureau of Justice Statistics, *Capital Punishment, 1990*. The data given in the main text were taken from this bulletin.
38. NAACP Legal Defense Fund, *Death Row, USA* (Baltimore, MD: 1991).
39. Ibid.
40. "Costs of Capital Punishment," *New York Times*, October 3, 1983, Sec. 2, p. 15. This reports on a study done by the New York Public Defender's Association. See also *Miami Herald*, July 10, 1988, Sec. A, p. 1.
41. Bureau of Justice Statistics, *Capital Punishment, 1985* (Washington, DC: U.S. Department of Justice, 1986).
42. Ibid., p. 3.

43. Ibid., p. 4.

44. Ibid., p. 4.

45. See Ernest van den Haag, "A Defense of the Death Penalty: A Legal-Practical-Moral Analysis," *Criminal Law Bulletin* 14 (January-February 1978): 51–68.

46. Hugo Bedau and Michael L. Radelet, "Miscarriages of Justice in Potentially Capital Cases," *Stanford Law Review* 37 (1987): 27–153.

47. See *Furman v. Georgia*.

48. See Thomas J. Keil and Gennaro F. Vito, "Race and the Death Penalty in Kentucky Murder Trials: An Analysis of Post-*Gregg* Outcomes," *Justice Quarterly* 7 (March 1, 1990): 189–207; Samuel R. Gross and Robert Mauro, *Death and Discrimination* (Boston: Northeastern University Press, 1988); Michael L. Radelet and Glenn L. Pierce, "Race and Prosecutorial Discretion in Homicide Cases," *Law and Society Review* 19: 587–621; Hans Zeisel, "Race Bias in the Administration of the Death Penalty: The Florida Experience," *Harvard Law Review* 95 (2) (1981): 456–468; Gary Kleck, "Racial Discrimination in Criminal Sentencing: A Critical Evaluation of the Evidence with Additional Evidence on the Death Penalty," *American Sociological Review* 46 (6) (1981): 783–805.

49. "Costs of Capital Punishment," *New York Times*, p. 15 (cited in Note 40).

50. Marvin E. Wolfgang and Franco Ferracuti, *Subcultures of Violence* (London: Tavistock, 1967).

SUGGESTED READINGS

Bedau, Hugo Adam (ed.). *The Death Penalty in America*. 3rd ed. New York: Oxford University Press, 1982.

Haas, Kenneth C., and James A. Inciardi (eds.). *Challenging Capital Punishment Legal and Social Science Approaches*. Newbury Park, CA: Sage, 1988.

Johnson, Robert. *Death Work: A Study of the Modern Execution Process*. Pacific Grove, CA: Brooks/Cole, 1989.

Sellin, Thorsten. *The Penalty of Death*. Beverly Hills, CA: Sage, 1980.

Van den Haag, Ernest, and John P. Conrad. *The Death Penalty: A Debate*. New York: Plenum Press, 1983.

Zimring, Franklin E., and Gordon Hawkins. *Capital Punishment and the American Agenda*. Cambridge, England: Cambridge University Press, 1986.

DISCUSSION QUESTIONS

1. Discuss the relative importance of capital punishment in American criminal justice compared with other types of punishment.

2. Trace the history of capital punishment in the United States.

3. Trace the evolution of case law regarding capital punishment in the United States.

4. Describe the two-stage trial process.

5. Compare and contrast aggravating and mitigating circumstances as they apply to capital cases.

6. Describe the death row population demographically in terms of age, race, sex, etc.

7. Describe the contemporary methods of capital punishment used today in the United States.

8. Compare and contrast the case *for* and the case *against* capital punishment.

13

Prisons and Correctional Institutions

The drug deal went sour. The promised transaction was to take place at 1 a.m. in the morning at the apartment of William Frost, a 28-year-old man who had made arrangements to purchase $800 worth of cocaine. When Christopher Malone and Bernard Spain, both college dropouts age 20, arrived with the drugs, Frost told them he had already made a purchase and was no longer interested in a deal. Two hours later, after Malone and Spain had been drinking whiskey and complaining to each other about the loss of the sale, they decided to take revenge. They prepared a molotov cocktail with a beer bottle filled with gasoline and a rag stuffed into the opening. The two drove back to Frost's apartment complex and quietly approached the ground-floor window to the apartment; Malone lit the rag with a cigarette lighter and threw the explosive device through the window. Immediately the gasoline exploded and flames soon engulfed the apartment. The two young men ran. Three months later they were arrested for arson and attempted murder.

Malone and Spain were sons of prominent families in their town, had no previous arrest records, and, other than being known among their friends as people who sold drugs, were considered to be average, middle-class young men with bright futures. They were unaware that the molotov cocktail they had thrown through the apartment window had caused severe burns to a man who had not been involved in the drug deal at all, but who was visiting Frost's apartment and was asleep on the couch when the fire was started.

Spain agreed to testify against Malone in exchange for the promise of leniency. Both young men were convicted of arson and aggravated assault. Lengthy presentence investigations revealed their relatively crime-free and trouble-free lives. Their families held to the hope that the sentencing judge would render light sentences, perhaps probation and community service. Both men were enrolled in drug and alcohol rehabilitation programs while they awaited trial and sentencing.

But, on the day of sentencing, Spain was given a 3-year term, and Malone was sentenced to a 10-year minimum in prison. The judge stated that the seriousness of the harm done, and the fact that the attack was with an "explosive device" mandated the maximum possible sentence. The young men, their families and friends, and defense attorneys were shocked at the severe sentences. Malone and Spain were handcuffed and led away to prison.

The two were separated in the jail and later sent to different institutions. Spain was sent to a youthful offender camp, complete with vocational training programs, recreational facilities, and rehabilitation opportunities. Malone, because of the severity of his sentence, was sent to a medium-custody prison.

Malone was loaded with other prisoners into a bus, all of them chained together, and taken to the prison. Experienced inmates were ready to welcome him, and the other newcomers, into their world, the society of captives. Three days after arrival, and after Malone had been processed through the prison classification procedure, a tough, older inmate walked up to him in the yard and stood directly in front of him, throwing a knife on the ground at his feet. "You have three choices," the older convict said. "One, you can pick up the knife and try to kill me. Or, two, I can pick up the knife and kill you. Or, three, you will be my whore." Frightening, isn't it?

ABOUT THIS CHAPTER

Not all stereotypes of prison are accurate. All prisons are not maximum security jungles. All inmates are not animals. All prisons are not dangerous. But the loss of freedom and loss of pleasures and privileges of normal life make the threat of prison deter us from crime. Right? Perhaps. For many, especially those who have been inside before, the incarceration experience is not so bad. And for others who have had no privileges or pleasure on the outside, prison offers security, care, associations, and an escape from the responsibilities of freedom.

This chapter deals with the incarceration of criminals in prisons, reformatories, and other correctional institutions. Christopher Malone, Bernard Spain, and the tough inmate are not the only types of prisoners, and deterrence is not the only goal or purpose of incarceration. Should prisons also rehabilitate offenders? Should prison authorities be allowed to punish inmates severely so as to make them pay for their crimes? These questions, and others, must be addressed. Prisons and correctional institutions present us with a number of difficult questions and problems. The reality of the prison world challenges the ideals of American society.

Life in prison is different from life in jails. Jails are local institutions designed for short-term confinement. Many people in jails are awaiting trial or sentencing. Jails do not have the range of rehabilitation programs found in prisons, and constant confinement in a cell is the normal condition in jails.

Prisons, on the other hand, are real-life "total institutions," not just dramatic sets on television or scenes in the movies. Prisons provide recreation, education, vocational training, libraries, leisure-time activities, religious services, and a great number of other elements of society in miniature. Prisons are complex social systems characterized by their own problems and heterogeneous populations.

Prisoners are classified and transferred as a means of keeping them from preying on one another. Prison discipline is maintained—a tough yet necessary part of prison life needed to prevent riots, killings, escapes, and the smuggling of contraband. Inmate rights are protected and prison actions are governed by leading court cases. And issues such as prison overcrowding regularly come before the Supreme Court.

The world of prison inmates is not pretty. It is the end of the line in our criminal justice process, and the maximum-security prison, historically as well as currently, is one of the harshest, most brutal, and most brutalizing structures created by human beings.

IMPRISONMENT AND THE CONSERVATIVE CRIME CONTROL MODEL

Conservatives believe a large amount of crime is committed by a small number of chronic offenders and that crime can be reduced by locking up those few chronic offenders.[1] We should identify those chronic offenders and selectively incapacitate them in secure institutions, provide self-help programs for those who wish to take advantage of them, but maximize the deterrence benefits of "tough but fair" prison environments. Rehabilitation programs are largely rejected by conservatives as ineffective for most criminals and a waste of taxpayers' money. Conservatives believe prisons have become too soft, too comfortable, and that the prisoners' rights movement has given prisoners benefits which many poor, law-abiding citizens do not have. Conservatives point out that since mandatory sentences began in the mid-1970s, crime rates have declined as the prison populations have increased.

IMPRISONMENT AND THE LIBERAL CRIME CONTROL MODEL

Liberals reject the notion that crime rates have come down as a result of the increased use of imprisonment; they point rather to demographics, to the recent decrease in the number of males in the 14- to 24-year age group. Liberals also reject the idea that society can accurately predict and identify chronic offenders. They point out the huge monetary costs of increased prison populations and the political costs of reducing prison terms for low-risk offenders which would be necessary to make room for high-risk offenders in the prison system. And liberals point out that conservative proposals about the prison system present a serious threat to Constitutional principles and are more suited to totalitarian regimes than to a democratic society. Liberals seek to develop and enhance vocational training and prison industries programs which will equip prisoners to find meaningful, well-paying employment after completion of their prison terms. And they believe nothing should be done which would violate the basic Constitutional rights and protections of prisoners.

THE HISTORY OF PRISONS

The increased reliance on confinement as a major means of dealing with criminals is of relatively recent origin, but the existence and use of confinement facilities is as old as the hills. Prisons exist in every state and federal jurisdiction of the United States, and in virtually every country in the world. Today almost all prisons in the United States are filled to overcapacity. Texas, for instance, has some inmates housed in tents. We have a record number of prison inmates, now approaching *1 million*—not only the highest number in history but the highest proportion of our population (number of inmates per 100,000 adult population) ever. (See Fig. 13.1*a* and 13.1*b*.)

Corrections is a growth industry; very few observers would predict a decline in *rates* of imprisonment, although the number of inmates may drop as the various "baby boomers" (and their children, the "echo boomers") grow older and move out of the typical inmate age group. And even if prison-prone populations decline, we may still maintain a large prison population because states have an enormous financial and political investment in institutions of confinement. Once a prison is constructed it tends to be used, and it is very rare for a prison to be closed, *ever*, no matter how old it

Many prisons in the United States are crowded, tension-filled, human warehouses. Here double bunks fill a dormitory, leaving very little room for prisoners to move around or otherwise pass their time without infringing on another prisoner's space.

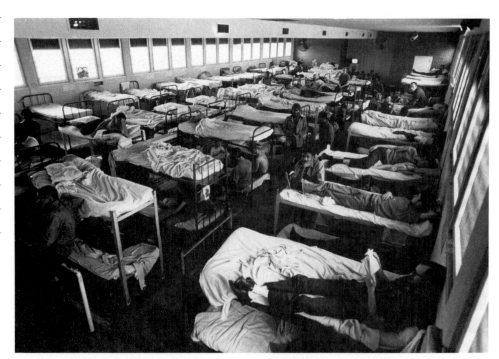

is. As a matter of fact, no sooner is a prison constructed than it becomes full—even overcrowded. We are bound to a policy of imprisonment due to some extent to the fact that we have built more and more facilities for confinement as additions to older prisons, not as replacements.[2] Also, prisons are relied on as a "last resort" after other less intrusive correctional measures have been exhausted. And prisons are major employers of full-time staff. For all these reasons, perhaps, the United States uses imprisonment more than any other country.[3]

The Earliest Prisons

Throughout history facilities for the detention and confinement of criminals have existed. References to "prisoners" are found in some of the world's earliest literature and, in antiquity, various natural and human-constructed structures were utilized to house prisoners. Ancient Semitic nomads utilized dry wells or cisterns to confine persons who, in one way or another, had deviated seriously enough from social norms to incur punishment. The offender would be lowered into the pit with ropes and left until further steps could be decided or until the prisoner died from exposure or starvation or from attack by wild animals. The use of pits or dry wells for confinement was common in many ancient cities. Early Egyptians housed prisoners in a walled, fortress-like tower until the king decided how to dispose of them. Moreover, underground prisons, "courtyard" prisons, and "house arrest" were all utilized in cultures thousands of years before the Greek and Roman eras.

Typically prisoners in antiquity were put to death or used as a slave labor force. But for most, a period of incarceration preceded either of these more drastic sanctions. In a fashion, early prisons were like the death rows of modern societies rather than prisons where incarceration, in itself, is the punishment.

Early Egyptian art depicts the transportation of prisoners in single file, hands bound behind them, each prisoner connected to the next by a rope tied to hooks run through the cheek or lip. For many, being condemned to hard labor in salt mines or on construction projects, such as the pyramids, was a death sentence, for they would die on the job. Prisoners were often transported to distant places of labor. At night, or when the prisoners were not otherwise engaged in labor, they were confined, sometimes bound, and almost always held in remote, hostile surroundings, making escape virtually impossible.[3]

Thus prior to relatively recent history, imprisonment was used primarily as a temporary holding action pending further decisions by the ruling authorities. Such confinement could last for years, but it was not considered, in itself, punishment for crimes; rather, it was detention prior to the imposition of official sanctions.

Origin of Modern Prisons

Maximum-security prisons and reformatories, as we know them today—and indeed the concept of imprisonment as the principal way of dealing with criminals—originated and developed in the United States.[4] While there were dungeons, gaols, workhouses, and similar facilities for criminals in medieval Europe and Asia, generally these were short-term lockup arrangements to hold offenders only until they could be executed, pilloried, branded, or transported to overseas penal colonies.[5]

Among other reasons for the development and spread of imprisonment was the lack of suitable new locations for penal colonies. Some early American settlements and Australia served as penal colonies early in their histories, receiving prisoners banished and transported from European countries. But for the most part such practices ended in the early 1800s, although there were a few exceptions such as Siberia, in the Soviet Union, and Devil's Island, owned by France and located off the coast of South

America. Boatloads of offenders from other societies became increasingly unwelcome on foreign shores.

In part prisons were developed as alternative, *internal*, penal colonies, receiving and holding "outlaws" banished from local communities and transported to the state-run, closed, walled communities called **penitentiaries**. The historic method of removal by banishment to foreign lands was no longer available, so a new form of removal was needed. "Of one thing there is little doubt: the necessity for the removal of the person defined as criminal has never been doubted by the proponents of these theories [of punishment]. Indeed it would seem that the criminal's exclusion is a deep societal need," one observer has written. [6]

We still practice the historic method of "**outlawry**" whereby criminals are simply driven out of organized society, placed outside the protection of the laws of civilized society, removed from the midst of honest citizens.

Indeed, the removal of criminals from society and the placing of them in secure facilities simply to get them away from the company of the noncriminal population is a very attractive solution to crime and what to do with criminals. Political leaders and legal authorities have traditionally dealt with unwanted problem people by forcibly removing them from the community—sometimes by banishment or transportation, sometimes by incarceration. Contemporary judges have been heard to justify a sentence of imprisonment by saying, "I just wanted to get him off the streets for a while." Or, as one of the inmates in the *Scared Straight* television depiction of hardened inmates trying to frighten juvenile delinquents said,

> What would your parents do with a dog that constantly pissed on the living room furniture? They'd get rid of it, that's what. Well, don't you know that every time you are brought into the court for a B & E, or mugging, or drugs that you are pissing on the judge's furniture and sooner or later the judge is going to get fed up with it and get rid of you? And then you go to prison!

Denial of freedom as punishment for crime had a particular attraction in the early years of our republic, for we had just emerged from a revolutionary struggle over freedom. What could be more punitive than taking freedom away from deviant citizens?

But restraint and punishment were not the only reasons used to support the idea of imprisonment. In the years between 1820 and 1840, when the first prisons were built in the United States, they came to be justified and rationalized on philosophical and moral grounds. Though it may seem strange today, early prisons were designed to be utopian societies, not only models for control and treatment of criminals, but also examples of a social order that could be generalized. David Rothman, a historian who has done extensive research into the origin of prisons, points out that the design of the prison originally attempted to eliminate the specific influences that were breeding crime in the community. As Rothman has written:

> Rather than stand as places of last resort, hidden and ignored, these institutions became the pride of the nation. A structure designed to join practicality to humanitarianism, reform the criminal, stabilize American society, and demonstrate how to improve the condition of mankind, deserved full publicity and close study . . . . [7]

Two types of prisons were developed in the United States, and for a number of years advocates of one kind argued with advocates of the other over their relative merits. One type was developed in Pennsylvania and reflected a strong Quaker influence. Its major characteristic was solitary confinement of prisoners; it is sometimes called the **segregate prison** and known generally as the **Pennsylvania Prison System**.

Inmates, held in solitary confinement, were isolated from the outside world and one another and were expected to remain in their cells, read the Bible, reflect on their crimes and "repent." Hence the term *penitentiary*.[8]

A different kind of prison was built at Auburn, New York. Known as the **Auburn Prison System**, this institution was characterized by a practice where prison inmates were held in cells at night but released in the daytime to work together at various forms of hard labor. This **congregate system** rested on the belief that the way to repentance and reform, as indeed the way to salvation, lies through hard work, in contrast to the Pennsylvania systems where repentance itself was the "way."

Both systems imposed total silence on prisoners, and in New York an elaborate form of marching—a shuffle called the **lock step**—was imposed on them as they moved, in silence, from their cells to their places of work. As Rothman pointed out, both types of prisons became world-famous, were visited and evaluated, and had their merits debated by scholars, politicians, and reformers. In this battle over the "best" system, the Auburn plan generally prevailed. The extended solitary confinement of the Pennsylvania system tended to drive prisoners insane and was very costly, whereas the congregate, work prison could help support itself by the labor of inmates.

Auburn Prison, built between 1819 and 1823, was quickly followed by similar prisons at Ossining (Sing Sing) and Dannemora (Clinton Prison), and eventually the Auburn plan spread nationwide and indeed became an international prototype of a maximum-security prison.

The **National Prison Association** was created and met for the first time in Cincinnati in 1870 in a spirit of progressive reform. The prison practices which had been generally accepted up to that time—lockstep, fixed sentence, isolation, silence—were now criticized and rejected by the majority in attendance. The famous Declaration of Principles called for major reforms. (See Box 13.1.)

In the 1870s a reformatory for young adult felons was established at Elmira, New York. Structurally, it was maximum-security, built very much like Auburn Prison, but its program included educational and vocational training opportunities as well as work. As Auburn became the prototype prison, so Elmira became the prototype reformatory, copied throughout the nation and the world.

Although the Pennsylvania segregation system did not become the basic pattern for prisons generally, its techniques and ideology are still very much in evidence. All maximum-security prisons contain within them other prisons, more severe forms of incarceration, for inmates who are troublemakers or who otherwise violate prison rules. Such prisoners are commonly placed in solitary confinement, segregated from the general prison population for periods of time under conditions similar to those found in the early Pennsylvania prisons. In fact, a common prison term for solitary confinement is "segregation."

Prisoners

At year-end 1980, there were 329,821 prisoners in state and federal prisons in the United States, and at year-end 1990, 771,243 inmates were incarcerated—a total increase of almost 134%. (See Fig. 13.1*a*.) Not only did the total number of prisoners increase dramatically, but the rate of prisoners per 100,000 U.S. residents doubled in those 10 years to almost 300 from 150 (see Fig. 13.1*b*). About two-thirds of the admissions to prison are new commitments, persons with no previous time served in prison.[10] As usual, males comprise the great majority of prisoners, about 94 percent. The median age for all admissions is 27 with 40 percent under the age of 24. Half of the robbers, burglars, and auto thieves were under age 24 at the time of admission. Young

---

BOX 13.1

Declaration of Principles
National Prison Association
Cincinnati, 1870

Reformation, not the vindictive infliction of suffering, should be the purpose of penal treatment.

Prisoners should be classified on the basis of a mark system patterned after the Irish system.

Rewards should be provided for good conduct.

Prisoners should be made to realize that their futures rest in their own hands.

Indeterminate sentences should be substituted for fixed sentences and disparities in sentences removed.

Religion and education are the most important agencies of reformation.

Discipline should be administered so that it gains the cooperation of the inmate and maintains his self-respect.

The goal of the prison should be to make industrious free citizens, not orderly and obedient prisoners.

Industrial training should be fully provided.

Prisons should be small; separate institutions should be provided for different types of offenders.

The social training of prisoners should be facilitated; silence rules should be abolished.

Society at large must realize that it is responsible for the conditions that breed crime.[9]

Prisoners in adult correctional facilities, 1925–1990 (*Sources: Bureau of Justice Statistics,* "Prisoners 1925–81," Washington DC: U.S. Department of Justice, December 1982 and *Bureau of Justice Statistics,* "Prisoners in 1990," Washington, DC: U.S. Department of Justice, May 1991.)

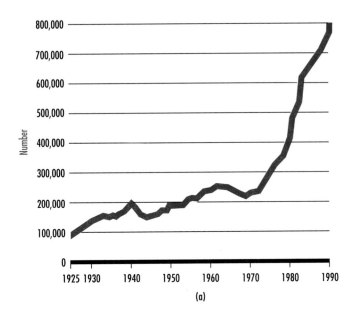

(a)

The incarceration rate for the entire U.S. population is also at an all-time high. (*Sources: Bureau of Justice Statistics: Bulletin,* "State and Federal Prisoners 1925–1985," Washington, DC: U.S. Department of Justice, October 1986 and *Bureau of Justice Statistics: Bulletin,* "Prisoners in 1990," Washington, DC: U.S. Department of Justice, May 1991.)

(b)

offenders (under age 18) and older offenders (over age 55) are more likely than other age groups to be violent offenders, with robbery the most frequent violent crime. Little difference exists between racial groups entering prison except that twice as many blacks as whites are imprisoned for robbery and almost three times as many whites as blacks are imprisoned for "other sexual assault," including child molestation of those incarcerated. Two-thirds have less than a high-school education.

Women in prison

351

**CHAPTER 13:
PRISONS AND
CORRECTIONAL
INSTITUTIONS**

The numer of women in state and federal prisons at the beginning of 1990 was 40,556, up from about 15,000 in 1980. (See Figure 13.2.) The rate of women serving prison sentences is 31 women per 100,000 which is considerably less than the rate of 549 for men. Women represent less than 6 percent of the total prison population. Almost a third of the women serving time for killing a relative or intimate have been victims of sexual or physical abuse. However, most women inmates are convicted of nonviolent offenses, and many were drug and alcohol abusers at the time they committed their offenses. More than 76 percent of the women in prison have children, and of those, 88 percent have one or more children under age 18 at the time of imprisonment; most of the mothers say they were living with their children at the time of arrest.[11]

Prison conditions

The conditions experienced by early prison inmates were at best drab and unpleasant, at worst degrading and brutal. In theory, however, prisons were not designed to be places *for* punishment but rather places *of* punishment; that is, merely being in prison was the punitive part of the sentence; additional punishment was used only for internal prison control—whippings for talking, for example, or segregation for striking a guard. Prisoner lifestyle was controlled by the **principle of least eligibility** applied in our society to all forms of "welfare" programs. This principle limits the kinds of food, housing, care, and treatment afforded prisoners to levels common to the poorest, "least eligible," free citizen. In short, prison conditions were not permitted to exceed bare minimum necessities. Both structurally and in their internal programs, prisons

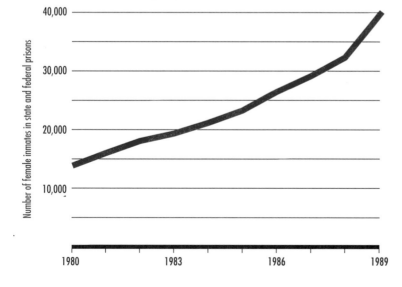

The female inmate population grew by more than 200% from 1980 to 1989

- The number of women under the jurisdiction of state and federal prison authorities at yearend 1989 was a record 40,556.
- Although female inmates are a relatively small part of the total prison population—5.7% in 1989—their share has been growing.

Number of female inmates in state and federal prisons

FIGURE 13.2

Nearly half of the women in state prisons for a violent crime in 1986 were under sentence for a homicide. (*Source: Bureau of Justice Statistics: Special Report,* "Women in Prison," Washington, DC: U.S. Department of Justice, April 1991.)

Cellblocks, such as this one at Marion Federal Prison in Illinois, keep prisoners locked in cells constantly except for brief periods when they may leave them to eat with other inmates, if they have earned the privilege through "good behavior."

were austere, stark, and uniform, providing minimum calorie diets and minimum standards of heat, light, education, training, and recreation.

How much have conditions of imprisonment changed since the early days of Auburn? Many of the prototype prisons built in the early 1800s still exist: Auburn, Sing Sing, and Dannemora are still operating in New York, modernized, of course, and now called **correctional facilities**. The lock step and silence systems are gone and the ready use of whip and lash to force conformity is no longer allowed. Yet incarceration in maximum-security prisons is still a harsh existence, unpleasant and degrading at best, brutal and brutalizing at worst. Modern medium- and minimum-security prisons have softened the architecture and reduced the drabness of steel bars and gray paint. Educational and training programs in many of these "pastel prisons" are better, more closely related to outside work opportunities than the original forms of hard labor. But they hold only a few selected prisoners. In the main, the walls, cellhouses, treeless yards, and regimented existence of early prisons remain the pattern in maximum-security institutions today. Measured against progress in society generally, changes in the conditions of imprisonment have been minimal. In the early days of Auburn even horses were a luxury in our society, and since then our technology has placed men on the moon. We have educated our population, increased life expectancy, become a leading world power; confronted Freud, Marx, and Darwin; changed in size and perhaps in morality. Yet prisons remain very much what they have always been. Any changes made have been made slowly and reluctantly.

PRISONS AND CORRECTIONAL INSTITUTIONS

Some states are building prisons at a break-neck pace. The explosion of the total number of prisoners, and the increasing use of mandatory prison sentencing, has created a need for large numbers of prison cells. However, as mentioned earlier, many older prisons are still in use. The Bureau of Justice Statistics reports that 43 percent of the prison population is housed in prisons *more than 50 years old*, and 12 percent of prisoners are confined to prisons more than 100 years old.[12]

Contemporary correctional jargon reserves the term "prison" for maximum-security, long-term institutions where the worst prisoners serving the longest terms are housed. Other facilities are referred to as "correctional institutions," or "correctional facilities." For instance, in Florida the Department of Corrections claims that only one prison exists in the state, the maximum-security institution at Raiford. Each of the other three dozen or more institutions for incarcerating felons are called correctional institutions. Moreover, a similar distinction is made in correctional jargon between "guards" and "correctional officers."

These distinctions in nomenclature emerged with the professionalization of the field of corrections during recent decades and the desire to modify the harsh images elicited by the terms "prison" and "guard." "Correctional institution" implies the presence of programs aimed at the improvement of inmates. These facilities house persons who will, with very few exceptions, be released one day and therefore are in need of some type of rehabilitation. But rehabilitation programs are deemed useless in real prison, where people are meant to live for long periods working at menial, hard labor not designed to develop postrelease employment skills. Indeed, quite a few maximum-security inmates will never be released or if released will be too elderly to compete in the outside job market. Why provide job training and clinical counseling to persons who will spend the rest of their lives in a cell?

Reformatories

Felons serve sentences in prisons or reformatories. Commonly, a reformatory is thought to be a place of incarceration for juvenile delinquents, but technically this is incorrect. Juveniles are housed in **training schools**, whereas **reformatories** hold young felons, generally those in the 18- to 21-year age group. In the past, prisons were sometimes called "penitentiaries" or "penal institutions." Today, as mentioned, the popular label is "correctional facility." These name changes reflect modifications in correctional philosophy from punishment to rehabilitation, or correction. Unfortunately, perhaps, many prisons simply changed the sign on the gates, leaving the inside conditions the same as before.

Prisons and other correctional institutions are usually located in sparsely populated areas. Older prisons may exist close to urban centers, but newly built and opened institutions generally are located far away from cities. This is because of the lower costs associated with buying undeveloped land and the relative absence of community opposition to constructing such facilities in less populated areas. Indeed, many prisons have proved to be the economic salvation of small towns. They become the major employer in the area, hiring their correctional officers and other staff from among the local residents. Prisons also contribute to local economies by purchasing many goods and services from nearby merchants, and that business is relatively unaffected by swings in the economy or seasonal changes. There are no off seasons or summer vacations among the criminal population.

Classification and Reception Centers

In years past, it was common for a sentencing judge to specify the prison or reformatory where an offender was to serve his or her sentence. Today judges generally do not name a particular prison but instead transfer custody of the offender to a department of correctional services. The offender is then transported to a **reception center**, a receiving prison, where he or she is classified and assigned to an available prison. Such institutions are quite common now. The convicted offender is normally housed there for a period of weeks while undergoing **preincarceration screening**, that is, observation and medical and psychological testing and evaluation, then presumably he or she is placed in the correctional institution within the state which has the proper programs to meet his or her set of needs.

Some critics say the reception process today is overemphasized, and that using such a large percentage of the state's budget allocated for prison psychologists simply on classifying prisoners rather than treating them is a misuse of resources, especially since most correctional institutions are more or less alike in how they function and what they do for prisoners. But classification has its importance.

Prisons must take who they get. The police can make discretionary decisions as to what laws to enforce and which offenders to arrest and move on to the prosecutor, the prosecutor has considerable discretion regarding which offenders to prosecute and for which crimes, and the judge has discretion regarding which of several alternative sentences to impose—but the correctional system *alone* has absolutely *no* discretion as to which offenders enter its gates. Correctional institutions, particularly prisons, serve as the end of the line of the criminal justice process, the receptacle of those offenders left over from the screening-out processes of the other agencies. The only discretionary decisions correctional institutions can make is where to place their prisoners, and those decisions are important for both prisoners and institutions, as detailed in the sections that follow.

Security Levels of Prisons

Because the first order of prisons is to have and to *hold*, the primary, foremost, and critical decision in classification is *security*. This has three dimensions: (1) the likelihood the inmate will escape or attempt to escape, (2) the likelihood the inmate will hurt correctional officers or other prisoners during the time he or she is incarcerated, and (3) the likelihood the prisoner will attempt to smuggle in contraband. Consider the cases described in Field Practice A and the classification issues found in each.

Prisoners, like the prisons themselves, are given overall maximum-, medium-, or minimum-security classifications, which do not necessarily dictate what type of prison they will be sent to. Maximum-security prisoners can be housed in medium- or minimum-security prisons and vice versa, depending on many other factors, including what proportion of a sentence has already been completed when a prisoner is transferred to a different prison setting, behavioral conformity (or misconduct) since reception, and so on. But security considerations do affect the types of jobs prisoners can be assigned to, where they are celled, and the amount of freedom they have to move around the institution without escort by correctional officers.

After classification according to custody requirements, inmates must be designated for transfer to a correctional institution to begin serving time in the general prison population. Today the federal and most state correctional systems have diversified facilities so that some choice of correctional setting is available (or at least a waiting list is available) at the time of classification. Prisons and reformatories are generally distinguished by their degree of security, which relates not only to perimeter control and internal gates and bars, but also to the types of industrial and treatment programs offered by the institution.

Maximum-security prisons are typically surrounded by high fences or walls, usually 18 to 25 feet tall, with gun towers placed at strategic intervals. Inmates are

This aerial view shows the prison at Taunton, Massachusetts, as a "total institution," with cellblocks, school and vocational training facilities, recreational spaces, and everything else necessary to operate a self-contained community.

Classification

1: Bank Robber

Price Gaudette, a 38-year-old man, arrived at the Classification and Reception Center facing a sentence of 30 years for the armed robbery of the Household Finance Loan Company of Austin, Texas. The FBI suspected Gaudette of a series of armed bank robberies throughout the Southwest but were unable to make a positive identification due to his unique talent for disguise. In the case for which he was convicted, his wig and mask had been blown off as he exited the loan company he had robbed and he was clearly seen by three citizens who later made positive identification. Gaudette was charming, likable, had a very positive attitude, and expressed a desire to devote his time in incar-ceration to the "improvement of his fellow man" in any way possible. He had served 2 years of a 5- to 8-year term for armed robbery when he was in his early twenties. No other arrest record was found.

2: Colombian Connection

George Engle, a 22-year-old man convicted of drug smuggling, was received by the department of corrections facing a 5-year term. Engle had no prior arrest record as a juvenile or adult. He had been caught unloading a fishing boat filled with bales of marijuana in what was reported as a "major drug bust." Engle stated that he was unemployed, broke, and when a friend offered him $5,000 for one night's work he agreed—only to get caught in what he said was his first and only experience in crime.

3: Dirty Harry

Harry Phelps, a 19-year veteran police officer, was received on a sentence of 15 years for extortion in a much publicized case in which Phelps had been involved in providing "protection" to an illegal gambling operation in Phoenix. Although he had no prior police record, his personnel record reflected a series of serious accusations by people he had "busted," ranging from alleged brutality to soliciting a bribe. Phelps was arrogant and hostile, and stated that he had been a scapegoat for corrupt politicians. ∎

---

housed in individual cells that rise in tiers (called galleries) in cellblocks, which do not touch the cellhouse walls. Prisons commonly operate industries, or shops, which produce goods used by state agencies. There may also be schools and other treatment programs designed for inmate rehabilitation and, of course, services for feeding and clothing and meeting the health needs of prisoners. Sections of maximum-security prisons are separated by gates, interior fences, and walls, and prison staff members are very concerned with preventing possible escapes, riots, and inmate possession of contraband. Some proportion of the population in any maximum-security prison is "locked down," that is, they remain in their cells continually except for twice-weekly showers. Any movement of inmates within the institution is closely regulated and monitored. Approximately 44 percent of the total prison population is housed in institutions like this.[13]

    Medium-security prisons are usually enclosed by chain-link fences topped with barbed wire, sometimes provide inmates with rooms instead of cells, and generally are much less regimented and security-oriented than walled institutions. Relative freedom of movement exists within the institution and inmates are allowed to move about to recreation areas, the library, and other areas of the institution. In some places inmates are permitted to wear civilian clothing, unlike prisoners in maximum-security facilities. Industries tend to be more modern—computer programming or television repair—in contrast to the laundries and auto-tag shops found in maximum-security prisons. Generally, medium-security institutions receive only prisoners who have been carefully screened for risk of escape or assault. Except in the federal system, these prisoners ordinarily do not come directly from the courts but are transferred from maximum-security prisons or reception centers. About 44 percent of all state prisoners are housed in medium-security prisons.[14]

Often white collar offenders
are incarcerated in federal
prisons which have individual
"spaces" instead of cells, and
offer some of the qualities of
life on the outside.

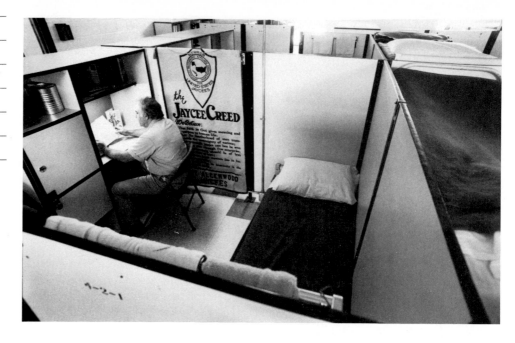

Minimum-security prisons typically do not have fences and the security around the perimeter is more relaxed. An escape from a minimum-security institution only requires a person to walk away. There are no armed guards, no gun towers, no barbed wire or electronic devices to make sure prisoners stay put. Generally, less dangerous prisoners are housed there—those with short sentences, those without lengthy criminal records, or those who are on their way out of the prison system after years served in more secure institutions without causing serious problems. The grounds resemble a school campus and a nearly normal lifestyle is experienced by inmates and staff alike. Family visits are more leisurely and take place more often. Housing arrangements are usually dormitory-style, sometimes even private or semiprivate rooms with more privacy than in more secure institutions. A wide range of programs exist to help inmates (sometimes called "residents") to prepare for life on the outside, including vocational training, academic education, psychiatric treatment, counseling, and, as in all institutions, drug and alcohol counseling. Work release and study release programs are encouraged whereby prisoners are allowed to travel away from the institution to attend school or to work. Only 12 percent of the total prison population is housed in minimum-security institutions.[15]

Prison Subculture

Sociologists, in particular, have conducted considerable research on the "prison community,"[16] often referred to as the **prison subculture**. Prisons, after all, are small, self-contained societies with rules, norms of behavior, ethical codes, formal and informal sanctions, and a whole range of complex relationships between keepers and inmates and inmates and other prisoners. Early studies of prison subculture concluded that the values held by it were in direct opposition to those found in free society. Prison subculture was a result of the conditions of incarceration, an adaptation to the prison environment. And in that environment a new language, specific group structure, and different sexual behavior emerge. Some characteristics of the subculture are imported from the streets, especially gang and ethnic groupings. But other elements are indigenous to the prison environment, created by people who have spent a majority of their lives behind bars.

Accommodations between guards and prisoners are necessary to allow the total institution to function. Guards comprise about 60 percent of the prison staff, their hours are long, and their pay is low. Job entry requirements are generally lower than for anyone else employed in the criminal justice system, and turnover rates are generally high. Inmates, of course, do not usually enjoy being guarded. And guards are impacted by the people they have to work with—convicted felons. So within the prison environment the subculture of prisoners also involves the presence of a custodial staff which is there to protect everyone, enforce rules, observe the inmates, and maintain order.

Inmate types—the "right guy," the "gorilla," the "merchant," the "punk," and the "rat"—have been identified and the "inmate code" has been described.[17] The inmate code represents a survival response, not only to the rigors of prison life but to the label of "criminal" and the damage to one's self-image brought about by the fact of incarceration.

Prisoners who exploit fellow prisoners are playing a dangerous game since they cannot escape the company of their victims. Eventually, anyone who successfully exploits a weaker individual is certain to lose to a more powerful or more skillful exploiter. Thus the main traits affirmed by the inmate code are dignity, composure, courage, and the ability to "take it" and "hand it out" when necessary.[18]

PRISON RULES AND REGULATIONS

The life of an inmate today, while certainly better in many ways than that of his early Auburn counterpart, is still one of strict regimentation, rigid rules, and conditions. It is often asserted that prison rules are imposed with malevolent intent, as part of a "degradation ceremony" required to satisfy the punishment goal of the incarceration of felons.[19] And there is little doubt that many present-day prison rules and regulations can be traced directly to earlier antecedents in the prisons at Auburn and in Pennsylvania, reflecting the beliefs then held about the nature and reform of criminal behavior. But a number of regulations, though abrasive in their impact, are simply the results of bureaucracy, the occasionally mindless rules of processing thousands of men and women.

Decisions were made early on about the sizes of prisons as well as their other features. Generally, maximum-security male prisons were designed to hold 1000 to 5000 inmates, with the average population being between 1000 and 2000 men, depending on state size and need. Women's prisons were (and are) smaller since adult female inmates have always been fewer than their male counterparts, today making up only about 5 percent of the national prison population.[20]

Prisons are often smaller than mental hospitals and similar institutions, yet their traditional size is criticized today as being too large and cumbersome to accomplish what is expected of a correctional facility. Prisons are "total institutions"[21] housing reluctant populations requiring intensive security measures as well as provisions for feeding, housing, work, recreation, and all other aspects of life in a single-sex community. Given the size and character of prisoner populations and the requirements to maintain security as well as to treat and rehabilitate inmates, prison rules and regulations have tended to proliferate simply to meet the requirements of mass care, feeding, and custody.

There is considerable variation in prison regulations and conditions from one place to another and among different types of facilities. Usually there are fewer rules and a more relaxed, less regimented lifestyle in medium- and minimum-security institutions. Nonetheless, even there prisoners are almost totally isolated from normal community contacts. Visits from approved family members are allowed but severely circumscribed. A few jurisdictions today permit some inmates to have conjugal visits with lawful wives. And increasingly prison systems are allowing selected prisoners to go home on short furloughs during their sentences. Prisoners may write and receive mail, though traditionally both outgoing and incoming mail is censored. Conferences with attorneys are not limited, and some prisons permit phone calls to families at specified intervals.

In a very real sense prison inmates are "outlaws." Their status places them outside many of the legal protections afforded ordinary citizens. They are subject to search without specific probable cause, they cannot vote, and they can be forced to comply with a wide assortment of restrictions on personal freedom ranging from type of clothing worn to where and when they can physically move around the institution. (See Field Practice B.)

Inmates in maximum-security prisons spend a good deal of time locked in their cells when they are not working in one of the prison industries. The locked cell is not only punishment, but protection, for it keeps other inmates out. Perhaps the worst and most dangerous aspect of imprisonment is forced association with other felons, for prisons hold some offenders who are aggressive and dangerous to other inmates within the prison as well as to people on the street.

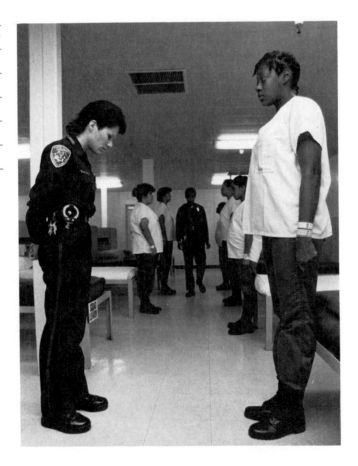

A female guard conducts morning inspection in a "Project Pride" program in a woman's prison. Boot camp-type programs are seen as one way to combat the inmate subculture which makes positive change difficult for many prisoners.

Security

1: Look What I Found

The cell house captain of D block in a maximum-security prison ordered the inmates in the four companies under his command held in their cells while other blocks fell out for work assignment. After the other companies marched off, D block officers searched every cell and subjected each inmate to a strip search. Extensive contraband, including twenty-seven homemade knives and sixteen blackjacks, was seized. Appropriate notations of contraband possession were written for inclusion in the inmates' files but no disciplinary reports were filed.

2: Watch This Guy!

An inmate with an extensive criminal history, including convictions for arson, bombing, and attempted escape, was classified as "Maximum Security" and placed in a "Restricted Company" by the classification committee of the prison. Whenever he leaves the vicinity of his company gallery (to meet with his attorney, report on sick call, meet with his family in the visiting room, or otherwise), standard operating procedures require him to be shackled with leg irons and handcuffs attached to a waist chain and escorted through the institution by two correctional officers.

PRISONERS' RIGHTS, DUE PROCESS, AND DISCIPLINE

In years past the outlaw status of prisoners was almost complete; they really were "outside the law." There was no way to protest conditions of imprisonment, for communication with the outside world was extremely curtailed and appellate courts, even if reached, would rarely respond to inmate petitions.[22] During the past three decades, however, this situation changed somewhat. Appellate courts mostly abandoned their **"hands-off" policy** and were increasingly willing to consider prisoner appeals, particularly where a Constitutional infringement was alleged.[23] While still recognizing the necessity for administrative discretion in maintaining custody of inmates, appellate decisions during recent years have tended to distinguish more sharply between the rights inmates lose through conviction and incarceration and those they retain. The scope of appellate court intervention has gone beyond curbing cruel and unusual punishment to such matters as censorship of mail, freedom of speech and religion, access to courts and counsel, the further deprivation of liberty resulting from placing unruly inmates in segregation, and a variety of other issues relating to internal prison control.[24]

However, a partial return to the hands-off doctrine seems currently in evidence as the U.S. Supreme Court has refused to grant *certiorari* for a significant number of cases involving prisoners' rights issues. The current Supreme Court does not appear to be eager to address matters relating to the treatment of prisoners. But the prisoners' rights cases most recently decided by the Court have served to tighten the control of prison administrators and to make legal redress of grievances more difficult for inmates.[25]

Disciplinary Hearings

While the full legal dimensions of the trend toward more comprehensive prisoners' rights have yet to be played out, it is clear that inmates today are afforded a greater measure of administrative due process in challenging decisions made about them while in prison. Hearings on such matters as segregation (solitary confinement), loss of **"good time"** (i.e., time off for good behavior), and similar matters, are now permitted in many jurisdictions.

A federal district court addressed the issue of in-prison discipline in 1971 in *Landman v. Royster*.[26] This decision was the result of a class action suit brought by Virginia prison inmates against correctional officials. Among other things, the prisoners alleged extensive use of solitary confinement and of other punishments for prison rule infractions including bread and water diets, placing inmates in chains, keeping prisoners nude in solitary confinement in unheated cells, and denial of medical treatment.

The court ruled that, first, the decision to punish must be made by an impartial tribunal. The officer who reported the violation cannot sit on the tribunal. Second, there must be a **disciplinary hearing** in which the accused has the right to present evidence in his or her defense, including the testimony of voluntary witnesses, to cross-examine adverse witnesses, to refute evidence submitted against him or her, and to select a *lay advisor* to present his or her case, who may be either a member of the noncustodial staff or another inmate. Moreover, the inmate must be informed of these rights when notice is given of the disciplinary hearing.

The court declared these minimum due process standards are necessary when solitary confinement, transfer to maximum-security confinement, or loss of good time are imposed, or when a prisoner is held in padlock confinement for longer than 10 days. The prison also must write out the specific rules relating to such disciplinary measures and post them throughout the institution.[27]

Loss of Good Time

The most significant form of discipline for prisoners is the loss of good time. Sentences are significantly reduced by good-time provisions, and when those days which have been deducted from the sentence a person is to serve are put back on for disciplinary reasons, the inmate's sentence is obviously lengthened. See Field Practice C.

In 1974 the U.S. Supreme Court decided a prisoners' rights case originating in the state of Nebraska, *Wolff v. McDonnell*.[28] The decision was sweeping and inclusive, dealing with such matters as due process requirements in loss-of-good-time proceedings and disciplinary procedures generally, including questions of an inmate's right to call and examine witnesses and to assistance of counsel. Other issues dealt with included mail censorship, the retroactivity of appellate court holdings in prisoners' rights cases, and various prison administration matters. (See Box 13.2).

The Court stated that prisoners are entitled to the following due process rights in disciplinary cases:

1. Advance written notice of the charges must be given the inmate at least 24 hours prior to the disciplinary hearing.
2. The disciplinary board must give a written statement as to the evidence relied on in their decision.
3. The accused inmate can call witnesses or provide documents for his or her defense providing doing so poses no undue hazard to institutional safety or correctional goals.
4. Either a staff member or a fellow inmate is to be provided as counsel for an illiterate inmate or in cases so complex the inmate may be unable to adequately comprehend or defend against the charge.
5. The prison disciplinary board must be impartial in its decisions.

Disciplinary Hearings

1: Heil Hitler

A 24-year-old white inmate appeared before a prison disciplinary board (called the "warden's court") charged by his cellhouse officer with "attempting to incite a riot." The inmate was reputed to be a leader of the Aryan Brotherhood, an inmate group devoted to white supremacy and support of a neo-Nazi ideology. After a fight between two other inmates, one white and the other black, this inmate agitated among his cellhouse colleagues for a massive retaliatory raid on a Black Muslim group, housed in a cellhouse nearby, who shared yard recreation time with this inmate and his cohorts. This inmate continued to shout "Cut the black mothers! Tomorrow we'll cut the black mothers!" after he was ordered to be silent and even after lights out. The disciplinary board ordered the inmate to be placed in solitary confinement for 30 days and to forfeit any and all "good time" (time off the maximum sentence for good behavior in prison) he had accumulated.

2: Pain in the Head

A 19-year-old inmate appeared at a prison disciplinary hearing charged with refusing to work (in the prison laundry) and talking back to a correctional officer. He explained he was sick at the time, plagued with a serious headache, although he had not reported for sick call. The board placed an official reprimand in his file and ordered loss of recreational privileges for 3 days.

3: Making Her Mark

A 20-year-old female inmate appeared before a prison disciplinary court accused of tattooing (with a needle, cigarette ashes, and ink) the word "owned" on the thigh of her female lover and with fighting. She explained that the other girl wanted the tattoo and indeed had insisted on mutual "branding," a common practice in the prison. However, this inmate had refused reciprocal tattooing and a fight ensued. Both "tattooing; self and others" and "fighting" violated prison rules. The disciplinary court ordered her held in "keeplock" (locked in her own room during the working day and during recreational periods as well as at night) for 1 week and the forfeiture of 2 months' good time. ■

Inmates do not, under *Wolff*, have the right to actual legal counsel or to confront and cross-examine accusers. Also, the rights specified in *Wolff* only apply to disciplinary cases which are *serious*, those that may result in confinement to solitary or the loss of good time.

After *Wolff*, other Supreme Court decisions addressed the issue of disciplinary hearings. ***Baxter v. Palmigiano***[29] affirmed *Wolff*'s decision that inmates charged in prison disciplinary hearings do not have the right to counsel or to confront and cross-examine witnesses. However, *Baxter* further held that an inmate's decision to remain silent and to invoke a Fifth Amendment right against self-incrimination could be used as an indication of the inmate's guilt in such proceedings, unlike in criminal cases in a court of law.

Then, in 1985 in ***Ponte v. Real***,[30] the U.S. Supreme Court ruled that if prison officials refuse an inmate's request to call witnesses on his or her behalf, and that refusal is challenged, the officials must explain their refusal either at the hearing or later in court if the inmate alleges the refusal resulted in a deprivation of liberty. Then, also in 1985, in ***Cleavinger v. Saxner***[31] the Court held that members of a disciplinary board may be held liable for what they do unless they can prove they acted in good faith.

Overcrowding

As we have seen, the prison population has grown very rapidly since 1980, and many prisons are bulging at the seams. In order to house more inmates in existing facilities, cells have been modified to create "bunk beds" instead of single beds for

Double-Bunking Crowded Prisons

The increase in state prison populations in recent years and the need to economize on state budgets forces prison administrators to maximize the use of available space. Other responses to the influx of prisoners, such as increased prison building and early release programs, are the responsibility of someone else, the legislature and governors for instance. But for the prison administrator who faces the constant stream of buses hauling new prisoners to the institution, the problem must be handled within existing facilities and release practices. As a result, every bit of space is used in the housing units of prisons, the areas in which inmates sleep.

Prison conditions prior to the second half of the twentieth century were generally horrible everywhere in the world. Despite the United States Constitution's prohibition against "cruel and unusual" punishment, prisoners have endured unrelentingly harsh conditions throughout most of the history of the United States. Prisons have typically been dirty, crowded, dangerous, depressing institutions. The prison administrator's familiar adage, "This ain't no hotel we're runnin'!", which characterized responses to complaints about prison conditions in previous decades and centuries, today must be tempered by requirements of Supreme Court decisions and other constraints on prison conditions.

Although living in prison today is a far cry from earlier days, prison life has yet to meet the standards set for it by American society. Perhaps the single largest problem to face the prison system in this country is the tremendous increase in the number of prisoners who must be housed in limited capacity institutions. In some states there truly is no more room in the inn. During the 1990s two factors have caused the serious overcrowding problems found in several states: tougher sentencing laws and high unemployment rates.

In some states, such as New York, all repeat offenders are required to serve at least one half of their sentences before becoming eligible for parole. This policy is a result of a mandatory sentencing law enacted in 1980 by a "get tough" legislature. In Texas a "three-time loser" statute has required that a person convicted for the third time for a felony crime, any felony crime, receive a mandatory life sentence without possibility of parole. The result is that a large percentage of prisoners now must be kept in prison longer than in previous years. And, if they are kept longer, fewer spaces are made available for new inmates. Simple mathematics tells us that if the rate in new inmate admissions exceeds the rate of existing inmate releases, the natural consequence is crowded prisons.

The unemployment rate also impacts state prisons. If a

Three inmates in a cell in the New York state prison in Watertown.

person cannot find employment outside the prison, he or she cannot be released. Parole rules require a "work plan" for those inmates who otherwise qualify for early release. But New York City's unemployment rate rose to 10.6 percent at the end of 1991, in Florida some counties experienced 14 percent unemployment, and Louisiana unemployment rates range above 20 percent. So, inmates who come from those areas find it very difficult to get jobs, especially with the added handicap of a prison record.

The need to use all available space has led to a practice called "double-bunking," arranging inmates' bunks in such a way that more, twice as many, inmates may be bunked than would otherwise be possible in a given amount of floor space. Since inmates in such facilities typically only spend their sleeping hours confined in such a space, such crowding has not been considered "cruel and unusual punishment." But for inmates, crowding means less privacy and a strain on facilities and staff of the institution. Disputes over television viewing, noise, body hygiene, and such otherwise nonproblematic issues increase, placing an added burden on the prison administration to maintain peace and order.

SOURCES: Patrick R. Anderson and C. Gary Pettigrew, "Effects of Doublebunking on Adult Male State Prisoners," *Corrective and Social Psychiatry* 31: 2, April 1985, pp. 46–54; and, Selwyn Raab, "New York to Install 3,000 More Prison Beds," *New York Times*, December 8, 1991, p. 52.

inmates, a process called **double-bunking**. This means that two inmates can be placed in a single cell, or eight inmates in a four-person cell, and so forth. Is such **overcrowding** of prisoners a violation of the Constitutional prohibition against cruel and unusual punishment?

In 1981, in *Rhodes v. Chapman*,[32] the U.S. Supreme Court concluded that double-bunking as such is not unconstitutional, but that if the totality of conditions in the prison is bad, if the staff is inadequate, or cell space too limited, or work programs nonexistent, or if recreation, medical care, or diets are inadequate, or if inmates are required to stay in crowded cells for too long each day . . . then, perhaps, the Constitution has been violated. In *Rhodes*, the Court concluded that the Southern Ohio Federal Correctional Facility, a medium-security prison built in the 1970s, was a quality institution with gymnasiums, workshops, school rooms, chapels, hospital ward, commissary, barber shop, library, visitation area, recreation field, and a garden. Each cell had approximately 63 square feet, hot and cold running water, a cabinet, a shelf, and a radio. The Court concluded that, although the inmates were double-bunked, the totality of conditions did not constitute cruel and unusual punishment. The Court stated that "the Constitution does not mandate comfortable prisons," and that harsh or restrictive conditions are "part of the penalty that criminal offenders pay for their offenses against society."[33]

Medical Care

Since a prisoner cannot secure medical care for himself or herself as needed as one would in the outside world, institutions have a legal obligation to provide inmates with adequate medical services. The absence or inadequacy of medical care is considered by the courts to be cruel and unusual punishment.

The leading decision regarding prison medical care was the 1976 *Estelle v. Gamble*[34] case, in which the Supreme Court held that "deliberate indifference" to the serious medical needs of inmates does constitute cruel and unusual punishment. By this the Court did not mean malpractice on the part of prison medical staff, but a deliberate indifference to the pain and suffering of inmates as demonstrated by (1) the failure of prison doctors to respond to a prisoner's needs, or by (2) prison guards who delay or deny intentionally an inmate's access to medical care, or by (3) guards who intentionally interfere with prescribed treatments of inmates. Medical care is defined as including mental health and dental care, as well as other medical needs.

The Treatment Mandate of Some Prison Sentences

For the most part, prison sentences are frankly used to punish offenders and incapacitate them, to hold them for long periods of time apart from society to protect the community from their predatory activities. There is rarely any clear legislative intent that such sentences are for the purpose of treatment or rehabilitation. Yet, especially where drug abuse or addiction is evident, treatment is expected.

A prisoner who is found to be psychotic is commonly transferred to a *hospital for the criminally insane*, often a maximum-security institution, for whatever psychiatric treatments are offered there. But many inmates under sentences with a **treatment mandate** are neither insane by legal standards nor psychotic by psychiatric diagnostic criteria. They remain in prison and are presumed to be receiving treatment for whatever condition led to the criminal behavior for which they were convicted. In general, appellate courts have recently shown an increased willingness to intervene in cases where it is alleged that the requirements for treatment in mental hospitals are not being carried out, but rarely have they addressed the question of whether correctional services have fulfilled, or can fulfill, whatever "specialized treatment" has been demanded by legislation.

Sometimes prisons are faced with the problem of having to treat inmates who do not want treatment, especially those who are dangerous and need antipsychotic medication. In 1990, in ***Washington v. Harper***,[35] the Supreme Court concluded that forcing such treatment is acceptable when the inmate is dangerous either to self or others, or when the treatment is in the best medical interests of the inmate.

The status of in-prison therapy has changed little over the years; although some states have opened special "diagnostic and treatment" centers or "medical facilities" for inmates. However, courts are still coping with prisoner allegations that legislative treatment and rehabilitative mandates are not being carried out in traditional prison settings. Even when special treatment programs are available, the issue is further complicated by inmate insistence on a right to refuse treatment or rehabilitative efforts if they wish. Is it possible to "rehabilitate" someone who does not wish to be rehabilitated?

Norval Morris, who advocates imprisonment only for repetitively violent criminals, also suggests that all treatment programs in these prisons be voluntary. He thinks the only required activities for inmates should be the assigned daily work stints and participation in a small "living group" in which treatment would be made available on a voluntary basis.[36] Likewise, the National Advisory Commission suggests that "No offender should be required or coerced to participate in programs of rehabilitation or treatment nor should the failure or refusal to participate be used to penalize an inmate in any way."[37]

Legal Trends

The field of administrative law dealing with **prisoners' rights** mushroomed during the 1970s and 1980s,[38] and as with many trends, the causes of this were varied but closely related. The increasing willingness of appellate courts to intervene at postsentence stages of the criminal justice process occurred in a cultural context of expanded legal services for the poor. This, coupled with an increased concern for the civil rights of racial and ethnic minorities, who are disproportionately overrepresented in prison populations, came at a time of widespread cynicism about governmental claims of benevolence or effectiveness. Prison riots focused public and professional attention on prisons and these riots were both cause and effect of an increasing political awareness among prisoners. One result of this was the creation of various commissions empowered not only to investigate prison conditions but to look at the whole concept of prisons and make suggestions for reform.[39]

Prisoners' rights decisions addressed a variety of failings in the prison system. Inmates were granted more access to lawyers and to legal documents and papers through prison law libraries.[40] Poor inmates were provided with writing materials to draft legal documents, with notary services, and with postage to mail documents to the courts. The limits on these resources are decided by the courts on a case-by-case basis.[41] Although prisons do not have to provide free lawyers to inmates filing appeals, prisoners cannot be denied access to the help of other inmates, known as "**jailhouse lawyers**," who are often quite knowledgeable about the law.[42]

Also, prisoners place a high value on visits by people from the outside; here the courts have generally given a higher priority to the right of inmates to receive visits from attorneys, ministers, and court officials than to their right to receive visits from family members and friends. Courts allow prison authorities to limit visiting hours, in the interests of prison security and order. And they can deny "contact visits"—visits in which the inmate can be face to face with a visitor to the point of touching—if such visits would raise legitimate fears for institutional security.[43]

The First Amendment rights of inmates have been litigated a great deal. *Freedom of religion* is recognized for inmates to the extent that they must be allowed to follow the rules of their religion, within reason. Nor can inmates be required to attend religious services if they do not wish to. *Freedom of the press* is recognized for inmates in that they must be allowed access to news and to members of the press who themselves wish to have access to the institution, although face-to-face interviews with journalists may be denied.[44]

Inmates have the right to send and receive mail, but prison authorities have wide-ranging powers to decide whether to reject incoming publications if they feel they may be detrimental to the prison's security.[45] However, the authorities can reject magazines for being obscene or pornographic, if they come directly from the publisher. All mail may be screened for contraband, but legal mail cannot be read by prison authorities. Prisoners have considerable rights to send mail outside the institution.

It is not just courts that scrutinize prisons in regard to how they treat their inmates. Because of the heightened awareness of life inside prison walls, various study groups charged with developing model rules and regulations concerning prisons and prisoners' rights have been organized. These model rules are too varied and extensive to be reproduced in full here. But in general, they call for greater attention to standards of evidence in decisions relating to the imposition of special punishments for infractions of prison rules, the right of prisoners to procedural due process, and other issues similar to those involved in dealing with suspects outside prison.[46]

Through the years a number of prisons have introduced **selected-inmate councils** to funnel prisoner complaints to administrative officials. In some correctional systems there are **ombudsmen**, persons neutral to the correctional system who hear and attempt to negotiate inmate complaints or demands.[47]

Despite such developments, incarceration in prisons and reformatories remains—aside from the death penalty—the most extreme and socially degrading example of the full power of the state to punish and force compliance. It is a vortex in our criminal justice system, a controversial method of control that is undergoing change but currently used to punish, restrain, and perhaps rehabilitate 1 million offenders.

PRISON RIOTS

Over the years American prisons have periodically experienced violent, damaging, and murderous inmate riots.[48] And the riots have often called forth violent and deadly reactions by prison officials, guards, police, and militia. In 1987 Cuban detainees in federal prisons near Atlanta and Baton Rouge took hostages and rioted when learning that Fidel Castro had agreed to their deportation back to Cuba. Most, if not all, of these detainees had been serving in Cuban prisons before they came to the United States. Apparently they preferred life in U.S. prisons to life in Cuban prisons.

As prison riots go, however, the Cuban detainee disturbances were not the worst—they did not result in loss of life. An extremely violent riot took place in the New Mexico State Prison in Santa Fe in 1980. Twelve correctional officers were held hostage and some were beaten. However, the inmates directed their worst violence toward themselves. Thirty-three inmates were killed by other prisoners, many by blowtorches. Homosexual rapes were common. The riot was eventually put down, but inmate murders (and the murders of some guards, too) continued in the New Mexico facility for some time.

In 1983 a riot occurred in Sing Sing Prison in New York. Hostages were taken, and for a while it looked like the situation could become as serious as what had happened at New York's Attica Prison 11 years earlier. At Attica, forty-three correctional officers and inmates lost their lives when the prison was stormed by guards and New York state troopers; at Sing Sing, however, the disturbance eventually ended without any deaths.

More than 300 prison riots have been documented in the United States since the first one in 1774, and 90 percent of them have occurred since 1952.[49] Since the early fifties, major riots have occurred in over a dozen states, often at different prisons in the same state. In addition, many other prisons have had disturbances that did not result in full-out rioting, but which nevertheless caused loss of life and extensive property damage. And in-prison gang fighting and murders occur even today on a regular basis in many prisons across the country.

Much has been written about and elaborate theories developed as to why prison riots break out in some prisons and not in others, or why a riot occurs at one particular time and not another, or, for that matter, why riots occur at all. Prison overcrowding has been blamed. Various power groups in inmate subcultures, including gangs, have been blamed. Racial tensions, sexual deprivations, sudden get-tough rule enforcement, poor food, lack of recreation, different child-rearing patterns in various ethnic groups, and a myriad of other factors and conditions have been blamed. Various experiments in prison management, including inmate participation in developing prison rules and enforcing regulations, have been tried. Hundreds of postriot reports have been written, wide-ranging recommendations have been made, training in human relations have been given to correctional officers, theories of crime causation have been constructed, race relations and cultural awareness seminars have been conducted to make officers more sensitive to the needs of and better able to communicate with inmates. But all to no, or little, avail.

A recent study of the governance of prisons showed a breakdown in warden and guard controls of prison security to be the common thread in all riots. This imaginative, well-documented analysis carefully reviewed all the complex reasons put forward as causes of prison conflicts and disorders—from power groups in inmate subcultures to the politicization of racial and ethnic minorities—and tested them against simple violations of sound security measures.[50] The conclusion it reached, so much simpler and more direct than the prison subculture type of analysis, was that the root factor behind these problems is the *loss of staff control*. The study compared maximum-security prisons in three prison systems, Michigan, California, and Texas, each of which has its own different management style. And on almost every variable, including cost of confinement, it rated prisons high on control as much better. The study's author, John J. DiIulio, Jr., concluded that in running a prison, *order* is the first item of importance, and that without order and control the other two major aspects of prison life—*amenities* (i.e., good food, cleanliness, and so forth) and *service* (i.e., programs for improving the life chances of inmates, from remedial reading to vocational training)—are bound to be inferior. Inmates in a prison that is unsafe and filled with predatory gangs out of control can hardly engage in rehabilitative or remedial efforts. Moreover, guards in prisons with a high level of control have much higher *esprit de corps* and much better job satisfaction (less turnover, etc.) than those in institutions with looser security. And riots almost always occur where there is sloppy, careless, and negligent security management.

Other models of prison riots exist, however. Martin and Zimmerman[51] suggest a **typology of prison riots**, which includes DiIulio's explanation, called (1) *collective behavior and social control*. The other prison riot types, or causative explanations, include (2) *environmental conditions*, including quality-of-life factors; (3) *spontaneous outburst*, such as in a pressure-packed situation where only a spark is needed to set off simmering hostilities; (4) *conflict*, in which the repressive power structure of the prison is directed against powerless inmates; (5) *power vacuum*, which may occur during abrupt changes in administration or power relationships; and (6) *rising expectations*, which occur when inmates expect more quality of life than the institution delivers.[52]

Regardless of the type of riot or its cause, though, effective prison management seems to be the best prevention, or hope of prevention.

SUMMARY

This chapter outlined the history of maximum-security prisons, which, as we know them, are very much an American invention. The first walled, turreted, congregate (inmates associating with one another) prison was built in Auburn, New York, in the early 1820s. It was copied across the country and around the world.

In 1876 the first reformatory was opened, also in New York, at Elmira. It too was copied widely around the world. The reformatory is very much a maximum-security prison, walled, with cellblocks and gun turrets. But reformatories are *not*, as commonly thought, institutions for juvenile delinquents. Instead they are places where young adult offenders are taught a trade and provided schooling (unlike adult prisons where inmates work in state-use factories or on prison farms when not in their cells).

Today, in addition to maximum-security prisons and reformatories, there are also medium-security prisons (fenced, not walled; rooms, not cells) and minimum-security prisons, forestry camps, farms, and other such institutions. All these are generally referred to as "correctional facilities."

Prisons serve many purposes, but the major one is to hold prisoners and prevent their escape for the terms assigned by the courts. Prisons are very successful in this "to have and to hold" function, for relatively few escapes occur. But they have other objectives also. They are designed as punishment. They take total freedom of choice away from inmates and keep them locked up, for years, in a single-sex community. And this loss of freedom, the absence from home and family, the disruption to employment and careers, and the enforced association with other inmates, some of whom are among the worst criminals in the state, is punishment indeed.

Prisons are also intended to protect the noncriminal members of society from those who would prey on them by removing criminals from their midst. Prisons are our modern substitute for the older practice of transporting offenders away from their communities to distant penal colonies. They are a form of internal exile.

The very existence of prisons, including their grim, forbidding appearance and the tales of the deprivations suffered by those inside them, is supposed to deter people from committing crimes should they be tempted. For all but those few murderers who are executed, prisons are the end of the line in the criminal justice decision network, the visible embodiment of the maxim that crime does not pay.

There has also been an attempt to make prisons serve a rehabilitative role. Early on these efforts arose from a religious context and were carried out through religious training; later prison systems began to offer psychological counseling, group therapy, vocational rehabilitation, and education from literacy training to college courses. The success or failure of these rehabilitative efforts was typically measured by whether inmates committed additional crimes when they were paroled or otherwise released. In these terms, rehabilitation has not proved very successful. Perhaps it was a misplaced hope to begin with. After all, prisons hold only criminals, who are in intimate contact with other criminals; perhaps no in-prison treatment can do much to affect the criminal mentality, and certainly it cannot change the street conditions the prisoner returns to upon release.

Prison inmates are classified according to escape risk and the dangers they pose to guards or other inmates, and are given tests to measure their vocational aptitudes and needs. In the past, prisoners had few rights, and their access to courts to appeal their cases was limited. Today, however, they have won some recognition from the U.S. Supreme Court in regard to their rights during imprisonment. Religious freedom is one, as are access to the courts and to a law library, the right to counsel under some circumstances, and the right to challenge a few conditions of confinement, including excessive in-prison punishment for violations of rules.

Prison communities have their own version of a criminal justice decision network. Prison rules and regulations are the laws; custodial officers exercise discretion in the enforcement of those rules; disciplinary hearings are conducted with certain due process safeguards. All maximum-security prisons have within them deeper prisons, called "segregation," where inmates found to have seriously violated prison rules, especially those involving violence and contraband, are placed in solitary confinement. As punishment, solitary confinement is indeed "hard time."

There are lesser punishments too: loss of recreational privileges, loss of job assignment, transfer to a tougher prison, loss of "good time" (time off one's term for good behavior). All legislatures make some provisions for good-time reductions in sentences, for it is believed that this helps keep the prisons under control and prevents riots, fights, and assaults on guards.

Today many prisons are overcrowded. In some states overcrowding is so serious that tents have been set up inside the prison walls to provide inmate bed space. In other states, earlier-than-usual release of more inmates makes room at the front end. Many states are now building new prisons.

Notes

1. See Samuel Walker, *Sense and Nonsense about Crime: A Policy Guide* (Pacific Grove, CA: Brooks/Cole, 1989), and Herbert L. Packer, *The Limits of the Criminal Sanction* (Stanford, CA: Stanford University Press, 1968).
2. See Donald J. Newman, "Critique of Prison Building," *New England Journal on Prison Law* 8 (1) (1982): 121–139.
3. Hans Jochen Boecker, *Law and the Administration of Justice in the Old Testament and Ancient East*, Jeremy Moiser (trans.) (Minneapolis, MN: Augsburg, 1980).
4. David J. Rothman, *The Discovery of the Asylum* (Boston: Little, Brown, 1971), pp. 79, 81.
5. John H. Langbein, "The Historical Origins of the Sanction of Imprisonment for Serious Crime," *Journal of Legal Studies* 5 (1976): 35–60.
6. Graeme R. Newman, "Theories of Punishment Reconsidered: Rationalizations for Removal," *International Journal of Criminology and Penology* 3 (1975): 180.
7. See Rothman, op. cit.
8. Ibid.
9. See E. C. Hines (ed.), *Transactions of the National Congress on Penitentiary and Reformatory Discipline* (Albany, NY: Argus, 1871).
10. Bureau of Justice Statistics, *Prisoners in 1990* (Washington, DC: U.S. Department of Justice, May 1991).
11. Bureau of Justice Statistics, *Women in Prison* (Washington, DC: U.S. Department of Justice, March 1991).
12. Bureau of Justice Statistics, *Population Density in State Prisons: Special Report* (Washington, DC: U.S. Department of Justice, 1986).

13. Bureau of Justice Statistics, *Correctional Populations in the United States, 1988* (Washington, DC: U.S. Department of Justice, March 1991).

14. Ibid.

15. Ibid.

16. Gresham Sykes, *Society of Captives* (Princeton, NJ: Princeton University Press, 1958). Also see Edward Zamble and Frank J. Porporino, *Coping, Behavior, and Adaptation in Prison Inmates* (Secaucus, NJ: Springer-Verlag, 1988).

17. See, for example, John Irwin, *The Felon* (Englewood Cliffs, NJ: Prentice-Hall, 1970).

18. Gresham Sykes and Sheldon L. Messinger, "Inmate Social System," in *Theoretical Studies in the Social Organization of the Prison* (New York: Social Science Research Council Pamphlet 15, 1960), pp. 14–15.

19. See, especially, Donald Clemmer, *The Prison Community*, rev. ed. (New York: Holt, Rinehart and Winston, 1958); Gresham Sykes, op. cit.; Donald R. Cressey (ed.), *The Prison: Studies in Institutional Organization and Change* (New York: Holt, Rinehart and Winston, 1961); and John Irwin and Donald R. Cressey, "Thieves, Convicts and the Inmate Culture," *Social Problems* 10 (1962): 143–155.

20. Bureau of Justice Statistics, *Women in Prison*.

21. Ervin Goffman, *Asylums* (Garden City, NY: Anchor Press, 1961).

22. See, generally, Note, "Beyond the Ken of the Courts: A Critique of Judicial Refusal to Review the Complaints of Convicts," *Yale Law Journal* 72 (1963): 506; and Note, "Constitutional Rights of Prisoners: The Developing Law," *University of Pennsylvania Law Review* 110 (1962): 985.

23. See Note, "Judicial Intervention in Corrections: The California Experience—An Empirical Study," *U.C.L.A. Law Review* 20 (1973): 452. See also Fred Cohen, *Legal Norms in Corrections* (Consultant Paper, President's Task Force on Corrections, 1967), and Edward L. Kimball and Donald J. Newman, "Judicial Intervention in Correctional Decisions: Threat and Response," *Journal of Research on Crime and Delinquency* 14 (1968): 1.

24. See Fred Cohen, "The Law of Prisoners' Rights: An Overview," *Criminal Law Bulletin* 24 (4) (July–August 1988): 321–349. Also see South Carolina Department of Corrections, *The Emerging Rights of the Confined* (Columbia: South Carolina Department of Corrections, 1972). See also Richard G. Singer, *Prisoners' Legal Rights: A Bibliography of Cases and Articles* (Boston: Warren, Gorham and Lamont, 1971).

25. Rolando V. del Carmen, *Civil Liabilities in American Policing: A Text for Law Enforcement Personnel* (Englewood Cliffs, NJ: Brady/Prentice-Hall, 1991) pp. 177–206. But for a recent exception see *Hudson v. McMillan* 60 U.S. Law Week 4151 (1992). pp. 177–206.

26. *Landman v. Royster*, 333 F. Supp. 1104 (E.D. Pa. 1974).

27. Ibid.

28. *Wolff v. McDonnell*, 418 U.S. 539 (1974).

29. *Baxter v. Palmigiano*, 425 U.S. 308 (1976).

30. *Ponte v. Real*, 37 CrL 3051 (1985).

31. *Cleavinger v. Saxner*, 106 S. Ct. 496 (1985).

32. *Rhodes v. Chapman*, 452 U.S. 337 (1981).

33. Ibid.

34. *Estelle v. Gamble*, 97 S. Ct. 285 (1976).

35. *Washington v. Harper*, 110 S. Ct. 1028 (1990).

36. Norval Morris, *The Future of Imprisonment* (Chicago: University of Chicago Press, 1974), p. 112.

37. National Advisory Commission on Criminal Justice Standards and Goals, *Corrections* (Washington, DC: U.S. Department of Justice, 1973), Standard 2.9(6), p. 45.

38. del Carmen, op. cit., p. 183.

39. *Attica: The Official Report of The New York Special Commission on Attica* (New

York: Bantam, 1972); See also Tom Wicker, *A Time to Die* (New York: Ballantine, 1975).

40. *Bounds v. Smith*, 430 U.S. 817 (1977).

41. *Gaines v. Lane*, 790 F. 2d. 1299 (7th Cir. 1986).

42. *Hooks v. Wainwright*, 775 F. 2d. 2433 (11th Cir. 1985), and *Johnson v. Avery*, 393 U.S. 483 (1969).

43. *Block v. Rutherford*, 104 S. Ct. 3227 (1984).

44. *Pell v. Procunier*, 417 U.S. 817 (1974), and *Houchins v. KQED*, 438 U.S. 1 (1978).

45. *Thornburg v. Abbott*, 109 S. Ct. 1874 (1989).

46. See Sheldon Krantz, Robert Bell, Jonathan Brant, and Michael Magruder, *Model Rules and Regulations on Prisoners' Rights and Responsibilities. Center for Criminal Justice, Boston University* (St. Paul, MN: West, 1973), pp. 63–64.

47. See Virginia McArthur, "Inmate Grievance Mechanisms: A Survey of 209 American Prisons," *Federal Probation* 38 (1974): 41; Timothy L. Fitzharris, *The Desirability of a Correctional Ombudsman* (Berkeley: University of California, Institute of Governmental Studies, 1973); and David D. Dillingham and Linda R. Singer, *Complaint Procedures in Prisons and Jails: An Examination of Recent Experience* (Washington, DC: U.S. National Institute of Corrections, 1980).

48. Randy Martin and Sherwood Zimmerman, "A Typology of the Causes of Prison Riots and an Analytical Extension to the 1986 West Virginia Riot," *Justice Quarterly* 7(4)(December 1990): 711–737.

49. Ibid.

50. John J. DiIulio, Jr., *Governing Prisons: A Comparative Study of Correctional Management* (New York: The Free Press, 1987).

51. Martin and Zimmerman, op. cit.

52. Ibid.

Suggested readings

Clemmer, Donald. *The Prison Community*. New York: Rinehart, 1958.

DiIulio, John J., Jr. *Governing Prisons*. New York: Free Press, 1987.

Drapkin, Israel. *Crime and Punishment in the Ancient World*. Lexington, MA.: Lexington Books, 1989.

Goffman, Erving. *Asylums*. Garden City, NY: Anchor, 1961.

Howard, John. *Prisons and Lazarettos*. Montclair, NJ: Patterson Smith, 1973 (two volumes).

Kauffman, Kelsey. *Prison Officers and Their World*. Cambridge, MA: Harvard University Press, 1988.

Lombardo, Lucien X. *Guards Imprisoned*, 2nd ed. Cincinnati: Anderson, 1989.

Martin, Steve J., and Sheldon Ekland-Olson. *Texas Prisons: The Walls Came Tumbling Down*. Austin: Texas Monthly Press, 1987.

Nagel, William G. *The New Red Barn: A Critical Look at the Modern American Prison*. New York: Walker, 1973.

Pollock-Byrne, Joycelyn M. *Women, Prison and Crime*. Pacific Grove, CA: Brooks-Cole, 1990.

Sykes, Gresham M. *The Society of Captives*. Princeton, NJ: Princeton University Press, 1971.

Useem, Bert, and Peter Kimball. *States of Siege: U.S. Prison Riots, 1971–1986*. New York: Oxford University Press, 1989.

Wicker, Tom. *A Time to Die*. New York: Ballantine, 1975.

Zamble, Edward, and Frank J. Porporino. *Coping, Behavior and Adaptation in Prison Inmates*. New York: Springer-Verlag, 1988.

DISCUSSION QUESTIONS

1. Describe the history of prisons and compare ancient methods of imprisonment with prisons in U.S. history.

2. Describe the process of incarceration and classification in prison and the various security levels of prisons.

3. Describe the types of inmates in prison and the various subcultures found in prison.

4. Discuss prisoners' rights and the evolution of case law regarding prisoners in the United States.

5. Describe the typology of prison riots proposed by Martin and Zimmerman. What causes prison riots? What can be done to prevent them?

14

Release from Prison and Revocation

Convicted murderer William

Horton, Jr.

Prisoners *have traditionally been released "cold turkey" after years in prison and deposited back into the community and among family and friends without jobs, current drivers' licenses, bank accounts, or any of the other necessary elements of life in freedom. Often an offender's family has adjusted to his or her absence, sometimes even preferring it. Weekend furloughs, work release, and parole supervision programs are designed to help people adjust to life on the outside after years in prison.*

Weekend furloughs enable prisoners to spend nights at home occasionally during the final few months of incarceration, thereby slowly weaning them away from prison and gradually acclimatizing them to life on the outside again. Forty-five states and the federal jurisdiction use furloughs and the program is widely acclaimed as a sensible way to relieve severe prison overcrowding.

Nevertheless, in 1988 furlough programs became infamous because of the Willie Horton case. Horton was the kind of criminal many people think of when they say "criminals should be locked up and the key thrown away." In 1974 he was convicted for murder in Massachusetts and sentenced to mandatory life in prison without parole. But in 1985 he was released on a "weekend furlough" and walked away to freedom. Ten months later he was arrested for breaking into a house in Maryland, raping a woman, and stabbing her companion.

Horton's escape was the first among first-degree murderers in nearly 5 years, and the violent crime rate in Massachusetts had actually dropped 13.4 percent while the national rate had risen 1.8 percent. Still, as a murderer condemned to life imprisonment without parole, Horton should not have been granted a furlough.

Willie Horton became a household name during the 1988 Presidential campaign when then Vice President George Bush used the "Willie Horton Case" against the Democratic candidate, Governor Michael Dukakis of Massachusetts, who had developed the furlough program. Campaign commercials on television and in print, produced by the Bush campaign managers, depicted Dukakis as a "soft-on-crime" liberal. Bush, on the other hand, was depicted in speeches and commercials as a man who would never consider letting a murderer out of prison. Willie Horton, a black committing crimes against white victims while he was supposed to be locked up, became a symbol, a powerful political tool. The events surrounding his case, however, also focused attention on how and when convicted criminals are released from prison.

ABOUT THIS CHAPTER

Most offenders who are sent to jails or prisons, even those with life sentences, are eventually released. Some inmates die of natural causes, while others kill themselves or are murdered in prison. A few very dangerous lifers are held in custody all their natural lives. Inmates who die or are killed while serving sentences are few, not more than a fraction of 1 percent.

Some offenders are repeatedly sent to prison, released, and returned on new convictions, in effect serving life sentences on a type of installment plan. While this sometimes occurs with criminals who persistently commit very serious crimes— successive homicides, rapes, armed robberies, and so on—for the most part *installment-plan lifers* are minor violators—check forgers, petty thieves—whose basic problems are alcoholism, addiction, or some deviant mental or emotional condition that may be untreatable, and who are not deterred by incarceration. Thus, most prison populations are composed of a mixture of "heavy," sometimes dangerous offenders, and a larger proportion of essentially minor but persistent violators.

This chapter deals with ways inmates are released from prison—by parole, by time off for good behavior, by serving a full sentence, and, more rarely, by pardon or commutation of sentence. It considers the issues of who makes the release decision, when the decision is made, and what the release criteria are. Release procedures are described, and the "rights" of inmates to be released, on parole or otherwise, are discussed. In Chap. 15 we discuss parole supervision in the community, but here we focus only on the decision to grant release.

An early release can be revoked, and the offender returned to prison to complete the sentence, if parole supervision rules are violated or the offender commits other crimes. Thus criteria for revocation, the procedures followed, and the way the Supreme Court has viewed both release and return to prison are also analyzed in this chapter.

Finally, the chapter deals with final discharge from sentence, which is the end point of the criminal justice process, along with the procedures by which a person's record may be expunged after sentence has been fully served.

TIME SENTENCED VERSUS TIME SERVED

Maximum prison sentences imposed on convicted felons in the United States are probably the longest in the world.[2] The length of maximum sentences is deceptive, however, if taken to mean the actual time spent in prison. While there is considerable variation from one state to the next, the overwhelming majority of the inmates released from prison have only served a part of their original sentences. (See Table 14.1.) Three-quarters of the released prisoners must continue to serve their sentences on parole or mandatory supervised release. And most of those released after their sentences have expired have had a considerable amount of time subtracted from their sentences due to "good-time" provisions. Good time is awarded for time served without disciplinary reports or other difficulties, as well as for participation in rehabilitative programs. (See Table 14.2.)

The drafters of the *Model Sentencing Act*, who proposed a 5-year maximum for all felons except those convicted of murder or atrocious crimes and those diagnosed as dangerous, argued that a 5-year maximum would not bring about any real difference in prison sentences, since the majority of inmates in *all* jurisdictions are released in less than 5 years anyway.[3] But with traditional sentences the offender is monitored after release and held accountable for the remainder of the maximum sentence. Therefore, if sentences were shortened the total amount of time under correctional supervision would be lessened even if the actual amount of time served in prison was not affected.

Advocates of Parole

In part parole became popular simply because it is more humanitarian than long prison sentences.[4] As already noted, prison sentences in the United States are among the longest in the world. Legislatures often enact unusually severe sentences during times of high publicity about crime. Likewise sentencing judges are commonly outraged and angry at the time of sentencing, when memory of the crime is still fresh. In such moments of anger or high publicity, judges have been known to impose extremely harsh prison terms. A system that permits parole allows tempers to cool and the actions of the offender to be viewed more dispassionately years later, thus offering an opportunity to mitigate sentences whose harshness appeared justified at the time they were handed down.

Parole also offers a chance to reduce the prison terms of offenders who, although guilty of serious crimes in the past, have aged and matured in prison and are no longer likely to violate the law again. Parole is also accepted as a way to control inmate behavior by offering the possibility of early release for those willing to participate in prison programs and cooperate with officials. All jurisdictions have some provisions

TABLE 14.1 *First releases from state prisons, over a one-year period;
sentence length and time served in prison by offense*

Most serious offense	First releases from State prison[a]			
	Maximum sentence length,[b] months		Time served in prison, months	
	Median[c]	Mean[d]	Median[c]	Mean[d]
All offenses	36	64.6	14	20.4
Violent offenses	60	90.1	23	30.3
Homicide[e]	120	133.7	35	40.9
Murder/nonnegligent manslaughter	120	142.2	42	47.4
Murder	240	218.6	78	71.4
Nonnegligent manslaughter	72	101.4	32	34.6
Negligent manslaughter	72	99.4	22	28.2
Unspecified homicide	180	187.1	50	54.3
Kidnaping	60	104.3	27	32.1
Rape	84	105.1	35	40.9
Other sexual assault	60	76.8	19	26.0
Robbery	60	95.2	25	31.6
Assault	36	61.1	16	21.7
Other violent offenses	36	58.3	16	19.6
Property offenses	36	55.6	12	16.8
Burglary	48	62.6	14	19.0
Larceny/theft	27	50.8	10	14.3
Motor vehicle theft	24	39.7	10	14.1
Arson	60	78.0	16	21.5
Fraud	36	46.8	10	14.4
Stolen property	36	44.9	11	15.2
Other property offenses	36	42.8	10	14.7
Drug offenses	36	49.8	11	14.1
Possession	34	47.4	9	11.7
Trafficking	36	51.6	12	15.6
Other drug offenses	24	48.5	10	13.2
Public-order offenses	24	37.0	8	11.9
Weapons	36	54.6	11	15.7
Other public-order offenses	24	31.8	7	10.8
Other offenses	24	49.5	10	14.1
Number of releases	71,121		71,121	

[a] *Note*: First releases are persons released for the first time on their current sentence. All data exclude persons released from prison by escape, death, transfer, appeal, or detainer. Data on sentence length are based on all first releases with a sentence of more than a year for whom the most serious offense and sentence length were reported. Data on time served in prison are based on all first releases for whom the most serious offense and time served were reported.
[b] Sentence length refers to the maximum sentence that an offender may be required to serve for the most serious offense.
[c] Includes sentences of "life without parole," "life plus additional years," "life," and "death."
[d] Excludes sentences of "life without parole," "life plus additional years," "life," and "death."
[e] Homicide includes all deaths where the offender intentionally killed someone without legal justification or accidentally killed someone through reckless or grossly negligent conduct.
Source: Bureau of Justice Statistics, *National Corrections Reporting Program, 1985* (Washington, DC: U.S. Department of Justice, December 1990), p. 24.

TABLE 14.2 *State prison releases,
one-year period; release type,
by method of release*

Method of release	Percent of releases	
	All releases	First releases[a]
All methods	100.0	100.0
Conditional releases	82.2	77.4
Parole board decision	41.0	36.5
Mandatory parole	36.8	35.2
Other conditional	4.4	5.7
Unconditional releases	12.2	16.4
Expiration of sentence	11.2	15.2
Commutation/pardon	0.4	0.6
Other unconditional	0.6	0.7
Death	0.5	0.5
Other releases	4.5	5.0
Not known	0.4	0.8
Number of releases	163,718	80,357

[a] *Note*: First releases are persons released for the first time on their current sentence. Data are based on releases from prison with a sentence of more than a year.
SOURCE: Bureau of Justice Statistics, *National Corrections Reporting Program, 1985* (Washington, DC: U.S. Department of Justice, December 1990), p. 22.

for granting "time off" for good behavior, although the time so granted is generally fairly limited. Parole offers more substantial reductions in sentences for offenders who behave and cooperate while in confinement.

Parole is also defended along economic lines since street supervision is much less costly than incarceration. The expense of holding an inmate in a maximum-security prison today is astronomical, up to $30,000 per year for each inmate for guarding, medical care, food, administrative costs, and a great deal more even in the most stark, overcrowded maximum-security prisons. In relatively uncrowded institutions with good educational and treatment programs, the costs are higher. Prisoners can be supervised on parole for only a small fraction of these amounts. And while on parole the offender can be gainfully employed, pay taxes, and support his or her family. Family welfare support is a significant cost to the community when a breadwinner is imprisoned.

Finally, advocates of parole point out its rehabilitative value, for supervised re-entry into the community is almost always safer and more effective than simply letting prisoners walk through the gates to freedom upon release. In general, according to parole advocates, giving due deference to critics of parole who see it as either too lenient or too harsh, years of experience with the practice have generally proved its effectiveness.

Critics of Parole

The history of parole in the United States has been stormy. The idea of releasing convicts before their sentences expire has been vigorously opposed from its beginnings to the present day. Interestingly, critics of parole tend to come from both ends of the liberal-conservative spectrum, even though they often argue against the practice from directly opposed points of views. Law enforcement groups have been particularly vocal in attacking parole as too lenient—a "bleeding heart" approach to criminals, as J. Edgar Hoover used to put it. Their view was, and perhaps still is, widely supported.

Very early in its growth the Constitutionality of parole was challenged on a number of grounds, among them that it was an infringement on judicial sentencing authority, that it usurped the pardoning powers of the chief executive, and even that it was an unlawful delegation of the legislative function. Generally these arguments were rejected by the courts, and the legal foundation for parole became well established. Only in the last few years, approximately a century after the introduction of parole at a correctional institution in Elmira, New York, has the concept come under attack again, this time by those criticizing correctional discretion and supporting a system of definite sentencing.

EARLY RELEASE AND THE CONSERVATIVE CRIME CONTROL MODEL

Conservatives argue that longer sentences have a greater deterrent effect, and that parole and good-time provisions allow prisoners to get out of prison too soon.[5] Judges should have the power to sentence dangerous offenders to long, even indeterminate sentences (10 years to life, for example) to maximize community protection and to send a message to potential criminals. According to conservatives, soft-hearted parole boards interfere with the judges' decisions by turning criminals loose on society to prey on law-abiding citizens. Moreover, criminals have begun to recognize that even if they get caught for crimes, they will be required to serve only a fraction of any sentence handed down by a judge, and this has resulted in even more crime.

EARLY RELEASE AND THE LIBERAL CRIME CONTROL MODEL

Liberals argue that prisoners who serve short prison sentences do just as well, or just as poorly, after release as offenders who serve longer sentences. They also argue that longer sentences place the United States in the dubious company of South Africa as the countries which give the longest sentences in the world. However, liberals do not favor the release decision processes currently used because of due process violations which result in those decisions often being made in an arbitrary way and in a discriminatory fashion. And since determinate sentences in the present political climate would mean even longer sentences, liberals believe, they favor early release provisions as a means of modifying the long sentences handed down by get-tough judges. They see early release as more humane, cheaper, and less harmful than lengthy imprisonment.

HOW PRISONERS ARE RELEASED FROM PRISON

Across the nation inmates are released from prisons in a number of ways: (1) on parole; (2) at a mandatory release date, which is generally the maximum sentence less time off for good behavior; (3) upon completion of the maximum sentence; and (4) by pardon or commutation of sentence. All the methods are used in each jurisdiction, but their frequency of use varies considerably. This variation stems from differences in legal requirements from one state to the next; organization of correctional systems, including differences in the quality of parole services; local customs; and the characteristics of inmate populations held in prisons. In states with strong and frequently used probation services, prison populations may be largely composed of "residue" violators or "heavies,"—those who are dangerous or so persistent in their criminality that probation supervision would place the community at risk and likely be ineffective. Parole boards in jurisdictions where probation is frequently used see different types of offenders from those in states where probation is less often used and where prisons hold more of a mix of less serious violators and "heavies."

Although many correctional facilities group various types of offenders together, every prison population is composed of a mixture of personalities, offense categories, age groupings, and lifestyles—a complexity regarding correctional populations not always recognized by the public. Individual offenders are diverse—they cannot be lumped together into one all-encompassing category. Some are disturbed and frustrated young adults, others are old and senile, while still others are alcoholics, drug addicts, or sex deviants. Some are committed to conventional values, others are not. Many prisoners come from urban slums and are members of minority groups that suffer economic and social discrimination.

Offenders also tend to lack education and vocational skills. Many have had failures in relationships with family and friends, and exhibit a pattern of cumulative failure that prevents them from developing a sense of self-respect. All this complicates decisions about release and creates obstacles to rehabilitation for the offenders themselves.

Parole

The word "parole" as we use it is derived from the French term for "word of honor." Most inmates, about 70 percent nationally, are released from prison under some type of supervision in the community. Most are released on *parole* by a parole board after the expiration of their minimum sentences but before a mandatory discharge date, and the rest are released on supervised mandatory release.[6]

History of Parole

The practice of allowing prisoners to leave confinement early upon giving their word that they will remain law-abiding had its early roots in Europe.[7] About the middle of the nineteenth century, various forms of parole were developed almost simultaneously in Spain, Germany, and the British Isles. In these early systems, prisoners were allowed to return to their communities, not because early release was particularly rehabilitative, but simply because letting them go home helped alleviate prison overcrowding. At home they were placed under the supervision of local police officers.[8]

In general the European "ticket-of-leave" system worked well—it did not seem to increase the danger to society in general and did, of course, lower "gaol" populations—and these positive effects were noticed in the United States. Since any parole system rests on an *indeterminate sentencing structure*, adapting parole to the United States required the introduction of a sentencing system with a time spread between the minimum and maximum term. The American tradition was *flat time*, determinate prison sentences like those currently imposed on misdemeanants and in several states for felonies as well.

An American prison reformer, **Zebulon E. Brockway**, was instrumental in establishing the first indeterminate sentencing law, in Michigan in 1869, where parole was first used with female convicts. However, shortly afterward the Michigan courts declared this law unconstitutional. Brockway later moved to New York, where he became superintendent of the newly constructed reformatory at Elmira. During the 1870s he succeeded in having an indeterminate sentence law adopted in New York. This became the basis for the first parole system for men in the United States when the Elmira Reformatory opened in 1876. Actually the entire reformatory idea put into practice at Elmira, including the use of indeterminate sentences and parole, was considered more of an experiment than a trend. Parole did not generally become a feature of prison sentences for older, ordinary felons until after the turn of the century. By 1925, however, indeterminate sentences and parole were found in most jurisdictions in the United States, and by 1970 every state and the federal government used it in some form.

In the 1970s, a number of states, under increasing pressure to "get tough on crime," adopted a presumptive system of flat-time (definite) sentences, and abolished parole as unnecessary for *future* inmates, though parole boards were retained to decide cases already sentenced. However, even some of the states that abolished parole (Maine, California, among others) have reintroduced early release primarily because of prison overcrowding. It is not called "parole" of course, for this term is too "soft" in a "get-tough-on-crime" environment. Instead, parole boards are commonly called Boards of Prison Terms, which sounds tougher and more restraint-oriented. So in spite of the popularity of flat sentences, parole still is the major way inmates are released from prison and is generally widely accepted as a viable and efficient correctional technique.

Making the Parole Release Decision

The actual paroling process, including the composition of the parole board, the caseloads, training, and authority of parole officers, and the procedures used to grant and revoke parole, varies markedly from one state to another. So does the comparative use of parole. These variations account in good part for the lack of agreement about the legal status of parole across the nation. Where parole is the common method of release from prison, it comes more often to be viewed by prisoners and their advocates as a "right"—and indeed it is the norm in such localities—than where it is granted reluctantly and rarely. And in jurisdictions with long statutory sentences, infrequent use of

Parolees usually are required to abide by certain rules and to keep officers informed about their residence and employment as part of their parole agreement. Here a parolee is interviewed by his parole officer.

Parole Hearing

COMMISSIONER: Take a seat please . . . your name is Charles Edward Robinson?

INMATE: Yes, sir.

COMMISSIONER: You were received here on December 2, 1990, is that right?

INMATE: Yes, sir.

COMMISSIONER: You received a sentence of from 3 to 7½ years for burglary while armed, to which you pleaded guilty. Is that correct?

INMATE: Yes, sir.

COMMISSIONER: The original charge was robbery, wasn't it?—Did you cop a plea?

INMATE: Well, I guess you could call it robbery—I took this money off this guy. I guess it was robbery or burglary.

COMMISSIONER: Now the record shows that you have a drinking problem, Charles, although you don't seem to have been in any serious trouble before.

INMATE: Yes, sir. I was drunk alright.

COMMISSIONER: What have you been doing about this problem? Are you in the AA group here?

INMATE: Yes, sir. I joined AA and have gone to every meeting since I've been here.

COMMISSIONER: Where are you working?

INMATE: Now I'm in the shoe factory. Before that I was in the laundry.

COMMISSIONER: Have you been involved in any other programs here?

INMATE: Yes, sir. I'm in Mr. Crawford's counseling group. I've taken an auto mechanics course in the school and I volunteered in the Blood Drive—

COMMISSIONER: What good has the group counseling done you?

INMATE: Well, I learned more about myself—my problems, I guess you'd call it. I learned to control myself.

COMMISSIONER: It says here that you intend to live with your sister if you make parole. Is this right?

INMATE: Yes, sir.

COMMISSIONER: And you have a job lined up as a mechanic's helper in this garage?

INMATE: Yes sir, They said they'd hire me right away—

COMMISSIONER: All right, Charles. That will be all. Thank you for coming. You will receive our decision in a day or two.

■

---

pardons, and no other alternatives to sentence mitigation, parole becomes crucial to inmates and an obvious focus of litigation.

The grant of parole at first was defined as an act of grace, of mercy, on the part of the state; it was a *privilege* afforded to a few but the right of none. Eligibility for parole was fixed by a statutory minimum sentence, or, where permitted by law, a minimum set by the judge at sentencing. In some places today a fixed minimum may be reduced a few months, even years, by good-time credits earned by a prisoner for good behavior while incarcerated. In this way the inmate's date for parole eligibility is made earlier than the sentence imposed by the judge. In some places, inmates must apply for parole consideration; in others, consideration for parole is automatic as the eligibility date approaches. In general, the grant, deferral, or denial of parole is discretionary with a *parole board*, commonly a panel of officials appointed by the governor and independent of both prisons and courts.

The brief dialogue in Field Practice A is not designed to illustrate an ideal *parole hearing*, nor is it offered as representative of hearings everywhere. Nonetheless, it is unusual neither in its shortness nor in the type of questions asked. Most hearings, especially in large states, are very brief and cursory.

In most states, members of the parole board personally interview an inmate at, or shortly before, the time he or she becomes eligible for parole. This is not a universal practice, however. In some states, instead of interviews the board reviews case file materials, and personal hearings are conducted only in selected cases.

In some jurisdictions, parole authorities employ a staff of "hearing officers" to conduct interviews and report their findings to the board, which then makes the actual decision about release. In these instances, the parole board acts as a policy-making body, monitors hearing officer interviews, and serves as an appellate body in cases where inmates are dissatisfied with hearing examiner decisions. The advantages of such a structure are that it makes individual hearings possible and promotes a more careful and deliberate procedure than often found in systems that do not have such interviews. It can be used where inmate populations are large or, in large states, where there are great distances between prisons. Many parole boards are small, and in large states they must travel constantly, often making the parole hearing a hurried experience.

The size of parole boards varies from 2 or 3 to 12 or more members. Some parole boards are composed of full-time members, others of part-time representatives whose major careers are elsewhere. In smaller states each parole applicant is heard by the full board *en banc*; in others, particularly in large states having many prisons, boards may be split into smaller panels with the hearings actually conducted by only one or two parole commissioners. In these jurisdictions, certain cases—those where a single member is in doubt, where there is a split opinion, or where the case is otherwise complex—the panel may refer the matter to the entire board.

The procedures of the hearing itself are variable, ranging from a few short questions to, more rarely, full-scale proceedings involving witnesses, lawyers, and evidence for or against release subject to adversary examination. Some boards may hear only a few inmate cases each day; others may handle 40 or more applications daily.

Careful and deliberate parole hearings can serve several important functions helpful to both the parole board and the prospective parolee. If the hearing has the appearance as well as the substance of fairness, it can enhance the prospects of successful completion of parole by promoting respect for the system of justice. Where the offender plays an active role in planning or deciding on his or her terms of parole, a greater commitment to the parole plan should follow. Conversely, where the person is dealt with abruptly, indirectly, or unfairly, or where arbitrary decisions are made without explanation, successful parole may be undermined. The hearing itself can provide an opportunity for both the inmate and the parole board to ascertain and discuss reliable information. Sometimes, however, inmates are encouraged to be truthful and frank in responding to questions at the parole interview, and then those statements are used to justify denial of parole. It has been suggested that certain due process protections, including *Miranda*-type warnings, should be extended to the parole interview.[9]

Criteria for Release on Parole

In deciding whether to grant or deny parole, the board does not rely solely on information from the interview, but has before it the complete correctional and police file on the prisoner (often including the presentence investigation) and some form of **parole plan** prepared by the prisoner with the assistance of the correctional staff. A typical parole plan contains information on where the parolee will be employed (or where he or she reasonably expects to obtain employment) and other intentions regarding lifestyle if returned to the community.

The traditional assumption has been that prisoners who are paroled are "good risks," that is, they have matured or have been rehabilitated and are not likely to commit any more crimes. However, the risk of recidivism must always be considered in any parole decision, and it is usually not all that easy to determine. An experienced parole board member once said to the authors:

> Everybody thinks a parole board's job is to let good-risk inmates out early. This is not the way it works. First, there are not any good-risk inmates; the way prisons are today all of them are lousy risks. The real function of the Board is to decide when, if ever, and under what conditions to let *bad*-risk inmates out. Remember, they are

going to come out anyway. We prefer to have some of them leave under field supervision.

The question, then, is the *degree* of risk a parole board faces that any released prisoner will break parole, and that often has to do with the nature of the crime for which the inmate was incarcerated. If it was murder, the risk of recidivism may be very low. If the crime was check forgery, the risk could be considerably higher, although release would probably be granted anyway.

It is important to remember that inmates who might be considered fairly good risks on the street may be denied parole for reasons unrelated to the possibility of recidivism. An inmate who constantly flouts prison rules and is otherwise a trouble-maker may have parole denied to support the prison disciplinary system. This is a strong message to other troublemakers that, if their disruptive behavior continues, their paroles will also be denied. In other situations inmates may be involved in educational or treatment programs when their parole dates arrive and may be held until they complete those programs. Furthermore, all parole boards have "hot cases" involving notorious or prominent inmates whose early parole would tend to bring intense criticism down on the entire parole system.

Sometimes the community is not ready to receive the released inmate. A chilling case of this type occurred in California in 1987. An inmate, convicted of raping and mutilating a young girl by cutting off both her hands, was paroled by the California Adult Authority. One community after another expressed outrage through demon-strations and citizens' committees about receiving a parolee convicted of such a repug-nant crime. The outcry was so great and the people in each of the many locations so adamant in not accepting this parolee that he was eventually returned to prison, still on parole, where he lived while seeking employment and a place to reside on the outside.

The factors parole boards must consider in their decisions in addition to the risk of recidivism can be summarized as follows:

1. The chances the inmate will conform to parole rules and regulations.
2. Whether release would be bad for overall prison morale, as in the case of an

383

A parole hearing is held in some states to determine whether to release a prisoner on parole based on the prisoner's performance in prison and answers given to parole board members at the hearing.

inmate who has been a serious disciplinary problem, where parole would appear to be a reward for such behavior.

3. The realistic chances of suitable employment and living conditions presented in the inmate's parole plan.
4. The community's willingness to have the parolee return.
5. Whether the release would promote disrespect for the law, as in the case of a serious offense or a notorious offender.
6. Whether the inmate has served about the average time for persons convicted for the same crime.
7. Whether the person could benefit from further involvement in prison training and educational or rehabilitative programs.[10]

The drafters of the *Model Penal Code* also suggest some additional factors, listed in Box 14.1.

The nature of the parole decision long has been the subject of research, and today some parole systems have adopted *parole guidelines* for parole decision-making based on research that determines the relative importance of various aspects of parole. In general, if an inmate meets the guideline criteria for release, he or she must be paroled unless the parole board can justify its denial in writing.[11] Parole, in short, is "presumptive" unless there are aggravating factors that the parole commissioners can identify and use to justify denial of release.

In recent years parole boards' decisions have been complicated by pressures to ease prison crowding. Every prison system in the United States has, to a varying degree, faced problems caused by the increasing dependence on incarceration as a crime control strategy. Most state prison systems are limited in their capacity to accommodate large numbers of prisoners. Prison capacity takes several forms: *cell capacity*, or the number of locked, secure, one-person cells; *bed capacity*, or the number of beds available in cells plus bunks in "dormitories," infirmaries, or even, as in Texas and Florida, tents; *program capacity*, or the number of work assignments, educational or vocational training opportunities, or group or individual therapy opportunities. Today all of these are in short supply.

Program capacity has been severely curtailed, so that most prisons today hold hundreds of idle inmates. There are too few in-prison jobs available for the numbers of inmates; indeed, there are waiting lists for the most menial tasks. Classrooms and treatment programs are full to overflowing. Work, education, or counseling in prison is not just a privilege that may be helpful in rehabilitation, but such programs help time pass. "Doing time" is what prisons are about, and idle time is doing hard time.

Cell capacity has been eroded as well. What little privacy and protection exist in a prison are provided by the individual cell, but cell space is limited. And sometimes cells are not even individual any longer as more and more prisoners are double-bunked. Even bed capacity is inadequate in many jurisdictions. Many states are holding sentenced felons in local jails awaiting openings in their prisons. There are over 18,000 prisoners nationally, or 2.4 percent of the total number of prisoners in the United States.[12]

Today we have the greatest number of prison inmates in the history of the United States, and the highest rate (number of inmates per 100,000 population) of prisoners in U.S. history as well. Many states are hurriedly building new prisons, but new construction simply cannot keep up with the need. While all of this is going on, legislatures almost everywhere are passing new *mandatory incarceration laws* for such crimes as driving while intoxicated, carrying a concealed weapon, and selling or trying to sell crack, cocaine, or other hard narcotics.

Some state's prison systems have become so full that correctional authorities have tried to "cap" the prison population, that is, to refuse to accept any new prisoners from the courts. But this enrages judges, legislators, sheriffs, and police, who normally have the task of delivering new inmates to the correctional system, and in general, capping the prison population has not worked.

The result of all this? Parole boards are being pressured to control the flow of inmates through *release*. In effect parole systems are being asked to relieve the overcrowding in prisons, and to make room for those convicted offenders awaiting transfer to prison by letting more prisoners out, and letting them out earlier in their sentences.

This relatively new pressure on parole boards adds a new dimension to the process of making release decisions, as each board grapples with the issues of recidivism risk, inmate and prison needs, and community safety in the face of intense prison space requirements. Field Practice B presents some typical parole cases. What would *you* decide given the circumstances just described?

Due Process at Parole Hearings

As mentioned near the beginning of this chapter, parole as currently practiced has come under attack, primarily on the ground that boards act arbitrarily and do not follow proper forms of due process and procedural regularity in their hearings. Commonly, proponents of parole abolition, mostly prisoners, have sought through higher court appeals to curb the discretion of parole boards. Challenges to denial of parole have raised a number of demands:

1. Parole boards should consider only proper and relevant information in making their decisions, and this information should be available to the inmate.
2. Reasons for denial of parole should be given and be appealable to a court.
3. Prisoners should have a right to representation by a lawyer at parole hearings.
4. Prisoners should be allowed to present witnesses in their own behalf and to cross examine hostile witnesses.

Court decisions have by no means always been favorable to inmates or parolees, but the hands-off doctrine has been abandoned. Appellate courts, including the U.S. Supreme Court, have intervened in the parole process where *revocation* of parole was

BOX 14.1

Model Penal Code

ADDITIONAL PAROLE CRITERIA Section 305.9 suggests that the parole board also consider:

1. The prisoner's personality, including his or her maturity, stability, sense of responsibility, and any apparent development in his or her personality that may promote or hinder a conformity to law.

2. The adequacy of the prisoner's parole plan.

3. The prisoner's ability and readiness to assume obligations and undertake responsibilities.

4. The prisoner's intelligence and training.

5. The prisoner's family status and whether he or she has relatives who display an interest in him or her, or whether he or she has other close and constructive associations in the community.

6. The prisoner's employment history, occupational skills, and the stability of past employment.

7. The type of residence, neighborhood, or community in which the prisoner plans to live.

8. The prisoner's past use of narcotics, or past habitual and excessive use of alcohol.

9. The prisoner's mental or physical makeup, including any disability or handicap that may affect a conformity to law.

10. The prisoner's prior criminal record, including the nature and circumstances, decency, and frequency of previous offenses.

11. The prisoner's attitude toward law and authority.

Parole Grant Decisions

1: Near the End

The inmate is a 29-year-old man serving a sentence of 1 to 10 years for burglary while armed. He has an extensive prior record of burglaries and assaults, has been on probation twice previously, and has served two prior terms, one in jail, the other in a prison. At the time of the hearing he has served 9 years of the 10-year sentence and has lost most of his good time for a series of minor but repetitive rule infractions while in prison. The parole board faced the dilemma of whether to hold him an additional year to his maximum discharge date or to parole him at the present time in order to provide supervision upon his return to the community.

2: Alcoholic

The inmate, a 47-year-old man, has served two years of a sentence of 1 to 7 years for forgery. He has a history of chronic alcoholism, with a record involving literally hundreds of arrests for public intoxication. He has served numerous short jail terms and was convicted of forgery (writing checks with insufficient funds) twice in the past. His adjustment in the institution has been good, but the program personnel reported him to be a chronic alcoholic with a negative prognosis.

3: Troublemaker

A 21-year-old inmate convicted of burglary received a sentence of 1 to 5 years. He has been in the institution exactly 12 months, and this is his first parole hearing. He has a minor prior juvenile record, but has maintained strong support from his family, and has a job awaiting him upon release. However, his institutional record shows three disciplinary infractions, two for contraband and one for refusing to work. He also was involved in a "scuffle" with other inmates that apparently was not serious enough to be labeled a "fight."

4: Murder without Motive

A 38-year-old inmate sentenced for murder has appeared before the parole board after having served 18 years in prison. At age 20 he had shot and killed his wife and then burned his house in an attempt to conceal the murder. The arson failed to hide the rifleshot death. He received a life sentence but became eligible for parole, as a model prisoner, after serving 15 years. An intensive investigation at the time of the murder failed to discover any clear motive for the killing. Apparently, it was a happy marriage. The partners were childhood sweethearts. There was no evidence of quarreling, drinking, drugs, or infidelity. The inmate had no explanation for the shooting except a "sudden impulse." Now, 18 years later, he still maintains he has no idea why, on a spring morning, he shot his young wife to death. He has always accounted for the arson as "panic" when he realized what he had done to her. He states, now as then, that he really loved his wife.

5: Swifty Jack

A 36-year-old inmate, serving 7 to 15 years for aggravated assault, has appeared before the board after 10 years in prison, having been denied parole twice earlier. The inmate, Swifty Jack Calhoun, was a reputed gangster and strongarm man, involved in corrupt construction union practices. His crime involved the brutal beating of a newspaper reporter who, at the time, was writing an expose of union corruption. The crime as well as the arrest and trial of Swifty Jack received widespread headline coverage at the time and is still widely remembered. Local newspapers carry stories periodically concerning Swifty Jack's progress through the prison system. On the other hand, correctional authorities report Swifty to be a model prisoner who regrets his prior lifestyle and who underwent a religious conversion as a "born-again Christian" about 4 years before this current board meeting.

6: Joan

This inmate, serving 5 to 15 years for manslaughter, has appeared before the board for the first time after serving 4 years and 11 months. She was convicted of killing her live-in boyfriend with a kitchen knife during a quarrel. She testified that the boyfriend, the father of one of her two small children, regularly beat her and that she had continually warned him that someday she would strike back. At her trial, she testified that the boyfriend was drunk, beating her, and threatening the children when she "defended herself" with the knife. In spite of this defense and evidence of bruises on her face, the jury convicted her of manslaughter in the first degree and the judge imposed the mandatory 5- to 15-year sentence. She has presented a parole plan that includes a job promise (as a waitress in a restaurant) from a former employer and living arrangements with her children and her mother in her mother's house.

the issue[13] but have been reluctant to interfere in parole *granting* procedures.[14] The distinction the courts have made between grant and revocation hearings evidently have rested on the concept of **vestment** in freedom. That is, parolees, having been released and returned to the community, have invested their energies and made their place in the outside world. They have a *vested interest* in remaining in the community, whereas prisoners at parole hearings, not yet having been released, have not vested themselves in the community. In other words, the courts held that it requires much more care, due process, and procedural regularity to *take away* freedom by revocation than to deny it in the first place.

Mandatory Release: Good-Time Laws

Mandatory release before the maximum sentence is served is possible in most states. It differs from parole in that the decision does not rest with a parole board and future risk is not a concern. Mandatory release laws are statutory (enacted by the legislature), allowing "time off for good behavior" in prison. Most states today allow prison inmates to earn **good time**, that is, a reduction in the *maximum* sentence for good behavior. **Specific-time statutes** give a formula by which a sentence is reduced by the number of days or weeks of good time a prisoner accummulates for each month served.[15]

The primary purpose of good time is prison control, for it gives inmates who conform with regulations hope of earlier release.[16] Another purpose is to provide supervised re-entry into the community for offenders who, for whatever reasons, were not paroled; thus mandatory release in some states requires the prisoner to agree to supervision until the court-imposed maximum sentence expires. However, in many jurisdictions the inmate on mandatory release walks free, without supervision, just as if he or she had served the maximum time.

Historically, good time was *given* by prison officials to particular inmates who demonstrated good behavior. These days, for the most part, good time is automatically calculated for all prisoners, though it can be *taken away*, in whole or in part, for misbehavior.

Depending on the statutes in a jurisdiction, good time reduces the minimum sentence, the maximum sentence, or both. When it is taken off the minimum, it simply makes the prisoner eligible for parole at an earlier date. But when taken from the maximum, it sets a mandatory release date at which time the prisoner *must* be released, though he or she is subject in some jurisdictions to supervision and the rules of parole until the court-imposed sentence runs out. Mandatory release has been called "parole-of-right" to distinguish it from parole granted at the discretion of a parole board. Like parolees, supervised offenders on mandatory release *can* have their freedom *revoked and be returned to prison* to complete their full sentences.

Persons sentenced to life imprisonment are not eligible for mandatory release, but good-time provisions may still affect them. In most jurisdictions a life sentence is translated into a minimum term, generally from 20 to 30 years, at which time lifers become eligible for parole. And lifers may earn good time to be deducted from this minimum, thereby becoming eligible for parole at an earlier date. For example, in Wisconsin a life sentence is interpreted to be 20 years, and a statute provides a formula for calculating the good time for sentences over 5 years. The formula is one-half the sentence, plus 1 year and 3 months. This means that Wisconsin lifers become eligible for parole (but not mandatory release) in 11 years, 3 months.

"Maxing Out"

Some prisoners, very few, serve every day of the maximum sentence handed down by the judge. This is called *"maxing out,"* and is rare today except for persons serving short-term misdemeanant sentences, felony inmates who have received very short maximum terms, a year or a year and a day, for example, and occasionally also longer-term inmates who are uncooperative, lose good time because of disciplinary reports, or otherwise fail to earn early release. Persons incarcerated for the first time

Executive Clemency

Executive clemency can function as a last chance for justice in cases where evidence or rules change after a decision is rendered. Consider the following story:

In 1979, in Norfolk, Virginia, Joe Giarratano, a drug addict, awoke in a stupor to find that a 44-year-old woman friend of his and her 15-year-old daughter had been brutally murdered. Giarratano confessed and was tried, convicted, and sentenced to death. But he began to have doubts about his confession and guilt. After receiving over 6000 pleas from Giarratano's supporters—including singer-activist Joan Baez and conservative columnist James J. Kilpatrick—Virginia Governor L. Douglas Wilder also became unsure of the conviction. Three days before the scheduled date of Giarratano's execution, Wilder used his power of executive clemency to commute the sentence to life imprisonment and offered Giarratano the chance to seek a new trial.

Or consider what happend in Ohio: Most states now recognize the validity of the "battered woman syndrome," a temporary psychological condition which may cause an abused woman to take violent action in self-defense against a long-time abuser. In 1990, the Ohio State Supreme Court ruled that women in the state are permitted to present evidence of the condition in their defense when being tried for the assault or murder of abusive mates. Shortly thereafter Ohio Governor Richard F. Celeste freed twenty-one women who had already spent 2 years in prison for killing or assaulting their husbands, and said four others could also leave as soon as they served 2 years. All of the women were ordered to perform 200 hours of community service. Women's rights groups hailed the mass commutations as a major victory for women.

Later, in 1991, Maryland Governor William D. Schaefer followed suit, and released eight women convicted of killing or assaulting men who had battered them.

are almost invariably released prior to completion of maximum sentence, either on parole or on mandatory release.[17] It should also be noted that the law requires inmates to be released on expiration of their maximum sentences no matter what their attitude or likelihood of committing additional crimes so long as they have not committed additional crimes while in prison.

Inmates in all jurisdictions can turn down the chance for parole, and in some places they can waive their good-time credits, thereby refusing mandatory release. This usually occurs in cases where the parole or mandatory release date is close to the sentence expiration date, and the inmate prefers to complete the time in prison to be totally clear, avoiding all community supervision upon release. Parole rules and conditions are often quite strict and act to curb parolees' freedom of movement and to cramp their lifestyles. Nevertheless, most prisoners welcome parole or mandatory release and have no wish to max out.

Executive Clemency: Pardon, Commutation, and Reprieve

The governor of any state, as well as the President of the United States, has power to pardon any prisoner in his or her jurisdiction or to reduce a sentence, making an inmate eligible for parole. This is known as *executive clemency*. One instance of executive clemency was President Ford's pardon of former President Nixon. This was an unusual case not only because a former President of the United States was the recipient but also because the pardon was granted *before* any trial of Mr. Nixon, either by the Senate or in the courts. The Nixon pardon raised a number of interesting questions, Constitutional and otherwise. Since Mr. Nixon was pardoned before he was convicted of any crime, does his acceptance of the pardon imply any admission of guilt? Could Mr. Nixon have pardoned himself? These and no doubt other questions will be the subject of debate for years, although most of them are legally moot and impossible to resolve with certainty.

Executive clemency has long historical roots. Early records of pardoning power are found in the Mosaic and Vedic laws. In 1066 William the Conqueror brought to England the view that pardoning power is the exclusive prerogative of the king. Over the years this became a very powerful common law tradition and has played an important role in the development of the U.S. legal system. Today executive clemency takes three major forms: pardons, commutations, and reprieves. A *pardon* generally restores a person convicted of a crime to noncriminal status by an act of executive clemency. Full pardons with complete restoration of civil rights are typically granted in cases where it is shown after trial that the person was totally innocent of the crime for which he or she was convicted. However, pardons are granted not only to the innocent. They also serve as acts of mercy and as rewards for meritorious deeds performed while under sentence, among other exceptional circumstances. In many jurisdictions pardons can be "conditional," that is, they can be used to restore only some of the rights lost by conviction.

A *commutation* is not a pardon but an executive order lowering an offender's minimum or maximum sentence to make the inmate eligible for parole. For example, a prisoner sentenced to life who has demonstrated an exceptional level of rehabilitation or performed some meritorious act may have his or her sentence commuted to a specific term of years less than life, which allows the parole board to consider an early release. The parole board, though appointed by the governor, does not necessarily grant parole every time the governor commutes a sentence. Recently, in New York state, Governor Mario Cuomo commuted the life sentence of an inmate convicted of killing a deputy sheriff. The commutation made the inmate eligible for parole, but the parole board refused to release him.

Reprieve is a form of executive clemency allowing a chief executive to halt executions that have been ordered by a judge and jury. A governor's reprieve may merely delay the execution or it may be accompanied by a commutation, reducing the sentence of the prisoner to life imprisonment. The reprieve power of governors has assumed new significance today in light of Supreme Court decisions affirming the

Presidents and governors have the power of executive clemency and pardon. President Gerald Ford signed a "full, free and absolute pardon" for former President Richard Nixon a month after Nixon resigned under the pressure of the Watergate scandal. President Ford later signed unconditional pardons for a number of Vietnam war resisters on the recommendation of his clemency board.

Constitutionality of death penalty provisions in a number of states. The number of prisoners on death row has become the largest in our history. Today, governors of states with large death house populations find themselves potentially confronting hundreds of reprieve decisions, a situation no governor faced for over a decade between 1972 and 1982 when the death penalty was temporarily not utilized following the U.S. Supreme Court decision, *Furman v. Georgia*.

Sometimes pardon, commutation, or reprieve is granted on the executive's own motion, but more commonly a prisoner files a formal petition with the governor. If it seems warranted, the governor may order the parole board, correctional authorities, or in some instances a special pardon board to investigate the case and make recommendations.

Although executive clemency is a very important power, often dramatic when used, pardon and commutation are not major methods of prisoner release. In most states only a handful of inmates are granted any form of executive clemency in any year.

Also, pardons, commutations, and reprieves may have *conditions attached* by the executive, which generally cannot be effectively challenged by the recipient. Reprieves may be temporary—for example, granting a pregnant woman convicted of murder a stay of execution in order to have her child and then reinstituting the order of execution. A well-known case of commutation with a condition attached was the parole of James R. Hoffa, former president of the International Brotherhood of Teamsters, where Hoffa was ordered to refrain from union management while on parole. Hoffa accepted his commutation and parole, then subsequently appealed the condition. However, it was upheld by the U.S. District Court for the District of Columbia.[18]

It may be that pardons and other forms of executive clemency will assume greater significance if the trend to definite sentences continues. Any correctional system housing an inmate population with no possibility of parole faces a good deal of pressure, not only from overcrowding, but from humanitarian considerations, and a more liberal pardoning system could become increasingly attractive. At present some states, like New York, are considering establishing full-time pardon commissions to investigate eligible inmates year round. If adopted, this would be a major change from the common practice of a few traditional "Christmas pardons" granted by the governor each year.

REVOCATION

Parole Revocation

Inmates released on parole or mandatory release are subject to supervision by field agents and must agree to abide by various rules and conditions. The rules and conditions of parole are drafted by the parole board, and the inmate must sign an agreement to follow those rules if he or she wishes to be released. There are two kinds of rules: *general*, which apply to all parolees, and *special*, which are set by the board in specific cases to assist the particular individuals in making it on the street. An example of a special rule might be to "receive regular outpatient psychiatric counseling" in a case where the board thinks the inmate is emotionally disturbed as well as criminal. Or an inmate with a long history of alcoholism may be required to regularly attend Alcoholics Anonymous meetings.

General conditions of parole may vary somewhat from state to state, but they are all quite similar. Parolees must agree not to associate with "known criminals," to

Parole Revocation Decisions

1: Murder and Beer

A homicide offender on parole after serving 17 years of a 15- to 25-year prison term was arrested and convicted of a misdemeanor. The new crime involved theft of beer from a supermarket. Although this was clearly a violation of parole, revocation meant a return to prison for the original maximum sentence, although a future reparole would be possible.

2: Schoolyard Lurker

Police observed a man, on parole after 8 years in prison for child molesting, loitering near a schoolyard. They took no action themselves but reported their observations to the offender's parole officer. Although there was no specific rule requiring the parolee to avoid the vicinity of schools, his crimes had generally occurred near schools and his victims were children on their way to or from school.

3: Bottoms Up

An armed robber, on parole after serving 4½ years of a 3- to 10-year sentence, was found to be heavily intoxicated on an "unannounced" home visit by his parole officer. Although drunkenness had played no part in his robberies, he had signed a parole agreement which, among other rules, forbade him to use alcoholic beverages "to excess."

4: In the Sunshine

A chronic shoplifter, on parole after serving 1½ years of a 1- to 3-year sentence, went on a "vacation" to Florida for 2 weeks with a boyfriend. She did not notify her parole officer or receive permission to leave the state, a requirement of her parole agreement.

5: Making a Deal

A prosecuting attorney approached the parole officer of an armed robber who had served 6 years of his 5- to 15-year sentence before being released on parole a year earlier. The prosecutor explained that the parolee was suspected of a series of burglaries but that the evidence, though strong, might not absolutely support a new conviction. The prosecutor offered to dismiss the burglary charges if the parolee were to be revoked on his present 5- to 15-year sentence, saying: "That way we're sure he's off the streets with no additional time to serve. Plus the record is cleaner this way." The parole officer knew it would be easy to revoke the parole; the individual had been reprimanded several times for minor parole rule infractions. Another conviction would make the parolee eligible for a "persistent felony" charge, sometimes called a "three-time loser" charge, which carried a life sentence. ∎

---

refrain from drinking to excess, not to use any mind-altering drugs, to keep a curfew (remain at home and be in bed by a certain time each night), not to change employment without prior approval by a parole officer, to support their families, not to leave the jurisdiction without prior permission from the parole authorities, not to possess firearms, to "cooperate" with the parole officer, including reporting regularly and being willing to have the parole officer make "unannounced" visits to the place of employment or the home of the parolee. And, of course, the parolee must agree to remain law-abiding.

Violation of these rules or the commission of new crimes makes the offender subject to *revocation* with subsequent incarceration or reincarceration. There is nothing automatic about revocation. It is a discretionary decision initiated by the supervising probation or parole officer. Field Practice C gives several examples. What would *you* decide in these cases?

In general, revocation of parole or mandatory release requires a more elaborate procedure than is necessary for initial sentence to community supervision. This is consistent with a general tradition in administrative law surrounding the removal of a privilege once granted, and in which the holder is considered to have a vested interest in the privilege so that its removal is protected by more procedural safeguards than are required for its denial in the first place. In an analogous manner, a university may deny a student admission in a much more cursory fashion than it could later expel him or her.

Not every violation of parole conditions results in revocation. Usually, a parolee is counseled to abide by the conditions of parole by the parole officer, who then typically "works with" the parolee to help him or her adjust to lawful living. Therefore, the parole officer enjoys broad discretion, and that discretion has resulted in some vague rules and regulations, such as parolees being required to avoid associating with "undesirable" people.

The parole revocation process begins when a parole officer discovers, or has reason to believe, a parolee has violated a rule or condition or when the parolee is arrested for a new crime. The parole officer makes an initial determination of whether the infraction or arrest is serious enough to call for revocation. If so, the decision to seek revocation is usually referred to a supervising parole officer for ratification. Then, depending on the requirements in the particular jurisdiction, an **administrative warrant** sufficient to detain the parolee may be sought from a parole board member or, if this is not required, the supervising field agent may issue a **hold order** to detain the parolee until a revocation hearing can be held.[19]

Until 1972 the common practice in many jurisdictions was for a parolee to be taken into custody and jailed when a revocation order was issued, and then returned from the community to a prison where, at some later date—days, weeks, or even months later—a hearing into the appropriateness of the revocation was held. This worked an obvious hardship on any parolee if it turned out that revocation was inappropriate because the charges were unfounded or otherwise unjust. In many ways it was comparable to denying bail to a person arrested for a crime, or refusing prehearing release to an alleged probation violator. But in the case of return to prison, the situation was more extreme. Removal from the community to the prison, even for a short duration, not only interrupted the parolee's family life and employment, but, since prisons are often distant from the scene of a violation, also created serious problems should witnesses, complainants, or others, including local counsel, be required or desirable at the hearing.

All this was changed by the Supreme Court in 1972 with the **Morrissey v. Brewer** decision (See Box 14.2). In that case, Morrissey admitted that he had violated his parole conditions by buying a car under an assumed name and operating it without permission, giving false statements to police concerning his address and insurance following a minor accident, obtaining credit under an assumed name, and failing to report his place of residence to his parole officer. The parole officer recommended that his parole be revoked for his continuing violation of parole rules. The Court established certain due process requirements for parole revocation, but stopped short of granting offenders the right to counsel.

One problem with parole revocation that has been rarely addressed is the availability of sanctions short of revocation for infractions of rules. In general, revocation has been handled as an either-or proposition: The parole officer who discovers rule infractions either does nothing or commences full-scale revocation proceedings. The drafters of the *Model Penal Code* suggest the following alternatives:

1. The parolee should receive a reprimand and warning from the board.
2. Parole supervision and reporting should be intensified.
3. Reductions for good behavior should be forfeited or withheld.
4. The parolee should be remanded, without revocation of parole, to a residence facility for such a period and under such supervision or treatment as the board may deem appropriate.
5. The parolee should be required to conform to one or more additional conditions of parole which may be imposed.

Morrissey v. Brewer, 408 U.S. 471 (1972)

. . . Our task is limited to deciding the minimum requirements (for parole revocation) of due process. They include a) written notice of the claimed violations of parole; b) disclosure to the parolee of evidence against him; c) opportunity to be heard in person and to present witnesses and documentary evidence; d) the right to confront and cross-examine adverse witnesses (unless the hearing officer specifically finds good cause for not allowing confrontation); e) a "neutral and detached" hearing body such as a traditional parole board, members of which need not be judicial officers or lawyers; and f) a written statement by the fact-finders as to the evidence relied on and reasons for revoking parole. We emphasize there is no thought to equate this second stage of parole revocation to a criminal prosecution in any sense; it is a narrow inquiry; the process should be flexible enough to consider evidence including letters, affidavits, and other material that would not be admissible in an adversary criminal trial.

6. The parolee should be arrested and returned to prison to await a hearing to determine whether his parole should be revoked.[20]

Perhaps parolees should be able to earn "good time" off the remainder of their supervision, much as prisoners earn good time off their maximum sentences. And perhaps parolees who no longer require supervision and guidance should be granted early discharge from parole if no foreseeable risk to the community exists.

DISCHARGE FROM SENTENCE

The formal criminal process ends when an offender has successfully completed the sentence, whether in jail, on probation, in prison, or on parole or mandatory release. Normally the "ex-offender's" conviction record remains on file, as does all of the other material and information gathered about him or her by the court and correctional authorities. Many of the corollary effects of felony conviction, including loss of voting rights and inability to obtain certain licenses or franchises or to enter certain occupations or professions, may affect offenders for many years after they have served their sentences. And the status of "ex-con" may haunt someone for a lifetime.

Today some jurisdictions have procedures for *restoration of rights* lost by conviction. In general, the ex-offender must apply to a court for restoration sometime after sentence completion (commonly 5 years), and cooperate in whatever investigation is ordered by the court.

There is an effort today to institute automatic restoration of lost rights to persons who have successfully served their sentences on the general grounds that the continuing negative effects of convictions work excessive hardship on many persons who have become fully law-abiding. To this end, there are provisions in some places for the *expunging of all records* of those who have successfully adjusted to life outside prison again. The National Council of Crime and Delinquency has proposed a model act in this regard which would annul the conviction of a person after discharge. Unless the person were to be convicted of another crime in the future, the previous record would not be used against the person under that proposed law. Employment applications would only be able to ask, "Have you ever been arrested for or convicted of a crime which has not been annulled by a court?"

Procedures for the restoration of rights or the expungement of records used today vary widely across the nation and are of limited success. Some damaging effects of conviction and serving a sentence may be diminished, but the negative status of having been convicted (or of having been a convict) tends to persist throughout the lifetime of the ex-offender.

SUMMARY

Most prisoners—even those sentenced to life terms or very long sentences—are eventually released. Those who are held in jail are released after serving the full term imposed at the sentencing hearing. Release from prison can come about in several ways: (1) by parole, after serving the minimum sentence; (2) after serving the maximum term less time off for good behavior, a process called mandatory release; (3) after serving a full, maximum sentence, called maxing out; or (4) following a pardon by a governor or the President of the United States.

The decision to grant or deny parole is made by a parole board after a review of the inmate's case file and, usually, a face-to-face interview. In deciding whether to grant parole, parole board members must evaluate both the probability that an inmate will commit a new offense and the type of offense he or she might commit.

Despite its widespread use, parole remains controversial. Conservatives argue that its use blunts the effectiveness of punishment; liberals contend that parole board members have too much unstructured discretion. The use of parole has several advantages: (1) It mitigates the harshness of long prison terms; (2) it allows officials to reduce the sentences of deserving offenders; (3) it is cheaper than long periods of confinement; and (4) it is somewhat safer than outright release since inmates live for a time under supervision in the community.

An offender's length of stay in prison is also affected by good-time provisions— a reduction in sentence granted for good behavior while in the institution. Good-time provisions function to preserve order in the institution, and they permit the supervised release of the offender back into the community. Unlike parole, mandatory release is not a discretionary decision made by a parole board. If the inmate behaves well in prison—usually measured by the absence of disciplinary reports—the maximum sentence imposed by the sentencing court is lessened by statutory provisions. The person on mandatory release must, however, obey parole rules and be supervised by a parole officer until the actual maximum term originally set by the judge is over.

Some prisoners, usually those with short sentences, waive parole and max out to avoid supervision following release. Parole or mandatory release can be revoked if the offender violates parole or mandatory release rules and regulations. In such instances, the offender can be sent back to prison to complete the sentence. The procedures for revocation today are subject to more due process requirements (a formal hearing, written notification of charges, presentation of evidence of rule violation or criminal offense, etc.) than a few years ago. However, revocation proceedings are not full-scale trials. For instance, parolees undergoing revocation do not have an absolute right to a lawyer. Attorneys need only be assigned where the parolee is mentally or educationally in manifest need of such assistance.

NOTES

1. Sources, Jacob V. Lamar, "The One That Got Away, Why an Escaped Murderer Haunts Michael Dukakis," *Time*, June 27, 1988, p. 22; and Jack E. White, "Bush's Most Valuable Player," *Time*, November 14, 1988, pp. 20–21.
2. Bureau of Justice Statistics, *Correctional Populations in the United States, 1988* (Washington, DC: U.S. Department of Justice, March 1991), p. 73.
3. Advisory Council of Judges of the National Council on Crime and Delinquency, *Model Sentencing Act* (Hackensack, NJ: National Council on Crime and Delinquency, 1963), p. 26.
4. For a discussion of problems involved in abolishing parole, see Andrew von Hirsch and Jay S. Albanese, "Problems With Abolishing Parole Release: The New York Case," *Criminal Law Bulletin* 15 (5) (1979): 416–435.
5. See Samuel Walker, *Sense and Nonsense about Crime: A Policy Guide* (Pacific Grove, CA: Brooks/Cole, 1989), pp. 223–228, and Herbert Packer, *The Limits of the Criminal Sanction* (Stanford, CA: Stanford University Press, 1968).
6. Bureau of Justice Statistics, *Probation and Parole 1990* (Washington, DC: U.S. Department of Justice, November 1991).
7. For historical developments of parole see Harry Elmer Barnes and Negley Teeters, *New Horizons in Criminology*, 2nd ed. (New York: Prentice-Hall, 1951); Frederick

Moran, "The Origins of Parole," *NPPA Yearbook* (1954): 71–98; Charles Newman, *Sourcebook on Probation, Parole and Pardons*, 2nd ed. (Springfield, IL: Charles C. Thomas, 1964); Sol Rubin, Henry Weihofen, George Edwards, and Simon Rosenzweig, *The Law of Criminal Corrections* (St. Paul, MN: West, 1963), Chap. 11.

8. Barnes and Teeters, op. cit., p. 351.

9. Cloud H. Miller and Patrick R. Anderson, "Postsentence Defense: The Presentence and Parole Hearing Interview and Implications of *Estelle v. Smith* in Postconviction Due Process," *The Champion: Journal of the National Association of Criminal Defense Lawyers* 8 (6) (1984): 18–22.

10. See Belinda R. McCarthy and Bernard McCarthy, *Community-Based Corrections* (Pacific Grove, CA: Brooks/Cole, 1990).

11. See P. B. Hoffman and S. Adelberg, "The Salient Factor-Score: A Non-technical Overview," *Federal Probation* 44 (1980).

12. Bureau of Justice Statistics, *Prisoners in 1990* (Washington, DC: U.S. Government Printing Office, May 1991), Table 7, p. 5.

13. See *Morrissey v. Brewer*, 408 U.S. 471 (1972). See also Comment, "Rights v. Results: Quo Vadis Due Process for Hearings in California and the Federal System," *California Western Law Review* 4 (1968): 18.

14. See Note, "Procedural Due Process in Parole Release Proceedings—Existing Rules, Recent Court Decisions, and Experience in the Prison," *Minnesota Law Review* 60 (1976): 341, in which the author states: "Although courts traditionally have adopted a 'hands off' approach to legal proceedings involving prisoners, the Supreme Court in the last decade has required prison officials to observe procedural due process in all significant areas of the correctional process except parole release decisionmaking. The Court has not addressed a claim for due process by a potential parolee. Such a claim would merit particularly close scrutiny, for a prisoner's interest in parole release may be as strong or stronger than any other prisoner interest that has been accorded procedural protection."

15. See Bureau of Justice Statistics, *Correctional Population in the United States, 1985* (Washington, DC: U.S. Department of Justice, 1987), for a survey of good-time practices in state correctional systems.

16. Jeffrey Nickerson, "Prisoner's Gain Time: Incentive, Deterrent, or Ritual Response?" *University of Florida Law Review* 21 (1968): 103; and Larry Kraft, "Prison Disciplinary Practices and Procedures: Is Due Process Provided?" *Harvard Law Review* 75 (1962): 904.

17. Bureau of Justice Statistics, *Probation and Parole 1989* (Washington, DC: U.S. Department of Justice, November 1990), p. 4.

18. *Hoffa v. Saxbe*, 378 F. Supp. 1221 (D.D.C. 1974).

19. Vincent O'Leary and Kathleen J. Hanrahan, *Parole Systems in the United States* (Hackensack, NJ: National Council on Crime and Delinquency, 1976), pp. 48–72.

20. American Law Institute, *Model Penal Code*, proposed official draft (Philadelphia: American Law Institute, 1962), Sec. 305.16.

SUGGESTED READINGS

Beck, James L., and Jody Klein-Saffran. *Community Control Project*. Report 44. Washington, DC: U.S. Parole Commission Research Unit, September 1989.

Citizen's Inquiry on Parole and Criminal Justice, Inc. *Prison without Walls: Report on New York Parole*. New York: Praeger, 1978.

Clear, Todd R., and Vincent O'Leary. *Controlling the Offender in the Community*. Lexington, MA: Lexington Books, 1983.

Glaser, Daniel, and V. O'Leary. *Personal Characteristics of Parole Outcome*. Washington, DC: U.S. Government Printing Office, 1966.

Hirsch, Andrew, and Kathleen J. Hanrahan. *Abolish Parole?* Washington, DC: U.S. Government Printing Office, 1978.

Stanley, David T. *Prisoners among Us—The Problem of Parole*. Washington, DC: The Brookings Institution, 1976.

McCleary, Richard. *Dangerous Men: The Sociology of Parole*. Beverly Hills, CA: Sage, 1978.

DISCUSSION QUESTIONS

1. Discuss the difference between the time served and the time sentenced.

2. Discuss the history and development of parole.

3. Compare and contrast parole according to the conservative crime control model and the liberal crime control model.

4. Explain the purposes of parole and factors which influence the decision to grant or deny it.

5. Discuss the revocation process.

15

Community Corrections

At 9:30 a.m. in the morning a man enters a downtown office building, walks through the hall to a door marked "Community Control," opens it, and goes in. The room is much like a doctor's office waiting room except the chairs are hard and there are no popular magazines or potted plants. A woman behind a window takes his name and tells him to have a seat. Soon, another woman holding a file folder opens a door leading to the inner offices and calls his name. After following her to her office, he allows her to inspect the small electronic monitor strapped to his left ankle. Then they talk about his efforts to find employment, his relationships with his wife and young son, and the drug treatment program he attends every Thursday. He is a probationer and she is his probation caseworker. He has been placed in an electronic surveillance program which restricts his movements from home to work to drug rehabilitation class and to the weekly appointment with his probation caseworker. If he strays from that routine, the electronic device on his ankle alerts the community control agent.

At 5:30 p.m. in the afternoon a city bus is crowded with people on their way home from work. One man in his mid-twenties, carrying an empty lunch box, exits the bus at the corner in a lower middle-class neighborhood and enters a large two-story house. There he signs the book near the door and notes the time of his arrival. Joining several other people, he then prepares for the evening meal and the routine of chores, television, and sleep before awaking the next morning to catch the bus for work. He is a convicted felon in a community-based half-way house, serving a 2-year sentence for burglary.

During the evening a young woman nervously waits for her turn to talk to her counselor. She keeps this appointment each Monday night after dinner in the work release center. This evening the counselor will help her fill out forms to arrange for a driver's test to reinstate her driver's license, which has expired after more than 6 years in prison. Previously the young woman opened checking and savings accounts at a local bank. She has been working in a downtown clothing store for several weeks and contributes $30 per week to the state for her room and board, sends $50 per week to her mother who has been caring for her two children since her arrest over 7 years ago, and places most of the rest of her earnings in the savings account. This weekend she will stay at her mother's house, with her children, for the first time since her arrest.

These convicted criminals are typical of thousands serving community-based sentences throughout the United States.

ABOUT THIS CHAPTER

Although many convicted criminals are removed from society to serve their sentences in jail or prison, the vast majority remain in the community, at home and at work, under the supervision of probation or parole agents. *Probation* is a sentence handed down by the judge to serve one's term entirely in the community without first going to jail or prison. It is not leniency. The sentence imposes rules and controls on the offender which are enforced by probation officers. *Parole*, as discussed in Chap. 14, is the part of a sentence served in the community after the offender has spent another part of it in prison. A major distinction, then, between probation and parole is that probation is a sentence ordered by the judge after a person has been convicted of a crime. Parole, on the other hand, is not a sentence from the court but a release decision made by a parole board after an offender has spent part of the sentence in an institution.

At present more than half of all sentenced offenders are placed on probation by courts,[1] and nationally about 70 percent of prison inmates are released on parole.[2] Community-based corrections is viewed as an alternative to incarceration, a less intrusive response to the criminal offense.

This chapter traces the history of probation, explains the advantages of *community-based corrections* over incarceration, and describes the world of supervised living while free from confinement. It deals with the conditions of community sentences, up to and including electronic monitoring and tracking. The rights of probationers and parolees are discussed, and a distinction is drawn between these two forms of community supervision in regard to permissible rules and conditions, the rights of authorities to search for and seize evidence, and the procedures and criteria for revocation.

HISTORY OF PROBATION

A cobbler from Boston named *John Augustus* is generally considered to be the "father of probation." In 1841 he provided bail and contributed to the reformation of a man accused of public drunkenness, an experience that began a lengthy period of similar efforts on the part of Augustus and that gave birth to the concept of probation. In his journal, Augustus wrote of that first encounter in the Boston City Court:

> In the month of August, 1841, I was in court one morning, when the door communicating with the lock-room was opened and an officer entered, followed by a ragged and wretched looking man, who took his seat upon the bench allotted to prisoners. I imagined from the man's appearance, that his offense was that of yielding to his appetite for intoxicating drinks. . . . The case was clearly made out, but before sentence had been passed out I conversed with him for a few moments, and found that he was not yet past all hope of reformation, although his appearance and his looks precluded a belief in the minds of others that he would ever become a man again. He told me that if he could be saved from the House of Correction, he never again would taste intoxicating liquors; there was such an earnestness in that tone, a look expressive of firm resolve, that I determined to aid him, I bailed him, by permission of the Court . . . at the expiration of this period of probation, I accompanied him into the court room; his whole appearance was changed and no one, not even the scrutinizing officers, could have believed that he was the same person who less than a month before, had stood trembling on the prisoner's stand. The Judge expressed himself much pleased with the account we gave of the man, and instead of the usual penalty,—imprisonment in the House of Correction,—he fined him one cent and costs, amounting in all to $3.76, which was immediately paid. The man continued industrious and sober, and without doubt has been by this treatment, saved from a drunkard's grave.[3]

Augustus was so encouraged by this experience that he devoted much of the remainder of his life and his material resources to the aid of men, women, and children caught up in the criminal justice system. He opened his own house to offenders he "perceived to be not beyond all hope of reformation," provided clothing and food, and assisted in securing employment. In addition to helping several thousand people in need of charity, in the 18 years remaining before his death in 1859, Augustus "bailed" approximately 2,000 persons "on probation."[4] After his death the work continued under the direction of *Rufus R. Cook*, the chaplain of the county gaol (jail) and a representative of the Boston Children's Aid Society.[5]

In 1878 Massachusetts passed the first probation statute and by 1920 every state in the union had a legislatively created probation system in operation. The *concept* of probation resembled the Augustus model in terms of offender screening, assistance, reformation, and benevolence. Early legislative discussions focused on that model, emphasizing the need for probation officers to be recruited from the ranks of ministers, social workers, psychologists, and other like-minded professionals. However, when probation was *implemented* as an agency of the state the emphasis became *surveillance* and *enforcement of rules.* The first state probation officers tended to be retired sheriffs and others concerned primarily with the strict control of offenders.[6] Today in every state probation efforts revolve around a combination of rule enforcement and surveillance. They also incorporate such casework techniques as counseling, job placement, and similar forms of assistance.

Probation received great impetus as a correctional technique with the spread of the juvenile court movement after the turn of the century. And while the history of community sentences for felons is a stormy one, since both probation and parole were, and remain, controversial, they have in general proven effective and are now widely used in most states.

COMMUNITY SENTENCES: OFFENDERS ON PROBATION AND PAROLE

The Case for *Community-Based Corrections*

Arguments in favor of community-based corrections usually rest on dissatisfaction with the state of affairs in prisons. Almost every argument *against* prisons can be restated as an argument *for* community-based programs.

Cost-effectiveness. The total expenses of incarceration are difficult to assess. Prison building costs have escalated in recent years toward "$70,000 per bed," meaning that a prison designed to house 1000 inmates can cost as much as $70 million, exclusive of the costs it requires to build the protective wall around it if one is desired.[7] In addition to building costs, the costs of operating a prison vary from a low of about $12,000 to above $30,000 per inmate per year.[8] Food, medical services, vocational and educational programming, 24-hour guarding year round, and the other necessities of prison life are very expensive. In fact, today it costs as much to send an inmate to a maximum-security prison as it does to send a student to Harvard or Yale. Nor do direct costs take into account the "invisible" costs of confinement—the loss of tax and social security revenues while an otherwise able-bodied person is confined, the social welfare costs of maintaining a prisoner's family, the loss of any major contribution to the overall economy.

Community-based programs, on the other hand, operate at a small fraction of the costs of incarceration. Capital costs are considerably lower, for there are no expensive security devices. Office space is all that is needed. The expense of providing social services and other correctional programs is much less than in prison, because they are provided by social service agencies within the community. Moreover, since the offender usually maintains employment while under community supervision, the "invisible" costs do not accrue. Instead, the offender contributes to his or her own upkeep as well as the upkeep of others through taxes, social security, family support, and in some cases even restitution to victims.

In short, prisons are financial liabilites, but community-based corrections can be assets.

Harmful effects of incarceration. Community-based programs help avoid the harmful effects incarceration can have on offenders. Disenchantment with imprisonment as a corrective measure has been widespread among criminologists for some time. Indeed, imprisonment has been found wanting as a rehabilitative device for inmates, a deterrent to other criminals, and a punitive response to criminal acts. And with the difficulties produced by the rapid increase of prison populations during the 1980s, the harmful effects of imprisonment have been further exacerbated.[9] Life in many institutions is at best barren and futile, at worst unspeakably brutal and degrading. Of course, prisoners in such institutions are unable to commit further crimes while serving their sentences, but the conditions in which they live are the poorest possible preparation for their successful re-entry into society, and often merely reinforce in them a pattern of manipulation or destructiveness.[10]

Prison existence does not resemble life outside of prison, and to assume that people will learn to live law-abiding lives in the "real" world by spending a period of years in prison is untenable. In prisons, we house together, in intimate interaction, the worst among us. To think that such an institution will rehabilitate anyone is ridiculous. Probably the worst behavioral treatment setting in the nation is the maximum-security prison.

Vernon Fox has written that American prisons, rather than reflecting the free society of which they are part, instead embody the following features of a totalitarian regime:

1. An ideology focused on custody.
2. A single mass-party, authoritarian, dictatorship.
3. Terroristic police control with a system of rewards and punishment to assure cohesiveness in implementing the ideology.
4. A monopoly on communications with the general public, including the use of censorship.
5. A monopoly on weapons to preclude armed combat between prisoners, but a well-armed force of perimeter guards.
6. A centrally controlled economy with expansion, conflicting staff, and infighting.[11]

Prisoners have virtually every decision made for them every day, from when to get up in the morning to what to wear to what to eat. Every physical need may be met, but they are not taught how to meet those needs themselves in a responsible way. Therefore, even with the considerable advances made in penological practices this century, one cannot avoid concluding that prisons often do more harm than good. At the very least, such treatment is poor preparation for the demands of living outside.

Community-based programs, on the other hand, are not "total institutions"; they maintain some semblance of the social qualities of free life. They do not degrade offenders, and allow them to have contact with the very type of law-abiding citizens society hopes they will become.

Community and family relationships. Community-based programs also help avoid social surgery, that is, the severing of a person's community and family relationships. Prison inmates are effectively cut off from spouses, children, employers, parents, friends, schools, churches, social service organizations, and fraternal and professional contacts. After release from prison, the re-establishment of any of these relationships is difficult. Prisons tend to be remote from the communities from which the prisoners come, making relationships with family and friends difficult to maintain. Community-based programs allow an offender to live with his or her family and to maintain other relationships including employment. And agencies within the community that may prove beneficial in rehabilitation such as Alcoholics Anonymous, drug treatment programs, marital and vocational counseling centers, and religious organizations can be utilized as well.

Success rates. In terms of recidivism, community-based programs are no less successful than prison. Recidivism rates among offenders are relatively high for all postconviction programs.[12] In fact, prison populations tend to be highly recidivist in nature since they are comprised of a sizable number of persons who have previously been incarcerated or who were on probation earlier and sent to prison for committing additional crimes or breaking the rules of their probation. Most probationers, on the other hand, do not go to prison.

Aside from recidivism rates, advocates of community-based programs point to other factors in favor of their approach: Community-based programs provide about the same level of community protection as prisons. Also, since community programs avoid the social surgery and harmful effects of imprisonment, offenders are usually not made worse by them. Scientific proof that incarceration of humans in prisons for any length of time has any beneficial effects is scarce. Yet the benefits of some community-based correctional programs have shown encouraging signs of success. At the very least, advocates argue, community programs are no worse than prisons and are significantly cheaper with fewer damaging side effects.

The Case Against Community-Based Corrections

The case against community-based correctional programs generally revolves around two themes:

1. Such programs are a form of "coddling" criminals; they are too lenient and do not serve as effective deterrents to crime for probationers themselves or for potential criminals in the general population.
2. Community-based corrections programs are usually unwelcome in most neighborhoods, especially when first proposed or instituted, because residents fear that unrestrained criminals will commit further crimes. As a result they often are located in high-crime, lower-class areas, which by their nature are criminogenic.

Moreover, opposition to such programs also comes from some offenders who feel that the traditional use of probation, as well as the traditional methods of selecting for parole, gives too much discretion to judges and parole boards. This creates uncertainty over actual sentence lengths and results in supervision conditions based on factors not related to the criminal conduct of the offenders. Some offenders argue that selection for both probation and parole is racially biased, so that minority offenders are disproportionately sentenced to prison.

The Future of Community-Based Corrections

Although cases of crimes committed by probationers and parolees can be found, as can illustrations of apparently unwarranted judicial or correctional leniency and abuses of discretion, most experienced observers of the criminal justice system support community sentences as safe and effective alternatives to incarceration.[13] Also, the records of probationers and parolees universally demonstrate a high success rate, in that they show the majority of probationers and parolees complete their sentences without committing further crimes.[14]

Faced with the current overcrowding in all our prison systems, there is little doubt that probation will become even more widely used in the future; there simply is no room in the prisons. And the emphasis today on determinate prison sentencing coupled with prison overcrowding means an increase in the number of early releases. If the prosecution and incarceration rates increase, or even if they continue at their present levels, correctional choices other than imprisonment will become even more important. The number of adults on probation has grown at a rate two and a half times that of offender populations in prisons.[15] And for several years states have been encouraged to develop plans and time-tables for implementing a range of alternatives to institutionalization.[16]

Even critics of the early release of prisoners recognize the need for postrelease supervision of offenders in the community. Likewise, few would deny the need for probation programs for those offenders who do not qualify for incarceration. Community supervision will continue to be valued as a means of helping offenders adjust to lawful living *and* of protecting the community. The emphases on work, restitution, and community service will continue to have an appeal as well. Probation will continue to be the most widely used criminal sanction because it is less costly, more humane, and no less effective for most offenders than incarceration.

COMMUNITY-BASED CORRECTIONAL PROGRAMS

Although probation and parole have been used for a century or more, most of the techniques and programs found in most communities today were unheard of until the 1970s. The need for less costly alternatives to incarceration, and the push for effective sanctions which benefit the offender while also protecting the community, have led to the creation of innovative programs. The foundation for all community-based programs, however, continues to be probation and parole casework.

Probation and Parole Casework

Offenders on probation or parole are under the supervision of a *field agent*, sometimes a fully trained social worker but more commonly a career professional selected for the job on the basis of a competitive examination. Often field agents have college degrees, and perhaps, but not necessarily, some training in behavioral science and clinical skills.[17] In general, probation and parole supervision involves some sur-

Probationers and parolees are required to meet with the officers assigned to their cases. Often the officers can help find employment or secure some other community service. Also, the officers clarify the requirements of supervised freedom.

veillance—the probation officer must somehow keep track of the "clients." In routine cases this entails only regular office visits. In addition, the field agent is generally charged with helping offenders adjust, to become "reintegrated" into all aspects of a law-abiding life, including relationships with family, work, and the use of leisure time. The probation or parole officer may provide counseling when needed or, as a kind of clinical "broker," refer cases to the appropriate clinical resources in the community. Field agents may also offer direct assistance by helping offenders find jobs or enroll in educational programs and otherwise guide and assist those who have any sort of adjustment problems. The task of supervising offenders involves both authority and helpfulness, a mixture that is not always easily reconciled. Probation and parole officers also have a duty to "protect the community" and inform the court of any deviation from rules and regulations. In fulfilling this responsibility, they have wide discretion to initiate revocation proceedings if offenders violate rules or conditions or otherwise fail to adjust satisfactorily to community living. This dual loyalty— to the interests of the community in general and to the offenders in their caseload— results in different "styles" of supervision. Some field agents use frequent threats of revocation to obtain conformity; others give priority to casework and counseling as a major supervisory style. There are disagreements among field agents over the importance of their law enforcement role in contrast to their social work functions. And the dual loyalty may lead to conflict with other criminal justice agencies, primarily the police.

The effectiveness of field supervision has been continually hampered by a shortage in staffing, often resulting in excessively large caseloads assigned to each agent. It is commonly agreed that a field agent should have no more than thirty-five or forty felony offenders in a caseload for effective surveillance and supervision. However, many probation officers have more than 100 persons under supervision. Very few carry caseloads of forty or fewer.[18]

Although it is common for offenders to be assigned at random to any probation or parole officer, some agencies are experimenting with caseloads of different sizes and matching specially trained officers with selected offenders. Many probationers and parolees present little risk of committing more crimes and have few adjustment needs, so their supervision need not be rigorous. In others, because they present higher risks or have complex adjustment problems, call for *intensive supervision*. In these cases, specially trained agents may be given reduced caseloads to permit very close surveillance and intensive counseling.[19]

Intensive Supervision Programs

Some offenders need more supervision, punishment, and control than standard casework provides, but not to the extent that they must be incarcerated. A middle ground, or intermediate sanction, is the **intensive supervision program (ISP)**. Georgia's ISP is well known and by 1985 had over 2300 offenders under supervision who otherwise would have had to be incarcerated, adding to the state's overcrowded prison problem. Mostly it is nonviolent offenders already sentenced to prison who are chosen for the program. Yet the offenders in the Georgia ISP have had a higher rate of successfully avoiding later sentences to prison than a comparison group of offenders who have served prison time.[20] The program has strict requirements:

1. Offenders must have five (5) face-to-face contacts per week with a field agent.
2. They must undertake 132 hours of mandatory community service.
3. They must observe a mandatory curfew.
4. They must be employed.

5. They are subject to a weekly check of local arrest records.
6. They are subject to automatic notification of arrest elsewhere via the state Crime Information Network Listing.
7. They must submit to routine and unannounced alcohol and drug testing.[21]

Most states have similar programs today. As in Georgia they provide supervision that is more focused, more intensive, and more aggressive than standard casework, along with swift and certain penalties for violating probationary rules and conditions such as curfews, drug and alcohol testing, and mandatory employment, among others.[22] It should be noted that intensive supervision programs only lessen prison crowding if persons placed in them would otherwise be prison-bound. If only offenders whose crimes would normally result in probation are placed in them, the program goals of saving money or reducing prison crowding are not achieved.

Halfway Houses

The traditional clear distinction between sentences served in the community and those served in correctional institutions is disappearing today. Many modern probation and parole services use a variety of **halfway houses** and **residential treatment centers**, which provide a mixture of partial institutionalization with community supervision.[23] Offenders in halfway houses live in special facilities similar to dormitories or motels rather than in their own homes. Typically, they are confined to these quarters nights and weekends but are allowed to leave during weekdays to go to (or look for) work or school or counseling sessions (**Work release/study release**). This type of program retains some of the security measures demanded of prisons while at the same time allowing selected offenders to retain some community ties, support their families, and gradually adjust to community living.[24]

The term *halfway house* indicates that those living there are half free and half confined, as described above. But halfway houses serve different functions depending on what type of offender one is talking about. They are *halfway-in houses* for offenders placed there in lieu of going to a prison or correctional institution; in such cases

Offenders on work release are required to live in custody when not at work. This is a work release dormitory in Danbury, Connecticut.

the full weight of criminal sanctions is mitigated and offenders are given an opportunity to "pay their debt to society" as well as to maintain societal contacts and receive needed services available in the community. The idea is to divert offenders away from prison.

Halfway-out houses, on the other hand, serve to gradually integrate offenders back into society after their terms in prison. Some inmates, especially those serving lengthy terms, have great difficulty adjusting to the free world, where they do not find the security and stability of the prison environment. Such institutionalized persons have historically had very high recidivism rates immediately after release. The common practice before the implementation of gradual release programs, or work/study release through halfway houses, was to provide an inmate whose term was completed with a new suit of prison-made clothes and a pair of shoes, a bus ticket to any city or town in the state, and $50 in cash. Often the newly released inmate, after years of separation from society, would arrive at a bus station alone, spend the $50, and soon be back to committing criminal acts. Work/study release allows an inmate to be eased back into society by spending the last 3 to 6 months of his or her sentence in a community-based halfway house where employment can be obtained, a bank account opened, one's driver's license renewed, and family and social relationships re-established—all with the support of the halfway house staff. Then, at the end of the sentence, the offender has a job, some savings, a place to live, and a chance to succeed on the outside as a law-abiding citizen.

Halfway-in house residents are typically under the supervision of probation officers or counselors. Halfway-out house residents are usually under the supervision of parole officers. In many jurisdictions probation and parole offices are combined so that a caseworker supervises a combination of persons on probation and parole. In such arrangements it is not uncommon for a counselor to supervise a person on parole who at an earlier time was on his or her probation caseload. In other jurisdictions the probation and parole functions are separated, often with probation operating as a county agency under the direction of the county judge and parole functioning as a state agency under the state department of corrections or the executive branch of the governor.

House Arrest

House arrest requires a person to remain at home during specified hours of the day and night. Permission to leave home is confined to emergencies and for necessary purposes such as employment and grocery shopping. Generally, house arrest is more stringent than intensive supervision programs but the purposes are much the same: to lessen prison crowding and lessen the financial costs of criminal sanctions.

Several states have house arrest programs, but Florida's Community Control Program (FCCP) is the largest.[25] Over 25,000 offenders have been supervised in this way since Florida began the program in the early 1980s. Generally, persons in the program are more serious offenders than those on either standard probation or ISP, but somewhat less serious than those sent to prison. In Florida, house arrest caseloads are no greater than twenty-five per field agent, and the agent is required to make twenty-eight contacts with each person he or she supervises each month. Some of the offenders are also monitored electronically, and most are required to perform community service and to pay restitution.[26]

Electronic Control of Probationers and Parolees

Relatively new and complex issues in probation and parole supervision involve the use of *electronic surveillance and monitoring* systems, which are being introduced

High-Tech Ball and Chain: Electronic Ankle Bracelet

Milton Avol a 63-year-old Beverly Hills neurosurgeon, was sentenced to 30 days. But rather than serving the sentence in jail, Los Angeles Municipal Judge Veronica Simmons McBeth required Avol to be confined inside a prison of his own making—a run-down apartment building he owned, complete with roaches, rats, and squalor. Avol had been charged with hundreds of health, fire, safety, and building code violations, and Judge McBeth decided the appropriate sentence was to keep the slumlord in one of his own buildings.

Rather than assigning guards to make sure Avol stayed in the building, an electronic system was used to monitor his movements so that, if he strayed more than 150 feet from a point inside one of the building's apartments, an alarm would go off in the offices of Trax Monitoring in Auburn, a small town in the foothills of the Sierras, northeast of Sacramento. Trax Monitoring President Jack Wood and his crew would then notify the Los Angeles County attorney, who would notify the judge that Avol had violated his sentence.

The system was fairly tamperproof. A small transmitter was encoded with Avol's name and identification number and attached to a plastic strap to be worn around the ankle. It sent a signal to a receiver in a small box, thereby telling Trax that Avol was at home. A 24-hour record was kept. The box was plugged into a wall socket to keep its battery pack charged, and was also connected to the telephone line. The field monitoring device was programmed to call the Trax Monitoring computer at intervals. If Avol attempted to cut the strap or slide it off his leg, or if he tried to disconnect the box, an alarm would go off at the Trax offices. And if Avol unplugged the telephone, or left it off the hook to keep the monitoring system from making a call, alarms would also be set off.

Several states use similar electronic monitoring systems. The costs range from $7 to $13 a person per day as compared to $40 to $60 a day per person in prison, or $20 to $28 per person per day for a work release program.

The system was the brainchild of Jack Love, a former district court judge in Albuquerque, New Mexico, who got the idea from a Spiderman comic book in which the villain put a bracelet on Spiderman to monitor his whereabouts. Electronics engineers put together a prototype system for Love, and founded a company to manufacture the devices which Milton Avol was required to wear.

SOURCE: J.E. Ferrell, "Electronic Ankle Bracelet Keeps Crooks Confined without Bars," *Birmingham Post Herald*, July 24, 1987, p. 3C. Reprinted in Belinda Rodgers McCarthy and Bernard J. McCarthy, Jr., *Community-Based Corrections*, 2nd ed. (Pacific Grove, CA: Brooks/ Cole, 1991), pp. 126–127, who reprinted it with permission from the *San Francisco Examiner*, 1987.

---

as prisons become more crowded, probation is granted to higher-risk inmates more frequently, and early parole is increasingly being used to alleviate prison overcrowding. Many sophisticated electronic devices are used today to track and to otherwise monitor probationers and parolees. All require the offender to wear (or to have medically inserted under the skin) some form of electronic beeper, microphone, or distance-activated alarm. One of the simplest such devices is a wristband or belt that sends a signal to a probation officer if the probationer strays more than a hundred yards or so from home. This has permitted a form of house incarceration as an alternative to jail or prison for those offenders who are not good risks for full community freedom. Devices fixed to the offender's telephone, which is randomly called five or six times a day, alert the probation staff if the offender fails to answer in a given amount of time.

Electronic tracking requires offenders to wear beeper devices that can be followed around the community by computer monitors. This provides information as to where the offender is at any given time and may lead to knowledge of companions or provide leads when crimes in a particular area of the community are reported.

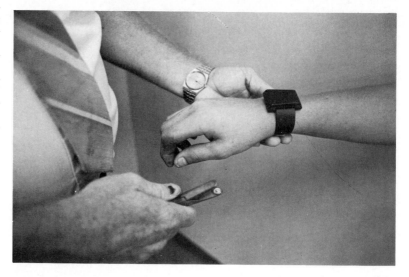

As of 1988, more than 2000 offenders in thirty-three states were being electronically supervised, and almost half of them were in Florida and Michigan.[27] Approximately one-third of them were property or drug offenders, about one-fourth were traffic offenders, and about 10 percent were convicted of violent crimes. Usually, offenders must pay the expenses of their own electronic monitoring according to a sliding scale based on the offender's ability to pay.[28]

The full use of electronic surveillance is still to be felt. Problems exist, of course, with the technology. For instance, locations close to radio stations, poor telephone wiring, special features on telephones such as call-waiting, along with power surges and other computer complications interfere with consistent and accurate telephonic communications.[29] Also, family members may be inconvenienced in their use of the telephone. And what are the ramifications of probationer tracking on others who are not criminal offenders? If a probationer under surveillance visits a friend not on probation, the visit and the relationship are still known to the probation staff and perhaps the police. If the probationer gets in trouble, can the electronic record of the visit be used legally to indict the friend in a conspiracy? These and other sticky issues have not yet been resolved.

Also, electronic devices cannot monitor some kinds of illegal activity. For example, offenders with beepers can still become intoxicated or sell drugs from their homes.[30]

Shock Incarceration and Boot Camp

One program with particular public appeal combines a relatively short period of imprisonment in a strictly regulated environment followed by another period of intensive supervision in the community. Known as **shock incarceration** or **boot camp**, it consists of 90 to 180 days in a military-like atmosphere in which offenders are required to participate in close-order drill, spit and polish military dress and behavior, physical fitness programs, and other activities which closely resemble *Marine boot camp*. Each offender is recommended for the program after being sentenced to a regular prison term, and generally must be a first-time prisoner serving a sentence of less than 7 years. Participation is voluntary and the prisoner may choose to leave the program at any time. Of course, prisoners may also be terminated from the program due to their lack of cooperation, misbehavior, or insufficient progress.[31]

The staff "drill instructors" are specially selected corrections officers who are expected to be good role models and counselors, and who must be able to provide positive reinforcement and support designed to bring about behavioral changes in the program's participants. The program seeks to develop personal pride in the prisoners. In addition to the other parts of the boot camp regimen, the prisoners are required to participate in group treatment programs, re-education programs, substance abuse education classes, and prerelease classes.[32]

Following the boot camp period, the offenders are released to an intensive supervision program where they serve the remainder of their sentence. Preliminary research indicates that prisoners who participate in this program are more positive about their prison experience than prisoners in the regular prison program. Of course, since the participants are carefully screened and selected, and are then allowed greater access to treatment opportunities than regular prison inmates, it is difficult to determine whether the discipline they receive in the boot camp or the opportunities for treatment are responsible for the positive results.

Restitution and Community Service

One of the failings of imprisonment is that the victims of crimes gain no benefit from the incarceration of those who perpetrated them other than being protected from further victimization during the period of incarceration. One solution to this problem is **restitution**, or requiring the criminal to repay the victim for his or her losses. The idea is to restore victims to the conditions they enjoyed prior to the crime by repairing the damage, replacing the stolen property, or in some other way "making it right." The amount of restitution is calculated based on the harm done, or the amount of money or property stolen or damaged. Also, the costs of medical treatment or the costs associated with lost time from employment can be calculated for restitution. Restitution can give the victim a sense that justice has been done, a feeling of equity which is not usually created by the traditional courtroom experience of trial and sentencing. Also, by making amends the offender enhances his or her own likelihood of rehabilitation.[33]

Similarly, when a person is locked up in a prison in order to pay his or her "debt to society," it is difficult to see how society is compensated. So, **community service** programs have been developed which require offenders to perform some work for, or make some definite contribution to, the community harmed by the criminal behavior. Usually the amount and type of community service is computed by the number of hours or days the offender is expected to perform some type of work in the community.

Restitution and community service programs have a universal appeal. The payment and work is viewed as punishment for the offender, but the victim or the community also gains some tangible benefit, or payment, in compensation for the crime. And this is accomplished with much less cost to the public than incarceration. Also, the emphasis on work and employment for the offender contributes to a belief that something good can result from the crime experience.

SPECIAL PROBLEMS AND NEEDS OF FEMALE OFFENDERS

Although only about 16 percent of all those on probation or parole are women, criminal justice scholars and professionals recognize that special problems and needs exist for female offenders. Over half of all female offenders have children, and many of them are divorced or single and carry the responsibility for the care and support of their children alone. This means these women are often poorly equipped to provide for the parenting needs of their children, either financially, physically, or emotionally.

These problems are especially acute for women sentenced to prison because incarceration always disrupts family relationships. Since women offenders are more likely to accept their family responsibilities than male offenders generally appear to be, the disruptions caused by their arrest, prosecution, and incarceration are especially problematic for family life.

It may be that the courts have in some measure already recognized the special needs of women. As we saw in Part I, female offenders comprise about 17 percent of the total number of arrests.[34] But as we also saw in Chap. 13, female inmates make up only 4 percent of the total prison population. Perhaps the discrepancy can be explained by the willingness of the courts to sentence female offenders to community-based correctional institutions more often than they do male offenders.

Community-based correctional programs certainly allow female offenders to maintain their family relationships, and when the full resources of community programs are made available to these women they are often able to secure the necessary education and training to obtain well-paying jobs. Economic independence and effective parenting skills, therefore, often are the focus of the community-based correctional approach for female offenders. Vocational training, job development and placement, and followup services are very helpful in the effort to divert female offenders away from prison.

Family services are also made available to female offenders more commonly than to male offenders. Temporary release, or furlough, programs allow mothers to receive the emotional rewards of child care while remaining under correctional supervision. Developing parenting skills is the focus of group training, and programs relating to spouse abuse and substance abuse are geared to address the special needs of female offenders. And aside from criminal entanglements, many women offenders must also deal with their own negative self-images, gender discrimination, and social disadvantages. These problems can be addressed in community-based programs better than by incarceration in a distant institution.

Community-based facilities for female offenders often resemble college dormitories, with space to hang clothes and other personal items.

In addition to supervision, probationers are subject to rules and conditions fixed by the courts, while parolees must abide by similar rules fixed by parole boards. Usually these are standard rules that apply to all probationers and parolees, but occasionally special rules or prohibitions are imposed if, in the opinion of a judge or a board, they are necessary to help a particular offender adjust and to prevent him or her from committing new crimes. For example, a sex offender may be required to participate in psychiatric counseling as a special condition of probation or parole.

Standard Rules and Conditions

The standard regulations for probation are virtually identical to those for parole. For the most part, they are enacted to control a wide variety of activities, particularly those that might lead the offender to commit new offenses.[35] For example, it is common to require probationers and parolees to refrain from associating with "known criminals," to abstain from liquor or to use it only in moderation, not to possess firearms, to remain in the community, not to change jobs, and not to marry or move without the permission of their field agents. In general, they must keep their activities and whereabouts known to the authorities and not change status in any way without the prior notification and consent of the probation or parole service. In addition, they may be required to maintain a "cooperative" posture with supervising officers. These rules and conditions, as well as any special conditions, are normally given to potential probationers and parolees in printed form with a requirement that they sign a document agreeing to abide by them if they wish community sentences.[36]

Whatever the specific set of rules and conditions imposed in any jurisdiction, a person on probation or parole is held to a higher standard of morality and is more restricted in his or her movements than citizens not under such a sentence. Violation of any rule or condition is grounds for **revocation** with subsequent incarceration. A probationer is under the control of both the probation officer and the sentencing judge, and like the Sword of Damocles, imprisonment constantly hangs over his or her head. Parolees also face possible return to prison for any infraction of the rules or conditions imposed on them.

Special Rules and Conditions

Both probationers and parolees are convicted felons—some courts view parolees as merely "inmates outside the walls"—and as such have lost many of the rights of free citizens and are subject to restraints and controls not applicable to law-abiding persons. This poses the problem of what kinds of rules and conditions may be imposed. Are there are limits, Constitutional or otherwise, on such restraints? Some experts argue that just about any rule is permissible, except those that violate the Eighth Amendment prohibition against cruel and unusual punishment, since both probationers and parolees are free to refuse community sentences and opt for prison if they object to the conditions. At best, this argument seems impractical and coercive. Initially, most probationers and parolees are willing to agree to almost any condition to escape confinement, preferring instead to challenge the appropriateness of various requirements once they are on the street.

Although there are exceptions, challenges to conditions are not normally over the common requirements that the offender remain law-abiding, sober, and keep his

Special Conditions

1: Essay

An offender convicted of assaulting a police officer was placed on probation for 2 years by the court. In addition to imposing the standard rules of supervision, the sentencing judge ordered the offender to pay the medical costs incurred by the victim and write an essay entitled "Why the Police Should Be Entitled to the Respect of the Citizenry," to be submitted to the court for approval.

2: Go to Church

A youthful offender convicted of robbery (purse snatching) was placed on probation for 3 years with a special condition that he "regularly attend a church of his choice" and present evidence to the court that he was complying with this condition.

3: Checks and Balances

A woman convicted for forgery, writing bad checks to a number of businesses in the community, was placed on 2 years probation by a judge with a special condition that she refrain from having any checking accounts during that time. ■

or her whereabouts known. More often litigated are the *special conditions* attached to the sentencing of a particular offender or class of offenders. Unique or peculiar interpretations of essentially vague conditions, such as a requirement to "cooperate with your probation officer," can also become the basis of litigation when given as the reasons for revocation. (See Field Practice A.)

It would appear that special, unusual, and possibly Constitutionally improper conditions are imposed more often on probationers than on parolees. At any rate, the frequency of litigation is greater in probation than in parole cases. The relative prevalence of unusual conditions in probation is perhaps explained by the fact that in most jurisdictions any sentencing judge can set whatever rules and conditions he or she deems fit, without review by any centralized authority. Although it is true that judges are trained in the law and normally are sensitive to Constitutional rights, there are literally hundreds of independent courts throughout the nation; consequently, probation conditions are set by many different individuals, even within a single state, resulting in much variation in content and purpose. In contrast, parole rules are usually standard within a particular state. They are set by a central paroling authority (the parole board) and offer little opportunity for individual parole agents to make rules. There are provisions in some places for setting special parole conditions for particular types of offenders (e.g., narcotics addicts), and in many places a parole agent has discretion to require some forms of unique performance under the general condition that the parolee must "cooperate" with his or her parole officer.

Some questionable conditions, some of them quite excessive, have occurred mostly in probation cases. Sometimes a probationer has challenged a rule in court claiming it is excessively "onerous," unrelated to the offense, and unnecessary as part of supervision; or a probationer may claim that a particular condition should be eliminated because it is "impossible" to comply with. Still other challenges seek relief from conditions that deny or chill Constitutional rights. The effective challenge of a probationary condition is often hampered by the contract the offender signed promising to obey the condition. And legislation in most states is silent regarding probation or parole conditions, making any challenge to them that much more difficult. However, a number of appeals have originated in California, which requires that conditions of community supervision be "reasonable."[37] In one case, the California Court of

Appeals of the Second District reversed the revocation of probation for an unmarried woman convicted of robbery who had become pregnant when one of the conditions of her probation was that she not become pregnant until she married. [38] The court applied the following test:

> A condition of probation which 1) has no relationship to the crime of which the offender was convicted, 2) related to conduct which is not in itself criminal, and 3) requires or forbids conduct which is not reasonably related to future criminality, does not serve the statutory ends of probation and is invalid. [39]

The court concluded that "appellant's future pregnancy was unrelated to robbery. Becoming pregnant while unmarried is a misfortune, not a crime." [40]

In the past it was a fairly common practice in some states to use *banishment*, called *sundown parole*, as a condition of probation. In these instances the offender would be placed on probation and instructed to leave the city or the state until his or her sentence expired. Appellate courts usually voided banishment orders. In the 1930s the Michigan Court, for example, held improper an order requiring a probationer to remove himself from the state for 5 years [41] and in another case voided an order requiring a defendant convicted of disturbing the peace to move from his neighborhood. [42]

Other special conditions that have been found improper have been varied. With respect to the probation conditions described in Field Practice A, a District of Columbia court found it improper to require an offender to write an essay on "Why the Police Should Be Entitled to the Respect of the Citizenry," [43] and conditions requiring compulsory church attendance generally have been held unconstitutional. However, conditions requiring a probationer to refrain from smoking or drinking alcoholic beverages have been upheld. [44]

An even more complex issue arises when a probationer or parolee is alleged to have violated some standard of behavior not specifically listed in the signed rules and conditions. Often the list of requirements ends with a broad, catch-all condition like "I agree to lead a clean, temperate, and honest life," which gives very wide discretion to the field agent.

SEARCHING PROBATIONERS AND PAROLEES

An offender sentenced to prison is totally under the physical control of the state. Inmates retain many of the Constitutional rights afforded to all citizens, but restrictions on search and seizure under the Fourth Amendment are not among them. Prison inmates can have their persons and cells searched at any time, randomly or at the whim of prison officials, without warrants and with no need on the part of the authorities to show probable cause. Whether the same broad right exists to search parolees and probationers under community sentence is not an easy question to answer because of different legal interpretations in different states and because the legal status of a parolee is not quite the same as that of a probationer. (See Field Practice B.)

A number of courts take the position that a parolee is an inmate serving part of his or her sentence on the street by the grace of the parole board. According to this view, parolees as "inmates outside the walls" can be searched in exactly the same way as prisoners still in confinement. Probationers, on the other hand, have never been inmates. For this reason, some courts allow parolees to be searched without probable

Legal Search?

1: Dorm Visit

Police suspected a college student on probation had committed the drug offense of selling marijuana. However, they did not have sufficient evidence to obtain a warrant to search his dormitory room. Detectives approached his probation officer and asked that they be allowed to accompany him on an "unannounced home visit" to the student's room. Such visits, though rarely carried out, were authorized as a condition of the probation agreement signed by the student. The probation officer, accompanied by two detectives, entered the student's room one night about 11 p.m. They discovered 2 pounds of marijuana and other drug paraphernalia in the small closet shared by the probationer and his roommate. This evidence was seized and the probationer was arrested. His roommate, a student not on probation and without a criminal record, was also arrested as an accomplice.

2: Bloodstains

Following a particularly brutal rape-murder, the police conducted a roundup of "known sex deviates" currently on parole. In each instance they searched the residence of the parolee. During one such search police discovered a piece of bloodstained clothing belonging to the parolee, seized it as evidence, and arrested the individual for the crime. ■

cause, along the inmate model, but require probationer searches to conform to Fourth Amendment restrictions the way they would for any law-abiding citizen.

This distinction is by no means universally accepted, however. On one occasion a New York court found being on probation insufficient grounds to deny the legality of a search. This occurred in *People v. Chinnici*, a case in which a probation officer caused a probationer, Chinnici, to be arrested for a traffic violation and his car searched after receiving an anonymous tip that he was in possession of a gun. If Chinnici had been on parole, the search would have raised no legal questions. But when the police officer found the gun in the trunk of Chinnici's car, and its presence there was then used as evidence against him, Chinnici moved to have the evidence suppressed on grounds that the search that discovered it was unconstitutional. The court nevertheless permitted the search, stating that the necessities of supervision and the potential danger to the public required that a probationer and his or her dwelling and automobile must be subject to search at any time.[45]

In regard to parole, in some parts of the country the authority of parole officers to search is justified by the written agreement paroled inmates are required to sign, giving permission in advance for parole authorities to search their persons or premises.[46] Under this agreement, it is assumed that the parolee has consented to any search, making a warrant or a valid arrest an unnecessary prerequisite.[47]

In about half the states, a parolee may only be searched, apprehended, or detained pursuant to an ***administrative warrant***, a parole board "hold" order issued in the belief that the parolee has violated some condition of supervision. Still other states allow field agents the discretion to do the same, sometimes with police assistance, without any such warrant or other document.

MODEL CONDITIONS OF COMMUNITY SUPERVISION

Because the conditions imposed on probationers and parolees vary so greatly from place to place, it is not possible to present a representative list of them. However, the drafters of the *Model Penal Code*[48] have prepared a set of "reasonable" conditions for probationers which courts might follow if they choose. (See Box 15.1.) Most of them are not unusual, although they are by no means uniformly imposed by courts across the nation and, although are specifically for probationers, apply to parolees as well. The most controversial condition is the final one, requiring any special condition to be related to rehabilitation and not unduly restrictive or "incompatible" with the probationer's "freedom of conscience."

The drafters of the American Bar Association's *Standards Relating to Probation* similarly suggest that no condition be imposed that is incompatible with the probationer's "freedom of religion."[48] The National Advisory Commission's standard, *Corrections* would require only those conditions "necessary to provide a benefit to the offender and protection to the public safety." It also recommends that the conditions imposed in an individual case be tailored to meet the particular needs of that offender and his or her community, and that the mechanical imposition of uniform conditions on all defendants be avoided.[49]

SUMMARY

This chapter dealt with the origins and history of probation as a major form of sentencing imposed on criminals in our society, and the differences between probation and parole. Probationers are sentenced directly to community correctional services under the supervision of a probation officer without serving prison terms, whereas parolees serve some time in prison and then are released back into the community under the supervision of a parole officer. Probation and parole together make up the major forms of community correctional services. The rules and conditions of probation and parole are virtually identical, and the differences in the supervisory duties of probation officers and parole field agents are minimal. In fact, in some jurisdictions the same officials handle both types of offenders and are called probation and parole officers depending on the role they play in regard to different offenders in their caseloads.

There are some important variations in community correctional practices. For example, many jurisdictions today support halfway houses (halfway in or out of prison), where offenders are locked in at night and/or on weekends but allowed to work in the community during weekdays. Halfway houses are not jails or prisons, but dormitory-like structures located in the communities where the offenders under supervision live. There are also house arrest, correctional "boot camps," and provisions for community service and victim restitution in many places. Some jurisdictions also use controls beyond simple supervision by case officers. Electronic devices, beepers of one kind or another, are affixed to some persons on probation or parole, and their movements tracked by electronic receivers. This provides close surveillance and allows somewhat higher-risk offenders to serve community sentences, and it is also cost-effective.

There are a number of arguments for and against community sentences. Those who oppose them generally feel that they are too lenient a punishment for what the criminals did and that their use does not protect the community at large from the risk of further crimes being committed by the offenders so sentenced. On the other hand, proponents of community corrections cite the greatly reduced costs of community sentencing in comparison to imprisonment, including the ability of probationers and parolees to support their families and pay taxes. Moreover, proponents of community corrections point to statistics showing the practice is no less successful in preventing

---

BOX 15.1

Conditions of . . . Probation

The Court, as a condition of its order, may require the defendant:

a. to meet his family responsibilities;

b. to devote himself to a specific employment or occupation;

c. to undergo available medical or psychiatric treatment and to enter and remain in a specified institution, when required for that purpose;

d. to pursue a prescribed secular course of study or vocational training;

e. to attend or reside in a facility established for the instruction, recreation or residence of persons on probation;

f. to refrain from frequenting unlawful or disreputable places or consorting with disreputable persons;

g. to have in his possession no firearm or other dangerous weapon unless granted written permission;

h. to make restitution of the fruits of his crime or to make reparation, in an amount he can afford to pay, for the loss or damage caused thereby;

i. to remain within the jurisdiction of the Court and to notify the Court or the probation officer of any change in his address or his employment;

j. to report as directed to the Court or the probation officer and to permit the officer to visit his home;

k. to post a bond, with or without surety, conditioned on the performance of any of the foregoing obligations;

l. to satisfy any other conditions reasonably related to the rehabilitation of the defendant and not unduly restrictive of his liberty or incompatible with his freedom of conscience.

---

repeat crimes than prison—that in most cases, in fact it is more successful in reducing such recidivism.

NOTES

1. U.S. Department of Justice, *Probation and Parole*, 1989 (Washington, DC: Bureau of Justice Statistics, November 1990).

2. Federal Bureau of Prisons, *National Prisoner Statistics* (Washington, DC: U.S. Department of Justice, 1990).

3. John Augustus, *A Report of the Labors of John Augustus, for the Last Ten Years, in the Aid of the Unfortunate* (Boston: Wright & Hasty, Printers, 1852), pp. 4–5. Reprinted as *John Augustus, First Probation Officer* (New York: National Probation Association, 1939).

4. Ibid., *John Augustus, First Probation Officer*, pp. 40–41.

5. Clemens Bartollas, *Introduction to Corrections* (New York: Harper & Row, 1981), p. 148.

6. David J. Rothman, *Conscience and Convenience: The Asylum and Its Alternatives in Progressive America* (Boston: Little, Brown, 1980), p. 85.

7. Bureau of Justice Statistics, *Report to the Nation on Crime and Justice* (Washington, DC: U.S. Department of Justice, 1988), p. 124.

8. Ibid., p. 123.

9. James Bonta and Paul Gendreau, "Re-examining the Cruel and Unusual Punishment of Prison Life," *Law and Human Behavior* 14 (1990): 347–372.

10. President's Commission on Law Enforcement and Administration of Justice, *The Challenge of Crime in a Free Society* (Washington, DC: U.S. Government Printing Office, 1967), p. 159.

11. Vernon Fox, *Introduction to Corrections*, 3rd ed. (Englewood Cliffs, NJ: Prentice-Hall, 1985), pp. 164–165.

12. See Bureau of Justice Statistics, *Examining Recidivism*, Special Report NC5-96501 (Washington, DC: U.S. Department of Justice, 1985).

13. Joan Petersilia et al., *Granting Felons Probation* (Santa Monica, CA: Rand Corp., 1985).

14. Bureau of Justice Statistics, *Examining Recidivism*.

15. Bureau of Justice Statistics, *Report to Nation on Crime and Justice* (Washington, DC: U.S. Department of Justice, 1988), p. 124.

16. National Advisory Commission on Criminal Justice Standards and Goals, *Corrections* (Washington, DC: U.S. Department of Justice, 1973), Standard 7.1, p. 237.

17. See Herman Piven and Abraham Alcabes, *The Crisis of Qualified Manpower for Criminal Justice: An Analytic Assessment with Guidelines for New Policy, Vol. I: Probation and Parole* (Washington, DC: U.S. Department of Health, Education, and Welfare, n.d.); and John Stratton, "Correctional Workers: Counseling Con Men?" *Federal Probation* 37 (1973): 14.

18. President's Commission, *Corrections*. See also Stuart Adams, "Some Findings from Correctional Caseload Research," in Robert M. Carter and Leslie T. Wilkins (eds.), *Probation and Parole* (New York: John Wiley and Sons, 1970), pp. 364–378.

19. See Edward J. Latessa, *Intensive Probation: An Evaluation of the Effectiveness of an Intensive Diversion Unit* (Ann Arbor, MI: University Microfilms International, 1979).

20. Billie Erwin and Lawrence A. Bennett, "New Dimensions in Probation: Georgia's Experience with Intensive Probation Supervision (IPS)," *Research in Brief* (Wash-

ington, DC: U.S. Government Printing Office, 1987); Billie S. Erwin, "Tools for the Modern Probation Officer," *Crime and Delinquency* 36 (1) (1990): 87–111. See also, generally, Belinda Rogers McCarthy and Bernard J. McCarthy, Jr., *Community-Based Corrections* (Pacific Grove, CA: Brooks/Cole, 1991).

21. Erwin and Bennett, op. cit., p. 2.

22. James M. Byrne, Arthur J. Lurigio, and Christopher Baird, "The Effectiveness of the New Intensive Supervision Programs, *Research in Corrections* 2 (2) (1989): 11.

23. Donald J. Thalheimer, *Cost Analysis of Correctional Standards: Halfway Houses* (Washington, DC: U.S. Department of Justice, 1975), Vols. I and II.

24. See Marguerite Q. Warren, *Correctional Treatment in Community Settings: A Report of Current Research* (Rockville, MD: National Institute of Mental Health, 1971); Oliver J. Keller, Jr., and Benedict S. Alper, *Halfway Houses: Community-Centered and Treatment* (Lexington, MA: Lexington Books, 1970); Bertram S. Griggs and Gary R. McCune, "Community-Based Correctional Programs: A Survey and Analysis," *Federal Probation* 36 (June 1972): 7; Robert M. Carter, Daniel Glaser, and Leslie T. Wilkins (eds.), *Correctional Institutions* (Philadelphia: Lippincott, 1972).

25. Byrne, Lurigio, and Baird, op. cit., p. 16; also, see S. Christopher Baird and Dennis Wagner, "Measuring Diversion: The Florida Community Control Program," *Crime and Delinquency* 36 (1) (1990): 112–125.

26. Baird and Wagner, op. cit.

27. Annesley Schmidt, *Electronic Monitoring of Offenders Increases*, NIJ Reports (Washington, DC: U.S. Government Printing Office, 1989), pp. 2–5.

28. Ibid., p. 4.

29. McCarthy and McCarthy, op. cit., pp. 126–127.

30. Erwin, "Tools for the Modern Probation Officer."

31. Doris L. McKenzie and James W. Shaw, *Inmate Adjustment and Change during Shock Incarceration*, Paper presented at the annual meeting of the American Society of Criminology, Chicago, 1988. Cited in McCarthy and McCarthy, op. cit.

32. Ibid.

33. Douglas C. McDonald, *Restitution and Community Service* (Washington, DC: U.S. Government Printing Office, 1988).

34. Bureau of Justice Statistics, *Women in Prison* (Washington, DC: U.S. Department of Justice, March 1991).

35. Walter L. Barkdull, "Probation: Call It Control and Mean It," *Federal Probation* 40 (1976): 5. See also *Rules* (Washington, DC: U.S. Parole Commission, 1979).

36. Nat R. Arluke, "A Summary of Parole Rules—Thirteen Years Later," *Crime and Delinquency* 15 (1969): 267.

37. California Penal Code, Sec. 203.1 (Supp. 1966).

38. *People v. Dominquez*, 256 Cal. App. 623, 64 Cal. Rptr. 290 (Ct. of App. 1967).

39. Ibid., p. 293.

40. Ibid.

41. *People v. Baum*, 251 Mich. 187, 231 N.W. 95 (1930).

42. *People v. Smith*, 252 Mich. 4, 232 N.W. 397 (1930). See also Note, "Banishment: A Medieval Tactic in Modern Criminal Law," *Utah Law Review* 5 (1957): 365.

43. *Butler v. District of Columbia*, 346 F. 2d 789 (D.C. Cir. 1965).

44. *Jones v. Commonwealth*, 185 Va. 335, 38 S.E. 2d 444 (1946).

45. *People v. Chinnici*, 273 N.Y.S. 2d 583 (1968).

46. See Arluke, op. cit., p. 274.

47. Note, "Striking the Balance between Privacy Supervision: The 4th Amendment and Parole and Probation Officer Searches of Parolees and Probationers," *N.Y.U. Law Review* 51 (1976): 803.

48. American Law Institute, *Model Penal Code*, proposed official draft (Philadelphia:

American Law Institute, 1962); American Bar Association, *Standards Relating to Probation*, approved draft (New York: Institute of Judicial Administration, 1970), Sec. 3.2, pp. 44–45.

49. National Advisory Commission, *Corrections*, Standard 5.4, p. 158.

Suggested Readings

Ball, Richard A., C. Ronald Huff, and J. Robert Lily. *House Arrest and Correctional Policy: Doing Time at Home*. Newbury Park, CA: Sage, 1988.

Cohen, Stanley. *Visions of Social Control*. Cambridge: Polity Press, 1985.

Giallombardo, Rose. *Society of Women*. New York: Wiley, 1966.

Keller, Oliver J., and Benedict S. Alper. *Halway Houses: Community Centered Corrections and Treatment*. Lexington, MA: Raytheon/Heath, 1970.

McCarthy, Belinda, and Bernard McCarthy. *Community-Based Corrections*, 2nd ed. Pacific Grove, CA: Brooks/Cole, 1991.

McCarthy, Belinda (ed.). *Intermediate Punishments: Intensive Supervision, Home Confinement and Electronic Monitoring*. Mousey, NJ: Criminal Justice Press, 1987.

Morris, Norval, and Michael Tonry. *Between Prison and Probation: Intermediate Punishments in a Rational Sentencing System*. Cary, NC: Oxford University Press, 1990.

Niederberger. W. V., and W. F. Wagner. *Electronic Monitoring of Convicted Offenders: A Field Test*. Washington, DC: National Institute of Justice, 1985.

Discussion Questions

1. Describe the history of probation.
2. Explain the cases for and the case against community corrections. Discuss the standard probation process and compare it with intensive supervision programs (ISP).
3. Discuss the usefulness and effectiveness of house arrest and electronic monitoring of offenders.
4. Explain restitution and community service programs and discuss their usefulness.
5. Describe the special problems and needs of female offenders.

The Juvenile Justice System

16

Juvenile Crime and Juvenile Justice

Acriminal justice professor in a class on juvenile delinquency described to the students some of her own behaviors as an adolescent which could be considered delinquent. She told of shoplifting candy from a neighborhood store at the age of 11, of running away from home at 14, of purchasing and consuming beer at the age of 16. Then, after that "confession," she asked the students to share with the class their own juvenile activities. Those students, several of whom were barely above juvenile age at the time, described a wide range of behaviors.

One girl told how she had punctured the tires of a former boyfriend's car and had scraped the length of the car with a key causing a deep scratch in the paint. A young man told how he and some friends had stolen cases of beer and other items and taken them out of the backdoor of a convenience store at which one of his friends was employed. Another told of setting fire to a vacant lot, another of purchasing and using marijuana, another of frequently sneaking in the backdoor of a neighborhood movie theater. A young woman told of entering a neighbor's house through an unlocked window and stealing cosmetics. A young man told of stealing an automobile and driving it until it ran out of gas and then abandoning it in a distant part of his hometown. Several students said they had shoplifted, illegally consumed alcohol, skipped school, and committed vandalism. No one in the class admitted to being arrested by the police for anything other than traffic violations.

After class, another student privately told the professor how he had committed several serious offenses, including armed robbery, as a juvenile and had spent 7 months in a state training school. Others subsequently also told her privately about being victimized in a variety of ways, including being raped.

While visiting the local juvenile detention center on the same day as the class discussion, the same professor learned that the youngsters there included a 13-year-old boy who had been arrested for the third time in a year for rape and sexual assault, an 11-year-old girl who was reported to be engaged in prostitution, a 16-year-old gang member who police said had fired a gun into a group of children in a school yard, and a 14-year-old girl who had reportedly stabbed another girl to death.

The youths at the detention center appeared to the professor to be very different from her students in the college classroom, different in their social backgrounds, educational opportunities, and prospects for the future. But was there really a difference? Are the experiences of you and your classmates consistent with those of the class described above? Do you believe the students told the truth about their own behavior? Is serious delinquent behavior rare—or is it so common that many, if not most, of those in your age group committed delinquent acts as juveniles? What is the difference between normal adolescent misconduct and juvenile delinquency? This chapter attempts to shed light on these and other issues related to juvenile delinquency and to explain how juveniles are handled in the criminal justice network through a group of agencies called the "juvenile justice system" that is separate from but related to the system that handles adult criminals.

About This Chapter: The Child-Savers' Movement

Until about a century ago, adolescent and child offenders, some admittedly capable of committing—or even guilty of committing—serious crimes, were processed through the adult criminal justice system, a practice having its roots in the early centuries of European common law. That system was brutal and stigmatizing, and not really effective in rehabilitating hardened adult criminals, let alone children, who were often victimized by it and turned into hardened adult criminals themselves because of its brutality.

Then in the early industrial years of American society, primarily the decades immediately after the Civil War, there started a movement to set up a separate juvenile justice system aimed more at rehabilitating young offenders than punishing them. This was part of a larger series of efforts collectively known as the *child-savers' movement*,[1] in which prominent American citizens—often women—set about improving the general living conditions of poor urban youngsters. Among other issues such as child labor and the treatment of orphans, these "child savers" felt that trying young offenders in adult criminal courts and imprisoning them in adult jails, workhouses, and penitentiaries was unnecessary and even counterproductive. Young offenders, they felt, were not yet hardened in their criminality—there was some hope that, if treated with a helping hand rather than a brutalizing one, they might reform and escape a life of crime.

The result of these efforts was the creation and establishment of the juvenile criminal justice system as we know it today, which began with the first juvenile court in Illinois in 1899 and spread from there to all the states in our nation.[2]

No system of state intervention ever built had higher hopes or more noble purposes. In contrast to the adult criminal justice system, which is punitive in its intent and stern and somber in its operations, the juvenile justice system was intended from the start to be "beneficent," to help youthful offenders, not punish them. Treatment, education, rehabilitation were its battle cries.

But the creation of a new system of justice is fraught with such problems as defining what crimes and what individuals are to be covered by it, what procedures to be used, and what outcomes from it are to be hoped for versus the outcomes actually realized. Moreover, in our society it involves the creation of a set of laws and procedures that ultimately must meet the various tests of Constitutionality under our system of government.

Like earlier chapters on adult criminal justice, this one traces the decision steps in delinquency processing from referral to aftercare. But it also examines issues such as the cutoff point between juvenile and adult and what juvenile behaviors other than outright criminality should be dealt with by the system, and how. It notes an important evolution of the system into two processes: one for dealing with children who commit acts that would be criminal if performed by adults, and one for dealing with children simply in need of state supervision or intervention.

Whether the high hopes of the early child savers have been realized is still being debated. Today, we preserve the philosophy of separate norms for juvenile justice yet find we must deal realistically with serious violent crimes committed by young people where juvenile processing seems too lenient on the one hand and too little able to protect the rest of us on the other. And as with all the other topics relating to criminal justice discussed in earlier chapters, there are conflicting views as to whether juvenile delinquency should be dealt with separately from adult criminality, and if so, to what extent juvenile criminals should be handled more or less harshly than adult criminals. We start our examination there.

JUVENILE DELINQUENCY AND THE CONSERVATIVE CRIME CONTROL MODEL[3]

Conservatives believe that lenient handling of juvenile offenders contributes to high rates of adult criminality. Much crime, they believe, is committed by a relatively small number of juvenile delinquents who believe they can get away with it because of their age. Conservatives point out that the seriousness of juvenile offenses has increased in recent years. No longer is juvenile delinquency a form of normal adolescent adventurism. Rather, serious crimes are committed by juveniles emboldened by their belief that, if caught, they will suffer only the wrist slap of a lenient juvenile justice system.

The conservative answer to this problem is to deter potential juvenile offenders by treating more harshly those who get caught. Detention of delinquents for longer periods of time in secure facilities, transfer of juvenile cases to the adult criminal justice system for more serious treatment, a crackdown on adolescent drug abuse, the removal of privacy protections for juvenile offenders, and a renewed commitment to discipline in the schools will help reduce the high rates of juvenile crime and will lessen the likelihood that juvenile offenders will become adult criminals. In the conservative view, even capital punishment for youthful criminals should be used as a deterrent.

JUVENILE DELINQUENCY AND THE LIBERAL CRIME CONTROL MODEL

According to the liberal view, juveniles who come to the attention of the police and juvenile authorities are deprived educationally and economically and lack opportunities to succeed legitimately. Liberals point out that most juveniles who are arrested have committed only minor offenses—often infractions so minor they would not even be considered illegal if committed by adults. But once arrested they are labeled delinquent by the police and other authorities in society, and then treated as criminals. Not only does this promote poor self-images for such youthful offenders, but it creates an atmosphere of antagonism between juveniles and adult authority figures. And incarcerating juveniles in adult institutions only escalates their fall into full-blown criminality.

The answer to the serious problem of juvenile delinquency proposed by liberals is to divert youthful offenders away from the damaging effects of the justice system, especially those produced by confinement facilities. Problem children should be treated through rehabilitation programs. An expanded use of juvenile probation programs staffed by caring, professional child care workers will reverse the harmful environmental effects the delinquent youngsters have encountered in their neighborhoods and families. In the liberal view, juveniles have been treated badly by the law historically, and are entitled to the full protection of due process and other Constitutional guarantees that are the right of every citizen.

We will see echoes of these arguments throughout this chapter.

THE NATURE AND SCOPE OF JUVENILE DELINQUENCY

Definitions of Delinquency

Juvenile delinquency represents many things to many people. To the police, delinquents may be merely underage criminals; to school authorities, they may be truants or the boy or girl who smokes in the washroom. To some parents, delinquents are other people's ungovernable children, and to some storekeepers delinquents are gangs loitering on the corner. Even experts who study and work with "problem children" lack consensus on the limits of the concept. Some authorities define delinquency as "emotionally disturbed behavior"; others see delinquency as "persistently antisocial behavior"; some define delinquency as "behavior in an adolescent disappointing beyond reasonable expectation"; and some pragmatists define delinquency as

"behavior which the police in any given community consider as deviant." In a strictly legal sense, juvenile delinquents are underage counterparts to adult "convicted criminals." That is, juvenile delinquency is a legal, court-assigned label.

The difficulty in defining the term does not revolve around deciding whose definition is more nearly correct, but rather is a matter of defining satisfactorily, in a few descriptive words, a form of social problem that is neither merely legal nor merely behavioral in its ramifications. Any definition may be correct in its own context, for example, a boy whom neighbors do not like. Such a child might be considered a delinquent *in that neighborhood* without his behavior qualifying as legal delinquency.

To be considered legally delinquent, a juvenile must have violated the law. It should be noted, however, that the law does not settle all the problems involved in determining that any given act is delinquent in nature. Variations in the kind of conduct defined in delinquency statutes, vagueness in the description of forbidden behavior, disagreements as to the cutoff age between juvenile and adult, and variations in court practices prevail across the country. Unfortunately, there is no universal precision and clarity in the law regarding just what constitutes legal juvenile delinquency.

Likewise, even greater subjectivity exists in regard to the social definition of delinquency, and the term as used in casual conversation can have a variety of meanings. Yet for the adolescent who has been labeled delinquent in any form, the consequences may be devastating, resulting in his or her exclusion from certain groups, disapproval from adults, and additional social stigmas that may force the child to associate with others who are also considered unacceptable.

The Age of Delinquency

In spite of Blackstone's comment that "one lad of eleven years old may have as much cunning as another of fourteen: in these cases our maxim is that *'malitia supplet aetaten'* [malice provides age],"[4] chronological age is universally used to distinguish between juvenile delinquency and either youthful offender status or adult criminality. Other measures of delinquency have failed. For instance, in an early Massachusetts case, *Commonwealth v. Trippi*, a 22-year-old defendant convicted of first-degree murder appealed by claiming and establishing that he had a "mental age" of only 13 years. His conviction was upheld, however, the court writing:

> When a man reaches manhood the presumption is that he possesses the ordinary mental capacity normally pertaining to his age. . . . The presumption of the lack of power of thought and capacity in favor of the child is due more to the number of years he has lived than to the character and development of his mind.[5]

Across the United States today all states have increased the maximum age limit for delinquency beyond puberty, generally placing it somewhere in the late teens. The most frequent legal upper age limit for "childhood" is 18, although in some states it is 16, in others 17, and in still others 21.[6] Some states specify different age limits for different types of delinquency and some make distinctions in the maximum delinquency ages for boys and for girls.

THE EXTENT OF JUVENILE CRIME

It is possible for juveniles to be prosecuted in juvenile court and adjudicated delinquent (or, found guilty) for a range of behaviors for which adults cannot be prosecuted, like truancy from school. These behaviors are called **status offenses**, signifying that the offense is peculiar to childhood status.

Status Offenses

Status offenses, although not particularly serious in themselves, are considered potential trouble areas for young people, predictive of future criminal behavior. The specific behaviors so labeled vary from state to state, and in many states are defined under a broader category variously called "persons in need of supervision" (**PINS**), "children in need of supervision" (**CINS**), or "minors in need of supervision" (**MINS**). Any acts that fall into these categories are considered "precriminal" behaviors. Status offenses comprise a large percentage of referrals to juvenile courts.

Status offense legislation often uses vague, or subjective, language. For instance, the California Welfare and Institutions Code states the following:

> Any person under the age of 18 years who persistently or habitually refuses to obey the reasonable and proper orders or directions of his parents, guardian, custodian or school authorities, or who is beyond the control of such person, or any person who is a habitual truant from school within the meaning of any law of this state, or who from any cause is in danger of leading an idle, dissolute, lewd, or immoral life, is within the jurisdiction of the juvenile court which may adjudge such person to be a ward of the court.[7]

Or the Georgia Juvenile Court Code of 1981:

> "Status offender" means a juvenile who is charged with or adjudicated of an offense which would not be a crime if it were committed by an adult, in other words, an act which is only an offense because of the perpetrator's status as a juvenile. Such offenses shall include, but are not limited to, truancy, running away from home, incorrigibility, and unruly behavior.[8]

Young Criminals

The sad fact is that young people—teenagers and those even younger—can and do commit the same types of conventional crimes as adults. Homicides, assaults, rapes, robberies, burglaries—the whole litany of ordinary crimes—are found in juvenile as well as adult criminal courts. Indeed, a substantial proportion of the total criminal activity reported in the official measures of crime involves juveniles. Victimization surveys, self-report studies, and official arrest data show that juvenile involvement in crime is considerably greater than the size of the juvenile population would predict.

Juveniles as Crime Victims

Victimization surveys show also that a disproportionate number of crime victims are adolescents. Persons between the ages of 12 and 19 have the highest rate per 1000 of those who are victims of robbery, assault, and rape. (See Fig. 16.1.) Indeed, victimization declines rapidly as people reach adulthood. In general, victim surveys belie the myth that juveniles prey on adults. While this does occur, of course, it is more likely that they prey on each other. High school students are frequently victimized in school or on school grounds.

Official Police Reports

Persons under the age of 18 account for 17 percent of all arrests and 31 percent of all *Uniform Crime Reports* (UCR) index arrests.[9] The vast majority of these arrests are of adolescents between the ages of 13 and 18, although this age group comprises a much smaller percent of the total population.

Participation in crime declines with age, according to arrest data. In sheer num-

Schoolyards are prime locations for delinquent acts and victimizations.

FIGURE 16.1

Victims of crime. Younger people are more likely than the elderly to be victims of crime. (*Source:* Bureau of Justice Statistics, *A National Crime Survey Report: Criminal Victimization, 1989,* U.S. Department of Justice, Washington, DC, October 1990.)

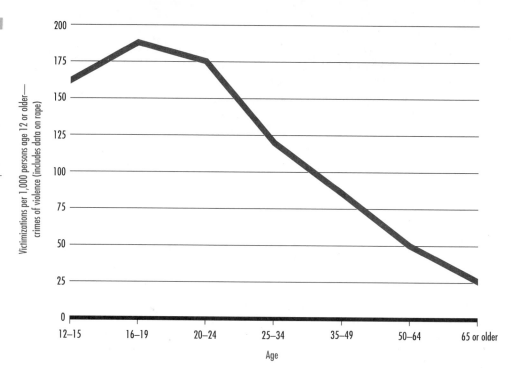

bers, property arrests peak among persons aged 16 and then drop dramatically, although the value of the property stolen by adults is much greater than that stolen by juveniles and the average amount stolen increases with age. Arrests for crimes against persons peak at age 18 and then also decline, although not as dramatically.[10] See Fig. 16.2.

The greater numbers of juvenile arrests may be the result of their lack of experience, or may be because the types of crimes juveniles commit are more visible and the perpetrators apprehended without much effort on the part of the police. The decline in arrest rates by age, on the other hand, may reflect the incapacitation of many offenders—that they have been caught and locked up. Or it may be due to the rehabilitation of many youthful offenders or their turning away from crime because of maturation.

There is little doubt that the major concern of the juvenile justice system today is young criminals, particularly young violent offenders, rather than status violators. PINS cases are still a serious responsibility of the juvenile court system, but the hopes of a century ago for the prevention of serious crime among young offenders have been pretty much dashed. What to do with bad kids, with criminal children, is the major problem faced by the juvenile system now.

Juvenile Crime as a Stepping Stone to Adult Crime

Juvenile delinquency often sets the stage for adult criminality. Although most juvenile delinquents do not go on to become adult criminals, many do. Studies have shown that many juvenile boys convicted of serious crimes were later convicted of serious crimes as adults.[11] Minor juvenile offenders tend not to develop into adult criminals.[12] But the more serious the juvenile crime career, the greater the likelihood of an adult criminal career.

THE JUVENILE COURT TODAY

For much of this century, juvenile courts faced two major problems: (1) the broad and almost uncontrolled discretionary power they exercised regarding problem children; and (2) the extreme informality of their procedures compared to those of criminal courts, leading to an absence of many due process safeguards. To a great extent these problems resulted from the courts lumping together three distinct categories of children that came before them:

1. Children in the juvenile age bracket who committed acts that would be crimes, sometimes very serious crimes, if committed by an adult
2. Children who committed status offenses, or offenses of childhood, that could be considered ''bad'' but would not be considered offenses if committed by an adult
3. Dependent and neglected children who were victims of abandonment or abuse to the extent that they became wards of the state

Because of the widespread lack of community resources to take care of children in need, those in all three categories were often mixed together by the courts when they placed them in community supervision, in foster homes, and in institutional settings. Delinquency therefore came to be a concept encompassing all three categories of children, although in the popular view the term was primarily associated with young criminals.

Most juveniles in trouble are status offenders rather than underage criminals. At first, however, the early juvenile courts did not distinguish between them very much, treating Huckleberry Finn, the truant, in much the same way, and with the severity, as young Mack the Knife. It was only later that greater distinctions began to be made, and the weight of the sentence made more proportionate to the offense. Today confinement in secure facilities may be recommended to prevent continual running away or continual violent behavior. And in general young criminals can be held longer and are eligible for waiver into the adult criminal justice system if the nature of their criminal activity warrants that move.

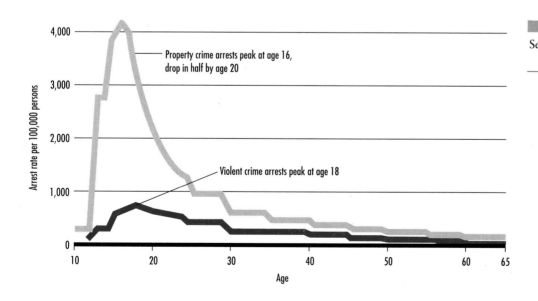

FIGURE 16.2

Serious crime rates are highest in young age groups.

For most of the first 60 years of the existence of juvenile court, attorneys for the child were rarely present because the proceedings were assumed to be nonadversarial in nature. Hearsay evidence was acceptable because it was thought to provide insight into the child's background and problem behavior. The court never attempted to *convict* and *punish* a juvenile, but rather, under the ***parens patriae*** philosophy, to act as a "father" to the child, to make determinations in the child's best interests and welfare.[13] There was therefore no need to prove the guilt of an alleged delinquent "beyond a reasonable doubt," as was the case for an adult accused of a crime in a criminal court. Rather, since the proceedings were conducted in the manner of a civil court, the commonly applied test was "preponderance of evidence." Furthermore, it was required only to establish that the child's *condition* was delinquent, not that some specific act had been committed.[14]

Historically, there has been no recognized right to a trial by jury in juvenile proceedings. This is justified on at least three grounds:

1. The confidential nature of juvenile court proceedings mitigates against involving citizens in the hearings, and a trial would merely ape the formality of criminal proceedings, in effect stigmatizing the juvenile as a criminal.
2. The concept of "a jury of one's peers" might be interpreted for juveniles to mean a jury of children, which would not be acceptable.
3. The common practice of conducting and writing a *predispositional report* on the child *before* the hearing (and sharing that information with the judge) makes a jury trial appear to be unnecessary. In the adult system, such a social investigation can be written only *after* conviction for a crime, to be used as presentence information for the judge. But in the juvenile system it has been customary to conduct that investigation *prior* to adjudication since the purpose is to assist the *parens patriae* process.

Because the juvenile court was designed to act in a child's best interests and the proceedings are civil, the actual in-court practices have remained quite informal. Juvenile proceedings generally take place in small courtrooms or conference rooms, sometimes even in the judge's chambers. The public and the press are not allowed to attend, and the judge typically does not wear a black robe. Much of the sternness and formality of the adult criminal court is absent.

However, several U.S. Supreme Court decisions during the past 25 years have brought more formality to juvenile court processes. With informality came lax adherence to some basic due process protections guaranteed by the U.S. Constitution, and cases which worked their way to the Supreme Court demonstrated a serious deprivation of rights for juveniles in some jurisdictions. So, although juvenile courts are still less formal than the adult criminal courts, the informality does not mean juveniles are denied procedural safeguards.

The Move Toward Due Process: Kent v. United States

The first landmark U.S. Supreme Court case to deal directly with the rights of juveniles was ***Kent v. United States***, decided in 1966 and based on a case originating in the District of Columbia.[15] This decision sent a warning to the juvenile justice system that the laxity of evidentiary and procedural standards of the *parens patriae* system would no longer be tolerated.

In this case, Kent, a 16-year-old boy, was charged with robbery, rape, and burglary.

The juvenile judge transferred Kent out of juvenile court and he was tried and convicted as an adult. Maximum confinement by the juvenile court would have been for "a period of time not to exceed his twenty-first birthday," or about 5 years. As an adult he faced the maximum sentence of death, although the court sentenced him to 30 to 90 years in prison. According to the District of Columbia statutes, there should have been a waiver hearing to determine whether Kent should be transferred to the adult court, but none was held. It was on this basis that the Supreme Court reversed Kent's conviction, so that technically it was a decision based on statutory interpretation rather than Constitutional rights. However, the justices went on to criticize many common practices of the juvenile justice system, in particular its inadequate detention and disposition facilities and its use of ineffective treatment techniques. They also pointed out that juveniles did not receive the same Constitutional protections given to adults or the care and treatment they were supposed to receive. The Court concluded that any waiver hearing must measure up to the essentials of due process and fair treatment. The consequence of *Kent* is that waiver hearings are now provided in juvenile courts across the land.

In most jurisdictions judges may at their discretion waive juveniles between the ages of 16 and 18 to adult criminal court for any offense, and in many states the waiver age is as low as 13 for violent crimes.

The Move Toward Due Process: In Re Gault

Sixteen months after the *Kent* decision, the Supreme Court decided another case that undoubtedly has had a greater impact on modern juvenile court proceedings than any other factor, *In Re Gault*.[16] The Gault story is worth telling:

Police officers received a verbal complaint by a woman, a Mrs. Cook, about a telephone call made to her in which the caller or callers made lewd, indecent, irritatingly offensive, dirty statements. On Monday, June 8, 1964, at about 10 a.m., Gerald Francis Gault and a friend, Ronald Lewis, were taken into custody by the Sheriff of Gila County (Arizona). Gerald Gault was then serving a 6 months' probation order as a result of having been in the company of another boy who had stolen a wallet from a lady's purse.

At the time Gerald was picked up, his mother and father were both at work. No notice that he was being taken into custody was left at the home. No other steps were taken to advise the parents that Gerald had, in effect, been arrested. The boy was taken to the Children's Detention Home. When his mother arrived home at about 6 p.m., Gerald was not there.

Gerald's older brother was sent to look for him. He learned that Gerald had been arrested. He and Mrs. Gault went to the Detention Home. The deputy probation officer, named Flagg, who was also superintendent of the Detention Home, told Mrs. Gault "why Jerry was there" and said that a hearing would be held in Juvenile Court at 3 p.m. the following day.

Officer Flagg filed a petition with the court on the hearing day, June 9, 1964. It was not served on the Gaults. Indeed, none of them saw this petition. It made no reference to any investigation, evidence, or any other basis for the judicial action which it initiated. It recited only that "said minor is under the age of eighteen years, and is in need of the protection of this Honorable Court; [and that] said minor is a delinquent minor."

On June 9, Gerald, his mother, his older brother, Flagg, and another probation officer named Henderson appeared before the juvenile judge in the judge's office. Gerald's father was not there. He was at work out of the city. Mrs. Cook, the complainant, was not there. No one was sworn at this hearing. No transcript or recording was made. No memorandum or record of the substance of the proceedings was prepared. Gerald was questioned by the judge about the telephone call. There was conflict as to what he said. At the conclusion of the hearing, the judge said he would "think about it." Gerald was taken back to the Detention Home. He was not sent to his own home with his parents.

On June 11 or 12, after having been detained since June 8, Gerald was released and driven home. There was no explanation in the record as to why he was kept, or why he was released. Mrs. Gault received a note, on plain paper saying "Judge McGhee has set Monday June 15, 1964 at 11:00 A.M. as the date and time for further Hearings on Gerald's delinquency."

At this appointed time, Gerald, his father and mother, Ronald Lewis and his father, and officers Flagg and Henderson were present before Judge McGhee. Again, the complainant, Mrs. Cook, was not present. Mrs. Gault asked that Mrs. Cook be present "so she could see which boy that done the talking, the dirty talking over the phone." The juvenile judge said "she didn't have to be present at that hearing." The judge did not speak to Mrs. Cook or communicate with her at any time. Probation Officer Flagg had talked to her—once over the telephone on June 9.

At the conclusion of the hearing, the judge committed Gerald as a juvenile delinquent to the State Industrial School "for a period of his minority [that is, until age 21], unless sooner discharged by due process of law."

No appeal was permitted by Arizona law in juvenile cases.

When this case finally reached the U.S. Supreme Court, the Court declared the basic due process rights citizens have come to expect, and which are guaranteed by the U.S. Constitution, to have been woefully absent in Gault's case. And the Gault case was shown to be the normal way juvenile processing was carried out in most states.

Specifically, the Supreme Court ruled that juvenile proceedings such as that described in *Gault* violated basic Constitutional rights, such as evidenced by the following:

1. No notice of specific charges against Gerald were given to him or his parents.
2. No attorney was offered or provided.
3. No witnesses were called, so Gerald was unable to confront or cross-examine his accuser.
4. No warning or notice of his right against self-incrimination was given to Gerald, and thus no waiver of that right took place.

The Court did not decide whether juvenile cases required transcripts of their proceedings or have the right to appellate review. But the *Gault* decision has had the effect of making juvenile courts more closely adhere to the principles of due process followed in adult criminal cases.

THE JUVENILE JUSTICE PROCESS

In general, the juvenile justice process flows through nine stages: (1) referral, (2) intake, (3) detention, (4) petition and adjudication, (5) disposition, (6) community supervision or placement, (7) revocation, (8) state training school, and (9) aftercare. (See Fig. 16.3.) It is differentiated from the criminal justice process for adults by its degree of formality and the labels assigned to the various stages of case processing.

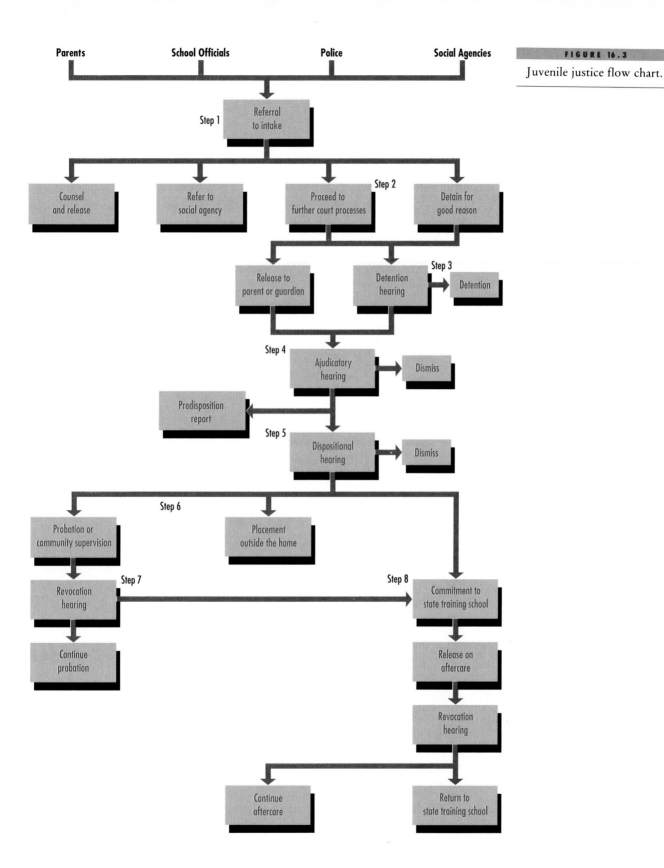

FIGURE 16.3

Juvenile justice flow chart.

Parents   School Officials   Police   Social Agencies

Step 1   Referral
          to intake

Counsel   Refer to   Proceed to   Step 2   Detain for
and release   social agency   further court processes   good reason

Release to   Detention   Step 3   Detention
parent or guardian   hearing

Step 4   Ajudicatory   Dismiss
          hearing

Predisposition
report

Step 5   Dispositional   Dismiss
          hearing

Step 6   Probation or   Placement
          community supervision outside the home

Revocation   Step 7   Step 8   Commitment to
hearing   state training school

Continue   Release on
probation   aftercare

                                                       Revocation
                                                       hearing

                              Continue   Return to
                              aftercare   state training school

Referral

The juvenile justice process begins at the point of **referral**; that is to say, the juvenile justice system does not go about looking for juveniles in trouble, but rather waits for the referral of problem juveniles to it by police and others. Most referrals are made by police officers who take a youngster into custody after either observing a delinquent act or receiving a complaint. Other referrals are made by school authorities, parents or guardians, or other social agencies.

Police Handling of Juveniles

Police generally favor handling juvenile cases, especially minor juvenile misconduct, in unofficial and informal ways, without moving the children through the justice system. The first choice of action by the police and school authorities is to send misbehaving children home to parents or guardians, or to take them there, *not* to take them to a police station. (See Field Practice A:2.) Such action by the police is called "diversion." This is not always possible, of course. If the juvenile is known to the police from prior encounters, if the offense is serious, or if the juvenile continues to give the cops or the school authorities a bad time, formal handling of the problem juvenile, that is, taking him or her into custody, is more likely.[17]

Many large police departments have separate units whose primary area of responsibility is to work with juvenile cases. These units are made up of specially trained juvenile officers (derogatorily called "diaper dicks," "kiddie cops," or "social workers") to whom patrol officers can refer cases of suspected delinquency arising in the normal course of patrol. Even small police departments sometimes have at least one officer assigned to handling juveniles. Specialized juvenile officers are much like detectives in the adult system. They ordinarily do not patrol but follow up on investigations brought to them by beat officers.

Studies of police response to juvenile suspects show that officers tend to divert most juveniles by returning them to their homes. However, police take custody and refer a child to juvenile officers or the juvenile court in cases in which one or more of the following circumstances is present:

Police handle juveniles daily for a variety of reasons. Here a teenage boy awaits questioning after a vandalism incident.

1. The act involved a serious criminal offense.
2. The juvenile has a number of prior contacts with the police and was returned home before.
3. The juvenile is at the upper age limit for juveniles.
4. The demeanor of the child is surly, defiant, or flippant.
5. The juvenile appears to be a gang member.

One study indicated that police almost uniformly took children into custody if they demanded a lawyer. The officers took this as evidence of "criminal sophistication" and almost never diverted such cases.[18] There is also some research evidence that children who appear to be poor and from deprived backgrounds or who are members of minority groups are more likely to be referred to the court.[19]

Police Concern for Due Process

If police are not able to divert juveniles away from the juvenile justice process, they are generally required to deal with the youngsters in the same manner in which they deal with adults. That is, Supreme Court decisions such as *Miranda, Terry, Mapp,* and others which have defined "defendants' rights" must be followed for juveniles just as they must for adults.[20] Also, forensic evidence and search procedures in juvenile cases must follow the same rules applicable in adult cases, with a few

Police Handling of Juveniles

1: Left Behind

While on routine patrol around midnight, a police officer observed a person standing outside an open window of a house which bordered an alley. As the officer continued to watch, undetected, a television was handed out through the window by a second unseen person. The officer turned on his flashing lights and approached down the alley, at which time the person standing outside the window dropped the television and ran. A young boy climbed out of the window and was caught by the officer. No one was home in the house. The boy gave his name and his age, which was 13. The police officer took the boy to the precinct house and referred the case to the juvenile division of the police department.

2: Break It Up!

At 11 p.m. on a Friday night a police officer was dispatched to a convenience store parking lot after the store manager called to complain about a group of teenagers congregating in front of the store. The manager stated that the teenagers and their cars hampered the access of customers to the store and that loud music and other noise were a nuisance. When the officer arrived, she ordered the teenagers to disperse and to "go on home before you get into trouble."

3: Saturday Night Drunks

While on routine patrol at 7:30 p.m. on a Saturday night, a sheriff's deputy observed a car full of young men swerving erratically on a country road. The deputy pulled up behind the swerving car and turned on his own car's flashing lights. The swerving car stopped and, as the officer approached, three teenage boys in the backseat were laughing and acting silly. When the driver, a 16-year-old boy recognized by the deputy to be a local high school athlete, opened the driver's door, a beer can rolled out of the car and onto the pavement. The officer could tell that he had been drinking. The boys were taken to the Sheriff's Department and their parents notified to come get them. No other action was taken.

4: Alternative School

A series of daytime household burglaries had occurred in a middle-class neighborhood in a medium-sized city. Two police officers on routine patrol observed two school-age boys sitting on a bench in a local playground during school hours. The officers approached the boys, determined that they were truant, and took them to their school. The principal told the police officers that the boys, both aged 14 and in the eighth grade, were absent a lot and had been suspended from school ear-

lier that year for repeatedly smoking in the restroom. One of the officers matched the dates the boys had been absent with those for several of the burglaries and discovered they were the same. The boys were taken to the police station for further investigation.

5: I Won't Do It Again, I Promise

Nadine Fishwater, a 16-year-old high school student, was stopped by department store security guards as she attempted to leave the store after security had observed her placing makeup and perfume inside her blouse. Nadine immediately began crying and offered to pay for the merchandise, saying she had "forgotten" to pay although she had intended to do so. Police were called to the store, a written report was prepared by store security, and Nadine was taken to police headquarters and her parents notified. Her parents stated that she was a "good" student, had never been in any kind of serious trouble before, requested that the police allow them to "work things out" with the department store, and asked them to release her in their custody. ∎

---

exceptions. For example, the police are prohibited from photographing or fingerprinting juveniles except in specific, rare cases in which serious felonies are involved. And even in such cases the fingerprints and photographs must be held in confidence by the local police and not forwarded to the Federal Bureau of Investigation's central files, as they are for adults.

Juvenile Intake

Assuming the police do not divert, and the child is taken into custody, that is, brought to the precinct house, the next step is referral of the child to the intake staff of the juvenile court (**intake**). The intake staff usually consists of juvenile probation

Intake

1: Mother Warned Her

Police took a 13-year-old girl to juvenile intake at 2 a.m. in the morning charged with public intoxication and disorderly conduct. According to the police report the girl was found in front of a convenience store, drunk and shouting at passersby. No record of previous referral was found. When contacted by phone, the girl's mother said, "I told her she had better quit drinking. Maybe now you can send her to a prison or something to teach her a lesson." The mother refused to come to the juvenile department.

2: Eagle Scouts

Two boys, both aged 16, were taken to intake by suburban police after the boys were caught inside a church dismantling the speakers and other sound system equipment. No previous record for either was located. The parents of both boys were horrified when notified of the arrest and came immediately to the juvenile detention center. One boy's father was a prominent dentist, the other an executive with a local lending institution. The boys were class officers in school and Eagle Scouts.

3: Cracked Up

Police referred a 15-year-old boy to intake after he had eluded police pursuit while driving his mother's car without permission. He had crashed the car through a chain-link fence after losing control turning a corner. The boy appeared to be unhurt but was incoherent. Medical examination revealed a high level of cocaine in his blood. One previous referral had been made 8 months earlier by police, who brought him in after he had been caught shoplifting by a store clerk. The boy's parents were divorced and the boy lived with his mother. She responded to the intake officer's call and came to the juvenile intake office. She reported that the boy was disobedient and unruly and, in effect, was beyond her control. She said the father lived in a distant state and seldom made efforts to see the boy. ∎

---

officers who are ideally (but only sometimes) trained as social workers. In urban jurisdictions the intake function is most often performed at a juvenile detention center or juvenile shelter, which is in operation 24 hours a day all year.

Intake essentially is a screening process to determine whether the court should intervene in a juvenile's life or whether it would be better to handle the matter in some other way. (For examples of the types of situations encountered, see Field Practice B.) Intake officers generally have the following options: (1) dismiss the complaint, or counsel the juvenile and release with no further action; (2) refer the case to another social agency, such as child welfare; (3) arrange for informal probation or voluntary supervision of the juvenile by an intake counselor for a few weeks or months; or (5) file a petition.

Juvenile Detention:

The Detention Decision

Although a certain amount of discretion is given to intake counselors regarding the detention decision, generally the decision is controlled by a well-defined policy in the form of guidelines or, in many jurisdictions, by a juvenile judge. Stringent criteria for detention has been established nationally for juveniles. **Juvenile detention** is roughly equivalent to adult jail, and, depending on the part of the country, is referred to as "juvenile hall," "juvenile shelter," or "juvenile detention center." Although no monetary bail is allowed in juvenile cases in most jurisdictions (juveniles usually cannot be fined either), the guidelines often require a **detention hearing** to be held before a juvenile judge within a reasonable amount of time in order to review and formalize the detention decision. In general, judges are aware that precautions must be taken to prevent juvenile detention centers from becoming the dumping grounds for the community's problem children. Detention should be reserved for those children who have specific needs to be held in a secure setting, such as:

1. Out-of-town runaways who need to be detained until arrangements can be made to return them home
2. Juveniles arrested for serious violations of the law who would pose an additional risk to society if released immediately and for whom no suitable alternative can be found
3. Juveniles who are chronic runaways and are likely to run away again
4. Juveniles already under probation or aftercare, where revocation must be considered
5. Serious juvenile offenders awaiting certification or waiver proceedings to adult court
6. Juveniles in some sort of danger, or who pose a danger to others

It is not uncommon for police, parents, or others to place pressure on the juvenile system to detain a child in order to ''teach him or her a lesson'' or to otherwise punish the child. Juvenile detention is not designed to be a place of punishment or a place of rehabilitation. It is a temporary holding facility designed to provide safe, humane, secure housing of juveniles awaiting future court proceedings or transfer to other settings. In a California case (*In Re William M.*) the State Supreme Court listed several *inappropriate* reasons to detain, including public outcry, nature of the offense

No release for this young man who was detained in the juvenile detention facility in Austin, Texas.

per se, the "need to crack down on juveniles," "convenience of the officers," "the belief that detention would have a salutary effect on the minor," and the juvenile's inability to give a good reason for release.[21]

Detention Facilities

Considerable variation exists regarding the type of detention facilities available for juveniles and the length of time they are allowed to be kept in detention. In most areas, especially urban communities, detention facilities for juveniles are separate from adult jails and lockups. In many small towns, however, juvenile detention may be permitted in a separate wing of the existing jail or in a few designated cells of the jail. It is never appropriate for juveniles to be housed with adult prisoners. The brutalizing nature of jails and the accompanying abuses of juveniles in adult jails have been well documented, occasionally by outraged news reporters. Many states have legislation similar to New York's, which makes it mandatory for authorities to do the following:

1. Provide foster family or group home type facilities for delinquents
2. Place children in one of four regional detention centers
3. Not use a jail for juvenile detention without the notification and approval of the New York State Division for Youth[22]

Those jurisdictions in which juveniles experience rape, suicide, assault, or other forms of victimization because they are housed in adult jails face the prospect of civil lawsuits. Juveniles should not be incarcerated in adult facilities, and where this procedure is not followed and moreover, if a juvenile is seriously injured or dies while confined in an adult facility, the jurisdiction which incarcerated him or her is vulnerable to accusations of gross negligence or disregard for the safety of the juvenile.

Recently constructed juvenile detention facilities are typically characterized by designs that "soften" the security aspects of incarceration. Usually they have single-bed rooms, not cells, each opening onto a common day room equipped with a television, table games, puzzles, and the like. Child care workers—not guards—are used to maintain order. Often activity rooms exist for arts and crafts. Sometimes school tutoring is offered along with outdoor recreation. Facilities for visits from families, attorneys, and caseworkers exist. Boys and girls are housed in separate wings of the same facility, although typically they share a common dining room.

Almost 90,000 children are being held in detention nationwide at any given time, and it is estimated that approximately 600,000 children are detained for some period of time each year. Since the population in detention is constantly fluid, with some children housed for only a few hours and others for much longer periods, it is very difficult to obtain accurate data on the characteristics of the detention population. Studies show that 18 percent of status offenders are detained, as are 34 percent of runaways.[23] Thirty percent of juveniles referred for property offenses are detained, and 38 percent of those referred for crimes against persons, drug violations, and public order offenses.[24]

In many states, statutes set a maximum length of time a juvenile may be held in detention prior to being released, diverted to a juvenile community placement without adjudication, or petitioned to the juvenile court for an adjudicatory hearing. In some states (New York, for instance) the maximum length of detention prior to further action is 3 days, but in other states (such as Ohio) 90 days is allowed. One survey has indicated that in some states every year a few juveniles are detained for as long as a year before they are seen by a court. *Most* detention facilities, however, hold juveniles for less than 1 month and insist that detention not continue beyond 48 hours without a petition for an adjudicatory hearing being filed by the authorities and a detention hearing being held to determine whether the juvenile should be detained prior to the adjudicatory hearing or released to parents who promise to return for the hearing (the detention hearing serves much the same function as a bail hearing minus the bail).[24] In cases where it is decided to detain the juvenile, the adjudicatory hearing must be scheduled relatively soon, no more than 21 days after the commencement of detention.

A type of informal probation is commonly used by the intake staff of the juvenile court as an alternative to either filing a petition for adjudication or releasing a child outright. The juvenile must consent to this placement. Informal probation is like formal probation in that the juvenile is under the supervision of a probation officer and is required to abide by the rules and conditions set by the intake staff. The advantage is that the juvenile avoids a record as a delinquent. In some jurisdictions, informal probation accounts for as much as 50 percent of all intake dispositions.[25]

The Adjudicatory Hearing

Since *Gault*, the **adjudicatory hearing** (or trial) is characterized by due process standards, beginning with the filing of a formal petition to request an adjudicatory hearing on the facts of the alleged delinquency. The petition originates with the prosecutor's office, but the intake section of the juvenile court is often its real instigator.

The petition is comparable to the information or indictment used in criminal court and contains the list of "charges" on which the child is referred (and perhaps has been detained) and on which he or she will be "tried." Upon the formal filing of the petition, the juvenile judge makes sure that the child is represented by an attorney (as required by both *Gideon* and *Gault*), who, whether retained by the child's family or appointed by the state, will represent the juvenile throughout the process from this point on.

In most instances the adjudicatory hearing is similar to a bench trial in criminal matters: The judge sits alone and makes final determinations without a jury. The vast majority of these cases are not adversarial; indeed they are much more like an adult arraignment in which the defendant pleads guilty. Often the "facts" in the case are not disputed and the child, through counsel, "stipulates" the facts and does not contest the charges. The role of the presiding judge at the adjudicatory hearing is to ensure that the proceedings meet statutory and Constitutional requirements.

The steps in the hearing usually include the presentation of the complaint by the prosecutor. Then the prosecutor presents whatever evidence has been gathered by the police or filed by the complainant, issues subpoenas, questions witnesses, and interprets the facts and the law from the perspective of "the people." When the juvenile stipulates the facts and does not contest the charges, the hearing is brief, with the judge often questioning the child directly concerning the alleged events. However, in a full-scale hearing, where the allegations are denied, the steps followed are very similar to those for an adult criminal trial. The prosecutor presents the state's case, which may include testimony by the arresting officer and witnesses along with all other evidence that has been legally obtained, and generally tries to prove that the charges are true. The defense counsel cross-examines the state's witnesses, challenges the state's evidence, presents defense witnesses, and generally tries to disprove the charges. The prosecutor then cross-examines the defense witnesses. Both sides present their summaries, and the judge then reaches a verdict.

The juvenile court judge has considerable discretion in adjudication. If the child is adjudicated delinquent, he or she may be returned to detention to await a **dispositional hearing** (a step similar to sentencing in the adult system). Alternatively, the child may be released in the custody of parents or a guardian to await further proceedings. In some cases in which the child has admitted the delinquency and the social investigation has been completed, the disposition hearing may follow immediately after adjudication.

The Predispositional Report Social Investigation

The most important outcome document prepared by the juvenile court is the social investigation. Sometimes called the **predispositional report**, this report in many ways resembles the presentence investigation used in criminal court. But for juveniles the focus of the report tends to be social work concerns, that is, the possibility of future rehabilitation, rather than past misconduct to determine the appropriate punishment. The function of the report is to acquaint the judge with the social conditions of the child's total environment to better provide a proper and helpful disposition of the case.

A carefully constructed social history is not limited to the manner in which the child has come into conflict with the law, although attention is given to previous delinquent history. The report also gives significant attention to family relationships; to peer groups; to the child's interests and activities; to his or her history of school performance and attendance, mental health, and areas of conflict; and to the identification of people who might prove helpful in the child's future development. In some cases psychological tests are administered and psychiatric evaluation may be deemed necessary. The report, when completed, includes all the factual information about the child as well as interpretative assessments, and a recommendation by the juvenile caseworker as to what disposition would be most suitable to help the child in question.

Dispositional Alternatives

At some time after the adjudicatory finding, a dispositional hearing is held before the juvenile judge. At this time a decision is made as to how the delinquency is to be resolved. The information contained in the predispositional report as well as the judge's own assessment of the situation guides this decision. Generally, the prosecutor and defense attorney attend the hearing, although their presence is not always required.

In making the disposition decision, the juvenile judge is generally required to first consider the *least restrictive alternative* of placement for the child which will serve his or her best interests and welfare. Of course, the best interests of the child must be balanced against the protection of the community from further depredations by any juvenile who has been found to have committed delinquent acts.

The dispositional alternatives available to the judge are:

1. Probation, the disposition most frequently chosen
2. Placement in a foster home or with a relative
3. Placement in a group home, private institution, or local treatment facility
4. Commitment to the state training school (the juvenile equivalent of prison)
5. Dismissal of the case

Which alternative is chosen can be of critical importance to the juvenile's future. Probation is generally the *first* disposition of choice throughout the country; it is certainly the least restrictive alternative compared to *any* secure setting. Juvenile judges usually consider state training schools to be the end of the line in the juvenile justice system and prefer not to place children in such facilities without giving them at least one opportunity at probation. The training schools often have a negative impact on the development of adolescents, as the number of adult felons who have been incarcerated for a portion of their younger years in juvenile institutions attests. Field

Dispositional Hearings

1: Mother and Son

Marvin Jones, a 13-year-old boy adjudicated delinquent after being arrested trying to sell marijuana to an undercover police officer, was brought before the juvenile judge for a dispositional hearing after spending 5 weeks in detention. Marvin had been referred twice to juvenile intake prior to this case, once by his mother 2 years earlier after he had been unaccountably gone from home for 3 days, and once by the police, who had apprehended him shooting at street lights with a BB gun. Marvin was 1 year behind in school after being retained in the first grade. His father had left him and Mrs. Jones when Marvin was an infant and had not been heard from since. Mrs. Jones was employed as a waitress at a local "family-style" restaurant and worked evenings. She stated that although Marvin was a "good boy," she had a difficult time providing the controls the boy needed.

2: Headed for Trouble

Willie Wilson, a 15-year-old boy adjudicated delinquent for the burglary of an auto parts store, was brought before the juvenile judge for a dispositional hearing. Willie had been arrested along with two adult males (ages 18 and 19) during the late-night burglary. He had four previous arrests for minor law infractions; this was the first time he had been adjudicated. He lived with his mother and an older sister (age 22) and a younger brother (age 13). Willie's school principal reported that, although he found the boy to be very likeable, he had had a series of difficul-

ties with Willie for cutting classes, disruptive behavior, and minor vandalism (writing on the bathroom walls). The adult coburglars were out on bail awaiting trial. The prosecutor's office requested that Willie be "put away" in the State Training School; the juvenile caseworker recommended probation. Willie had been in detention for 2 ½ months.

3: Country Club Delinquent

Timothy Fairchild, a 16-year-old boy from an upper-middle-class family, came before the juvenile judge for a dispositional hearing accompanied by his father, his mother, and the family's attorney. Timothy was a very intelligent, well-mannered, articulate young man who had been arrested seven times since age 12 for a variety of offenses including possession of barbiturates at school, stealing money from a teacher's purse, vandalism of a green on the country club's golf course, auto theft, and runaway (he had taken his girlfriend and her mother's car without permission to the beach for a long weekend). In the immediate instance, Timothy was charged with possession of several items that had been taken from neighborhood homes in recent burglaries. He denied the burglaries but admitted that he "bought and sold" various items from "friends" not knowing that they were stolen. The case had brought about phone calls to the juvenile department from burglary victims wanting the boy "put away" as well as from friends of the family who wished to serve as "character witnesses" for the boy and his family. Mr. Fairchild, an executive with a large manufactur-

ing company, offered to send the boy to military school, to assist in the return of any stolen items, and to make restitution even though he did not feel that his son was guilty of burglary.

4: Stepdaughter

Melissa Smith, a 15-year-old girl with a past history of repeated runaways and staying out all night with young adult males, was adjudicated as a PINS and was now before the juvenile judge for a dispositional hearing. She lived with her mother and stepfather; her own father had died when she was an infant. Melissa told caseworkers that her stepfather had made repeated sexual advances toward her and that her runaways were the result of those advances. She stated that she had been molested by the stepfather "more than once" and that if she were made to live with him again she would just run away again. Her mother and stepfather denied the accusations and claimed that the girl was emotionally confused and did not respond appropriately to their guidance and discipline, that she was spoiled. Melissa had no record of felony arrests and was well liked by her schoolteachers, although her poor class attendance resulted in failing grades. Melissa asked if she could be allowed to live with her deceased father's elderly parents (her paternal grandparents) in a neighboring state. Her mother objected to this. ∎

Practice C gives some examples of the kinds of situations juvenile judges are faced with.

Juvenile Probation

A major advantage of **juvenile probation** is that the child is allowed to remain in his or her own social environment. This can work to the disadvantage of successful casework since harmful factors in that environment will continue to exert powerful

Innovative Program Unpopular With Police Officers

The Tulsa Police Department was faced with a dramatic increase in auto thefts in 1990, many by juveniles. Convinced that the courts and reformatories could not provide the shock, or the role models, the young juvenile delinquents needed, Tulsa police chief Drew Diamond developed the Youth Intervention Program (YIP), an innovative attempt to straighten out young offenders.

The centerpiece of the plan was that juveniles between the ages of 12 and 14 were sentenced to a period of probation during which they were assigned to ride with a police officer on patrol for about 150 hours over a period of several months. The kid and the cop would become buddies, more or less, according to Chief Diamond's plan. And, the theory was that the nightly drama on the streets of Tulsa would be a sobering experience for the juvenile offenders.

However, since the program was devised by the police chief, alone and without significant input from the patrol officers themselves, it was met with apathy and resistance on the part of many police officers. Chief Diamond was unpopular with the rank and file officers, and they resented the fact that the program was imposed on them by him.

Corporal Julie Harris pointed out that officers were uncomfortable with the fact that juveniles who were allowed to ride with police officers on routine patrol were made privy to the officers' routines, that they could see when and where officers left weapons in patrol cars while booking suspects, investigating crimes, or taking meal breaks. Officers also disliked the fact that the juveniles would learn police radio jargon, and be able to translate the private code of the officers and dispatchers. They objected to the fact that the juveniles selected for the program were multiple offenders, with lengthy records of auto theft and other police contacts.

Foot patrol officers were also required to participate in the program, taking juvenile offenders with them as they walked their beats. The juveniles wore special T shirts with a "YIP" logo prominently displayed on them, and the police chief believed that a good rapport could be developed with the delinquents as they strolled through the neighborhoods.

Youth Intervention Program (YIP) juvenile and patrol officer.

However, some officers pointed out that the T shirts and the close relationships with uniformed beat officers were not beneficial to the kids. The T shirts caused negative labels ("bad kid") to be attached to the juveniles, which was damaging to their self-esteem. The special recognition of their delinquent status was more harmful than helpful, some officers concluded. Also, some other juvenile offenders not in the program believed that the YIP kids were informants, snitches for the cops.

Despite the good intentions, the YIP program was suspended following Chief Diamond's resignation as Chief of Police. Nevertheless, Tulsa police officers, as well as police everywhere, continue their quest for a good, effective, cheap, innovative way to solve juvenile delinquency.

SOURCES: Interview with Corporal Julie Harris, Tulsa Police Department, March 24, 1992; Richard Woodbury, "Putting the Brakes on Crime," *Time*, September 2, 1991.

influences on the youth. But the fact is that the child will ultimately have to learn to live in a law-abiding fashion in his or her own social and family environment anyway. Even if he or she is placed in a state training school, the child will undoubtedly return, and rather quickly at that, to the same home environment. Probation, in its best form, attempts to provide the child with better guidance and coping resources than those provided by parents, teachers, guardians, and others. It is also an additional set of controls placed on the child, which may not be all that bad since being out of control is a common correlate of delinquency. Well-trained probation caseworkers may be able to provide excellent counseling and guidance to troubled juveniles who have not been able to find the special help they need in their normal family or school situations prior to their court experiences. In essence, juvenile probation is an opportunity to help youthful offenders overcome the delinquency-producing factors they find inside themselves and in their day-to-day environments.

Placement Outside the Home

In the main, juvenile judges avoid commiting juveniles to training schools if at all possible. **Placement outside the home** but short of state school commitment is often seen as a viable alternative. This is a middle ground between probation and commitment. It is a more restrictive sanction than normal probation and generally rests on the belief that the parents or guardians of the juvenile are unwilling or unable to cope with the child's misbehavior or neglected condition. Sometimes a placement is arranged by a child's parent or parents, with the advice of counsel, to avoid a more severe disposition. For instance, a teenage boy living with his divorced mother may be placed in the father's custody in a different city or state. Mama may lose him but at least he will not be in lockup. In the case of more affluent families, a private placement in a relative's home or a boarding school may be arranged. Out-of-home and out-of-neighborhood placements allow a child to break the cycle of peer involvement and offer a new environment and a new opportunity to start over with a clean slate.

Placement in a **foster home** is common in most jurisdictions.[26] Foster parents are volunteers, rather than professional employees of the juvenile justice process, but are generally reimbursed for expenses by the city or county to open their homes to delinquents or to children needing parental supervision. They are usually carefully selected by the staff of the juvenile court and are closely monitored. A foster home substitutes a new set of surrogate parents and a new family setting for the old, and, depending on the location of the foster home, the child may be required to enter a new school district and to make new friends.

A **group home** is a type of foster home that allows a number of juveniles to be placed with a single pair of foster parents. The juveniles then live with their new "parents" as a "substitute family." Group homes vary in size—there may be as many as 12 children in a single home, depending on the size of the house and the capabilities of the foster parents. These arrangements are generally more economical than single-child foster homes and, depending on the skills of the adults involved, may be more effective in developing a positive environment of group support for learning how to live according to law-abiding norms. Group homes utilize treatment methods that emphasize peer pressure and collective support, and if the proper ambience can be developed, dramatic improvements can be noted in behavior of otherwise delinquent children. The negative consequences that might result from such children living together intimately and joining together in more delinquencies can be eliminated and the experience turned into a positive influence on the juveniles through skillful group therapy methods.

A number of private institutions exist which will take a limited number of delinquent children as placements. Throughout the country "boys' ranches" and "girls' villas" are operated by organizations ranging from sheriffs' associations to religious groups. Some of these specialize in long-term placements and are intended to serve as the home of the children who live there until they reach adulthood. In situations where parental custody has been terminated or children have been orphaned, these homes often provide outstanding nurture within a group living framework. Some facilities specialize in the temporary care of children for periods of up to a year or two, with the parents pursuing independently their own avenues of family improvement in anticipation of the time when they will be reunited with their children.

Incarceration in a State Training School

Commitment to a secure **state training school** is the most severe outcome of the juvenile justice process. Although training schools differ from prisons in terms of size, type of structures, degree of security, and variations in internal programming, they are the juvenile equivalent to prisons.

Moreover, no matter what the rhetoric of rehabilitation, commitment to a training school serves as a *punishment* of juvenile offenders, and is generally viewed as such by the court, the child, the police, the parents, and everyone else familiar with any particular instance of such commitment. It is also aimed at deterring other youthful offenders, especially in communities experiencing juvenile gang activities and plagued by juvenile crime. Sending away a gang member or a notorious juvenile offender may be frankly intended as a clear message to others in similar situations that incarceration is possible for them as well, and it is not unusual for judges to say so in the course of committing juveniles to state training schools. In fact, commitment to a training school serves the purpose of deterring juvenile crime better than severe prison or death sentences serve to deter adult crime. This is because juveniles often misbehave in gangs or cliques, and the judge's deterrent message can be directed to a specific subpopulation rather than to the diffuse and nebulous population of "potential lawbreakers" in society as a whole.

In comparison with prisons, most training schools are small (housing an average of 100 to 300 "residents") and are medium or minimum security. Although they are single-sex secure facilities, they resemble college campuses: no walls and gun turrets, no austere and highly secure cellblocks, no uniformed guards. Most modern training schools have ample recreation facilities, "dormitory"-type arrangements rather than cells, houseparents rather than guards, and little perimeter security except perhaps being enclosed by a chain-link fence. Many of them are, on the surface, quite attractive, with grass, shrubs, classrooms, gymnasiums, and sometimes even swimming pools.

Training schools emphasize *education* and *training*. The juveniles have certain work assignments, but their major daily activities revolve around school. If prisons can be considered walled factories or warehouses, state training schools can be considered fenced junior high or vocational schools. But even though they look less austere than prisons, like prisons, their primary function is to have and to hold. Their internal ambience is less punitive, less bleak, and less depressing than that of maximum-security adult prisons, but the authorities running them must take whatever steps are necessary to prevent escapes and to maintain internal discipline and order.

Most states appropriate a higher proportion of state resources to juvenile offender rehabilitation than to adult rehabilitation, no doubt because juveniles are seen as more likely to be rehabilitated. States with limited funds for institutional correctional practices generally opt to give more per capita for juveniles than for adults. In most states a greater proportion of trained psychologists, clinical social workers, teachers, and other professional "rehabilitation experts" is placed in juvenile institutions than in prisons. Likewise many states provide juvenile institutions with state-of-the-art vocational and educational training equipment and facilities. Vocational training tends to emphasize blue-collar skills. Educational programs tend to be largely remedial and basic since most juveniles committed to state training schools are behind in school attainment or limited in their academic potential. The assumption seems to be that state training school inmates are not college-bound and should be trained to enter the job market as early as possible upon release.

Juveniles committed to state training schools tend to be among the worst and most disturbed youths in their communities. And since they are forced into close association with other such juveniles, the effects of peer contamination, as well as the negative influences of institutionalization, exist in training schools, just as they do in adult prisons. Teenage populations are difficult to work with under the best of circumstances, but several hundred delinquents enclosed together in an institutional setting provide a real challenge to the best and brightest social therapists assigned to—and even devoted to—working with juvenile delinquents. In fact, successful therapeutic efforts under these conditions appear almost miraculous, and there is a long and sordid history of abuses within juvenile institutions. Also, the fact that in some states training schools—like prisons—are placed far away from urban areas often makes it difficult to recruit and retain qualified staff to work there.

Release and Aftercare

In theory, each juvenile offender is released from the training school at the optimal point of his or her rehabilitation in terms of educational advancement and treatment goals. In practice, though, because of overcrowding, many institutions release juveniles not at their maximum treatment points, but simply to make room for new youths sent to them by the courts. Release usually depends on recommendations by the institutional staff made to a releasing authority comparable in function to an adult parole board.

In all jurisdictions today juveniles come out of training schools under the supervision of juvenile aftercare caseworkers, the juvenile equivalent to parole officers. **Aftercare** is a less legalistic and stigmatizing term than parole, implying a greater emphasis on counseling and casework. Ideally, aftercare provides not only general supervision in the home and community, but also a continuation of vocational training, school guidance, and counseling.

Also ideally, aftercare caseworkers are trained social workers or psychologists able to monitor the behavior of the children and provide assistance in their readjustment to their communities. Unfortunately, in practice, many aftercare caseworkers are as overloaded as probation and parole officers. In such situations, the most they can do is to make nominal checks on the juveniles under their supervision, periodically reviewing each child's adjustment to school, family, and community. If a child successfully completes aftercare supervision without revocation, he or she is discharged from the juvenile process.

Revocation

Like parole for adults, juvenile aftercare is subject to **revocation** under certain circumstances, in which case the child is returned to the training school for further incarceration not to exceed his or her twenty-first birthday. In some jurisdictions state legislatures have voluntarily adopted revocation hearing procedures similar to those court-mandated for adults, including the right to counsel. In many cases, juveniles on aftercare who are arrested for further serious law violations, especially if they are older

Revocation

1: Here We Go Again

Fourteen-year-old Harry Thorsten was released on aftercare from the state training school after having been sent there for participating, along with an 18-year-old cousin, in the armed robbery of a liquor store. Harry had spent 10 months at the school and was 6 months into aftercare when he was arrested for car theft. He and two other boys took a car parked in a shopping center parking lot with its keys still in the ignition and drove around town until police apprehended them.

Other than this offense there had been no indication of trouble; Harry had been attending school regularly, had complied with his counselor's program of group therapy, and had been involved in activities at the local boys' club.

2: Boy Criminal

Bernie McNeeley, an 11-year-old boy, was arrested by vice officers for soliciting adult men in a public rest room as a homosexual prostitute. Bernie was an attractive, street-wise boy who had been recently placed on probation on a PINS after a series of reported runaways and truancies. His parents were both alcoholics and his father had been unemployed for a long time. Police suspected that Bernie had been involved with some local drug dealers as a courier and also that he was now being used as a model for pornographic magazines. The boy was flippant, cocky, and seemingly out of control. ■

adolescents, are certified under the *Kent* procedures and moved to the adult court system. Field Practice D gives two examples of juveniles arrested while on aftercare.

THE DREAM AND THE REALITY

After almost a century of experience with the juvenile justice system started by the child savers' movement, its success or failure is still being debated. And as with debates about most social experiments, there is no simple answer. There is little doubt that most of the youngsters who have had contact with the juvenile system have *not* progressed to adult criminal careers. But is this because the juvenile court system works? Because probation or social casework intervention is effective? Perhaps. Who can say for sure? Maybe most young offenders would stop misbehaving before adulthood even if the juvenile justice systems had never been created. Perhaps maturation would naturally result in their reform. However, most informed observers think the juvenile system has contributed something to some prevention of adult criminality. If nothing else, the system's alternatives—short of its training schools—have been less brutal and brutalizing than the adult criminal processing of juveniles that preceded it.

Successes

Juvenile justice processing was set up to be deliberately less stigmatizing than the criminal court system. Names of delinquents are withheld from the press, records are sealed, hearings are closed to the public. There is a school of thought called "labeling theory" which holds that deviation is caused, or at least hardened and made worse, by the attachment of such negative labels as "criminal," "psychotic," or "sex deviate" to persons by the formal system handling them—sort of a self-fulfilling prophecy theory. At any rate, the juvenile system has very conscientiously avoided negative labeling and the ruining of reputations that comes with it.

Many practices in juvenile justice have been adapted to adult criminal processing as "reforms." Diversion, a basic tenet of the juvenile system, has become much more common in the adult system. And the newest prison architecture, a long way from the walled and turreted traditional maximum-security look, owes much to the minimal perimeter restraints and comparatively attractive interiors of juvenile training schools.

On balance, and overall, the juvenile justice system has probably met many of the hopes and dreams of its founders. It is more humane, less punitive, and less degrading than criminal processing. Over the years it has increasingly separated the treatment of young criminals from that of those unfortunate non- or precriminal children in need of adult supervision (PINS or CINS). Somewhat different procedures have come to be used for criminal versus status offenders, including much shorter in-custody restrictions on status offender PINS. More recently, different procedures have been applied to delinquents who have committed property offenses and those who have committed violent and aggressive crimes. And most delinquents and PINS begin and end their experiences with the law within the juvenile system; they never move on to the adult criminal system.

Failures

Having said all this, it is still important to note that the system is far from a complete success; perhaps some of its virtues even contribute to its failures. In certain cases it overprotects the violator at the expense of the victim. Perhaps it does not provide enough security, for long enough, to offer maximum protection to the communities from predatory juveniles. And the advantages of the informality of its procedures may be offset by less attention paid to due process and procedural regularity.

Moreover, in spite of all the developments that have occurred in terms of counseling, foster homes, diversion of various sorts, and modern up-to-date training schools, delinquency remains a major problem in our society. Today drugs, particularly crack cocaine, are epidemic in some youth subcultures. Teenage pregnancy continues to increase, and the rate of school dropouts perpetuates an undereducated social class of the downtrodden and poor among us. Terrible homicides, brutal rapes, robberies, and muggings are still committed by many young people in our society. And increasingly in many jurisdictions the age of exclusive juvenile court jurisdiction over violent juveniles is being *lowered*. Today in many places violent, dangerous children can be tried, convicted, and sentenced in the adult system as young as 13 or 14 years old. So, in a way, where violent youngsters are involved, the system is moving backward. They remain untouched by juvenile processing and, except for longer periods of incarceration, are not effectively handled by the adult system either.

A Lesson

The hopes and dreams for a better world deriving from our juvenile justice system have not been entirely fulfilled. Much has been accomplished, but serious delinquency remains. Perhaps no system can achieve a delinquentless society. But one lesson learned from the changes in the way courts have looked at juvenile processing over the years is that no system of justice, either for children or adults, no matter how well-intentioned, can exist in our society without appropriate attention to Constitutional rights and the due process of law.

Summary

This chapter started with the child-savers' movement of the late 1800s and dealt with one of its results, the American juvenile court system. The outcry against treating children as adult criminals resulted, in 1899, in a separate juvenile court for young offenders established in Chicago. From that beginning, a separate juvenile justice system eventually developed and spread to all the jurisdictions in the United States. The juvenile justice system is designed to rehabilitate young law violators, not to punish them. Through juvenile court, the state acts as a substitute parent for children in trouble and those in need of supervision beyond that which parents or guardians can provide. This means the juvenile system has come to have jurisdiction over three types of sharply distinguished "problem children": those who have committed no criminal acts but need state intervention, such as children who are orphaned or abused; those who commit status offenses, or acts considered violations solely because of the youthful status of their perpetrators, such as truancy or running away from home; and those who commit acts considered criminal by statutes applicable to adults as well.

At first, because the juvenile system supposedly acts in the best interests of young people, much as their parents do, these juvenile offenders had none of the rights afforded to adult criminal defendants. In recent years, however, the U.S. Supreme Court has decided juveniles are entitled to virtually the same Constitutional rights as the rest of us, such as a right to legal representation during the processing of their cases.

This chapter described the steps of the juvenile justice process from referral and intake to community supervision, detention, release, and aftercare. It tracked the decision network for young criminals and young status offenders much as earlier chapters tracked the decision network for adult criminals.

The juvenile process is less punitive, less adversarial, less rigid, and less bound by procedural regularity than adult criminal justice processing. Designed primarily to *help* the child, it stresses rehabilitation, not punishment or deterrence. It is less formal than criminal court processing, preferring instead to handle young people in trouble informally and favoring diversion home to parents or guardians rather than full-scale processing through the official juvenile justice system. Some of its distinctive features have been adapted for use in the adult criminal justice system.

Notes

1. See Anthony M. Platt, *The Child Savers* (Chicago: University of Chicago Press, 1969).
2. See Robert M. Mennel, *Thorns and Thistles: Juvenile Delinquents in the United States, 1825–1940* (Hanover, NH: University Press of New England, 1973); Steven L. Schlossman, *Love and the American Delinquent: The Theory and Practice of "Progressive" Juvenile Justice, 1825–1920* (Chicago: University of Chicago Press, 1977).
3. See Samuel Walker, *Sense and Nonsense about Crime: A Policy Guide* (Pacific Grove, CA: Brooks/Cole, 1989), and Herbert L. Packer, *The Limits of the Criminal Sanction* (Stanford, CA: Stanford University Press, 1968).
4. Sir William Blackstone, *Commentaries on the Laws of England,* Thomas M. Cooley (Chicago: Callaghan, 1899), vol. I, p. 1230.
5. *Commonwealth v. Trippi*, 268 Mass. 227, 167 N.E. 354 (1929), p. 148.
6. Howard N. Snyder, John L. Hutzler, and Terrence A. Finnegan, *Delinquency in the United States, 1983* (Pittsburgh, PA: National Center for Juvenile Justice, 1985), p. 85. See also Paula Downey, *Legal Status of Adolescents, 1980* (Washington, DC:

Department of Health and Human Services, 1983). Also, see Linda A. Szymnaski, *Upper Age of Juvenile Court Jurisdiction Statutes Analysis* (Pittsburg: National Center for Juvenile Justice, March 1987).

7. *California Welfare and Institutions Code*, Section 601 (West Supplement, 1971).

8. *Georgia Juvenile Court Code*, cited in Frank W. Miller, Robert O. Dawson, George E. Dix, and Raymond I. Parnas, *The Juvenile Justice Process*, 3rd ed. (Mineola, NY: The Foundation Press, 1985), p. 112.

9. Uniform Crime Reporting Program, *Age-Specific Arrest Rates and Race-Specific Arrest Rates for Selected Offenses 1965–85* (Washington, DC: U.S. Government Printing Office, 1986).

10. Bureau of Justice Statistics, *Report to the Nation on Crime and Justice* (Washington, DC: U.S. Government Printing Office, 1990).

11. Ibid.

12. Ibid.

13. See Douglas R. Rendleman, "Parens Patriae: From Chancery to the Juvenile Court," in F. Faust and Paul Brantingham (eds.), *Juvenile Justice Philosophy* (St. Paul, MN: West, 1974).

14. *In Re Winship*, 397 U.S. 358 (1970), and *McKeiver v. Pennsylvania* 403 U.S. 528 (1971).

15. *Kent v. United States*, 383 U.S. 541 (1966).

16. *In Re Gault*, 387 U.S. 1 (1967)

17. Bureau of Justice Statistics, op. cit.

18. Nathan Goldman, *The Differential Selection of Juvenile Offenders for Court Appearance* (New York: Council on Crime and Delinquency, 1963); see also John P. Kenney and Dan G. Pursuit, *Police Work with Juveniles and the Administration of Justice* (Springfield, IL: Charles C. Thomas, 1975).

19. National Advisory Committee for Juvenile Justice and Delinquency Prevention, *Standards for the Administration of Juvenile Justice* (Washington, DC: U.S. Department of Justice, 1980).

20. See Miller, Dawson, Dix, and Parnas, op. cit.

21. *In Re William M.*, 3 Cal. 3d 16 (24 August 1970); see also Thomas R. Phelps, *Juvenile Delinquency: A Contemporary View* (Pacific Palisades, CA: Goodyear, 1976), pp. 155–187. The National Council on Crime and Delinquency offered the following criteria for the use of detention: "Children apprehended for delinquency should be detained for the juvenile court when, after proper intake interviews, it appears that casework by a probation officer would not enable the parents to maintain custody and control, or would not enable the child to control his own behavior. Such children fall into the following groups: (a) Children who are almost certain to run away during the period the court is studying their case, or between disposition and transfer to an institution or another jurisdiction. (b) Children who are almost certain to commit an offense dangerous to themselves or to the community before court disposition or between disposition and transfer to an institution or another jurisdiction. (c) Children who must be held for another jurisdiction; e.g., parole (aftercare) violators, runaways from institutions to which they were committed by a court, or certain material witnesses."

22. *NCCD News*, 51, no. 4 (September-October, 1972): 13; see also Juvenile Justice Standards Project, *Standards Relating to Interim Status: The Release, Control, and Detention of Accused Juvenile Offenders between Arrest and Disposition* (Boston: Ballinger, 1980); regarding bail for juveniles see *Doe v. State*, Supreme Court of Alaska, 487, P. 2d 47 (1971).

23. Bureau of Justice Statistics, *Children in Custody 1975–1985* (Washington, DC: U.S. Department of Justice, 1989); H. Snyder, T. Finnegan, E. Nimick, M. Sickmund, D. Sullivan, and N. Tierney, *Juvenile Court Statistics, 1985* (Pittsburg: National Center

for Juvenile Justice, 1989); also see *Report to the Nation on Crime and Justice*, cited in Note 10 above.

24. *Report to the Nation on Crime and Justice*, cited in Note 10.

25. Charles Frazier and Donna Bishop, "The Pretrial Detention of Juveniles and Its Impact on Case Dispositions," *Journal of Criminal Law and Criminology* 76 (1986): 1132–1152; also, Belinda McCarthy, "An Analysis of Detention," *Juvenile and Family Court Journal* 36 (1985): 49–50.

26. See *Doe v. State*, already cited in Note 22; also see Samuel M. Davis, *Rights of Juveniles: The Juvenile Justice System Today* (New York: Clark Boardman, 1974); and see Claudia Worrell, "Pretrial Detention of Juveniles: Denial of Equal Protection Marked by the *Parens Patriae* Doctrine," *Yale Law Review* 95 (1985): 174–193.

Suggested readings

Child Abuse: Prelude to Delinquency? Findings of a Research Conference Conducted by the National Committee for Prevention of Child Abuse. Washington, DC: U.S. Department of Justice, Office of Juvenile Justice and Delinquency Prevention, 1986.

Giallombardo, Rose. *The Social World of Imprisoned Girls.* New York: Wiley, 1974.

Glasser, William. *Schools without Failure.* New York: Harper & Row, 1969.

Glueck, Sheldon, and Eleanor Glueck. *Unraveling Juvenile Delinquency.* Cambridge, MA: Harvard University Press, 1950.

Jackson, Robert K., and Wesley D. McBride. *Understanding Street Gangs.* Sacramento: Custom Publishing Company, 1985.

Jankowski, Martin Sánchez. *Islands in the Street: Gangs and American Urban Society* (Berkeley, CA: University of California Press, 1991).

Metropolitan Court Judges Committee. *Deprived Children: A Judicial Response.* Reno: National Council of Juvenile and Family Court Judges, 1985.

National School Safety Center. *Gangs in Schools: Breaking Up is Hard to Do.* Malibu: Pepperdine University Press, 1988.

Platt, Anthony M. *The Childsavers: The Invention of Delinquency.* Chicago: University of Chicago Press, 1969.

Schur, E. M. *Radical Non-Intervention: Rethinking the Delinquency Problem.* Englewood Cliffs, NJ: Prentice-Hall, 1973.

Schwartz, Ira M. *Reinvesting Youth Corrections Resources: A Tale of Three States.* Minneapolis: Humphrey Institute, Center for the Study of Youth Policy, 1987.

Springer, Charles E. *Justice for Juveniles.* Washington, DC: U.S. Government Printing Office, U.S. Department of Justice, Office of Juvenile Justice and Delinquency Prevention.

Discussion questions

1. In what ways does the juvenile court system differ from the criminal court system in philosophy and practice?

2. Discuss the definition of juvenile delinquency.

3. Compare and contrast the conservative and liberal approaches to juvenile delinquency.

4. Describe the different types of cases brought before juvenile courts and discuss the implications of each.

5. Why have juveniles traditionally not had the right to jury trials?

6. Describe the due process shortcomings of the Gerald Gault case.

7. Describe the juvenile justice process.

8. Describe police handling of juveniles. How does it differ from police handling of adults?

9. Explain the role of detention in juvenile case processing.

10. Describe the dispositional hearing and explain the options available to the juvenile judge.

11. Describe state training schools for juveniles.

Glossary

AA Alcoholics Anonymous, a self-help organization for chronic alcoholics.

accessory Any person who aids, advises on, or conceals a criminal.

actus reus A wrongful act; an element of a crime.

ADA Assistant District Attorney.

adjudication The formal decision of a court in a case.

affirm The decision of an appeals court to let stand a conviction or sentence of a trial court.

aftercare A form of parole for juvenile delinquency.

aggravated assault An unlawful attack by one person on another for the purpose of inflicting severe bodily injury, usually accompanied by the use of a weapon or other means likely to produce death or serious bodily harm.

aggressive patrol A controversial police practice usually involving the saturation of a high-crime area with police officers who stop, question, frisk, and search pedestrians and motorists, almost at random, in an effort to prevent crimes and confiscate weapons.

AIDS Acquired Immune Deficiency Syndrome. A fatal blood disease usually caused by sexual contacts or contaminated needle use; sometimes the result of birth to AIDS-infected mothers.

alias A name different from a person's legal name; usually employed for illegal purposes.

allocution The right of a convicted person to address the court before sentence is passed.

American Bar Association (ABA) A national professional organization of lawyers.

American Bar Foundation (ABF) A research wing of the ABA.

American Law Institute (ALI) A national association of prominent lawyers and legal scholars who voluntarily draft model laws, such as the *Model Penal Code*.

amicus curiae A friend of the court.

anarchy The absence of law or supreme authority. Anarchism regards any form of politically organized government as unnecessary and undersirable.

anomie A state of normlessness, uncertainty of goals, purposes, and norms that are necessary for a properly ordered society to function.

Apodica v. Oregon (1972) Supreme Court decision upholding an Oregon statute allowing conviction by a twelve-member jury which voted 10 to 2 for conviction. Held that nonunanimous jury verdicts for conviction are permissible.

appeal The process whereby a higher court reviews a decision of a lower court.

appellant One who appeals a legal decision to a higher court.

appellate courts Courts of appeal that interpret and apply statutes to specific criminal cases, but ordinarily do not conduct trials, accept guilty pleas, or impose sentences. Their primary purpose is to settle legal controversies arising from litigation in the lower courts.

Argersinger v. Hamlin (1972) Supreme Court decision expanding the Gideon decision (right to counsel) to indigent defendants charged with any crime (misdemeanor, felony, violation, petty offense) which may result in a term of incarceration.

arraignment The pleading process; legal proceedings at which formal charges are read, the defendant is notified of his or her rights, and a plea to the charges is requested.

arrest The physical taking into custody of a person believed to have committed a crime.

Aryan Brotherhood White supremacy racist gang active in prisons.

assembly-line justice The operation of any segment of

the criminal justice system with such speed and impersonality that defendants are treated as objects to be processed rather than individuals.

assigned council   An attorney in private practice who is assigned by a court to represent an indigent defendent and whose fee is paid by the government that has jurisdiction over the case.

Augustus, John   Nineteenth-century American; commonly known as the "Father of Probation."

auxiliary police   Trained and uniformed (but unarmed) volunteer civilians who work with local police.

bail   A method that allows pretrial release of an accused by means of having him/her post financial security to ensure appearance at later proceedings, such as trial.

bailbondesman   Person in the business of posting bail for criminal suspects; usually charges a percentage of whatever bail has been set.

bailiff   A court officer who announces the arrival and departure of the judge and maintains order in the court.

Bail Reform Act of 1984   Act authorizing pretrial detention of those accused of crimes; made bail requirement adjustments and other changes relating to bail.

banishment   Form of punishment where an offender is ostracized from the community to a remote location.

bargain, explicit or overt   An arrangement by the state with a defendant whereby the defendant agrees to plead guilty in exchange for some concession by the state, such as a reduction in the seriousness of the crime or a more lenient sentence than usual for the crime.

baton   A police officer's nightstick or club.

Batson v. Kentucky (1986)   Supreme Court decision holding that prosecutors may not exclude members of one race from a jury because they believe they may favor a member of their own race.

Beccaria, Cesare (1738–1794)   Developed classical school of criminology; "father of classical criminology;" wrote *Essays on Crimes and Punishments*.

Bell v. Wolfish (1979)   Supreme Court decision allowing certain security measures, such as body cavity searches, restrictions on packages from the outside, cell assignments, etc., for pretrial prisoners held in a jail in order to maintain order and security.

bench trial   Adversarial proceeding where the judge determines the guilt or innocence of the defendant after hearing the evidence.

Betts v. Brady (1942)   Supreme Court decision limiting the right to counsel, stating that counsel is not necessary for a fair trial in all felony cases and that the states need not appoint counsel for indigent defendants in noncapital cases. Overturned by Gideon v. Wainwright (1963).

bigtop   Maximum security prison. Also known as big house.

bit   A sentence.

booking   The official registering of an arrest by the police, occurring at a police station house and requiring the physical presence of the person arrested for fingerprinting, etc.

box   Segregation (solitary confinement) unit in a prison.

Bresolin v. Morris (1977)   Washington State supreme court ruling that drug rehabilitation programs in Walla Walla prison, while "minimal" did not violate Constitutional principles for not being more extensive or successful.

Brewer v. Williams (1977)   Supreme Court decision upholding the Miranda ruling.

burglary   Some states define burglary as "breaking and entering," while others merely require the lesser action of "unlawful entry with intent to commit a crime."

burn   To inform on or identify an offender. To expose an undercover officer or informant.

bust   To arrest.

capital punishment   Use of death penalty to punish criminals.

CERT team   Correctional emergency response team. A unit of correctional officers trained to deal with inmate disturbances, riots, and escapes.

charging   The process of formal criminal accusation, usually involving the prosecutor and sometimes a grand jury. The term is also used to mean the judge's instruction of a jury on matters of law.

child-saver movement   Nineteenth-century reformers who developed programs for troubled youth and influenced the creation of the juvenile justice system.

chronic criminals   Persons who have been arrested three or more times. This small proportion of the offending population is believed to be responsible for a significant portion of all criminal behavior.

citation   An order, issued by the police, to appear before a magistrate or judge at a later date. Usually used for minor violations; avoids the taking of a suspect into immediate physical custody.

classical criminology   Theoretical perspective suggesting that (1) people have free will, (2) people choose to commit crimes for reasons of greed or personal need, (3) crime can be deterred through fear of punishment.

coercion   Compulsion by force or by threat; constraint.

cohort analysis   The study over a period of time of a number of persons possessing some common characteristic.

Coker v. Georgia (1977)   Supreme Court decision ruling that the death penalty for raping an adult female is unconstitutional if the rape does not result in death for the victim.

Coleman v. Alabama (1970)   Supreme Court decision establishing the Constitutional right to counsel at "critical stages" of the process, includes the preliminary hearing.

collar   (n.) An arrest; (v.) to arrest.

common law   Court decisions from prior times that have not been enacted into statutes by legislatures.

community-based corrections   The location and operation of correctional services in offenders' neighborhoods or other places outside prisons or jail, usually accompanied by the input of community opinion and decision making.

community-oriented policing   Police strategy that emphasizes fear reduction, community organization, and order maintenance rather than crime fighting.

community service   A sentence requiring that the criminal perform some specific service to the community for some specified period of time.

commutation   Reduction of a sentence by a local chief executive, state governor, of the President of the United States in felony cases. Usually involves reduction of a life sentence to one that makes the prisoner eligible for parole.

conflict theory   View that conflict among interest groups, especially those of opposing socioeconomic classes, is the main determinant of human behavior.

congregate   A penitentiary system, developed in Auburn, New York, in which each inmate was held in isolation during the night but worked with fellow prisoners during the day under a rule of silence.

cop out   To plead guilty, often in return for a lesser charge.

court   A prison term meaning a section of the prison yard or gymnasium claimed by a clique of inmates as their "turf" or a space where only they may stand.

courts, trial   Federal, state, or local courts with jurisdiction to conduct trials, accept guilty pleas, and act as fact finders and sentencers of persons convicted of crimes.

cowboys   Police who are members of tactical units used for aggressive preventive patrol.

crack   A highly addictive, crystalline form of cocaine which is smoked.

criminal intelligence   Information concerning alleged criminals that is not necessarily substantiated by a determination of guilt or the result of a public proceeding.

criminalistics   The science of crime detection, based on the application of chemistry, physics, physiology, psychology, or other sciences. Involves extensive laboratory work and is a highly specialized field.

criminal justice   A system for the enforcement of traditional penal laws, analysis of which involves describing the structural interreelationships of legislatures, appellate courts, and enforcement and administrative agen-

cies as well as their corresponding processes of decision making from arrest of suspects through charging, adjudication, sentencing, imprisonment, and release on parole.

criminology   The scientific study of crime and criminal behavior; the body of knowledge regarding crime as a social phenomenon, largely concerned with finding "causes" of criminal behavior and measuring the extent of crime.

critical state   A stage of the criminal justice process which the courts have determined to be a crucial point capable of affecting the outcome of a criminal case.

cruel and unusual punishment   The Eighth Amendment guarantees freedom from cruel and unusual punishment; however, the definition has rested with the courts.

dangerousness   Term designating the ranking of offenders and offenses along some sort of "seriousness" or violence-prone continuum.

DEA   Drug Enforcement Administration. Federal agency charged with enforcing laws against unlawful narcotics.

death row   Cells holding inmates condemned to die by execution.

detention   Preadjudication, or predispositional lockup of juveniles.

detention hearing   A hearing in juvenile court to determine whether a juvenile is to be detained or released pending further juvenile proceedings.

determinate sentence   A sentence to incarcerate for a specific amount of time, whereas an indeterminate sentence has a minimum and maximum period of time between which the incarcerated person may be released on parole.

deterrence, general   The threat of punishment which is directed toward all members of society, and which seeks to restrain them from engaging in future criminal conduct. Punishing one criminal is assumed to deter others who might be inclined to commit similar crimes.

deterrence, specific   The preventive effect of actual punishment on the offender so that the crime is not repeated.

diaper dicks   Juvenile police officers. Also known as kiddie kops.

differential association   The theory that criminal behavior depends on personal associations.

dime   Ten-year prison sentence.

directed verdict   Acquittal of a case by the trail judge after the jury has heard all the evidence but before it deliberates, on the grounds that the evidence does not prove guilt beyond a reasonable doubt.

discretion The authority to choose among alternative actions or not to act at all.

disparity Arbitrary or capricious differences in sentences between similar offenders convicted of the same crime.

dispositional hearing A hearing to determine what should follow findings of delinquency.

District Attorney (DA) Chief prosecutor of a district (usually a county). Most DAs are elected but some, including all federal DAs, are appointed by the jurisdiction's the chief executive.

diversion A decision or program designed to divert offenders from official processing to less formal, less adversarial, and noninstutitionalized community-based settings.

double jeopardy The common-law and Constitutional prohibition against trying a defendant more than once for the same crime.

drive through (drive by) A practice whereby fighting street gang members in cars drive through a rival gang's "turf" shooting at buildings and anyone believed to be an enemy gang member.

drop a dime Inform the police about a crime or a suspect.

due process The fundamental yet ambiguous Constitutional principle stating that no person shall be deprived of life, liberty, or property without due process of law.

Duncan v. Louisiana (1968) Supreme Court decision ruling that the right to trial by jury does not apply to crimes punishable by incarceration for less than 6 months.

effectiveness The extent to which the criminal justice process (or any agency or individual functionary therein) achieves its objectives in a manner consistent with its long-range responsibilities.

efficiency A variable in the measurement of effectiveness, involving evaluation of the effectiveness within existing constraints of budget, personnel, and other resources over time.

en banc "In the bench." Refers to a session of a court, usually an appellate court, where all judges assigned to the court participate.

entrapment A defense against criminal responsibility based on claims of improper acts committed against the accused by another, usually by police undercover agents. A situation where police encouragement plays upon the weaknesses of an innocent person and beguiles him/her to commit crimes he/she would normally not attempt.

equal protection The Constitutional principle asserting that the law must be applied equally and impartially to all, regardless of race, economic class, sex, and so on.

Escobedo v. Illinois (1964) Supreme Court decision ruling that persons in custody, after arrest, have the right to counsel prior to, or during, any interrogation.

exclusionary rules Legal rules, established by the U.S. Supreme Court and state courts, which hold that the Fourth Amendment prohibition against unreasonable searches and seizures requires that illegally obtained evidence is impermissible and must be excluded as evidence at trial.

ex parte On one side only, done for, or in behalf of, one party only.

ex post facto A retroactive law criminalizing actions that were innocent at the time they were done or increasing the punishment for a criminal act after it was committed.

expunge The act of physically destroying information—including criminal records—in files, computers, or other depositories.

extradition The surrender and transportation of a person accused of or convicted of a crime in one state by another state holding the person in custody.

felony A serious criminal offense punishable by at least 1 year in prison.

felony murder The legal rule that if the death of a person occurs during commission of another felony crime, the person committing the felony can be charged with first-degree murder, and, if convicted, be sentenced as if the killing were intentional and premeditated.

fence (v.) The selling of stolen goods; (n.) a receiver of stolen property.

fink An informer.

fix Pay off, bribe, corrupt. A fixer is one who can arrange to have a criminal charge dropped by means of bribery.

foster home A family, not the child's own natural parents, paid by the state to care for a juvenile.

fraud Theft by false pretenses, trick, or misrepresentation.

frisk A pat-down search of a suspect by police, designed to discover weapons, not to recover contraband. The scope of a frisk has been limited by the courts to be less than a full-scale search; it can occur only under specified conditions where the officer has reason to believe he/she is "in danger of life or limb."

fundamental fairness This basic principle, essential under a democratic system, rests on the belief that crime control efforts must be fair even if it means an impairment of enforcement efficiency.

Furman v. Geogia (1972) Supreme Court decision overturning the death penalty statutes as they were then applied for being in violation of the Eighth Amendment prohibition against cruel and unusual punishment. The door was left open for the states and the federal jurisdiction to rewrite death penalty statutes which the U.S. Supreme Court could approve as Constitutional. Many states have now done so.

Gagnon v. Scarpelli (1973) Supreme Court decision holding that probationers have certain due process rights at an administrative hearing to consider revocation of probation.

gatekeeping A process of simple tabulation or head counting, as when prison authorities count the number of prisoners who enter and leave an institution.

Gault, in re (1967) Supreme Court decision in which due process rights, including the right to counsel, written notification of charges, confrontation of accusers, and protection from self-incrimination, were extended to juveniles.

Gideon v. Wainwright (1963) Supreme Court case which held that the Constitutional right to counsel extends to all defendants in felony cases. Indigent defendants must have attorneys provided without expense to them.

good time Credit allowed on the sentence which is given for satisfactory conduct in prison. It may reduce the minimum or maximum sentence or both. Accumulated days of good time may be taken away from inmates if they violate prison rules.

grand jury, charging The grand jury attached to a court whose purpose is to ratify or reject the prosecutor's request for a formal charge to be levied against a specific defendant.

grand jury, investigatory The grand jury attached to a court empowered to conduct investigations into possible crimes or corruption.

Gregg v. Georgia (1976) Supreme Court decision finding that Georgia's death penalty statute for felony homicide did not violate the Constitutional right to life.

habeas corpus A writ that directs a person holding a prisoner to bring the person held before a court to determine if the imprisonment is lawful.

habitual offender A legal category effective in some states by which severe penalties up to life imprisonment can be imposed on criminals convicted the third or fourth time of the same or any crime.

hard case A tough, experienced prison inmate.

hard time Sentence served in a maximum-security prison.

harness bulls Uniformed police officers. Also known as bulls, jakes, portables, uniforms, blues.

Holt v. Sarver (1970) Supreme Court decision finding that conditions in the Arkansas prison system were in violation of the Eighth Amendment prohibition against cruel and unusual punishment.

homicide This offense includes all willful killings without due process (e.g., murder and nonnegligent manslaughter).

hung jury A trial jury unable to reach a verdict.

Huratdo v. California (1984) Supreme Court decision upholding the conviction and death penalty of a man convicted without being indicted by a grand jury on grounds that use of a grand jury, although required by the U.S. Constitution, is merely a procedure which the states may abolish at will.

IAD Internal Affairs Division. Police officers in a specific unit charged with investigating other police for evidence of corruption, brutality, or other misconduct.

incapacitation An objective of sentencing, the aim of which is to restrain a potential offender from committing new and/or different crimes, usually by holding him or her in a maximum-security prison.

incarceration Imprisonment in a state, federal, or local institution.

indeterminate sentence A prison sentence having a spread of years between fixed minimum and maximum terms.

index offenses Term designating the eight classes of offenses reported annually by the FBI in its *Uniform Crime Reports;* they include willful homicide, forcible rape, robbery, burglary, aggravated assault, arson, larceny over $50, and motor vehicle theft.

indictment A written accusation presented by a grand jury to the court in which it is impaneled, charging that a person or persons named has (have) done some specified criminal act. An indictment is a formal charging instrument.

information A formal charging document similar to an indictment; this is the most common method of bringing formal charges. An information is drafted by a prosecutor and tested before a magistrate at a preliminary hearing, not before a grand jury.

insane A legal classification meaning a defendant is not guilty (technically not responsible) because of court determination that he/she lacked control over his/her actions, could not tell right from wrong, and so on, at the time he/she committed the offense.

initial appearance The first time an arrested suspect is taken before a court for consideration of bail or other forms of pretrial release.

intermittent sentence A sentence to jail on weekends and holidays with freedom to live at home and to work in the community on working days.

jacket A criminal record file.

jury, grand A jury of inquiry impaneled for the term of the court, whose functions include investigation of alleged crime and corruption and the ratification or rejection of the prosecutor's request for a formal charge (indictment). Grand juries usually consist of 23 members and serve for a fixed term as opposed to the smaller trial jury which functions only for the duration of the trial. A working quorum for a grand jury is commonly 16, and an indictment is issued on the affirmative vote of 12 members.

just deserts   The philosophy that the punishment appropriate to the particular crime of which an individual is convicted should be the only consideration in sentencing.

juvenile delinquent   A youth who has not yet reached a specific age and who has been adjudicated by a juvenile court to have committed a crime or to be incorrigible or in need of supervision by the state.

K-9 squad   Police dog unit; the name is a play on the word "canine."

***Katz v. United States* (1967)**   Supreme Court decision holding that the Fourth Amendment protection from unreasonable searches and seizures extends to public phones and any areas "accessible to the public," if a person using them reasonable seeks to preserve conversation as private.

keep lock   Prison disciplinary measure where an inmate is locked in his or her own cell 23 hours a day while other prisoners work or go to school, the mess hall, or recreation.

***Kent v. United States* (1966)**   Supreme Court decision that juveniles are entitled to due process rights, including the right to counsel and procedural safeguards, before the juvenile court can waive its jurisdiction and transfer a juvenile to criminal court to be tried as an adult.

***Landman v. Royster* (1971)**   Supreme Court decision holding that prison inmates have rights to administrative due process in prison disciplinary hearings.

larceny (theft)   The unlawful taking or stealing of property or articles of value without the use of violence or fraud.

Law Enforcement Assistance Administration (LEAA)   Agency of the U.S. Department of Justice responsible for administering law enforcement grants and loans under terms of the Omnibus Crime Control and Safe Streets Act of 1968. LEAA was abolished in 1981.

lineup   A police identification procedure by which the suspect in a crime is exhibited before victims or witnesses to determine if he/she committed the offense.

mala in se   The common law term meaning "evil in themselves."

mala prohibita   Term designating crimes that are largely legislative creations.

mandamus   A writ issued by a court ordering a lower court or any other agency to perform a particular act.

mandatory release   Release from prison at a maximum sentence less time off for good behavior.

***Mapp v. Ohio* (1961)**   Supreme Court decision establishing the principle that illegally obtained evidence cannot be used against a person in court or any state or federal jurisdiction. This is the "exclusionary rule."

max out   Serve a full sentence without parole.

***Maxwell v. Bishop* (1968)**   Arkansas state supreme court decision holding that the suspicion that the death penalty for rape may have been applied discriminatorily in the past or in some places does not automatically render present procedures invalid.

***Meachum v. Fano* (1976)**   Prison inmates are not entitled to due process safeguards when corrections authorities decide to transfer them to more secure facilities.

mens rea   The mental element of a crime, the intent to commit an act.

middle stages   Stages of the criminal justice process where formal charges are brought and innocence or guilt determined, and where convicted offenders are sentenced.

***Miranda v. Arizona* (1966)**   Established the "Miranda warning," which informs suspects of their Constitutional rights to silence, counsel, and protection against self-incrimination; the warning must be read to suspects under arrest before the start of any interrogation.

misdemeanor   A criminal offense which is less serious than a felony, and which is usually punishable by no more than a year in a county jail, and/or a fine, restitution, or some other minor penalty.

Missouri Plan   A system of electing judges who run for office on their past record, not against another candidate.

Model Penal Code (MPC)   Model legislation prepared in 1962 by the American Law Institute, containing suggested revisions of the substantive criminal law and proposing a model sentencing structure.

Model Sentencing Act (MSA)   Drafted in 1963 by the Advisory Council of Judges of the National Council on Crime and Delinquency (NCCD), this 35-page document proposed model sentencing structures.

***Morrissey v. Brewer* (1972)**   Supreme Court decision holding that parolees are entitled to certain due process rights at an administration hearing at which revocation of parole is being considered.

mugger   A street robber. Hit-and-run assaulter who

steals purses, jewelry, or wallets. The act itself is known as mugging.

narc Undercover police officer working on narcotics cases.

National Council on Crime and Delinquency (NCCD) A private research organization.

***Newman v. United States* (1967)** Supreme Court decision holding that different persons arrested for the same crime are not entitled to equal plea bargains because the Fourteenth Amendment guarantees "equal protection before the law" does not include the requirement that prosecutors treat every offense and every offender alike.

nickel 5-year prison sentence.

nolle prosequi The prosecutor's decision not to initiate prosecution even when there is sufficient evidence to do so.

nolo contendere Latin term meaning "I will not contest it." Has the same legal effect as a plea of guilty, but not the same repercussions in any subsequent civil suit.

norm, social A rule or standard of behavior within a group or society that is defined by the shared expectations of the dominant members of that group or society. Social norms provide guidelines regarding the range of permissible behaviors appropriate in a given situation.

***Oliver v. United States* (1984)** Supreme Court ruling that "open fields" are not protected from search and seizure under the right to privacy because the Fourth Amendment only protects privacy that "society is prepared to recognize as resonable."

Ordinance Local laws enacted by a city or county legislative body.

on-line agencies Crime control agencies responsible for the everyday processing of cases, police, courts, prisons etc.

parens patriae Power of the state to act in behalf of the child and provide care and protection equivalent to that of a parent.

parole The conditional release of a prisoner from his/her uncompleted sentence of incarceration, to community supervision by state agents. The parole decision is made administratively, by a parole board, and is the dominant means by which convicts are released from prison.

parole board The state administrative agency empowered to decide whether inmates shall be conditionally released from prison before completion of their sentences.

Part I offenses Eight index crimes whose incidence is reported to the FBI by police: murder, rape, robbery, aggravated assault, burglary, larceny, motor vehicle theft, and arson.

Part II offenses All other crimes other than Part I offenses.

pat down A physical search of the suspect's outer clothing (not inside pockets) which is conducted to protect the officer from a possible weapon.

***People v. Chinnici* (1968)** Supreme Court ruling that probationers may be searched without warrant.

per curiam Literally, "by the court." An opinion of the full court, as opposed to one with some judges affirming and others dissenting. Usually a brief decision, without detailed argument.

perp Perpetrator; used by police to indicate a suspect or an offender.

petition An order to report to a juvenile court for an adjudication hearing. Comparable to an indictment or information for an adult.

pimp Procurer and protector of prostitutes.

plaintiff The complaining party in any litigation, such as the state in a criminal case.

plea bargaining The practice involving negotiation between prosecutor and defendant and/or his or her attorney, which often results in the defendant's entering of a guilty plea in exchange for the state's reduction of charges, or for the prosecutor's promise to recommend a more lenient sentence than the offender would ordinarily receive.

PO Depending on the context, this stands for probation officer, parole officer, or police officer.

Police Advisory Board A citizens' group organized to react to general police policy matters; sometimes organized on a neighborhood basis.

Police Review Board A citizens' group composed of representatives of particular ethnic, racial, or other groups whose task is to investigate allegations of police misconduct.

***Powell v. Alabama* (1932)** Supreme Court decision establishing the right to counsel for indigent defendants charged with capital crimes.

preliminary hearing A court proceeding serving as the testing ground for an information brought by a prosecutor against a criminal defendant. Unlike grand jury proceedings, it is open to the public and may be attended by the defendant and his or her attorney. At this hearing, the prosecutor seeks to convince the judge that there is probable cause to believe the defendant committed a crime and should be held over for trial.

presentence investigation (PSI) Investigation of the relevant background of a convicted offender, usually conducted by a probation officer attached to a court, designed to act as a sentencing guide for the sentencing judge.

presentence report The report prepared from the presentence investigation, which is designed to assist the judge in passing sentence on a convicted defendant. Presentence reports vary in scope and focus, but most include information on the criminal history, employment, school background, and so on of the defendant.

presentment A charge issued by a grand jury on its own motion, as opposed to an indictment, which is a charge requested by a prosecutor.

presumption of innocence Evidentiary standard at trial. Defendant is innocent unless state can prove guilt of all elements of the crime beyond a reasonable doubt.

pretrial screens Stages in the criminal justice process that are designed to exert quality control over police arrests and prosecutors charging decisions in order to reduce the chances of unwarranted and unnecessary trials.

prima facie Latin term meaning "at first sight." It refers to evidence presumably sufficient to indicate a crime has been committed by a particular person unless otherwise contradicted.

prison A correctional facility designed to hold felons. Prisons vary from maximum security to minimum security.

prisonization A process by which the prison inmate comes to strongly identify with and gain status within the inmate culture.

probable cause Reasonable cause, less than beyond a reasonable doubt and more than suspicion. This evidentiary standard requires enough facts to convince a reasonable intelligent prudent man to believe that an offense has been committed and that the accused person committed it.

probation A sentence served in the community without incarceration, under supervision of a probation officer and conditional upon adherence to rules established by the courts.

Procunier v. Martinez (1974) Supreme Court decision holding that prisoners' Constitutional right of freedom of speech cannot be infringed upon through mail censorship of prison inmates, nor can prisoners' access to the courts be restricted by limitations on the use of paraprofessionals and law students by inmates.

Project SEARCH Launched in 1969, the System for Electronic Analysis and Retrieval of Criminal Histories is a major, federally funded program, designed to integrate the criminal statistical reporting system of all the states. SEARCH was established to explore the potentialities and feasibility of an on-line system which would per-

mit interstate exchange of offender history files maintained by state and local criminal justice agencies.

propriety This basic principle, somewhat related to standards of fundamental fairness, assets that law enforcement must conduct itself in a proper fashion in obtaining confessions, guilty pleas, etc., that are trustworthy and accurate, and in providing humane treatment to all suspects or defendants. The basic mandate for fairness and propriety rests on Constitutional guarantees of protection against unreasonable search and seizure, freedom from self-incrimination, equal protection under the law, due process of law, and freedom from cruel and unusual punishment.

prosecutor An attorney, often elected, who represents the state and conducts investigations and charges suspects with crimes. Also known as the District Attorney.

public defender An attorney attached to a court jurisdiction whose job involves the defense of indigents.

punk prison slang that usually refers to homosexual inmates.

quick justice Extremely fast procedures from arrest through conviction to sentencing of a defendant willing to waive all proceedings and plead guilty.

rap, rap sheet Rap is slang for a conviction and sentence. Rap sheet is an offender's official criminal record listing prior arrests, convictions, and sentences. Rap partner is a codefendant, convicted and sentenced for the same crime.

rape, forcible The carnal knowledge of another person through the use of force or the threat of force.

rape, statutory The carnal knowledge of another person who has not yet reached a certain age, not requiring the use of force or lack of consent.

reformatory State incarcerative institution for young felons, usually those 18 to 21 years old, although many reformatories hold inmates up to age 30. Similar in security to prisons, but with more vocational programs.

reintegration A correctional goal or style that stresses the merging of correctional agencies with community resources and the necessity of on-the-street adjustment of offenders. The aim is to promote the offender's reentry into the community, and to this end, both the offender and the community are viewed as change targets.

release on own recognizance (ROR) The pretrial release of an arrested person on his/her stated promise to appear for trial at a later date, and after a determination that he/she is likely to appear. Used primarily with indigent defendants as an alternative to monetary bail, ROR was initially developed in the 1960s by the Vera Institute of Justice in New York City.

reprieve Last-minute stay of an execution by action of the chief executive.

research, applied As opposed to pure research, this kind of inquiry is directed toward the formulation or discovery of scientific principles that can be used to solve some practical problem.

research, pure As opposed to applied research, this kind of inquiry is conducted for the purpose of formulating scientific principles and theories, rather than for the purpose of solving a specific problem. Pure research seeks to lay an essential foundation for further scientific research.

restitution The act of restoring, or making good; or giving equivalent for any loss, damage, or injury committed. Although seldom used as a dispositional alternative in the U.S. criminal justice system, it is primarily employed in minor property offenses and vandalism involving juveniles.

revocation Probation or parole may be revoked (withdrawn) for commission of a new offense or for violation of any condition of the parole or probation. Revocation is decided by the same agency that granted the conditional release.

robbery A felony involving theft of property from a person by the use of force or the threat of force. Examples are mugging, holdups, yoking, and so on.

Roberts v. Louisiana (1977) Supreme Court decision that declared unconstitutional a statute requiring mandatory capital punishment for persons convicted of killing police officers while the officers were acting in their line of duty.

Robinson v. California (1960) Supreme Court case that struck down a California statute making narcotics addiction a criminal offense.

rumble A street battle between fighting youth gangs.

sally port A large back gate in a prison wall used for admitting trucks and other large supply vehicles.

Santobello v. New York (1971) Supreme Court case that approved the practice of plea bargaining and condemned the practice of broken promises by prosecutors.

screw A correctional officer or guard.

segregation A secure unit in prison where inmates are held in solitary confinement as punishment for prison-rule infraction or for their own protection from other prisoners. In prison slang, segregation is called the box, or solitary.

self-report studies A modern survey technique designed to measure the number of criminals by asking respondents if they have committed crimes with a specific period. Although their validity may be somewhat suspect, even with firm pledges of confidentiality, as many as 91 percent of the respondents surveyed by some studies have admitted to committing one or more criminal acts.

sentence, flat (straight) A fixed sentence without a maximum or minimum length spread.

sentence, indeterminate A sentence to incarceration with a spread of time between a minimum date of parole eligibility and a maximum discharge date. A completely indeterminate sentence has a minimum of 1 day and a maximum of natural life.

sentence, maximum A maximum sentence sets the outer limit beyond which a prisoner cannot be held in custody.

sentence, minimum The time that an offender must spend in prison before becoming eligible for parole.

sentence, suspended Technically a "sentence," but involving unconditional, unsupervised release of the convicted defendant.

sentencing The postconviction stage of the criminal justice process in which the defendant is brought before the court for imposition of sentence. Usually a trial judge imposes sentence, but in some jurisdictions sentencing is performed by jury or by sentencing councils.

sentencing councils A panel of three or more judges that confers to determine a criminal sentence. Sentencing councils are not as commonly used as sentencing by a trial judge, though there appears to be a greater trend toward the council approach, in an effort to reduce sentence disparity.

sentencing juries Trial juries attached to a court that impose sentence.

serial murderer A repeat killer of random victims.

severance The separation in criminal proceedings of co-defendants accused of the same crime for separate proceedings or trials. It also refers to the separation of multiple charges against a single defendant for separate trials on each charge.

sidearm A police officer's pistol.

Stack v. Boyle (1951) Supreme Court decision upholding the Constitutional right to reasonable bail.

stakeout Hidden police keeping premises or vehicles under constant surveillance.

stare decisis Literally, "let the decision stand." This judicial principle guides courts to consistently follow legal precedent from former cases.

subculture The culture of an identifiable segment or subgroup of a society, which is part of the larger culture but which differs in certain important respects (e.g., values, language, social norms, etc.). This sociological term is generally applied to subcultures of criminals, delinquents, police, etc.

subpoena A written order from a judge, prosecutor, grand jury, or defense counsel requiring a specific person to appear in a designated court at a specified time to testify in a matter under the jurisdiction of that court. Records, such as tax returns, may also be subpoenaed and thereby ordered to be produced in court.

sundown parole Unlawful banishment of an offender from the community by the sheriff or local police.

suppression hearing A hearing before a judge (without the jury present) to consider whether physical evidence or statements, admissions, or confessions were properly obtained and therefore can be introduced at trial or, if improperly obtained, cannot be shown to the jury.

surveillance Police investigative technique involving visual or electronic observation or listening directed at a person or place (e.g., stakeout, tailing suspects, wiretapping, etc.). Its objective is to gather evidence of a crime or merely to accumulate intelligence about suspected criminal activity.

Swain v. Alabama (1965) Supreme Court decision upholding the practice of using peremptory challenges to exclude jurors based on race.

SWAT team Special Weapons Attack Team or Special Weapons and Tactics Team. A police unit that deals with hostage situations, snipers, barricaded offenders, and other situations where surprise, attack, and firepower are needed.

tail To follow a person, keeping him/her under hidden surveillance.

Tennessee v. Garner (1985) Supreme Court decision holding "Constitutionally unreasonable" the shooting of a fleeing felon by a police officer for the purpose of preventing him/her from "getting away."

Terry v. Ohio (1968) Supreme Court decision holding that police officers may stop and frisk a person if they have a reasonable suspicion that he/she has committed or is about to commit a crime or that he/she is armed and dangerous.

throwdown A junk pistol carried by some police officers and dropped near a suspect to justify a dubious shooting.

ticket-of-leave Alternative term (British) for parole.

tier A floor of cells in a cellhouse of a maximum-security prison. Also company, a group of inmates living on the same tier.

tracking The following of an individual through the entire criminal justice process; this technique is rarely employed. Also known as cohort analysis, which involves starting with a sample of persons at a specific point—all citizens questioned by police in a given period, for example—and tracking these persons as they flow through the system and are dropped or diverted from it, or carried further into it. (See cohort analysis.)

training school State institutions housing juvenile delinquents on court order; designed to offer educational and vocational training programs.

trial, bench A trial before a judge sitting without a jury.

trial jury The jury participating in the trial of a given case; ordinarily composed of 12 members; a petit jury as opposed to the larger, grand jury composed of 23 members.

typology A classification schema composed of two or more ideal types that provide abstract categories in terms of which individual or group phenomena are analyzed. A typology of criminal behavior, for example, seeks to organize data about different types of criminals for the purpose of aiding research efforts and developing general theories of criminal behavior. As a conceptual tool, typologies are potentially useful constructs.

Uniform Crime Reports (UCR) National crime statistics maintained by the Federal Bureau of Investigation, they are based on data concerning eight "Index" offenses: willful homicide, forcible rape, aggravated assault, arson, robbery, larceny over $50, and motor-vehicle theft. Their basic statistic is "crimes known to the police," that is, those that are reported to the police or discovered by the police, but not necessarily solved. The UCR published annually by the U.S. Department of Justice.

United States v. Ammidown (1973) Supreme Court decision stating that a judge may not withhold approval of a plea agreement if the prosecutor is found to have given consideration to "public interest" matters such as the deterrent aspects of the law, and the necessity for convicting the most serious perpetrator.

United States v. Jackson (1968) Supreme Court decision holding that a procedure by which defendants who plead guilty to a crime (kidnapping) were subject only to a sentence of life imprisonment and those who contested the charges at trial were subject to capital punishment violated the Fifth Amendment right against self-incrimination and the Sixth Amendment right to trial by jury.

United States v. Latimer (1969) Supreme Court disapproving of a sentencing judge considering the evidence of charges on which the defendant had been acquitted.

United States v. Leon (1984) Supreme Court decision accepting "good faith" exception to the exclusionary rule in a case in which officers seized evidence based on warrants issued by a magistrate which later turned out to be defective.

United States v. Wiley (1980) Supreme Court ruling that a defendant should not be given a more severe sentence merely because he or she exercised the right to a trial before a judge or jury.

venue The location of an alleged crime; place from which the jury is drawn, and where the trial occurs.

vice squad Police officers specializing in enforcing laws against gambling, prostitution, and narcotics.

victimization survey A technique for measuring crime more precisely than it is measured by official crimes known to the police, this survey method attempts to discover how many persons claim to have been victimized by crime over a specific period of time. Some of the most famous victimization surveys conducted within recent years included studies performed for the President's Commission on Law Enforcement and Administration of Justice. Virtually all of these studies indicate that the incidence of crime is several times greater than reported by the police in the FBI's *Uniform Crime Reports.*

victimless crimes Crime for which there is no nonofficial complainant or victim (e.g., drug law violations, prostitution, homosexual acts between consenting adults, drunkenness, etc.). This class of offenses comprises the bulk of crimes handled by the criminal justice system.

voir dire The selection of jurors in court through examination by defense counsel and prosecutor, intended as a screening device to weed out persons who might be biased or otherwise incompetent to render a fair verdict. In addition to the judge's removal of jury candidates following the *voir dire,* the prosecutor and defense counsel each have the option to make a specific number of peremptory challenges which can result in the removal of jury candidates without demonstrated cause.

Wade v. United States (1967) Supreme Court ruling that an accused person has the right to an attorney at various stages of criminal processing, including a lineup after an indictment has been issued.

waiver The voluntary decision of a defendant to give up some rights to which he/she is entitled. For instance, a preliminary hearing may be waived and a guilty plea constitutes a waiver of the right to a trial.

warrant, search A warrant obtained from a judge empowering the police to search a specified premise on the belief that it contains criminal evidence.

white-collar crime Introduced in 1939 by the late criminologist, Edwin H. Sutherland, this term usually signifies law violations by corporations or individuals, including theft or fraud and other violations of trust, committed in the course of the offender's occupation (e.g., embezzlement, price fixing, antitrust violations, etc.).

Williams v. Florida (1970) Supreme Court decision upholding the conviction of a man for armed robbery by a six-member jury, ruling that there is no Constitutional requirement for a twelve-member jury.

Winship, in re (1970) Supreme Court ruling that the standard of proof in juvenile adjudicatory hearings must be "beyond a reasonable doubt" as in the criminal court, not the "preponderance of evidence" standard commonly used in civil procedures.

wiretapping A form of electronic eavesdropping where, upon court order, enforcement officials surreptitiously listen to phone calls.

wise guy Member of organized crime.

Witherspoon v. Illinois (1968) Supreme Court ruling that the conviction and death sentence of a person by a jury "qualified" on the basis of their support for capital punishment violated due process of law, that a person executed by such a "stacked deck" would be deprived of his life without due process of law.

Wolff v. McDonell (1974) Supreme Court ruling that prison disciplinary proceedings which could result in the loss of good time or in solitary confinement must be accompanied by certain due process protections, including written notification of charges and a transcript of proceedings.

work release Correctional programs that allow an inmate to leave the instituton for the purpose of continuing regular employment during the daytime, but reporting back to lockup nights and weekends.

writ of certiorari A method of obtaining review of a case by the U.S. Supreme Court; a writ issued by a superior court to an inferior court, directing that the record of a case be delivered for review.

writ of Habeas Corpus Literally, "You have the body." A common-law instrument designed to bring a person held in custody in a lockup, jail, prison, or other institution before a court or judge, to force the state to "show cause" why custody should continue; an instrument initiating an appeal of custody.

yard Outdoor recreation area in a prison.

Name Index

Subject Index

Photo Credits